For years, this has be
for anyone planning a ski or snowboard
vacation to Europe

"Facts, prices and advice on choosing a ski package, getting around Europe and finding friends to ski with."   —New York Times

"Everything skiers need to know but the weather forecast."
—Robb Report

"Tips and money-saving ideas for skiing in Europe."
—San Francisco Examiner

"Detailed information on lift ticket prices, cross-country facilities, nightlife and more."
—Powder Magazine

"The flavor, feel and personality of each resort."
—Boston Globe

"It provides independent evaluation of the ski terrain and offers more extensive information than found in other guides."
—Skier News

"Start your planning with SkiSnowboard Europe. It includes everything needed to make an educated decision about which slopes to hit."
—PhysiciansFinancial News

"Get it before you ski off."   —Endless Vacations

"I've been using SkiSnowboard Europe since the first edition appeared to select destinations for my club and then to organize the trips."
—RN, Washington DC

"We live about two hours from Chamonix and we love your SkiSnow-board Europe book."   —JM, Thoiry, France

Help us do a better job

Research for this book is an ongoing process. We have been at it for more than a decade. Each year we revisit many of these resorts, and every winter we speak with locals from every resort.

If you find a new restaurant, hotel, bar or disco that you feel we should include, please let us know. If you find anything in these pages that is misleading or has changed, please let us know. If we use your suggestion, we will send you a copy of next year's edition.

Send your suggestions and comments to:
Charlie Leocha, *Ski Snowboard Europe*, World Leisure Corporation
P.O. Box 160, Hampstead NH 03841, USA
or send e-mail to leocha@worldleisure.com

Copyright © 2008 by World Leisure Corporation

Front cover photos courtesy Kitzbühel Tourism, Austria.
Back cover photos, (clockwise from top) Chairlift courtesy of Lech-Zürs, Austria; Chalets courtesy Les Menuires, France; Sledding courtesy Kitzbühel Tourism; Rotating restaurant courtesy Saas Fee, Switzerland; Snowboarder courtesy Lech-Zürs, Austria.

Chapter heading illustrations by Len Shalansky,
59 Darling St., Warwick, RI 02886, (401) 738-3215

Distributed to the trade in the U.S.A. by
Midpoint Trade Books, Inc., 27 W. 20th Street, Suite 1102,
New York, NY 10011, Tel. (212) 727-0190, fax (212) 727-0195.
Internet: www.midpointtradebooks.com

Distributed to the trade in U.K. by
Portfolio, Unit 5, Perivale Industrial Park, Perivale, Middlesex, UB6 7RL
Tel. (020) 8997-9000, fax (020) 8997-9097.
Internet: www.portfoliobooks.com

Mail Order, Catalog, other International sales and rights, and Special Sales by
World Leisure Corporation, 177 Paris Street, Boston, MA 02128.
Tel. (617) 569-1966, fax (603) 947-0838
E-mail: leocha@worldleisure.com;
Internet: www.worldleisure.com or skisnowboard.com
ISBN: 0-915009-86-2 (978-0-915009-86-2)
ISSN: 1072-8996   LCCN: 93-643935

SKI
SNOWBOARD
EUROPE

16th Edition

by Charles Leocha
with
Karen Cummings
Iseult Devlin
James Kitfield
Hilary Nangle
Peggy McKay Shinn
Zahlen, Xtehn, Rohre & Vehro Titcomb
William Walker

WORLD LEISURE CORPORATION
Hampstead, NH

Contents

Contents

Contributors to Ski Europe (16th edition)

Charlie Leocha has been skiing worldwide for over two decades. In addition to *Ski Snowboard Europe*, he is author of *Ski Snowboard America,* an annually updated guidebook to North America's top ski resorts. He has skied, eaten, slept and partied at virtually every major international resort. He writes about travel and skiing for scores of magazines. newspapers and websites. His commentary can be read at tripso.com.

Karen Cummings, whose skiing heritage began in North Conway, N.H., has had the good fortune to be shown around the slopes by St. Anton native, Herbert Schneider (son of Hannes Schneider, the father of modern skiing). She also visited Norway and Iceland in preparation for this guide.

Iseult Devlin, a former editor at *Skiing Magazine* and *Skiing Trade News*, is now a freelance writer. She has written about winter sports and gear for *Sports Illustrated for Women, Outside, Skiing for Women, Ski, Skiing* and other publications. Devlin is also the author of, *Winter Sports, A Ragged Mountain Press Woman's Guide.* She taught skiing for two years in Kitzbuhel, Austria (a former Rote Teufel!) and raced on her college ski team.

James Kitfield has been awarded the Gerald R. Ford prize twice for distinguished reporting, and the Jesse H. Neal award for excellence in reporting. His book, *Prodigal Soldiers*, was published by Simon & Schuster. He skis whenever and wherever he has a chance. He first met Charlie Leocha dancing in a conga line through a bar in Verbier.

Hilary Nangle, a nationally recognized travel writer, normally skis in Maine, but will manage a foray into the Alps whenever the opportunity avails.

Peggy McKay Shinn who grew up in the West and raced on skis, now lives in Vermont still enjoys a few turns in European snow.

Zahlen Titcomb, Xtehn Titcomb, Vehro Titcomb and **Rohre Titcomb** are lucky enough to split living and skiing between the U.S.A., Italy, France and China. They are all accomplished snowboarders, skiers and ultimate Frisbee players. They write about snowboarding and skiing specializing on discovering the young, hip places to stay and play. They updated Verbier, Megève, Morzine/Avoriaz and Tignes in France.

William Walker is one of the founding co-authors of this book. A skiing journalist, he has been writing and living in Germany for almost 30 years. He was an editor with European *Stars and Stripes* and has written for many international publications.

Vanessa Reese, a virtual skier, pulls information from the corners of the Alps and the Pyrenees and makes sure this project and our Web site, www.skisnowboardeurope. com, stays up-to-date.

Peter Aiken, Andrew Bill, Cindy Bohl, Claudia Carbone, Christopher Elliott, Kari Haugeto, Steve Giordano and **Lynn Rosen** all contributed updates to various chapters.

Ski Snowboard Europe

Getting the most out of this guidebook

Skiing in Europe is the dream of just about every American skier and for British skiers it is normally the most cost effective ski holiday available. Today, with easy flights across the Atlantic and the Channel and tour packages to dozens of the resorts that nestle in the Alps, the dream is easy to fulfill. This book is designed to help give you the information you'll need to plan your trip and get the most out of it.

For Alpine veterans who return year after year, this book will help you to make your own arrangements, or at least to decide which resorts you want to visit. We believe that you won't find another guide with as many useful numbers and addresses for a European ski vacation. And this is a guidebook that is useful on the ground, with details about dining, nightlife, day care, snowboarding, cross-country skiing, ski schools and other activities that will help to make your European ski vacation a totally enjoyable experience.

Time and money

Unfortunately, too many Americans don't seriously consider skiing in Europe. They may seriously dream about it, but dismiss the idea as too costly or too time-consuming. Skiing in Europe is neither.

Consider the average urban skier in the United States: reaching the nearest destination resort will take him five, six or seven hours and that travel is normally during daytime. Skiers and snowboarders heading to Europe, normally board a flight in the evening and land the next morning. Transfers to the Alps are only a couple of hours and this puts you in the resort the following afternoon. Voilà!—on the average, you spend about the same travel time.

As far as money goes, European ski packages average about $1,200 to $1,500 per person for a week of skiing, including seven nights of first-class lodging, transatlantic airfare, transfers to resorts, breakfast and dinner every day, lift tickets in some cases and all taxes. This is about the same as you would spend taking a vacation to a Rocky Mountain resort from the East Coast or from California.

Even a one-week vacation within driving distance from home in the United States can end up costing more than $700. Some tours cost less than $1,000 for a week in Innsbruck, Austria, for example, including air, breakfast, dinner and transfers from the East Coast.

Also, with the advent of direct flights from the West Coast to Europe and code sharing, time and expense are no longer the major factors they once were for people living in once non-gateway cities.

Chapter organization

The resort chapters are divided into several sections. We begin by sketching the personality of the place, to give you a feel for the overall resort—is it old and quaint or modern and high-rise? Clustered at the base of the slopes, or a few miles down the road? Remote and isolated, or around the bend from another resort? Is it family-oriented or catering to singles, walkable with good shuttlebuses or requiring a car, filled with happy, friendly faces or with an aloof herd of "beautiful" skiers?

A detailed description of the mountain layout is next, followed by a mountain rating. In mountain layout, we suggest an approach to exploring the mountain based on your abilities and in the mountain rating we describe what the mountain has to offer for beginner, intermediate, advanced or expert; more importantly, this section also suggests which resorts the beginner looking for the mellow might try or the expert looking for the extreme may choose to avoid. Snowboarding terrain parks and halfpipes are included for many resorts as well as some expanded cross-country ski coverage.

The major ski school programs are outlined, together with prices for group and private lessons.

Lift ticket prices are listed for adults, children and seniors. The price lists in most cases include single-day passes, as well as multiday tickets where available. Where possible we list the 2007/08 prices; where no date is noted, assume the prices are from the 2006/07 season.

Under Accommodations we list the most luxurious places to stay as well as many of the ski area bargains. In the Condos and flats section we list many private homes that are available for rent during the winter season.

The dining recommendations always include the best gourmet restaurants in town, where money is no object—but we don't leave out affordable places where a hungry family, or a broke college kid, can chow down and relax. There are also plenty of in-between restaurants suggested. These suggestions have been compiled from interviews with locals and tourists, gleaned from the top gourmet guidebooks, then combined with our own dining experiences.

Après-ski/nightlife describes places to go once the lifts begin to close and where to find entertainment later in the evening. We discuss, for example, which bars are packed with celebrants for immediate après-ski, likewise where to find an inviting, cozy spot in front of a fireplace. We'll help you find pulsing disco on a packed dance floor, or soft music and quiet after-dinner talk.

Details on resort child care facilities are given with prices, times and ages of children accepted.

Activities and facilities, such as tennis and squash, fitness clubs, skating, sleigh rides, hot-air ballooning, curling and festivals, are included under other activities.

Finally, we give detailed Getting There instructions on how to reach the resort either by plane, car or train and finish with the most important phone numbers and addresses for tourist information.

Using the Internet

One of the most significant changes in making reservations at and gathering information about ski resorts has been the development of the Internet. Virtually every world-class resort now has an Internet site with basic information about the resort including latest snow conditions, statistics, lift tickets, ski school prices, some lodging and contact information.

This Internet information is an excellent addition to the material in this guidebook. If there are any changes to the pricing and scheduled events, they are normally posted on the skisnowboardeurope.com site.

Skisnowboardeurope.com provides the most detailed destination information available on the Internet for European winter resorts. It will include more up-to-the-minute snow condition and weather reports, snow cams and late-breaking bargains. The site is online with basic resort information contained in this book.

Skisnowboard.com presents the most comprehensive information on destination resorts in North America gleaned from the pages of *SkiSnowboard America and Canada*. Check out either site and join our mailing list for breaking news about ski and snowboard resorts in the USA, Canada and Europe.

Getting To & Getting Around Europe

The first step in planning a European ski vacation is to get across the Atlantic. Crossing the ocean and getting to the resort is the major cost to be borne: for example, while transportation to Aspen, Colorado, from New York City constitutes about 37 percent of a typical week's ski vacation budget, the travel segment of a similar ski trip to Austria represents about 50 percent of the total cost. But transatlantic air travel is also where a clever traveler can save the most money.

If you are a do-it-yourselfer, even the transfer from the airport to the resort can be used to save both time and money, if you plan ahead. Remember, though, that there are tradeoffs between cost and convenience: you want to go to Europe to ski and see as much as possible, not to spend endless hours in bus or train stations waiting for connections. It's worth doing a little homework to get the best deal and a travel agent or tour operator can help out with the specifics.

After studying pricing at ski resorts and airlines, we feel that the best overall values are available through tour operators or when making arrangements through the Web. These "packages," whether organized by an operator or created dynamically on the Internet, are not group tours where everyone is herded onto a bus together, but rather tours which take advantage of group discounts and negotiated air and hotel rates. You will fly with friends you choose and will receive coupons or passes for transportation to the resorts. Some operators use buses, others trains and some even provide rental cars, all for remarkably low prices.

Getting across the Atlantic

There is plenty of capacity and service from almost every area of the country, which makes getting to Europe more convenient and easier than ever. And, of course, winter air travel works to a skier's advantage, because prices are often 40 to 50 percent lower than in the peak summer months.

A travel agent and tour operator can be extremely helpful at this stage. But supplement the agent's information by doing some investigating on your own. Airline fare structures are complicated and seem to change daily—even with scheduled airlines. And when charters and group tour flights are included, the options can become phenomenally complex.

Tell your travel agent exactly what you are looking for and explain what you think you should have to pay, based on ads you have seen. The agent will either confirm your opinions or let you know what has changed since your last information. Try to find an agent who will guarantee the lowest possible fare.

These agents often will let you know exactly what is available and then you can make a decision, even if it's to take a more expensive flight based on convenience or better connections. A good travel agent can save both time and money.

Tour operators specializing in European ski and snowboard vacations make the process of making air and hotel reservations simple. Most of these organizations allow selection from dozens of hotels and chalets and work together with several airlines.

Online travel agencies, such as Expedia and Travelocity, also provide good sources of winter vacation arrangements. On the Web, travelers can create a "dynamic tour package" with very low prices. In some cases the prices created on the Web are just as low at those negotiated by tour operators, months before the winter season.

Lessen jet lag – stopover in Iceland

If you're on your way to ski in Europe and want to ease into the time change, stopover in Iceland, either on the way over or way back. Or both.

Located in the North Atlantic, Iceland is four hours ahead of the U.S. Eastern Standard Time zone, and two hours behind most of the skiing destinations in the rest of Europe. The rugged 40,000-square-mile (103,000-square-kilometer) island provides the perfect break for a transatlantic flight as it is roughly five to six flying hours from the East Coast and two to three hours from Europe.

Visitors get to see Mother Nature at her most forceful in Iceland. This is partly because its location brings strong prevailing winds and some dramatic weather — during a leisurely lunch one March, the view went from sunny, to horizontal snow, to driving rain, back to sunny, many times, actually. But, it's also because Iceland sits right on the "constructive" junction of the African and American tectonic plates.

What does that mean? It means active volcanoes (last eruption was in 2004), steaming hot springs (which heat the buildings in Iceland and ensure the country is pollution-free), and occasional earthquakes (rest assured that all construction is required to be built to withstand these earth tremors). This is a country that's still forming. The two plates are gradually moving away from each other — at a rate of nearly an inch (2 cm.) a year. Viewing the resultant rift in relatively recent lava fields shows a huge slash in the surface of the earth that runs from the southwest to the northeast of Iceland. Standing in it, with waterfalls plunging here and there over the edge of one plate, which looms 25 feet higher and at least the same distance away from the other, can make even the most macho among us understand why you don't mess with Mother Nature.

Many who stop in Iceland only get to visit Reykjavik, the world's northernmost capital and a 45-minute drive past gray, dreary lava fields from the airport at Keflavik. More than 60 percent of Iceland's total population, which is less than 300,000, live in Greater Reykjavik. Don't let the concrete apartment and office buildings surrounding the city fool you. The center is quaint, colorful, fun to stroll through and boasts of lively nightlife.

The main shopping street is Laugavegur, with stores featuring books, Icelandic designs, the latest fashions from Europe, trinkets, and music — please note that Icelanders have bizarre taste in music (case in point: Björk) so be sure and stroll through and check it out. Cafes and restaurants are found all along the way. For a taste of traditional Iceland, meaning lamb and fish, a stop at Laekjarbrekka is a must. While it seems touristy, the atmosphere is delightfully quaint and the food surprisingly delicious.

Museums and art galleries abound within walking distance in the city. The short days during the winter must bring out the creativeness of the Icelanders as amazing artwork can be found displayed in even relatively plebian motels.

Much as the city has to offer, it's the countryside that is not to be missed, even if it's just a day trip to Blue Lagoon. These are public therapeutic thermal pools to help skiers prepare for demanding days on the slopes or to ease weary muscles following their ski trip. Local tour companies can take visitors on day trips from Reykjavik to places like Pinvellir National Park to view the Great Atlantic rift, the magnificent Gullfoss waterfall and the Geysir hot spring area, or the South Shore area past lush farmland, glaciers, and looming waterfalls. Or, visitors can rent a car and strike out on their own. Be sure to leave time to enjoy the scenery — steam rising from hot springs or spray from waterfalls and cone-shaped mountain ridges. There is one photo op after another along the way.

For more information about traveling or staying in Iceland, consult www.icelandair.com, www.icelandadventure.com, or www.icelandtravel.is.

Car rental

For the independent skier who wants to get the most out of a European ski vacation, a rental car offers the most flexibility and is a bargain—especially when two skiers share expenses. Rental cars can be picked up directly at the airport upon arrival. Aside from making it a breeze to get to the ski resort, a rental car gives you the freedom to explore the surrounding area or take a short side trip when ski conditions aren't perfect or you just want a break from skiing.

What license do you need?

The driver of the car usually must be at least 19 years old and must have a valid driver's license that has been in effect for at least one year. (The age requirement increases for some more luxurious automobiles.) It is not necessary to have an International Driving Permit when driving in Europe—your home state license is acceptable—but it is a good idea. The AAA issues them and they are good for a year. Fill out an application and give them two passport-type portrait snapshots. By mail, start the process a month before your departure. If you live near an AAA office, you can accomplish the entire process there, including photos, in less than an hour. International Driving Permits cost $10. Call AAA for details and the location for the nearest office issuing International Driving Permits at (800) AAA-HELP. Remember, even with the International Driving Permit you will still need your U.S. state license as well. Canadians can call (800) 336-HELP for information on the nearest location to pick up an international license. You can get an application over the Web from www.aaa.com.

BEWARE: We checked out the Internet for International Driver's Licenses. Watch out! There are scores of sites claiming to issue international driver licenses, but none are as inexpensive as the AAA license deal. We found pricing for $34, $40 and $230.

NOTE: In Europe, especially in the Alpine countries, you need to have what is called a Green Card (carte verte) for insurance. This is provided by rental companies, but it is best to make a quick check of the documents when you pick up your car.

Getting the best rates

If you make reservations two to seven days in advance of your arrival with any of the major car rental companies, you qualify for special European vacation rates. These run about $200 to $250 a week, excluding taxes. (If you're comparing car rentals to possible train travel, this will mean that each person will pay about $400 for a full month's automobile use—plus gasoline, which even in an extreme case shouldn't run more than $200 apiece.) The only requirement for this rate is that you keep the car for at least five days. If you return it before that, you will be charged at the daily rate, which often can cost more than keeping the car the entire week.

While all car rental companies may offer reasonable rates throughout the year for tourism, only Auto Europe (800-223-5555) guarantees that they will find the lowest rate. Auto Europe also can organize camper van rentals, handicap vehicles and chauffeur services.

Another tip: If the need to rent a car comes up while traveling in Europe, it is normally less expensive to call back to the U.S.A. (or go on the Web) and make your reservations with the U.S.-based office. Auto Europe's rates require a minimum rental of three days, however, even the three-day rate from Auto Europe is often less expensive than renting a car through a European rental car office for a single day. Check the Auto Europe Web site at www.autoeurope.com for a list of toll-free numbers that will connect directly to the Auto Europe call stateside center.

Drop-off charges

Generally, there are no drop-off charges if a rental car is returned in the country where it was picked up. Some rental companies will allow rental cars to be dropped off in other countries for no drop-off charge if the rental is for at least 21 days. There are some companies that will allow one-way rentals, but only to a limited group of cities. Ask whether your case falls into one of these categories and if not, pick up and drop off in the same country.

Collision damage waiver/insurance

If you rent your car with a credit card which provides collision damage waiver (CDW) you have adequate protection. Diners Club, American Express, MasterCard Gold and Business and VISA Gold and Business all provide this coverage automatically **as long as you decline the CDW option on the rental contract.**

This credit card coverage covers the card holder and additional drivers as long as they are signed up properly with the rental company and appear on the contract. Read the fine print. Some credit card companies do not cover your car if you were driving on a dirt road or in the case of hit and run accidents and so on. Check also to see whether this is primary or secondary coverage. Primary coverage is what you want. Secondary coverage only comes into play after your own insurance company pays for damages ... then the credit card company pays the difference. Most credit card collision damage is primary in Europe, while back in the U.S. it is normally secondary.

In the U.S. most collision insurance coverage applies to rental cars as well as to your own automobile, but in Europe most American coverage is not valid. You should have some form of collision damage insurance. According to Auto Europe the normal rental contract deductibles in Europe range from $2,000 to $5,000.

Even with your credit card coverage, your rental car company may demand a security deposit to cover the deductible until everything is settled. You must, in most cases, settle with your credit card company and then reimburse the rental company. Taking the European collision damage insurance allows you to walk away from any accident without mountains of follow-up paperwork.

If you are planning on renting a luxury or four-wheel-drive vehicle, check with the credit card to make sure that the car you are renting is insured under their CDW plan. Some makes and models of automobiles are excluded from coverage.

Rental car operators highly recommend the purchase of CDW for anywhere from €3 to €30 a day depending on the make of car. It makes your life easier in the event of an accident. If you can handle the hassles of doing some of your own accident paperwork during the settlement, credit card companies allow you to save money.

Theft insurance

Collision damage used to include other types of damage such as theft of the vehicle. These days, theft insurance has been separated from collision—you must purchase it separately.

According to Auto Europe many countries have made theft insurance mandatory. Where theft insurance is mandatory it is included in Auto Europe rental charges at a discounted rate.

When theft insurance is not required, we recommend purchasing it even if you are covered for collision through your credit card CDW.

Other charges

Most major airports now assess an airport pickup surcharge.

Additional driver charges of around €22 per rental or about €10 a day will be added to your bill if you need to have an extra driver listed on the contract.

Child seats cost approximately €35 per rental.

Heading into Eastern Europe

If you are planning to take a rental car into Eastern Europe make sure to inform the company. Many rental car companies will not allow cars to be brought into Eastern Europe because of high rates of theft. Auto Europe has the largest selection of vehicles available for travel into the former Soviet Bloc, however, rates are higher than regular rentals.

Ask for a ski rack and check your chains

When you make reservations, be sure to tell the agent that you will require a ski rack and chains. Chains are usually provided free when ordered in advance, however in Austria there will be an extra charge. Ski racks cost extra (for example €35 per rental in Austria) in some countries. When you pick up the car, the ski rack will be easy to see, but you'll have to check closer for the chains. Make sure the chains provided are the correct size for the car. You are the one who will be putting the blasted things on, so you should take a great interest in making sure they are the right size. Check the number on the box carefully against the size of the tires. There is nothing more disconcerting than finding out that the chains are one size too small when you are stuck only a few hundred meters from the top of a pass.

Special airline car-rental deals

Airlines often offer reduced price cars or "free" cars with many promotions to Europe. You may be able to take advantage of them.

• You normally must travel with another person for the deal.

• Your deal is only for one week, or three days in many cases and then you begin paying the regular rates—either weekly or daily. These may be high enough to wipe out the original savings if you remain in Europe for a week or two.

• You will have to pay the insurance, taxes, gasoline and any drop-off charges in most cases.

• Ski racks and snow tires are much harder to come by with these deals.

Autobahn tolls

The superhighway systems in Italy, Spain and France are — simply put — expensive. However, the time they save is normally worth the money spent.

NOTE: In Switzerland cars must pay an annual autobahn toll to be permitted on the superhighways. If you rent a car outside of Switzerland and plan to drive on the superhighways, make sure your rental car has the appropriate up-to-date Swiss highway toll sticker before you drive on the Swiss superhighways. The police will not let transgressions go unfined. The hassles can easily ruin a vacation.

Germany has no tolls and no speed limits.

Austria charges about 75¢ per day for a toll sticker payable to the local rental car company. If your car does not have a highway sticker you may be fined if you are caught on the superhighways. You can purchase a temporary sticker good for the length of time you will be in Austria at the border.

Taking the train

There are good train transfers from Munich to Garmisch; from Zürich and Geneva to most of the Swiss resorts; from Milan to some of the Italian resorts; and from the Austrian resorts. The major problem with rail travel is the hassle of dragging equipment on and off the train, compounded by the usual need to change trains at least once on a trip to an out-of-the-way resort. The Swiss railways are the only ones with a workable luggage transportation system: baggage can be checked in at the train station at Geneva or Zürich airport and then delivered to your resort. The system works in reverse, with the luggage actually checked through to your final destination—New York, London or anywhere. Cost for the service is about SFr20 per piece of luggage.

Virtually every Swiss resort except Champéry, Cran-Montana and Flims are easily reached by train. If you plan to stay in your resort, you can be comfortable taking the train and confident that your luggage will be at your hotel when you arrive.

Four people sharing a car always save money over a train and, in many cases, two people can save money, or they will find the price difference so small that car rental is the way to go. Renting a car provides much more freedom and allows side trips in case of bad weather on the mountain.

The Eurailpass and other national train passes are not much good for a ski vacation. It is better to purchase a second-class ticket to the resort; remember, since skiing is your object, you probably will not be on the train long enough to justify buying a long-term pass.

European Skiing Basics

What should a skier expect when arriving at a European resort? Culture shock aside, there shouldn't be too many surprises, because the U.S. ski industry has been modeled to a great extent on the long-established European resorts.

In most cases you will be able to ski into the town or village where you are staying. Of course, this doesn't apply if you are staying in a city such as Innsbruck, Salzburg or Interlaken.

General snow conditions

Snow in Europe is not as dry as Utah or Colorado snow, owing to lower elevations and milder climate. Nor is it ice half the time as in New England, because of more constant temperatures.

Most of the trails are well above treeline and are only defined by grooming machine tracks and signs posted to help out in white-out conditions.

The best snowfall seems to take place in January, making both January and February good months for skiing. Plan to go in January, since February and March are also the most expensive times to ski or snowboard, except for the Christmas, New Year's and Easter holiday periods. The week before Christmas is normally a pretty good time to go, but chancy in terms of snow.

Spring skiing sees the Alps at their finest, with prices at most resorts again at low-season levels. If you want an adventure, head off-piste with an instructor for spring skiing. In his company you will learn the best times to ski different areas as the day progresses and the sun warms the snow. The secret is to get onto the run just before you begin breaking through the crust and then move to the next part of the mountain.

Insurance

Before you go, take a close look at your health insurance to be certain you are covered in case of an accident. Most policies provide worldwide coverage, some are limited in the case of skiing accidents and others group skiing accidents under the broad category of "accidental injury," which may mean that your deductible will be waived. Know what coverage you have. If you do not have enough, arrange to buy special ski insurance. Your agent should be able to point you in the right direction.

Several companies offer this insurance and surprisingly (amazing what you can find in the fine print) some credit cards include similar insurance if you purchase your airline ticket or pay for your vacation with the card. In addition, you can purchase ski insurance once you arrive at the resort. *Carte Neige* in France is easy to purchase at most resorts. Local tourist offices have details, and it is often sold with lift tickets — buy it.

Accommodations and meals

Where you sleep, live and eat constitutes the most expensive part of your stay at a European ski resort. Lodging and meals vary widely, not only with the type of hotel or restaurant but also with the season.

Use this guide to select a hotel or apartment that is near the slopes and near the center of town. Or if you want a quiet spot on the outskirts of the village we'll help to point you in the right direction.

Choosing a hotel

If you take a package tour or make your arrangements on the Web, your decisions are made long before you arrive at the resort. Most of the popular hotels used by tour packagers and available on the Internet are included in this guide; the descriptions should help.

If you arrive in a resort without reservations, plan ample time to select a hotel. This means taking about a half hour to check out what the room situation is like.

The local tourist office will steer you in the right direction and will tell you which hotels have rooms available. Ask for three or four recommendations, then check out the rooms in person. In low season—January or April—don't be pressured into taking a room you don't want; in most cases, there are plenty available.

Many times rates at hotels and pensions vary significantly even within the same categories. After choosing where you want to stay, you'll need to decide whether to take full or half board, or only breakfast (see below). Make sure to ask if any reductions are available. You may get a special rate by staying a full week or by staying through Friday night and leaving on Saturday, the day most ski weeks turn over.

Make sure that you understand exactly what the room rate includes. Are the listed prices for the room or are they per person? Are the prices with breakfast only, half pension (see below) or full pension. If you insist on getting clear information at the start, it makes your trip much more pleasant.

Staying in British-style ski chalets

Ski Chalets have recently become one of the most popular ways for British skiers to stay and ski in style, without paying whopping hotel rates. What the rest of the skiers of the world haven't yet realized is that they can use them, too.

A chalet takes the convenience and informality of an apartment and the amenities and gourmet cuisine of a hotel and lumps them all into one fantastic package. Chalets are often converted private homes or small hotels, fully catered (breakfast, afternoon tea and snack and three-course dinner with wine) and run by professional hosts who cook, clean and do the shopping. Many are ski-in/ski-out or near the slopes and even employ their own ski guides to get their guests acquainted with the mountain.

Chalets are best suited for young, sociable skiers looking for an easy way to form a group of friends to eat, ski and party with (some chalets sleep up to 35 people!). Chalet-goers should be easy-going and not too squeamish about sharing bedrooms (there is a charge for unused beds or rooms), but in return you will stay in some of the nicest accommodations around with a group of people who may challenge even your après-ski and nightlife stamina.

Staying in a chalet, you'll also be able to customize your own vacation. While the meals and service included in the basic price are first-rate, there are a number of extras for you to choose from if the basic package just isn't enough. When you book your vacation, be prepared to specify if you want vegetarian meals, premier service (with even more amenities and gourmet cuisine!), or even, packed lunches for the slopes, etc.

One thing to remember: chalets can be a great alternative for families (with discounts for children and nanny services at an extra charge); however, many of the chalets listed by various travel companies do not accept children under age 16 unless you book the entire chalet. If you are travelling with children, you will probably need to look for smaller chalets for your family or inquire about special family chalets that will cater to your needs.

Chalets are available at most major French resorts and at a few Austrian, Swiss and Italian areas as well. There are a number of tour holiday operators to call or write to for information. Be aware that most prices they will quote include one-week's lodging, food, ski guides plus round-trip airfare from London (or snowtrain from Calais), so be sure to tell the sales agent if you are not travelling from the U.K. All companies below have discounts for large groups and for children. The major tour operators are as follows (individual resort chapters list which ones provide chalets in the area):

Crystal Holidays (Internet: http://www.crystalholidays.co.uk E-mail: travel@crystalholidays.co.ukor Phone: 0870 848 7000) claims to have the largest service, with chalets in almost all resorts in Europe.

Inghams (020 8780 4433; e-mail Travel@inghams.co.uk) has an impressively long list of chalets at major ski resorts in France, Austria, Switzerland, Italy and Andorra.

Thomas Cook/Neilson (08705 141414; E-mail sales@neilson.co.uk; Web site www.neilson.co.uk) has chalets in 11 of these resorts. Or contact your travel agent.

Simply Ski (020 8742 2541; E-mail ski@simply-travel.com) and Chalet World (01952 840 462) have chalets for rent at most French resorts and a very limited number in Switzerland and Austria. First Choice (0990 557755) also has chalets in France and Austria.

Thompson (0870 606 1470) has chalets in 15 of these resorts.

We mention Ski Chalet availability in each resort, however please refer back to these pages for phone, fax and Internet connections.

Country by country

Hotels in different European countries are organized and run by different standards. These standards affect how the hotels are listed and what amenities you can expect within their various categories.

Accommodation in Italy, Spain and France is controlled by a government rating system which is too difficult to explain and often seems to make no sense. Hotels grouped within the same category with similar room rates often vary greatly. Some regulations produce confusion, such as a requirement in Italy that to be classified as first class, a hotel must have at least 40 rooms. Thus, some 36-room super-luxurious hotels with fabulous rooms and perfect service are listed as second class.

Hotels and other accommodations in the mountains are usually far cleaner and the service far superior to what you normally find in the rest of France and Italy.

Switzerland, Austria and Germany are no-nonsense countries. The hotels are clean and neat. The rating system is based on stars, with the highest rating being five stars, which means luxury class. The hotels tend to be accurately rated. In these countries it is actually hard to find a real dive.

One fact of life in the mountains during the winter season is the requirement to take at least two meals, or half pension (see below), in the hotel where you are staying. During high season this requirement is firm and some hotels may even insist on full pension. The price is well worth it in most cases. In your hotel search, however, ask several locals which hotels or pensions have the best food. This research should also enter into your decision on where to spend your week in the resort.

Season by season

For the lowest prices, the best season to stay in any resort hotel—and to eat at any restaurant—is low season. This is normally from December 1 through the weekend before Christmas, then again from the weekend after New Year's through the first weekend in February and again from the end of March through the month of April. The exact dates vary. Be sure to check to see when the low season starts and finishes.

The bargains in January are wonderful. Resorts are virtually guaranteed to have snow and facilities will not be crowded. In low season the resorts are not packed to capacity, so the kitchen and hotel staff have time to provide exceptional service. In addition, the on-site facilities, such as sauna, steamroom, pool or exercise room tend to be less crowded.

Early-season and late-season bargains are always a bit dicey in terms of finding good snow. Should anyone be making decisions on whether to visit the Alps before Christmas or after Easter, opt for a trip in the Spring. The experience is delightful and the certainty of snow is far higher than in December.

Pensions

Pensions are usually smaller, family-run affairs that cost significantly less than hotels. The pension guest in many cases feels a part of the family.

Some lodgings have a bath and toilet in the room, others have the bath and toilet down the hall or just next door. Most pensions recommended in this book have rooms available with private bath and toilet. If you do not mind a semi-private arrangement, you can request that type of room and save even more.

Many pensions, especially in the mountains, offer full restaurant service and will include all three meals in the price during the ski season. Many require that you take at least half board (see below) when staying for a week. It usually is well worth the price.

Bed & Breakfasts and Garni

Bed & Breakfast (B&B) and Garni mean the same thing. A B&B is what the name implies: room with breakfast only. Normally, you cannot take lunch or dinner there. This means heading out to discover local restaurants.

The Bed & Breakfast arrangement is often the least expensive in a mountain town, other than staying in private homes or apartments. Do not let yourself be fooled by the low price, though. Remember, you will have to pay for your meals in restaurants, which will add significantly to your costs. Although pensions and hotels may appear to cost more, when meal prices are taken into consideration, they may really be a bargain.

Garnis and Bed & Breakfasts do offer several advantages. First, you have a chance to try different restaurants and different styles of cooking during your stay. Second, you can often save money by eating less. Hotel menus include a full meal with all the trimmings and each is priced on the assumption that you eat everything on the daily menu. You may only want to eat a plate of spaghetti and be on your way. In other words, you pay only for what you eat.

"Full pension/full board" or "Half pension/half board"
That is the question

Full pension, or full board, means that your hotel will provide breakfast, lunch and dinner each day of your stay.

The meals are served at set times in most hotels and pensions. If you miss the mealtime, the establishment is not required to provide an alternative meal (but some of the better hotels will offer you a meal in a smaller grill rather than in the main dining room).

When you agree to full pension, ask whether the hotel has either a box lunch to take with you or a coupon arrangement with a restaurant on the slopes. If the hotel does not have such an arrangement, you will be required to return to the hotel for every meal, which can really cut into skiing time. (Or, simply forgo the meal even though you are paying for it.) This could be an important consideration when deciding between hotels.

Half pension means that the hotel will offer breakfast, plus one additional meal, normally dinner, every day of your stay. Often referred to as half board, this is often the best arrangement. You are free to eat what you want and where you want during the day while on the slopes. If you plan to go out on the town to dine at a special restaurant, you can arrange to have lunch at the hotel that day and be free for dinner elsewhere.

In high season many hotels require you to take full pension. But in low season you can often get the room at half pension only, or with breakfast only.

The basic meal is all that is included in the full- or half-pension price. Any wine, water, extras, changes from the menu, coffee or liqueurs are billed as extra charges.

Staying in condos, flats or chalets

An economical alternative to staying in a hotel, pension or B&B is to take a condominium, flat (apartment) or chalet. They are often scattered through the town and offer reasonably priced accommodations.

Apartments (condos) are most popular in Switzerland and France and the Italians are now beginning to get their condominium rental arrangements organized.

They come in all sizes. You can rent a studio, which is perfect for a couple, or an apartment for four, five, six or eight people. The price per person drops considerably as the size increases. These are fantastic bargains: the daily cost can be as low as €20 to €30 per person if two share an apartment.

Units are normally rented with a fully equipped kitchen, all utensils and a dishwasher. Bed linen and a clean-up are sometimes included; in other cases there are charges for them. Check also for a utility fee: it may be included, or you may pay for the electricity used at the end of the stay.

If you decide that you would like to stay in a flat or chalet, contact the resort tourist office and ask for a listing of the units that will be free when you're going to visit. The tourist office will send you a list; make your choice and return the information to the tourist office. You will usually have your confirming correspondence with the owners.

If you arrive with no arrangements, the tourist office will make several calls and send you off to see several apartments and speak with the owners.

Staying in a private home

Private homes at many resorts will rent out rooms. These rooms are normally very inexpensive, with prices ranging between those of a B&B and an apartment. If you are traveling alone, a private home is often the best bargain you can get.

Staying in a private home can give you a better feel for the local scene: you pick up hints on the best places to go on the slopes and in town and in many cases you will find yourself treated like a friend of the family.

Start at the local tourist office. It has addresses and phone numbers of the families who rent out rooms. The tourist office often will call and make arrangements. Ask to see several rooms and then make your choice. These rooms normally do not have private bath and shower. You share with the family in many cases.

In some cases, the room price includes breakfast but the arrangements vary from house to house. Expect to pay €20 to €30 a night, depending on the resort and season.

Make sure that baths or showers are included in the price; if not, ask for the price and the best time of day to take a bath or shower. (Hot water can be at a premium just after the slopes close for the day.)

Calling from Europe to the U.S.

It is easy to direct-dial from any European country to the U.S.A. The prefix for the U.S. is 001 in most countries. Then dial the area code and your local number.

Purchase a telephone card overseas. They are easy to use and charges for calls to the U.S.A. are often less than using a stateside telephone card.

Internet connections

There are scores of Internet cafes in Europe. They can be found at virtually every resort mentioned in this guidebook. Prices are amazingly inexpensive. If you are an email junky, you can rest assured that you will not have to bring your laptop along to access your messages.

Credit cards and travelers checks

Most large resorts and full-fledged hotels accept major credit cards, but don't expect the smaller pensions and hotels to accept them. The normally accepted cards are American Express, Diners Club, Visa and MasterCard (called "Eurocard" in Europe). You can leave store credit cards and Discover cards at home.

Some resorts allow skiers to pay for lift tickets with credit cards but not all. It is best to come prepared with adequate cash. In Germany, Switzerland and Austria credit cards are accepted by restaurants and hotels but not with the frequency they are taken in the U.S. In France, Italy and Spain, however, credit cards are accepted for virtually all transactions from car rentals to highway tolls to some taxi cabs.

Credit cards often have advantages you wouldn't think about. They offer toll-free numbers for assistance in finding doctors and lawyers should you need them. Most credit cards also have a buyers protection plan that may insure gifts you buy from theft and damage during your travels. And some cards will help with arrangements back home should you have an unfortunate accident. Read your fine print.

Changing money

The basic rule of changing money at a bank applies at ski resorts—even more so than in most places. Hotels and restaurants that accept travelers checks almost never give you a rate of exchange equal to the one you can get from a bank. Plan ahead and save yourself the difference. To change a small amount of money, it is often better to exchange it at your hotel, because there is no minimum exchange fee.

The most advantageous exchange rates are available when receiving a cash advance using a credit card. However, make sure the credit card does not charge an "overseas charge fee" or have an exhorbitant "cash advance fee." These fees can add up to seven percent. Normally, credit cards issued by credit unions and a handful of smaller banks do not assess cash-advance fees or overseas charge fees.

That said, you can get cash advances in local currency with a MasterCard or Visa at most banks in the Alps. In France and Spain cash machines are the most convenient means of getting Euros and often provide the best exchange rates (if you use a low-fee credit card). Plan ahead—there is a limit on daily withdrawals. Don't wait until the last day when you have to settle your bills to head to the cash machine.

Again, beware the extra charges many credit cards add for overseas charges and pay attention to your card's cash advance fee. If your card charges a two percent overseas fee, it will be no better bargain than using travelers checks or exchanging cash.

Austria

If one were to ask Americans, Canadians or Brits what they think of when they hear "Austria", chances are, they will say "skiing". Austria has marketed the concept of cozy Alpine villages and trails winding through forested mountains so well that many people imagine perpetual snow whenever they hear the name. Reality is as enchanting as the marketing images. For skiers, Austria is a wonderful mix of old-world, chalet-studded villages; lift-linked ski areas; lively mountain huts; rustic wood-paneled restaurants and exceptional nightlife and après-ski.

For Americans making their first trip to Europe and finding their way into an Austrian village, there is a sense of *déjà-vu*. When Americans and Canadians want to create the perfect ski resort, they send experts to study Austria. And when they build, they mimic Austria. Look at the town of Vail in Colorado, the Austrian-style condos throughout New England and the massive wooden chalet hotels constructed in Sun Valley. Though others may try to copy the Austrian style, the essence of Austria cannot be canned or crated and taken to a new mountain. It needs to steep in deep valleys and evolve over centuries in hidden villages.

As important as atmosphere, mountains, chalets and skiing may be, Austria has another secret ingredient. This is a country where sincere hospitality is deemed as important as great skiing. Austrians seem to go out of their way to make visitors feel at home. From the ski instructors to the hotel managers to the restaurant owners, they seem to take genuine pleasure in knowing that you have enjoyed yourself in their country. Their word for this feeling of warmth and congeniality, *Gemütlichkeit*, sums up what they strive for as hosts.

Theories abound as to why certain Austrian resorts are touted by veteran skiers as the most friendly and fun in the Alps, and the simplest probably strikes closest to the truth—the locals are comparatively unspoiled by success. The chances are better in Austria than in any other Alpine country that your ski instructor or Bed & Breakfast hostess either works on a farm in the summer, or did until recent years. Switzerland is more efficient; France is more sophisticated and Italy has a greater flair for food, but Austria is down-home friendly.

After countless visits to ski resorts around the world, every contributor to this ski guide can attest that no one knows how to have fun like the Austrians. In our après-ski sections, we outline the traditions of schnapps on the slopes, tea time after skiing and late night partying.

Although Austria is one of the skiing capitals of the world, it is very affordable; this, with the hospitality you'll encounter, will help to insure a fond memory of your trip.

Austria's Alps

The Austrian Alps have three major chains—the Northern Limestone Alps, the High Alps and the Southern Limestone Alps. The Northern Limestone Alps have many natural valleys and are home of resorts such as Lech, St. Anton, Ischgl and Kitzbühl. The High Alps are anchored by the Oetztal resorts of Sölden and Obergurgl and stretch to Innsbruck, Zell am See and Kaprun. These High Alps have few easy passes across them. Passes like the Brenner Pass and the Grossglockner are famous for their road, tunnel and bridge engineering which allows traffic to move north and south. The Southern Limestone Alps form the border with Italy and Slovenia.

The mountain elevation in Austria is lower than that found in Switzerland, France or Western Italy. But Austria gets plenty of snow since the winters get colder the further east one travels in the Alps. However, in the early winter and spring seasons, make sure to check the snow cover before planning a major skiing vacation.

Home of the Arlberg Method

Austria's name has forever been linked with the development of modern skiing. It was in the Arlberg that a unified system of skiing was devised. Previously, skiers used a form of telemarking, but Hannes Schneider based his ski technique on the snowplow which allowed skiers to maintain control in all phases of skiing.

His methods were popularized through movies, and he set up the first organized ski race, the Arlberg-Kandahar. Later Hannes Schneider would travel to the United States, after being released from Nazi prison for banking concessions, and start the first ski school in the Mt. Washington Valley, the Eastern Slope Ski School.

Driving in Austria

The Austrian highway system has a program of highway toll stickers somewhat similar to that used in Switzerland, but more flexible. Anyone driving on the Autobahn must purchase this sticker. Drivers of automobiles can purchase the toll sticker at automobile associations before arriving in Austria or at a gas station near the border. Once inside Austria, additional stickers can be purchased for periods from one week to one year at post offices, tobacco shops and most gas stations throughout the country.

Most rental car companies have decided that they will be passing along the tolls to customers renting cars in Austria. See the rental car/Autobahn toll section page 18.

When is high season?

High season: Christmas to New Year's, February through late March.

Low season: Before Christmas, January after New Year, and from late March through April closing.

For the exact high/low season weeks outside of holiday periods, check with the individual resorts. Their dates may vary because of local school holidays.

Telephone country code for Austria is 0043.

The Arlberg

Lech, Zürs, St. Anton, St. Christoph, Stuben

If you were to question a group of aficionados about the top Austrian ski destination, odds are they would say the Arlberg or mention one of the resorts in this region. This is, after all, where Austria's skiing took its first faltering steps in 1907 and where legendary ski hall-of-famer Hannes Schneider perfected the Arlberg Method which was brought to the U.S. in the 1930s.

Traditional in style yet modern in service and amenities, this region is what newer resorts in the U.S. try to emulate when they strive for the Austrian "look." Able to absorb thousands of guests at any one time, the towns of the Arlberg have determinedly retained their village atmospheres—"The only high-rise buildings are the churches," one local proudly told us—while at the same time providing a totally modern ski experience. And because so many British frequent the area, U.S. visitors will feel very much at home in this still very Austrian destination.

So dense are the skiing opportunities, the area has been broken down in the collective skiing consciousness into the various town-resorts that compose the region. St. Anton, St. Christoph and St. Jakob are normally discussed as a unit spread along the southern side of the Arlberg massif. Lech and Zürs hold down the west-facing side of the mountain and the small village of Stuben sits beside the road at the far western edge of the region where the Lech and St. Anton valleys go their separate ways.

Separated by miles of snow fields, peaks and passes, these towns are all linked by shuttlebuses, lifts and a single Arlberg ski pass to form a skiing wonderland for intermediate and expert skiers. Once remote—and inaccessible after heavy snow—the area is now only a two-and-a-half hour drive from Zürich Airport and less than two hours from Innsbruck.

Strictly speaking, St. Anton, St. Christoph and St. Jakob belong to the Austrian state of Tyrol, while Lech, Zürs and Stuben are part of Vorarlberg. Most skiers, however, skip such technicalities and simply call them the Arlberg slopes.

One of the allures of the region is that, while the individual resorts share the same snow, they all have a totally different flavor. Picking from them, you are sure to find your ideal.

St. Anton, the largest, is a bustling and fun resort, and could be considered the most egalitarian of the three with its wide range—from low cost to ritzy—of accommodations and dining. This historic ski town is dramatically different now that the main rail line has been moved and no longer separates the village from the slopes. The station is just outside the village, across the highway, next to the Tennis Center. No more waving to the Orient Express, but also no waiting for trains to pass to get to or from the lifts. New pedestrian areas are opening up and there are now more facilities for visitors, such as a public, heated outdoor swimming pool and an activity center. With "something for everyone," the town fills up, especially on weekends. Lift lines getting up to the skiing in the morning used to be long, but new lifts have cut the waiting time dramatically. And once up on the mountain, the vastness of the slopes spreads everyone out and lift lines are minimal.

The quieter, St. Anton neighborhood of **St. Jakob**, just down the valley and comprised mainly of guest houses and restaurants, is now more accessible to skiers thanks to the new Nassereinbahn gondola.

St. Christoph, the highest Arlberg village at 5,400 feet, is a smaller, more exclusive and more expensive version of St. Anton. It's a good place to get away from it all. New high speed lifts have erased the lines prevalant just a few years ago.

Only a few miles apart at the point where the Flexen Pass ends in a snow wall in winter are **Lech** and **Zürs**. Don't miss Sporthaus Strolz (Zürs) where you can buy custom-foamed boots, designer jeans, home décor and Austrian crafts all under the one roof. Offering a more exclusive feel (Princess Diana often stayed here), Lech is a full-fledged town with more nightlife and shopping than Zürs. On the shoulder of the hill and accessible only by cable car, one of its satellites—Oberlech—is called the "ski resort of the future" by the local tourist board because the only means of transportation are on foot, on skis or on the lifts. Small and contained, lift ticket sales are limited so the slopes never get too busy. Oberlech features hotels and restaurants that are connected by a series of tunnels that keep the mundane deliveries of luggage and supplies completely out of sight of the vacationer. The other, Zug, is a tiny, quaint village hidden away down a tree-lined lane and perfect for families with small children and those seeking peace after 21:00 p.m. It is not a ski-in, ski-out area except for experts. Zürs, only minutes up the valley, is a compact cluster of only 25 buildings, most of them luxury hotels. When celebrities go skiing in Austria, this is where they often stay.

Thanks to their location at the end of the valley and their exclusive air, Lech and Zürs have shorter lift lines and less crowded slopes than the St. Anton side of the Arlberg. From any hotel it's less than a few minutes' amble to the nearest lift and from there you can tour the four resorts until you find one that suits the moment's mood.

Stuben, a tiny and unpretentious village on the fringe of the Arlberg, is proportionately quieter, with more moderately priced hotels. Thanks to the Albona lift, which rises in two stages, the connection with St. Christoph/St. Anton is easy. Because of its altitude it can be colder than the other resorts, but Stuben has an advantage in the spring: Its snow is still good when the snow in Lech and Zürs is tapering off.

The Arlberg resorts may be ranked from most to least expensive: Zürs, Lech, St. Christoph, St. Anton and Stuben.

Mountain layout

The available ski area is significant. More than 50 grooming vehicles prowl the slopes included in the Arlberg ski pass, creating 163 miles of piste and leaving 112 miles of deep snow. The area is served by 85 lifts and cable cars. The main Galzig tram has been updated with a Funital lift featuring 28 mini-gondolas, each holding 24 passengers, which is triple the capacity of before.

Perhaps the resort that best characterizes the Arlberg is **St. Anton** (or Stanton, as many Americans pronounce it). In mood it's an endearing mix of Alpine rusticity and the most modern elements of international ski high life.

Throughout the Arlberg you'll encounter guest houses, shops and perhaps a *Würst* stand or two named for the Valluga, the 9,220-foot rocky pinnacle—the high point in St. Anton skiing.

It is from near the Valluga summit, reached by cablecar, that one of the great intermediate skiing cruises in Europe begins. The slope from the Vallugagrat (8,692 feet) is filled with hundreds of turns as you work your way down for at least an hour to the valley floor.

Experts can take the final section of the cable car to the top of the Valluga. After a difficult climb—accompanied by a guide only—they can ski down to Zürs.

You'll find less nerve-rattling skiing further down. We recommend the massive mogul field off the Tanzboden lift, where you'll see the best skiers bouncing from bump to bump, throwing in the occasional 360-degree turn for flair. Or take the Schindlergrat triple and choose to ski the groomed Ulmerhutte or challenge yourself on the ungroomed Schindler Kar or the Mattun. The village of **St. Christoph**, which sits along the crown of the Arlberg Pass at 5,904 feet, is the other ground station for skiing this side of St. Anton.

The blue and red runs are cruises that offer great enjoyment, and there's good skiing for beginners from the base at St. Christoph. Once served only by T-bars and a tram, St. Christoph now has quad chairs taking skiers up to the Galzig area.

The other ski area on this side of St. Anton is the Kapall, a 7,629-foot summit where you'll enjoy the two blue runs to the Gampen midstation at 6,068 feet. From Gampen continue through the trees into town, or drop over the ridge into the Steissbachtal and take the last half of the Valluga run.

When the crowds are too much or the snow turns to mashed potatoes, head to St. Anton's third ski area, the Rendl (6,888 feet). It's less crowded because the single gondola that serves these slopes is a longer walk than the cable cars to the other areas. It is also served by a good shuttlebus system.

The mountain is shaded in the morning, which means it can be icy; however, by afternoon the snow is in better shape than in the rest of St. Anton, especially in the spring. The powder lasts longer here as well and there is some steep challenging terrain especially off of the top. The best intermediate run is from the Gampberg summit (7,895 feet) back into the village. Snowboarders will want to test their skills in the fun park.

This area is also the scene for après-ski activities. Sun worshippers flock to Rendl Beach to catch the afternoon rays and sip "Absolut Dream," a Rendl Beach concoction made of peach schnapps and vodka.

Zürs and **Lech** can be easily skied together, but there is no real connection between St. Anton and Zürs and between Stuben and Zürs. However, as noted, guides take experienced skiers—experts with guts—from the Valluga down the Lech/Zürs side. To get back you have to depend on your car. The free shuttlebus from Lech to Alpe Rauz or the public bus from Lech to St. Anton costs about €3 per person one way.

Telephone prefixes: St. Anton: 05446; Stuben: 05582; Lech and Zürs: 05583

Either Lech or Zürs would qualify for resort status by itself, even if their lift passes didn't cover the entire Arlberg. In Lech skiing is centered on the Oberlech region. This section of the mountain can be easily reached by a cable car and two chair lifts from the center of the town. A system of 16 lifts takes skiers further up to 7,799 feet. This area will keep an intermediate busy for two days, and off-slope skiing will challenge experts. Opposite Oberlech is the Rüfikopf area, reached by a high-speed cable car. From here experts—real experts—can drop straight down the face to Lech, while intermediates can loop around or cruise down to Zürs.

Zürs is a bit tougher as far as marked trails go. All the runs from the top of the Trittkopf (7,985 feet) are rated intermediate, but most would rate a black diamond in U.S. resorts. Once again, experts can make their own trails straight into town. The Madloch side of the valley has six long intermediate runs and three long beginner runs. However, after the area is well skied, you can venture almost anywhere on this side.

One of the great runs of the area is known as the White Ring, a three-hour circuit that swings around both sides of the valley, connecting Lech, Zug, Oberlech and Zürs. Take the lifts to the 7,997-foot-high Madloch Joch and then ski the red (intermediate) Madloch run around the back into Lech. To complete the circle, take the cable car from the middle of town to Rüfikopf and ski down and across to the base of the Hexenboden lift and then to Zürs. For Zug, detour off the Madloch and then come back up on the Zugerberg lifts. From there, it's a red-rated (intermediate) cruise down into Oberlech.

Stuben, tiny with only a few lifts, is our favorite bargain village in the region. It's inexpensive, but a bit out of the way. The best run is intermediate—from the Albona Grat (7,872 feet). Stuben is connected with St. Anton/St. Christoph by the blue-rated trail from the Albona midstation to a crossover tow at Alpe Rauz. From there, take the chair lift to Pfannenkopf and work your way down into St. Anton.

Snowboarding: The best areas are off-piste. In Lech, there is the Snowpark/Easypark at the Schlegelkopf and St. Anton has the Fly-IN Rendl Park.

Mountain rating

Intermediates run the show in the Arlberg region. St. Anton is overwhelmingly red and blue on the ski map, with plenty of challenges that merit expert skills.

Although Lech and Zürs cover all the levels, prepared runs favor the intermediates on up. Experts will never get bored thanks to the wide-open expanses of off-trail powder that are among the best in all Europe.

Real experts can find off-piste and out of bounds places that will take their breath away. There is really something for everyone here.

Cross-Country

The St. Anton am Arlberg area has around 40 km. cross-country trails. Skating tracks can be found in **St. Jakob, St. Cristoph, Ganderau** and **Pettneu.** If there are heavy snowfalls, the skating tracks won't be laid until the day after. St. Christoph has a 2.5-km. high-altitude track for intermediate cross-country skiers and skaters. Because of its 1,800 meter altitude, it's also used as a meeting place by some alpine skiers so be prepared for a few extra bodies. **Stanzertal** has 22 km of easy scenic groomed trails for beginners. **Lech** and **Zürs** have a combined 26 km of cross-country tracks. In Lech, trails start next to the bridge near the Aparthotel Flomena.

Ski school (2007/08 prices)

St. Anton prides itself on teaching skiing to all levels and has two ski schools, Skischule Arlberg with over 300 instructors and Skischule St. Anton with 60 instructors. This is the home of the Arlberg Method, the standard for ski instruction throughout the world. The school classes form in amazing numbers each morning at the base of the Gampen. Lech and Zürs also have 300 instructors, with classes forming at the base of the Schlegelkopf lift, in Oberlech and in Zürs. Ski school prices are approximately the same throughout the region.

If you can swing it, hire a private instructor for at least a day. One contributor noted, "In less than five minutes and without having to look back at me once, my instructor pinpointed my many bad habits. We spent the rest of the day hammering them out of my system. In the process, I easily skied slopes I'd have thought twice about before. And I lost my American-bred fear of mass mogul fields after I learned the right techniques for attacking them."

Ski school prices for St. Anton/St. Christoph:

Private lessons cost €227–€303 per day, with €20 per each additional person.

Group lessons are €59 a day; €139 for three days.

Snowboarding lessons for one day are €63, lessons for three days cost €146 and a snowboard college for five days will run €198.

The **cross-country** ski school prices are the same as for Alpine lessons. Also ask about special family and senior rates.

Ski school prices for Lech/Zürs are normally within a few Euros of the prices in St. Anton.

Lift tickets (2007/08 prices)

The bargain is the Arlberg pass. These are high season rates.

High Season Rates	Adults	Senior/Youth (16-19)	Child (7–15)
one day	€41.50	€38	€25
three days	€114	€101	€68
six days	€199	€173	€119
seven days	€224	€194	€134
fourteen days	€363	€313	€218

Senior discounts are for men older than 65 and women older than 60. There is also approximately a 10 percent discount in middle season (January and April).

Accommodations

Based on high season, per person/double occupancy with half board: €€€—€125+; €€—€75–€124; €—less than €74.

St. Anton (telephone prefix 05446)

Hotel Schwarzer Adler (2244, fax 224462; €€€) Great traditional atmosphere in a four-star hotel proudly doing business since 1570. After a day on the slopes, relax in the indoor pool, spa, whirlpool and steamroom.

St. Antoner Hof (2910; fax 3551; €€€) is one of two five-star hotels in St. Anton. The hotel is away from the main downtown street, but close to the slopes and the new location of the train station.

Hotel Post (22130; fax 2343; €€€) Hardly need to leave this beautifully com-

Telephone prefixes: St. Anton: 05446; Stuben: 05582; Lech and Zürs: 05583

fortable hotel in the center of town, with a deck for lunch, a choice of nightlife in the basement and a redone health spa that offers progressive steam rooms and saunas. Very friendly and thorough service with a lovely restaurant.

Sporthotel (3111; fax 311170; €€€) In the pedestrian zone. Here you can arrange a week's lodging, dance in the nightclub and enjoy a steak in the restaurant. It also has an indoor swimming pool and sauna.

Hotel Mooserkreuz (2230; fax 3306; €€–€€€) On the edge of town. Sauna and indoor swimming pool, plus at the end of the day, you can ski back to the hotel.

Grieshof (2331; fax 202417; €€€) Located across the street from the Mössmer. This four-star hotel boasts an indoor swimming pool and friendly service.

Montjola (2302; fax 23029; €€€) A cozy lodge with excellent dining. About a five-minute walk (uphill) from the town center. The fondue capital of the Arlberg.

Hotel Fahrner (22360; fax 223622; €€–€€€) Another uphill climb from the village center, but a lovely, family-run inn with its own hand-constructed wine cellar and a traditional Austrian atmosphere.

Kertess (tel. 20050; fax 200656; €€€) This four-star establishment is located in a quiet area just a 10-minute walk from the town center. Excellent dining and quality service. Offers a shuttle bus. At the end of the day, ski right to the door. Sauna and massage available.

Hotel Pension Rendlhof (3100; fax 310050; €€€) This hotel has received rave reviews from readers. It is only minutes from the center of St. Anton and out of the range of the late-night singing as revelers stagger home.

Hotel Mössmer (2727; fax 272750; €) Off the pedestrian zone in an area that's quiet and close to the action. Ask for a room in the recently added wing and pay due homage to the Mössmers' guard dog, Tino. B&B only.

Hotel Sailer (2673; 267310; €€) Affordable, homey and a local hang-out—a favorite haunt of ski instructors after a long day on the slopes. The rooms are utilitarian, but it's a quick stroll to the lifts.

Ehrenreich (2353; fax 23538; €€–€€€). Just minutes away from the lifts but away from the crowd, this quaint lodge looks over a mountain stream and the Ferienpark.

Zur Pfeffermuhle (3740; fax 37415; €€€) Among the most expensive in the neighborhood of St. Jakob, but still affordable compared to comparable hotels just a mile up the road in St. Anton proper. This four-star hotel offers spa facities and is child friendly.

Hotel Tirolerhof (2448; fax 2915; €€) One of the larger establishments in quiet and quaint St. Jakob offering lots of activities.

Bellamonte (3137; 313720; €) and **Haus Rosa** (3252; fax 3252; €) both small and affordable B&B options. The neighborhood of St. Jakob has many.

Ski Chalets: Inghams/Bladon, Chalet World, Ski Mark Warner, First Choice. (See page 20 for phone, fax and internet addresses.)

St. Christoph (telephone prefix 05446)

Arlberg-Hospiz (2611; fax 3773; €€€) The most exclusive spot on this side of the Arlberg. The restaurant is one of Austria's best with a world-famous wine cellar. The five-star hotel has a top-notch spa with indoor swimming pool and fitness center. Newly renovated on-slope apartments with all amenities are also ideal for families; a breakfast room in the facility serves a generous buffet assortment daily.

Maiensee (2804; fax 280456; €€€) Next to lifts with all amenities.

Lech (telephone prefix 05583)

Hotels in exclusive locations shift around in terms of which one gathers the celebrities and which one slips a bit in the gossip sheets.

The top hotel in Lech these days is the **Hotel Arlberg** (21340; fax 2134–25; €€€) which is conveniently located and oozing old elegance. This five-star hotel was where Princess Diana used to stay. The lobby recreates an old hunting lodge and log fires crackle in front of overstuffed couches and chairs.

Gasthof Post (22060; €€€) A Relais & Chateaux five-star hotel which attracts a slightly older upscale crowd and is beautiful and cozy. Once actually the post office in Lech, this hotel still has its stuccoed-and-painted facade and is filled with antiques. It is worth a visit, if only to soak up the old-money atmosphere, to at least stop in and have a drink at the bar.

Goldener Berg (22050; 250513) This four-star sport hotel in Oberlech features a Kiddy Club with activities for children from ages three and up. The service is free. The hotel is known for its gourmet cuisine and famous wine cellar. A new spa offers such niceties as a swimming pool, steam bath, Finnish sauna and organic sauna. A mud pack treatment features local ingredients.

Angela (2407; fax 240715; €€€) is beautifully appointed and ideally positioned—a real ski-in/ski-out spot with plenty of solitude in Lech. Supervised children's program in the afternoons and evenings.

Burg Hotel (22910; fax. 229112; €€€) Top quality with sauna, whirlpool and tennis. It is only steps from the cable-car station and is a center of après-ski action.

Krone (2551; fax 255281; €€€) An European Romantic Hotel with every modern amenity and with an award-winning restaurant; its sauna and pool overlook the ski slopes. It still looks much the way it did 100 years ago. The rugged chalet building is set between the church and the river.

Kristiania (2561; fax 3550; €€€) A bit out of the mainstream but nice, this hotel is owned by the 1952 Olympian Othmar Schneider. The hotel is a member of the Small Luxury Hotels of the World. The family's private art collection appears throughout the hotel and greatly adds to the ambience.

Sonnenburg (2147; €€€) in Oberlech, is made up of twin chalets with the traditional wood/stucco facade. The terrace overlooking Lech below is a hot spot for tea-time après-ski. There is childcare for children younger than age four.

Haldenhof (24440; fax. 2444-21; €€–€€€) A friendly, family-owned and family-run hotel—the perfect Austrian inn with delicious traditional cuisine.

Alpensport Hotel Lech (22890, fax 2727; €€) and **Pension Chesa Rosa** (22890; fax 2727; €€€) are two of the more popular guest houses.

Kristall (2422; fax 24223; €€€) is behind the church; an ideal location for beginning skiers. Friendly service.

Pension Sursilva (2970; fax 31760; €€€) Good value and modern facilities.

Just outside Lech, in Zug, **Gasthof Rote Wand** (3435 ; fax 343540; €€€) has a traditional atmosphere with a heavy wood interior and many antiques. It has an indoor pool, health club, sauna and so on. There's also a children's playroom and babysitting service.

The tiny **Gasthof Alpenblick** (2755, fax 27668; €) is a real family bargain in Zug, near the Rote Wand and the special family area.

For less expensive lodging in Lech near the lifts try **Alpenland** (2351, fax 23515; €€), **Arabell** (2181, fax 218192; €€), **Acerina** (3320, fax 332040; €€), **Bianca** (2829, fax 282915; €€), **Odo** (2358, fax 394315; €€), **Montfort** (2478, fax 247825; €€+), **Sursilva** (29700, fax 297022; €€) and **Grissemann** (2221, 222116; €€).

In Oberlech check out **Astoria** (2979, fax 297929; €–€€); **Michaela** (2617, fax 3015; €€-), **Berger** (2839, fax 29397; B&B only, €).

Telephone prefixes: St. Anton: 05446; Stuben: 05582;
Lech and Zürs: 05583

Ski Chalets: Inghams, Total, Thompson, Simply Ski. (See page 18 for phone, fax and internet addresses.)

Zürs (telephone prefix 05583)

The top spot here is:

Zürserhof (2513; fax 3165; €€€) This is one of the most luxurious hotels in the Alps, in a class with the Palace in St. Moritz. This is the hotel that made the tiny village famous. It is a series of five chalets joined together and filled with the ultimate in Tyrolean luxury. Wood paneling surrounds you and oriental carpets cover the floors.

The four-star **Albona Nova** (2341; fax 234112; €€€) is tucked round the back, away from the road and right by a lift. This charming and splendid hotel has carved-wood ceilings and an intimate appeal. German-speaking critics have called it "Klein und fein." That translates to small and fine. The restaurant is fabulous.

Arlberghaus (2258; fax 225855; €€€) and the **Schweizerhaus** (2463; fax 42128; €€) are some of the less expensive (Bed & Breakfast or Half Board only).

Stuben (telephone prefix 05582)

Post Hotel (761; fax 7626; €€) A good choice for uncomplicated skiing with on-site ski rental, ski school and a bank.

Haus Erzberg (tel. 520; fax 7294; €) Small hotel (13 beds), B&B only.

Hotel Mondschein (tel. 511; fax 736; €€€) Excellent hotel in historic 1739 building. Indoor pool, friendly atmosphere.

Apartments, condominiums, flats

If you want to rent a vacation apartment, ask for the apartment listing brochure from each of the tourist offices in the Arlberg. They maintain a complete list of hundreds of apartments and chalets available in season.

In Lech, apartments can be rented with four beds for about €150 a day, high season. In St. Anton, a four-bed apartment can be rented for about €160 a day. These prices are about average.

Dining—St. Anton and St. Christoph

Here, appropriately so, most of the best restaurants are up on the mountain. Heading the list is the **Galzig Verwall-Stube** (2352501, fax 2352502) where sitting at what seems like the top of the world you can dine on lobster ravioli, baked monkfish, saltimbocca, nutty spinach leaves and finish with fresh fruit sorbets. The daily menu ranges from €30–€110. Watch your choice and you can have some of the world's best cooking in a spectacular setting for very affordable prices.

The other great dining experiences on the mountain are in St. Christoph. The **Arlberg Hospiz Ski-Club Stube** (2611, fax 3773) is a bit more luxurious than its sister restaurant the **Hospiz-Alm** (3625, fax 362510). Both establishments are owned by the same family. At the Ski-Club Stube the lunch menu is not as sumptuous as the dinner menu. Try the veal filet with vegetable canneloni and have the orange pancakes with homemade toppings for desert. At the Hospiz-Alm the lederhosen-clad waitstaff sets the tone. Feast on pickled salmon terrine, then sip the lobster cream soup, move on to the lamb and finish with chocolate mousse. The fixed menus normally are €32–€60.

Down in the village of St. Anton, the best restaurant is in the only five-star hotel in the town. The St. Antonerhof's rustic **Rafflstube** (2910, fax 3551) is top of the line, but not at the top of the mountain.

The king of fondue lives at the **Hotel Montjola** (2302), ten minutes above town.

Step through a painted door and enjoy any of eight different fondues in cozy, low-ceiling rooms. They also serve normal fare in monster portions. Their "Giant Wiener Schnitzle" lives up to its name.

The **Alte Post** (25530) has fine local cooking served in a 17th century setting.

Museum (2475), upstairs above the Ski and Folk Museum, has three rooms where gourmet Austrian meals are served. One room is the original room of a 90-year-old mansion and it has a huge marble fireplace with oak paneling from the Czech Republic. Meals will cost €25–€35.

For a romantic evening head out to the **Verwall** (3249) for Tyrolean specialties by candlelight. Make reservations and call a taxi or take a horse-drawn sled and bring along some schnapps. The food is good but the experience is better. This is also a favorite stop for cross-country skiers during the day.

Another very traditional place to have Austrian fare is the **Sailer** (2673) where you can fill up with the locals without breaking the bank. **Schindler** (2207) has a motto, "Simple, yet exquisite." Locals and Michelin report that the food here is the real traditional stuff such as salbeileber and apfelschmarrn. **The Schwarzer Adler** (2244) sets a table that brims with Austrian specialties. Prices start at €12.

Reasonably priced meals are always on the menu at the **Aquila Café** (2217), **Testarossa** (29685) and **Grieswirt** (2965). The fondue, pigs knuckles and chicken wings at the **Robis Rodelstall** (0699-10858855) are good and affordable. It is at the bottom of the lighted toboggan run and has tables around a big open fireplace. At the top of the toboggan run, go to the **Rodelalm** and have local specialties before beginning your two-km., eight-minute toboggan ride down the floodlit track.

Hazienda (2968) serves excellent steaks and seafood.

Don't leave St. Anton without a pizza from the **Pomodoro** (3333) if only to say you had one. It's cheap and friendly, and you may see your ski instructor there. But we would spend our pizza and pasta money at **San Antonio** (3474).

The **Funky Chicken** has the cheapest eats in town—hard to miss as you come down off the slopes. It's open to 2 a.m. and has take out. There are couches in front of the fireplace. It is a great place to people-watch over a margarita or a beer. Half a chicken sets you back less than €4.50.

For breakfast, head to **Häferl** for the best pastries and cakes in town. **Aquila** also has good pastries and coffee.

Lech and Zürs dining

In Lech, many restaurants have instituted a children's menu with a fixed price of €10 or so. For good food try the restaurants in **Hotel Montana** (2460), which has the best wine cellar in town. The **Arlberg** (21340) is highly recommended with an Austrian influenced gourmet menu. **Hotel Salome** (23060) gets good recommendations. **Hotel Krone** (2551) is a shrine of local cooking with exceptional use of local ingredients.

For nouvelle Austrian cuisine, try the **Goldener Berg** (22050), also known for its romantic fondue; or **Brunnenhof** (2349). The **Hotel Post** (22060) and the **Almhof Schneider** (3155) serve traditional recipes. **Hûs Nr. 8** (3322), an intimate restaurant offering Austrian fare at a median price, is in a cute old house with low doorways.

Restaurant Italiener (3734) has the best, inexpensive Italian in town with a fabulous antipasta buffet. Plus, its bar downstairs is quite a scene after 10 p.m. For those with a sweet tooth, head to the **Olympia Café** (2311) at the base of the tram to Oberlech for some real Austrian apple strudel or "Kaiserschmarrn"—don't ask, just order it.

Fux (2992) not only has the town's hot bar, it has an excellent restaurant with heavy Asian influences. Try chicken satay, miso soup, sushi, tempura and dim sum.

Telephone prefixes: St. Anton: 05446; Stuben: 05582; Lech and Zürs: 05583

Just outside Lech, in Zug (normally reached by a sleigh ride from Lech), the **Gasthof Hotel Rote Wand** (3435) offers excellent food in the best of Austrian tradition. Its specialty is an excellent fondue bourguignon with dozens of different dipping sauces, starting with soup and finishing with strudel. **Restaurant Klösterle** (3190), in a small, former monastery, is expensive but worth it with fondue specialties in an historic setting. **Gasthaus Alphorn** (2750) also has excellent meals.

For cheaper eats, try **Pizza Charly** (2339) for good Italian food and head up to **Gasthof Omesberg** (2212) for great traditional Austrian fare.

In Zürs, **Albona Nova** (2341, fax 234112) has been recognized by the top critics in Europe and has a serious following. Make reservations. Try the wild duck with polenta, the goose liver ravioli, the lamb with eggplant. Between courses, clear your taste buds with cocoa sorbet. Then finish with spectacular cheeses or a soft creme brûlée.

The **Edelweiss** (2662, fax 3533) is another phenomenal dining experience with its a la carte Chesa restaurant, a Gault Millaut rated spot. Start with a tomato mousse with carparccio, move to the roast lamb with ratatouille and risotto and finish with a tart chocolate drizzled over mangos and papayas.

You can depend on great meals in the **Zürserhof** (2516). Also, try **Hirlanda** (2262), for excellent meals. The **Flexenhüsle** (4143) has enjoyable fondue nights.

Mountain restaurants

On the mountain, of course, you can ski over to the Galzig or the two gourmet spots in St. Christoph. But, heck, even food lovers need to take a break from big meals and the gourmet stuff.

In that case head to **Griabli** (3673) for a fun lunch on the mountain in real Austrian style. **Gampen** (2352532) has a good self-service with a nice terrace.

In Stuben, try the **Restaurant Berghaus**, right near the base of the lift, with German specialties and pizza.

In Lech many of the Oberlech restaurants can be considered "on-mountain." And in Zürs, every restaurant is on the moutain. But otherwise, head to the **Rüfikopf Panorama Restaurant** for good eating and a great view.

 # Après-ski/nightlife

St. Anton and St. Christoph

In St. Anton's pedestrian zone, you'll be able to find something that suits your night tastes by simply taking a stroll. There are dozens of small bars and gasthofs. Drinking tends toward beer and schnapps. Anywhere you go, expect to pay between €4.50 and €7.70 for a drink and a coat check fee of about €1.50.

At the **Mooserwirt**, happy hour (or tea-time) has skiers bouncing off the walls and the outside terrace. It's tough to reach on foot; partyers who can't stand on their own two skis have been known to take the tops of the picnic tables and sled back into town.

Stop by the **Krazy Kanguruh**, with its reputation as one of the region's two wildest watering holes. We can't praise it wholeheartedly: It's wild, but away from the center of town and Bo don't know crowded till he gets there. Buy a "bullet" from a scantily-clad waitress, which she will pour down your throat to the cheers of onlookers.

Closer to town and somewhat more sedate are the hangouts at the **Alte Post Hotel** and the **Hotel Post**. On the Alte Post's outside terrace, you can sip Glühwein and watch the last of the sun's rays climb up the peaks, or you can sweat it out in the Hotel Post's two basement bars. Both feature live music, but one attracts the heavy drinking, heavy smoking, young crowd, while in the other a slightly older group disco and polka their ski kinks away.

Check out the traditional and cozy **Sennhütte** with live music. Try a Little Willy, a ski pole filled with Williams schnapps. Don't think this place is quiet and peaceful, it can get crazy at tea-time. The **Hotel Anton** opposite the Galzigbahn is getting pretty trendy and is a place to see and be seen. If you are looking for a place where you can gaze longingly into your spouse's eyes, head into one of the hotel bars. They tend to be much quieter. You'll also find it at **Jacksy's**, and the **Alibi**, a small, offbeat bar with the enticing sign, "Men—No Shirt, No Service, Women—No Shirt, Free Drinks!"

Late night discos and karaoke bars are everywhere—try your best off-slope maneuvers in the **Picadilly** or the **Hazienda**.

Après-ski/nightlife—Lech and Zürs

In Lech, après-ski begins on the slopes in Oberlech and often includes champagne as the drink of choice, especially at **Hotel Montana**. You'll find fun and friendly tea-time crowds of all ages at **Hotel Burg** and **Hotel Sonnenburg**, both located thankfully close to the tram.

Once down in Lech, choose wild and crazy at the **Tannbergerhof**—be prepared to dance in your ski boots outside at the ice bar to oompah music—or more sedate (relatively speaking) at the **s'Pfefferkörndl**, which gets going later in the evening.

After dinner, head to the jazz café and night club with the unfortunate name (in English anyway), **Fux,** right on the river. It has become quite the "cool" spot. The avant-garde wooden architecture is a real contrast to conservative Lech. It has two different bars all beating to disco and an excellent cigar bar.

A more chic after-hours address is the Hotel Krone where there is the **Side Step** disco and a local crowd. Disco action pulses at the **Scotch Club** in the Hotel Arlberg and zither music is played Sundays in the **Gasthof Post** that is much quieter, and fun.

Zürs has the **Zurserl** disco in the **Hotel Edelweiss**. The insider spot is **Vernissage**. The **piano bar** in the Hotel Thurnhers Alpenhof is pleasant and **Ambiente** fills up for tea time and après-ski in the Sporthotel Zürsersee.

Child care (2007/08 prices)

Ski courses for kids from age 5 (special courses for kids from age 3–5) are offered, as are a ski kindergarten, and babysitting services (from 2 1/2 upward). Supervised lunch is €14 a day.

Kindergartens, for children 2 1/2 and older, are available in all the resorts. In St. Anton you'll pay €59 a day and €224 for six days including lunch. Prices in Lech and Oberlech are about €50 a day and €145 for six days. Lunch is about €8 per day extra. Open from 9:30 a.m.–4 p.m. Babysitting on a weekly, daily or hourly basis can be arranged through the tourist office.

In Lech, hotels Austria, Goldener Berg, Rote Wand and Sonnenburg all have private kindergartens.

These are the ski school rates. The ski school does not include lunch but lunch can be arranged and your child can be supervised for lunch. There are reductions if parents are also enrolled in the ski school. Hours are 9 a.m. – 4 p.m

Ski school rates	St. Anton	Lech/Zürs
one day	€73	€52
three days	€181	€110.50
six days	€301	€166

Telephone prefixes: St. Anton: 05446; Stuben: 05582; Lech and Zürs: 05583

Other activities

In addition to downhill skiing, there's **toboganning, cross-country skiing, snowboarding, paragliding, walking** and **skating. Heliskiing** is available in Lech and Zürs. On Tuesday and Thursday the cable car takes rodelers (**tobogganers**) to Gampen.

An adventure for those from the modest U.S. is to partake of the glorious **spas** in the more luxurious hotels. While hot tubs, steam rooms and saunas are a civilized way to end a ski day and sooth tired muscles, Americans need to be forewarned that Europeans enjoy these in the altogether. Nobody minds if you wear a bathing suit or cover yourself modestly with a towel, but you will be the one who stands out in the crowd.

St. Anton (2380) and Lech offer **horse-drawn sleigh rides** through the forest. The price for up to five people is around €70 for about an hour. Other activities include **swimming, tennis** and **sightseeing. Shopping** in the resorts includes authentic Austrian garb, designer wear in Lech, but is limited to ski wear and souvenirs elsewhere.

 ## Getting there

You'll probably fly into Zürich, although the trip can be just as easy from Munich or Innsbruck.

Driving from Zürich, take the autobahn to St. Gallen, then to Feldkirch and the Arlberg Pass. Tunnel toll each way is €8.50. From Munich and Stuttgart, it is easiest to drive to Bregenz, then to Feldkirch and the Arlberg. From Zürich, it's a little over two hours by car, or take the train to St. Anton am Arlberg or Langen am Arlberg.

Lech and Zürs lie further up the Flexen Pass. Get off the train in Langen and take a bus up the hill, or get off the train in St. Anton and take a different bus.

Direct trains connect Langen with Cologne, Dortmund, Munich, Innsbruck, Salzburg, Zürich, Paris, Brussels and Calais. The Orient Express (800-237-1236) also makes a stop in St. Anton during the off-season (beginning in late March).

More convenient than the train is direct ski bus service from Zürich Airport to all the Arlberg resorts that runs on Fridays, Saturdays and Sundays. On Fridays, departure is at 12:30 p.m.and 6:30 p.m. On Saturdays, buses leave at 10 a.m., 12:30 p.m. and 3:30 p.m. On Sundays, two buses leave at 12:30 p.m. and 6:30 p.m. Fares are about €45 one way and €75 round trip. The bus trip takes about three hours and at times can be quicker than driving since the bus drivers know how to avoid the weekend traffic jams. Make reservations through Arlberg Express (05582-226, fax 05582-580).

There is a bus connecting the Munich airport with St. Anton. Call Four Seasons Travel at 0512-584157. Local taxi companies will also pick up at the airport: Taxi Harry (2315), Taxi Lami (2806) or Arlberg Car (3730).

 ## Tourist information

St. Anton: Tourismusverband, A-6580 St. Anton am Arlberg; Telephone 05446-22690, fax 2532.
Internet: www.stantonamarlberg.com.
E-mail: info@stantonamarlberg.com

Stuben: Verkehrsverein, A-6762 Stuben; 05582-399, fax 3994.
Internet: www.stuben.com. E-mail: info@stuben.at
Lech and Zürs: Tourist Office, A-6764 Lech; 05583-2161, fax 3155.
Internet: www.lech-zuers.at. Email: info@lech-zuers.at
Zürs: Zürs Tourist Office, A-6763 Zürs; 05583-2245, fax 2982.

Bad Gastein

Skiing may be the number one pastime in the Gasteiner valley, but the area's popularity as a meeting place for European vacationers keeps it lively the year round. Austrians from all parts of the country head up the valley in winter. The area is a group of four ski systems: Bad Gastein, Sportgastein, Bad Hofgastein and Dorfgastein.

If you are looking for ski-in/ski-out, this is not the place to come. You will have to do plenty of klomping around in your ski boots. This town perched on the side of the mountain was not designed for skiing. The town has set up good storage facilities to allow skiers to keep equipment near the slope, but that also limits your skiing since you always have to return to the point where you started. An excellent system of shuttlebuses helps move skiers between the different resort towns.

Bad Gastein first gained fame as a thermal spa. It is still Austria's top spa and one of the best-known in Europe. The therapy is based on submersion in radon-laced water. A curious hot spring-fed pool has been carved into rock for this therapy. Another form of the treatment takes place in the nearby town of Heilstollen. Here small trains carry those seeking the cure deep into abandoned mines where different chambers with high radon content and differing temperatures above 100 degrees Fahrenheit are visited according to doctor's orders.

Because of the spas, the resort attracted the upper crust of society and a rather etiquette-conscious clientele. The formality that developed over the years, especially in the grand hotels—many of which still have private thermal pools—continues today. The winter coat of preference will probably be fur, and the lineup of shiny automobiles in front of the casino often makes it look like a Mercedes or BMW showroom. Although spa visitors still cling to protocol, the modern skiing tourist has softened the stiff rules of decorum. This is a town where you can live elegantly, complete with black tie, or casually, never changing from your ski jacket.

 ## Mountain layout

The best skiing is from the top station on the Stubnerkogel at 7,373 feet, where an exceptional intermediate run stretches nearly seven miles. This run, the Angertal, drops 4,264 feet. From the ground there is a lift connection to the Schlossalm area above Bad Hofgastein.

There's a challenging World Cup run from the sides of the Graukogel opposite the Stubner. The lift takes you up to 6,556 feet, and the black run takes you down. (A side trail accommodates intermediates).

For 80 km. of cruising trails, head up to the Skischaukel Dorfgastein-Großarl area. Take the cable car to the Fulseck and ski down to Großarl and back down again to Dorfgastein.

Also try Sport Gastein, about six miles away and easily accessible by bus. The best of the runs is from the top of the Kreuzkogel. The eight-seater Goldberg-Bahn gondola takes you to the top in 14 minutes. At the top, a choice of four different trails awaits you. The best of them is the north trail, which is left unprepared and provides great powder skiing, given the right conditions. The nearly five-mile run covers a vertical drop of almost 4,950 feet.

Snowboarders tend to congregate in Dorfgastein-Großarl with its excellent snowpark that has a bordercross course though there are snowparks in other areas.

This is not a good resort for beginners. Movement is not convenient with the beginner slopes a bus ride away. After the easy trails, the step up in difficulty is daunting.

Mountain rating

The valley, particularly Bad Gastein, is intermediate country, with the most notable exception being the World Cup course. It is a good place to tune up one's ski legs, leaving some spring in them for partying later. Solid experts will enjoy about a dozen black runs, but once finished with them, they'll be ready to move on. Experts should check out an off-trail group or a guide for a morning. Both will offer little-known runs down unprepared sections of the resort, and these should provide most of the challenge.

Cross-Country and snowshoeing

There are over 90km of prepared cross-country tracks in the Gastein area. Cross country skiing is guaranteed until spring in Sport Gastein on a snow secure high trail system 1,600 metres above sea level. Night Owls can take advantage of the floodlit track in Bad Gastein (Böckstein District).

Snowshoeing

Bad Gastein: Choose the time of the walk that suits you when registering. Prices depend on the size of the group participating. Register with the Cross Country Skiing School Böckstein (0664-4571250).

Bad Hofgastein: Snowshoers meet every Tuesday from 1-4 p.m., in the Ski Centre Angertal (between Bad Gastein and Bad Hofgastein) directly in the Ski School Office. Contribution towards the cost of the equipment is €4.00. Advance registration is available at the Spa and Tourist Office in Bad Hofgastein (6432-3393260).

Dorfgastein: Tours run every Tuesday 1– 4 p.m. Equipment and guide cost €5 with guest card. Register at the Tourism office Dorfgastein (6433-20048).

Lift tickets (2007/08 prices)

The Ski Amadé lift ticket cover this valley's main regions. Each town in the region offers single-day limited-lift tickets. But this lift ticket does more. It also allows skiing in a phenomenal region. The resorts are not connected, nor are they really all that close, but your lift ticket is good wherever you go in these areas. Daily rates are for individual sectors.

Here are the additional regions and the towns where the lifts are included in the ski pass: Salzburger Sportwelt (Flachau-Wagrain-St. Johann/Alpendorf, Zauchensee-

Flachauwinkel-Kleinarl, Radstadt-Altenmarkt, Eben, Filzmoos, Goldegg), Dachstein-Tauern-Region (Schladming-Planai, Rohrmoos-Hochwurzen, Ramsau am Dachstein, Haus im Ennstal, Pichl-Reiteralm, Forstau-Fageralm, Gröbming-Stoderzinken, Pruggern-Galsterbergalm) plus, Hochkönigs Winterreich und das Großarltal.

The lift rates are based on main season, mid season and pre- and post-season.Main season is 12/22/07 - 01/ 11/ 08 and 01/26/08 - 03/28/08. Mid season is 01/12/08-01/25/08. Pre- and post-season is from resort opening to 12/21/07 and from 03/29/08 until the resort closes. Special family rates are also available.

Main season	Adult	Youth (16–18)	Child (15 and younger)
Two days	€74	€62	€38.50
Six days	€182	€153	€94.50
Fourteen days	€315	€264.50	€164

Photo ID is required for youths and children. Youth are those born 1989 to 1991; children are those born 1992 to 2001. Children born before 2002 ski free (only in the attendance of an adult - specific local and regional regulations may apply).

Photos are also required for any ski pass for 8 days or longer. Photo machines at all cashpoints. Existing photos may not be used.

A €3 keycard is required. The deposit is refunded when you return the keycard.

Ski school (2007/08 prices)

Three area ski schools have a total of 130 instructors. The Snow Sport School Gastein has locations in Dorfgastein (06433-7538), in Bad Hofgastein (6432-6339) and in Bad Gastein (6434-2260). The Ski and Snowboarding School Dorf-Aktiv (6433-20048) is in Dorfgastein. The Ski School Schlossalm (6432-3298) is in Bad Hofgastein.

These prices are for ski and snowboard lessons at Ski- und Snowboardschule DORFAKTIV. They are comparable to the prices of the other ski schools in the Gastein Valley. One hour of private lessons for one person is €45; for two people, €55; for three people, €65; and for four people, €75. Group lessons cost: one day, €53; three days, €130; and five days, €150.

Accommodations

Choose from a great selection of hotels in Bad Gastein and Bad Hofgastein. There is less variety in Dorfgastein nearer the entrance to the valley. Of the three, Bad Gastein probably offers the most European ski atmosphere, including a healthy helping of nightlife.

Based on high season, per person/double occupancy, with half board: €€€—more than €125+; €€—€75-€124; €—less than €75.

Arcotel Elisabethpark (25510, fax 255110 ; €€€) has plenty of amenities, but not much Austrian flavor. **Hoteldorf Grüner Baum** (tel./fax 25160; €€€) was once the Archduke's hunting lodge. It is set five km. outside of town and is one of the great Austrian hotels. **Kurhotel Salzburgerhof** (6230, fax 623070; €€€) comes highly recommended by Americans and British alike. **Hotel Wildbad** (37610, fax 376170 ; €€–€€€) has a spa and is located in the center of town.

These hotels are all convenient to the lifts: **Bärenhof** (3366; €€), **Hotel Eden** (2076; €€), **Pension Gabriele** (4411) and **Kur- und Sportpension Kerschbaumer** (2433, fax 243319; €€). **Chalet Wetzlgut** (2065, fax 206570 ; €€) is an apartment group right under the lift. **Haus Elfi** (4662, fax 46622; €) is a B&B right at the base of the Stubnerkogelbahn.

Telephone prefix: Bad Gastein, 06434;
for Bad Hofgastein, 06432; Dorfgastein. 06433

Bad Hofgastein

Try the **Hotel Alpina** (06432-8475, fax 06432-847570; €€€), **Hotel Oster-reichischer Hof** (06432-6216, fax 06432-621651; €€+) with a country manor atmosphere, and **Hotel St. Georg** (61000, fax 610061; €€€).

Good and less expensive hotels are **Kurpark Hotel** (6301; €€), **Bayrischer Hof** (86460; €€), **Hotel Austria** (6223; €€), and **Berglift** (6219, fax 85044; €).

B&Bs with excellent locations are **Pension Angerer** (tel./fax2020; €), **Gstrein** (6485, fax 648527; €), **Haus Lenk** (6740; €) and **Haus Regina** (3130, fax 3129; €).

Apartments, condominiums, flats

Details on chalet and apartment rentals are available through the tourist offices in any of the resorts. Write or fax to the office with the dates of your vacation and they will send you back several apartments from which to choose.

Dining

Gault Millau recommends some of Bad Gastein's top restaurants. The **Hoteldorf Grüner Baum** (25160), virtually a private village tucked in a nearby side valley, serves excellent Austrian mainstays amidst wonderful scenery. **Hotel Rader** has fine dining.

The **Bellevue Alm** has good fondue. For a traditional, inexpensive Austrian meal, try the **Orania Stuben**. **Mozartstude** and the restaurant in Hotel Nussdorferhof are both recommended.

The top eatery in the region by some accounts is **Römerhof** (7777) in Dorfgastein. Here try a roast with asparagus and spring onions or test the au gratin potatoes.

Après-ski/nightlife

For aprés-ski the elite choose the tables at the **Casino** in Bad Gastein or retire immediately to the bar near the playing tables. **Zentrale, Gatz. -Silverbullet** and **Haeggbloms** are packed after skiing. Beyond 11 p.m. the evening grows progressively wilder at the **Ritz** in the Salzburger Hof, the **Central Park** and **Kir Royal** in Bad Gastein. **Gatz** and **Hägblom's** are also very popular after skiing. The **Glocknerkeller** in Bad Hofgastein is a typical Austrian pub with music and dancing each night. Other hot spots are **Salute** and **Disco Almstadl**.

Child care (2007/08 prices)

Child care is offered for children three years and older in Bad Gastein (06434-2260) and Bad Hofgastein (06432-6339). The The Snow Sport School Gastein offers ski school lessons as well as a newly created 8,000-meter Kids' Park in the Angertal.

In Dorfgastein, children age 3 and older who are guests of a Pongi hotel can join the Pongi Children's Club. Children who do not stay in hotels and guesthouses which are affiliated with the Pongi Club must pay a membership fee. Individual babysitting service is also offered. Get more information through the tourist office.

The Pongi Club member card also gives you a 10% discount on Bambini course at the Ski- und Snowboardschule DORF-AKTIV (0664/2029793). The ski school provides lessons and child care from 9:30 a.m. to 3:30 p.m. for children ages 3 and older. Prices for children ages 3-4 (without the Pongi card) are €40 for a half day; €100 for three half days; €25 for a test day; €160 for three days; and €200 for five days. Please note that these prices include the cost of care, lunch and beverage unless otherwise noted.

Other activities

The three towns have a great variety of outdoor recreation. A day trip to Salzburg with a tour down the **salt mines** is one of the preferred outings. Bad Gastein and Bad Hofgastein are famed thermal spring resorts. Take time to enjoy the **hot springs** during your visit.

For non-skiers, the view from the Schlossalm at 7,000 feet is worth the ride up from Bad Hofgastein. In Bad Gastein, visit the Nikolauskirche built in the 15th century. This church, now not in use, has an unusual star-shaped vaulted nave, several interesting murals and is built around a central pillar.

In Bad Hofgastein the Gothic church with its high vaulted ceiling is worth a visit. Dorfgastein also has an interesting parish church dating back to the 14th century.

Getting there

The best international airport connections are through Salzburg or Munich. The best way to get to the resorts is by car, driving south, along the magnificent Tauernautobahn to Bischofshofen and on to the Gastein valley. Expect about an hour's drive. Train connections from Europe are also excellent. Once there, you will need a car to get the most of the experience.

Tourist information

Kur- und Tourismusverband, Kaiser-Franz-Josef-Strasse 27, A-5640 Bad Gastein; 06432-3393537; fax 06432-3393537.
E-mail: info@badgastein.at. Internet: www.badgastein.at.
Kurverwaltung, A-5630 Bad Hofgastein; 06432-3393-260, fax 06432-3393232. Email: info@badhofgastein.com
Internet: www.badhofgastein.com
Tourismusverband, A-5632 Dorfgastein; 06432-3393460, fax 06432-3393437.
Email: info@dorfgastein.com. Internet: www.dorfgastein.com

Telephone prefix: Bad Gastein, 06434; for Bad Hofgastein, 06432; Dorfgastein. 06433

Innsbruck

Innsbruck, sometimes known as "The Capital of the Alps", has twice hosted the Winter Olympic Games (1964 and 1976). However, Innsbruck, capital of the Austrian Tyrol, is no quaint ski village. This city of more than 130,000 residents in the valley of the emerald-green Inn River has such a collection of cultural attractions that skiing is not the dominant factor. Innsbruck just happens to be surrounded by a group of resorts with excellent skiing and it has linked its ski package offerings with two of the most famous resorts in Austria—St. Anton and Kitzbühel.

For centuries, Innsbruck has been a crossroads of civilizations. The bridge from which the city gets its name has linked the north and south of Europe since the time of the Romans, who regularly used the Brenner Pass. New rail links made Innsbruck a major junction on the east-west rail links between the Alps and central Europe. And the silver mines made this a rich and busy commercial center.

In the ancient days, this was the center of the Holy Roman Empire, which ruled over most of Europe, from Italy to the Pyrenees and to the English Channel. When you look at a city map it is easy to see where the old castle walls once stood. Colorfully restored buildings give the town center a cheerful yet medieval feel. Old inn and shop signs still hang, arcades still shelter travelers from the storms, traditional restaurants still serve patrons today as they did in Mozart's day and merchants (all be they modern) still line the cobblestone streets.

Innsbruck is a great place to try out a lot of Austria's skiing to get an idea of where to spend more time next season.

With a major university and lots of cultural history—castles, cathedrals, palaces and the like—Innsbruck has many sightseeing opportunities as well. It also has a great deal of beauty and charm, with the Inn River flowing through the city and good walking areas in the old city center, up and down the river banks and parks. There is a good tram and bus system up to Igls, to the Hungerburgbahn and to the winter hiking trails.

Those looking for the best restaurants and cafes will not be disappointed. Those looking for rollicking good all-night dancing and drinking can find it here. The city is also a good family environment, with lots of affordable restaurants and activities for kids like the zoo, gondolas and trains going up into the mountains.

Igls, (a part of Innsbruck) a small village on the south side of the Inn Valley, is only a 20-minute bus ride (or 30-minute tram ride) from the city. Commercialism hasn't taken over. Attractive walking paths through meadows leading to nearby villages add to the relaxed charm and genuine sense of retreat. Not prohibitively expensive, it attracts a slightly older and sedate crowd. There are a few local nightspots, but this is more a place for a quiet dinner with drinks afterward than for a rocking party night of disco and barhopping.

Note: The Club Innsbruck Card covers everything from reductions on sightseeing and free lantern-lit hikes to free child-minding services in the ski kindergartens in Igls and Kühtai and reductions on lift passes. It is available free of charge from your place of accommodation provided that you are staying in Innsbruck or one of the holiday villages. If you stay in the city you have a longish ride to the lifts, but you can ski eight nearby areas, and can also strike out for a day to St. Anton or Kitzbühel. The free ski bus system has been perfected over the years and makes getting to the slopes quick and easy. Innsbruck is a great place to try out a lot of Austria's skiing to get an idea of where to spend more time next season.

Mountain layout–Skiing

Olympia SkiWorld, the ski areas ringing the city, is made up of (in descending order of difficulty) Patscherkofel, Axamer Lizum, Kühtai, Rangger Köpfl, Glungezer, Schlick 2000 and (in a class of its own) the Stubai glacier. Altogether, nearly 285 kilometers of trails for downhill skiers.

Experts should strike out north across the Inn River to Nordpark-Seegrube, which is the gateway to the great black trails of the Hafelekar. Wend your way down the mogul-studded steep black run from the 7,658-foot-high summit. It's one of the most challenging in Austria and a good test of expert status.

Of the Olympic slopes, the Axamer-Lizum is best known. The slopes of Axams, a village about six miles outside Innsbruck, start at the 5,192-foot level. Here you can find every major resort amenity short of lodging.

Even though it's considered heresy in Axams to say, we liked three other runs better than the famous Olympic course, the Hoadl (7,677 feet). The first two, from the nearby 7,336-foot Pleisen and slightly lower Kögele, take you back to the valley floor. The Kögele is the better of the two, with a great four miles of skiing. The run down the Birgitzköpfl on the opposite side of the valley was the demanding in the area. The moguls pound a skier's thighs and the steep slopes test an intermediate's courage.

At Tulfes-Glungezer, nearly eight miles from Innsbruck, trails start at 7,557-foot. For powder and off-trail skiing, we highly recommend the area around the Glungezer summit. The hardcore climb half an hour to enjoy the best off-trail variations.

Igls, at 3,024 feet, is in the shadow of the Patscherkofel, the 7,658-foot summit for the FIS men's downhill run. You can ski the same 2.4-mile course traveled by Franz Klammer to win a gold medal at the 1976 Games and you have the added advantage of new snow-making equipment that will keep the entire descent white, no matter what the weather. The bobsled run is also at Igls and visitors are allowed to try bobsledding on the Olympic course for €30 per person.

Stubaital, home of one of Europe's top summer skiing areas, guarantees Innsbruck skiable terrain throughout the year. This area, about an hour from downtown Innsbruck, is one of the best glacier skiing areas in the world. It offers something for every skier from beginners to experts as well as a chance to experience some of Austria's most beautiful countryside. (*see Neustift-Stubaital chapter*)

Mountain rating

As a twice-Olympic city, Innsbruck offers plenty for the expert. Each of the major ski areas will give the intermediate countless tests. Beginners need have no fear. All those Austrians had to learn how to ski too and the beginner trails are at the bottom of the longer chairlifts. The moment you're ready, so is the mountain.

Mountain layout–Snowboarding

The Olympia SkiWorld Innsbruck is the home of two-time snowboard world champion Martin Freinademetz. The region has five snowboard fun parks, making it ride-heaven for trick-happy boarders.

Axamer Lizum: The Axamer Lizum Snowpark was recently added to the Speed Area. If you get a little hungry after experiencing the park's curved box, kicker, kinked box, flat box, flat rail, kicker, easy wall-ride and corner, you can head right over to Cafe-Restaurant Lizum which is also a new addition to the Speed Area.

Schlick 2000: In the backcountry, a short hike from the Kreuzjochbahn mountain station is a virtual freeride arena. It's a natural snow park with cliffs, rollers and pillows, but boarders should check with the Avalanche Warning Service to make sure that the area is safe before heading up. The northeast slopes are an avalanche risk during warmer temperatures. Boarders who ride the backcountry are required to have beepers, shovels, beacons and at least one other skier accompanying him or her. If this area is deemed unsafe, try exploring the slopes directly off the Kabinenbahn which usually still has some pockets of powder left well after the last snowfall, or riding the natural halfpipes and jumps above Wächten, or going to the Snow Park SennJoch.

Nordpark-Seegrube (also known as "The Snowboard Mecca": The "Grubn" is perfect for freeriders and the Skyline Fun park has a massive 120-meter superpipe.

Stubai Glacier: The area has wide, open bowls for powderhounds and numerous natural kickers and a halfpipe in its snow park.

Rangger Köpfl: The resort added this snow park and has been making steady improvements on it since it's construction.

Lift tickets (2007/08 prices)

The **Innsbruck Super Ski Pass** is your key to 715 kilometers of skiable terrain serviced by 110 ski lifts. This multi-day ticket is valid at the eight resorts of the Olympic SkiWorld Innsbruck (plus Stubai Glacier) and gives you the option of skiing the renowned and prestigious resorts of Kitzbühel and/or Arlberg (St. Anton, St. Christoph, Stuben, Zürs, Lech). The pass must be purchased from Tourist Information.

Skiers can also purchase the **Innsbruck Glacier Ski Pass** at the Innsbruck Information, the Axams Tourist Information Office, Mair Ski School of Götzens and at the ticket counters of the mountain railway bottom stations. The multi-day Innsbruck Glacier Ski Pass allows you to experience eight of Tirol's finest resorts (Nordpark-Seegrube, Patscherkofel, Axamer Lizum, Kühtai, Rangger Köpfl, Glungezer, Schlick 2000 and Stubai Glacier). A total of 75 ski lifts serves a skiable terrain of 285 kilometers. These are the prices. These are prices for the Innsbruck area lift tickets.

	Adult	Youth/Seniors	Children (age 6-15)
three days	€99	€78	€59
six days	€170	€136	€102
three of four days	€105	€83	€62
three of six days	€108	€86	€72

These prices are for the Super Ski Pass that includes a day in Kitzbuhel or St. Anton, plus the skier shuttle to the resorts.

	Adult	Children (age 6-15)
four of six days	€159	€106
five of six days	€210	€143

Children up to 6 years (if accompanied by an adult) – ski free with both the Innsbruck Glacier Pass and the Innsbruck Super Ski Pass.

Your CLUB INNSBRUCK CARD includes transportation between the ski areas and Innsbruck every day. Call Tourist Information for more information.

Ski school (2007/08 prices)

Each area has organized instruction with a total of approximately 180 instructors and 15 different ski and snowboard schools working in the region daily. Private and group lessons for downhill and cross-country are given. School courses meet on the slopes, which you can reach by shuttlebus. The following prices are for the Ski- und Snowboardschule Innsbruck, Leopoldstraße 4, (0512-58174217 or 0699-101 28 730, fax 0512-5817422) and represent the average price for ski lessons in the area.

4-hour private lesson	€155 (one person)	€170 (two persons)
one day group lesson	€44	**
three day group lesson	€98	**
· five day group lesson	€135	**

Cross-country

With 146 kilometers (91 miles) of well-groomed trails cross-country enthusiasts will also get their money's worth in Innsbruck's skiing region. Here, cross-country skiing is both a tour of the holiday villages around Innsbruck and a commune with nature as you enjoy the unspoiled landscape. The eye-level views of the surrounding mountains when moving along the 4.5 km (2.8 miles) track at the Stubai Glacier and the 3.5 km (2.2 miles) long one in the Schlick 2000 are magnificent. On the plateaus of the lower mountains overlooking Innsbruck, the cross-country regions Rinn, Natters and Axams offer a total of about 56 kilometres (35 miles) of tracks, partly covered with artificial snow to ensure perfect conditions.

However, if you long for altitude, there are numerous trails on higher ground too, for instance in Oberperfuss, in Kühtai and in St. Sigmund-Praxmar, where the trails run along the romantic Mellach stream to the head of the valley at the foot of the glacier, the Lüsener Ferner. And if you prefer to reach even higher heights, try out Kühtai at 2,020 metres (6700 feet) above sea level.

At an altitude of 1,640 metres (5300 feet), Lüsens in the Sellraintal valley is about 45 minutes from Innsbruck in a high mountain pass, with about 15.5 km (9.7 miles) of trails, groomed in two basic loops. The longer loop encircles a lake and passes through woods and the shorter begins at the nearby downhill ski area. Both offer beautiful high mountain scenery but no real backcountry or wilderness travel. It is also hard to lose the crowd. A couple of good inns make handy lunch stops. Trails are well-groomed and the lake loop can offer some thrills for advanced beginners and intermediates.

The daily cross-country ski-bus gives the guest the possibility to explore different trails around Innsbruck.

Accommodations

While it may be more romantic to stay in one of the neighboring villages, the attraction of Innsbruck is that you can enjoy the benefits of a major city and one of Europe's cultural capitals.

Rates shown here are per person based on double occupancy with half board in February. €€€—€125+; €€—€75-€124; €—€less than €75.

Europa-Tyrol (5931, fax 587800; €€€) On Südtiroler Platz across from the train station, this is the quality choice for Innsbruck. It is only a short distance from the old city and near the top attractions.

Romantik Hotel Schwazer Adler (587109, fax 561697; €€€) is not normally part of tour operator inventory, but is perfect for the discriminating upscale traveler.

Hilton Hotel (5935, fax 5935220; €€€) is Innsbruck's other top hotel. It's next to the casino and close to the ski shuttlebus stop.

Goldener Adler (571111; €€€) A four-star hotel in the city center operating since 1390 with a good Tyrolean restaurant.

Central Hotel (5920, fax 580310; €€–€€€) Another Innsbruck tradition on the Sparkassenplatz. Modernized lobby with classically Austrian rooms.

Weisses Kreuz (59479, fax 5947990; €€) Has nice single rates for comfortable rooms right in the old center. This a wonderful hotel hosting visitors since the 1400s. Known for possibly the best breakfast buffet in Innsbruck. A good deal.

Goldene Krone (586160, fax 5801896; €€) Traditional Austrian hotel at the arch; rooms are a little more contemporary but hotel is also an old Innsbruck mainstay.

Weisses Rössl (583057, fax 5830575; €€) A family run small hotel, which guarantees good value in the Altstadt with a traditional restaurant serving local food.

Hotel Innsbruck (59868, fax 572280; €€–€€€) A more modern hotel. Not much character or charm, but very central location and a good view of the river and mountains across the way and a back door that opens into the old town.

Hotel Grauer Bär (59240, fax 574535; €€) Large, newly renovated hotel across from the Jesuitenkirche with a very modern lobby, restaurant and rooms.

Igls

This is a pleasant spot but for vacationers, it doesn't offer a complete package. It is just too small, spread out and isolated. If you plan to stay there check out these hotels. Bring a car. You'll need it to keep from suffering from cabin fever and to move around the village. Bus connections to downtown Innsbruck are OK. Getting elsewhere is problematical with most buses requiring a connection in downtown Innsbruck. If you want this type of Alpine atmosphere, it is best to head to nearby Seefeld or Neustift where the village is concentrated and cohesive.

Sporthotel Igls (377241, fax 378679; €€€) In the center, directly across from the bus stop. One of the top places in Igls with an outdoor terrace for drinks and lunch as well as another at night for drinks and dancing. Restaurant is upscale Austrian.

Schlosshotel (377217, fax 378679; €€€), Villersteig, has the ambiance of a retreat surrounded by woods and lawns on the edge of town, but it's a 10-minute walk (at most) from the center.

Apartments, condominiums, flats

Lodging in Innsbruck is primarily in hotels and pensions. For information on chalet and apartment rentals nearer the slopes, contact the Innsbruck tourist office.

There are more apartments in Igls. Send your requirements to the tourist office and it will send back a list of available apartments. Private rooms in Igls, with breakfast, cost about €30 per person a night.

Dining

Restaurants listed below are in the heart of the city, where you'll also find the best lodging. In the individual towns and villages there are countless dining establishments and mountain restaurants.

Price coding (without wine) is €€€—€36+, €€—€16–35. €—€15-.

We start with the top restaurants for Austrian/Tyrolean cuisine. The top restaurants based on locals' recommendations and awards are all outside of the old center. Fax numbers are included since reservations, far in advance, are recommended. **Kapeller** (Philippine-Welser-Strasse 96; 343106 fax 34310668; €€€) in the Amras section of Innsbruck serves great steak with a mustard onion crust. For dessert, try the flaming raspberries. **Schwarzer Adler** (Kaiserjägerstrasse 2; 587109 fax 561697; €€€) at the corner of Universitätsstrasse has menu wonders such as smoked halibut with red onions, potatoes and creative applestrudel. **Europa-Stüberl** (Brixnerstrasse 6; 5931 fax 587800; €€€) across from the train station offers a wonderful calf liver cooked in calvados and great plum creations for dessert.

The close runners up are all excellent restaurants and are oozing with Austrian atmosphere. Reservations are recommended.

Dengg (Riesengasse 13; 582347; €€) holds a Gault Millau toque, Michelin fork and is always mentioned by locals. Go for the unusual polenta cream soup, then crayfish with vegetables in sour cream sauce. At **Riese Haymon** (Haymongasse 4; 566800; €–€€), try the young onion soup and the lamb carpaccio with pesto. The **Goldener Adler** (Herzog-Friedrich-Strasse 6; 571111; €–€€€) has served a whole list of luminaries engraved in marble outside the door. Try the cream soup with parsley, the roast goose and top it off with ice cream with plum sauce or enjoy bananas in Grand Marnier. Lunch menus are very affordable.

Fischerhäusl (Herrengasse 8; 583535; €€) claims to be one of the oldest. Other good Tyrolean restaurants in the old town include **Ottoburg** (Herzog-Friedrich-Strasse 1; 584338; €€) and **Weisses Rössl** (Kiebachgasse 8; 583057; €€).

Outside of the old town try **Bierwirt** (Bichlweg 2; 342143; €€) in Amras around the corner from Kapeller Restaurant. Locals swear this is the area's best regional cooking. In Igls enjoy a meal at **Batzenhäusl** (Lanserstrasse 12; 38618; €€). In Lans, not far from Igls is the award-winning **Wilder Mann** (Römerstrasse, Lans; 379696; €€–€€€) featuring exceptional Austrian meals. In Patsch try **Grünwalderhof** (Römerstraße 1, 377 304, €€) and enjoy great panoramic views of Stubai valley from the garden. For a special panoramic meal on Friday and Saturday, take the cablecar up to Seegrube and enjoy a meal in the restaurant at the cablecar station with the lights of Innsbruck glittering far below you. Call 293375 for reservations. The cablecar runs at a reduced rate for the dinner guests.

Back in town, here are some more suggestions.

Thai Li Ba (Rathausgalerien, 567888, €€) has a great vegetarian selection, making for a good break from its heavier Austrian competitors. It is very popular with locals; you'll be seated next to smartly dressed Austrians chatting on their cell phones over a plate of Thai Noodles or Lemon Pepper Yellow Fin Tuna. Expect to pay about €10-20 for main dishes; their fine selection of Austrian wines begins at €20. If forced to wait go next door to the cocktail bar **Havanna** or the bar on the 5th floor of **Hotel The Penz** for a smooth drink before dinner.

Cammerlander (Innrain 2; 586398; €–€€) is a bright family place right on the riverbank just outside the old city center. Enjoy pizzas and pasta dishes, some Asian soups and steaks in a nice setting.

Papa Joe's (Saillergasse 12, 583046; €–€€) serves Americanized buffalo wings, Caribbean jambalaya and Texas steaks just inside the Altstadt. It's a younger, single, sports bar spot.

You can't beat Italian restaurants for good meals at good prices. Innsbruck has plenty of them. The best in Innsbruck is **Da Peppino** (Kirschentalgasse 6; 275699; €€) open only for dinner. Try the spaghetti with baby octopus or have your fish filleted by the table and top it all off with profiteroles filled with mascapone. This is an experience—not your Mama's red sauce pasta. **Pizzeria Romantica** (Kiebachgasse 11; 586828; €) is a typical pizzeria with a bit of rustic Italian ambiance. **Solo Pasta** (Universitätsstrasse 15, 87206; €) serves more than two dozen different and very reasonable pasta dishes from lasagna to spaghetti to rigatoni. Must be good—it's packed at night. Almost next door **Il Dottore Pizza & Pasta** (Kaiserjägerstrasse 1; €) is packed as well with locals. **Al Dente** (Meranerstrasse 7; €) has very interesting creative pasta dishes with lots of variations and a good salad bar as well. **Panini** (Herzog-Friedrich-Strasse 17; €) is a good lunch stop, in the Altestadt, near the Goldenes Dachl. It's a step above Au Bon Pain. You'll find good pizza squares, sandwiches, soups and desserts.

Sahib (Sillgasse 3; 571468; €) serves good Indian meals from hot and spicy curry to creamy sags. **Canton China** (Maria-Theresien-Strasse 37; €) is a good Chinese spot, with €4.50 midweek specials (Monday to Thursday, not holidays). This has attractive, upscale decor and prices are quite reasonable. It is not at all your run-of-the-mill Chinese food. This may be the best Chinese food in town.

If you need a hometown fix there are the ubiquitous **McDonalds** (Maria Theresien-Strasse and Herzog-Friedrich-Strasse; €) and **Burger King** (Südtirolerplatz 16, 575143. But even though the names are American, the prices are not and seem to be a little high, even for Austrians.

Après-ski/nightlife
We recommend you walk through the old city for just about every version of nightlife you could desire. The view is beautiful and you'll find small pubs and bars hidden in alleys and under archways.

Check with the tourist office for a list of concerts taking place around town or go to www.webticket.at—tickets are also sold at the information office. You never know who's touring Europe while you're on vacation.

Innsbruck has a bit of something for everyone. Here's the lowdown:

Innsbruck's Casino, the largest in Austria, attached to the Hilton Innsbruck at Salurner Strasse 15, is open for elegant gaming. Jackets are required.

The **Europa-Bar** in the Europa Hotel and the 5th floor bar at the modern **Hotel The Penz** in the city-centre are popular spots, but the hottest meeting places in town are the bars that fill the town hall gallery which include **Gössers** and **Havanna**. **The Roof Top Wine Bar 360°** gives you a spectacular view from Innsbruck & the surrounding mountains.

For the young crowd, hot spots with a pub and beer atmosphere are the **Theresienbräu** and the **Elferhaus**.

Piano Café/Bar (Herzog-Friedrich-Strasse 5) is definitely for an older (40s and older), upscale crowd. It is relaxed and comfortable with an antique interior and paintings that cover the walls. Look carefully—it's easy to miss.

Café Club Dine & Dance (Siftgasse 12) is a large Victorian bar with high ceilings and a smoking club atmosphere. Ring the bell to enter. The club has a large and spacious interior with seating in a loft over the main floor and a quieter, more intimate bar to the side. The crowd is mixed, but leans toward older side clientele.

Limerick Bill's (Maria-Theresien-Strasse 9) is an Irish Pub with three upper levels and a basement. On Friday and Saturday there are bands and dance-till-you-drop evenings that can last until the wee hours of the morning.

Treibhaus tucked in a back alley behind China Restaurant, just outside the Altstadt, is Innsbruck's real bohemian hangout for all ages and types, tourists and locals alike. A spacious upstairs has a kitchen serving mediocre pizza and the basement is known for hot local jazz and ethnic music on most nights and Sunday mornings.

Krahvogel (Anichstrasse 12) is a very trendy "in" bar with live music.

For a spectacular place to sip coffee and drinks, try **Segafredo Sky** (on the top floor of Universitatsstrasse 15) just across the street from the Jesuitenkirche. It is nice to see the city from rooftop level. You have the mountains in one direction and the twin church towers of the Jesuitenkirche on the other.

On the ground level of the same building check out **Proseccheria Mionetto**, a sparkling wine bar, featuring the Italian version of dry champagne.

Other recommended spots are: **Toscana**, a creative, old-fashioned bar and hangout for artists and intellectuals; **Ebi' s Cocktail Bar**; and **Bögen-Lokale** where you can dance and party until morning

Bacchus is a former 80s disco now one of the gay/lesbian meeting places in town and open until dawn.

Austria prides itself on great cafes. These are some of the best in Innsbruck.

Café Sacher at the entrance of the Hofburg serves coffees and rich chocolate cakes and pastries under crystal chandeliers. Try also **Cafe Mundig, Café Katzung, Murauer Cafe** and **Café Kröll.**

Just outside the center (worth a pilgrimage for pastry and coffee lovers)

Valier (Maximilianstrasse 27) won the "Golden Coffee Bean" in 1999. Critics rave about the pastries and the creams created by this cafe artist.

Gritsch (Anichstrasse 18) combines an excellent cafe with a bar and a bistro. This is a great place for a drink or snack as well. Ask for any of the following that will cure any sweet tooth—Schwarzwälder Kirsch, Apfelstrudel or Indianer mit Schlag.

Cafe Central (Central Hotel/Boznerplatz) is a true Viennese music cafe offering live piano music and Tango on Sunday evenings (8–11 p.m.). It also has a meal menu with elaborate pastries and desserts. Eat amidst a semi-grand interior and enjoy a large collection of newspapers. This is *the* traditional coffeehouse of Innsbruck.

Child care (2007/08 prices)

Child care and ski kindergarten courses (age 3-1/2 and older) are available in Innsbruck's ski areas and at the Nurserien-Ski Kindergarten. Contact the tourist office for details.

In the heart of Innsbruck is the Kinderpark (0676 93 88 564 for reservations) run by Maria-Theresien-Straße. This new facility can be used by locals as well as guests in Innsbruck; your children are cared for by professional kinder garden teachers. It costs €1 for the first hour, €2 for every further hour. The Kinderpark is open Monday - Friday from 9 a.m. - 6 p.m. and Saturday from 9 a.m.- 5 p.m.

In nearby Igls, Snowsports Igls (phone/fax: 0512-377377) has Bobo's which is divided into several programs for children age 4 and older (space is available for children younger than 4 upon request). Bobos Punktejagd is a relaxed and flexible way for children age 3-5 to learn to ski. Children can begin on any day; there's no time limit and children are able to learn at their own pace. Access to this mini ski area costs only €5 per card and is open every day, except Thursday, from 2-4 p.m.

Bobo's Kindergarten is for children, usually age 4 and older, who don't want to learn to ski or snowboard, but still want to play in the snow. Activities include sledging, tobogganing, snowman building and indoor play. The kindergarten is open from 9:15 a.m. to 5 p.m., Sunday to Friday. Reservations are required. The program is free (not including lunch which is €8).

Bobo's Kinder-Club also offers ski instruction for children age 4 and older. Classes can start on either Monday or Sunday and end on Friday, 9:30 a.m. - noon and 1 p.m. - 2:30 p.m. One day costs €50; a half day costs €35. Three days cost €110; three half days cost €80. Six days cost €146; six half day, € 104. Lunch is an extra €8.

Bobo's Mini-Club is a variation of the kinder-club. It's a morning course that can start on either Monday or Sunday and end on Friday, 9:30 a.m. - noon (afternoon courses can be requested). It is designed to give parents the chance to be present for the first hour of the course and ease children into the program. One day costs €35. Three days cost € 80. Five days cost €96. Lunch costs an extra €8.

SchiSchule Kühtai (05239-5231; fax 05239-5371) runs a kindergarten for children age 3 and younger with snowplay. Hours are from 10 a.m. –noon and from 2–4 p.m. and cost €10 each day; €5 each half day. Midday care (noon - 2 p.m.) with lunch is €13. Children ages 4 and older are eligible for group ski lessons. Courses start on Sunday at 9:30 a.m. and run to Thursday with classes from 10 a.m.–noon and from 2–4 p.m. Cost is €47 for one day; €110 for three days; and €144 for six days.

Other activities

Innsbruck shares with Grenoble the distinction of being a town in the Alps with more than 130,000 residents; as noted, it's a provincial capital and has a wealth of art and historical treasures. It is also on the way to the Brenner Pass, gateway to the Italian Lakes and Venice.

Innsbruck is accustomed to visitors in ski outfits, whether inside a museum or at a fine restaurant. Visitors always head for the heart of town along the Maria-Theresien-Strasse for the outstanding view of the Karwendel mountain range.

The best way to see Innsbruck is to walk through the old town. Allow about two hours. The most photographed house in the old city is Goldenes Dachl, a former royal building from the 16th century, with gold-plated copper shingles on the roof.

Visit the **Hofburg Palace** where Maria-Theresia lived and Marie Antoinette was born. At **St. Jakob's Cathedral** baroque illusion is fascinating. Look at the façade—though it looks like there are five round windows over the door, there are only three; two are painted. Plus, the ceiling of the cathedral appears to be a series of domes—all but the one over the altar are flat as a pancake. The **Hofkirche** houses the tomb of Maximilian I, comparable to the burial spots of ancient pharaohs. The massive tomb is surrounded by 28 large bronze statues of the emperor's heroes, friends and family the emperor wanted to have escort him in death—both of his wives made the list. The **Tyrolean folklore museum** gives a glimpse into the rustic small huts you see sprinkled on the mountain side. On the south edge of town, the terrace and coffee shop on the top of the modern ski jump built by the famous architect Zaha Hadid is very popular. People come for the apple strudel as well as the magnificent view of Innsbruck and the surrounding mountain ranges.

The money-saving Innsbruck Card costs €24 for 24 hours or €29 for 48 hours and €34 for 72 hours. These passes are discounted by 50 percent for children ages 6–15. The card provides limited access to cablecars and public transportation around Innsbruck/Igls and Halls. It also gives entrance to 18 major sightseeing attractions in and near the city. These include the Imperial Palace, the Museum of Tyrolean Folk Art, the Provincial Museum, Ambras Castle, The Bergisel ski jump, the Alpine Zoo, the Court Church and the multimedia displays at the Swarovski Crystal Worlds. Contact the Innsbruck Ticket Service (5356) for more information.

A good selection of classical music concerts takes place at the Concert House, the Konservatoriumsaal (music school) and at different festivals like the traditional and famous Innsbruck Festival Weeks in August.

Cinematograph and Leokino are good art cinemas, offering relatively contemporary and classic films in original language, not dubbed. The only cinemas in Innsbruck for this and something of a rarity in Austria.

Just outside Innsbruck, the Swarovski Crystal Worlds (05224-51080) features a spectacular array of the colorful glass, from the world's largest crystal (alas, at 300,000 carats, it is a bit large for Elizabeth Taylor's neck), collections of costumes and artifacts made with innumerous pieces of crystal and a 122-meter long wall filled with 12 tons of brilliant crystal.

For an unique experience head to Sinne which has a dark museum, through which you are led by blind people.

 ## Getting there

Innsbruck airport has daily jet service throughout Europe. Munich is the international airport most often used by travelers from the United States, but traffic through Innsbruck airport is increasing. Austrian Airways and Austrian Airlines have scheduled services from Frankfurt and Vienna, offering a perfect alternative to trains, buses, or a long drive by car.

By car from Munich, take the Autobahn to the Inntal autobahn and then to Innsbruck—no more than three hours. A more scenic drive is from Munich to Garmisch-Partenkirchen and then about 70 minutes over the mountains to Innsbruck. Add at least two hours for sightseeing in Garmisch.

Shuttlebuses connect Munich Airport with Innsbruckwith departures every day from Munich at 11:30 a.m. Limousines are also available through Four Seasons Travel (584157, fax 585767) but require advance reservations. They leave Munich Airport daily every two hours.

Tourist information

Innsbruck Tourismus
A-6021 Innsbruck, Burggraben 3, Austria;
Telephone: 0512-59850, fax 0512-59850107.
Internet: www.innsbruck.info
E-mail: office@innsbruck.info

Telephone prefix: 0512

Ischgl, Galtür and the Paznaun Valley

Ischgl (pronounced Ish-gull) is an extensive ski resort high in the Alps (4,592 feet), on the border with Switzerland and is almost unknown by non-Europeans. If you like the charm of truly being on an "European vacation," this valley is perfect.

The town itself is a small Alpine resort built on a knoll in a deep valley and is easily walkable from one end to the other, thanks to elevators and short-cut tunnels. No high-rise construction seriously mars the small village effect. The ski area is far above and out of sight from the road, the base stations and the town. Eleven smaller hamlets complete the region.

Ischgl has it all—40 lifts, more than 230 km. of wide trails, cross-border runs into Switzerland, off-trail areas, cross-country, Alpine village atmosphere, inviting local cuisine, both luxury and affordable lodging options, and some of the wildest après-ski and nightlife in Austria. There is so much fun to be had in Ischgl we recommend resting up *before* you go. Be forewarned, nearly 50 percent of Ischgl's skiers are from Germany, so if you want to meet people, it helps to speak some German. If that's not an option, you'll fit in if you just practice dancing in your ski boots.

With 90 percent of its ski area over 6,600 feet, snow is virtually assured until the beginning of May. From the slopes above Ischgl, you can cross into Switzerland and visit duty-free Samnaun.

Twenty minutes up the valley is Galtür, a picturesque village of only 730 residents and 20 restaurants, which is spread out around a late-baroque church. Although connected to Ischgl by bus (and the Silvretta ski pass), it's much smaller and quieter with a correspondingly smaller ski area (40 km. of runs). It is particularly known for its cross-country and ski-touring opportunities. Since Galtür is the highest village in the Silvretta-Paznaun region, it has a long snow season (December to April).

Generation after generation has been drawn to Galtür by its quiet charms and unhurried pace. Families will find the resort caters to their needs.

Mountain layout–Skiing

Ischgl's slopes are the most extensive in the valley, with neighboring See, Kappl and Galtür servicing smaller areas. Across the mountains to the south, in Switzerland, Samnaun is connected by lifts.

From Ischgl three gondola lifts rise to the main skiing area 3,280 feet above the town. The Silvrettabahn and the Fimbabahn take skiers from opposite ends of town to the Idalp area (7,582 feet). The Pardatschgratbahn goes from the eastern section of town to Pardatschgrat at 8,609 feet. A new double-decker cable car Alp Trida and a new eight-seat chair lift now brings skiers from Samnaun back to Ischgl, meaning no more bottlenecks on the Swiss side of the border. A new trail now winds between the Pardatschgrat to the middle station of the Silvretta lift.

From the Idalp sector, lifts fan out to all corners of the resort. Skiers choosing to go directly to the higher Pardatschgrat still have to pass through the Idalp area. The immediate Idalp area is a small valley in the midst of the peaks with runs and lifts radiating on all sides from its floor. It serves as the learning area, offering long, very easy swaths with excellent lift support.

From Idalp, take the chairlift up to Idjoch. The Idjochbahn was the first bubble-covered eight-person lift in the world. Here, drop down into the Swiss Alp Trida section for long intermediate runs. Or continue up to the Greitspitz for more challenging skiing in the Austrian section beneath the Palinkopf into the Hölltal or over another ridge to the Paznauner Taja. The slopes are so extensive, it's an adventure just finding your way around—each lift summit reveals another valley (and unbelievable vistas) and another set of runs to explore. The trail from Greitspitz into the Höllenkar, has opened a previously virgin face of the mountain.

At the end of the day, take one of the runs from the Idalp or down the Velilltal for beautiful, wide-open, intermediate cruising. Or if you want to end the day with a challenge, drop from the Pardatschgrat. If you are staying near the Silvrettabahn, you will want to head left toward the middle station, then follow the No. 1 trail into town. For those closer to the Fimba or Pardatschgratbahn stations, keep going straight down into town. Where the trail forks, ski to the right.

Determined off-trail skiers can arrange for a snowcat to take them to the Piz Val Gronda or the Heidelberger-hütte with a guide for a day of skiing across untracked snow. This area is scheduled for lift development, but it still seems to be a few years away. The Swiss must first construct an additional lift from Samnaun before the Austrian lift-builders can raise a wrench.

Over the border to Samnaun, Switzerland

Swiss Samnaun is the target of many Ischgl skiers because they are either determined to experience skiing over the border to a Swiss town, or they are hot on the trail of duty-free cigarettes, perfume or whisky. In any case, the run from the back side of the Palinkopf is relatively tame and the town itself hardly more interesting than the nearest airport duty-free store.

Duty-free here is big business. If one smokes or wants to fill up the hot toddy cabinet, Samnaun is wonderful, but once is more than enough for the run from Palinkopf. A new cable car takes skiers from the center of Samnaun-Dorf back to the slopes above Ischgl. There is normally about a half-hour wait for the tiny, slower Ravaisch cable car that used to be the only way to return.

There is another trail from Alp Trida down to Compatsch. This trail is rather difficult and often closed because of avalanches (too much snow) or rocks (too little). If you do get down, a postbus will carry you back up to the Ravaisch cable car.

Telephone prefix: Ischgl 05444; Galtür 05443

Galtür

A three-minute shuttlebus ride takes you from the village to Wirl, a collection of on-piste hotels and the gateway to the slopes. The skiing here is mellow-to-intermediate, better than Ischgl for beginners and families who want to ski together.

A quad-chair carries skiers up from the base at Wirl to Birkhahnkopf. From there, take the Ballunspitz lift to a choice of three easy expert runs or a good intermediate trail. A couple of log-cabin restaurants dot the surrounding slopes. From there you can ski down to the frozen reservoir, the Kopssee, or traverse round the back of the mountain to the Innere Kopsalpe, which offers the toughest runs. On a sunny day, this back bowl offers an advanced intermediate fun for an entire morning or afternoon.

Galtür also has night skiing on Wednesday from 7:30 p.m. to 10:30 p.m. Rates for night skiing are €10.50 for adults, €6.50 for children and €8 for seniors.

Mountain layout—Snowboarding

Take the 8-person chairlift Idjoch (B3) or the 4-seater chairlift Flimjoch (B2) to the Rennstrecke (Paradise) Funpark at Idjoch which claims to be the largest dedicated snowboard park in Europe. It has 30 obstacles and something for every skill level including a variety of jumps; a quarterpipe; rails; funbox; boardercross with snakes and waves; a timed giant slalom run; a speed run which is measured in kilometers per hour; and even a kindercross which has a boardercross for children with snakes, waves and a jump.

Mountain rating

Intermediates and experts will have a wonderful time in Ischgl. The area offers wide-ranging, well-prepared trails and 50 miles of off-trail challenges. Experts looking for super-steep terrain will be disappointed.

The resort is perfect for a mixed intermediate and expert group, but is not recommended for absolute beginners. English at the ski school is limited to technical ski jargon, and the nursery slopes are far above the town. Galtür, with its wide-open slopes and relaxed atmosphere, is better for younger skiers, beginners and intermediates.

Cross-Country

Ischgl has three main cross-country routes. The first route, the Trisannaloipe, starts next to the large car park (opposite the Silvretta Seilbahn) and leads 5.2 km. along the Trisanna to the Ostloipe in Galtür. The 8.7-km. Ostloipe (East-Trail) connects to the Trisannaloipe and finishes at the leisure centre in Galtür. And lastly, the 6.6-km. Westloipe (West-Trail) is actually a loop that gives skiers a tour of the Galtür Leisure Centre (1,580 meters).

Galtür has a total of 74 km. of cross-country ski tracks groomed for both classic and skate skiing. Besides the Westloipe and Ostloipe which are mentioned above there are also four other routes from which to choose: the 4.5-km. Schiwanderweg Zeinis; the 8.15-km. Schiwanderweg Bielerhöhe; the 5.2-km. Anschlußloipe Ischgl; and the 5-km. Schiwanderweg Jamtal.

Ski school (2006/07 prices)

Ischgl has the largest ski school. Both Galtür and Ischgl teach the Austrian method.

The following prices are for the Snowsport-Academy Ischgl (05444 5257 or 5404, fax 05444 5752).

Private lessons for 90 minutes (9:30 a.m. - 11 a.m.) are €102; each additional person is €16. Lessons for 90 minutes (1:30 p.m. - 3:30 p.m.) are €97; each additional person is €16. Lessons for two hours (9:30 a.m. - 12:30 p.m. or 11:15 a.m. - 2:15 p.m.) are €176; each additional person is €20. Lessons for three hours (9.30 a.m. - noon and 1 - 3 p.m.) are €216; each additional person is €28. After three of any of these courses, the price is reduced by €10.

Group lessons have a minimum of 6 people. Lessons are from 11:15 a.m. to 2:15 p.m. Prices for one day are €49; for three days are €118; and for five days cost €158.

Silvretta Galtür Ski and Snowboard School prices (05443 85 65 or 0664 514 63 41, fax: 05443 85 65):

Private lessons for one hour cost €52; each additional person is €15. A full day (4 hours; Sunday–Tuesday) is €175. A full day (4 hours Wednesday – Saturday) is €162. Each additional skier costs €19 apiece per day.

Group lessons for one day are €49; two days, €88; three days, €120; five days €154. Group lessons for a half day are €34; two half days, €67; three half days, €95; five half days €118.

 # Lift tickets (2007/08 prices)

All skiers except beginners should buy the Silvretta ski pass, good for all area lifts (Ischgl, Galtür, Samnaun and the entire valley), plus shuttlebus transport.

	High Season	Low Season
three days	€120.50	€103.50
six days	€219.50	€189
seven days	€247	€212.50
thirteen days	€383.50	€330

Individual area day tickets in Ischgl cost €37. In Galtür the price is €32. These are prices with the guest card for Galtür/Ischgl visitors.

Children born after September 1, 1999 ski free when accompanied by an adult. Seniors older than age 60 receive about a 15 percent discount. At press time, children born after September 1, 1990 are entitled to the children's discount. Official picture identification is required for the purchase of discounted tickets for seniors and children.

 # Accommodations

Based on high season, per person/double occupancy with breakfast: €€€—more than €80; €€—€50–79; €—less than €50.

Ischgl

The **Trofana Royal** (05444-601; €€€) is the top spot in town.

The **Hotel Elisabeth** (05444-5411; €€€) is at the base stations of the Fimbabahn and the Pardatschgratbahn and has the perfect location, plus pool, sauna and solarium. The hosts speak English well.

Madlein (05444-5226; €€€) has a central location with Zen theme and a selected number of designer rooms, pool, sauna and solarium. The hotel also features two of the best nightclubs in town.

The **Hotel Post** (05444-5232; €€€) has been completely upgraded and features all the amenities including a swimming pool, spa, English-speaking service, and a tasteful bar. It has more sedate après-ski, but rather wild nightlife. Staff at the **Sonne** (05444-5302; €€€) is good with English. The Sonne also has excellent après-ski.

Gasthöfe Goldener Adler (05444-5217; €€€) boasts one of the best kitchens in town, a sauna and steambath. The **Olympia** (05444-5432; €€€) near Fimba and

Telephone prefix: Ischgl 05444; Galtür 05443

Pardatschgrat lifts; **Yscla** (5275; €€€) near the Silvretta lift; and **Charly** (05444-5434; €€€) are convenient to everything.

The best B&B or garni in town is **Christine** (05444-5346; €€–€€€). A moderate B&B is **Sporthotel Ischgl** (05444-5351; €€) is a bit out of the way, but a good haven for English speakers. As is the **Alpenblick** (05444-5311; €€)—ask for Martin, he also teaches skiing.

The recommended lower-priced B&Bs—**Palin** (05444-5445; €€), **Lasalt** (05444-5121; €€), and **Erna** (05444-5262; €€).

Galtür

Prices in Galtür are lower than those in Ischgl. Be sure to ask about the guest card when you arrive. It identifies you for discounts in the town for the swimming pool, and other activities. The telephone prefix is 05443. Many of the hotels have special prices for children. Also note: Galtür has dozens of excellent B&Bs.

Based on high season (February), per person/double occupancy, half-board: €€€—more than €125; €€—€75–124; €—less than €75.

The best lodging here may be the **Gasthof Zum Rössle** right on the center square. It has a fine, traditional restaurant and spa facilities (05443-8232; €€–€€€).

The **Alpenhotel Tirol** (05443-8206; €€) is another four-star. **Fluchthorn** (05443-8202; €€) is in the center of the village. **Almhof** (05443-8253) and the **Alpenromantikhotel Wirlerhof** (05443-8231) are in the midst of the ski area in Wirl. **Zum Silbertaler** (05443-8256; €€) is a three-star near the tennis center and pool. Try **Gampelerhof** (05443-8307; €€), **Bergfried** (05443-8208; €), or **Luggl** (05443-8386; €€).

For bed & breakfasts head to: **Alpenhaus Salner** (05443-8288; €); **Dr. Köck** (05443-8226; €) or **Belvedere** (05443-8219; €), plus many more.

Apartments, condominiums, flats

The rental apartment business is well organized and bookings can be arranged through the tourist information office. When writing, provide details about when you plan to arrive, how many people will be sharing the apartment and what facilities you desire. In return you will receive a list with several choices. Make your selection and notify the individual owner, depending on the instructions you get.

Normally, linens and kitchen utensils are included in every apartment. Heat, taxes, electricity and cleaning services may be extra. Expect to pay €30 per person a night, depending on how many are sharing the apartment, where it's located and its relative position on the luxury scale.

Dining

First head to the **Trofana Royal** (05444-600; fax 05444-60090) for its five-star restaurant, which is considered one of the best in all of Europe. The chef here was selected as Chef of the Year in Austria in 2000. Try the deer with mountain berries and chestnut-filled ravioli. Finish up with soufflé made with Williams pear schnapps. Make reservations early.

Also recommended is the traditional kitchen of the **Goldener Adler** (05444-5217). Locals also highly recommend the **Trofana Alm** (after après-ski is over; 0544-602) for good international cooking (and pizzas as well). The **Hotel Post** restaurant (05444-5232) is elegant and sumptuous. Try the authentic-looking **Kitzloch** (05444-5618), built 15 years ago out of 300-year-old logs. It serves traditional food. In fact, it's so traditional that the spread for the bread is gramnel schmalz, which translates to "fat," but it tastes good. **Yscla** (05444-5275) has a good French and local menu. Don't ignore the on-mountain dining when joining Ischgl's regulars for a long lunch break. Recommended stops include the **Alp Trida** in Switzerland for the excellent food and the **Eisbar Gampen** on the Austrian side for the fun.

In Galtür, be sure to eat once at the **Rössle** (ask for the local schnapps), **Landle** and at **Zum Silbertaler**. The **Fluchthorn** also serves hearty affordable meals.

In Samnaun, enjoy a meal at the **Hotel Post**. It's pricey but one of the best.

Après-ski/nightlife

Here Ischgl shines. It has one of the best après-ski scenes from 3–7 p.m., then excellent nightlife from 10 p.m.–2 a.m.

The best après-ski spots include the **Trofana Alm** and the **Kuhstall**, just up from the Silvrettabahn and near the Post and Goldener Adler, and the **Kitzloch** at the opposite end of town near Hotel Elisabeth and the Fimba and Pardatschgratbahn. These spots rock from about 4–7 p.m., with a disc jockey spinning music, the bar serving half-liter beers and the crowd singing and dancing in ski suits and ski boots. The **Sonne** also has a lively crowd with live bands and dancing.

The three major discos begin to crank at about 10 p.m. or 11 p.m. The **Tenne** in the basement of Hotel Trofana (go to the side door) offers the most crowded venue, with dancing and wild contests alternately competing for attention. The **Pacha** in Hotel Madlein is for a younger crowd. **Posthorndl**, in the basement of Hotel Post, has been decorated like a Gothic dungeon, complete with flickering chandeliers, marble gargoyles, and blue-lit disc jockeys. You'll find yourself wanting to shift with the crowd, depending on which club has the best entertainment.

Galtür
Almhof and **Alpenromantikhotel Wirlerhof** have lively après-ski at the bottom of the lifts. After skiing, the "in" place for action is the **Weiberhimmel** (woman's heaven) where dancing on the balcony in ski boots is an art form. The music varies from Austrian songs to 70/80s rock. After dinner most head to the **Pyramide** in the Hotel Luggi, or to one of the other hotel bars.

 ## Child care (2006/07 prices)

Child care services are available. Contact the Paznaun-Ischgl Tourist Office (05444-52660) for assistance.

There is a guest kindergarten without ski school at Idalp. The price is €29 a day, and, €19 for a half day. Supervised lunch costs €7.

Snowsport-Academy Ischgl (05444 5257 or 5404, fax 05444 5752) runs a children's program with lessons for kids 3–5. Course times are from 10:30 a.m.–12:30 p.m. and 1:30 p.m.–3:30 p.m. Costs are €46 (4 hours) and €30 (2 hours) for a half day. Add €7 for supervised lunch (only with whole day skipass).

The normal children's ski school with lessons for kids 5 and older are €45 for a full day, €113 for three days and €162 for six days. Prices do not vary much between high and low season. Add €7 for supervised lunch. Course times are from 10:30 a.m.–12:30 p.m. and 1:30pm – 3:30 p.m. with a minimum of 6 children.

There is a kindergarten for non-skiing children ages 3–4. Course times: 10:00 a.m.–4:00 p.m. Prices per child are €29 for a full day and €19 for a half day. Add €7 for supervised lunch (only with whole day skipass).

Silvretta Galtür Ski and Snowboard School (05443 85 65 or 20046, fax: 05443 85 65) has babysitting and special programs for children age 3 and older. Upon request your children will be cared for for the whole day or for a half day by Margit, the child care teacher.

Telephone prefix: Ischgl 05444; Galtür 05443

The Children and Bambini Courses (ages 3–4 Years) are a combination of skiing lessons and snowplay. It costs €30 per half day.

The Galtür ski school has Siggi's Kinderland where children ages 3–14 years old can learn to ski in a sheltered area. This ski-play area has its own cable lift, wonder carpet, carousel, warm up hut, wave run and much more. It is ideally near the Valley station and the bus stop right next to the parking lot.

It is not necessary to use a chair lift or a t-bar lift to get to the children's area. Siggiland is a fenced off area. Snowboarding and adult beginners are not permitted to use the Kinderland. Parents and friends can watch their children from outside the area. Prices are: €30 for a half day; €85 for three half days; €47 for a full day; €109 for three full days; €135 for five full days. A supervised lunch costs €9.

Other activities

Winter merely enhances rather than disguises the beauty of Galtür, a mountain village some 5,197 feet high. Galtür is the gateway to the Silvretta Alpine Highway, which is open in warm-weather months. If taking photographs of beautiful buildings is one of your hobbies, visit the spired parish church Maria Geburt in Galtür.

A **swimming** pool has opened in Galtür. Entrance fees for guests staying in Galtür are €6 for adults, €3.50 for children and €5 for seniors.

In Galtür, the Tennishalle is open from 11 a.m.– 9 p.m. with charges of €16–18.50 per hour. Galtür also has Kegelbahnen, an Austrian version of **bowling** which costs €10 per hour.

Landeck, an Alpine crossroads near the entrance to the valley, is a regional **shopping** center and is distinguished by the towering Fortress Landeck.

As additional excursions, you can travel to Innsbruck and Munich.

Getting there

The nearest international airport is in Munich. From there, the easiest highway route is Garmisch, Fern Pass to Landeck or Innsbruck, and on to Ischgl. The train stops in Landeck which is served by regular bus service.

Tourist information

Paznaun-Ischgl Tourismusverband, A-6561 Ischgl, Austria.
Telephone: 05444-5266-0; fax 05444-5636.
Internet: www.ischgl.com. E-mail: info@ischgl.com

Tourismusverband, A-6563 Galtür/Tirol, Austria.
Telephone: 05443-8521, fax 05443-852176.
Internet: www.galtuer.com Email: info@galtuer.com

Kitzbühel and Kirchberg

Framed by rugged mountains, Kitzbühel dates back to the ninth century, when it landed on the map as a copper mining and trading town. With storybook snow-covered scenery, it's hard to believe that skiing is relatively new here. It wasn't until 1892 that skis were first introduced. But the sport rapidly gained popularity, and two years later a large consignment of skis arrived from Norway, paving the slopes for Kitzbühel's first ski championship.

This once quaint village has been growing by leaps and bounds over the past decade. Today it is a real town with benign sprawl, well outside the old limits of the traditional village center (which is thankfully still its quaint self). Among the Austrian resorts, Kitzbühel is the most commercial, glamorous and expensive. New lifts like the 3S gondola connecting Pengelstein and Jochberg have made travel between villages faster. The new detachable 8-passenger Steinbergkogel (C6) chairlift will help eliminate long lines at the bottom of the bowl. Kitzbuhel has also made significant investments to further expand its snowmaking systems.

The biggest news is the new connection of Kitzbühel and Kirchberg with the interconnected region of Ski Welt. This means now a skipass can be purchased that connects 250 lifts and 700 km. of trails.

If possible arrive in Kitzbühel before nightfall, when the wrought-iron entranceway lamps and flickering candles in the restaurant windows lend a special charm to the streets. You'll hear the jingle of bells on a horse-drawn sleigh, and in the distance someone in a gasthaus will let out a hearty laugh that rises above the sound of a piano or zither. The exterior of Kitzbühel is old, lovely and quite romantic. The interior is modern and efficient. The atmosphere is bright, boisterous and never dull.

In Kitzbühel the skiing day is long enough to tire you out, and it's followed by nightlife that can last forever. This is Austria's winter entertainment capital, with top European performers appearing throughout the season. In January, during the famed Hahnenkamm Downhill World Cup (usually the middle weekend), Kitzbühel vibrates with action. The streets are filled even at midnight with music and laughter that ripple through the narrow alleyways. This is the perfect time (albeit the most expensive) to be in Kitzbühel.

Kitzbühel is a resort that a vacationer with plenty of pecuniary resources should consider. As at Aspen or Vail, you'll rub shoulders with the rich and famous and be treated like royalty but at about half the cost. This is a town where tour operators can save you a bundle and one that careful planning can make very affordable.

Kirchberg, a smaller town 5 km. to the west, shares the same mountain and has become a major player in the area. Everything here is within easy walking distance. Filled with a younger crowd, attracting families and more dedicated skiers, Kirchberg has some of the wildest après-ski in Austria and somewhat lower prices than its flashier neighbor. The strongest contingent of tourists in Kirchberg comes from Holland. They know how to have a good time and can define the best of wild après-skiers. If you are looking for that touch to a vacation, this is the place. Upvalley from Kirchberg the connection lift to Ski Welt provides connections to one of Austria's largest interconneted areas. See the *Ski Welt Chapter*.

Mountain layout–Skiing

If you ski well, Kitzbühel is close to unbeatable. You can spend all day on its slopes and not use the same lift or ski on the same run twice. There are more than 56 prepared runs across an amazing 168 km. of mountain. This is the site of one of the first ski safaris, where skiers travel 30 km. by lift and descend 35 km. between Kitzbühel and Pass Thurn. It's marked by round signs with an elephant on skis pointing the way and the entire route can be made on skis. Start early. The trip takes a full day.

The main area is a north/south ridge that is defined by a pass headed to Pass Thurn strung with the villages of Aurach and Jochberg. The valley used to defining the eastern side of the area finds Kirchberg and Aschau. A new lift over Pass Thurn connects the Kitzbühel/Kirchberg area with the Brixental and another rising from the Kirchberg valley links the area with Westendorf in the Ski Welt.

There is more skiing on the opposite side of each valley. To the southwest there is the Kitzbüheler Horn that has become a snowboarder's mountain. To the east, on the other side of Kirchberg, is the Gaisberg area with its new quad-chairlift. The Fleckalmbahn goes to the Ehrenbachhöhe above the Hahnenkamm race circuit.

Real experts can always find good skiing just off the marked trails. Some of the best spots are beyond the Pengelstein peak where the Hochsauerkaser trail drops to the west and the Schwarzkogel runs to the east. Both provide off-piste possibilities at any point an expert wants to turn his or her skis. The Steinbergkogel bowl is another expert playground with an old single chair and a new 8-passenger chair bringing skiers back to the top of the bowl. Trails like Powder Heaven and Direttissima are aptly named with the right snow. Way up the valley the Bärenbadkogel peak has plenty of expert drops where anyone with real skill can pick their own trail down the mountain.

Off the Kitzbüheler Horn, experts can take the Larchenhang then Horn Standard trails from the peak with thousands of off-piste possibilities all along the way. Gaisberg is more of a practice mountain for intermediates and beginners.

Pengelstein is an intermediate peak with short trails dropping to the west and a long trail into Kirchberg. The Kirchberg trail is a good morning sun route.

The best runs are a closely guarded secret. Guides are tight-lipped about where to find good powder and empty runs. For a long uninterrupted slope try the Niedere Fleckalm, which in the morning is uncrowded and offers a very fast gondola. In the afternoon stick to the Ehrenbachhöhe, which provides a variety of terrain from intermediate to challenging. The Giggling (off the single chair near the Steinbergkogel bowl) is one of the longest runs and a good way to end the day. At the bottom walk to the bus stop, find a cab or stop in for a drink at one of the bars.

Mountain rating

Trail skiing in Kitzbühel and Kirchberg is strictly intermediate with a few black stretches. There are enough smooth, mellow crusing runs for the beginner and lower intermediate to keep harmony in any mixed-skill group.

 Experts, except those concentrating on their times down the Hahnenkamm run or the Gaisberg course above Kirchberg, should ski on something more challenging than the prepared runs. Guides can take serious skiers on off-trail expeditions from Kitzbühel or Kirchberg that will delight even the most hardened experts.

Mountain layout–Snowboarding

The Kitzbüheler Horn has received top ratings from European snowboard magazines. Freestylers, freeriders and alpine snowboarders all have a blast. There is a permanent 450-meter-long boardercross course with almost 300 feet of vertical and 14 obstacles for competition on Brunellenfeld. They also have an excellent 100-meter-long halfpipe and a snowboard rental area.

The Hahnenkamm is also a good area for snowboarders as well as the Pengelstein and Hieslegg where terrain attracts fewer skiers.

The Snowboard Center at the Kitzbühler Horn (2701) rents boards. Rote Teufel holds special all-inclusive courses in snowboarding, starting at €60 per day. Three full days costs €130.

Kirchberg ski schools have three-day snowboarding lessons for €134 and a snowboard weekly lesson for €165.

 ## Cross-country and snowshoeing

Cross country skiers carrying their skis can use the entire Kirchberg/Kitzbühel bus system without charge. Overall there are 120 km. of cross-country trails in the region.

There are four primary trails ranging from easy to difficult and stretching some 36 km. just around Kitzbühel itself. But a short ride on the free ski bus gives you access to more trails in the region. If you include Reith, Aurach and Jochberg with Kitzbühel, there is a total of 45 km. with seven trails of various difficulty levels and breathtaking Alpine views far removed from the frenetic pace of the downhill slopes.

Kirchberg has new track-setting equipment to maintain three primary tracks in the area, the longest of which is a 30 km, loop from Kirchberg to the Brixental.

Snowshoeing: The Kitzbühel Tourist Office organizes guided hiking trips and snowshoe walks from Monday to Friday. Meeting point: 9:45 a.m. in front of the office Kitzbühel Tourismus in the part of the town near the cinema. No need to register in advance. Free of charge for all hiking fans who have the Kitzbühel guests' ticket, otherwise it's €5 per person.

Two highly recommended tours are the 3-S continuous loop gondola tour and to the water storage ponds at the Resterhöhe/Pass Thurn. There's a minimum of 4 persons.

Telephone prefix: Kitzbühel, 05356; Kirchberg, 05357

Guestcard holders can take these tours. The Spectacular 3-S continuous loop gondola hiking tour meets every Wednesday at 9:30 a.m. in front of the Kitzbühel tourist office. Cost is €52 per person including snowshoes and sticks. The Resterhöhe/Pass Thurn tour costs €14.80 per person for the gondola and skibus.

Ski school (2007/08 prices)

Group Lessons generally cost about €60–€70 per day and are a good way to sharpen your skills if you're out of practice, to get to know the mountain and to find the best snow conditions.

Six ski schools compete for the **Kitzbühel** vacationer: Ski School Reith (65496), Ski School Aurach (65804) and Rote Teufel also known as Red Devils (62500).

Rote Teufel is the main ski school in Kitzbuhel. Costs run about €60 for one day of lessons. Three days are about €130. Six days will set you back around €170. Rote Teufel teaches special group and racing schools. One day of racing school is €70 and three days €150.

In **Kirchberg**, choose from Skischule Kirchberg (2209) and Skischule Kirchberg Aktiv (35230). Prices are more or less the same, with full day group lessons costing about €52, three-day lessons about €125, and five-day lessons €137.

Private lessons are one of the best ways to discover the beauty of these mountains while improving your technique is to hire a private guide. Costs vary: most instructors for one to two people cost between €200-€225 per day; €150-€175 for a half day.

Lift tickets (2007/08 prices)

Kitzbühel offers a variety of lift tickets, including senior citizens' discounts. High season includes Christmas and New Year weeks to mid-March. Before Christmas and late March on are low seasons.

	High Season	Low Season
one day	€38.50	€33.50
three days	€101	€88
six days	€180	€156.50
seven days	€2022	€175.50

Children born 1992-2001 and youth born from 1989-1991 get a discount. Children born after 2002 ski free.

Accommodations

At first blush, Kitzbühel's hotels might easily be mistaken for well-kept farmhouses, with their sloping roofs and white façades. On the inside, however, they are as efficient and elegant as they are clean. We have chosen these places because they speak English and they are in the old town or very close to the Hahnenkamm gondola. Some of the smaller hotels, gasthöfe and apartments do not take credit cards. Ask before it is too late. Many will take a check.

Based on high season, per person/double occupancy with breakfast: €€€—more than €80; €€—€50–79; €—less than €50.

The **Hotel Goldener Greif** (64311, fax 65001; €€€) bills itself as an ancient Tyrolean inn dating back to 1271. However, the property was completely redesigned and redecorated and now features such modern amenities as a casino next door, sauna, swimming pool, solarium and Turkish steam bath.

With its sliding glass doors and wide-open lobby, the **Sporthotel Reisch** (63366, fax 63291; €€€) is by far the brightest of the Kitzbühel hotels. Also offered is a spa where trained therapists provide massages, facials, treatments and relaxation programs.

At the **Schweizerhof** (62735, fax 6273557; €€€), one of the few ski-in/ski-out inns, guests can also enjoy a full-service spa. Live après-ski entertainment is the order of the day in high season.

Another excellent ski-in/ski-out spot is the **Hotel Rasmushof** (652520, fax 6525249; €€€) right at the finish of the Hahnenkamm course. This hotel is pure quality and quiet luxury. It is about a hundred steps from the town and all the charm, plus nice touches like indoor pool, sauna, steamroom and fitness center.

The **Hotel Zur Tenne** (64444, fax 6480356; €€€) leaves the guest with the impression of living inside a giant ark, with heavy wood walls and ceilings It features some of the nicest antiques. Because it's in the town center, the hotel's lovely and bright Wintergarten dining area looks right onto the main street.

The stained-glass windows and mounted antlers in the **Tiefenbrunner Hotel** (66680, fax 6668080; €€€) tell a story of its Tyrolean heritage. Paintings and carvings lining the lobby wall narrate the history of this part of Austria. The cozy bar is often packed with a mix of locals and tourists. Treat yourself to a fine vintage from the 800-year-old wine cellar. Unwind in the newly renovated heated pool, sauna, and steam room. Most rooms have been recently renovated and there's a brand new spa.

Schloss Lebenberg (6901, fax 64405; €€€) has always been a hotel where you could live like a king, so it's no surprise that during the 2007/08 season this converted castle on the outskirts of the town is being renovated and extended to include a spa.

Kaiserhof (75503, fax 7550355; €€€), formerly the Montana, is steps from the Hahnenkamm gondola. Ski right down to this hotel at end of the day. The Kaiserhof is a brand-new property owned by Best Western featuring a pool and sauna. Children under 5 are free (in parents room) and there is a playroom called the Mausefalle.

Hotel Ehrenbachhöhe (621510; €€ half board only) has rooms and an indoor swimming pool up on the mountain, in the midst of the Hahnenkamm area. If you are here for the skiing, this is a perfect place to be. No credit cards accepted.

Hotel Resch (62294, fax 65006; €€) The hotel has a good location near town and the lifts. Rooms vary in size but all are pretty large, however some have tables and sitting areas.

Eggerwirt (62455, fax 6243722; €€) A find with a great eatery. You'll love it.

Licht (62293, fax 62293-33; €€€) B&B but also has apartments.

These affordable B&Bs have great locations: **Haselberger** (62866; €) and **Hochfilzer Gästehaus** (62217, fax 05355/5864; €).

These apartments are on the slopes and within a few minutes' walk of downtown: **Maurachbauer** (tel/fax 72358; €€, sleeps up to eight people in a farmhouse); **Pension Johanna** (64856, fax 640547; €€, sleeps two to four people, breakfast extra); **Apartmentpension Dr. Hillebrand KEG** (62614, fax 6261426) sleeps two to or five people, breakfast included); **Hof Oberhaus** (73267, fax 73267; €€-€€€) sleeps two or four people in a farmhouse).

Kitzbühel has scores of other very affordable B&Bs that are perfect for anyone traveling on a budget. Contact the tourist office for reservations and information.

Ski Chalets: Inghams. (See page 18 for phone, fax and internet addresses.)

Kirchberg

The accommodations here are not as luxurious as the five-stars in Kitzbühel nor as expensive. If traveling with your family, Kirchberg is a perfect place to stay. The clientele is also a bit younger in Kirchberg. (Note: Telephone prefix for Kirchberg is 05357.)

Hotel Alexander (05357/2222, fax 3407; €€€) the top spot in the center of Kirchberg with sauna, steam room, whirlpool, and Internet connections.

Telephone prefix: Kitzbühel, 05356; Kirchberg, 05357

Hotel Sonnalp (05357/2741, fax 2741200; €€) has sauna and pool. It is great for families. The long walk back from town after a night out can be daunting.

Hotel Sonne (05357/24020, fax 2402-88) is a four-star property located close to the slopes. It has a pool, sauna, steam room, and spa treatments.

Hotel Klausen (05357/2128, fax 3612; €€) is outside of town right next to the Fleckalmbahn. It is the perfect for those concentrating on skiing and not partying.

Hotel Metzgerwirt (05357/2325, fax 232549; €€) is a solid four-star hotel right in the center of Kirchberg.

Hotel Cordial Vitalhotel (05357/2842, fax 2842406; €€€) is a good four-star hotel with heated outdoor pool, sauna, whirlpool, steam room, fitness center, and children's club.

Hotel Seehof (05357/2228, fax 22288; €) Beautifully redone rooms in a three-star hotel, great location. A real bargain.

Gasthof Kirchenwirt (05357/2852, fax 3773; €) Well-run, inexpensive gasthof right in town center with good food. What more can one ask for?

If you want to stay up on the mountain call Alpengasthof Filzerhof (05357/2587, fax 258752)

There are scores of B&Bs in Kirchberg with prices in the €18–€33 per night range. Contact the Kirchberg tourist office for more information and for reservations.

Ski Chalets: Crystal, Inghams/Bladon, First Choice. (See page 16 for phone, fax and internet addresses.)

Apartments, condominiums, flats

A list of apartments is available from the Kitzbühel and the Kirchberg tourist office.

A number of pensions allow visitors to rent rooms with kitchens in ski season, but as always, it's best to check with the tourist office.

Read the directory carefully and ask the property for a *Prospekt* or brochure, before deciding where to stay.

Prices per night per person for four people sharing an apartment range from farmhouse inexpensive—about €14 a night in high season—to downtown expensive, €35 a night in the same time period. Prices in Kitzbühel and Kirchberg are about the same.

In most apartments in Europe you will be charged for various services. Meals, cleaning, linen and often utilities can all add up. Ask about what is and isn't included.

 ## Dining

Prices (without wine) €€€—€40+, €€—€21–40, €—€20-.

For the best meals in the area try the following Gault Millau two-toque rated eateries. Tennerhof Restaurant (63181; €€€) gets rave reviews for everything from main courses to avant-garde desserts. Schwedenkapelle (65870; €€€), actually closer to Kirchberg near the Fleckalmbahn, is exceptional and has dinner served on Saturday with musical accompaniment.

For an out of the ordinary experience try the candlelight dinner at Restaurant Hochkitzbühel (6957230; at the top of the Hahnenkamm Gondola; €€€). It is continental gourmet cooking with all the bells and whistles. Disappointingly, though you would expect it, there is no view of the town of Kitzbühel from the restaurant. Take time to enjoy the view on the ride up.

Finally, head to Lois Stern (74882; €€), just outside the old town, for creative cooking in an open kitchen where you can watch Lois cook. He is a master of cuisine tending toward Italian and also brings strong influences of Japan to his kitchen. When you have had enough meat, cheese and potatoes, this is a fascinating change.

For those of us who like quantity and traditional meals rather than dining on rarified gourmet creations, check out these spots:

The **Landhäusl** (64007; €€) serves the largest portions in the area. Make reservations! Most tables seat six to eight people, and the staff won't hesitate to seat you next to someone else—not a good idea if you want a romantic dinner for two. Worth recommending: the Wienerschnitzel and Kaiserschmarren, a pancake-style dish. Dinner for two costs about €35. Credit cards accepted.

Locals gravitate toward the **Huberbrau-Stuberl** (65677; €–€€), for Tyrolean specialties as well as Austrian fare. Eat early or late to avoid a wait.

Insomniacs should drop by **Zinnkrug** (62613; €–€€) which is the closest thing to an all-night diner. Open all the time and recommended by every local we asked, it serves a good basic Austrian meals and spare ribs and takes credit cards.

Looking for Mexican cuisine? You're in luck; there are two restaurants that dish out tacos and cold Coronas. The most popular is **La Fonda** (73673). Service is slow, but you'll eventually get your chimichangas. Dinner for two costs about €25. Credit cards aren't taken, but there's an automatic teller machine around the corner.

In Kitzbühel, it's pizza, not schnitzel, that seems to be everywhere. Most bars serve small single-size pizzas, but they're not what you might expect—an Austrian pizza has a thinner crust and less topping than its American cousin.

Barique (Hinterstradt 19; 62658) has a lively bar scene. It also serves an excellent selection of spaghetti dishes, as does **Il Gusto** (Hinterstadt 19; 72790).

On the mountain stop in for lunch or at least a beer and schnapps at the **Seidlalm** where the World Cup races were founded and at **Sonnbergstub'n** where there is a singing chef. Coming to Kirchberg make sure not to miss **Gasthof Maierl** at the top of the Maierl lift. Try the rustic Tyrolean *Blutwurst, Groest'l mit Spiegelei or Kasespätzle mit Röstzwiebel.* Or head to **Gasthof Schroll** for *Kaiserschmarren aus der Pfanne.* **Rasmushof** has lunch specials just off the trails, cheap!

Fine dining just outside Kitzbühel is worth the taxi ride to the nearby towns of Reith and Aurach. In Reith head to **Tischlerwirt** (65416; €€) and feast on meals like deer with blackberry balsamic sauce and desserts such as cherry cake with rum. In Aurach go straight to **Giggling-Stube** (64888; €€) where you will be overjoyed with your meal. Try the creative wild game and lamb dishes.

Heading up the valley in the direction of Pass Thurn in Jochberg try **Bärnbichl-Stube** (Bärenbühelweg 35, Jochberg; 05355/5347; €€) for acclaimed Austrian meals. The Gröst'l and trout are wonderful. This is a great place to stop for lunch while on the ski safari. Also in Jochberg is **Schwarzer Adler** (05355/6911; €€).

In Kirchberg, most group arrangements are for full pension. If you want to go out on the town, one of the best restaurants is the **Pfeffermühle** (05357/2222; €–€€) attached to the Hotel Alexander, that the owner calls Austrian with a touch of Italian. It features a wood-fired pizza oven and its specialty is meat that you grill on a hot stone set in the middle of the table. It's great fun. Cost is between €14–20 depending on the cut of meat.

Geniesserrestaurant Rosengarten (05357/2527; €€€), in Hotel Taxacherhof, the award-winning chef Simon Taxacher creates his versions of nouvelle Austrian cuisine and continental gourmet meals. Call for reservations. Candlelight dinner here with a lover is the perfect setup for a great dessert.

For a real traditional experience head to the **Kupferstuben** (05357/2335; €€) where you can fill up very affordably on rustic Tyrolean meals in the perfect atmosphere. Make reservations, it's packed. There is actually an Italian working at the **Nabucco**

Telephone prefix: Kitzbühel, 05356; Kirchberg, 05357

(05357/35099; €) that serves pizza and pasta. For excellent wild game, try the **Kirchenwirt** (05357/2852; €–€€).

 ## Après-ski/nightlife

What you do in Kitzbühel after skiing is as important as the skiing itself. The nightlife should be renamed morning life, because things don't really get underway until 2 a.m. or so. That's when you can hear the whoops, yells, laughter and song of bar-crawling skiers as they slide down the sidewalks.

Amazingly, there are only a few bars that cater to the after-hours crowd. Jet-laggers searching for a cold brew and a warm pizza should follow the stairs in the cellar of **Mangoes** (0664/2410600) open 10 p.m.–2 a.m., "but we really don't close until five or so," says the bartender. Watch out for the darts! British expatriates can rely on their instincts to find the **Londoner** (71427) and **Big Ben** (71100), two almost authentic pubs. The Londoner is across from McDonald's. For Irish singing, head to **Flannigan's Irish Pub** (63237) at Jochberger Strasse 4. You'll find **Jimmy's** if you wander along the town square in the *Fussgängerzone* (pedestrian zone). **s'Lichtl Pub** (63924) is right on the main drag across the street from the Hotel Tenne. **Seppi's Pub** (64662) is also a fun spot. **Grieserl** (72752) beneath the Tieffenbrunner is a good meeting spot for drinks and has excellent Internet connections.

There are four discos in the town square area. **Club Take 5** at Hinterstadt 22 (74131), **Olympia** at Hinterstadt 6 (72143), **Club Python** at Hinterstadt 6 (63001) and **Royal** at Hinterstadt 9 (75901) which features the only English-speaking disc jockey. Generally, discos don't open until 9 p.m., and often close at dawn.

Hotel Goldener Greif's **Casino Kitzbühel** is open 7 p.m. until 2 a.m. daily. Visitors may try their luck at baccarat, blackjack, wheel of fortune and slot machines.

Kirchberg is one of the party centers of Austria with a strong Dutch contingent of party animals. It claims one of the wildest après-ski bars in Europe, **The London Pub**. This bar has been copied in other towns, but this is the original. It's dance-til-you-melt, dance-on-the-tables time from about 4 p.m.–8 p.m.. This is the wild après-ski party you've dreamed of. If you haven't tried it yet knock back a couple of "Der Flugels," made with Red Bull and flavored vodka.

Later at night the party continues there or moves to the **Tiroler** (4455) that is decorated like a giant country barn. Or head to the **Fuchslöchl** for dancing.

 ## Child care (2007/08 prices)

The **Kitzbühel** tourist office (62155-0 or 62272) keeps a list of licensed, multilingual babysitters. Ski schools also offer full-day lessons for ski kindergarten for kids from ages 3 to 5. Costs are €60 for a day, €110 for two days, ranging to €160 for five days.

Anita Halder (75063), a nurse, also watches children for an hourly charge.

In **Kirchberg** there is the Krabbelstube (4255), a kindergarten for children from age 6 or younger, open Monday to Friday, 7:15 a.m.–6 p.m. and Saturdays from 7:15 a.m.–noon. Prices are approximately €51 for a day and €119 for three days. Babysitting service is available through the tourist office.

The ski school in Kirchberg also has special children's programs. Rates are the same as for the normal ski school, with an additional €8 for lunch. The Children's Mini Club Total for kids 2–4 years of age has care for about €28 for a day and about €50 for a half day. Lunch is an additional €6.

Other activities

The **Aquarena** (64385) is the indoor sports area, with a swimming pool, sauna, steam room and solarium. New slides give it a waterpark feel. Admission is €9 for adults (with guest card €8) and €5.60 for children (with guest card €5).

Element3 – Adventure Center (0664-1000580) offers parasailing flights. A flight from the Hahnenkamm costs €99 per person; the Hike and Fly Safari which lets you sail from three mountains in one day costs €300 per person.

For **balloon trips** call Ballooning Tyrol in St. Johann (05352/5666). Balloon flights cost cost €291 for about 2 hours.

You can go **ice skating** at Schwarzsee Lake or at the Sportpark Kitzbuhel (20222). At the Sportpark adults pay €5.50; children pay €2. There is also curling, climbing, ice hockey and Austrian bowling facilities at the Sportpark.

Horse-drawn sleigh rides are available through Henntalhof at Unterbrunnweg 21, (64624) for €60 per hour, and one sleigh can seat up to six people. Rides are also offered by Eberl Hubert at Innerstaudach 58 (66380). Carriages seat up to five people and cost €50.

Kirchberg has a 3.5-km.-long **toboggan-run** that stays open until 10 p.m. With your ski pass it's free during the day. The cost in the evening is about €8 for adults and €4.50 for children. The Gaisberg lift takes you up and you slide down. After drinks the steep trail takes on an added challenge. There is a Gasthof at the top and one in the middle of the run that serve libations to lubricate the runners.

Getting there

The most common route to Kitzbühel and Kirchberg is via Munich. Innsbruck and Salzburg are also popular arrival points. Although train service is available, many prefer the easy 1-1/2-hour drive from Munich in a rental car. Express trains ease the hassles of driving and leave twice a day from Munich.

Tourist information

Kitzbühel Tourism (Kitzbühel-Reith-Aurach Tourism), A-6370 Kitz-bühel, Austria; Telephone 05356-7770, fax 05356-77777. Internet: www.kitzbuehel.com.   E-mail: info@kitzbuehel.com.

Toursimusverband Kirchberg, Hauptstrasse 8, A-6365 Kirchberg, Austria; Telephone 05357-2309, fax 05357-3732. Internet: www.kitzbuehel-alpen.com or www.kirchberg.at. E-mail: info@kitzbuehel-alpen.at or info@kirchberg.at.

Mayrhofen

Hintertux and Tuxertal in the upper Zillertal

Mayrhofen is one of the most beautifully situated resorts in Austria. The towering mountains seem to surround the town as you drive up the wide valley. This is not a place one would happen upon by accident and comment, "This would be nice to come back and visit." The only villages further up the mountain pass lead to dead-end glaciers. If you arrive in Mayrhofen, you probably want to be there. The locals will surely do their best to keep you in their valley.

The village, about a 15-minute walk across, could be a Hollywood set. The church steeple towers over wooden façades and balconies on whitewashed mountain houses. Konditorei display tempting pastries. The latest Tyrolean fashions—still harking back to tradition—fill dress shop windows Bakeries emit mouthwatering smells of fresh bread. Dogs chase each other. Restaurant candles glisten through hazy windows and hearty laughter echoes from gasthausen.

The road south to Hintertux rises steeply through narrow gaps in the mountains. After passing through 10-kilometer-long Tuxertal (connected by lifts with Mayrhofen) you'll reach the Hintertuxer Glacier which is isolated at the end of the road. This glacier provides year-round skiing laced with one of Europe's most modern ski lift systems.

Five main ski regions are connected to Mayrhofen—Penken, Finkenberg, Horberg/Gerent, Rastkogel and Eggalm. They tend to keep their snow longer than most Austrian resorts because of their altitude (about 5,900 to 8,200 feet). However little of the skiable snow reaches down to the town of Mayrhofen lying at an altitude of only 2,067 feet above sea level. This is a resort where the ski runs are high above the town. Skiers normally come back to town by the gondolas or by bus from one of the outlying higher-altitude villages.

English is spoken by most natives, but most visitors to Mayrhofen originate from Germany and the Netherlands, with a strong contingent of Brits and Australians and an occasional American.

In February, Austria is Mayrhofen's biggest customer, offering a steady flow of visitors on holiday. Check before making vacation plans so you don't hit a busy week.

The other villages of the Tuxertal are in the next valley up the mountain road on the way to the Hintertuxer glacier. They are all cute but without the amenities offered by Mayrhofen. Finkenberg with its steep streets hugs the mountain road connecting Mayrhofen with the Tuxertal.

Of the villages in Tuxertal, Lanersbach is the largest and provides some village atmosphere. If you blink, you will miss Juns and Madseit. Hintertux is far up in the Tuxertal Valley at the base of one of the best glaciers for summer skiing. It makes no pretense of being anything but a glacier ski resort. If it had sidewalks, they would be rolled up when the lifts close. However there are good restaurants and some good bars at the base of the lifts and in the nearby town.

 # Mountain layout–Skiing

This area has some of the most modern lifts in Austria. Considering that many feel Austria is the last bastion of T-bars, virtually all of Mayrhofen can be skied using only chairlifts, gondolas and cable cars. In December 2006, the ski-lift company completed a major upgrade in the Ahorn, one of the few remain sectors that had been dominated by T-bars. The newly installed Ahorn cable car is the biggest in Austria. The 160-person gondola zips skiers up to the 2,000 meter plateau is six minutes. Also for the 2007/08 season, the two main T-bars will also be replaced by an eight-person chair lift. These lifts, and the entire new mountain faces that they open, change everything. Much of the new terrain was once the province of only backcountry skiers.

The Ahorn sector his best suited for beginners and lower intermediates though more advanced skiers may also enjoy skiing here. At the end of the day, you can drop right back into town.

From Mayrhofen, you can access the main ski area by either the Penkenbahn or the Horbergbahn high-speed gondolas. Both are connected with all the hotels in the town by a shuttlebus every 15 minutes during the winter.

Once at the top of the Penken those interested in the children's center and beginner lessons only have to step off the lift. From the top of the high-speed, six-seater Penken Express, beginners can swing to their left to avoid the steeper sections and drop back to the top station of the gondola. Intermediate and advanced skiers will love the steeper sections off this lift. They can drop down to the top of the Horbergbahn and take the lifts to the wide-open, off-piste, powder-filled terrain of the Gerent.

Further up the Horberg Hallow, experts and intermediates looking to push themselves should take the 150-person cable car up to 7,217 feet where there is wide-open skiing. Experts looking for a real challenge should try the Hikari.

Hintertux and the Tuxertal

Skiers in Tuxertal can drop into the Rastkogel and Eggalm areas. Both are excellent beginner and intermediate areas with plenty of off-piste for experts. After a day of skiing either take the bus back to Mayrhofen or they can ride the Rastkogelbahn and then another six-person high-speed chair lift back up to the top of the ridge. From there cruise down the Hofberg/Gerent area to return to Mayrhofen. Both of these areas now connect with the main Mayrhofen ski areas.

The Hintertuxer glacier opens at the end of the valley rising from 4,921 feet to top out at 10,564 feet—that's an amazing 5,443 feet of vertical. This is one of the top training areas for ski and snowboard teams from all over the world. From the ground station you can see most of the nearly 50 miles of trails above. The lift system is superb

Telephone prefix: 05285

and the small mountain huts on the runs are great fun.

The best run is the trail from the Grosser Kaserer (10,700 feet) down over a great steep field of bumps to the gondola. A nice intermediate run leads from the top of the Gefrorene Wand to the Spannagel house, which is cozy and serves excellent food.

Mountain rating

This is a region that has something for everyone. Experts will delight in the Horberg/Gerent area. They have an enormous area to explore and enjoy.

Intermediates have Eggalm and Raskogel in the Tuxertal that are a blast and the Penken is a phenomenal intermediate area with super fast lifts. Intermediates can also head over to the Horberg/Gerent area where the slopes are wide open and they have plenty of room to test themselves.

Beginners have the benefit of one of the best ski schools in Austria. They have excellent learning areas at the top of the Penkenbahn and in the Penkenjoch at the top of the Finkenberger Almbahn.

For snow reports, call 62373.

 ## Mountain layout–Snowboarding

This is becoming a real destination for snowboarders. Austria's top free riders come here to hang and hundreds of boarders attend summer boarding camps held on the glacier, but they stay in Mayrhofen.

The area has wide-open, above-treeline snow that drops into tight trees offering plenty of challenge.

The resort caters to boarders with Burton Park and its lift system that makes the hassle of T-bars a thing of the past. It's the only snowpark with its own four-seater lift. The park has five jumps. Two of the jumps are beginner's tables. The others are a professional and medium line which are built up as three large jumps and one spine. The spine is built so that riders can duck out of the 20-meter table, which is considered a pro jump. There's a halfpipe and a few rail lines, which include a rail strictly for beginners and a truly unique rail that allow boarders to ride five rails in one ride!

 ## Ski school (2006/07 prices)

There are four ski schools in Mayrhofen with over 150 instructors to teach all grades of skiers. The Austrian ski method is used on all courses.

Group Lessons—Prices are uniform, and competition for the skier is tight.

Regardless of the school you select, you'll pay €55 for one day of lessons, €115 for three days. Six days will amount to €130.

Children's lessons are slightly less and include lunch. The schools are: Ski School Manfred Gager (63800), Ski School Mayrhofen Total (63939), Ski School Mayrhofen 3000 (64015) and Peter Habeler Ski and Alpine School (62829).

The following prices are for the Ski School Mayrhofen 3000: Private Lessons—Mayrhofen's private lessons for one or two students cost €48 for one hour; €90 for two hours from Thurs. to Sat. and €99 for two hours from Sun. to Wed.; and €150 for two hours from Thurs. to Sat. and €173 for two hours from Sun. to Wed..

Snowboarding lessons — Again, prices seem to vary little from school to school. Classes cost €36 a day; €87 for three days; €122 for five days. Some four-hour private lessons are also available. Contact the ski school for prices.

Cross-country

If you left your cross-country equipment at home, don't worry. Rentals are less expensive than downhill equipme. Weekly discounts are always available.

Mayrhofen offers nine trails for a total of 30 km. All trails are rated easy, making this an ideal place to learn. Overall, cross-country opportunities are not really outstanding, especially for the more advanced. There can be a problem with snow cover at the low altitude. We suggest that cross-country skiers take the bus up to Tuxertal and cross-country ski on those trails. They normally have more snow cover.

Lessons cost about the same as downhill, and are usually offered privately.

Lift tickets (2007/08 prices)

Buying a lift ticket can be a perplexing task. Mayrhofen sells a variety of passes with a complex price structure. Want to ski exclusively at Mayrhofen, or at all 167 Ziller Valley lifts? Tickets for each individual resort are available, as well as for the regional Zillertaler-Superskipass. With the connection of Mayrhofen and Tuxertal, there is more than enough skiing for a week.

Mayrhofen/Tuxertal area lifts

	Adult	Youth	Child
half day (starting at 11 a.m.)	€31.50	€25	€15.50
one day	€36	€29	€18

Zillertaler–Superskipass

	Adult	Youth	Child
four days	€126	€100.50	€63
seven days	€197.50	€158	€99
fourteen days	€344	€275	€172

Youth are those born after January 1, 1989 and children born after January 1, 1993. Proof of age is required to receive the child and youth rates. Children, born after January 1, 2002 can ski free with an accompanying adult.

A fee of €2 is charged for the chip card, which will be refunded in full when you return the card fully intact to one of the resort's drop-off points.

Accommodations

When considering an appropriate hotel or apartment in Mayrhofen, keep a few points in mind. First, the number of stars on a property only means you'll pay more, and not always get more. Second, price is dictated less by proximity to lifts than by which bank of the Ziller river it sits on. Cross the bridge to the west bank and you'll pay less—not just for lodging but food and drink as well. Third, for peace and quiet at night, avoid the route between Scotland Yard Pub, the Ice Bar and Nikki's. Revellers wander between the bars, then stagger and sing later in the night.

These selections based on spoken Engish, amenities and then location.

Based on high season, per person/double occupancy with breakfast: €€€—more than €80; €€—€50–79; €—less than €50.

American visitors usually prefer the **Hotel Neuhaus** (6703; €€). Guests are treated to authentic Alpine motif lobbies, with nicely furnished rooms and an indoor pool. Visitors may watch a movie, go bowling, shoot pool or get a massage in the spa.

The **Hotel Zillertaler Hof** (62265; €–€€), a quiet and modern property, also features an indoor pool. With its venerable antiques and wood carvings on display, this inn emanates style. Rates don't reflect the impressive list of amenities.

For a little extra room, try the **Hotel Neue Post** (62131; €), with its airy lobby and generous-sized rooms. One of Mayrhofen's earliest guest houses, it includes sauna, whirlpools, solarium, extensive restaurants and dining rooms. **Hotel St. Georg** (627920, fax 62792406; €€–€€€) has an indoor pool, and excellent rooms. **Apparthotel König** (62235, fax 620665; €) is a good place to check out if you are traveling with four or five friends. **Pension Austria** (62647, fax 6264711; €) is another inexpensive, cozy place about 100 yards from the town center and the Pengenbahn.

If you want to be in the middle of the après-ski action head to one of these spots. The **Hotel Strass** (6705; €€) prides itself in its historic furniture and decorations. But its prices are very up-to-date. Three other properties are also owned by the same family: **Sporthotel Strass, Villa/Aparthotel Strass** and **Hotel Garni Strass**. These are at the epicenter of the Ice Bar and Arena Disco. Across the Ziller River is the **Gasthof Brücke** (62232; €), which is also a big après-ski attraction. It has a nice lobby and medium-size rooms with antique furniture and beautiful tiled floors. The Gasthof plays host to a decidedly younger crowd. Many skiers take a short stroll from here to the town's only outdoor watering hole, Nikki Schirmbar.

Hintertux has several hotels right at the base of the glacier. If you're intent on skiing and little else, they're a good choice. **Hotel Rindererhof** (05287-501, fax 50210; €€–€€€) has an excellent location right at the gondola going up to the glacier. **Hotel Neu Hintertux** (05287-318, fax 318409; €€€) is almost as close to the lifts as the Rindererhof but more luxurious and has a swimming pool. **Badhotel Kirchler** (05287-312; €€€) is beautiful, expensive and comfortable. **Pension Rosengarten** (05287-87413, fax same; €€) is a comfortable, medium-priced spot in Lanersbach.

Contact the Tux tourist board (A-6293 Tux-Lanersbach 472; 5287-8506, fax 05287-8508) for more information.

Apartments, condominiums, flats

The quality of apartments varies. Some double as hotels in peak season and offer a long list of amenities; others are simple rooms. Prices vary dramatically. Some properties will charge €15 in peak season for a no-frills room, while others ask for €50 per night. Usually, the farther from town they are, the less you'll pay. The Ziller River remains an important natural boundary—on the west bank the cost of a room drops.

A directory of apartments is available from the Mayrhofen tourist office.

Dining

Mayrhofen is not one of the dining meccas of Austria. The restaurants, though not gourmet, are excellent and resonably priced. Many of them exude Austrian charm filled with wood paneling and lined with antlers. Note: Do not assume that Austrian restaurants take credit cards—many do not. Check before you dine or carry cash. Where we know the establishment takes cards, we let you know.

Prices (without wine) €€€—€36+, €€—€16–35, €—€15-.

Wirtshaus zum Griena (62778; €€) is the most authentic Tyrolean restaurant in town. Come here for all the specialties. It is a bit out of town across the river.

If you're looking for a romantic dining spot with real Austrian cuisine, try the **Hotel Neuhaus Restaurant** (6703; €€). Be sure to make early reservations to get into one of the small Stube, a dining area with wonderful ambiance. Credit cards accepted.

Neue Post (62131; €€) has a series of very cozy and romantic Stuben (small dining areas) and the cooking is almost as good as the Neuhaus.

Andrea (62601; €€) serves excellent Austrian and Italian meals.

Zillergrund (62377; €–€€) gets good reviews from the locals, but you will need a car or have to take a taxi. It's worth the ride.

A good Austrian restaurant is **Karlsteg** (05286/5250; €€) but it is a drive.

Ländenhof (63451; €–€€) is a family-run Austrian place.

The **Grillküchl** (36126; €) is a small, cozy restaurant with only about five tables. The kitchen is open and prices certainly don't match the rich and intricate wood decor. Show up early to get a table. No credit cards.

Mamma Mia (6768; €) in the Hotel Elisabeth serves good pizza and pasta.

At the **Fleishhauerei Perauer** (literally: The Butcher Shop; €), across the river along Ahornstrasse, patrons order native meat dishes with a decent Spätzle, an Austrian pasta specialty with cheese. During the evening, witness locals wagering on card games. It's probably more entertaining to watch than play. No credit cards.

The **Singapore Restaurant** (63912; €) dishes out authentic hot and sour soup and flavorful main courses that will jump-start your taste buds. Credit cards welcome.

The slopes Mayrhofen has excellent restaurants as well. Two that are good for having lunch with non-skiers are **Bergrast** (easy to get to for non-skiers) and **Gschosswandhaus** (about a ten-minute walk). Otherwise take your choice of dozens. **Christa's Skialm** is packed and noisy. **Schneekar** is hard to miss—it is a wooden pyramid. **Gschossalm** is a stopping place for schnapps on the way home and a favorite of the local ski instructors. **Sunalm** has a great sun deck which is especially bright in the spring. **Grillhofalm** serves fresh pizza. It's a favorite of snowboarders because it's right next to the fun park and snowboard jumps. Crowds gather to oooh and aaaah..

Cafes are a part of life in Austria. The best in town is **Café Kostner** on the Hauptstrasse. It is in the Viennese style and gets rave reviews by the critics.

 ## Après-ski/nightlife

Most bars get hopping about an hour before the lifts close. They are packed till around 7 p.m. or 10 p.m. when everyone seems to leave to eat. Discos open around 10 p.m. and usually close at 4 a.m. on the dot.

Après-ski is wild in Mayrhofen. **The Ice Bar** and **Nikki's Schirmbar** are the two places to be for skiers right after coming off the slopes. **The Ice Bar** claims to serve more Grolsch beer than any other bar in Europe. At **Nikki's Schirmbar**, an outdoor watering hole with loud music, just across the river along Ahornstrasse. Expect to see skiers dancing on tables in their boots. The fun starts around 3:30 p.m. If you're looking for a specialty drink, avoid the main bar (under the umbrella) and head to the side bar where Schnapps Shots (say that three times fast) in edible wafer shot-glasses are prepared for around €1. Don't forget the napkin!

Snowboarders congregate at **Scotland Yard** (Scotti to the locals). This is a British-style pub complete with an operating British phone booth. The selection of on-tap beers is extensive. It gets packed. Later in the evening many of the snowboarders wander down to the **Apropos Bar.**

If looking for something a bit more sedate, head to **Mo's Esscafé & Musikroom** right on the main drag, or try the **Happy End** which serves good wines.

There are two discos in town — the **Sports Arena Disco** (6705) and **Schlüsselalm** (62232). Cover charges can vary from €1–€1.50.

Sporthotel Strass (6705) serves more reasonably priced drinks and features excellent après-ski entertainment. The crowd packs the inside and outdoor bars. After 9:30 p.m. it's an unbelievably crowded madhouse, even on weekdays.

From what we've heard, the new **White Lounge** near the Mayrhofen cable car will be one of the hottest hangouts for the 2007/08 season. It's a six-meter tall ice cave which houses a bar.

In Hintertux, try the **Batzenkeller**, the **Almbar**, the **Nostalschi Bar** in the Hotel Berghof, or the **Papperla-Pub**.

Child care (2006/07 prices)

This is an area of resort expertise where Mayrhofen excels. Ski schools provide day care and ski instruction for children.

Approximate ski school cost without lunch is €55 for one day; for two days, €95; for three days, €115; and for six days, €130. Lunch costs €12. The ski school also takes children from age 2 for the same rates as the group lessons.

Mayrhofen's Guest Kindergarten, called **Wuppy's Kinderland,** takes children from 3 months to 7 years of age. It is open Monday–Friday from 9 a.m.–5 p.m. Price for a full day of supervision is €29, and for five consecutive days, €135. Lunch costs €4 per day. The kindergarten also hires out strollers, prams, and cots for children. It has a swimming pool, nursery school facilities and other activities. Private baby-sitters are also available.

The Mayrhofen Tourist Office (6760) provides a babysitting referral service. They also publish a directory of services, which includes information about child care.

Other activities

Mayrhofen has an excellent indoor **swimming pool** and an **ice skating rink**. Skating is approximately €3 per hour for adults and €2.50 per hour for youths (age 16–19) and €2 for those age 15 and younger. **Tobogganing** is the extracurricular activity of choice here, perhaps because it includes heavy drinking. Sledders hitch a ride to the Tuxer Valley in a motorcoach and ascend to the top of a 6-km. run at the Höllenstein Hütte (which appropriately means the hut built on hell's stone). There, they imbibe mulled wine before zipping down the mountain. For more information, call Action Club Zillertal at 62977. Cost is €25 per person.

Snowtubing is another enjoyable alternative to skiing. Again, drinking is recommended for adults. You bounce down the slope on inner tubes. Call Action Club Zillertal at 62977. Cost is €25 per hour.

Skiers who feel a little *lebensmüde* (tired of life) can try heart-stopping **flights** over the Zillertal. About €65 will get you airborne. Three operators provide the tours.

Getting there

Mayrhofen is nestled in the Ziller valley, about 190 km. from Munich and 170 km. from Salzburg. Rail connections are available, but the most popular way of getting to Mayrhofen is by bus or car. Since the train operates on a single small track, and direct rail service is not available from either airport, passengers must switch to a train or bus at Jenbach. For more information on rail or bus connections, call the Mayrhofen train station at 62362.

Tourist information

The Mayrhofen Tourism is located at the Europahaus in Mayrhofen, Dursterstrasse 225, A-6290 Mayrhofen, Austria; (05285) 6760, fax (05285) 676033.
E-mail: info@mayrhofen.at
Web site: www.mayrhofen.at

Neustift - Stubaital

Neustift is a pretty, picture-prefect Austrian village in the Stubai Valley south of Innsbruck. The village is one of about a dozen or so (depending on your definition of village) that lie in this valley that leads to the Stubai Glacier, the largest glacier in Austria, and one that is open year-round for skiing and riding.

Each village is as pretty as the next. The main villages—Neustift, Schonberg, Mieders, Telfes and Fulpmes—have their own character. A free shuttle plies the route between the glacier base station and Schonberg.

This valley was instrumental in the foundation of mountain tourism by the Austrian and German Alpine Clubs. Neustift was one of the first series of villages in Austria to construct a network of mountain paths and huts. As far back as 1891, Neustift established a mountain guide association.

 ## Mountain layout–Skiing

The altitude here ranges from approximately 1,000 meters in Neustift to 3,340 meters at the top of the glacier. That means the upper stations of the glacier are more than two miles high.

Another characteristic is the variation in the weather and conditions. When the wind is howling and blowing snow creates white-out conditions on the glacier, the trails down in Neustift, Mieders and Fulpmes may be serene and sunny. Crowds can vary dramatically between each of the resorts.

The smaller mountain, the Elfer, is served by a gondola rising from Neustift. Three additional lifts serve almost 3,250 feet of vertical. This would be a complete resort in the U.S.A. The trails are best suited for advanced and intermediate skiers. Beginner terrain here is limited.

The expansive skiing and riding is up on the glacier — all year long. This is wide-open, above treeline skiing. Some trails allow skiers and riders to cruise 14 km. down almost 2,400 feet of non-stop vertical. The lift takes skiers from the parking lot at 5,600 feet up 1,788 feet to a snowfield where four lifts fan out reaching different areas of the glaciers. There are groomed runs, but the mountain begs to be discovered.

Experts can find steep trails from Jochdohle and beneath Wildspitze and Daunkogle. The Wildspitzschuss and Eisnase are exciting. Then there is the Wilde Grubn route that provides 10 km. of ungroomed adventure. You had better be in shape. A guide can take real experts to chutes and drops that will make them pucker up a bit.

The off-trail hut-to-hut experience here is excellent along the ring of peaks behind the glacier. There are hundreds of km. of trails that are a blast but require hiking.

Intermediates have excellent long cruising trails from every lift. With good weather, this area is a delight. Try to stick to the upper mountain. Dropping back to the middle station (the upper part of the cable car from the parking lot) finds longer lines.

Beginners have their own learning area at Gamsgarten. This is also where the children's center is located. But there are easy trails from almost every point here, unless you end up off-piste.

The trails at Fulpmes are known as excellent sheltered learning slopes and those above Mieders are gentle and run through the woods.

Mountain rating

For beginners, this is an excellent place to learn to ski. If beginners stay down-valley in Fulpmes they can have a blast until they are a bit more confident and can tackle the glacier. Any way you look at it, this is spectacular, big mountain skiing accessible to beginners.

Intermediates will be inspired to sing if they hit the glacier in good weather. This area can be explored by a competent intermediate all day long.

Experts — real experts — as always, can find skiing to keep them busy. The off-trail drops from Wildspitz and Daunkogel take some hiking but are exciting. The long ungroomed Wilde Grubn is inspiring.

Mountain layout–Snowboarding

Snowboarders come here for carving big turns on wide runs. There is also a halfpipe and a speed course for snowboarders. The natural chutes on the glacier are like nirvana. Some of Europe's champions come from this area.

Fulpmes' Schlick 2000 has a terrain park and halfpipe as well.

Cross-country

The Stubaital is an excellent spot for cross-country skiing. Trails link all the villages in the valley from Fulpmes to Neustift to Milders to Falbeson. In all there are about 130 km. of groomed trails.

Ski school (2007/08 prices)

Private lessons for one person cost €46 for one hour, €90 for two hours, €135 for three hours and €170 for four hours. There are additional charges for extra students.

Group lessons for adults are four hours long — two hours in the morning and two in the afternoon — available from Sunday to Thursday. One day costs €60; two days, €95; three days, €125; four days, €135; five days €145.

Snowboarding lessons are "4 hours 4 you" on Sunday, Wednesday and Thursday. One day costs €60; two days cost €115; three days cost €135.

Cross-country lessons cost €50 for a half day, €83 for two half days, and €105 for three half days.

Lift tickets (2007/08 prices)

The Stubai Super Ski Pass allows skiing and riding on all the trails in the the valley, including the Stubai Glacier, Neustift-Elfer, Fulpmes-Schlick 2000, and Hochserles, plus free shuttlebus service in the valley and the use of swimmng pools in Neustift and Fulpmes. Available for four days or more. The one-day price is for the Stubai Glacier pass.

	Adults	Youth (15–18)	Child (10–14)
one day (Stubai Glacier Pass)	€36	€23.40	€18
four days	€128.50	€83.50	€64.30
six days	€169	€109	€84.50

Children age 9 and younger ski free.

Accommodations

Rates here are based on high season, per person/double occupancy with half board: €€€—€125+; €€—€75-€124; €—less than €75. This is a bargain region when it comes to excellent hotels.

Spa-Hotel Jagdhof (2666; fax 2666503; €€€) is the most luxurious in town. It is everything Tirolean from the lobby to the restaurant. It has a spa and a heated pool.

Sport Wellnesshotel Neustift (3899; fax 389955; €€) has Tirolean-style rooms, a heated indoor/outdoor pool and massive lobby.

Schönherr Apartments (3530; fax 353030; €-€€) in the center of the village, has beautiful suites and flats with B&B.

For the best of the bargains in Neustift make reservations at **The Hoferwirt** (22010; fax 220122; €) that has excellent half-board, or check into **Sportpension Elisabeth** (2232; fax 3496; €) a quality bargain B&B.

In Neustift-Kampl, the **Hotel Steuxner** (2242; fax 28317; €) has great prices and wonderful views.

Neustift-Stackler has the beautiful **Stacklerhof** (3666; fax 36666; €) that is very affordable and has wonderful Tirolean decorations in the public areas and the guestrooms.

Apartments, condominiums, flats

A list of apartments and B&Bs is available from the tourist office. Write ahead of time and ask for the size you require and the dates that you are planning on being at the resort. Either the tourist office or the apartment landlords will contact you with several possibilities. Make your selections and get back to them.

Prices per night per apartment are between €40–€100 for a two-room apartment during high season and €50–€150 for a three-room apartment. Prices do not normally include local taxes and the cleaning charge.

Dining

The Stubai Valley has some exceptional Tirolean restaurants.

The best is the **Silberdistl** (3171) that has a rustic atmosphere and wonderful classic Austrian meals. The **Jagdhütte** (2668) dining room is set in dark wood with a rugged character. **Kratzerwirt** (3152) is just outside of town in a pretty Alpine house.

In nearby Kampl, try dinner at the **Hotel Steuxner** (2242); and in Fulpmes, it is worth the trip to have a meal at **Gasthof Dorfkrug** (05225-62488) in the heart of the small town.

Après-ski/nightlife

Austrians love apres-ski and this valley is no different from the rest of the country. Beware, if you have been practicing your drinking with

Telephone prefix: 05226

American light beers and shift to the real Austrian stuff, you may feel the effects a bit more quickly.

Stubaital is not one of the party capitals of Austria, however the bars and pubs get packed and there are a few discos and live bands. **Dorfpub** in the middle of town has bands and is an institution. **Nook Bar** gets packed. **Bierfassl** and **Aumi's Pub** fill up with locals. The discos, all within walking distance, are the **Nachtkastl** and **Rumpl**. Pick your poison. They open at 9 p.m. or so and don't start getting packed until nearer to midnight. For the voyeurs, there is the **Apres-ski** that is a strip and gogo bar.

Child care (2007/08 prices)

The Micky Maus ski school (2540) is right up on the Stubai glacier. It has snowplay for children from age 3 and a 'tiny tots' ski course for kids from age 4. The programs run from 10 a.m. to 1–3 p.m. The rates for the snowplay program are €22 a day and €15 for a half day. The ski school program costs €60 for a day; three days, €125; and five days, €145. These rates include two hours of lessons.

Other activities

The valley has five long **toboggan runs** that are a blast, especially after an evening of wine, beer and schnapps. Elferrodelbahn in Neustift village is lighted for night sledding.

There is **ice climbing, hang gliding, parasailing, hot air ballooning, dog sledding, sleigh rides** and **ice skating**.

There are **two indoor pools** that have free entrance included on the guest card.

Plus, **Innsbruck** is only 18 miles away (*See Innsbruck Chapter*)

Getting there

The closest international airports are Innsbruck (25 km.) and Munich (200 km.). There is a shuttle service from the Munich airport called Four Season Travel (0043-512-584157). Check with your hotel to see if they offer a free shuttle from the Innsbruck station.

The closest train station is Innsbruck. The Stubai Bus leaves the Innsbruck station approximately every hour and takes about 45 minutes.

If driving, take the Brennerautobahn A 13 to Exit 10 (Schönberg), then follow Stubaitalstrasse B183. There is an extra toll for the Brennerautobahn.

To avoid the extra toll from Innsbruck, take Exit 3 (Innsbruck Sud) and continue on Brennerbundesstrasse B182 and take the exit for Stubaital.

Tourist information

Neustift Tourist and Travel Office, Dorf 3, A-6167 Neustift im Stubaital, Austria.
Telephone (05226) 2228, fax (05226) 2529.
For lodging reservations call the tourist office.
Internet: www.neustift.com E-mail: info@neustift.com

Oetztal
Sölden, Hochsölden, Obergurgl, Hochgurgl

If it's great skiing you want with unforgettable scenery, the Oetztal is in a class with only a handful of European ski valleys. The tall, jagged mountains are an effective barrier to severe weather, and help preserve good snow conditions during the end of the year. To the south, across Timmelsjoch, which is a road passable only in summer, lies Italy. To the north, a winding road spills out of the Oetz Valley after numerous tunnels and bridges.

With the possible exception of a few warm weeks in August and September, these mountains are always skiable. When the snow disappears in the lower elevations, vacationers ascend to the glacier and ride its eternally frozen runs.

The two main resorts in respective valleys are Sölden and Obergurgl. Hochsölden is a suburb of Sölden, huddled above the larger town. Hochgurgl is merely a cluster of six hotels up the mountain from Obergurgl.

Sölden is stretched along the main road that traverses the valley. The road is bustling with foot and auto traffic, but gives visitors easy access to all services such as rentals, restaurants, nightlife and lifts. This energetic resort provides the on-the-go traveler with endless skiing, a snow guarantee, entertainment and culinary options. In contrast, the smaller villages of Hochsölden, Zwieselstein and Vent are quiet bedroom hamlets sporting excellent hotels and restaurants.

Obergurgl and Hochgurgl are both a 15-minute drive from Sölden. Obergurgl is a picture-perfect Alpine town tucked into the mountains, complete with old church steeple and chalets. Another part of the village, Pill/Angern, is even smaller and less expensive with its own rural charm. It is not within walking distance of the town's center; however, it is adjacent to one of the main cross-country systems and is lift accessible.

Obergurgl is, unlike Sölden, virtually traffic-free. It has a tradition of serving British clientele. You will quickly realize you are in a true Austrian village where time-tested tradition reigns. The smaller dorf of Hochgurgl is a clutch of remote, excellent hotels clinging to the side of steep slopes.

Mountain layout

Sölden

Let's look first at the ski slopes above Sölden. They are split into three areas—the Giggijoch-Hochsölden, the Gaislachkogl and Golden Gate to the glacier. The skiing overall is wide open. Though there are trails marked on the map, with good snow, you can ski virtually anywhere, which makes Sölden a favorite of powderhounds and means plenty of skiing above the treeline. The area lends itself to various levels of intermediate with some expert off-piste runs thrown in for good measure. In fact, an adventurous expert will have no trouble keeping busy above Sölden and in the Obergurgl/Hochgurgl areas. Beginners will be limited in their choice of trails.

Access to the slopes is either by cable car at the the Giggijoch station, at the north end of Sölden, or by gondola at the Gaislachkoglbahn station, at the south end of town. The cable car ascends past Hochsölden and up to the Giggijoch Bergstation. This contemporary top station is also host to five lifts that fan out into a wide bowl. The difficulty ranges from corduroy groomed beginner to off-piste expert trails.

Great fun for a day of skiing and riding is to start at the Giggijoch area and traverse over to the Gaislachkogl summit. This intermediate to expert terrain is a wonderful adventure guaranteed to fulfill your wildest dreams about skiing and riding in the Alps. For a delicious hearty stew or to quench your thirst, stop at the Gampealm on trail 11.

The Gratlift and Stabele doublechairs, halfway up the Gaislachkogl summit, access a wonderful variety of intermediate trails and tons of off-piste riding and skiing.

The trails off of the Gaislachkogl summit are narrow and the sides of the trails drop off to nowhere, making this solid intermediate terrain. However, because the ultra-modern Gaislachkogl gondola carries both up and downhill traffic, even beginners can enjoy the views from one of the highest peaks in the Alps. On a clear day you can see the highest peak in Italy. Just a few kilometers from where you're staying, the famous site where the 5,000-year-old frozen body of Oetzi (known to some as the Iceman) was discovered several years ago.

Though the Austrians are meticulous groomers, there are ravines everywhere sporting headwalls with enough powder to make any rider or expert happy. Areas of special note are off the Langegg six-passenger lift, as well as the off-piste runs off of the Rosskirplbahn quad. Snowboarding is extremely popular in the Oetztal. A new boarders'park has been created to international standards at the Giggijoch. It includes a halfpipe, bordercross, quarterpipe high jump, rails, diamonds, half-diamonds, fried egg, fun-box spins and jumps.

Obergurgl and Hochgurgl

The skiing above Obergurgl and Hochgurgl is more extensive than Sölden, and thanks to a recently added lift, skiers can cruise down from Hochgurgl to Obergurgl, and ride back up to the Hochgurgl trails. Above Obergurgl, the Festkogl lift opens to a wide face with unlimited intermediate skiing. Experts can drop to the right-hand side of the lift and take the unprepared run through the Verwalltal back to the lower lift station. This area is high (6,369 to 10,015 feet) with good, crisp snow. For a change, traverse over to the Hohe Mut area, which has a good unprepared run from the Hohe Mut Restaurant and a group of shorter lifts and runs.

You can access Hochgurgl by the gondola from Pill/Angern or by car, if you aren't staying there. This town has developed into a relatively upscale community anchored by one of the best luxury Alpine hotels, the Top Hotel Hochgurgl. Lifts peak out at 10,170 feet, where a mountain restaurant provides spectacular views. The skiing for experts is down the Königstal; for beginners in the center of the area; for intermediates under the Kirchenkarlift. Like Obergurgl, this area is perfect for continuous off-piste cruising.

Both Obergurgl and Hochgurgl have good beginner slopes.

If you want to concentrate on cross-country skiing, choose another area. Some trails exist, but not the network you'll need to ensure variety.

One last hot tip: ski on Saturday. German visitors, like clockwork, consistently and predictably use Saturday as a travel day and leave the slopes practically abandoned.

Mountain rating

With a few exceptions, particularly from the Gaislachkogl, these runs are for intermediates. Some of our contributors have rated every marked run some variation of intermediate.

There are enough training areas at the bottom for ski schools. The beginner has plenty of terrain to ski, especially in the center of the Giggijoch/Hochsölden sector.

Experts looking for wild steeps in the Oetztal and to dive into the off-piste will find a dream come true. In summer, when skiing is a real luxury, this is one of Europe's finest areas.

Slopes are well-marked and considerably wider than at other Austrian resorts.

Obergurgl-Hochgurgl offer wonderful above-treeline skiing where if you see it, you can ski it. There is skiing for every level of skier. Beginners have plenty of room and experts can look for wide open spaces but without much extreme challenge.

Ski school (2007/08 prices)

There are five ski and snowboad schools in Sölden and Hochsölden. They are Ski School Sölden-Hochsölden (5254 2364, fax 5254 3171), Ski School Yellow Power Sölden (5254 2203-500, fax 5254 30010), Ski- & Snowboard School Vacancia (5254 3100, fax 5254 2939), Freeride Center Tirol Markus Morandell (650 2665292) and Ski- and Snowboard School Aktiv (5253 6313, fax 5253 6313).

Sölden

Group Lessons — At the Ski School Sölden-Hochsölden: A day of lessons is €56, three days is €129. The weekly (6 days) charge is €189. Group snowboarding lessons are the same price as skiing lessons.

Children's skiing and snowboarding lessons are €51 for a full day (4 hr.); and are €174 for 6 days. Lunch is an additional €9 per day.

Private Lessons — One of the best ways to tour the Oetztal is to hire a guide. As elsewhere, the more people to join your private group, the less you'll end up paying. A four-hour private lesson for two people, for instance, costs about €190, but for each additional person, add €25. Three hours costs €160 and two hours cost €125.

Cross-country Lessons are two hours per day. One day costs about €39, two days cost €70 and three days cost €100.

Obergurgl-Hochgurgl

The Obergurgl Skischule (tel. 05256-6305) has about 100 instructors and is considered on of Austria's best.

Group lessons cost €55 for a full day, €132 for three days, and €174 for five days. There is no significant reduction for children.

Private lessons for one or two skiers are provided in two-, three-, four-, five-, and six-hour intervals. Call the school for a complete list of prices. There are 3 two-hour lessons which take place from 9 a.m. to 2:30 p.m. with 15-minute breaks in between lessons. Two hour lessons cost between €113-€123. Each additional person costs €8. There are 2 three-hour sessions from 9 a.m. to 4 p.m. with an hour break between. Each session costs €162 with any addtional people being €12. There is one 5-hour session which costs €240 with any addtional people being €20.

Obergurgl snowboard lessons cost €65 for a day, and €156 for three days.

Cross-country lessons are €33 for groups of at least four skiers for two hours. Snowshoe walks of about 2 hours (including snowshoes and lamps at night) cost €33.

The Hochgurgl Skischule (05256-6265) is much smaller with just over a dozen instructors. Its reputation is not as polished nor its courses as organized. Group lessons cost €55 for a full day, €132 for three days, and €192 for five days. Private lessons cost €130 for a two hours and €205 for four hours. Snowboard lessons cost €65 for a full day, and €156 for three days.

Lift tickets (2007/08 prices)
Sölden/Hochsölden

Because Sölden is a year-round ski area, a variety of passes and tickets are sold. The costs can seem even more confusing than the trail map. All ski passes are hands-free SWATCH Access or Key Cards (Key Card deposit is €2).

These are the high season rates for the Sölden-Hochsölden ski pass, valid for all operating ski lifts in Sölden and Hochsölden, Gaislachkogl, Innerwald, Gampealm, Golden Gate and both glaciers, but not in Vent or Obergurgl/Hochgurgl. High season lasts from Dec. 22, 2007 - Jan. 11, 2008 and from Jan. 26, 2008 - Apr. 06, 2008. Midseason lasts from Jan. 12, 2008 - Jan. 25, 2008 and from Apr. 07, 2008 - May 4, 2008.

	Adults	Children (8–14)	Youth (15-19)	Seniors*
one day	€41.50	€26	€33	€35
three days	€112	€63.50	€80.50	€92.50
six days	€205.50	€111	€143	€169.50
fourteen days	€356.50	€169.50	€252.50	€293

*Seniors are men older than age 65 and women older than age 60.

Skiers may also buy a Rettungskarte (mountain patrol card) for about €10. If you get lost and require assistance from the patrol, or if you're injured in an accident, the card acts as insurance. Without the card, the charge is €110 or more.

A photo I.D. is required for tickets for 8 or more days of skiing and for any reduced ski passes (children, youth, seniors, handicapped).

Obergurgl-Hochgurgl (high season)
  Season B– Dec 23, 2007 to Jan 12, 2008/
  Season C– Jan 13, 2008 to Feb 26, 2008

	Adults	Children (8-16)*	Seniors (60+)*
half-day (from noon)	€32.50/€30.50	€19	€24.50
one day	€41.50/€40	€26	€35
three days	€112/€102	€66.50	€92.50
six days	€205.50/€184.50	€112	€169.50
fourteen days	€356.50/€323.50	€206	€293

*Same price during both seasons.
Physically disabled persons and children 8 years old and younger ski free.

Cross-country skiing

There is a 16-km. loop around the Sölden region. However, 50 km. of tracks are accessible via the cross-country ski bus to Langenfeld. Rentals are available at all sport shops in the area. The daily charge for rentals is €10–25 per day, depending on the store. Weekly discounts are always available.

There is both skating and classic skiing in Niederthai, a 5 km. skating course between Umhausen and Tumpen, plus a 3 km. skating trail from Umhausen to Arzwinkel for intermediates and to Köfels for experts.

Obergurgl-Hochgurgl has 12 k.m. of cross-country tracks near each village.

Accommodations

The prices are per person, with breakfast, based on double occupancy. €€€=more than €300; €€=€100–300; €=less than €100.

The most lavish and beautifully decorated hotel in Sölden is the **Central Hotel** (22600, fax 2260511; €€€). Even its pool is a cut above anything else in Austria. With Roman architecture, tall ceilings and classic paintings, it is unique.

The **Sonnenhaus Tamara** (5040, fax 50460; €€–€€€) offers what may be the friendliest concierge service in Sölden. The furniture is new but the antiques are real.

At the **Hotel Liebe Sonne** (22030, fax 2423; €€–€€€) modern mixes with the old. A large rock fountain, marble floors and modern art combine with minimalist furniture. Apartments are available. They have their own ski school.

Hotel Erhart (2020, fax 20205; €€–€€€) is a four-star with a great restaurant. Franz, the owner and generous host, features ski safari and dinner/toboggan ride to entertain guests. The ski safari starts with schnapps and then skiing. Guests are grouped by skiing ability. On Thursday nights Franz takes the guests up the mountain to a hut for dinner and a toboggan ride down. The hotel is 5-10 minutes from the Gaislachkoglbahn.

Hotel am Hof (2241, fax 2121111; €€–€€€) has rustic post-and-beam construction, with wooden floors, fitness and massage room, sauna and steam bath, parking garage and ski room. It is off of the main road and central to town.

Hotel Sölderhof (5030, fax 50360; €€) Some rooms have showers and some have baths—if you have a preference, please request. This hotel hosts weekly activites for guests from a ski safari to curling instructions and games. Sauna, whirlpool, solarium and ski room round out the amenities. The restaurant also serves the public.

Hotel Hochsölden (2229, fax 225951; €€–€€€) is halfway up the mountain, in Hochsölden. This is a ski-in/ski-out property for most of the season. There are few extras, but the location is unbeatable. They have their own ski school.

Frühstückpensions — B&Bs

Wildespitze (2341, fax 234140; €) Britta Riml runs this 20-bed guesthouse only five minutes from the Giggijoch cable car. She speaks good English. Rooms all have private baths. **Prantl Stefan** (2525, fax 2525; €) is more intimate with only six rooms in a working farmhouse. The only British-style chalet is **Gustl's Farienhausl** (2090, fax 2090-15; €) with eight beds. **Montana** (5080, fax 50806; €) is a B&B with apartments, sauna, tanning bed, TV and radio in the rooms. It is at the base of the Giggijochbahn. **Arnold Andre** (2269, fax 2954; €) is a B&B owned and operated by World Cup ski racer Andre Arnold and his wife. **Gastehaus Larchenpark** (2386, fax 2386; €) is a B&B with stained glass and crystal displays near the Giggijoch lift. All 22 rooms have a toilet with either a shower or bath.

Obergurgl and Hochgurgl

Top Hotel Hochgurgl (05256-6265, fax 26510; €€€+) is perhaps one of the best hotels in the Alps, by any measure. It matches elegance with the Zürserhof in Zürs and the Palace in St. Moritz.

Hotel Wiesental (05256-6263, fax 63583; €€€) is very convenient to the lifts in the old town. It has an atmospheric, rustic restaurant.

Hotel Edelweiss and Gurgl (05256-6223, fax 6449; €€€+) is close to the lifts.

Hotel Madeleine (05256-3540, fax 354355; €€€+).

Hotel Josl (05256-6205; 6460; €€) is in the town center with Fen Shui-influenced design and a good après-ski bar and restaurant.

Hotel Gamper (05256-65450, fax 631760; €€€) is in the center of the town with an excellent kitchen. Special Week: €610–€655.

Hotel Ideal (05256-62900, fax 6302; €€€) is the bargain of Hochgurgl with all the amenities—sauna, fitness room, and garage.

Hotel Wurmkogel (05256-6246; fax 6307; €€).

Dining

Sölden has over fifty different restaurants, plus the hotels offer excellent meals as part of their full- and half-board options. Dining here is strictly by the clock when not on the mountain. Lunch is served until 2 p.m., après-ski is from 4 p.m.–7 p.m. and dinner follows. Tipping at après-ski is either round up to the next Euro or pay €2–4 over the tab.

Prices (without wine) €€€—€36+; €€—16–35; €—€15-.

Restaurant Dominic (2646; €) provides a religious experience, with stained glass ceilings, ornate wood carvings and pew-like chairs. Bring your credit card.

The **Parkhotel** restaurant (2250; €) specializes in grilled food such as steaks and lamb chops at reasonable prices. No credit cards.

These next three places have great traditional Tyrolean meals. The traditionally costumed waiters at **Die Alm** (2401; €€) serve meals amidst stuffed wildlife, train tracks and churning ceiling fans. The **s'Pfandl** (3607; €€) in Ausserwald and **Grüner's Almstube** (€€) serve Ripplan, Kasspatzn, Knedlan and Gröstl.

In Hochgurgl, the **Top Hotel Hochgurgl** has a wonderful **Tiroler Stuben**. The **Hotel Ideal, Hotel Laurin, Hotel Angerer Alm, Hotel Riml, Hotel Olymp** and the **Wurmkogl** all serve good basic cooking as well.

In Obergurgl head to the **Romantik** and **Belmonte** for Italian food. Try the **Gamper** and then the **Mathiesn** for good Tyrolean cooking. The **Josl** is known for its wild game. **Hotel Deutschmann** has good fondue, raclette and tyrolean specialties. The **Wiesental** also serves excellent meals in the center of town.

Après-ski/nightlife

Après-ski activities in Sölden start after 3 p.m. and last until promptly 7 p.m. when all bars empty of guests who head home to ready for dinner and nights filled with dancing, drinking, and smoking. Expect to pay a cover charge of €4-€5 to get into most bars for the later nightlife.

Philipps in Innerwald is a favorite outdoor bar on the Number 11 trail back into town. **Heiner's Adabei** is a good place to stop along trails 21 or 22. The **Hinterher** at the base of the Giggijoch cable car is a loud, fun, friendly bar always filled beyond capacity. **Shirmbar** outside of the Hotel Liebe Sonne is yet another outdoor bar overflowing with partiers dancing in their ski boots and singing to the cranking music.

Joker — Da ist die Hölle los (We're raising hell here) is decked out in an infernal motif, with flames, goblins and demons. Old chairlifts converted into restaurant chairs are suspended from the ceiling. The early crowd is teenage and the later clients are older. They offer a selection of specialty drinks, and a climbable cliff leads to the **Bierhimml** (Beer Heaven), decorated with angels and clouds. Loud music and pizza are served up. Some credit cards are accepted at both establishments.

Another hot spot is the glass-enclosed **Bla-Bla Eisbar** that opens at 3 p.m. just in time for the first après-skier. It attracts a young snowboarder crowd. **Lawine** blasts live rock'n'roll music and has pool tables.

Crave mixed drinks with ballroom dancing? The upscale **Alibi Bar** at the Central Hotel is home to the €11 margarita—not for the faint of wallet. Credit cards accepted. At **Jacob's Weinfassl** (5030) taste a variety of Austrian and Italian wines.

In Obergurgl, the **Nederhütte** rocks with accordian and guitar for après-ski. A stop at the **Edelweiss Bar** at the base of the Gaisberg lift is then in order. Later head to the **Joslkeller** with country music. Then discover the **Hexenkuch'l** in the Hotel Jenewein, the **Krumpn's Stadl** at Hotel Schöne Aussicht, and the **Austria Keller** in the Hotel Austria with oom-pa-pa music and mugs of beer.

In Hochgurgl the place to be seen is the either the **African Bar** in the Hotel Hochgurgl, the **Putt In Bar** at the Hotel Riml or **Toni's Almhutte** at Sporthotel Olymp.

Child care (2007/08 prices)
Sölden Region
The tourist information center in Sölden keeps a list of qualified babysitters and care providers, which is available upon request.

The **Ski School Sölden/Hochsölden** (2364) has the Gigglijoch ski kindergarten that accepts children ages 6 months to 8 years old and is open Sunday through Friday, 10 a.m.–3 p.m. There are baby lifts, magic carpets, carousels, play-corners, and a kid's ski bus. Bobo's Kids Club is for children who want to learn to ski. Meals are €9 per day. A full day costs €51; three days are €123; and six days are €174.

Ski School Total Vacancia has Kid's Club Total which includes child care during lunch, a terrain garden and children's racing school for children ages 3 to 14. The school is open 10 a.m. to 12 p.m. and 1 p.m.–3 p.m. A full day costs €46; three days are €107; and six days are €157.

Ski Kindergarten Yellow Power (2203-500, fax 30010) has a kindergarten that is open from 10 a.m. to 12 p.m. and from 1 p.m.–3 p.m. Lunch is €9 per day. A full day is €49; three days, €123; and six days, €168.

Nursery services are offered.

Obergurgl-Hochgurgl

In Obergurgl the Obergurgl Ski School (05256-6305, fax 05256-6503) runs a special course for nonskiing children ages 3 and older from Sunday to Friday, 9:45 a.m. to noon and from 1:30 p.m. to 3:30 p.m. The cost for two hours of care is €20.

Children's snow day care costs the same as ski school. For children 3–5 yrs. old, the ski school's Bobo's Mini Club is open from 9:30 a.m.–12:30 p.m. and 1:30 p.m.–4:30 p.m. and costs €30 for half day and €55 for a full day.

Only children ages 4 and older have the option of taking the supervised lunch which costs €14.

Other activities
Tobogganing tops the list of extracurricular activities in Sölden. Tradition calls for lots of drinks beforehand. Call Hotel Alpenland at 2365 or Gasthof Silbertal at 2987.

Telephone prefix: Sölden, Hochsölden, Vent 05254; Hochgurgl and Obergurgl 05256

At the Freizeit Arena, a hot spot on cold and snowy days, visitors can **swim**; soak in a **steambath**; bake in a **sauna**; tan in the **solarium**; work out on an **indoor tennis court** or play **volleyball**, **badminton** or **bowl**. For more information call 2514.

Tandem hang-gliding provides a birds-eye view of the entire mountain range. Jump off a cliff in a parachute and hang for hours on thermal currents. Call Outdoor Vacancia at 3100. One trip costs roughly €100.

Horse-drawn sleigh rides leave from the Hotel Liebe Sionne. Call 2203-0.

The **Stuibenfall** is Tyrol's highest waterfall with a drop of 150 meters. The **Piburger See** is a mountain lake with phenomenal reflections on a good day. The hamlet of **Farst** is the steepest and most daring settlement on the mountain. Viewed from below it appears that the buildings of the village are tied to the mountainside.

Getting there

Train service is not available to the Sölden area, making the bus and car the fastest way to get there. Sölden is about 225 km. from Munich (3-1/2 hour drive in good conditions) and 266 km. from Salzburg. This remote Alpine region along the Italian border offers a scenic, but at times difficult to traverse, 20-minute stretch of winding roads from the Autobahn. Bus service is also available every hour from Innsbruck. Prices start at about €15, but phone the bus company at 05266-89200 before buying a ticket.

Tourist information

Ötztal Tourismus, Information Sölden, A-6450 Sölden, Austria; 057200-200, fax 57200-201.
Internet: www.soelden.com or www.oetztal.com
E-mail: info@soelden.com or info@oetztal.com

Ötztal Tourismus, Information Obergurgl-Hochgurgl, A-6456 Obergurgl, Austria; 057200-100, fax 057200-201. Internet: www. obergurgl.com E-mail: info@obergurgl.com

Ötztal Tourismus, Information Vent, A-6458 Vent, Austria; tel. 057200-260. Internet: www.vent.at E-Mail: vent@oetztal.com.

Saalbach-Hinterglemm

You may have heard of Saalbach's reputation as an après-ski "Animal House," but nothing can prepare you for the reality.

You have stopped to enter the dark, woodsy Hinterhagalm tea bar on the last run down, having worked up a thirst on the nearly two-mile Asterabfahrt trail into Saalbach. By the time the first beer arrives, the waitress has to swing her tray to adjust to the unspoken rhythm of the overflow crowd and the clumping of ski boots keeping time to the beat of traditional Austrian folksongs from the live band. Even before the T-bar outside the door closes for the day, the entire chalet is transformed into a dance floor. Legs dangling over the upstairs balcony jig to the two-step. By the time you're ready to locate your skis for the final 300-yard glide into the village, the way out is blocked by a swaying mass of bodies. You have to literally get down on your hands and knees and make a crawl for it. No one seems to notice. Then, just before you make it between the last set of legs separating you from the door outside, you hit your head on something. Looking up, you see you've bumped heads with someone crawling in.

Saalbach forms the epicenter of the activity. Squeezed in the narrow throat of the valley, with mountains crowding in as a backdrop for the chalet-style hotels and their carved wood balconies, the village is as quaint as any you could picture in the Alps. The custard-yellow steeple of an old church dominates the packed rooftops, and a mountain stream rushes soothingly through the town.

The valley floor broadens considerably just a mile up the road at Hinterglemm. Here hotels are larger and the village fans out over a wider area. Because it is as central to the main ski crossroads of the valley as Saalbach and has more mid- to upper-level hotels with full amenities, Hinterglemm loses some of the coziness that you find in Saalbach. While Hinterglemm has the look and feel of a resort, everything about Saalbach says that it was an Alpine village in its own right before the ski rush began.

Mountain layout—Skiing

Saalbach Hinterglemm offers one of the best interconnected lift systems in Austria. Even expert skiers determined to put as many miles under their skis as possible, would find themselves hard-pressed to cover the area from one end to the other in a single day—never mind stopping along the way to enjoy the skiing.

Lifts cover both sides of a long valley. The most central spot is Saalbach. Go up the valley for one day's ski excursion and down the next.

Experts should head directly for the Schattberg X-Press gondola. The black run directly beneath the lift is a good example of why expert skiers keep coming back. It has good grade, it's bumpy and it's long.

For another uniquely European experience, turn left at the top of the Schattberg cablecar down the Limberg-Jausern trail. This is the longest trail in the area and worth taking just for the sake of adventure. Vorderglemm at the bottom of this run represents the southern boundary of the area. You can cross up to the other side of the valley on the Schönleiten cablecar.

Experts who turn right at the top of Schattberg (Schattberg-East) and go up the short Westgipfel gondola to Schattberg-West can enjoy a mountainside of advanced trails leading down into Hinterglemm. There's plenty of tree skiing on this broad swath of mountain, and the run all the way down is worthy indeed of an expert's interest. Rather than heading back up the two lifts to Schattberg-West, cross over to the Zwölfer and let the cablecars take you back to the summit. Ski down and continue up-valley.

The runs down to the midstation from the top of Zwölfer (6,509 feet) are nice and very bumpy. There are lots of fine cutovers into untouched sugar for powder monkeys (snow permitting, of course). From the top, cut over to the Seekar T-bar, which has advanced runs from the top and an excellent powder bowl off to the right.

The entire north side of the valley is one intermediate run after another down an open mountainside. Spend a day in the Hasenauerköpfl and Reiterkogel area. If you head further to the left up the valley toward Spieleckkogel, you will stand about as high as you can in the valley (6,522 feet).

Advanced intermediates will enjoy taking the long Kohlmais cablecar, which begins in Saalbach near the old church. From the top, there's a long 3-km. advanced run down into Saalbach. Because of the relatively low height (5,886 feet from the top) of this area, all the runs seem to skirt or cut through beautiful forests. And at every juncture, there's the ubiquitous hut where you can enjoy a drink and a spectacular view.

For a top-to-bottom basher, cut over to the Bergeralm chair lift. From the top, enjoy the challenging 7-km. Bergeralm-Schönleiten run (Nos. 57 and 67 on the trail map) down to the valley floor to the Schönleiten cablecar. The eight-person cablecars will whisk you all the way to the top of Schonleiten. From the restaurant in Schonleiten, you can enjoy the most spectacular view in the entire valley and one of the truly memorable panoramas in the Alps. If you care to digest your lunch over some bumps, round the ridge toward Leogang and ski the three T-bar lifts. They're short but sweet.

Beginners should take the Bernkogel chair lift from Saalbach and change lifts to make it all the way to the top of Bernkogel. The run from the top to the midstation is gentle, wide and very confidence inspiring. In fact, this is where the Austrian ski instructors take their classes of first-timers. The adventurous will find manageable, broad runs down from the top of both the Kohlmaiskopf and Bründkopf lifts.

 ## Mountain layout—Snowboarding

There is a professional terrain park at the Unterschwarzachlift in Hinterglemm and a snow park at the Asitzmuldenbahn in Leogang. The professional terrainpark has a funbox, a corner, a wellenbahn, a big air jump, two straight jumps and seven rails.

The Nitro Snowpark in Leogang has a large variety of rails, corners, kickers, jumps and banks in its flood-lit area. There's even a 14-meter pool with a slide. And if you're in need of some pointers on your techinique, check out Nitro's free weekend boarder workshops.

Mountain rating

There are only a few runs that are strictly for experts, but there's plenty of challenging terrain in the Skicircus to keep excellent skiers occupied. There always seems to be a tree glade beckoning somewhere.

Intermediates have discovered Nirvana. The north side of the valley is a canvas of intermediate runs for the intermediate skier to choose his or her favorite brushstroke. There is really no part of the Skicircus that is off-limits to the intermediate with the exception of the run under the Schattberg X-Press gondola. You can enjoy all the pleasures of exploring the entire circuit without hitting a dead end.

Beginners and advanced beginners will find Saalbach Hinterglemm much to their liking. There are plenty of broad slopes, even from the top, that lead them on a gentle curve miles down into the valley.

Cross-Country and snowshoeing (2007/08 prices)

This is not a major cross-country area. There are two groomed trails with a total of 11 km. of tracks. The first track is in Hinterglemm village and is 8 kms. The second track is Höhenloipe Hinterglemm which is 4 kms. long and starts near the top of the Reiterkogel lift.

There is a three-hour snowshoe tour through the Glemm Valley offered every Friday at 2 p.m. The meeting place is at the Lengau bus stop. Snowshoes will be provided for you, but you must bring hiking boots and sticks. The tour costs €15 per person. Contact Hans Eder, qualified guide, (699 11105629) for more information.

Ski school (2007/08 prices)

There are nine major ski schools in both Saalbach and Hinterglemm. Combined, there are over 200 instructors in the area.

The following are the prices for skiing and snowboarding lessons at the Skischule Aamadall (668256, fax 668212) and are representative of ski school prices in Saalbach.

Group lessons (four hours, 10 a.m.–12 p.m. and 1:30 p.m.–3:30 p.m.) are €61 for a full day, €141 for three days, and €161 for four to six days.

Private Lessons for one or two people vary in price depending on the time that you take the lesson. An Early Bird lesson (9-10 a.m.) costs €53. A Double Private I lesson (9-11 a.m.) costs €102 A Double Private II lesson (10 a.m. to noon) costs €114. A Double Private III lesson (1-3 p.m.) costs €111. A Single Private lesson (noon to 1 p.m..) costs €61. Each addtional skier costs €11.

Lift tickets (2007/08 prices)

These are Skicircus Saalbach Hinterglemm Leogang main season rates (10% VAT included). Main season is from Dec. 22, 2007 to Jan. 5, 2008 and from Jan. 26, 2008 to Mar. 24, 2008. All skipasses are given out on KeyCards which cost €3. For skipasses valid 9 days or more a photo is necessary.

	Adults	Child (6–15)	Youth (16–18)
One day	€38.50	€19.30	€30.80
Three days	€106.60	€53.30	€85.30
Six days	€186	€93	€148.80
Fourteen days	€318.10	€159.10	€254.50

Telephone prefix: 06541

Accommodations

Based on high season, per person/double occupancy, with half board: €€€—more than €125+; €€—€75–€125; €—€75-.

Alpenhotel (6666; €€€) This is Saalbach's flagship hotel. The big red arch dominates the entrance of the village and announces that the Alpenhotel caters to all whims—sauna, solarium, massage, exercise room, indoor swimming pool, whirlpool and so on. It also houses the most exclusive disco in Saalbach, the Arena.

Haider (6228; €€€) Not as fancy or as large as the Alpenhotel, the Haider is quaint in the traditional Austrian mold, with carved wood headboards on the beds and shutters. There's a sauna, solarium and a hot whirlpool, as well a hideaway lounge with fireplace. Besides an excellent restaurant serving traditional Austrian fare, there's also an informal pizzeria—always a plus for carbo-hungry skiers.

Sporthotel Ellmau (72260; €€€) and **Hotel Glemmtalerhof** (7135; €€€) in Hinterglemm are excellent and offer full amenities, such as sauna, solarium and indoor swimming pool. There's also babysitting on the premises.

The upscale **Wellness-Hotel-Kendler** (62250, fax 6335; €€€) in Saalbach, is packed with health facilities, saunas, steambaths, fitness room and spa.

Scharnagl (6284; €–€€) is too new to rate as quaint. This pension scores high because of its location next to the old church and across the street from both the Kohlmais gondola and the Bauer's Schi-Alm. The rooms are clean and airy, and the proprietress, Frau Brudermann, is always willing to help. It has the best après-ski bar in town.

Another recommended pension in Saalbach is the **Berger** (7140; €). In Hinterglemm, try the **Flora** (7100; €).

Ski Chalets: Crystal, Inghams/Bladon, Neilson (see page 16 for phone, fax and internet addresses).

Apartments, condominiums, flats

Saalbach has hundreds of apartments for rent. Contact the tourist office for apartment information: Tourism Association Holiday Service (6800-30, fax: 6800-39; holiday@saalbach.com). Give them your arrival and departure dates and level of luxury you desire.

Dining

Austrian cooking mirrors the country and its people—hearty, simple and unpretentious. Few sights are more welcome after a full day's skiing than a generous pork filet with mushroom gravy and a heaping portion of *Spätzle*, Austria's unbeatable doughy noodles. For a sweet treat on the mountain, try *Germknödel* (a sweet doughy bread filled with jam and covered with warm vanilla sauce).

The **Hinterhagalm** (7282 or 6291) just at the top of the Turm T-bar is something of a local legend. Its 5 p.m. tea bar is one of the most notable après-ski events in the valley, yet at night this beautiful old lodge serves traditional Austrian dishes with old-world atmosphere. This restaurant was a backdrop for "The Sound of Music."

Nearly all the major hotels in both Saalbach and Hinterglemm feature good restaurants, where you'll find menus with prices conveniently posted outside. Those with large appetites should try the restaurant in the **Hotel Sonne** (7202) which features more than five different steak dinners. **Restaurant Kendler** (6225) is highly rated by the critics and filled with rustic atmosphere. Try the sole or the very Austrian onion roast venison. Bring cash.

No ski resort is complete unless it has an informal pizzeria with good food and reasonable prices. In Saalbach, the pizzeria in the **Hotel Haider** (6228) gets our vote.

No less than 40 mountain chalets serve food, and each lift seems to have one of these either at the top or bottom—or both. Two mountain huts deserve special mention—the **Wildenkarhütte** at the top of the Schönleiten gondola for its spectacular panoramic view, and the rustic **Thurner Alm** (8418) on the trail midway up new Bergeralm chairlift for its hunting lodge flavor and ski-up bar.

We've also heard good things about **Goaßstall** (8705), a lodge in Hinterglemm at the bottom of the Reiterkogel gondola, which serves a special dinner called "Hot Goat". It's a fillet of steak served on a traditional wooden platter in the shape of a goat.

 ## Après-ski/nightlife

Saalbach Hinterglemm's reputation for great nightlife has more to do with the atmosphere and attitude of the area than the number of discos (officially only five). Along with the wild-and-crazy Austrians you're bound to meet, there's also a healthy contingent of British and Scandinavians (especially Swedes).

The **Arena** disco in the Alpenhotel is the upscale nightspot. The action inside doesn't start until after 11 p.m. Expect to pay a cover (it varies depending on the entertainment) and about €8 for a mixed drink. There are two bars, a live band and plenty of overstuffed couches and tucked-away alcoves for a break from the dancing.

The disco in the **Sporthotel**, just up the main street from the centrally located Alpenhotel, is where the young and adventurous let their collective hair down. There's a circular balcony that overlooks the dance floor. You need only pick out the partner of your choice from this vantage point and then leap merrily into the crowded fray.

Cross the stream just off the main street and walk uphill to the **Backstatt Stall**. The upstairs disco is on two levels, with another balcony for scoping the dance action. The atmosphere is a little more woodsy and mellower than the spots mentioned above, and it's easier to find room on the dance floor.

Après-ski has to be witnessed to be understood. Where else, except inside the **Bauers Schi-Alm** (at the bottom of the Turm T-bar, across from the old church), can you see Austrians dancing the can-can to "New York, New York," stacked three on top of one another and swaying like demented totem poles? The bedlam at the **Hinterhagalm** tea bar just up the slope is a rival for honors as Après-Ski Madhouse of the Mountain.

The **Harley Davidson and Bikers' Pub**, in the basement of the Hotel Zur Dorfschmiede, features a shiny selection of full-size Harleys and motorcycle memorabilia, lots of leather and studs, and an owner who dishes "hog" talk with the best of them. Hokey, but a lot of fun.

 ## Child care (2007/08 prices)

There is no organized nursery. The only programs are organized through the ski schools in Saalbach.

Skischule Aamadall (668256, fax 668212) has the Mini-Clown World Programme for children age 4 and older. Along with ski techniques, the children also have the opportunity to race, drive snow mobiles, snowblade and snowtube. There's even a little disco. Choose between half and full day lessons (with or without lunch break). Two-hours lessons are only for advanced skiers. Half-day lessons cost €43 for one day; €102 for three days; and €122 for six days. Full-day lessons cost €61 for one day; €141 for three days; and €159 for six days.

Group skiing courses for teenagers 13-17 years old are also available. In the morning, the students are tutored in Alpine Ski Technique and in the afternoon there are fun activities and lessons on technique for carving, snowblading and snowshoeing. There's also a Ski Race. Full-day lessons cost €61 for one day; €141 for three days and; €159 for six days.

Telephone prefix: 06541

Other activities

Try an afternoon excursion by horse-drawn **sleigh**. Lindlingalm offers tours that include a stop for a traditional Austrian lunch (7190). For an hour the ride costs €10.50 per person. For a half-hour ride the price is €6 per person. Lengauerhof is another option for **sleigh rides**. Prices (minimum 5 persons): one hour costs €11 per person and a half hour costs €6 per person. Contact Fam. Breitfuss, Hotel Lengauerhof, (72550) for further details. Sleigh rides are also offered by Taxi Schmidhofer (7163) and Lengauerwirt (7255).

Ice-skaters and ice-hockey players should head past the Zwölferkogel gondola to the **skating rink** (Fam. Telawetz 7403, fax: 7403) at the end of the valley on the left. The entrance fee is only €3.

Speed Demons should definitely try **toboganning**. There are several options in the Saalbach area: The 4.5 km.- longSimalalm toboggan run (8772, fax 87724) costs €13. The 3 km.-long Spielberghaus run (7253, fax: 72534) is a 45-minute walk to the Spielberghaus and costs approximately €11. The 1.5 km.-long Maisalm run (7409, fax: 74093) is a 25-minute walk to the Maisalm. Reiterkogel has a new flood-lit toboggan run for night skiing. Toboggan rental: € 5/evening - Deposit: € 20.

Getting there

By train: There are direct trains to nearby Zell am See from both Munich and Salzburg. You can either take a cab the remaining 18 km. to Saalbach or wait for the regularly scheduled bus, which makes the trip to Saalbach nine times a day from the train station.

By car: The drive from the Munich airport to Saalbach takes about two and a half hours. From the Salzburg autobahn take the Siegsdorf exit, then follow signs to Lofer-Maishofen, then signs to Saalbach Hinterglemm.

Some hotels offer parking, or you can park in the multideck garage on the outskirts of town. Once in Saalbach you won't need a car.

Tourist information

Contact the Informationscenter, A-5753 Saalbach, Austria; (06541) 680068; fax (06541) 680069.
E-mail: contact@saalbach.com
Internet: www.saalbach.com

Schladming/Ramsau

with Dachstein-Tauern Region

This is the area in Europe where Arnold Schwarzenegger comes to ski, but more on that later. Whether you are looking for the challenge of the fastest World Cup downhill or wide beginner and intermediate runs through thick pine forests; whether you seek the excitement of skiing on the Dachstein Glacier or the serenity of one of the most extensive cross-country areas in Austria, it's all in Schladming.

Schladming, in the center of Austria about an hour's drive from Salzburg, hosts thousands of Austrian, German, Swedish, Danish, British and Dutch tourists. Already one of the leading vacation centers for the Austrians, the region has completed an extensive series of developments that have turned the valley into a world-class resort. The local term for this area is *Sportregion Schladming Dachstein-Tauern*.

Schladming, the hub of the area, is nestled around a old town center, with shopping, nightlife and restaurants—all within a five-minute walk from the main lifts.

Rohrmoos, about a five-minute drive up the mountain, features more hotel rooms than Schladming, and guests can step out their door, put on their skis and set off down the mountain. Rohrmoos is spread out and a long walk from the Schladming village.

Ramsau lies on the opposite side of the valley, with a southern exposure. It is settled on a long plateau that features some of the most interesting cross-country skiing in Austria: the 1999 Nordic World Championships were held here. Accommodations are extensive but dispersed. At the top of the Dachstein cable car (elevation 8,850 feet) you overlook the entire Schladminger Tauern region mountain range and the Enns River Valley. Haus im Ennstal, a short drive along the valley from Schladming, is perhaps the most picturesque of the main villages in the region. It remains traditional, anchoring the Hauser Kaibling ski area.

The Schladming Dachstein Tauern ski pass also allows skiing in the Gasteiner Valley, Hochkönigs and Grossarltal. That brings the total available skiing and riding option in the region to 270 lifts covering 860 km. of trails. Though the lifts are not interconnected, there is a shuttlebus system that links the various resorts as well as parking at each resort.

Mountain layout–Skiing

The *SkiAmadé* pass opens hundreds of km. of prepared runs at the nine ski areas along the Sportregion Schladming-Dachstein Tauern valley.

The major areas are Planai (6,214 feet) above Schladming; Hauser Kaibling (6,610 feet) above Haus; Hochwurzen (6,069 feet) above Rohrmoos; and the Reiteralm (6,102 feet) above Pichl. Each area offers plenty of skiing for a day and summer skiing is available on the Dachstein glacier.

The Planai is served by an efficient gondola—waiting time in the valley is minimal even on Sundays. A quad chairlift adds to the lift capacity in this region. T-bars open the back bowls of the Planai area and the valley face of the mountain is crisscrossed by beginner and intermediate runs. The No. 1 run, from the top of the cable car to the bottom station, is the longest on the mountain and an absolutely joyful experience. Intermediates can cruise, and beginners can handle the entire run.

The Hochwurzen area is reached through a series of T-bars, chairlifts and a gondola from the Reiteralm area. New high-speed lifts make the trip quick from the Planai area. For people staying in Rohrmoos or coming by shuttlebus, a gondola whisks skiers to the top or take the quad chairlift. The upper areas are intermediate and the lower ones, around Rohrmoos are a beginner's paradise.

Hauser Kaibling, rising above Haus, is normally not so crowded as Schladming. At times you'll find yourself alone on a beautiful mountain with some of the best intermediate slopes under your skis. Intermediate is the main focus of this mountain. Take the Schischaukel to the base of the Hauser Kaibling cable car just outside town. A new gondola now adds dramatically to the uphill capacity from this village.

Reiteralm, above the towns of Pichl and Gleiming, provides a good day's worth of skiing for intermediates. Beginners have too limited an area to make the half-hour series of lifts worthwhile unless they are staying in one of the base towns.

Overall, the area uses up a week of skiing without repeating a section. Even good skiers will be hard-pressed to cover every trail in six days of all-out skiing.

Mountain rating

The area is an intermediate paradise. Beginners should center their efforts on Rohrmoos, although all sections have beginner runs. After three days of lessons, beginners can make their way all the way down each of the mountains with their instructors.

Experts should keep an eye out for good powder and test themselves high up on Hauser Kaibling or on the lower sections of the World Cup downhill runs both in Haus and Schladming. The real experts should hire a guide to take them off trai.

Mountain layout–Snowboarding

There is a Burton Super Park on Dachstein glacier and the area is perfect for freeriding and big carving. A massive halfpipe drops from the Galsterbergalm at 2,700 meters of altitude, making it one of the highest in Europe. Together with the halfpipe the resort has created a massive snow park with jumps and hits to keep riders busy for hours. Another halfpipe can be found in the middle of the Planai sector and another at the top of the gondola at Reiteralm.

In the summer this is a good snowboard training spot with riding on the glacier. The halfpipe is open even in June, July, October and November. There is night riding in Rohrmoos on the World Cup run into the stadium.

Boarders gather at the Lärchkogel trail. This is one of the favorite spots for boarders. There are also interesting natural obstacle courses on the Fageralm and at Stoderzinken at opposite ends of the valley.

Cross-Country (2006/07 prices)

The cross-country ski eldorado between Dachstein and Tauern features a network of 484 km. of groomed classic and skating tracks that are second to none in Austria.

The elevated plateau of Ramsau am Dachstein is well known for its first class range of trails. There are 150 km. of skate and classic cross-country slopes in the area. Many national teams take advantage of the tracks on the Dachstein glacier on 2.700-meter elevation for their year in/year out training. The majority of this terrain can be skied by most intermediate skiers, but be advised that 18 km. of this area is strictly rated expert. If you're up for a challenge, give the Dachstein Gletscher's World Cup runs a try. Prices: One half day and a map costs €5. A full day and a map costs €6. Three days costs €10. Seven days cost €20.

Schladming-Rohrmoos has about 60 km. of quality cross-country ski trails with shimmering names like "Crystal trail" and "Silverstone trail" in a very romantic atmosphere. Untertal, Obertal and Enns valleys define high-altitude, deep-wood cross-country skiing without being too remote. A good number of inns and snack bars are dotted along the trails. Most of the trails are skiable until late spring. Prices are: €4 for a full day ticket and €15 for a muliday ticket. A season ticket for Schladming-Rohrmoos costs €2. A season ticket for Schladming-Rohrmoos-Ramsau costs €60.

Ski school (2006/07 prices)

There are 18 schools. Ski School Hochwurzen-Planai (61268, fax 61343), Ski School Tritscher (22647, fax 611426), and Blue Tomato Snowboard School (24223-16, fax 22474) are the biggest.

The following prices are for skiing lessons from the Ski School Hochwurzen-Planai. Prices are competitve between the schools.

Private lessons for one or two people in the morning cost €95; in the afternoon, €85 and for 4 hours, €180 per person.

Group lessons for one day cost €45, for two days €90; for three days, €115.

Children's group lessons with lunch break and playtime —€60, one day; €160, three days and €200, five days.

Snowboard lessons are available from the Blue Tomato (24223-16, fax 22474). Beginners with their own equipment pay €115 for three days;; he price including boot and board is €172. For a five-day course adults cost €146; the price including boot and board is €219.

Private lessons costs €46 for an hour; €88 for two hours and €170 for a full day (four hours).

A three-day **freestyle snowboard course** for those with their own equipment is around €115 and the five-day freestyle program is €146. There are courses for carving and twin tip skiing as well.

Lift tickets (2007/08 prices)

The lift tickets cover this valley's nine mountains and 97 lifts. Each town in the region offers single-day limited-lift tickets. But the nine-mountain lift ticket allows skiing and snowboarding throughout this Salzburg region. The resorts are not internconnected by lifts, nor are they really all that close, but your lift ticket is good wherever you go in these areas. Here are the additional regions and the towns where the lifts are included in the ski pass: Salzburger Sportwelt (Flachau-Wagrain-St. Johann/Alpendorf, Zauchensee-Flachauwinkel-Kleinarl, Radstadt-Altenmarkt, Eben, Filzmoos, Goldegg), Gastein Region (Bad Gastein,

Telephone prefix: Schladming, Ramsau, Planai, 03687;
Hauser Kaibling, 03686; Reiteralm, 06454;

Bad Hofgastein, Dorfgastein, Sportgastein), plus Hochkönigs Winterreich and the Grossarltal.

The lift rates are based on high season which is from Dec. 22, 2007 – Jan. 11, 2008 and Jan. 26, - Mar. 28, 2008.

	Adult	Youth (16–18)	Child (15 and younger)
one day	€38.50	€32.50	€20
three days	€106	€89	€55
six days	€182	€153	€94.50
fourteen days	€315	€264.50	€164

Keycard is required. Deposit €3.00 (refunded upon return).Photo is required for passes of 8 days or longer. A free digital photo is taken at the resort.

Accommodations

Rates are based on high season, per person/double occupancy with half board: €€€—more than €125; €€—€75-€124; €—less than €75.

Sporthotel Royer (200, fax 20094; €€)is a four-star hotel in Schladming. This is a modern hotel with pool, indoor tennis and squash courts, sauna and pony rides. It is the favorite of Arnold Schwarzenegger, who grew up in a village not far away. Guestrooms have plenty of closet space, CNN on the television, hair dryers and showers over the tub.

Posthotel Schladming (22571, fax 225718; €€), in Schladming, is the oldest, most traditional hotel on the main square. It's only a three-minute walk from the Planai lift and has a new sauna area.

Hotel Zum Stadttor (24525; fax 2452550, €€) is also in Schladming. The hotel has a whirlpool and sauna and is about a five-minute walk from the Planai lift.

Hotel Pichlmayrgut (06454-7305; €€) If you want to stay in an old Austrian estate, this fills the bill. Amenities include indoor tennis, pool, sauna and steambath. Pichl lifts and the 4 Mountain Schischaukel are a five-minute walk from the hotel.

Hotel Neue Post (22105, fax 221055; €) is smack in the middle of town.

Right across from the Planai lift station is **Gästehaus Handlos** (22633, 226333; €€). Though it is B&B only, it can't get much more convenient.

Gasthof Kirchenwirt/Tritscher (22435, fax 2243516;€) is in the town center.

The **Schloss Moosheim** (03685-23231; €€) is a bit out of the way, but you sleep in a real castle. It adds to your vacation stories and has good transport to the lifts.

Gasthof Herrschaftstaverne (03686-2392; €€) is a good family spot only 200 meters from the base of the cable car. It has an indoor pool, sauna and curling alley.

For those looking to save money, try staying at **Jugend & Familiengastehaus** (24531, fax 2453188; €). Plus there are dozens of B&Bs cost between €20 and €30 per person. Stay near the top of the Hauser Kaibling in the **Krummholzhütte**, where you have to share a bathroom and shower, for €26–€31 a day, half pension. You get a room near the summit and about a 10-minute schuss down the mountain right out the door.

One of the best hotels in the area is **Alpengasthof Peter Rosegger** (03687-81223; €€) in Ramsau. It's perfect for those planning cross-country skiing or snowshoeing. The restaurant (only for hotel guests) is considered one of the best in the area.

The Dachstein-Tauern Region has a series of lodging deals that include seven nights lodging, half pension or breakfast only, six days of lifts and pool access. Prices are per person based on double occupancy during mid January.

Apartments, condominiums, flats

There are hundreds of units available in all shapes and sizes. Depending on the number of people in your group and the time of the year, prices per person should range from €15-€30 a night. In most cases linens and towels are extra (€25 for the week).

Contact the tourist office and describe what you want and how much you will pay. The office has a computer system that tracks all bookings in the area.

 ## Dining

The best restaurants in town are the **Posthotel**, **Sporthotel Royer** and the restaurant in the **Stadttor**. The place to spend the least money and still eat well is **Kirchenwirt**.

For great ski-slope meals on the Planai, stop in at **Schafalm** also known as **Onkel Willi's Hütte** (yes, Uncle Willi's Hut), only a few ski glides from the top of the main Planai lift. On the Hauser Kaibling, the **Krummholzhütte** at the top, and the **Stöckl-hütte** where the three lifts meet, are good. Try **Gasthof Steger** in Haus/Ennstal.

At the base of Schladming's Planai is a small inn called **Charly's Treff** owned by Charly Kahr, the Austrian who coached the national team at the 1960 Squaw Valley Olympics and the British women's team in the early 1970s. He also coached Olympic and World Cup champion Franz Klammer, a local hero. In his restaurant, savoring a schnapps, Charly regales visitors with stories of the skiers he has trained.

Many visit Charly's Treff to sample hearty dishes Aus Oma's Kochbuch (From Grandmother's Cookbook). The Geschnetzeltes (pork and noodles, €10) was very good and you don't leave hungry. Steirer Käsnock (cheese and spätzle noodles) at €7 is another favorite. Charly retired from coaching in 1985 and now spends his time overseeing his restaurant, visiting with friends like Schwarzenegger, and skiing. "I like the tree skiing and village atmosphere of Schladming," says Kahr.

The **Brand Alm,** a classic mountain hut about halfway down from the base of the Dachstein glacier cable car, is the quintessential Alpine hut. You'll see customers in lederhosen, since many people hike up from Ramsau for lunch. The Teller Erbsensuppen (split pea soup) is hearty and the Krainer sausage, served with the best sauerkraut we've ever eaten, should not be missed.

 ## Après-ski/nightlife

For wine and quiet talk, try the **Marias – The Mexican Bar.** The best dancing is at the **Sonderbar** or **WM-Arena** Hauser Kaibling. Other cozy meeting places include **Bacis** and **The Beisl**, both just off the main square. The Beisl is in the passageway at 12 Main Square and is a good place to meet people. Check out **La Porta**, near the town's old gateway.

The two main discos outside town, and also the best spots for meeting European skiers, are the **Sport Alm** in Ramsau and the **Erlebniswelt** in Rohrmoos. In Haus/Ennstal, stop into the new **Pub Remise** in the old castle.

 ## Child care (2006/07 prices)

Children age 3 and older can sign up for ski school. At the Ski School Hochwurzen-Planai (61268, fax 613434), there are two-hour morning lessons. One day costs €30. Two days cost €60. Three days cost €80.

Ski School Tritscher (22137, fax 611426) has a Mini Club for children age 3 to 4 which costs €30 for a half day and €80 for three half days. The Kinder Club is for

Telephone prefix: Schladming, Ramsau, Planai, 03687;
Hauser Kaibling, 03686; Reiteralm, 06454;

children age 4 and older. Including a supervised lunch, it costs €60 for a trial day; €160 for three days; and €200 for five days.

Other activities

Visit Salzburg. The **Loden fabric factory** in Ramsau gives tours—arrange them in advance by calling 81930. The factory and outlet are only about 10 minutes from Schladming.

Snowshoeing, wildlife watching and **horse-drawn sleigh rides** are offered by many of Schladming's smaller surrounding villages. **Horse-drawn sleigh rides** are available in Ramsau/Dachstein. **Ice skating rinks** are open in Rohrmoos and Gröbminger Land, and there are public **swimming** pools in Schladming and Ramsau.

There are also a variety of outback adventures, such as **climbing frozen waterfalls** or snow covered peaks, with overnight stays in mountain huts or igloos.

Getting there

There are good train connections from Munich and Salzburg. Both have international airports. Salzburg is a 93-km. drive from Schladming. Take the Ennstal exit.

Tourist information

The central tourist office for the region is Regionalverband Dachstein-Tauern, Ramsauer Str. 756, A-8970 Schladming, Austria; tel. 03687-23310, fax 23232.

Internet: www.dachstein-tauern.at
E-Mail: info@dachstein-tauern.at
Note: This is the central tourist office for the 9 winter sports resorts (Pichl-Reiteralm; Schladming-Rohrmoos, Ramsau am Dachstein, Haus im Ennstal, GröbmingerLand – Pruggern, Naturpark Sölktäler, Vitaldörfer Öblarn & Niederöblarn, Donnersbachwald, Bergregion Grimming). It handles reservation requests for any town in the area. There are also local tourist offices in all sport resorts.

Seefeld

If you've come to get away from it all, you have found the right spot. If you had your mind set on wild skiing and late-night partying, you are in the wrong place.

Seefeld is a purpose-built Austrian resort that was developed far before modern architecture came into fashion and ski lifts made downhill skiing an end in itself. It was created more than 50 years ago. This resort was designed as a place to get away from the pressure of everyday life and work. It still is a place to relax and to refresh one's spirit.

The village has been laid out with almost no through traffic and with a town center where vacationers can meet, talk, have a coffee or drink, and enjoy events. The look is pure modern Alpine with lots of peaked roofs and wooden balconies, but without the large barns that dotted the original Alpine resorts.

Seefeld also doesn't present itself as a go-for-broke downhill ski and snowboarding resort. This is a resort where relaxation is *de rigueur* on the slopes and off of them. Enjoyment, not excitement is the aim.

This resort is the capital of cross-country skiing in Austria, and many claim that it is one of the premier spots for skinny skiing in the world. Indeed, the cross-country and biathlon Olympic competitions have been held here twice when the international winter games were headquartered in Innsbruck.

Seefeld also offers 143 km. of walking trails and plenty of additional activities for families. Between cross-country skiing, Nordic walking, mellow slopes, swimming, ice skating, tobogganing and dining most visitors and their families succeed in escaping the pressures of the outside world, if only for a few days.

Nearby Garmisch and Mittenwald in Germany provide additional skiing and activities. Innsbruck is only 20 minutes away by car and about a half-hour away by a spectacular train ride. Go there for plenty of cultural action, shopping and skiing. And for those with travel on their minds, the Brenner Pass crossing into Italy, with its shopping and dining, is less than an hour's drive.

Mountain layout—Skiing

There is not much exciting to say about the skiing, except that the visuals and natural beauty are spectacular. The Seefeld skiing areas are on two separate mountains that are connected by local ski buses.

The Gschwandtkopf is the first area and where most of the beginners start. It only has about 1,000 feet of vertical. It has a quad chair taking skiers and riders to the top from the valley station, a single chair lift rising from Reith, and then after that there are only drag lifts. If you are a thrill-seeking skier or rider, a day spent here will feel like eternity. If you are a beginner or intermediate this is the place to learn.

On the other side of town is the Rosshütte/Härmelekopf area with a vertical drop of more than 2,500 feet. The old Rosshütte lift rolls skiers up the first 1,600 feet then one cable car glides to the peak of the Seefelder Joch. Long, snowmaking-covered, cruising trails open up before you and drop the full vertical of the sector. A second cable car leaves from the top of the Rosshütte rail and spans a valley reaching to the ridge just below the Härmelekopf. Most skiers wind their way along the ridge back to the base station; however, intrepid experts and advanced skiers climb the last 150 feet of vertical to the top of Härmelekopf and drop down the backcountry flanks of the mountain.

The regional lift ticket includes all the lifts in Garmisch-Partenkirchen, together with the Zugspitze (see our Garmisch chapter). It also covers lifts in Mittenwald where an ancient cable car takes skiers to the tip top of the Karwendelspitz where Germany's only free-riding descent starts. The descent drops more than 1,400 feet of unprepared (but avalanche controlled) vertical.

Mountain rating

For beginners, this may be one of the best places in Europe to learn to ski. The instructors speak excellent English. Their sense of humor is contagious. Their smiles warm. And the terrain is perfect to take skiers and boarders from the first awkward snowplow turns of an initiate to the confident parallel turns of an intermediate.

Intermediates have the perfect place to start to make parallel turns. This is the place to learn to set your weight on those shaped skis and make them zip you around your turns.

Experts—real experts—as always, can find skiing to keep them busy. If you are into cruising or if you are planning on keeping your knees in one piece this is a great resort where you can let them rip. However, there will not be wild descents here at this place. The best is above the Härmelekopf cable car. You might consider a trip to the nearby Zugspitze in Germany. It's included in the Happy Ski Card.

Mountain layout–Snowboarding

This is a place to learn. If you are looking for places to do jumps and for terrain parks head to Rosshütte where there is a snow park and a halfpipe called the Crazy Hole.

Riders who really want to strut their stuff should head to Mittenwald and do the drop down the Karwendel or go play on the Zugspitze. If you stay in Seefeld, you may get restless, but there is no reason not to strike out for resorts only about 20 minutes away that are included with your lift tickets.

Cross-country

Seefeld is Europe's (maybe the world's) capital of cross-country skiing. As mentioned in the introduction, this was the site of the events for two Olympics. The Nordic Ski World Championships took place here in 1985, a Cross-Country Skiing World Cup was held here in 1999 and Nordic Combination World Cups are held here every January.

The cross-country office is at the Olympia Sports Center (3060). It is open from

9 a.m. to 2:30 p.m. (Closed for lunch from 12:30–1:30 p.m.). On Sunday, they open 45 minutes later and close 30 minutes earlier.

There is an interconnected network of 262 km. of trails —152 km. are classic trails and 110 km. are skating trails — that includes something for every level of skier and skater.

The trails are free for anyone holding a guest card (meaning that they are staying in a hotel, B&B or apartment in the village). Trails are set and groomed daily.

This cross-country paradise offers lots of possibilities on beginner and intermediate runs extending into backcountry woods, deep forest and meadows; skating lanes are also available. It's generally rolling terrain, but with enough turns, dips and downhill runs to keep it interesting for most skinny-skiers. There are a few restaurants and inns along the way for rest stops and lunch.Trails are extremely well laid out and groomed. In complicated backcountry areas, a map would be handy because many trails intersect and directions are not always well marked. Here, as elsewhere in Austria, trails tend to be overrated for difficulty, at least by American standards. An intermediate trail is usually just a little beyond beginner level, and an intermediate can easily handle trails marked difficult.

Ski school (2006/07 prices)

Schischule Seefeld (5212-2412, fax 5212 2412 4) caters to real learning. This is the perfect spot to really get the feel of carving and where to learn new tricks on your board. This is a perfect place to learn to ski.

Private lessons (for skiing and snowboarding) for one person cost €40 for one hour (9 a.m. to 10 a.m.) and €42 for one hour (12 p.m. to 1.p.m. or 1 p.m. to 2 p.m.); €84 for 1 hour 45 minutes (12 p.m. to 1:45 p.m.) for 1-2 persons; €114-€132 for two hours for 1-2 persons; and €189 for four hours for 1-2 persons. Each additional person pays €10.

Group lessons (skiing) for adults are four hours long. One day costs €48; two days cost €96; four days cost €134; six days cost €165.

Snowboarding lessons are two hours per day with a maximum of 8 people. One day costs €48; two days cost €96; three days cost €109; five days cost €144.

Cross-country lessons are four hours long. One day costs €48; two days cost €96; four days cost €134; five days €149. Beginners can get a two-hour lesson for five days, €103; or for four days, €92.

Lift tickets (2007/08 prices)

The Happy Ski Card multiday ski pass is valid in Seefeld, Neuleutasch, Mösern, Reith bei Seefeld and in the Zugspitze region (Garmisch-Zugspitze, Mittenwald, Ehrwald, Lermoos, Biberwier, Bichlbach, Berwang, Heiterwang, Grainau).

	Adults	**Youth** (16-17)	**Children** (5-15)
three days	€91	€83.50	€54.50
six days	€169	€156	€101.50
thirteen days	€298.50	€275	€179

Children age 6 and younger ski for half the normal child ticket price.

Accommodations

Rates here are based on high season, per person/double occupancy with half board: €€€—€125+; €€—€75-€124; €—less than €75.

Telephone prefix: 05212

It is hard to go wrong here in Seefeld. The most expensive in town are **Hotel Klosterbräu** (26210, fax 3885; €€€) and **Hotel Astoria** (2272, fax 2272100, €€€) both with indoor pool, sauna and steam grotto.

The four-star **Viktoria** (4441, fax 4443; €–€€) has rooms based on different historical time periods and places. Try the Tibet, New York, or the Modern Times room.

The **Lärchenhof** (23830, fax 238383; €€), also a four-star hotel, combines luxury with Austrian hospitality. Food is great here, and there is entertainment organized most nights with Tyrolean nights, dancing and fashion shows.

The **Casinohotel Karwendelhof** (2655, fax 2201-500; €€–€€€) has a spectacular lobby and sits just across from the train station. It is part of Best Western reservations.

The **Waldhotel** (22070, fax 200130; €–€€) is directly across from the Rosshütte lift. It caters to families and is a member of the Children's Hotels of Austria.

Die Post (22010, fax 2201500; €€–€€€), the **Hiltpolt** (2253, fax 284553; €€€), and the **Diana** (2060, fax 2188; €–€€) are smack in the middle of the village.

Apartments, condominiums, flats

A list of apartments and B&Bs is available from the tourist office. Write ahead of time and ask for the apartment size you require and the dates that you are planning on being at the resort. Either the tourist office or the apartment landlords will contact you with several possibilities. Make your selections and get back to them.

Prices per night per apartment are between €70–€100 for a two-room apartment during high season and €80–€150 for a three-room apartment. Local taxes aare €1.20 per person per day and do not include the cleaning charge.

 # Dining

Seefeld is a town where the visitors enjoy a good meal. This resort has an embarrassment of riches when it comes to fine dining. The top four restaurants have won various awards The first mentioned are highly rated by Gault Millau and the next two are unique and delicious in their own way.

Number 1 on many critics' lists is the **Ritter-Oswald-Stube** in the Klosterbräu (26210). This space is filled with atmosphere and the food is delectable as well. It is packed every evening. From the starter, salmon tartar, to the dessert, mint-chocolate sorbet, your taste buds will dance. Meals here will run about €40–€50.

Finally, take time to enjoy a meal at **Kracherle Moos** (4680) where the chef creates specials in a unique setting. Two ancient farm buildings were transported here and connected to create this restaurant. The daily menu is €16–€20.

Dinner or lunch at the **Triendlsäge** (2580) is fun and reasonable. Take time to see the old original 1848 sawmill that has been preserved. At the **S'Alte Wirtshaus** (4824) dine in an old building dating back to the 1300s. A fun spot is the **Alten Schmiede** in the Hotel Hiltpolt.

 # Après-ski/nightlife

Good après-ski can be found throughout the village. Tea-time festivities take place at the the **Alt Seefeld Restaurant**, or at **Tenne** in the Kaltschmid. Head to the **Pirate Club** for dancing or try the new **"Wildfang"-Bar** for a glass of champagne or a cocktail. Stop in the **Beisl Pub** for beers or a good glass of wine. The **Siglu** serves libations. At night head back to the **Kanne** or the **Buffalo Westersaloon** or **Fun Disco Jeep**.

Child care (2006/07 prices)

Schischule Seefeld (2412) has programs for different age groups. Gizzi's Children's Club, open Monday through Friday from 9 a.m. to 5 p.m., cares for children age 18 months to 8 years. There's a large playroom which is divided into different areas with different toys, a changing room and a bedroom for napping. Children also play outside in the snow in the playground. A half day (less than 4 hours) costs €25 and each additional child pays €5. A full day (4 hours or more) costs €35 with each additional child paying €10. A supervised lunch costs €5.

Tiny Tots is a beginners' ski course for kids ages 3–5 with a maximum of 8 per group. The program hours are from 9:30–11:30 a.m. and 12–2 p.m.. Children are guaranteed two hours of lessons per day and there's a Tiny Tot's race that's held every Friday which is followed by a prize-giving ceremony. The rates are: three days, €79; four days, €94; and five days, €102. Supervised lunch costs €12 per day. A five-day program combining lunch and lessons costs €184.

Group lessons for kids ages 3–15 are divided into a beginner's and an advanced section. Each section has classes that are four hours long, with a maximum of 10 children per group. One day costs €48; two days , €96; four days, €128; five days, €140. Supervised lunch costs €12 per day.

Other activities

The village's Olympia indoor **swimming pool** is open daily from 9:30 a.m. to 10 p.m. Entry is €11 for adults. For a pool and sauna entry the price is approximately €14.50. Children pay about half price. There is a small increase in prices on Sunday. There are also indoor pools open to the public at Hotel Bergland, Vital Royal Dorint Sofitel and Kronenhotel.

Ice skating is available on the Olympia indoor rink for €5 for adults and €3.50 for children ages 14 and younger, for a half day. **Snow rafting** is great fun. Ride a blow-up boat or a banana boat for €9.50. Play **tennis** at the Casino Tennis Hall for an hour for €17 or get a block of ten entries for €146.

Seefeld also has a **casino**, a German language **movie theater**, a **library, Tyrolean evenings, paragliding, tobogganing, curling, ice climbing** and **indoor golf**.

Read the Innsbruck chapter and the Garmisch chapter for most nearby activities and excursions.

Getting there

Munich's Airport is only two hours away by car on the autobahn. Get to the airport early when leaving—it's massive. Innsbruck is about half an hour's drive. Rail and bus travelers will find connections to Garmisch and to Innsbruck, where they can connect to any town in Europe.

Tourist information

Seefeld Information Office, Klosterstraße 43, A-6100 Seefeld, Tyrol, Austria.
Telephone (050) 8800, fax (050) 88051.
For lodging reservations call the tourist office Monday–Saturday, 8:30 a.m.–8 p.m..
Internet: www.seefeld.com
E-mail: region@seefeld.com

Telephone prefix: 05212

SkiWelt • Ellmau, Söll, Westendorf

SkiWelt Wilder Kaiser-Brixental, surrounding the Hohe Salve, is Austria's largest interconnected ski area. Not only is the region the largest interconnected group of lifts in the country, it's also one of the most affordable. The wide expanse of slopes with the backdrop of the rocky Wilder Kaiser boasts 90 lifts, 250 km. of trails, and 180 km. of snowmaking spread above nine villages. Guests come from across Europe, but English-speakers tend to cluster in a few of the villages.

The entire ski area is perhaps the most accessible in Austria to skiers coming in from Germany. It's only 20 minutes from the Kufstein border crossing, which is about an hour from Munich.

The main villages are Going, Ellmau, Scheffau, Söll, Hopfgarten, Westendorf and Brixen im Thale. We will focus on Ellmau, Söll and Westendorf since these have the preponderance of English-speaking skiers.

Ellmau and Söll have a large group of British skiers, but Ellmau has more families and less party animals than Söll just down the road. In Ellmau, you can find some of Austria's best dining and beautiful chalets. The small town has very convenient access to the lifts and is easy to reach from Germany or Innsbruck.

Söll has much more of the party animals with British and Swedes mixing for a great fun-time atmosphere. Westendorf also has a core of British skiers who make this their resort of choice. All these towns share the same massive interconnected series of trails.

Söll carefully cultivates its small-town image with little shops whose operators are overwhelmingly friendly and strike up a conversation in English at the first opportunity. The main street is full of visitors at almost any hour of the day or night. While traffic is heavy, pedestrians have taken priority, causing motorists to wait, sometimes impatiently, as the shoppers stroll across the roadway to browse.

It's quite clear from the heavy traffic in the local grocery stores that not everyone takes full pension. Full shopping bags mean a lot of picnic lunches and breakfasts prepared back in the room. Everywhere you encounter young couples strolling hand in hand, a change from the more elegant and expensive European resorts where the crowd is older and not always so affectionate.

Söll becomes little U.K. during the winter with a predominant number of the guests coming from the British Islands. Some vacationers who want to soak up the Austrian culture will be disappointed, however those who want to have an easy time with the language will find this village perfect.

On the other side of the Hohe Salve, in the Brixental, is the village of Westendorf. It is a small place, conveniently just up out of the reach of the main road. The town church presides over a series of chalets that provide the picture-perfect Alpine scene. The British and Australians return to this perfect setting year after year. They are joined by a strong Dutch contingent. The mix is most pleasant and the partying is not overbearing. The only major drawback is that the connection to the lifts of SkiWelt is by bus. There is no skiing into town at the end of the day.

There are plans in the works to link Brixen to Westendorf and to link Westendorf with Kirchberg on the other side of the Gampen. When these trails are linked with those of Kitzbühel and Kirchberg, this interconnected system will be even more amazing.

Mountain layout–Skiing

The best skiing is concentrated in the valley headed by Söll which includes Itter, Scheffau, Ellmau and finally Going. Around the mountains, in the Brixental valley, you will find Hopfgarten, Kelchsau, Westendorf and Brixen im Thale. All but Westendorf and Kelchsau are on an interconnected circuit. Free bus service is provided from Westendorf, providing skiers with a two-valley network of lifts and hundreds of trails.

Ellmau/Going access to the slopes is via a high-speed quad, a train or a double chair. Taking the high-speed lift is the best bet. At the top there are two six-seat high-speed chairlifts that fill the backside of the Hartkaiser with intermediate skiers.

One thing you will realize quickly is that this region has made a concerted effort to build fast efficient access to the mountains. What they may lack in expert terrain, them make up in speed to the slopes. There are still drag lifts, but you can ski all day, stick to the chairlifts and never need to take a T-bar.

About a 15-minute walk from Söll (connected by a frequent and free shuttle), an eight-passenger gondola carries skiers up the mountain. Further access to the skiing area is provided by the four-passenger gondola of Itter and the eight-passenger gondola of Hopfgarten.

From the top of the Hohe Salve (5,670 feet) at Söll, you can appreciate the massive dimensions of the Wilder Kaiser area which is officially called the SkiWelt Wilder Kaiser-Brixental, but is known to the English and Austrians as simply the SkiWelt. Your view includes the 5,115-foot Brandstadl summit at Scheffau, the 4,820-foot Hartkaiser at Ellmau-Going and further to your right the town of Kirchberg, gateway to Kitzbühel. On the skyline you see ski slopes as far as Pass Thurn, and the famed Grossglockner is on the distant skyline.

Good parallel skiers should do the SkiWelt tour, which begins and ends in Söll (of course you can begin and end wherever you want to). Skiers work their way up and down the ridges, visiting Itter, Hopfgarten, the outskirts of Brixen, then back up to Zinsberg, and finally back to Brandstadl and over to Hartkaiser, stopping along the way in Scheffau, Ellmau and perhaps Going.

The black run from the summit of Hohe Salve above Söll will challenge a good skier. It's a 4-km. trail with a vertical drop of about 2,200 feet. The best intermediate run is the Rigi along the back side and then around the Hohe Salve, all the way down to the Gasthof Kraftalm where they serve a *Jägertee* (Hunter's Tea) that will blast your ski boots off. The recipe, according to the Gasthof owner, is tea, some rum, red wine, plenty of schnapps, a goodly amount of sugar and some herbs for aroma. He adds, "Don't light a match near it while it's hot."

There is also good night skiing and riding in Söll. It's available from Wednesday to Saturday from 7:30 p.m to 9:30 p.m.

Westendorf skiers need to take the free ski bus to the gondola in Brixen im Thale to reach the flanks of Hohe Salve. From the top of the gondola, a six-person high-speed lift makes the final ascent. The slopes above the town are also quite good. They have a vertical drop of around 1,500 feet and the gondola links with a quad chairlift, a triple and a couple of old single chairs to open up some nice high terrain that holds snow quite well. In fact, when conditions stink in the rest of the region, Westendorf gets packed with riders and skiers.

Mountain layout–Snowboarding

This has been rated as a good place to try snowboarding. The slopes are relatively gentle. There is a fun park in Westendorf and a halfpipe in Hopfgarten. There's also a terrain park in Ellmau. The snowboard schools here get accolades for their beginning and carving programs.

Most boarders will stay on the north side of Hohe Salve. That's where the best snow stays as well as the most interesting trails. Some of the steepest terrain is around Scheffau, but other than that is all easy stuff. Pray for a big snowfall the day before you arrive.

Mountain rating

The Wilder Kaiser is intermediate country with a capital "I." You can head down any slope without hesitation and enjoy moderately challenging, well-groomed runs. A fine place to hone your skiing skills. This area is not recommended for the demanding skier craving black-trail thrills.

Cross-country & snowshoe (2007/08 prices)

The SkiWelt Wilder Kaiser–Brixental is a cross-country paradise, with approximately 170 km. of tracks that link Söll with Itter, Scheffau, Ellmau, Going, and continue on to St. Johann. Along the connecting track on the 225-km. "Koasa-Loipen," cross-country skiers can discover even more new and challenging terrain.

In the Brixental, the trails link Westendorf with Brixen im Thale and then continue to the end of the valley and Kirchberg making 170 km. of circular routes and high altitude tracks with guaranteed snow which wind through Brixen im Thale and Kelchsau.

Guided tours are organised for beginners and more advanced skiers. Hire a guide for a multi-day or weekend tour in open terrain featuring superb ascents and unforgettable descents. Trial courses are available for €37. The fee for equipment hire is €9.

Ski bus service within the resorts is free with the guest card. The local post bus is also available at an added cost.

SkiWelt Wilder Kaiser – Brixental can offer you even more winter Nordic fun in the form of snowshoeing. Snowshoeing for 5 to 7 people including equipment, snack and transfer costs €48. Söll Westendorf and Brixen also have guided snowshoe walks.

Ski school (2007/08 prices)

The SkiWelt has thirteen ski schools. Ski & Snowboardschule Söll/Hochsöll (5454), in Söll has approximately 60 instructors, most of them are English-speaking - a strength in the Wilder Kaiser region.

Their prices are similar to other ski schools in the region.

Lessons are daily. Week-long lessons begin on Sundays and Mondays. Instruction is 10 a.m. to noon and 2–4 p.m. No group lessons held on Fridays or Saturdays.

Private lessons are also offered through the ski school office for €55 per hour for one, with €20 for each additional person. Beginner lessons take place on the beginners slope directly across from the ski school office before going up the mountain after a couple of days.

Private instructor for a day (4 hrs) is €195, with €25 for each additional skier.

Group lessons: A full-day session (4 hours) costs €63. Three days cost €130. Five days is €138. A special half-day (two hours a day) course for intermediate skiers and above is available for €83 for three days and €90 for five days.

Snowboarding lessons: People age 10 and older can take two-hour lessons. One day costs €48; two days, €85; and three days, €95.

Lift tickets (2007/08 prices)

These SkiWelt Wilder Kaiser-Brixental tickets are good for the entire interconnected area including Going, Ellmau, Scheffau, Söll, Itter, Kelchsau, Hopfgarten, Westendorf and Brixen im Thale.

Peak Season: Dec. 22, 2007 - March 24, 2008
Off-Peak Season: Opening until Dec. 21, 2007 and March 25, 2008 until Closing

	Peak/Off-Peak Adults*	Youth*	Children*
one day	€35.50/€32	€28.50/€25.50	€18/€16
three days	€99/€84	€79/€67.50	€49.50/€42
six days	€173/€147	€138.50/€117.50	€86.50/€73.50
fourteen days	€298/€253.50	€238.50/€202.50	€149/€126.50

*Adults are those born in 1988 and before. Youth are those born 1989–1991. ID is requested. Children Tare those born 1992–2000. Children born in 2002 and after ski free. Identification is requested for teens and children.

Accommodations

For reservations contact Tourist Office Söll (tel. 05333-5216, fax 05333-6180) or SkiWelt Wilder Kaiser-Brixental (05358-505, fax 05358-50555).

Rates: Based on double occupancy with half board in February. €€€—€125+; €€—€75–€124; €€—less than €75.

Two of the best hotels in the area are in Ellmau. **Hotel Bär** (05358-2395, fax 239596; €€€) and the **Kaiserhof** (05358-2022, fax 220260; €€€) both have all the amenities including indoor pool, saunas and steam baths.

For the most part it is hard to find many hotels that will cost more than about €100 for half board during the ski season.

Hotel Greil (5289; €€) a 10-minute walk from the center of town, is quiet. The food, both tasty and filling, is served by a friendly staff.

The best hotel in town is **Postwirt** (5081; €€), a renovated, beautiful building near the local tourist office. Equally attractive and historic is **Feldwebel** (5224;€€), a 57-room hotel just down the street. **Hotel Tyrol** (5273; €€) is about halfway between the Greil and the center of town.

Hotel Alpenschlössl (6400) approximately three kilometers outside of Söll, and **Hotel Alpenpanorama** (5309) situated on the "Sonnbichl," are recommended four-star hotels. On the mountain we liked the **Salvenmoos** (5351; €) for skiers who want to hit the slopes immediately and don't need to go into town often.

There are over two dozen hotels in Söll. Private rooms and bed & breakfasts are numerous. The tourist office can arrange rooms in all price ranges (5216).

In Brixen im Thale, **Gasthof Hoferwirt** (05334-6742, fax 30094; €) is almost across the street from the gondola. **Pension Sonnhof** (05334-8532, fax 6064; €) is the chalet most imagine when heading to the Austrian Alps. **Reitlwirt** (05334-8119; €) has excellent service and a good restaurant.

In Westendorf, head to **Vital-Landhotel Schermer** (05334-6268, fax 2384; €) where you get a covered pool and covered parking. At the **Hotel Jakobwirt** (05334-6245, fax 2467; €) there is another covered pool and the place is perfect for families. The **Hotel Glockenstuhl** (05334-6175, fax 2462; €) also has an indoor swimming pool, sauna and its own restaurant. There are also three **youth hostels** where young skiers can stay for as little as €21 a night with half board.

Ski Chalets: Crystal. (See page 16 for address, phone and fax.)

Dining

One of the best restaurants in Austria is the **Schindlhaus** (516136) in Söll. A young chef has swept in, creating exciting meals. The Mediterranean influences are blended with local mountain foods and it gets a star in Michelin.

Hotel Bär (05358-2395, fax 239596) and the **Kaiserhof** (05358-2022, fax 220260) are also excellent. At the Bär try the homemade gnocchi, the appetizer bar, the grilled specialties with a strong garlic sauce and finish off with a fine cheese. The Kaiserhof sometimes serves salmon tartar followed by fine seafood with cream polenta. Costs are in the range of €23–€50 at any of these three award-winning restaurants.

Another top restaurant in the region is **Brixner Thalhof** (05334-8468) in Brixen im Thale. This restaurant is proof positive that good simple cooking is sometimes the best. Even the most expensive meal doesn't break €25. We could eat here every night.

Stallhäusl (05332-76342) comes highly recommended as does the **Stöcklalm** (05333-5127). **Gasthof Hochfilzer** (05333-5491) is about one-and-a-half kilometers out of town but is well worth the walk.

The **Stube** of the Postwirt has the most atmosphere, complete with a group of old timers at the big front table who puff on their pipes and argue loudly about everything. The food is good and filling. The Stube came in second for best apple strudel in town. It was good but not quite as fine as **Cafe Mirabel's**, up the street.

Après-ski/nightlife

The ski instructors and longtime visitors gather after skiing in the small bar at the **Gasthof Postwirt**. Also popular with guests and locals alike are **Leo's Bella Vita** and **Rossini** in the resort centre.

There's a younger crowd and louder music at the **PartyHouse Whiskey Mühle** and **Western Saloon: Buffalo** at the Pizzeria Venezia. **Salvenstadl** rocks just across the main road from the gondola. A couple of igloos serving schnapps and hosting games of nageln, a drinking game in which the participants compete to see who can drive a nail into a tree stump with the narrow end of an hatchet first, make for merriment on the trails back to town from the gondola base.

In Westendorf, the Dutch gather at **Gerry's Bar**. The best tea-time is at **Kibo Bar** and the **Wunderbar** can be fun. Also recommended are the bowling alley in **Theresianna, Bruchstall, Moskitobar** and **Karat-Bar**.

Child care [2007/08 prices]

KinderKaiserland run by the Ski- & Snowboardschule Scheffau (5358 8308, fax: 5358 84708) is a winter adventure park with more than 7,000 square meters of safe skiing terrain for children. It's open from December to Easter, every day from 9:45 a.m. to 3:30 p.m.

Unsure if your child is ready for ski instruction? KinderKaiserland offers a 45-minute trial program for children age 2-4 for €20 that runs every day from 12:05 p.m. to 12:50 p.m. A one-hour trial program for children age 4-12 that costs €15.

Otherwise, a half day (2 hours) costs €35; three half days are €75; and six half days are €95. One full day (4 hours) costs €45; three days are €100; and six days are €130. A supervised lunch from noon to 1:30 p.m. costs €10.

Ski & Snowboardschule Söll/Hochsöll runs Monti's Kinderwelt and Monti's Mini-Club. The ski kindergarten (Monti's Kinderwelt 5 – 14 Jahre), across the street from the ski school building, takes children from ages 5 to 14 (05333 5454; fax 05333 5556). Prices are similar in the other resorts of the SkiWelt Wilder Kaiser-Brixental.

These are the prices for Monti's Kinderwelt in Söll: Five-day (4 hours per day) cost €138, a three-day program will cost €130, and two-day will cost €100. Additional cost for lunch and supervision is €10 per day.

Monti's Minis is next to the gondola station for non-skiing kids ages 3-5. A full day of care (9:30 a.m. to 4 p.m.) including snack and lunch will cost €45; a half day (9:30 a.m. to 1:30 p.m.) including snack and lunch is €30. Two hours of care costs €15; two hours with lunch costs €20.

Other activities

Söll has a well-developed recreation complex with a beautiful **indoor pool** with a heated outdoor extension, sauna, bio-sauna, steambath and solarium. Check out different activities with the tourist office. There are **toboggan runs**, **snowshoe tours**, **rustic cabin evenings**, **horse-drawn sleigh rides**, **torchlight hikes** and much more.

Both Salzburg and Innsbruck, with a wide range of **museums** and scenic outdoor attractions, are within an hour's drive.

In addition, it is not unusual for the visitor with a car to visit Innsbruck and then venture down the Brenner motorway for a short excursion into Italy. The same is true for a visit to Munich for those who arrive from Innsbruck or Milan.

Getting there

The main arrival airport is Munich, about 90 minutes by bus from Söll and other towns in the area. If you're driving, take the Salzburg autobahn out of Munich and then the Rosenheim cutoff (called the Inntal autobahn). You cross the border near Kufstein and take the second exit, Kufstein Süd. Söll will be marked on the autobahn exit sign. From the turnoff, it's about 15-minute drive over one slight uphill grade to Söll.

Tourist Information

Ski Welt Tourist Office, Stockach 38, A-6306 Söll, Austria.
Telephone 05333-400, fax: 05333-400-9100.
Email: office@skiwelt.at   Internet: www.skiwelt.at.

Telephone prefix: Söll, 05333; Ellmau, Scheffau and Going, 05358
Westendorf and Brixen im Thale, 05334

St. Johann in Tirol

St. Johann in Tirol along with Oberndorf, Kirchdorf and Erpfendorf, is a part of the Ferienrgion valley area known as the Holiday Region. St. Johann in Tirol in winter is a Tyrolean resort town just far enough from the lifts to keep locals aware of the need to welcome visitors with a smile. The town is afloat in a sea of snow, lending a special atmosphere to a place that can't decide whether it is a resort village or a valley town.

Although St. Johann is only 2,297 feet above sea level, the snowfall here is certain and heavy from Christmas to March. That, together with north-facing slopes, pleases serious skiers. The setting is picturesque, with the familiar outline of the Kitzbüheler Horn forming part of the panorama. Kitzbühel is about 9.6 km. away.

The typical Tyrolean hotels here are large and have a deserved reputation for the hospitality which is sometimes missing in bigger, better known resorts. At night you'll know immediately from the lower decibel levels that this is not a party town. The streets don't exactly fold up at 8 p.m., but the nightlife is quieter.

The region has an excellent shuttlebus system that links hotels and apartments with the lifts and all the villages in the valley.

St. Johann is the shopping center for the region and caters to lots of locals as well as the tourists who come to ski. The mix of visitors is fairly well balanced between British, Germans, Dutch and Swedes. It creates a real international atmosphere that adds to the vacation.

One of the year's biggest events is the Tiroler Koasalauf, an international cross-country race staged in mid-February. It begins at the Koasa Stadium cross-country center in St. Johann. The event has its own Web site at www.koasalauf.at. The Holiday Region offers more than 275 km. of cross-country runs.

 ## Mountain Layout

The trails of St. Johann and Oberndorf run along the flanks of the Kitzbüheler Horn. You can reach them by gondolas from St. Johann and from neighboring Oberndorf.

The runs lie on the north-facing side of the Kitzbüheler Horn so they maintain their snow cover for the entire season. Snowmaking now spreads the white stuff over three wide top-to-bottom swatches of the mountain. Though the resort has spent money on snowmaking, they, like Kitzbühel, did it at the expense of lifts. It is one of the drag-lift capitals of Austria.

The top station is Harschbichl at 5,577 feet. From there you have a choice of blue and red runs and one black trail.

We enjoyed the black run, which really begins from Penzing at 4,799 feet and swings down through mogul fields to the parking lot above Oberndorf. A new gondola now serves this section of the mountain non-stop from the parking lot. As with any Austrian resort, the off-piste possibilities are endless.

Intermediates can go wild. Some say that the whole mountain is dedicated to intermediate pleasures. Start with the run from the Eichenhof drag lift on the far side of St. Johann for a good downhill cruise and small crowds. From there you can work your way to the Jodlalm chairlift that will take you to just below the Harschbichl. From the top of the Jodlalm chair, cruise to the middle station of the gondola to reach the summit. You can follow the lines of a dozen different trails cut into the mountain.

Beginner slopes are at the bottom of the mountain.

Snowboarders have a halfpipe at Eichenhof and a snowboard jump set up about halfway up the Harschbichl gondola from St. Johann in Tirol.

An expanded pass, Schneewinkel, opens more than 55 lifts serving 170 km. of runs through two adjacent valleys. The St. Johann pass is valid on these lifts when purchased for four days or longer. Though they claim 8 different towns included in the pass, there are only five worth noting—St. Johann in Tirol, Oberndorf, Waidring, St. Ulrich am Pillersee, and Fieberbrunn.

Again, all are drag-lift heavy and have trails for intermediates and beginners. The longest run in the other areas is in Fieberbrunn tracing a 5 km. length and dropping 2,624 feet. The most difficult trail in the area is Buckelpiste Reckmoos under the Reckmoos lift. Fieberbrunn opens up lots of expert off-piste possibilities, but go with a guide.

Mountain rating

St. Johann and Oberndorf are for intermediates. The slopes are rarely challenging unless you go off-piste, and only beginners and the intermediates will find the skiing interesting enough for a week. Mainly family-friendly skiing is found in Kirchdorf and Erpfendorf. However, with the regional ski pass advanced intermediates and experts can try a number of challenging slopes in the area, in particular those in the Fieberbrunn off-piste areas and on the Steinplatte above Waidring, about 16 km.

Cross-country

Well-laid-out, groomed trails extend in two opposite directions from St. Johann. The Koasastadion Ski Touring Center provides good maps, rentals and a starting base. The trails offer pleasant rolling terrain, a taste of backcountry woods (if not all that extensive) and plenty of traditional inns along the way for lunch, rest and refreshment. The Holiday Region which includes St. Johann, Oberndorf, Kirchdorf and Erpfendorf has a total of 275 km. of set trails that are basically divided equally between expert, intermediate and beginner. Then there are the adjoining trails to Going and Ellmau which can link another 60 km. of trails to the area. No cross-country skier can cruise all these trails in a dedicated week.

Telephone prefix: St. Johann 05352

Lift tickets (2007/08 prices)

The Ski St. Johann in Tirol & Oberndorf pass offers lift access to the entire St. Johann-Oberndorf-Eichenhof region. The one-, two- or three-day St. Johann pass covers 17 lifts serving 60 km. of prepared trails on the north side of the Kitzbüheler Horn. Lifts include three gondolas, a quad chair, one triple chair, two double chair, and 10 surface lifts.

Note: High Season is from Dec. 22, 2007 - March 24, 2008. Normal Season is from the start of the season to Dec. 21, 2007 and Mar. 25, 2008 to the end of the season.

Skipass St. Johann in Tirol / Oberndorf / Eichenhof

	High/Normal		
	Adults	Juniors	Children
half-day (from noon)	€28/€24	€15/€20.50	€14/€12
one day	€33/28.50	€27/€23.50	€16.50/€14.50
two days	€64/€54	€52/€43	€32/€27
three days	€93/€80	€75/€65	€46.50/€40

For skiing for four or more consecutive days, there's the Schneewinkel area pass. The pass covers 170 km. of runs in St. Johann in Tirol, Oberndorf, Kirchdorf in Tirol, Erpfendorf, Fieberbrunn, St. Jakob im Haus, St. Ulrich am Pillersee, Hochfilzen, Waidring und Kössen. The lifts are not currently interconnected; however buses link areas where lifts do not.

Skipass Schneewinkel

	High/Normal		
	Adults	Juniors	Children
four days	€120.50/103	€97/€83	€61/€52
six days	€166/€142	€133/€114	€83/€71
fourteen days	€278/€237	€223/€190	€139/€98

These are the prices for the Kitzbüheler Alpenskipass. This pass includes 249 ski lifts and 704 k.m. of ski pistes.

Kitzbüheler Alpenskipass

	Adults	Juniors	Children
one day	€41	€33	€20.50
three days	€112	€89	€56
six days	€196	€156	€98

Ski school (2007/08 prices)

St. Johann has approximately 130 of the 240 instructors teaching in the Holiday Region. One of the main ski schools is the Ski- & Snow-boardschool St. Johann in Tirol – The Original (5352-64777). Prices are competitive at the other regional ski schools.

Private lessons for skiing and snowboarding (for 1 to 2 persons) cost between €90 and €95 for a half-day morning lesson and €85 for a half-day afternoon lesson. Each additional person pays €20. It costs between €175 and €165 for a full day. Each additional person pays €20. From Wednesday to the end of the week, the school offers a discount on full day lessons. One day is €165 with each additional person being €20. *Note*: Half day equals 2 hours of lessons and a full day equals 4 hours.

Group lessons for skiing and snowboarding for one day are €58; for three days, €103; for five days, €123; and for six days, €133.

Freestyle, mono skiing and **telemark lessons** are available by request only.

www.skisnowboardeurope.com

Accommodations

St. Johann has one of the best organized accommodation services in Austria. By using the hotel-apartment list or searching for accommodations at www.ferienregion.at, you can arrange for any type of accommodation—from simple B&B to apartment rental.

We recommend that you come in January or March when the maximum price reductions are offered. Two sport packages are outstanding. Variation A includes a Schneewinkel six-day ski pass. Variation A has a starting cost of €250 for B&B and €405 for half board. Variation B includes a Schneewinkel six-day ski pass and six days of lessons. Variation B has a starting cost of €365 for B&B and €520 with half board. The sport package price for a first-class hotel or guesthouse is about what you'd pay just for accommodations at some resorts. St. Johann hotels and guesthouses offer the mid-range, all-inclusive package.

Based on high season, per person/double occupancy with breakfast: €€€—more than €80; €€—€50–79; €—less than €50.

Our favorite deluxe hotels are the **Hotel Bruckenwirt** (Kaiserstrasse 18, 62585, fax 6258514; €€-€€€) with the town center right outside your door; **Sporthotel Austria** (Winterstellerweg 3, 62507, fax 65137; €€-€€€) with a hotel swimming pool; **Hotel Crystal** (Hornweg 5, 62630, fax 6263013; €€) right along the ski runs; **Goldener Löwe** (Speckbacherstrasse 23, 62251, fax 62981; €–€€) the town's largest with lots of package groups; and **Hotel Dorfschmiede** (Speckbacherstrasse 24, 62323, fax 621678; €€-€€€) with a heated swimming pool and only a three-minute trek to the lifts and the downtown.

For one of Austria's best experiences try **Hotel Gruber** (Gasteigerstrasse 18; 61461, fax 6146133; €€-€€€). It is recommended for its atmosphere and service.

Hotel Schöne Aussicht (Berglehen 23, 62270, fax 64626; €€-€€€) with an excellent location on the slopes.

If you stay at the **Gästeheim Aloisia** (Schwimmbadweg 8, 62419, fax 64485; €) you will have the Panoramabad right outside your door. It's almost like having a swimming pool right in your hotel for a fraction of the cost.

The Ferienregion St. Johann in Tirol has a multitude of excellent accommodations; we've never been disappointed. The tourist offices can provide a full list and help with reservations. There are scores of Garni, Gasthöfe and Pensionen that have room and breakfast for less than €50 a night. That's a steal.

Apartments, condominiums, flats

Apartment rental is as easy as finding hotel or pension lodging in St. Johann. Contact the tourist office and tell them your arrival date. They will send a list of available apartments. You then contact the apartment owner directly. Apartments that sleep four range in price from €45–€200 a night.

Dining

For Austrian specialties head to one of the three following restaurants. The **Post** (62230), smack in the middle of town, oozes charm. **Hotel Bruckenwirt/Restaurant Ambiente** (62585) is the upscale place in St Johann in Tirol. The restaurant is top of the line and an elegant piano lounge offers an authentic English tea service. One is expected to dress up a little for dinner in the restaurant, but things can be more casual in the lounge and bar. **Park Hotel** (62226) offers Tyrolean and Austrian specialties in a not-so-formal atmosphere. **Römerhof** (63516) has recommended Tyrolean meals.

Telephone prefix: St. Johann 05352

For the best in Italian, head to **Villa Masianco** (64630), an affordable pizzeria serving Italian meals that the locals love. This place has grown from a small pizza joint to a big restaurant over the past decade. It must be doing something right.

Pizzeria Rialto (64168). Pizza and the rest right at the station in what may have been the old station house. Pleasant and charming northern Italian/Tyrolean decor.

La Rustica (62843) serves meals from wood-fired pizza to pasta to scallopini.

Café Platzl (62380) has a very good ice cream bar and family restaurant upstairs. Lively but not too rowdy bar for the twenty-somethings downstairs. Easy to find right on the main plaza in the center of town.

Café Rainer (62235) is the best cafe in town and doubles as a family restaurant with live local (but not Tyrolean) music on the main street. It even fills up for lunch with locals who munch on treats from the impressive pastry shop attached.

Eateries with great views include **Gasthof Hochfeld** (62985) at an altitude of 3,280 feet, which also organizes sledding evenings, and **Schöne Aussicht** (62270). **Gasthof Rummlerhof** (63650) is a perfect spot for lunch or dinner if you are on the cross-country trails. For great pastries, head to the **Café-Konditorei Pranzl** at Kaiserstrasse 26.

Après-ski/nightlife

One of the nice things about skiing here is that the runs drop right into the town which makes starting après-ski very convenient and most people can walk back to their hotels.

Café Rainer has the best tea-time, après-ski atmosphere. It kicks into full gear about 3:30 p.m. and carries on until 7 p.m. or so.

The Brewery behind the Hotel Goldener Löwe can be lots of fun.

The recently enlarged **Bunny's Pub**, one of the livelier places to go, is easygoing and casual. This pub is good for après-ski with a happy hour, karaoke and live music later in the night. It is filled with Brits and Aussies.

Max Pub is a fairly lively, open-air bar at the foot of the slopes which is frequented by a young crowd. The music is LOUD. There is karaoke and live music at night.

Chez Paul Bar and Café serves small meals just a short walk from the town center. This pleasant and informal place is slightly yuppified and is more suited for a thirty-something crowd than the disco set.

Michi's in the Hotel Fischer is also a good place to meet after skiing and for late night revelry.

Crowded House is a hopping disco/dance hall near the Hotel Goldener Löwe. It's a younger hangout for those who like the music turned UP.

Child care (2007/08 prices)

Ski instruction is offered for children ages 3 and 4 at the Bobo Mini-Club run by the **Ski & Snowboardschool St Johann in Tirol – The Original** (5352-64777). Classes are small with groups for three to five children and take place for two hours in the morning. A half day including ski and boot rental costs €25. A half-day extension costs €20. Older children can join the ski school's Kid's Club. Prices are the same as adult group skiing lessons.

Ski & Snowboardschool Eichenhof (5352 65930, 61548, fax 61548-4) has both racing and traditional ski school programs. The traditional program provides a protected, sunny area with a ski roundabout and a moving carpet where children age 5 and younger can learn at their own pace. The racing school is for more experienced skiers who are interested in learning racing or how to ski moguls or in deep snow. Price: €140 for six days. A supervised lunch costs €8.

Ski & Snowboardschool Wilder Kaiser (5352 64888) has several programs for children. The first is Bambini which teaches children age 3 to 5 how to ski in groups of no larger than five. Bambini costs €195 for six days. With the "Kinder" program (twelve children maximum per group), children age 5 to 12 first begin their instruction in a separated child-only area. The Anfänger program costs €132 for six days. Kinder Fortgeschritten is another week-long program for children who can confidently snow plow, turn and stop. The entire couse takes place on the blue runs of St. Johann where children are coached in technique and work up to parallel skiing. Special activities take place on Thursday and Friday. Kinder/Jugend - Meisterklasse is a six-day masterclass in techniques such as jumping, powder skiing and freeriding. For further pricing contact the ski school.

Other activities

The Holiday Region St. Johann has pushed hard to expand its recreational activities. The Panoramabad complex features a 25-meter **heated pool, a wellness area** with **sauna** and **steamrooms**, a long **water slide** to keep kids and the kids-in-us happy, a **wading pool** and an **ice skating rink**. The **Kaiserquell** in Kirchdorf offers sauna and steambath with all kinds of wellness features as well as massages at the Vital & Beauty Center.

Indoor tennis (62625 or 63156 or 8138) is a popular activity.

Horse-drawn sleigh rides cost approximately €12 per person at the Hinterkaiser (63325). Horse drawn sleigh rides also leave from St. Johanner Hof (05352/62207), Othmar Krisch (05352/62759), Landgut Furtherwirt (63150), Kramerhof (6901, Oberhabachhof (63168) Tischlerhof (64135) and Hanneshof (8186).

In St. Johann, there is a great lighted **toboggan/rodel run** from Hochfeld/Hirschberg down the mountain. It is open until midnight everyday, with lifts operating from 7–9:30 p.m. on Monday, Wednesday and Friday.

Night skiing is available on Monday, Wednesday and Friday from 7-9:30 p.m from the Hochfeld double chairlift and on the Rueppen-run. It's also available on Wednesday from 7-9 p.m. off the Eichenhof drag lift I on the Eichenhof run I.

There are **Kegelbahns** in the Hotel Goldener Löwe (62251) and in the Tennis Kegel Center (63377). For **hot-air balloon rides** call Ballooning Tyrol (0664/3420115). They cost €180 per person. For tandem **paragliding**, try Mountain High (0664/2415561) for €99 per person.

The town itself is beautiful to look at, with one Tyrolean house after another presenting traditional Austrian scenes and motifs painted on the exterior walls.

Getting there

St. Johann is about 68 miles from Munich and 59 miles from Innsbruck; most visitors arrive from Munich. Take the Inntal autobahn and exit at Felbertauern/St. Johann in Tirol. Train service connects St. Johann with Innsbruck and Munich.

Tourist information

Tourismusverband St. Johann in Tirol, A-6380 St. Johann in Tirol, Austria; 05352-633350, fax 05352-65200.

For snow conditions call 05352-64358.

Internet: www.ferienregion.at

E-mail: info@ferienregion.at

Telephone prefix: St. Johann 05352

Zell am See-Kaprun

Here is an Alpine combination as compatible as beer and pretzels. Yes, these two neighboring resorts fit together hand in glove, like a finely tuned dance team where both partners have learned to subtly complement each other for the best possible performance. Above the low-key village of Kaprun, the Kitzsteinhorn glacier guarantees wide-open bowl skiing the year round, while the majority of Zell am See's Schmittenhöhe slopes sweep down through the trees, more reminiscent of Colorado's Breckenridge or classic New Hampshire trails.

Together they comprise the Europa Sports Region, a land rich with winter and summer outdoor activities. In the spring, high-energy types can ski in the morning and windsurf the lake in the afternoon. Austrian and European skiers have long known the Europa Sports Region as an ideal location for skiing. The area was one of the first resorts in Austria with descents recorded as far back as 1893.

Lake Zell serves as the region's focal point. This long narrow body of water sprawls 13 km. along a picturesque valley shadowed by the Hohentauern, Austria's highest mountain range. When the lake freezes in winter, townspeople fish through the ice, go ice-boating, or skate across Zell's surface to the village of Thumersbach on the other side.

Zell am See sits on a flat semicircular piece of land that juts into the lake, squeezed from the mountains ringing the shore. Cream-colored buildings huddle around the well-preserved 13th-century church of St. Hippolyt, and the Vogtturm (city tower) which dominate Zell's skyline, giving it the air of a medieval mountain town rather than a bustling ski village. One could wander for hours through the town's winding streets and have no trouble envisioning merchants and traders from bygone days going about their business.

Today the streets are still lined with unpretentious shops—sport stores, well-stocked markets, intriguing crafts shops. You'll also find cozy cafes, gasthauses and restaurants filled with locals and tourists alike. Zell am See, with a year-round population of almost 10,000, has honed the fine art of balancing the fantasy sought by tourists with the real needs of its citizens.

On the surface, Kaprun puts on a quieter face than does Zell am See, partly because it is much smaller in scale. But its laid-back atmosphere sets a more relaxing pace, and the village common gives it the air of a small New England college town. The Kitsteinhorn was Austria's first glacial ski area.

On the mountain, Kaprun has completed a new Alpine Center at the top of the old Gletscherbahn.

 ## Mountain layout—Skiing

There are two major areas: Zell am See's Schmittenhöhe lifts take skiers to the 6,500-foot level, while Kaprun is famed as a year-round ski area with runs on the glacier beneath the peak of the 10,506-foot Kitzsteinhorn. This year is has a new six-pax chairlift move even more skiers.

To ski the Schmittenhöhe, avoid the main cablecar from town and take either the Sonnenalmbahn or better still, the newly-extended Areit gondola from neighboring Schüttdorf direct to the Breiteck peak. You can also take the Zeller Bergbahn and work your way up the left side of the mountain.

The runs are good for intermediates with some expert challenges too, particularly the two runs used in the World Cup and regional downhill races. Our favorite is the trail from the Kapellenlift summit to Breiteckalm and then down a wonderful turning slope parallel to the woods. From there, it's black to the bottom. Locals call this run the Trass. Intermediate skiers may enjoy the Standard—it drops from the top to Breiteck but then breaks back to the right over the Hirschkögel trail.

Kaprun is about six miles from Zell am See and it's another 3-1/2 miles to the base of the area's lifts. Take the two-stage cablecar up to the glacier to Alpincenter. A third section of the aerial cablecar continues to the top of the Kitzsteinhorn at 9,935 feet.

Kaprun's skiing is for the most part intermediate. Experts will want to tackle the final part of the run from the top of the Gletscherbahn to the Langwied midstation, run 8 from the Sonnenkarbahn, or run 2 on the left side of the glacier. While up at the peak of the Kitzsheinhorn, take your skis off and walk the 360-meter-long tunnel for a 360-degree panorama view of the Hohe Tauern National Park and the Grossglockner, a 12,460-foot-high giant of a mountain.

Finally, for the area's ultimate in off-piste expert skiing, hire a guide (contact any ski school) and leave the back side of the Kitzsteinhorn glacier and ski to the valley of Niedernsill.

 ## Mountain layout—Snowboarding

Competitive snowboarders should head to the Gipfelbahn area to find the boardercross, a gnarly race course made up of gates, bumps, gaps and a 360-degree ramp. Access the halfpipe and quarterpipes on the Kitzsteinhorn glacier via the Keeslift. Intermediate and Alpine snowboarders will be happiest riding down the wide cruisers of the Schmittenhohe and riding the aerial lifts, rather than riding T-bars to the relatively flat terrain of the glacier. Expert boarders should hire a guide from any ski school and ride off-piste both at the Kitzsteinhorn and Schmittenhöhe. Schmittehöhe also has a halfpipe at the Glocknerbahn and an area called Jumping City at the top station of Areit III that expert boarders will also enjoy.

Mountain rating

Zell am See is outstanding for intermediates; its network of trails and connecting lifts offers new challenges and different aspects to the slopes as you work your way across the area. For the beginner there are training slopes and plenty of room to take a fall or two without serious suffering. Experts will head for the glacier at Kaprun, where there are also challenging intermediate runs. The combined ski region offers 54 lifts and 130 km. (80 miles) of trails. A very efficient bus system, included with your Europa Sport Region ski pass, serves both areas.

The Kitzsteinhorn glacier is an easy intermediate area. Though there are ultra wide, gradual runs, the vast number of skiers and the altitude make it an intimidating experience for the beginner. Experts will have to search for ravines (*renne*) or gullies (*wassarkar*) to the sides of the groomed pistes for bumps and steeps filled with powder.

 ## Lift tickets (2007/08 prices)
Tickets for the Europa Sports Region Pass:

	High Season	Intermediate Season	Pre-Season
two days	€73	€73	€68.50
three days	€106	€106	€96
four days	€134.50	€134.50	€121
five days	€160	€151	€145
six days	€184	€173	€166.50

Youth born from 1987 to 1989 get a discount of about 20 percent. Children born in 1990 to 1999 get a 50 percent discount. Children younger than 5 ski free.

Shuttlebuses and local transport between Kaprun and Zell am See are free if you buy the regional ski pass.

Daily rates at the separate sections of the Europa Sports Region are €38.50. Zell am See Schmittenhöhe daily rates are also €38.50.

 ## Ski school (2007/08 prices)
Zell am See/Kaprun ski school has approximately 260 instructors. Courses range from beginner through competition racing techniques.

Information is available through the ski school office in the valley station of the Sonnenalmbahn (73207).

Private lessons cost €165–200 for one day (four hours) or €45–€50 per hour, €28 per additional persons.

Group lessons for a day (four hours) are €56; three days cost €139; and for four to five days run €154.

 ## Cross-country
There are 200 km. of prepared trails in the Europa Sports Region circling the lake and going into nearby valleys. These trails are directly connected to the Saalachtal and Pinzgau cross-country ski-runs.

With its 40 km., Zell am See has the largest trail network of the region and one of the most scenic. Starting from the indoor tennis courts via Königshof to Thumersbach, trails lead from town to town across the region. One of the most notable is the track that takes you past Erlberg via Schüttdorf to Högmoos, passing by the towns of Bruck and St. Georgen.

The Fischhornloipe is one of the prettiest trail systems. Taking the West Loop is a 5 km. loop suitable for beginners. The 9 km. Zell Loop along the southern lakeshoree is for intermediates. The Zell Loop along the north shore is 25 km. through fields. It is also perfect for intermediate skiers.

The 5 km. Westloipe cross-country ski-run is very well suited for beginners. It leads from Kaprun to Piesendorf. The 3 km. Höhenloipe cross-country ski-run on

Kitzsteinhorn is open all around the year. At a height of 2,800 meters, you can closely experience nature in the middle of the glacier. Among the cross-country specialties of the 'Europa-Sportregion' are its two lit-up nighttime cross-country ski-runs (each about 4 km. long) called Nachtloipe in Schüttdorf/Zell am See and in Kaprun respectively.

However, other communities offer multi-faceted trails, as well. In Kaprun, cross-country ski-runs towards the Oberpinzgau are also available to the winter sportsmen. Along the river Salzach, the trail leads up to Mittersill via Piesendorf, Niedernsill, and Uttendorf-Weisssee. Mittersill prepares 33 km. of trails for its cross-country skiers. In Uttendorf, the cross-country ski-run is 25 km. and in Piesendorf it is 27 km.. Taxenbach, Kaprun, Bruck/Fusch, and Niedernsill also come up with noteworthy figures: They can offer their guests trails which are between 14 and 19 km. Together with the connection to the Pinzgau and Saalachtal cross-country ski-runs, it is a paradise of 200 km. worth of trails for cross-country skiers of all kinds.

Accommodations

Zell am See (telephone prefix is 06542)

Many of Zell's hotels and pensions are near the lifts. In addition, for those who want to be closer to the Kaprun glacier, there are accommodations in Kaprun.

Thumersbach, across the lake, is separated from the best skiing but quite scenic. Check with the tourist office in Zell for further information.

Zell also offers 24-hour service to individuals who come without reservations. Visitors can use an information board similar to those used at airports: push a button next to the hotel name, and its location is illuminated on the map. You can then telephone the hotel directly and check on room availability.

The all-in-one-week package is called Schnee-Okay, and is available in low and middle season. A Schnee-Okay package in a four star hotel with half board is available in January at the starting price of €511. Schnee-Okay includes seven days accommodation, a six-day regional pass, unlimited use of the ski shuttlebus and six days' admittance to swimming pools in Zell and Kaprun. Schnee-Okay also includes six days' use of the indoor ice rink in Zell, a 10 percent discount on ski rental and a €10 discount on a four- or five-day ski course at either the Zell am See or Kaprun ski school. At the other end of the price scale is the simple B&B starting at €345 a week.

Rates below are per person based on double occupancy with half board in February. €€€—€125+; €€—€75–€124; €—less than €75.

Lodges are plentiful in Zell am See. One of the most romantic is the **Grand Hotel** at Esplanade 4 (806; €€) on the shores of Lake Zell. This stylish beauty was built to be enjoyed from bottom to top. Dine in its casually elegant restaurant, then head upstairs to the glass-domed Wunderbar for a nightcap.

The Hotel Salzburgerhof, Auerspergstrasse 11 (765; €€€) is Zell am See's only five-star hotel. Lodging at this large, chalet-style hotel includes a Wellness Center with a whirlpool, sauna, swimming pool, solarium, massage facilities and exceptional cuisine in its award-winning restaurant.

A very nice four-star hotel is the **Hotel Neue Post**, Schlossplatz 2 (73773; €€€). Well-located and handy to shops and restaurants, this family-owned condominium property features an outdoor hot tub, sauna, massage, fitness room, and television in all rooms. The lobby bar is a good place to meet friends. Friendly desk clerks will have your laundry done for a very reasonable price.

Closer to the slopes, the **Hotel Berner**, at Nikolaus-Gassner-Promenade 1 (779; €€€) sits just a block or so off the main thoroughfares, a short walk from the Zeller

Bergbahn gondolas. The warm friendly personalities of the Berner family will make you feel very much at home.

Other recommended four-star hotels are: **Hotel Zum Hirschen,** Dreifaltigkeitgasse (774; €€€); **Hotel St. Georg** Schillerstrasse (768; €€€); **Romantikhotel zum Metzgerwirt** Sebastian Horl Str. 11 (72520; €€€); and **Hotel Alpenblick** Alte Landstrasse (5433; €€€).

Three-star recommendations:

The Sporthotel Lebzelter, Dreifaltigkeitgasse 7 (06542/ 776; €€) is one of Zell am See's most conveniently located lodges, right in the heart of town and just a few steps away from prime shopping.

Hotel Krone Kitzsteinhornstrasse 16 (57421; €€).

Gasthof Steinerwirt, Schlossplatz 1 (72502; €) is an excellent two-star.

For B&Bs or Frühstückspension try **Alpenrose** (72570; €), **Landhaus Buchner** (72062; €), **Hubertus** (72427; €), or **Klothilde** (72660; €), all of which have English-speaking employees, who are quite interested in interaction with tourists.

Kaprun (telephone prefix is 06547)

For its size, **Kaprun** boasts an array of accommodations you would expect to find at much larger resorts, and the Kaprun/Zell am See transportation system has so many pickup spots that location isn't really an issue.

Sporthotel Falkenstein (8625; €€€) is one of the better full-service lodges. At the south end of town, it offers a panoramic view of the village from its north-facing side and a dazzling look at the Kitzsteinhorn from the other. Sit on the terrace in early morning and watch the sun dance off the Kitzsteinhorn's peaks. Hearty buffet breakfasts are served each morning. Lunch and dinner are also served in the hotel's spacious dining room.

One of the best four-star "downtown" hotels is the **Orgler** (8205; €€€). You'll want to tiptoe over the fine oriental rugs scattered about its light pine-paneled lobby.

Other recommended four-star hotels: **Steigenberger Kaprun,** Schlossstrasse 751 (7647, fax 7680; €€€). **Hotel Antonius,** Schlossstrasse 744, (7670, fax 76706; €€€). **The Hotel Zur Burgruine** (8306, fax 830660; €€€) is near the Kaprun fortress ruins. The hotel's cheerful dining room is excellent for dinner whether you stay here or not. **The Hotel Sonnblick** (8301, fax 830166; €€€), just off town central, is another outstanding spot if only for its wide balconies made for enjoying the views.

Other three- & two-star recommendations are: **Katharinehof** (8866; € B&B), **Alpenrose** (7240; €€ B&B), **Eschenhof** (8674; € B&B), **Alpenblick** (8477; € B&B), **Jaga-Hias** (8345; € B&B) and **Heidi,** near town center (8223; €).

Ski Chalets: Inghams/Bladon. (See page 16 for phone, fax and Internet addresses.)

Apartments, condominiums, flats

The tourist office will provide a list of available apartments and chalets in the area. In addition, you can book directly through agencies in the area. For more information, call Apartmentservice (80480). Apartments large enough to sleep four will range in price from €60–90 per night.

 ## Dining

Schloss Prielau (72609) is acknowleged to be the top restaurant in the area. It serves internationally recognized award-winning continental cuisine. Call for reservations.

The Bar "Einkehr" (72363) at Schmittenstr. 12, Zell am See, is a chic bistro with a horseshoe bar complete with electric generator and the main dining room upstairs. Recommended by Gault Millau. The **Landhotel Erlhof** (566370) is also highly rated by Gault Millau for gourmet cuisine.

The next restaurants all serve excellent Austrian cuisine. For the best combination of fine dining in a comfortable atmosphere (lots of wood carvings and unusual wall lights), try the **Steinerwirt** in Zell am See. It specializes in sirloin steak Vienna style (with onions and small dumplings), and the Salzburger Nockerl (a tasty soufflé) is not to be missed for dessert.

The **Guggengbichl** hut features Kasnocken (noodles, cheese and butter) baked and served in a huge skillet. Scraping out the bottom of the pan for the crusted delicacy is fun for the whole table. The inn rises above Kaprun and diners are allowed to climb 5,280 feet above and slide down to the entrance in sleds provided for the thrill. It's a good way to work up an appetite or work off the huge dinner.

Jagawirt (8737) near Kaprun is a charming inn, owned and operated by Hans and Theresia Nindl, which provides an outstanding dining experience. We enjoyed wild goat (Gamsgebraten) in mushroom sauce with black bread dumplings (Schwartzbrot-knodel) and cranberries (Pieiselbeen). A venison filet (Hirschrunckenfilet) is cooked medium (Rosabebraten) with mushrooms (Steinpilen) in Burgundy sauce, €20. Nindl is an avid hunter and he takes some of the local game (venison, antelope, goat) for the restaurant. Two delicious desserts are blueberries heated with flour and eggs with vanilla ice cream (Moosbeernocking) for €6, and Mandelecken, a light almond cake floating in blueberry and kiwi sauce for €6. The inn is also a popular après-ski stop for skiers coming down from the Kitzsteinhorn glacier. African art and artifacts decorate the walls of the restaurant, attesting to the Nindls' living in Rhodesia part time. Jagawirt is only open September through May.

Limberghof, just outside Zell am See, serves rich fried pork, veal and beef steaks on wooden planks. Tropfen Amelner, about 90 proof, is a perfect *digestif*.

Dorfstadl is the locals' favorite restaurant in the region. The setting is hand-hewn post-and-beam and the food is spectacular not only in taste but in presentation. Try the garlic soup for an appetizer and apple strudel for dessert. For a main course any selection will please.

Once you have had your fill of Austrian fare, try Italian or Tex-Mex.

Delicious cordon bleu and pepper steak top the fare at **Traubenstube**. For a light meal, sample **Pizzeria Giuseppe** and **Zum Casar** (47257). **Crazy Restaurant**, in the "Villa Crazy Daisy," is a Scandinavian-owned Mexican restaurant with an inexpensive menu featuring among other items "breath killer" garlic bread.

The **Café Konditorei Mosshammer** and **Café Feinschmeck** are your best bets for a late afternoon snack, especially for mouth-watering pastries and chocolates. **Vanini** on Banhofstrasse has the best and largest variety of Austrian and other pastries.

In Kaprun, dining is good at the large hotels. Two favorites: **Kaprunerhof** and **Hotel Zur Burg**. The **Cafe Konditorei** has wonderful pastries in Kaprun.

On the mountain, at the top of the Schmittenhöhe, **Breiteckalm** is the lunch choice. Here Peter Radcher, owner, chef, waiter, bartender and perfect Austrian host, serves a hearty traditional Austrian fare.

Gletschermühle on the glacier is a good luncheon spot with its Tyrolean fare, spectacular views, huge deck and sun chairs for rent.

Telephone prefix: Zell am See 06542; Kaprun 06547

Après-ski/nightlife

Come evening, intimate taverns and rollicking discos open their doors. For quieter entertainment, elegance and perfect location head for the **Wunderbar** on the top floor of the Grand Hotel overlooking Lake Zell.

The **Sportstüberl**, in the Hotel Lebzelter, is an après-ski bar built in the 1700s, and its bartenders wear lederhosen. It is open 4 p.m.–4 a.m. and offers an atmosphere where locals and tourists gather for a cold beer or a hot Jägertee. Here townsfolk sometimes challenge each other at *Stocknagaln*, a game where the object is to hit a thin nail imbedded in a block of wood with the sharp blade of an ax.

The **Jagawirt** is one of the most picturesque après-ski gathering spots.

Curiously, the largest (and the most lively) night haunt in the region lies on the outskirts of tiny Kaprun, not in Zell am See: **The Baum Bar** burned to the ground a few years ago, and when it was rebuilt it bounded back better than ever. A huge dance floor is usually packed by midnight. Partygoers boogie till closing time at 6 a.m.

Entertainment is harder to find in Kaprun, but it is there. The **Kitsch & Bitter** and the **Paletti Pub** are perfect. Another good disco is **La Bomba**. The **Vine Bar de Vino, Killy's Bar** and the **Music Pub Pavillion** are recent additions to the Kaprun nightlife.

In Zell am See, one of the most popular stops for vacationing Europeans is the **Villa Crazy Daisy Pub**, Salzmannstr. 8, which is usually full of Brits, Dutch, Swedes and other party-hardy types. Bands play seven nights a week. Order drinks like "No Thanks I'm Fine," "Against the Wall," "Orgasm" and "Slippery Nipples." The **Pinzgauer Diele** has great après-ski 'till 7 p.m., then after 11 p.m. it's considered the top disco. It's often loud with ski movies. The **Bierstadl** features 33 different kinds of beer and is where the locals gather. **Classics** features live music, but can be a bit smoky. **Hirschenkeller** is a blues, rock and reggae bar across the street from the post office under Hotel Zum Hirschen. **Viva Club** disco heats up after 1 a.m. at 4 Kirchengasse. Après-ski can be enjoyed at the outside bar atop **Schmittenhöhe**, overlooking the church and at **"Einkehr"** near the Zeller Bergbahn.

 ## Child care (2007/08 prices)

Kindergarten for children ages 2 adn older costs €55 for one day, €122 for three days and €173 for four or five days.

The children's ski school is open daily from 10 a.m. to 3 p.m. Lunch can be arranged for €11. Children age 4 to 10 are accepted for €56 for a day, €139 for three days. €154 for four or five days.

In Kaprun, call 7582 or 8232 or 0664-3425317 for children's ski school information; in Zell the number is 72320 or 0664-4531417 or 0664-2530381.

 ## Other activities

A visit to nearby **Salzburg**, made famous a generation ago by the movie *The Sound of Music* and always famous as Mozart's home, attracts hundreds of thousands of tourists each year.

The Zell skyline is distinguished by the outlines of the St. Hippolyt church and the Vogtturm (city tower). Even nonskiers will enjoy the Schmittenhöhe on a clear day when you can see at least thirty 3,000-meter (9,843-foot) or higher peaks in the region.

On Sunday evenings in Kaprun, the tourist office stages **folk entertainment** and **storytelling** around a bonfire within the ruins of an old fortress. You'll enjoy the music, though the stories are in German.

At Kaprun, visit the Gothic Pfarrkirche in the middle of town and the castle ruins, even if you're not there for the storytelling and music.

The Kaprun Optimum with an indoor and outdoor **swimming pool** and **fitness center** is packed with fitness-minded Europeans and is a great place to meet other skiers. The pool is open from 11 a.m.–10 p.m. Entrance is €7.40 for adults. The pool sauna costs €12.60 per session.

Castles are in Prielau and Kaprun.

For **Alpine sightseeing flights** call 757937. Try **bowling** at Schlossstrasse (8222). For **horse-drawn sleigh rides** check out Mrs. Schernthaner Anni (0676-6435814) or Family Hörfarter (06547-8484).

There is an illuminated **toboggan** run from Jausenstation Guggenbichl, Kaprun and one in Zell am See from Gasthof Köhlergraben.

For **ice-skating** head to the Sports and Leisure Center (785) in Zell am See or at the small natural ice skating place in Kaprun. But for a fantastically picturesque experience, try skating on the frozen Lake Zell.

For a fine selection of Austrian crafts and ceramics stop in at Hierner & Co. Stadtplatz 6, Zell am See. For souvenirs there are a plenty of choices in the village.

Getting there

Zell is about 56 miles from Salzburg, which has jet service from other European airports. The usual airport for international arrivals is Munich, about 143 miles away. Vienna is about 240 miles.

Zell has regular national and international train service and bus service to Kaprun.

By automobile from Munich, drive to Salzburg by autobahn, and head toward Bischofshofen. Rental cars are available in Salzburg or Munich.

Tourist information

Europa Sportregion Zell am See - Kaprun
A-5700 Zell am See, Austria
tel. 06542-770, fax 06542-72032.
E-mail: welcome@europasportregion.info.
Internet: www.europasportregion.info.

Kaprun Information, A-5710 Kaprun, Austria;
tel. 06542-7700, fax 06542-72032.

Telephone prefix: Zell am See 06542; Kaprun 06547

France

Thanks to the Winter Olympics, France is now a well-known skiing region. Albertville, the largest town in the area—one without any skiing, ironically—anchored the events, but the real scene was at the resorts of Courchevel, Méribel, Val d'Isère, Tignes, Les Arc and La Plagne.

While the 1992 Olympic Games focused world attention on French ski areas, surprising many viewers that French skiing was so well established, the French have been on the slopes for a long time. Resorts like Chamonix, Megève and Val d'Isère shared in the initial development of Alpine skiing half a century ago. Many of the modern French resorts have been purpose-built for skiing: entire villages, such as Avoriaz, Tignes, Courchevel, Flaine, La Plagne and Les Arcs, have been created with skiing uppermost in the designers' minds. The result has been thousands of apartments and hotels that give you the convenience of walking out your door, stepping into your skis and skiing some of the most extensive slopes in the world. In addition, the après-ski life is great and the food and wine reflect France at its best.

France is home of the most elaborate ski networks found anywhere in the world. The Les Trois Vallées region, the Portes du Soleil (shared with Switzerland) and the l'Espace Killy region of Val d'Isère and Tignes are unparalleled in the skiing universe for wide open spaces and dramatic skiing.

The French skiers that vacationers will meet in the mountains are also some of the friendliest people one can meet. The abrupt manner some tourists associate with French locals just won't be found here. In the mountains, everyone comes to enjoy life and share the wonderful beauty of the environment.

From breakfast with croissants and café au lait, to a lunch *picnique* on a sunny terrace, to sumptuous dinners, no one will forget the love affair the French have with cuisine and the passion with which they enjoy the culinary life. Don't feel that to get the most out of French cooking, one has to spend for gourmet haute cuisine. Here in the French Alps, some of the best local meals in France can be found. Meats from cattle grazing in mountain pastures, fish from sparkling unspoiled streams and lakes, cheese aged in hidden caves, and liquors fermented in local barrels, all make up dining that is hard to beat. Start with *Kir*; test the *charcuterie*—paté, sausage, dried ham; enjoy the local cheeses—Beaufort, Rublechon, Chêvre; savor crêpes with Grand Marnier; and drink local wines—Gamay and Crépys.

The French add a bit of drama and love to have Fondue Savoyarde—tradition says, when a woman loses her bread in the fondue cheese pot, she must kiss her neighbor to her right (imagine the jockeying for places at some fondue tables); when the man loses his bread, he must buy a round of drinks.

Getting apartments and flats in France

Apartments are the way to go in France. They are inexpensive and often right on the slopes; however, they are small from an American's point of view. If you want space, get the next larger sized apartment than you would normally reserve. Studios are one large room. *Deux pièces* means two rooms or one bedroom with a living room that can sleep two more people; *trois pièces* is three rooms, usually two bedrooms plus a living room.

The seasons

High season: Christmas and New Years, then all of February and March to mid-April.

Low season: January after the New Year holiday, then late April.

Use these as general guidelines, because some resorts may have slightly adjusted seasons owing to local school holidays. Check with your destination resort to get the exact dates if you are planning your trip on a season borderline.

Telephone notes

In France you will notice that there is no city prefix. It is included in the eight digits which make up the number. Only Paris has an additional prefix. Most of our phone numbers are listed as xxx xx xx xx. When you call from outside of France dial the country code, 0033, then dial the number as we show it in the book. When calling within France you must always dial zero first.

Les Arcs
Bourg-St. Maurice

Les Arcs is not a town or village. It is a group of modern complexes high above the Savoy transportation hub of Bourg St. Maurice. It was designed expressly as a ski resort; a purpose-built collection of large sprawling hillside buildings with an unusual swooping roof design and an new modern faux-Savoyard village.

This resort has become part of one of the largest interconnected ski and snowboard areas in the world. Les Arcs recently linked its trail system with that of La Plagne via Plan-Peisey. The combined area, Paradiski, has 425 km. of trails. The enormity is mind-boggling. The joint resorts boast 144 ski lifts: a funicular, four light-weight cablecars, a twin-cable cablecar, 10 sections of gondola lifts, 18 detachable chairlifts, 44 chairlifts, 28 ski lifts suitable for walkers and 25 ski lifts accessible free of charge.

A cablecar, Le Vanoise Express, with 200-person cabins spans the valley from Plan-Peisey on the Les Arcs side to Les Coches on the La Plagne side. The span is 3,000 meters and the cablecar hangs 380 meters above the valley floor. The trip from station to station, takes four minutes. The La Plagne (the largest individual ski area in France) trails are detailed in a separate chapter.

Les Arcs has had a remarkable unity, not only in its modern architecture, but also in its infrastructure and support systems. A new village, Les Arc 1950, takes a different tack. It is a modern collection of hotels and U.S.-sized condominiums built in the guise of a traditional Savoyard village.

Of the other three high-altitude complexes that comprise Les Arcs (each named for its altitude in meters). Arc 1600 is a family-orientated area. It was the first built, with three hotels, shops and a nursery that cares for children four months or older. Rooms tend to be functional and more moderately priced, and the nightlife is minimal. Arc 1800 is the largest complex, with the biggest selection of restaurants and shops. Arc 2000 was constructed when the lift system expanded to reach the higher elevations. It offers skiing and riding for every level and easy access to the glacier. Its surrounding expert terrain has made it a famous shrine for serious skiers.

Overall, the resort is decidedly international with a little less than half its clientele arriving from outside France. You'll have no difficulty finding someone who speaks English if you need help, nor will it be a problem striking up conversations.

Included in the ski pass for the area (see Lift tickets) are lifts originating in the lower villages of Peisey-Nancroix, Vallandry and Villaroger. These hamlets are century-old settlements that offer a strong contrast to Les Arcs.

For visitors who want to combine a bit of local flavor with their high-tech ski adventure, a seven-minute funicular ride down the steep slope from Arc 1600 to Bourg St. Maurice offers a chance to spend a few hours in the shops, museums, and restaurants of a Savoyard town. A bustling open-air market on Saturdays offers Savoy specialties, such as mountain ham, wine and rich, creamy Reblochon and Beaufort cheeses.

 ## Mountain layout–Skiing

Les Arcs is glorious for the ski-till-you-drop-and-then-do-it-some-more crowd. Snowboarders come from all over the northern hemisphere because, as one American enthusiast was heard to say, "In France you have the right to die." This doesn't detract from France's excellent safety records, but the French are not saddled with the onerous liability problems faced by American resorts. Trails are marked, but this is generally seen as a formality or as a handy guide in white-out conditions. Otherwise, ski at your own risk.

Les Arcs has three large sections and two smaller ones. The sectors all are linked. The first major area is the face above Arcs 1800 and 1600, with 28 lifts servicing six expert trails, 15 intermediate runs and 19 beginner slopes.

The second major area is a massive valley above and beyond Arc 2000 bounded by the 10,484-foot peak and ridge formed by the Col du Grand Renard and the Arpette. The 15 lifts in this area service 10 expert, 10 intermediate and 11 beginner trails, as well as plenty of off-piste possibilities.

Peisey-Nancroix Vallandry has one expert trail, a baker's dozen of intermediate runs, and 10 beginner runs. In cloudy or windy weather, these tree-lined slopes offer good visibility. This wide-open area drops down to the Vanoise Express.

The Vanoise Express connects Les Arcs to La Plagne and creates the Paradiski Ski Area. The 425-square-km. Paradiski area opens three glaciers and two summits — each above 3,000 meters high. Skiers will have their pick of 232 pistes served by 175 ski lifts. Boarders will enjoy two boardercross areas, four snow parks and two halfpipes. Connections are arduous on the La Plagne side of the cablecar.

Finally, there is the Villaroger sector, at the end of the 7 km.-long Aiguille Rouge runs. It has only three direct lifts back to the crest above Arc 2000. Another lift allows those who have skied below Arc 2000 to reach Villaroger without returning to the top of the Aiguille Rouge.

Mountain rating

This is one of the best Alpine areas and features something for everyone. There is great intermediate skiing all across the face above Arc 1800 descending from Arpette, Col des Frettes and Col du Grand Renard. Advanced intermediates will love the runs from the Aiguille Rouge across the glacier and down the Piste du Grand Col. Beginners and intermediates will have plenty of area at the bottom of the valley between Aiguille Rouge and Arpette. Experts face some exhilarating runs from the Aiguille Rouge across the glacier and then can drop down the massive face above Arc 2000.

Above Peisey-Nancroix Vallandry are relatively gentle beginner and intermediate runs ideal for carving. The drop along the ridge to Villaroger is for strong intermediates and experts. Experts should sign up with a guide and tackle the off-trail tours circling behind the Aiguille Grive and the Aiguille Rousse or ski an itinerary off the backside of the Aiguille Rouge looping around to Villaroger.

Mountain layout–Snowboarding

Like all major ski areas, Les Arcs has terrain for all levels of snowboarders. With a large portion of boarding above treeline, Les Arcs has tons of open spaces for cruising but relatively little tree boarding. If you are looking for tree boarding, the best place you'll find will be above Plan Peisey and Vallandry.

Never-ever boarders should head to the free bunny lifts at Arcs 1600, 1800 and 2000 (1600 lifts—TK Pierre Blanche, TS Combettes, TK Millerette; 1800 lifts—TS Chantel, TS Jardin Alpin; and 2000 lifts—TS Saint Jacques, TK La Combes 1-2, TK Rhodos). There you will find open, easy terrain perfect for your first few turns.

Beginners will benefit most from the first half of the Transarc gondola and the upper sections of Plan Peisey and Vallandry, where the trails are wider than they are lower in the valley.

Intermediate riders can tackle most of the upper portions of Arcs 1600 and 1800 except for L'Arpette and Col Des Frettes, which are steep and sometimes covered in moguls. Starting from Arc 2000, intermediates should stay on Plagnettes and Bosses or Bois De L'Ours and Comborciere, but should think twice when deciding whether or not to hit Grand Col, Aiguille Rouge or Varet.

Advanced and expert boarders can search all over the mountain but will find the best stuff in Grand Col or off Aiguille Rouge. If you're looking for a real adventure, go to a local ski school and ask about the awesome backcountry opportunities starting from the top of the Aiguille Rouge and Le Grand Col.

At the L'Arpette terrain park you'll find a boardercross and three different itineraries with some sweet tabletop jumps perfect for huge air. The combined Paradiski region has two boardercross, four snowparks and two halfpipes.

Cross-Country

The Société des Montagnes de l'Arc maintains the 30 km. of cross-country trails in Les Arcs. The trails are free and there are various routes from Arcs 1600, 1800, 2000 and Bourg St. Maurice.

Arc 1600 has a 5-km. loop, starting in Courbaton. Arc 1800 has a 5-km. loop, starting from the Jardin Alpin. Arc 2000 has a 5-km. loop (near the ESF 2000). In favorable snow conditions, there's also a 15-km. loop in Bourg Saint Maurice that can be accessed using the funicular from Les Arcs.

Ski school (2007/08 prices)

Darentasia (tel/fax 0479 04 16 81), **Privilège** (0479 07 23 38, fax 0479 07 68 31) and **Initial Snow** (0612 45 72 91, fax 0479 40 09 61), **Arc Adventures** (International Ski School 0479 07 41 28) **French Ski School** (ESF), and **Spirit 1950** all have programs in the villages. They offer guides/instructors for paragliding, snowshoeing, snowmobiling and backcountry skiing/boarding.

French Ski School (ESF) has bases at Arc 1600 (0479 07 43 09), Arc 1800 (0479 07 40 31), and Arc 2000 (0479 07 47 52) for a combined total of 250 instructors. Group and private lessons are offered to skiers and boarders older than 3 years. Group lessons run from €133. Private lessons cost approximately €38-€46 an hour for one to two people.

Ecole de Ski Snowboard School Spirit 1950 (0479 04 25 72) is in Arc 1950. Six half-day skiing lessons cost €145-€155 and six half-day boarding lessons cost €170.

 # Lift tickets (2006/07 prices)

These lift tickets allow skiers/boarders to go anywhere in **Les Arcs**. Tickets for six days or more include a lift pass for L'Espace Killy,, Les Trois Vallees, La Plagne, Prolognan La Vanoise, and Les Saises; also, you have one free day at La Rosiere/La Thuile (in Italy).

	Adults (age 14-59)	Children (age 6-13)	Senior (age 60-72)
Half day	€31	€23.50	€25.50
One day	€43.50	€33.50	€34.50
Six days	€198	€148.50	€148.50

At the very beginning and end of the season, all tickets are discounted about 40 percent; other than this, there is no high or low season. A child younger than 6 skis free. Skiers/boarders older than 72 who buy a one- to fifteen-day pass ski for €5. Insurance per day costs adults €2.50 and children €2. There is free night skiing/boarding at the base of each Arc on Tuesdays and Thursdays.

The Sample Paradiski with the Les Arcs six-day skipass allows one day of skiing/boarding in La Plagne. Adults pay €211; children and seniors, €158.50.

These prices are the prices for **Paradiski ski-pass** that includes Les Arcs / La Plagne. Plus, with a six-day pass visitors get access to the Savoie Olympic ski-area for a day of skiing at Espace Killy, the 3 Valleys, Les Saisies and Pralognan La Vanoise.

	Adult (age 14-59)	Children (age 6-13)	Senior (age 60-72)
One day	€46	€34.50	€39
Six days	€237	€178	€178
Seven days	€264	€198	€224.50

 # Accommodations

Rates are based on double occupancy during high season (February) with half board: €€€=€125+; €€=€75-€125; €=less than €75.

Grand Hotel Paradiso (0479 07 65 00, fax 0479 07 64 08; €€€) at Arc 1800 is the top of the line and recommended by Michelin.

Hotel du Golf (0479 41 43 43; fax 0479 07 34 28; €€€) was the first constructed in Arc 1800 and is still the flagship hotel. Rooms are simple, functional, clean and comfortable with exceptional views. It has a new 400-meter spa and regular entertainment. Its restaurant/bar/nightclub draws guests from all over Arc 1800.

Radisson SAS Hotel and HMC Arc 1950 (0479 04 04 85; €€€) are luxury in stone and wood. They have two-, three- and four-bedroom apartments with shops, bars and restaurants plus sauna, swimming pool and fitness center access.

Les Melezes Hotel Club (0479 07 50 50; fax 0479 07 36 26; €€) at Arc 2000 has 140 alike rooms. Watch out for the solo rooms sold to singles "with no supplement." With this arrangement, you will be sharing your toilet and bath.

L'Aiguille Rouge (0479 07 57 07; fax 0479 07 39 61; €€), also in Arc 2000, seems just as comfortable as the rest. Here the rooms are offered in packages with half-board (drinks included) and six-day lift tickets.

La Cachette (0479 07 70 50; fax 0479 07 74 01; €€) in the more family-oriented Arc 1600 has a fitness center and a child-care center.

Bourg-St-Maurice at the base of the funicular has an excellent collection of hotels (rated two stars or less) at bargain prices.

Apartments, condominiums, flats

Les Arcs is oriented more toward apartments than hotels; there are thousands more apartments. An apartment is a better bargain if you're willing to do without the amenities of a hotel. But if you like amenities, stay at the HMC or Radisson residences in Arc 1950 which have condos with hotel service and many of the village amenities.

Despite some horror stories about tiny French apartments, there is enough room unless you try to pack four people into one studio. Stay in Arcs 1600, 1800, 1950, 2000 and Bourg-St. Maurice. The best way to go is with a package (includes seven nights and a six-day lift pass). Per-person prices based on two sharing a small apartment are approximately €190 during low season in January, €250 during February and €200 during Christmas. Not included in these prices is the €10 booking fee (per reservation) and the daily residence tax.

You can make plans by calling the Booking Service at 0479 07 68 00 (fax: 0479 07 68 99) or emailing reservations@lesarcs.com.

 ## Dining

Here the focus is on the functional—just like the architecture. When we asked locals about the restaurants, the response was usually a puzzled look and a smile after ponderous thought. Here what we think are Les Arcs' best:

In **Arc 1600** try **Chez Fernand** (0479 07 78 14) with fondue and other specialties created by the owner; and nearby **La Rive** (0479 07 70 50). Also try **Au Petit Loup** (0479 07 74 50) and **Le Cairn** (0479 07 79 85) serving Savoyard specialities.

In **Arc 1800**: The **Hotel du Golf** main restaurant (0479 41 43 43) is the nicest restaurant in Les Arcs. The atmosphere is modern elegance. Meals cost around €38–€40 a person before considering wine.

Le Chalet Bouvier (0479 04 14 68) has good food and good atmosphere.

La Marmite (0479 07 44 28) is a small, cozy, friendly place with a €17–€20 menu and child's menu for €7.

Le Plante d'Baton (0479 07 45 13) is a very traditional French-looking restaurant with meals for €15–€21 and a child's meal for €7.

SOS Pizza (0479 07 51 65) makes great, inexpensive pizza for takeout only. It is a hop downstairs from the tourism office. **Casa Mia** (0479 07 05 75) and **Gargantus** (0479 07 44 99) also make good pizza.

In **Arc 1950**: **La Casa** (0479 07 56 48) serves a collection of pizzas, salads and dried ham inside and on their patio. **Hemingway's** (0479 04 25 51) is a good across-the-board eatery with an outdoor dining area as well. **La Cantina** (0479 04 04 85) is the Mexican/Spanish place in the Ramada SAS Hotel. **Chez Anne** (0479 06 43 11) serves Savoyard specialties. **Le Chalet de Luigi** (0479 00 15 36) serves northern Italian specialties. **Les Belles Pinte** (0479 07 35 42) is an Irish pub with pub fare.

In **Arc 2000**: **Chez Eux** (0479 07 34 36) serves fine fondue and raclette as well as great semi-gastro food. **Red Rock Café** (0479 07 10 58) serves good burgers. And **El Latino Loco** (0479 07 79 49) is OK. Little else can be heartily recommended.

For a special lunch on the mountain don't miss **Belliou La Fumée** (0479 07 29 13), named after a Jack London story, in the valley of Arc 2000. This unique family-run restaurant was built in the 15th century by King Victor Emmanuel of Italy as a bear-hunting lodge. Omelets cooked over an open fire are served in the pan, and other regional specialties are prepared and served with care. Or after a long ski down to the bottom of the Villaroger lift, visit **La Ferme** with excellent mountainside food.

Le Chalet de L'Arc (0479 04 15 40) serves up atmosphere. This chalet on the slopes compliments its menu with its own freshly baked bread. You can go by ski or foot.

La Creche (0479 07 55 47), at the top of the Transarc Gondola, serves inexpensive cafeteria-style grilled food downstairs with a sit-down restaurant upstairs. The restaurant menu runs €16–€22.

Since many of the best restaurants are in far-flung places surrounding Les Arcs, visit **L'Ancolie** (0479 07 93 20), reported to be a beautiful little restaurant in Peisey.

Child care [2007/08 prices]

There are excellent child care centers at the four Arcs. Each center includes outdoor outings such as snow walks, snowsports and indoor activities such arts and crafts, trampolines, videos, etc. A health certificate and BCG vaccine record is required. The prices for the centers are similar and approximate.

Arc 1600: La Cachette (0479 07 70 50; fax 0479 07 74 01) is actually a hotel daycare and gives priority to the its child guests. Children age 4 months and older can take part in the Kids Club open daily (except Saturday) from 8:30 a.m. to 6 p.m. Children ages 7-12 have all day skiing with the ESF and dinner.

Arc 1800: Les Pommes de Pin (0479 04 15 30; fax 0479 04 15 31) runs a nursery for ages 1-2 years old from Sunday to Friday which costs €155 for six half days and €205 for six full days; a childcare center for ages 3-6 from Sunday to Friday which costs €145 for six mornings, €145 for six afternoons and €195 for six full days. There's also a Mini Club with ski lessons for ages 3-8 where price varies according to the age of the child from €255 for a half day and €336 for six full days.

Arc 1950: Cariboo's club (0479 07 05 57) looks after children ages 3-15 years old which cost €190 for six half days and €230 for six full days.

Arc 2000: Garderie (tel/fax: 0479 07 64 25) looks after children age 18 months to 6 years from Sunday to Friday, 8:45 a.m. to 5 p.m. Parents must provide children with snacks. It costs €205 for six-day playgroup, €137 for six half days €180 for six half days with ski lessons, €290 for six full days.

Après-ski/nightlife

In Arc 1800, the ski instructors head to **Bar Le Gabotte** in the center of Le Charvet, as does the majority of the English-speakers when the lifts shut down. The overflow congregates in **Bar le Thuria** across the square. Also try the small **Arc Café** (0614 73 44 56). Stop in at **Le J.O. Live Rock Café** (0479 07 40 42) for live music and dancing starting at 10:30 p.m. every night.

In the Les Villards section of Arc 1800, the best après-ski is in **L'Ambiente** (0479 07 49 51) and in the **Jungle Café** (0479 07 19 62) with its funky jungle decor and pumping beats. Also try the **Be 4 Café**.

There are discos in Arcs 2000, 1600 and 1800. They all follow the French disco formula: drinks in the €12.50 range and opening times around midnight, closing about four in the morning. For live music and dancing, make sure you take a look at the **Red Hot Saloon** to see who is performing when. **Apokalypse** is *the* disco in the Arc 1800 Les Villards section. If you are staying in Arc 2000, disco **K.L.92** normally is the place of choice for visitors of all ages. Also at Arc 2000, **El Latino Loco** is a bar/hangout that is open day and night.

At Arc 1950, head to **Les Belles Pintes** for a good Irish pub and to **Bachal** in Luigi's for dancing.

Other activities

There are almost 200 shops, bars, and restaurants; **floodlit nighttime skiing; dog sledding; fitness centers; horse-drawn sleigh rides; mountaineering; horseback riding** and **squash courts.**

Bourg-Saint-Maurice has one hundred and fifty shops, bars, and restaurants; **fitness centers; museum; horse-sleigh rides; covered swimming pool; horseback riding** and more.

Also contact tourism for information about **helicopter rides** or reservations for **snowshoeing** and other guided activities. Les Arcs is home to the **Speed Skiing track**, built for the 1992 Olympics. For a mere €13, you can test your courage by blitzing down the lower part of the one-mile slope in a timed run; €20 gets you two runs; €25 pays for three. This price includes special helmet, goggles and skis.

Getting there

Les Arcs in directly above Bourg-St. Maurice, which is linked to Paris by TGV speed train service, Eurostar and Thaly's. The nearest major international airport is in Geneva. There are four buses a day that travel from the Geneva airport to Les Arcs. Other nearby airports are Lyon, Chambery and Grenoble.

By car, take the Albertville exit on the autoroute, then follow the signs to Bourg-St. Maurice. Les Arcs is a 30-minute ride by car, or a seven-minute ride on the funicular, from Bourg-St. Maurice to Arc 1600 every 20 minutes, 7:40 a.m. to 7:20 p.m.

Arcs 1600 and 1800 have free parking in most of their indoor and outdoor lots. You can park outdoors for free 5 km. from Arc 2000 (free shuttles will run you to Arc 2000 on every hour). There is pay indoor and outdoor parking at Arc 2000.

Arc 1950 has underground parking for all the accommodations. Park your car, then take an elevator right to your condo or hotel room. All shuttles stop at Arc 1950 as well.

Tourist information

There are tourism offices in all 4 Arcs and in Bourg-St. Maurice. They are open daily from 9 a.m. to 7 p.m.

Bourg Saint Maurice Tourist Office (Main Office)
105 Place de la Gare, 73700 Les Arcs/Bourg Saint Maurice

Le Charvet, Les Sapins, 73700 Arc 1800, France
Tel. : 0479 07 12 57 Fax : 0479 07 24 90
Email : lesarcs@lesarcs.com Internet: www.lesarcs.com

Central Booking Office
B.P. 58, 73706 Les Arcs Cedex, France
Tel : 0479 07 68 00 Fax : 0479 07 68 99
Email : reservation@lesarcs.com

Chamonix Mont-Blanc

Chamonix is the most famous ski town in France. It also breaks every normal European rule for a resort. None of the trails drop directly into town; instead, the ski areas are spread along a valley almost 10 miles long. Only two of the areas are interconnected. Some lift lines can be long, especially for the Grand Montet. Shuttlebuses are crowded and erratic but eventually arrive. The weather can change in a matter of hours from sunshine to a stormy whiteout. But what Chamonix does offer is perhaps the world's best expert and advanced skiing on spectacular mountains rising more than 12,500 feet above the valley. And Chamonix itself has a strong Alpine flair. You won't find the space-age structures that set the tone for so many of France's other resorts. The world's best expert skiing and one of the world's most picturesque settings, in the shadow of 15,767-foot Mont Blanc creates an experience that is hard to beat.

Small-town coziness is the rule, with plenty of restaurants, narrow streets for shopping and good hotels. This atmosphere can make one forget about the logistics of getting on the trails. But remember, to fully enjoy Chamonix, you'll need a car or a bus to get to its slopes that are spread out for miles along the valley floor. There is an erratic shuttlebus service from Chamonix center to the outlying areas; some hotels provide bus service.

In Chamonix you can ski hard all day long, then sit at a café in a small square and sip a *kir*, wine or beer. The bars are crowded with an international group. You are surrounded with other skiers who are here not for the ritz and the glitz, but for the challenge and the exhilaration of testing themselves against Europe's most spectacular slopes.

 ## Mountain layout

From the slopes of Chamonix and on to Argentière and Le Tour, a string of lifts takes skiers up both sides of the valley. On the Mont Blanc side you ascend above outcroppings and slopes of this magnificent peak, while on the opposite side you enjoy the Mont Blanc panorama as the lifts take you to outstanding runs.

In Chamonix, most skiers choose the challenges of **Le Brévent** at 8,288 feet. The cable car rises from the town to Planpraz where the skiing really begins. The second section of the cable car takes experts and hardy intermediates to the top of Le Brévent, and a chair lift carries the less advanced intermediates to the Les Vioz area. Try the black run from the back of Le Brévent with a buddy. If after the first few hundred feet you're not confident, you can cut to the left and take an advanced intermediate trail.

Intermediates may prefer the midstation slopes at Plan Praz, especially the chair lifts that reach 6,560 feet. In addition, work your way to the right and take the chair up to the Col Cornu's 7,488-foot level for a good intermediate run and off-trail skiing.

Ten minutes away by car is **Les Praz,** ground station for the cable car to La Flégère midstation. From here, a chair lift takes you to L'Index at 7,822 feet, where the skiing is outstanding for intermediates. There are off-trail challenges to the right and the left of the upper gondola.

The intermediate run from L'Index to Les Praz base is a challenging, advanced intermediate 30-minute romp. However, in high season you can wait as long as 45 minutes at the bottom to get back on the cable car. You'll want to stay on the upper mountain unless you're moving to another slope or making the last run of the day.

For our money, the best skiing in the valley is reached by driving 10 minutes up the valley to **Argentière**. The wait at the cable car base station at Argentière should not be more than a half hour, even in high season. From the midstation there are only three main lifts. But these lifts open up excellent skiing. As one instructor observes, "Why ride lifts when you can ski?" Here, you can really ski. A gondola and a chair lift offer excellent intermediate terrain and plenty of off-trail skiing for experts.

Advanced and expert skiers should head up the second stage of the cable car. You'll have to pay an additional €10 to take the second car. (Trips are included on a six-day Mont Blanc pass.) For experts, the skiing is definitely worth the extra cost. At the top of Les Grands Montets take time to ascend the observation deck for one of the most spectacular views in the Alps. When you are ready to ski you have two basic choices—both offer 4,200 feet of vertical skiing. This part of the mountain has never seen a grooming machine. You can drop down a black trail across the Argentière glacier to Croix de Lognan, or go around the other side of Les Grands Montets and ski under the cable car. There are wide-open, off-trail opportunities for any skier willing to go for it. In fact, the "trails" offer only a general direction to the midstation. The red-rated (intermediate) trail branches off from the glacier route and then drops beneath the cable car to the midstation. It is often almost as much of a challenge as the expert-rated runs.

At **Le Tour** there is a system comprised of two gondolas and five other lifts at the end of the valley. The second eight-seat gondola links Le Tour to the village of Vallorcine. This area is perfect for beginners and intermediates and families who are looking for comfortable cruising in the sun.

The most talked-about adventure in Chamonix—not necessarily the most challenging —is the 14-mile-long glacier run from the Aiguille du Midi (12,601 feet) back into Chamonix (3,363 feet). The scenery is magnificent, and the memory of the Vallée Blanche and the Mer de Glace will remain forever.

The **Vallée Blanche** expedition could be more appropriately called ski mountaineering than simple skiing. Go prepared for changing weather and changing terrain: the weather in town may be balmy, with a howling wind at the top of the Aiguille du Midi and zero visibility. Be ready for freezing, windy weather. Pack goggles or mountaineering glasses, good gloves, a warm jacket with a hood if possible, and your ski hat.

You start by climbing—roped to your guide and holding your skis tied together— down a narrow windy ridge. At the end of the ridge, you break the tether with the guide and, sheltered from the wind, step into your skis. Groups are separated from one another by several hundred meters. You may be skiing on trails for a time, then turn off for powder if your guide finds it. Sometimes the trail simply ends, which means climbing over rocks or ice chunks with your skis on your shoulder or balancing over a snowbridge spanning a deep crevasse.

The mountains surrounding you are all famous in the annals of climbing. The Vallée Blanche starts on the upper, smooth portion of the glacier. As it begins to break up and crevasses block the route, skiers sideslip down narrow chutes in a region called the Seracs. At the end of the Seracs and after almost two hours descending on skis, there is often a stop at the Refuge du Requin for a warm drink. From the refuge the run enters a wide-open area called the Salle à Manger (dining room).

The needlelike Aiguille des Drus, with Europe's longest climbing vertical, towers above the glacier. From this point the Mer de Glace begins its drop into the valley. As the glacier ends, another refuge, Les Mottets, offers snacks and drinks. Then it's back into the town, the entire trip having taken all day.

Although guides are not required, they are strongly recommended. In fact, unless you are an expert mountaineer, you'd be crazy to attempt this adventure without one. If the clouds close in, the guides bring you down by compass and you're assured of having someone to belay you when crossing over crevasses and during the initial windy climb down the ridge. As an extra precaution, each participant receives a beeper. Guides cost about €260 (without a skipass) for one to four skiers. Add about €16 for each additional person. If traveling alone, check with the guide office in town to register for a group. With a group the cost is about €70.

What level of skier can handle the Vallée Blanche? A solid intermediate, comfortable on skis, who can sideslip easily and make quick turns can make the trip. You need to be in good enough condition to tour more than four hours at high altitudes.

An additional feature of Chamonix is the chance to travel through the Mont Blanc tunnel into Courmayeur, Italy, on the opposite side of the massif, where skiing is very good. There's often good weather here when Chamonix is clouded over.

Mountain rating

Beginners should stick to Le Tour and Le Brevent. Though experts rave about the resort, thousands learn to ski here every year. But realize that this is not a walk-to-your-lesson resort.

Intermediates choose Chamonix year after year as an ideal area to increase their skills on challenging terrain.

Experts need never worry that there may not be a bigger challenge over the mountain: here, there always is.

Chamonix can best be enjoyed by all skiers with a guide to take them to their most suitable level. Chamonix Ski Fun Tours, part of the French Ski School, and Compagnie des Guides, have weekly packages that include a guide for small groups.

 ## Ski school (2007/08 prices)

A total of 300 instructors offer courses in the French Ski School Chamonix (450 53 22 57), French Ski School Argentière (450 54 00 12), Evolution 2 (450 55 90 22) and Ski Sensations (450 53 56 46). The schools offer a variety of programs so call and find out what's best for you.

The ski schools are competitive and prices are usually with a few euros of each other. The following are the prices for the French Ski School Chamonix.

Private lessons for skiing, cross-country skiing and snowboarding (one to two people) cost €38 an hour; three or four skiers cost €48. A day of private instruction is €275 for one to six people and €25 for each extra person. There is a maximum limit of eight people.

Group lessons for a half day (four hours) cost €56. A four-day course, consisting of daily morning or afternoon instruction (four hours a day), is €130; a six-day course is €172. For snowboarding classes, adults and juniors (ages 13 and older) cost €56 for a half day and €172 for six half days. For cross country classes, adults and juniors cost €31 for two-and-a-half hours and €145 for six days of two-and-a-half hour classes.

Out-of-bounds ski guides for up to six skiers can be hired for €290 (full day).

 # Lift tickets (2007/08 prices)

The normal Chamonix lift ticket, called **Chamonix Le Pass**, gives access to Brévent-Flégère area, Domaine de Balme, Les Grands Montets area (cable car from Lognan to Grands-Montes NOT included), Les Planards, le Savoy, les Chosalets and la Vormaine. Access to the Grands-Montets cable car costs €10 and a reservation is required. Photo ID without sunglasses or ski hat is required to purchase ski pass of 10 days or more. With the purchase of pass that is 3 days or more you may take one day off during the entire duration of the skipass.

Chamonix Le Pass	Adults	Children (4-15))/ Senior (60+ yrs)
one day	€37	€30
three days	€104	€83
six days	€185	€148

You may exchange the Chamonix Le Pass for a **Mont-Blanc Unlimited Pass** by paying the difference between the two.

The Mont-Blanc Unlimited Pass gives access to Chamonix Le Pass areas plus the Aiguille du Midi and Helbronner cable car, the Montenvers train, the Lognan-Grands Montets cable car, the Les Houches ski area and one day of skiing at Courmayeur. Reservations are required in order to enjoy access to the Grands-Montets. Photo ID without sunglasses or ski hat is required to purchase ski pass of 10 days or more.

Chamonix now uses an electronic ski-pass system. The Hands Free Badge costs €3, which will be refunded to you when you return the badge.

Mont-Blanc Unlimited Pass	Adults	Children (4-15))/ Senior (60+ yrs)
one day	€47	€38
three days	€136	€109
six days	€225	€180

 # Accommodations

The Chamonix reservation service (which also has listings for Argentière and Les Houches) is run by the tourist office, Place de L'Eglise, (450 53 23 33). Nearly 90 hotels provide a range of accommodations from luxury suites to dormitory-like rooms. Because of the many restaurants and snack bars, don't hesitate to book a hotel without a half-pension plan.

Rates are per person per day, based on double occupancy with half pension in February. €€€=€125+ ; €€=€75–€124; €=less than €75.

Mont Blanc (450 53 05 64; €€€) A grand old hotel with renovated suites that offer upscale accommodations not found elsewhere in the town. The restaurant is one of the best in the region.

Auberge du Bois-Prin (450 53 33 51; €€€) A Chateau and Relais Hotel, this is best in town for quiet and coziness but is a long walk uphill from the center of town. Rooms are decorated in dark wood with fixtures in brass and gold. The views of Mont Blanc from most rooms are spectacular, with Chamonix spread out below.

Hôtel du Jeu de Paume (450 54 03 76; €€€) Above the village of Le Lavancher, this hotel is understated, quiet luxury built in the wooden chalet style. It has an indoor/outdoor pool and well-appointed rooms.

Le Prieuré (450 53 20 72; €€–€€€) This is an excellent, functional hotel with some Alpine touches. It is large, short on quaintness and long on convenience. It also has a private shuttle to the ski areas, as well as covered parking.

Hôtel Savoyard (450 53 00 77; €€–€€€) This small hotel is created with a French-country motif. It oozes charm and management is very helpful. It sits next to Le Brévant gondola, a steep climb from town. Great for skiing Le Brévant.

Hôtel des Aiglons (450 55 90 93; €€–€€€) is modern with a beautiful, soaring lobby and great views of Mont Blanc. It is near the popular Restaurant Impossible.

Alpina (450 53 47 77; €€) This place could just as easily be a high-rise business hotel, but the views from the rooms across the valley to Mont Blanc are spectacular. It is in the center of town and the rooms are among the largest in town.

Sapinière Montana (450 53 07 63; €€) is only a five-minute walk from the center of town. Rooms are basic and slightly aging.

De la Croix Blanche (450 53 00 11; €€) Centrally located, this property has decades-old interiors that are nonetheless well maintained and pleasant. (B&B only)

La Vallée Blanche (450 53 04 50; €€) This freshly renovated small hotel is next to the churning river running through town and steps from Chamonix's center. Rooms feature beautiful, locally-made Alpine furniture. Breakfasts are a feast. Fills fast, so book early.

Ski Chalets: Simply Ski, Neilson (see page 16 for contact information).

Apartments, condominiums, flats

Chamonix has hundreds of furnished chalets and apartments offered through several agencies. Prices for a studio with sleeping arrangements for two to four: €224–€510. A two-room apartment housing six people will cost €368–€1201. The tourist office provides direct booking. Call 450 53 23 33.

Dining

Chamonix's excellent dining is augmented by the fact that it's a real town, not a resort, so prices are generally very reasonable. And it has its share of excellent, top-quality restaurants. Prices listed here are all approximate and vary depending on beverage and meal.

Albert Ist et Milan (450 53 05 09) is Chamonix's best, where the chef mixes nouvelle cuisine with local mountain cooking. The giant dining room features expansive views of Mont Blanc. The food is praised equally by France's top critics and the locals, who are most pleased by the size of the portions. The menu is an exceptional value—about €60.

Le Matafan (450 53 05 64) in the Mont Blanc Hotel is laid out around a large fireplace. Try the foie gras and the veal with figs. The wine cellar is one of the best in the region, with over 14,000 bottles priced from €3–€680. Gourmet menu is €60.

Auberge du Bois-Prin (450 53 33 51) is in an intimate, old home. Dinner is served by waitresses in local costume. The restaurant is noted for taking the normal and making it special. Meals cost €33–€43, with a gourmet menu at about €60.

Eden Restaurant (450 53 06 40), in Hôtel Eden, is a bit out of the center of Chamonix in the suburb of La Praz. The views of Mont Blanc and the Drus are spectacular. Specialties are trout amandine and lobster au gratin. The menu costs €23–€53.

La Cabana (450 53 23 27) is next to the golf course and a few minutes' drive outside town. It is a highly rated (Michelin two forks) rustic chalet with regional meat and potatoes. Expect to pay €40 for a full dinner.

For a quaint evening in a picture-postcard setting, dine at **Maison Carrier** (450 53 00 03) set in a reconstructed Savoyard farm house. Meals are about €35.

Sarpé (450 53 29 31) a few kilometers out of town is a destination for many serious gourmands. A meal here is about €35–€40.

Restaurant L'Impossible (450 53 20 36) This eatery is built in an ancient barn and is as rustic as it gets. You'll dine around an open grill and get buzzed on peach kirs. Make reservations. This is an experience you will remember. Expect to pay around €22 for a meal.

Atmosphere (450 55 97 97) is a very jazz-and-blues oriented, riverbank café-esque, Michelin two-fork rated, restaurant decorated in subdued tones. Try to get a table in the sunroom overlooking the river for a truly romantic spot. Dinner will cost about €22 without wine.

Calèche (450 55 94 68) is an elegant, regional restaurant with the traditional, mountain wood tastefully mixed with flowered fabrics and stuffed chairs. They serve everything from fondue and raclette to full dinners. A very reasonable €25 evening menu offers choices of nine appetizers, five main courses and six desserts.

Chaudron (450 53 40 34), on Rue des Moulins, is very rustic. A heavy, stone wall lines the small restaurant. You dine under wooden beams while farm tools and a giant wagon wheel add a country flavor. Specialties are regional dishes, grilled meats and brochettes. Fixed-price menu for dinner will run about €22.

Hotel Les Lanchers (450 53 47 19) in Praz-de-Chamonix has a fine restaurant.

Boccalatte (450 53 52 14) serves Savoyard meals in a blond wood setting. Prices are reasonable. Fondues cost €13–€15, and the Alsace Choucroute about the same.

L'M is a brasserie serving low-ticket crêpes, galletes and meals in the middle of town. In the spring a large terrace opens, which makes snacking and nursing a long drink most enjoyable. Most selections with a drink will range between €8–€15.

 ## Après-ski/nightlife

The immediate après-ski usually consists of having drinks in one of the bars in the center of town. Try the **Chamouny**, the **Brasserie du Rond Point** and the **Irish Coffee**. In spring the outdoor tables in the center of town fill up with skiers. **La Cabolée** attracts skiers coming down Le Brévent. For basic bars head to the **Bumble Bee** and **Mill Street**.

In Argentière, the **Office Bar** is packed with English speakers. For immersion in French, head to the **Savoie** or to **Rusticana** for drinks.

Nightlife devotees have plenty of choices here besides gambling. **Arbat** has live music and is hot these days. The **Blue** is excellent, with occasional live jazz or country & western. **Le Pèle** disco is large, loud and packed with teenagers. One of the main meeting spots for English-speakers is the **Choucas Video Bar**, which is normally packed, dark and smoky.

The hard-partying crowd heads out to **Jeckl and Hyde,** which has a touch of Irish influence and is located between Hotel Des Aiglons and Restaurant Impossible. Other good spots are **Ice Rock Café** and **Cantina**. The new king of nightlife may be **Wild Wallabies Bar** where the owner whips the British and Scandinavian crowd into a drinking, singing, burping and dancing frenzy.

Child care (2007/08 prices)

The **Chamonix Ski School** (450 53 22 57) takes children 3–12 years into their Kid's Club. From December to February 10, lessons (two 2-hour lessons), child care and lunch are included for €70 a day or for €295 for six consecutive days. From February 11 to April, lessons (two 2.5-hour lessons), child care and lunch are included for €74 a day or for €330 for six consecutive days.

Child-care services are available at the larger hotels, and babysitting services are available for around €20 (half day) or €35 (full day). For more information, contact the tourist office.

Maison Pour Tous kindergarten on Place du Mont Blanc (450 53 12 24) takes children 3 to 6 years. It's open 7:45 a.m. to 6:30 p.m. Monday to Friday. Reservations strongly recommended.

The Panda Club (450 54 08 88 for the Bureau/Office) has kindergarten with ski instruction in both downtown Chamonix (450 55 86 12) and in Argentière at the cable car station (450 54 04 76). These child care centers have games, crafts, ski lessons with videos and outdoor snow games. Children ages 3-12 can receive care, supervision and lunch for €60 for a half day, €80 for a full day, €255 for five half days, and €310 for five full days, €285 for six half days, and €340 for six full days.

The **MJC, Maison des Jeunes et de la Culture**, (450 531 224; fax 450 534 441) provides care for children age 3 to 12 years old. The activities are theme-based and include sports, tournaments, theater and educational trips.

Other activities

More than any other area you may visit, this one merits an aerial tour. The Mont Blanc massif and the stunning surrounding peaks are best seen from the air. Choose from four different trips ranging from €25–€95 per person. Call **Air Mont Blanc** at 450 58 13 31.

The **swimming center** has three pools, all heated, plus **sauna** and **turkish baths**. There is also an **ice rink, indoor tennis, bowling** and a **casino**.

Getting there

Nearly everyone arrives by the autoroute or by train from Geneva. However, Chamonix—with Courmayeur on the other side of Mont Blanc—is ideal for visitors who have skied in Italy and who want to work their way up through Switzerland and France.

The TGV leaves Paris at around 8 a.m. and arrives in Sallanches at about 1 p.m. There is also a special train/bus combination, with the train departing from Paris just after 7 a.m., a change to bus in Annecy and arrival in Chamonix before 1 p.m.

A taxi from the Geneva airport will cost about €120, and a bus from the airport to the resort costs about €30.

Tourist information

Tourist Office, 85, place du triangle de l'Amitié BP 25, 74400 Chamonix Mont-Blanc Cedex; Telephone 450 53 00 24; fax 450 53 58 90.
Internet: www.chamonix.com
E-mail: info@chamonix.com

Flaine

Flaine is an all-or-nothing proposition: either you take to this purpose-built, concrete-and-steel, French resort in the Haute Savoie, or you search deeper into the Alps for quaint chalets and sleighs as backdrop to your downhill adventures. You may or may not like Flaine's exterior appearance, but its skiing, which is overwhelmingly intermediate, is bountiful and good. And this car-free resort is great for families.

Let's face it: to anyone expecting an Alpine village, Flaine is an odd sight. The rectangular flat-topped buildings — reputedly designed by Marcel Breuer — clinging to the slopes of this narrow valley appear to have all been poured from the same grey cement. However, in terms of practicality, they seem to serve the purpose. Cars are unnecessary, and housing and services are clustered to provide maximum convenience for skiers. There is also a cluster of Scandinavian-style chalets. Le Hameau de Flaine is only a kilometer from the base area and served by a regular, free shuttlebus.

Everything here is designed with winter sports in mind, and at 5,183 feet (almost a mile high), snow is practically guaranteed from December to May. When the blue piste of la Cascade is open, Flaine is connected by a system of lifts to the more traditional lower-altitude towns of Les Carroz, Morillon and Samoens, and by bus to Sixt. Together they form a wide-ranging ski circus of 78 lifts and more than a hundred marked trails totalling 257 km. of downhill adventure. Marked runs are predominantly intermediate and upper intermediate, but adventurous experts will find numerous possibilities just off-piste.

Mountain layout–Skiing

First, all but beginners should take the cable car to the top of Les Grandes Platières to drink in the magnificent views of Mont Blanc and the jagged-toothed range running north (to your left) from the Aguille du Midi. Here on the treeless top of the world you can get a feel for the distances and the variety of terrain spreading out in three directions. Behind you, down the cable car route, are a black run and several alternate intermediate routes running directly back into Flaine or connecting with the chair and surface lifts in this section.

To your right is the Lindars section, reached by "The Eggs," cable system. There's also a chair to the top.

To your left stretches another whole system of lifts and trails, served by an eight-seat chair. The trails drop down on the near side to the gentle beginner area at Flaine center. The trails on the far side drop to the Gers expert terrain, and further left to the long, winding trails down to Samoens, Morillon or Les Carroz. Each of these villages is at the bottom of its own system of trails and lifts, so plan one or two all-day excursions on this side. Leave yourself enough time to explore, stop for lunch and wend your way back to Flaine before the lifts close.

Les Carroz, Morillon and the valley town, Samoens, are Flaine's supporting cast, but their attraction lies in their more traditional Alpine accommodations.

Of the runs above these towns, we liked the blue-rated trail from Cupoire summit (6,166 feet) to the chair near the parking lot in Morillon. With easy turns, a few moguls, and trees for orientation, it's a fine cruise. The runs on this side are almost invariably intermediate. One exception to try is the black trail from Plateau des Saix summit to the Grand Massif Express (formerly the Vercland lift station).

 ## Mountain layout–Snowboarding

The Jampark, on the Calcédoine run over the Aujon ski area, has terrain of varying difficulties. The snowpark has one boardercross track that can accommodate up to four competitors with big jumps, spines lines, rails, quarters and separate tables for beginner and more advanced boarders. It also has a chalet reception area, sound system and cool zone (offering all the gear you need to take care of your board on a self-service basis). Free events and activities with barbecues and snowparties with D.J. music are held throughout the season.

The Jampark Kids of Morillon is a snowpark designed for future freestylers from ages 5 to 12. There you will find whoops and banked turns on a mellow slope.

Mountain rating

Beginners will find great training slopes and excellent ski instruction.

Intermediates are in the majority here, and the slopes are laid out with that in mind. Les Grandes Platières is an intermediate's mountain, offering at least 15 different red-rated variations.

Experts will find plenty of challenges, particularly if they enjoy off-trail skiing.

 ## Cross-Country

At 1,844 meters, Le Col de Pierre Carrée offers the highest cross-country skiing area, in the Alps which usually means good snow cover even in early spring. There are 17 km. of marked tracks for skating and traditional cross-country skiing. A free skibus serves the area. In the Agy area, a half-hour away from Flaine, is an additional 30 km. of tracks.

Contact the cross-country reception chalet (450 90 14 63) for more information.

Ski school (2007/08)

Flaine excels in ski instruction. There are two schools here: the French Ski School (450 90 81 00) and Ski Ecole International (450 90 84 41). Prices between the two are about the same.

Private lessons cost €38 per hour for one or two skiers.

Group lessons: The ESF guarantees a limit of not more than 9 people. Group lesson prices for six half days of instruction (two hours per day) are €132 for adults; €115 for children age 3–11.

An extended ski school with four hours a day for six days costs €140 for adults, €115 for children age 3–11.

Lift tickets (2007/08 prices)

These prices are for the entire Grand Massif area which includes Flaine - Les Carroz - Morillon - Samoëns - Sixt.

Note: Seniors age 50 and older ski for the same price as juniors.

Who skis free: Children younger than age 5 and senior older than age 75.

	Adults	Children (5-11)	Junior (12-15)
half day	€34	€25.50	€26.50
one day	€38	€28	€30
two days	€68	€51	€53
four days	€136	€102	€106
six days	€187.20	€135	€147

Accommodations

Flaine primarily offers apartments, although you also can choose from the hotels listed below near the Forum Square. Most hotels have been taken over by tour operators except the Chalet La Cascade.

Rates: high season, half-board for one based on double occupancy; €€€=€125+, €€=€75–€124, €=less than €75.

Hotel Totem (450 53 88 88; fax: 450 53 88 77; €€) is run by Crystal Holidays.

Hotel Club Le Flaine (1 45 77 52 62; fax: 4 92 12 62 20; €€) and **Hotel Aujon** (450 90 80 10; fax: 450 90 88 21; €€) are both run by Mer Montagne Vacances.

Chalet La Cascade (phone/fax: 450 90 87 66; €).

Le Hameau de Flaine is a village of Scandinavian chalets. Weekly rates are from €645 for a two-room apartment that sleeps four (or six in a squeeze) during January low season to €1,350 during the high season. A five-room chalet, for eight to 10, costs €1,370 during January low season and €2,300 during high season.

Apartments, condominiums, flats

Apartment complexes in Flaine have been built on three levels. Above the Forum on the hillside are the units of Flaine Forêt. These are the better apartments, many privately owned. Apartment buildings are also clustered around the main Forum square, and there are more below the Forum level at Front de Neige. The most convenient are those in the Forum area.

The least expensive studio apartment on the Forum level in middle season (first two weeks of February) costs about €290 a week, and in high season (end of February and holidays) about €725.

For rental bookings there are several agencies: Pierre et Vacances (450 90 87 99); Agence Renand (450 90 81 40); Agence Home International (450 90 82 93); Agence Astrid (450 90 86 41); Agence Flaine Immobilier (450 90 46 70); and Agence Flaine Réservation (450 90 89 09).

Dining

Restaurants are limited because most guests are on full-pension plans with tour operators and apartment guests cook in their own kitchens.

Dine in a rustic chalet atmosphere in the restaurant **Les Chalets du Michet** (450 90 80 08) which serves good food in a converted cow shed, or try **La Perdrix Noire** (450 90 81 81) for excellent basic French food. At **Chez Daniel** (450 90 81 87) try raclette or fondue, or sizzle your meat on hot rocks. The restaurant in the **Aujon Hotel** (450 90 80 10) serves local Savoyard specialties. Reservations suggested. Pizza can be found at **Chez la Jeanne** (450 90 80 06) or **La Pizzeria** (450 90 84 56).

On the mountains, lunchtime offerings are pretty much standardized; you pay less on the Samoëns-Morillon side. Halfway down the Morillon side, **L'Beu** (450 90 17 89) serves simple, good regional specialties.

Après-ski/nightlife

Plan on staying in Flaine, because the road down the mountain can become treacherous, particularly after the sun goes down. Hotel bars are good meeting spots. Try the very British (and nice) **White Grouse Pub** or strike out for **Le Sub** if you are looking for disco action. **Les Cimes** has karaoke twice a week.

Child care (2007/08 prices)

Les Petits Loups (450 90 87 82) in the Syndicat Intercommunal Building — Flaine-Forum in Crèche takes children age 6 months to 3 years old. Both the MMV Hôtel Club Le Flaine (450 90 47 36) and the MMV Hôtel Club Aujon (450 90 80 10) have programs for children ages 18 months to 14. Call 492 12 62 12 for reservations.

Hotel Le Totem (Crystal Holidays) and Les Lindars (Club Med) offer childcare.

The Ski Ecole International's Green Mouse Club (450 90 84 41, fax 450 90 88 07), ski kindergarten for kids 3 to 5 years, is conducted Sunday to Friday. The cost is about €138 for six half-days .

The Rabbit Club and Fantaski (450 90 81 00, fax 450 90 81 54) are run by Ecole du Ski Francais. Fantaski is a special kids' area with a baby rope tow where they can learn to ski while having fun. Both facilites cost approximately €243 for six days with lunch (€189 without lunch).

Other activities

There is an **ice-driving school** (450 90 82 59) with one- to three-day lessons. **Helicopter rides** (450 90 80 01), a **climbing wall** (450 90 62 91), **paragliding** (450 90 81 00, 450 90 01 80 or 660 08 81 79) and a **cinema** are available. The **swimming pool** (450 90 84 99) is open three mornings a week and every afternoon. Entry is €4.20 for adults for six swims and €2.60 for children.

Getting there

Geneva airport, about 45 miles away by the Geneva-Chamonix autoroute, is the closest. Take the Cluses exit.

There are three shuttles to Flaine daily from the Geneva airport or the downtown Geneva bus station. Tickets are €37-€43.50 one way and €63-€74 round trip.

You can also take the train to Cluses and then a Transport Alpbus (450 03 70 09) to Flaine. The bus costs €11.

Tourist information

Office du Tourisme Flaine, F-74300 Flaine, France
Telephone 450 90 80 01, fax 450 90 86 26.
Internet: www.flaine.com
E-mail: welcome@flaine.com
Internet: www.flaine.com

Le Grand-Bornand

Le Grand-Bornand is a pleasant little resort set in a rambling valley. It is an intermediate area great for family getaways. It has two centers; one is town center Le Grand-Bornand village at 3,250 feet (1000 meters) and the other is what the tourist board refers to as the second floor of the resort, Chinaillon, set at 4,225 feet (1,300 meters). The village of Le Grand-Bornand functions like any European resort, but instead of being clustered around a central point, it is set along a skirting road that eventually winds up the Vallée du Bouchet. A farmer's market still is held every Wednesday morning in the town center defined by the church.

Access to skiing/boarding from the village is a bit convoluted, but once aboard one of the two gondolas, everything falls into place. We recommend that visitors choosing to stay in Le Grand-Bornand village try to select one of the hotels or B&Bs near the lifts. It will make life much more convenient.

Chinaillon, 6 km. from Le Grand-Bornand village, is more a modern collection of hotels and restaurants than a traditional village. It has the best access to the downhill slopes and slightly better nightlife than the village does

 ## Mountain Layout–Skiing

Le Grand-Bornand is split into four sections. These sections are not as large nor as defined as those of La Clusaz. The bulk of the skiable terrain is pastureland in the summer, so excellent skiing is possible even when snow depths seem low. There are no large rocks to cover.

La Joyère area is directly above Le Grand-Bornand village facing southwest and garners maximum sunshine. The skiing here is mellow and perfect for families and beginners. There is a special beginner ski pass for this area.

Chinaillon has a north and northwest exposure with trails for all levels of skiers. This is also where much of the snowmaking has been focused and where the snowboarding facilities have been located.

Lachat is the top of the resort at 6,825 feet (2,100 meters). From this point, strong intermediates and experts will find plenty of challenge. The Noire du Lachat slope is considered one of France's most difficult runs (when it is open).

Maroly is the section with the surest snow and the best views. It is an intermediate playground with long cruising trails and plenty of snowmaking.

Mountain layout–Snowboarding

Snowboarders will not have a hard time getting around Le Grand Bornand. There are only a couple long, flat cat tracks that should be bearable for even beginner boarders. There is good range of difficulty in the runs here, and it is not a pain to access the more difficult ones. However, in shabby conditions, there are very few options for advanced and expert boarders.

The snow park consists of ten or so well maintained flat tops alongside a boarder-cross course, with a fairly steep 150-foot halfpipe at the bottom. It is in the Vallee du Maroly area. Boarders can reach it by taking the Chouly Poma lift or the Terres Rouges chairlift.

First-timer snowboarders should start out in the area at the top of the Rosay gondola or off the quad chair, Les Gettiers. Here the runs are wide and flat. Be careful not to take the Lachat chairlift; the easiest way down will probably be via the same chairlift you ride up in.

Beginner and lower intermediate boarders can venture almost anywhere at Le Grand Bornand. There are wide runs in the Vallee du Maroly area. The three chairlifts that meet at La Floria (1800 m) lead to more challenging terrain. There still may not be an easy enough way down Le Lachat for beginners.

Intermediate and advanced riders will enjoy the steeper, ungroomed terrain on La Floria. On these runs there are many turnoffs that lead to ungroomed snow fields. From the top of the Maroly Poma lift, boarders can reach a vast area of ungroomed terrain with many fun land features. Plenty of ungroomed terrain can be reached from the top of the Lachat chairlift, but sometimes these runs are covered in moguls. Also, snow permitting, there is some good tree boarding on the Tete des Annes.

Experts should stick to the two peaks, La Floria and Le Lachat. The marked runs are mostly ungroomed, and the terrain is steeper than it appears on the map. Also, there are many opportunities to drop into bowls or chutes; just beware of cliffs. The bottoms of these steep runs merge into the intermediate runs that the lower lifts serve; in order to get back to the steep stuff, boarders must take these flatter, more crowded runs.

Mountain Rating

Beginners and intermediates will have a swell time in either La Clusaz or Le Grand-Bornand. These are wonderful places for a romantic getaway for a mixed-ability couple. Many lifts offer side-by-side beginner and intermediate trails meeting at the bottom, perfect for families or friends of differing abilities.

Experts who know the area or who ski with a guide will find some toothy terrain with patches of difficulty

Cross-country (2007/08 prices)

The 62 km. of scenic cross-country trails in the Grand-Bornand area follow paths through clusters of winter farms and century old chapels. With varied trails in the Valley du Bouchet and Chinaillon, cross-country skiers of all abilities will have plenty of terrain to tackle.

In the Valley du Bouchet, circuits range from 3 to 20 km. in length and are quite scenic, running along the river and farmhouses. The 3-, 5-, 10-, 15- and 20-km. circuits are set for classic and skating styles and lead from the village toward the Bouchet valley. In addition, there's also a 2-1/2-km. beginners run.

Other trails include the 14-km return link circuit with La Clusaz (Confins area) and the 12-km skating training circuit. Skiers can also take a turn in the biathlon stadium (cross country and shooting).

In Chinaillon, beginners can find their own stadium near the village. More experienced skiers can try the 2-, 5-, 8- and 12-km circuits leading out from the old village.

	Adults	Child (16 and younger)
half day (afternoon)	€6	€3
one day	€7	€3.50
eight days	€28	€16

Ski school (2007/08 prices)

There are four ski schools: **International Ski and Snowboard School "Starski"** (450 27 04 69, fax 450 09 28 46); **Aravis Ski School "Aravis Ski Concept"** (680 57 08 03); **French Ski School ESF** (450 02 79 10; and **"Ecole 2 Ski"** (450 09 00 45).

Le Grand-Bornand French Ski School (ESF) is in the village (0450 02 79 10) at the tourist office, and at Chinaillon (0450 27 01 83) under the chairlift La Floria.

Private lessons are held from 9-10 a.m. or from 1-2:30 p.m. or from 1- 3 p.m or from 3-5 p.m. An hour lesson for one or two is € 33;

Group lessons: Six adult half-day lessons cost €118.

Children's lessons: For children ages 3-6 years the ski school's Piou Piou program is available. Lesson times are 9:45 a.m. to 12:15 p.m. or 2:15 p.m. To 5 p.m.. Six lessons cost €112. Children ages 6-12 years can take six half-day lessons for €102.

Snowboarding lessons: Six half-day lessons from 2-5 p.m are €144. Three half-day lessons from 10-12h15 a.m are €65.

The **Le Grand-Bornand Cross-Country and Snowshoe School** has two locations — Tourist house (450 02 78 17, fax 450 02 36 02; open every day) in the Village and at Chinaillon (450 09 60 66; open weekends and French holidays). Adult prices: €21 for a half day; €56 for three half days; €85 for five half days; and €128 for six full days .Child prices: €19 for a half day; €87 for six half days; and €112 for six full days .

Lift Tickets (2007/08 prices)

The Aravis ticket includes Le Grand-Bornand and La Clusaz, Manigod and Saint-Jean-de-Sixt; shuttles are free between resorts and the bus stations with this ski pass. Below are the high/low season prices for the Aravis lift ticket and the Le Grand Bornand-only lift ticket.

	Adults	Child (age 5-15)	Senior (60 and older)
two days	€59/59	€49.50	€54
five days	€129/127	€108	€124
seven days	€173.50/161.50	€128.50	€157

Le Grand-Bornand only

	Adults	Child (14 and younger)	Senior (61 and older)
half-day	€20	€16	€18.50
one day	€25.50	€20	€23
six days	€122.20/110.30	€101.30/91	€113.20/107

Children younger than age 5 and senior citizens older than 75 ski free.
Children younger than age 8 have the Bambin Ski Pass.
Note: High season is from Dec. 22 2007 to Jan. 4, 2008 and Feb. 2 to Mar. 14 2008. Low Season is before Dec. 21, 2007, from Jan.5 to Feb. 1 2008, after Mar. 15 2008.

Accommodations

Le Grand-Bornand has two three-star hotels and nine two-star hotels. For information or reservations, call the tourist office (04 50 02 78 00). Rates listed are based on per-person half-board, double occupancy: €—€75 and less; €€—€75–€125; €€€—€125+. Credit cards are accepted at all hotels.

Les Glaieuls (450 02 20 23; €), known for its good food, is the closest you will get to the gondolas in the village.

Best Western Chalet Les Saytels (04 50 02 20 16) Near the church, Chalet Les Saytels offers a bar, restaurant, satellite TV, a sauna, Jacuzzi, and billiards.

Les Cîmes (450 27 00 38) Relatively near the slopes at Chinaillon, Les Cîmes is a three-star hotel. It is small and cozy with lots of blond wood furnishings and only 10 rooms.

Le Vermont (450 02 36 22) is a chalet-style two-star hotel with a Jacuzzi, sauna and swimming pool, close to the two main gondolas in the village.

In Chinaillon, check out **Les Flocons** (450 27 00 89), a two-star right on the slopes where you will have to walk across the snow to reach your room.

Apartments, condominiums, flats

In Le Grand-Bornand there are 500 chalet apartments. Contact Le Grand-Bornand tourist office by phone or e-mail. For two people, expect to pay at least €350 in high season and €160 in low season. For 3–5 people, it will cost at least €500 in high season and €185 in low season. For 6 or more people, it will be at least €650 in high season and €300 in low season. (These are per-person rates.)

Dining

Le Traîneau d'Angeline (450 63 27 64) is an interesting place to eat, as it blends modern art with the antique French style, and then adds techno music to the background. Daily menu costs €17–€20.

Aux Deux Guides (450 02 23 65) is like stepping back in time into a dark stonewall castle. Daily menu is €15.10–€17.50.

L'Auberge du Pré Vieux (450 02 23 66) has excellent meals in a wonderful woodsy atmosphere. The daily menu is €23–€25; child's menu is €7.

At **Au Bon Vieux Temps** (450 02 32 38) you can watch your dish cook over an open fire. The atmosphere in this cozy farm house is friendly and active. Daily menu is €15.20–€19.80.

Apres-ski/nightlife

This resort is know for its family atmosphere. Nightlife is gentle by any stretch of the imagination. From **La Bournerie** above Le Chinaillon they have sledding runs — always exciting after "la grole."

Les Deux Guides has lots of ski and snowboard videos going and excellent cocktails. **Maurice's Bar** serves lots of beer. In Chinaillon, **Le Baron Noir** is the place to be.

Child Care (2006/07 prices)

Garderie Les P'tits Maringouins has locations in Le Grand Bornand village and also in Chinaillon.

Garderie Les P'tits Maringouins au Village (4 50 02 79 05; fax: 4 50 02 28 01) is in its own building "L'Espace Grand-Bo" in Le Grand Bornand village near the center of the village. There are play rooms, a motor-exercise room, a book corner, a mini climbing wall, a ball-swimming pool and even a trampoline. They accept children 3 months to 5 years old. Children ages 2-1/2 and older can also participate in Les P'tits Bouts De Glisse where they can learn to ski on the nursery slope.

The Garderie Les P'tits Maringouins Le Chinaillon (450 09 60 80) accepts children 8 months to 5 years. It is open only in the winter.

Both the garderie in the village and in Le Chinaillon are open from 9 a.m. until 5:30 p.m.; however, the center in Le Chinaillon is only open Monday through Saturday while the center in Le Grand Bornand village is open every day.

These are the prices for both of the Les P'tits Maringouins locations. A morning without meal costs €16,50 (with meal, €26); an afternoon without meal costs €21 (with meal, €30,50). A full day with meal costs €34. Three consecutive days cost €95. Six mornings (Sunday through Friday) without meal costs €82,50; six afternoons without meal costs €105. Six full days (Sunday through Friday) with meal costs €170. There is also a €2.50 enrollment charge.

The hour-long introductory course to Jardin des Neiges "Les P'tits Bouts de Glisse" costs €11.

Other activities

The region is proud of their farming heritage. Livestock in this valley still outnumber the inhabitants. Grand Bornand has set up farm visits where they demonstrate their way of life and show Rebochon cheese making.

Ice skating, **paragliding**, **snowmobiling**, **snowshoeing**, **heliski**, **ice-climbing**, **horse-drawn carriage**, **hiking** and **Vallee Blanche** (skiing/boarding a glacier on Mont Blanc) programs are all available. For more information call the tourism office.

Getting there

From Geneva airport, a round-trip bus ticket costs €54. Taxi from Geneva airport to Grand Bornand costs about €105 or €150 nights, weekends and holidays. The bus to Annecy costs about €10. The train (TGV) from Paris to Annecy takes three hours and costs around €70. From there Le Grand-Bornand is reached by bus or taxi (a taxi from Annecy is about €55).

Tourist Information

Office de Tourisme Le Grand-Bornand
74450 Le Grand-Bornand
tel. 0450 02 78 00; fax. 0450 02 78 01
Internet: www.legrandbornand.com
E-mail: infos@legrandbornand.com
In Chinaillon tel. 450 09 60 09

La Clusaz

The center of town is easy to find in La Clusaz. The church on the central square can be seen for miles around, its sturdy-looking tower topped by a distinctive clock and graduated wedding-cake steeple reaching high above the surrounding wood-shingled rooftops. Newly restored and modernized with excellent acoustic properties, it doubles as a concert and lecture hall for visiting dignitaries and performers. During a good winter, this town is hard to beat for intermediate family skiing.

La Clusaz has been a bustling village since the 16th century, but today in the peak season, its 2,050 year-round inhabitants open their doors and hearts to as many as 22,000 visitors. The first ski lift here was built in 1935, but La Clusaz has succeeded in keeping its lived-in, workday atmosphere. Visitors are initiated into the traditions and customs of "Les Cluses," as they call themselves, rather than the other way around. In winter on Mondays, farmers turned innkeepers and local merchants put on humorous welcome-night races that end in convivial silliness on the village green (now white), a large snow-play area adjacent to the skating rink and cable car and flanked by restaurants and outdoor tables. During the day it provides a safe playground and sledding slope for children.

The compactness of the village, its wraparound views of ski runs, forests and peaks, its old winding side streets and leisurely pace make La Clusaz a winner for skiers or boarders who wish to get away from the hustle of modern life. Children are welcomed, and families will find this resort easier to manage than most. Don't expect to find noisy, swinging nightlife except on weekends—here the emphasis is on lingering over dinner with family and friends, and the traditional French Alpine atmosphere makes it hard to believe that Geneva is actually a 60-minute drive away. (On weekends it becomes much easier to believe when the city-dwellers stream in.)

Mountain Layout–Skiing

La Clusaz has five different areas to ski. Visitors can ski a different section each day. Just a cablecar ride above the town, intermediate and beginner terrain allow wide open cruising. Here Beauregard Mountain rises to 5,544 feet and, true to its name, offers beautiful views and cruising trails through magical forest terrain. On the right side of Beauregard Mountain (looking down the mountain) is a good expert trail. Beyond Beauregard, Massif de Manigod offers a network of 15 lifts serving mostly beginner and intermediate trails. Moving around the valley to massif de L'Etale, the runs become steeper and longer. Massif de L'Aguille has excellent advanced terrain and a long plunge through Combe du Fernuy for strong skiers.

Massif de Balme offers good bump skiing and usually has the best snow. Here skiers will find some of the best expert stuff. La Clusaz has good bump skiing as well as freestyle. There are two ways to get back from La Balme. The return to the village is a 4 km. trail alongside a mountain road through the woods. A cable car runs skiers and boarders from the base of La Balme to halfway up Massif de L'Aguille.

Mountain Rating

Beginners and intermediates will have a swell time in La Clusaz. This is a wonderful place for a romantic getaway for a mixed-ability couple. Many lifts offer side-by-side beginner and intermediate trails meeting at the bottom, perfect for families or friends of different abilities. Experts who know the area or ski with a guide will find some toothy terrain with patches of difficulty especially on Massif de Balme.

 ## Mountain layout–Snowboarding

Las Clusaz is known as a center for freeriding and new glide.

Boarders at every ability level will find a part of the mountain just right for them. Try out the terrain park—with a halfpipe and a couple tabletop jumps—halfway up the Massif de L'Aguille. Take any of the Loup lifts to get to the top of the park.

Never-evers could make their first turns on the Poma lift (Champ Bleu) or the gondola (TC de La Patinoire) at the edge of town. Otherwise, take the new gondola from La Clusaz to the top of Massif de Beauregard for wide slopes. (Learning how to use Poma lifts shouldn't be more difficult than strapping yourself to your snowboard.)

Beginners could spend time at Massif de Manigod; it is easiest to get there by car or shuttle bus. Here, there are two chair lifts and an assortment of Poma lifts. With enough snow, you can take the scenic cat track back to town.

Intermediate boarders will enjoy cruising the slopes on Massif de Beauregard or Massif de Manigod. However, the face of Massif de L'Etale or any of the eight lifts above the town provide steeper runs. At the La Balme area the groomed trails will probably suit intermediates best.

Advanced/expert boarders can go just about anywhere and have a great time. The Aguille chair lift provides wide, fairly steep groomed and ungroomed terrain (beware, though, for at some point after every snowfall, this face turns into a mogul field). At the top of the Aguille lift, take a right and board at your own risk down the Combe de Borderan, an expansive off-piste bowl. Also, at the top of Massif de l'Etale there are some pretty steep, open terrain, along with a few off-piste trails through the trees.

For a full plate, head to La Balme (with the higher elevation and lower temperatures, powder lasts longer here than the rest of La Clusaz). Enjoy the vast, ungroomed fields of snow and the many natural land features. Xavier, the head of snowboarding at La Clusaz said, "La Balme is a natural terrain park." Countless mounds and ridges provide great big air jumps with even better landings.

For expert snowboarders, there are backcountry opportunities. Above the Aguille chair lift, a 30-minute hike will lead to La Creuze, a challenging bowl that eventually funnels down to marked trails. Above the L'Etale chair lift, one can hike and reach off-piste terrain. From the top of Col de Balme chair lift, one can take a long hike over a ridge and into the Combe de Bellechat, an extremely wide valley with snow as good as at La Balme. Boarders should consult local experts before venturing into any of this terrain (in most cases, hiring a guide is the safest and smartest thing to do). Information on backcountry boarding (and guides) is available at 450 32 66 05.

Cross-Country (2007/08 prices)

There is excellent cross-country in La Clusaz, with 70 km. of prepared trails, Plateau des Confins (1,450 meters) and the Plateau de Beauregard (1,690 meters).

The 52 km. on the Plateau des Confins (4 km. from town) includes 10 circuits ranging in length from 0.5 km. to 10 km. ringing a frozen lake. On the site there are an info center, first-aid station, picnic room, French ski school (ESF), sports shops, hotels, restaurants and parking.

There is also a 7 km. trail connecting Plateau des Confins with the 30 km. of trails of Le Grand-Bornand. Confins is accessible by ski-bus or by car.

The 18 km. on the Plateau de Beauregard includes 8 circuits ranging from 1 to 4 km. long, some of which are shared with the downhillers. The plateau is accessible from the village via the Beauregard gondola lift, or by car or shuttle from the Col de La Croix Fry. On site there are a first-aid station, picnic room, ski lessons, sport shops, hotels, restaurants, parking. The area is open from 9 a.m. to 5 p.m.

These prices are for the Plateau des Confins and Beauregard.

	Adults	Child
half day	€6 (€5.50 Beauregard)	€3
one day	€7	€3.50
one week	€28	€16
(valid for all of France)		

Ski School (2006/08 prices)

La Clusaz has seven ski schools with more than 200 instructors: **Alter Ego** (06 07 39 72 53); **Evolution 2** (04 50 23 52 77); **Dimension Freeride** (04 50 03 54 39); **International Snowboard and Ski School Sno-Academie** (04 50 32 66 05); **Ski School Aravis Challenge** (04 50 02 81 29); **Bureau des Guides** (04 50 63 35 99); and **La Clusaz French Ski School (ESF)** (450 02 40 83).

Prices at each of the programs are about the same. These are high season prices. At **La Clusaz French Ski School (ESF)** rates are:

Private lessons: A one-hour lesson for one to two people costs €37; for three to four people, €49. A guide for a full day costs €294 (high season) and €252 (low season).

Group lessons: Six days for adults are €167; children younger than 12, €162.

Sno Academie (0450 32 66 05) teaches exclusively snowboarders. It offers two-hour private lessons starting at €66. Sno Academie also offers multi-day lessons, and snowboarding camps for beginner and advanced boarders, in addition to lessons for handicapped people.

Lift Tickets (2007/08 prices)

These prices are for La Clusaz only during the high season. High season is December 17-30 and January 28 to March 10.

Those younger than 5 and older than 75 ski/board for free. High season is December 17–30 and January 28–March 10. For the rest of the season, tickets for two days or more of skiing cost 10–15 percent less.

	Adults	**Child** (5–15)
two days (high season)	€55	€44.50
three days (high season)	€79	€63
six days (high season)	€149.50	€107
fourteen days (high season)	€265	€186

Accommodations

La Clusaz has eight three-star and 11 two-star hotels. For information or reservations, call the tourist office (0450 32 65 00). All the rates listed below are based on per-person half-board, double occupancy with half board: € is €75 and less; €€ is €75–€125; €€€ is €125+. Credit cards are accepted at all these hotels.

The **Alp'Hotel** (450 02 40 06; fax 450 02 60 16; €€€) offers a covered pool and sauna. It is the top-rated by Michelin. We liked the **Beauregard** (450 32 68 00; fax 450 02 59 00; €€€) at the foot of the slopes, with a covered pool, Jacuzzi, sauna, game room and nightly entertainment. The **Alpen'Roc** (450 02 58 96; fax 450 02 57 49; €€), just 150 meters from the slopes offers a covered pool, hot tub and sauna.

Les Chalets de la Serraz (0450 02 48 29; fax 0450 02 64 12; €€€) 4 km. out of town is a typical mountain chalet a bit above the town with a wonderful restaurant. **Hotel Carlina** (450 02 43 48; fax 450 02 63 02; €€) has great south-facing balconies and offers a covered pool, sauna and game room. **Sapins** (450 63 33 33; fax 450 63 33 34; €) is a fine place in the center of the village at prices that are hard to beat.

Les Airelles (450 02 40 51; fax 450 32 35 33; €€) is in the village and has one of the better restaurants and a sauna. It is a great value. **Floralp** (450 02 41 46; fax 450 02 63 94; €€) is only steps from the lifts with a fine restaurant. **Le Vieux Chalet** (450 02 41 53; fax 450 32 33 99; €) is a small, quite rustic, cozy hotel on the edge of the slopes. It is a walk from town, but ski-in/ski-out. The **Beaulieu** (450 02 43 48; fax 450 02 63 02; €), just on the edge of town, offers a covered pool, sauna and game room. **La Piste Bleue Hotel** and **Telepherique Hotel** are at the top of the Beauregard cable car. They offer the best views in the area and are the cheapest. Half board goes for about €46. Beware, though, for there is no access if you miss the last cable car.

Apartments

In La Clusaz, there are 1500 apartments and chalets. **La Clusaz Tour** (04 50 32 38 33; fax 04 50 32 38 34) has information and package rates.

The "all-inclusive" apartment package has a starting price of €185 per skier per week during regular season and a starting price of €252 per skier per week during holiday season. Rates based on a four-person studio.

Dining

While you're in the Haute Savoie region, try some of the great local specialties. Most restaurants in La Clusaz will serve Raclette, a fun dish that drips melted cheese over potatoes; Tartiflette, a dish of potatoes with tasty, creamy Reblochon cheese melted over it; Matafan, big potato fritters; Farcon, a mixture of mashed potatoes, cabbage, pears, raisons, and chestnuts; Les Diots, little pork sausages prepared in white wine; Les Atriaux, roasted pieces of pork wrapped in 'voilettes'; or La Tomme Blanche, reblochon cheese that is not yet mature.

Le Bercail (450 02 43 75) on the Massif de L'Aiguille is one of the finest dining experiences that can be found at any international ski resort. It is accessible by skis and at night by sleigh or snowcat. Unforgettable dinners, available only by reservation, include typical Savoyard dishes served in a rustic farm setting around two blazing fireplaces. The fixed menu offers plenty of options for a good deal. The *Degustation* Menu offers a palate-expanding meal with many, many courses

L'Arbé (450 02 60 54) is the place to go for cheese dishes. For a great fondue or raclette you will spend around €20–€25 with wine.

Le Grenier (450 32 36 06) is a very cozy, wooden place just around the corner from the church. This restaurant specializes in raclette. Huge half-wheels of Reblochon cheese are melted by an interesting contraption. Meals can go for €16–€30.

There are plenty of other excellent restaurants in La Clusaz. **Le Symphonie** (450 32 68 00), in Hotel Beauregard, is a classic French and nouvelle restaurant. **Restaurant de Savoie, Alp Hotel Restaurant, Hotel Des Aravis Restaurant, La Caleche** (450 02 42 60) and **L'Ecuelle** (450 02 42 03) are cozy, beautiful, old places where wood burns and regional specialties are served.

These restaurants serve tasty dishes for a little less than the rest. **La Bergerie** (450 02 63 40), offers a €7 child's meal and dinners for €12–€25. It is a small, cozy pizzeria that also serves regional specialties and Reblochon plates. **La Braise** (450 02 68 75) serves child's meals for €7.50, plate-of-the-day for €12–€17, pizza for €8–€10 and for tartiflette €5–€6 . **La Scierie** (450 63 34 68) is a well lit, open restaurant with a fireplace. It serves children's meals for less than €10 and tasty dinners for €11–€12.

If you cannot decide on a restaurant, check in at any of the inexpensive creperies or pizzerias in town. You can also save by eating a full meal at lunch, when meals generally cost less, or by picking up some bulk food at the supermarket. Sometimes, good French bread and cheese can do the job; this should cost no more than €4.

Aprés-ski/nightlife

The nightlife in La Clusaz is happening on weekends, but, shall we say, dead on some weekdays. The older, more mature crowd hangs out at **Le Salto** or **Le Pressoir**, video bars with many beer choices; they are open until about 2 a.m. **Le Caves du Pacally** is comfortable, casual, hangout; open until 2 a.m. **Bar Roc Café** is a dim, cozy place in town groovin' to '80s disco music. **Bali Bar** is a fun little bar that is usually packed with friendly people dancing to island music. **Panama Café** is a Tex-Mex bar with Cuban music.

Boarders and skiers of all ages head to either of the two disco/pub/nightclubs, both open until 5 a.m. **Club 18** blasts loud music and is great for chilling or close quarter dancing. **L'Ecluse** is also a great late-night hangout. The dance floor in this disco is not a floor but a thick sheet of glass, revealing the flowing waters of the town's river. Both of these exclusive nightclubs have cover charges of about €12.

Child care (2007/08 prices)

Le Club des Mouflets (450 02 48 91, fax: 450 32 65 21)is right above the tourism office. It takes children from 8 months to 4 1/2 years. There are different rooms for different aged children; it offers many indoor activities such as musical games, collages and crafts. Rates are as follows: €15.50 for a half day, €22.50 for full day (with lunch), €79 for six half days, €144 for six full days (with lunch). A supervised lunch is €4.50.

Le Club des Champions (450 32 69 50, fax: 450 32 69 51) accepts children ages 3–6. They offer one-hour ski lessons to children ages 3–4, and two-hour lessons to children 5 and older. The other outdoor activities include snowman-making, sledding and other snow games. Indoor activities are also offered. Rates: €15.70 for a half day, €23.60 for full day, €81 for six half days, €121 for six full days (without lunch). Lunch is available from noon to 2 p.m. for an extra €10.80 per day.

Both Le Club des Mouflets and Le Club des Champions are a few steps away from the church. They are both open every day in the morning and afternoon.

Other activities

There is a **swimming complex** (04 50 02 43 01) with various open-air and covered pools, a hot tub, sauna, steam room, solarium, and fitness center; from December 20 to April 30, it is open every afternoon 13:30 p.m.-19:30 p.m. Entrance to the pools costs approximately €6.50 for adults and €5.50 for children; entrance to the fitness room, sauna, and steam room costs €14.

The town's **ice skating** rink is open in the morning from 10 a.m. to 12:30 p.m., and in the afternoon from 2:30 p.m.-6 p.m., and at night from 5 p.m.–11 p.m. Entrance is €3 and skate rentals cost €4. Occasionally there are **ice hockey** or **skating competitions** (450 02 48 45). From 5:30 p.m.–7 p.m., every Wednesday, Thursday and Friday, ice karting is available; €11 for a 10-minute round.

Paragliding (450 02 66 51) or (450 02 68 96) is available for €55 per person. **Snowmobiling** (450 32 35 37) costs €95 per hour for two people. There are **snowshoeing**, **heliski**, **ice-climbing**, **four-wheeling**, **husky sleigh rides**, **quad biking**, **hiking**, and **Vallée Blanche** (skiing/boarding a glacier on Mont Blanc) programs. For more information call the tourism office.

Getting there

From the Geneva airport, a bus costs about €60 and a daytime taxi ride costs €110 (€160 at night). The bus from Annecy to La Clusaz costs €10. The train (TGV) from Paris to Annecy takes 3-1/2 hours and costs about €75. A taxi from Annecy to La Clusaz costs about €60.

Alpine skiers and snowboarders will not need a car in La Clusaz, except to get to the one or two out-of-town restaurants or to Manigod, (a small complex of apartments up the valley past Massif de Beauregard). Everything in town is within walking distance.

Tourist information

La Clusaz Tourist Office,
Place de L'Eglise, 74220 La Clusaz, France; 04 50 32 65 00,
fax 04 50 32 65 01
Internet: www.laclusaz.com; Email: infos@laclusaz.com

La Plagne

This is the largest single ski resort in Europe, if you base such a superlative on the number of lifts and lift capacity. Other ski regions, such as the Trois Vallées, the Dolomites or the Portes du Soleil, may be larger, but they are formed by combining several independent resorts .

That said, as large as it is, it wanted to be bigger. La Plagne recently linked its trail system with that of Les Arcs via Plan-Peisey. The combined area is called Paradiski and has 425 km. of trails. The enormity is mindboggling. The joint resorts boast 142 ski lifts: a funicular, twin-cable cablecar, three cablecars, 12 sections of gondola lifts, 66 chairlifts, 58 draglifts, 28 skilifts available for walkers, 26 free-ski lifts and six moving walkways.

A cablecar, Le Vanoise Express, with 200-person cabins spans the valley from Plan-Peisey on the Les Arcs side to Les Coches on the La Plagne side. The span is 3,000 meters and the futuristic cablecar is 380 meters above the valley floor. The trip, from station to station, takes four minutes. A new eight-seat chairlift at Arpette will allow easier transfers from Plagne Bellecote to the trails down to the Vanois Express. The Les Arcs trails are detailed in a separate chapter.

La Plagne claims a vertical of 6,500 feet. The lower 1,700 feet of that is through trees and along winding roads. Still, when the snow is good a skier can start out from Roche de Mio at 8,775 feet and drop to Montchavin at 4,062 feet, which means more than 4,700 feet of working vertical. Another vertical drop across the western face of Bellecote down to Les Bauches provides almost 4,000 feet of nonstop vertical that will challenge any skier.

Even in the modest upper ranges of the area, the working vertical is about 2,500 feet. Since it is one of the highest resorts on the continent, La Plagne can't be beat for certainty of snow; there will be snow up on the glacier, even in the middle of August.

La Plagne revolves around apartment life. It offers about 47,000 beds in small apartments and only about 1,500 beds in the eleven hotels in the region. The purpose-built sections of La Plagne consist of the six high-altitude modern clusters, connected by a creative series of public conveyances called telemetro, telebus, and telecabine, and traditional shuttlebuses. Each complex has apartments, with stores and ski shops all interconnected by tunnels and walkways. These underground passages, while extremely practical in snow country, give several of the areas an oddly urban feel, reminiscent of a subway shopping mall. Four lower villages are also connected to the lift system.

Plagne Centre at 6,463 feet is the original, constructed 40 years ago as one of France's first built-for-skiing villages. What the buildings lack in charm they make up for in convenience—two hotels, dozens of restaurants, scores of shops, a cinema and apartments are all connected by underground passages with 20 lifts fanning out from the just outside its doors.

Plagne Villages at 6,726 feet is a cluster of small apartment houses and Alpine-style buildings with wooden features and peaked roofs. There are no hotels, only apartments and shops.

Plagne 1800 is a consistently designed neo-Savoyard mountain village with wooden chalets and peaked roofs. This grouping contains squash courts.

Aime La Plagne, also sometimes called Aime 2000, is a newer purpose-built complex above Plagne Centre. Many consider it the most convenient, with many of the best apartments in the resort. There are a cinema and a good collection of shops and restaurants. A cablecar connects Aime La Plagne with Plagne Centre.

Plagne Bellecote is a group of massive, interconnected, high-rise buildings over an underground shopping mall. There are no hotels in this group, but it has La Plagne's only heated outdoor swimming pool and is the starting point of the gondola to the glacier at 8,858 feet.

Belle Plagne, built in the Savoyard chalet style, is the newest of La Plagne's centers. An underground garage system allows one to reach each of the chalet groups. A multilevel shopping arcade with covered walkways provides a touch of Alpine charm. There is also a fitness center.

Villages that are part of the complex have ski schools and ski kindergartens for children plus ski rentals.

Plagne Montalbert at 4,429 feet with a couple of two-star hotels, a selection of apartments and eleven restaurants has its own lift system that connects with the rest of the La Plagne region.

Montchavin and Les Coches are at 4,101 feet and 4,757 feet respectively. Les Coches is the new station of the Vanoise Express that will link to Les Arcs. These villages have lift tickets, which may be purchased separately, as well as a two-star hotel, some chalets and apartments and 14 restaurants.

Champagny-en-Vanoise at the top of a valley separating La Plagne from the Trois Vallées area is a picturesque town clinging to the mountain walls. A cablecar takes skiers up to giant snowfields that connect with all the other resorts. During the past two years, new lifts have made the connections between Champagny and Bellecote Glacier very easy. Skiers staying in Champagny-en-Vanoise can ski into town down two challenging intermediate trails with plenty of off-piste possibilities.

Mountain layout—Skiing

There are 134 trails, including 10 black and 34 red, covering 225 km. of ski area with 105 ski lifts, eight of which are gondolas, and one that connects Bellecote and Belle Plagne with the glaciers.

What you see, you can ski. Just take off and explore different sections of the resort on different days. Intermediates will not get into any trouble here if they stick to the upper slopes and stay off the glacier. This is one of the best intermediate resorts in the world. The distances here are extreme. Be sure to plan your day before finding yourself on the wrong side of the resort when lifts start to close.

Adventurous skiers can find plenty of challenge along the fringes of the resort. Experts will want to drop behind the ridge above Aime La Plagne, follow the Morbleu and Les Etroits trails that loop around to the Les Coqs lift, and then challenge the Les Coqs and the Emile Alais trails.

Another expert adventure is to take the Bellecote cablecar from the peak of Roche de Mio to the Glacier of Bellecote at 10,662 feet. This spectacular ride takes skiers down 500 feet before rising almost 1,640 feet. From the glacier, advanced skiers in tip-top shape can follow the lazy Bellecote or Le Rochu runs down more than 2,000 feet of vertical to the Chalet de Bellecote lift. Skiers with guides will take the Traversé lift and set off across the face of Bellecote and drop towards Les Bauches some 1,200 meters (3,900 feet) of vertical below. It is a daunting ski afternoon or morning. The restaurant at Les Bauches certainly seems welcoming after that descent. From here, lifts reconnect skiers with the network.

A similarly challenging descent can be made from the Bellecote Glacier to Champagny-le-Haut along the Cul du Nant with a guide. A shuttlebus (registration necessary 479 55 05 28) takes skiers back to the cablecar at Champagny-en-Vanoise.

Experts can drop alongside the bobsled run for some good skiing through trees and across pastures down toward Plagne Montalbert. Snow is fine during most of the season, but in the spring ask about coverage.

The combined Les Arc/La Plagne Paradiski region has two boardercross courses, four snowparks and two halfpipes.

Mountain layout—Snowboarding

La Plagne is equipped with three outstanding snowparks in Bellecôte, Montchavin and Champagny en Vanoise (complete with sound systems) and 3 boardercross circuits.

The SnowPark in Plagne Centre is on the la Capella piste. The Colorado, Funiplagne gives you access to this 25,000-square meter area with 20 different modules and 4 circuits.

To get to the Snowpark of Montchavin-Les Coches take the Dos Rond chairlift or the or the Vanoise Express (the cable care that links La Plagne and Les Arcs). The Snowpark is split into three different play areas: a beginner's area with small obstacles, an intermediate and an expert area. It's a good place for groups of varying skill levels.

At Bellecôte there is a naturally occuring halfpipe that snakes between pine and larch trees with numerous handrails and jumps.

Mountain rating

La Plagne is an intermediate and beginner mountain, at least as far as the prepared trails go in the Bellecote, Belle Plagne, Grand Rochette, Montchavin, Les Coches, Plagne Montalbert and Champagny sectors.

Intermediates will think they have died and gone to skier heaven. The rolling mountains offer acceptable steeps where intermediates can play, and mellow, off-trail areas to develop deep-snow skills. The Champagny section is pretty tame, but the run into the town and return ride make a great outing.

Beginners and lower intermediates are in one of the best European resorts for learning to ski. Here beginners can have the experience of taking a lift to the highest point, with all the thrill of the spectacular views, and still be able to get back down the mountain safely.

Advanced skiers will find challenging skiing on the back of the Biolley sector. There are plenty of spots for creative experts to go off trail and find more than enough to keep them busy for a week. Any expert will be challenged by the runs down the glacier. The more skill you have, the further off the basic trails you can venture. With good snow this glacier area is fantastic for even the best skiers.

Cross-country and snowshoe

The resort also has 80 km. of excellent cross-country trails. The cross country trails can be found running all along the base of the Alpine ski area from Les Coches to Plan Bois to Les Frasses to Plagne Bellecote to Plagne Centre to Le Fornelet to Plagne Montalbert and Longefoy.

On the Champagny-en-Vanoise side of the range, extensive cross-country skiing is available at Champagny le Haut with trails going into the Parc National de la Vanoise.

Plagne Montalbert and Montchavin-Les Coches also have a few cross-country skiing trails. Plagne Montalbert even has a themed trail where you can learn all there is to know about the mountain environment.

The ESF Champagny en Venoise provides snowhoe tours that cost €15 for two hours and €29 for four hours. There's also a night tour which includes a tradional meal at the Refuge du Bois that costs €36. Note: There is a minimum of five people to take the tour and these prices do not include the cost of equipment rental.

Ski school (2007/08 prices)

The La Plagne ski schools have 550 instructors available throughout the various village complexes. Prices vary depending on which program and village you select for lessons.

The following prices are for the **Ecole du Ski Francais de Champagny en Vanoise** (479 55 06 40, fax 479 55 07 55) and are similar to the prices of other ski schools in the area.

Private lessons for skiing, snowboarding, cross country and telemark for one to two people cost €35 per hour. For every month except February, private lessons for five or fewer people cost €95 for two hours; €165 for a half day; and €285 for a full day. For every month except February, private lessons for six to ten people cost €195 for a half day; and €335 for a full day.

Group lessons are for a three-day course from 9:30 a.m. to 1:30 p.m. cost €107. Lessons for six half days are also €107. Group snowboarding lessons cost €102 for a three-day course and €160 for a six-day course. Cross-country lessons (5-person minimum) costs €90 for five half days.

Lift tickets (2007/08 prices)

The La Plagne region has a lift ticket system that is made up of four sectors. Lift passes may be purchased for only the villages of Montchavin/Les Coches, Plagne Montalbert or Champagny. The La Plagne overall pass prices are below. Together with an inter-resort shuttle pass, the ticket will allow skiers to go virtually anywhere in the area.

	Adults	**Children (ages 6-13) & Seniors (ages 65-71)**
One day	€41	€31
Six days	€197.50	€148.50
Seven days	€223	€167.50

Who skis free: Children younger than age 6 and seniors age 71 and older.

There is a separate pass for Paradiski. It covers 425 km. of pistes and 2 glaciers in La Plagne, Les Arcs, Peisey-Vallandy and unlimited use of the Vanoise Express cablecar. Photo identification is required for passes of six days or more.

	Adults	Children (ages 6-13) & Seniors (ages 65-71)
One day	€46	€34.50
Six days	€237	€178
Seven days	€265	€199

This is just a basic price listing for the ski areas, but La Plagne has a variety of passes and discounts including some for families, freestylers, boarders, etc. Contact the resort for the best deal on the right ticket for you.

Accommodations

Rates here are daily rates for half-board based on double occupancy in February, unless otherwise indicated: €€€=€125+; €€=€57–€124; €=less than €75.

Hotel Mercure (479 09 12 09; fax 479 09 29 52; €–€€) Overall the atmosphere in Belle Plagne makes Mercure's location desirable, but what one gains in atmosphere one loses in choice of restaurants and shops. If you are a single and someone tells you that there will be no supplement, beware. "Half rooms" for singles with no supplement mean you share a shower and toilet with another unfortunate half-roomer.

Hotel Les Alpes in Aime (479 09 70 24; €) This small hotel has only 14 rooms.

The new **Chalet/Hotel Les Montagnettes** (479 55 12 00; fax 479 55 12 19; €€) in Belle Plagne has some wonderful apartments with more space than the older apartments in Plagne Centre. This is an upscale choice in the region.

In the villages there are two-star hotels. **Hotel l'Ancolie** (479 55 05 00; fax 479 55 04 42; €–€€) in Champagny has a great location right at the base of the cablecar. **Les Glières** (479 55 05 52; fax 479 55 04 84; €–€€) is also in Champagny. **Hotel Bellecote** (479 07 83 30; fax 479 07 80 63; €) in Montchavin has rooms by the week. **Hotel l'Aigle Rouge** (479 55 51 05; fax 479 55 51 14; €) in Plagne Montalbertis a good value. Children normally get a 30 to 50 percent discount in most hotels.

Ski Chalets: Crystal, Simply Ski, Thompson, Neilson (see page 16 for phone, fax and Internet addresses).

Apartments, condominiums, flats

Apartments are by far the most popular form of accommodation in La Plagne. There are more than 20 times the number of apartment beds than hotel beds. Accommodations range from tiny 17-square-meter rooms to spacious quarters. Two can make it without any trouble in a normal two-person French apartment but will be much more comfortable if they can afford to rent a place advertised for four. In Belle Plagne, a studio or one-bedroom apartment with plenty of room for two will run €255–€300 a week in January. There also are bargain weekly rates starting from only €210 per person, including ski lifts, lessons and equipment rental discounts (if more people share) in January. Such rates are hard to beat. For information call 479 09 79 79.

 ## Dining

Most of the restaurants listed below are in Plagne Center. Since Plagne Center is connected with both Aime La Plagne and Plagne Villages by cablecar and telebus, it serves as a center for these three complexes. The restaurants here prove that even in modern surroundings, small, cozy eating spots can be created with all the atmosphere and charm one might expect to find in a traditional town bistro. Although La Plagne is considered an economical resort by French standards, meals can still cost a bundle. Top restaurants here will run about €32–€35 for a full meal, excluding wine. The moderate restaurant meals run about €18–€25, including wine, and the inexpensive ones will have a fixed-price menu at about €15 without wine. For those looking for less expensive meals, try one of the crêperies or a pizzeria where a meal can end up costing as little as €10 with a beer.

Plagne Center

Le Bec Fin (479 09 10 86) offers excellent French cooking for a fixed-price menu of €10–€25. The decor is best by candlelight. English is spoken.

Le Chaudron (479 09 23 33), in the open field in the middle of Plagne Center, presents excellent grilled specialties cooked over an open fire in the middle of the dining room. Expect your meal to cost €20–€30.

Le Refuge (479 09 00 13) is the oldest in the resort. Photographs of bobsled champions cover the walls in the very local, very French bar out front. In the dining room each table is centered under a telescoping copper hood, which vents smoke while guests barbecue their own steaks at the table. Expect to spend about €10–€25.

Follow the Rue de la Gaité to discover three moderate to inexpensive restaurants: **L'Estaminet** (479 09 12 69) serves Alsatian specialties in huge portions; **La Metairie** (479 09 11 08) has Savoyard specialties on wooden tables with a fixed-priced menu of €13; and **L'Etable** serves excellent meat and Savoyard specialities as well in a very charming atmosphere (479 09 04 82).

Walk to the end of the hall and pick up—would you believe—a pizza to go at **Pizzeria Domino**.

Aime La Plagne

Here, our favorite is **l'Arlequin** (479 09 05 29). After winding down a circular staircase you will have the chance to sample pizza if you insist, but with a difference. They make a pizza *quattro formaggio* with four French cheeses; its owners also have created a smoked salmon pizza. One unique creation you've probably never tasted—*tagliatelli foie gras* — is served. Try the normal raclette and fondue or the special *rouergat*, a duck fondue where the duck is cooked in liver oil. Or order the "royal stone," a superheated rock upon which you grill mixed meat and foie gras. For the atmosphere, unique food and good service you'll end up spending €25–€35 and leave stuffed.

Au Bon Vleux Temps (479 09 20 57) on the slopes above Aime 2000 in a charming old chalet, offers specialties from €12 for lunch, or about €15 for dinner.

Belle Plagne

The most popular restaurant is **Le Matafan** (479 09 09 19), which is normally packed. Tables fan out around an open fire, country cupboards stand against the wall and lace curtains drape the windows. A series of eleven different luncheon plates are offered, including mountain ham, paté and cheese for €10 or an omelet with bacon, salad and fries for €11. Dinner portions are mountain-sized.

La Face Nord and **La Cloche** serves up good food in a less formal atmosphere. **K2**, which offers a meal plan for the Résidence Carene, has a €14 menu for good regional specialties.

Head to **The Cheyenne Café** for a taste of Tex/Mex at affordable prices.

Plagne 1800

La Mine (479 09 07 75) is perhaps the best gourmet-type restaurant with the average meal in the €32 range before you add wine. The elegant dining room with open fireplace and beamed ceiling accompany the upscale meals and price. **Loup Garou** (479 09 20 17) also offers tasty dinners. Be careful not to confuse the Loup Garou with Loup Blanc, which doesn't offer dishes quite as tasty.

Plagne Bellecote

La Ferme (479 09 29 32) has good local food with fish specialties.

On the slopes

There are 21 different mountain restaurants not including the restaurants in the complexes themselves, which offer excellent midday dining. Included are **Le Vega** (479 09 00 61), **La Galerne** (479 09 17 94) and **Le Chaudron** (479 09 23 33) in Plagne Center. Most of the mountain restaurants are self-service. **Le Biolley** (479 09 07 52) above Aime La Plagne gets the most sun. For sitdown meals, try **Le Val Sante** at the far left edge of the resort area and be ready to ski home slowly, stuffed with lots of great food. **L'Arpette** (479 09 15 40), just above Belle Plagne and recognizable by the motorbike hanging from the rafters, serves up good mountain food. **La Bergerie** (479 09 07 95) above Plagne Bellecote has a rustic atmosphere and pricey mid-mountain dining. **La Grande Rochette** (479 09 09 08), at the top of the gondola from Plagne Center, offers spectacular views at lunch and dinners on Thursday.

 ## Après-ski/nightlife

The **Showtime Cafe** (479 09 15 69) in Plagne Bellecote has live music some nights and karaoke on others.

The **No'Blem** (479 09 10 78) in Plagne Center is a coffee house offering concerts and a gathering place for the young crowd.

 ## Child care (2006/07 prices)

The ESF offers so many kindergartens, snow nurseries and clubs for kids and teens that we do not have room to list them all. More than 550 instructors conduct programs that take care of children ranging from 10 weeks to 18 years old. Programs and prices depend on which village you select. Contact the ESF for further information: Plagne Center (479 09 00 40, fax 479 09 20 87 for Place de la cheminée and 479 09 12 05, fax 479 09 16 36 for Immeuble Nanda Devi place de la Cheminée); Montchavin (4 79 07 83 54, fax 479 07 82 04); Montalbert (479 09 77 24, fax 479 09 71 00); Belle Plagne (479 09 06 68, fax 479 55 10 08); Champagny en Vanoise (479 55 06 40, fax 479 55 07 55); Plagne Villages (479 09 04 40, fax : 479 09 17 46); Aime la Plagne (479 09 04 75, fax 479 09 12 77); Plagne Bellecote (479 09 01 33; fax 479 09 05 91); Les Coches (479 07 80 33, fax 479 07 82 37); and Plagne Soleil (479 09 20 95, fax 479 09 16 45).

Nursery Marie-Christine in Plagne Center (479 09 11 81) takes children age 2-6 for about €40 a day, without meals, or €25 for a half day.

Belle Plagne nursery (479 09 06 68) accepts children eighteen months to 6 years. The nursery is closed on Saturday.

Children ages 18 months to 3 are welcomed at the nursery where they can enjoy themselves with drawing, games and toys, singing, videos and snowplay. One half day without meal is €35; one day without meal is €65; one day with meal is €95; six half days without meals are €151; six days without meals are €225; six days with meals are €340.

Children age 3–6 old have a ski kindergarten called Club Piou Piou. One morning is €49 and one afternoon is €46; six days without meals are €188; six days with meals are €338.

For older children (age 3-13), the ski school has special programs designed for young skiers. Never-evers can take a course that includes lifts for six days for €237. Six full-day lessons will cost €188.

Other activities

The **heated pool** in Plagne Bellecote is open from 3:30 p.m. to 7 p.m. The **ice rinks** in Plagne Bellecote, Aime la Plagne and Les Coches are open from 2:30 p.m. to 7 p.m.; on Wednesdays and Fridays they're open to 11:30 p.m.

In Champagny en Vanoise, there is a 22-meter artificial ice tower for advanced training in **climbing**. You can also **paraglide** over the skiable terrain.

Rent **squash courts** in Plagne 1800 at Maeva reception.

The Olympic **bobsled run** for the 1992 games, makes La Plagne the official bobsled capital of the Alps. Visitors can take a hair-raising, 80-kilometer-per-hour plunge down the 19 curves of the track in a special (safe) sled when the track is not being used for competition. There is also the option of **taxi-bobbing** — taking a 90-kilometer per hour ride with a professional — or going it alone in a **mono-bob**.

There are English-speaking doctors in the Plagne Centre medical center. It is open 8:30 a.m.–7 p.m.

Getting there

Local transport: Plagne Centre to Aime La Plagne is served by a telemetro 8 a.m.–1 a.m. Plagne Center and Plagne Village has a telebus from 8 a.m.–1 a.m. Plagne Center and Plagne 1800/Bellecote are connected by shuttlebus on the hour and half hour, 8:30 a.m.–12:30 a.m. Bellecote–Belle Plagne cablecar links Belle Plagne from 8 a.m.–1 a.m. Bellecote–Plagne 1800–Plagne Center are connected by a shuttlebus at quarter past and quarter to the hour, 8:45 a.m.–12:45 a.m. **Telebus** is approximately €3 for two trips. The Telemetro and shuttlebus are free.
Taxi: Christian Bouzon (479 09 03 41); Taxi Silvestre (479 09 70 58); or Champagny Taxi (479 55 05 28).

Tourist information

La Plagne Tourist Information and Reservations:
The tourist information office is in Aime, in the valley. Send mail to Bureau de Tourisme de La Plagne, BP 36, 73210 La Plagne, France.
Country code: 0033
Telephone: 479 09 79 79
Fax: 479 09 70 10
Internet: www.la-plagne.com
E-mail:bienvenue@la-plagne.com

Megève

Megève exudes old-fashioned charm with narrow streets, small squares, trendy boutiques, quality antique shops, crowded bistros, dozens of small hotels, even an old-style bakery filling the town square with the fragrance of fresh bread. The small village is huddled around the old church, a medieval tower and the town hall. The upper crust of Europe and especially France make Megève their winter home when cold weather forces them to abandon the Riviera. Furs are the coats of choice for strolling past shop windows. The latest fashions are found on the slopes during the day, in expensive gourmet restaurants and some of France's best discos and nightclubs after dark. You can spend your nights bouncing to the beat in packed jazz clubs or wandering the romantic streets listening to the jingle of bells and the clip-clop of horses.

Like Zermatt, Megève has a look that Walt Disney might have imagined had he created a ski resort. The atmosphere is almost storybook: from its Old World town buildings to its narrow streets, from its art deco deluxe hotels to its perfect French country inns, and from its gourmet restaurants to its pulsing late-night casinos and discos. Megève hits all the notes between hedonistic excess and traditional ski-village delight.

For skiers, Megève's own ski area is relatively uninspiring, but the town has leveraged its ambiance with the slopes of neighboring towns, creating an area with exceptional variety of terrain. It links the slopes of neighboring Saint-Gervais-les-Bains, St. Nicolas de Véroce, Les Contamines, La Giettaz and Combloux. There's something for every level of skier with an overall skiing domain of almost 278 miles of trails including 43 km. of cross-country pistes.

Mountain layout—Skiing

When the snow cooperates, the region has some of the most varied skiing you can find in Europe. Megève lies at a low elevation, which can be a serious drawback in winters with little snow. But this can also be a blessing, offering more comfortable skiing for the entire winter without the chilling cold found in higher resorts. With this in mind, Megève has one of the most extensive snowmaking operations in France.

Priority areas on any expert's list should be Mont Joly and Mont Joux. Both peaks are actually in the St. Gervais area, but the St. Gervais and the Megève ski runs are so well-integrated that the connection is seamless. The two peaks separating Megève from St. Gervais are lined with black- and red-rated runs, as well as excellent off-trail drops down toward Le Gouet in St. Nicolas de Véroce. A favorite from the top of Mont Joly is the liftline, which starts from the 7,637-foot summit of the lift and drops precipitously to the base at 6,107 feet. You have one real choice coming down, and it's black all the way. Nearby, a shorter run that descends from the Epaule lift is also rated black. To the right and left of both runs are wide open steeps with off-trail action.

From atop the Mont Joux lift there are a half dozen runs down to St. Nicolas. These runs shift from steep to mellow, starting from wide-open snowfields and ending in tree-lined trails. You can also descend the other side of Mont Joux and back into Megève.

The Mont d'Arbois summit offers a mix of black, red and blue runs. The summit is served by four lifts on the Megève side and by another four climbing up from St. Gervais. The eight-person gondola serving the Princesse area has many great cruising runs perfect to warm up your edges before hitting the more challenging slopes over towards Mont Joly.

Across the plateau from Mont d'Arbois rising above Megève are three peaks—Rochebrune, Alpette and Cote 2000. This series of peaks offers another varied system of runs. The best is a descent from the Rochebrune summit through the trees and back to the valley station. Experts can test themselves skiing from Cote 2000 down to the altiport on black and red runs. Beginners and basic intermediates can enjoy a field day with the swooping runs from the Alpette peak.

The third area served by the Megève pass is Le Jaillet. This lift system is half owned by the town of Combloux. It is best suited to beginners and lower intermediates who are gaining confidence or for experienced skiers who want to spend some time playing and cruising down mellow slopes. Advanced beginners and lower intermediates will find Le Jaillet, at 5,576 feet, ideal.

There are also four black-rated runs. Most scenic of the black runs is the mile-long trail (6,133 feet) from Christomet. Our favorite on this side is the run through the woods along the Creve Coeur lifts just below Le Jaillet summit.

Skiers who are looking for more of a challenge than the Jaillet should head over to the steep slopes in the 25-km. expansion area that extends from the Jaillet side to La Giettaz.

If you find yourself lost or in need of directions, look around for the blue and yellow jacketed "ambassadeurs". Two of these locals are on the slopes of each section of Megève (Mt. d'Arbois, Rochebrune, Jaillet) every day. They are at your service. Most of them speak both French and English.

Mountain layout—Snowboarding

Megève generally caters to beginning and intermediate snowboarders, but advanced riders can find enough to keep busy in the terrain parks or off piste on the Cote 2000 chairlift. All of the trails are groomed, so moguls aren't a problem. There are two snow parks: one on Mont Joux and the other is on the Combloux section. The better of the two parks is on Mont Joux, which has a manmade pipe and an on-duty pro lending shovels to the kids constantly modifying and doctoring the jumps. On weekends the park offers music and the best local tricksters showing off their big air skills. Though Megève is generally not a destination for the younger crowd, as the final cost of even a few days vacation can substantially dent a budget, there are pubs and discos for anyone looking for a late-night party. Rental and tuning shops are abundant, and snowboarding lessons are readily available with the ski school.

Mountain rating

Taken together, Megève's mountains offer several challenges and make the area an acceptable destination for the expert skier who realizes that this is no Chamonix or Val d'Isère. (Although if you're skiing on a Mont Blanc ski pass, Chamonix is a possibility any day of the week.) Intermediates and those trying to push to the advanced level should find this a great place to improve and test their skills.

Beginners should go to Megève without hesitation. There's enough good skiing at the lower ability level to keep them going until the improvements come. Then it's on up the mountain with the big boys and girls.

Ski school (2007/08 prices)

About 200 teachers are registered in the Megève area. Large ski classes are conducted by schools in Megève, notably the French Ski School (450 21 00 97), Ski School International (450 58 78 88), St. Gervais (450 47 76 08) and Combloux (450 58 60 49).

Group lessons: Five two-and-a-half hour morning lessons will cost €142.

Snowboarding: Five three-hour courses are €142. Six four-hour courses are €252. Six two-an-a-half lessons cost €180.

Private lessons: One to two people cost €39 for one hour. Three to five people cost €50 for one hour. One to five people cost €330 for a full day.

Cross-country instruction costs the same as downhill. There is also the Ecole Freeride (450 93 03 52) that offers lessons for children from 4–12 years individually or in groups (six people maximum).

Lift tickets (2007/08 prices)

The Megève only pass is €26 for a half day and €33 for a full day. To access any of the lifts, you must first pass through a gate that verifies that you have bought a ticket. Megève is one of the few resorts that offer the "no-hands" system: as you pass through the gate, it detects your ticket, which can be in your pocket or in your wallet.

For cross-country skiing, a child under 16 can discover all the resort has to offer for about €4 per day. An adult's ticket will cost about €6.

Note: The Evasion Mont-Blanc ski pass also includes the Megève area. It is by far the best lift-ticket bargain. In addition to Megève, it covers St. Gervais Bettex, St. Nicolas, La Giettaz, Combloux and Les Contamines. It comprises 111 lifts, more than 445 km. of prepared runs and free skibus shuttle service within Megève and Combloux. Children are ages 5–14. Seniors are age 60 and older. Here are the prices.

	Adults	**Children**	**Seniors**
One day	€34.50	€27.50	€31.50
Two days	€65.50	€52.50	€59.50
Six days	€166	€133	€149.50
Six days "liberty"	€187	€149.50	€169

Accommodations

Megève has the best collection of upscale, beautiful, elegant hotels of any ski resort in Europe or in the world, for that matter. In style they range from avant-garde and art deco palaces to gilt-and-velvet luxury to rustic French provincial. Rates based on one person double occupancy in February €€€=€125+; €€=€75–€124; €=less than €74.

Chalet du Mont d'Arbois (450 21 25 03, fax 450 21 24 79; €€€) is a small, super-luxurious, chalet/hotel owned by the Baron and Baroness Rothschild. Guests are treated like personal guests rather than hotel residents. Imagine yourself moving into your own mountain chalet with a lot of mountain wood and priceless antiques.

Lodge Park (450 93 05 03, fax 450 93 09 52; €€€) provides the style of a North American lodge. It has a very classy bar and a warm and comfortable atmosphere.

Les Fermes de Marie (450 93 03 10, fax 450 93 09 84; €€€) is not just a hotel; it is a phenomenon. Jocelyne (a painter and designer) and Jean-Louis Sibuet (a builder) have created a private hamlet just five minutes from the town center. Farmhouses from across France were painstakingly taken apart and reassembled here. There are 69 bedrooms, three restaurants, living rooms, a library and bar, and a spa with an indoor pool along with a wide range of spa treatments. The food is excellent. One restaurant specializes in cheese dishes with hearty, local tartiflette and fondue always on the menu. The rooms and suites are tastefully decorated, often with paintings by Jocelyn Sibuet.

In addition to the main hotel complex, the owners, who also operate Au Coin du Feu, have opened two large luxury residences just outside of town called **Les Fermes du Grand Champ** (450 93 03 10, fax 450 93 09 84; €€€+) that can be rented by one or more families. These residences are spacious and decorated with antiques. They have saunas, swimming pool, garage, private meal service and other amenities. The larger chalet sleeps eight to 10 people and includes an office, covered swimming pool and fitness room. It rents for €6,900 to €10,500 per week, depending on the season.

Hotel le Fer à Cheval (450 21 30 39, fax 450 93 07 60; €€€) is like a French country cottage. Every highlight is rendered in wood. The furniture is rustic. The walls are covered in country-patterned fabrics and stencils. Even the doors are hand-painted.

Au Coin du Feu (450 21 04 94, fax 450 21 20 15; €€–€€€) is a country-perfect setting, owned by the brother of the Fer à Cheval's proprietor, with similar French country touches. In the restaurant, wooden cupboards line the walls, alternating with stone arches around a fireplace. The hotel has 23 rooms many of which are minisuites.

Hotel La Prairie (450 21 48 55, fax 450 21 42 13; €€) is an excellent, three-star B&B in Megève. The chalet-style building is bright and spacious. The rooms are simple with heavy wooden doors and pine highlights. Every room has a TV, and you are an easy five-minute walk from the center of town.

Week-End (450 21 26 49, fax 450 21 26 51; €–€€) is a B&B next door to Coin du Feu, about a five-minute walk up a relatively steep hill from the town center. The rooms have been redone and almost every room has an extra bed for a child or third person. Perhaps something as simple as getting rid of the chenille bedspreads would make the Week-End look more up-scale, as it should be. The owner speaks excellent English.

La Chaumine (450 21 37 05, fax 450 21 37 21; €–€€), just a short walk from the center of town near the Chamoir cablecar, is an inexpensive, newly renovated, two-star hotel. This old restored farm B&B is cozy and charming.

Another excellent possibility for rooms in a newer, very attractive Alpine hotel is **La Grange d'Arly** (450 58 77 88, fax 450 93 07 13; €).

Megève Reservation books rooms, apartments or chalets (450 21 29 52, fax 450 91 85 67). Altogether there are 35 hotels in town, although not all are open year-round.

Apartments, condominiums, flats

Write to the Megève tourist office (see Tourist Information), which will contact the major rental organizations in town. You will hear from several—make your pick and let the agencies know your decision. Mid-January, expect to pay about €330–€500 a week for a three-star apartment. In February the price will be €650–€1,200 a week. During the Christmas holiday apartments are rented for two-week periods and will cost €1,300–€1,600 for a four-star apartment. Linen is an additional €22 a week.

Dining

You won't have any problem getting excellent food—there are eight Michelin-rated and 11 Gault Millau-listed restaurants.

Flocons de Sel (450 21 49 99) is an upscale restaurant with cuisine from all over France. It has gained a great reputation, rating one star in the Michelin Guide. Clients drive from hours away to dine there. Reservations are highly recommended.

Chalet du Mont d'Arbois (450 21 25 03) belongs to Baron Rothschild. Enjoy Michelin two-fork meals in a country atmosphere created by heavy beams and soaring, stuccoed arches. The chalet claims one of the best wine cellars in Megève. A meal will cost €40–€60.

Le Prieure (450 21 01 79) is nestled between the church and the priory on the main square. This spot is as cozy a dining atmosphere as it gets.

Les Fermes de Marie (450 93 03 10) serves fine French meals and cheese specialties in a French country atmosphere.

Le Cintra (450 21 02 60) has a seafood bar in a lively ambiance.

St. Nicolas (450 21 41 79) is a restaurant in the basement of the Hotel Au Coin du Feu. Giant wooden cupboards, armoires and stone basement arches provide a real country touch. The chef serves up Savoyard country specialties. Expect to pay €40.

Fer à Cheval Restaurant (450 21 30 39) in the hotel of the same name also has a very rustic country feel. Country cooking with a Savoyard gourmet flair will cost about €35–€40 per person for dinner.

Les Drets (450 21 31 78), better known as "Chez Lou-Lou," gets a lot of repeat customers who claim they return because of the owners. Driving there is easiest. It's on the road to Cote 2000 just before you get to the altiport (a small area on the mountain with runway and lot for pilots who have their own small planes). Pilots must have special training to use the altiport, but you can also get there from the slopes if you're willing to take a short walk. It is open only for lunch, which starts at €15.

For local mountain specialties of fondue, raclette and *pela* (a regional country dish of pan-fried potatoes and bacon covered with melted cheese and served in the pan with a selection of mountain-dried beef and sausages), make sure to visit the following two small restaurants within a one-minute walk of each other.

Le Chamois (450 21 25 01), next to the church and old town tower, specializes in cheese fondue at about €15.50 per person. Unlike most restaurants, Le Chamois will serve a single guest who arrives with a fondue craving.

Les Marronniers (450 21 22 01) is a tiny rustic cafe at the opposite end of the building that houses Le Chamois. Wooden walls are lined with hundreds of colorful old pastel coffee pots. Raclette is served the old-fashioned way—scraped off with a knife—for about €18. They also serve crêpes, gallettes (thick pancakes) and omelettes.

For eating on the mountain we have recommendations for each area. The best overall is **L'Alpette** between Rochebrune and Cote 2000 (450 21 03 69). **La Petite Coterie** in Le Bettex (450 93 14 40) is also excellent. Both will be crowded in high season, so you should make reservations. On the top of Mont d'Arbois, choose from refined dining at **Ideal 1850** (450 21 31 26) with its south-facing terrace or try the **Igloo** self-service (450 93 53 36) next to the upper station of the Princesse lift. On top of Mont Joux, the **Espace Mont Joux** (450 58 99 67) has great views of Mont Blanc, and **La Cote 2000** (450 21 31 84) near the altiport. **Super Megève** (450 21 22 05) at the top of Rochebrune has a 360-degree view and a big terrace for lunches in the sun.

Across the valley on the Jaillet Massif, try **La P'tite Ravine** (450 21 38 67). It's right on the slopes and has a cozy, familiar atmosphere.

Head to **La Ferme de Chateluy** (06 09 30 54 15), a restored historic farm, where the toilet is literally in the woodshed and the salads and desserts are top-notch. It is off the Chateluy blue run from the top of the Bettex gondola. Follow the little sign to the left of the blue run—a tiny path leads directly to the restaurant.

Also notable for its straight-on view of Mont Blanc, **Au Petit Montagnard** (450 93 25 09) offers a tomato fondue specialty.

Near the bottom of the ladies' Olympic downhill course and on the cross-country trails, the **Cote 2000** (450 21 31 84) offers local specialties in a Savoyard chalet.

For the best bread for miles, head to "Le Refuge du Boulanger" where the bread is made before your eyes. If you're out late one night, drop by and you may get some "pain au chocolat" fresh from the oven.

Après-ski/nightlife

Despite the rustic atmosphere, Megève is modern in all aspects. Discos pulse and lights flash, keeping beat with the thumping music. The live entertainment ranges from France's top singers and entertainers to local musicians and bands. It all continues until at least 4 a.m.

At **Bar Cocoon**, there's a small dance floor and if you're lucky you might stumble upon some live music. For a little pasta and some tapas try **La Wake Up**.

Discos don't get rolling until after midnight, so don't plan to tackle Megève nightlife after an eight o'clock dinner. If you're looking for packed dance floors, you're going to have to wait until about 1:30 a.m.

About 7 p.m., head to the **Jazz Club Les 5 Rues** in the tiny back streets of Megève and prepare yourself for great jazz. The **Cave de Megève** also has jazz.

The recently redecorated **casino** opens at 5 p.m. but doesn't really get going until about midnight.

The two main discos are **White Pearl** and **Palo Alto**, situated right in the center of town so club hopping is easy. Be aware that visitors are expected to be dressed nicely in high season, White Pearl is a standard disco; check the posters around town for theme nights. If you're looking for action, reserve a table at Palo Alto (450 91 82 58) which is always ready to accommodate more people thanks to the walls, which expand and contract depending on the amount of people inside.

Child care (2007/08 prices)

Meg' Accueil Enfance (450 58 77 84) kindergarten near the Jaillet runs is for children 12 months to 12 years old and costs €40 with lunch.

Club des Piou-Piou De La Caboche (450 58 97 65), on the Rochebrune slope next to the Caboche cablecar, gives beginning ski lessons to kids ages 3–6. Prices range from €87 for a full day with lunch and €33 for a half day without lunch. Reservations are required.

The tourist office maintains a list of multilingual babysitting services.

Other activities

Megève and the neighboring villages draw many nonskiers who walk throughout the area. **Walkways** are better kept than most you'll encounter at other Alpine resorts. Stores are perfect for **window shopping**, but prices can destroy budgets. **Day outings** to Chamonix or Geneva are popular—both are only about an hour away.

Megève has an excellent sports center with **skating**, **swimming** in your choice of two covered pools, **saunas**, **fitness rooms**, covered **tennis** and **golf** practice ranges, **indoor climbing** wall and **curling**. Rates for adults for the Sports Center are normally €4.60 for skating and swimming. For children, the entrance fee is €3.60. Tennis courts can be reserved by calling 450 21 15 71 and will cost €13 per court-hour or €60 for six coupons which are good for six hours of court time.

The outdoor **skating rink** in the center of town costs €4.60 for adults and €3.60 for kids. If you are lucky, you may have a chance to enjoy **ice bumper cars**.

Paragliding is available through the "Compagnie des Guides" (450 21 55 11) for €65. They also offer **snowshoeing**. Ask for the trek full of breathtaking views once traveled by the Romans. (450 21 55 11). **Sightseeing airplane flights** over the Mont Blanc range are also popular and cost about €29 per person for a 10-minute flight to €116 for a 40-minute flight. The **bowling** alley (450 21 18 40) is a three-minute drive from the center of town right next to the major supermarket.

There are a variety of **dogsledding** adventures (450 21 37 03) for those who want to just sit back and enjoy the ride and those who want to grab hold of the reigns.

An annual **"polo sur neige"** tournament takes place during the second week in January. In mid-March players travel from all over the world to play in the only **golf tournament held in the snow**. The golf course opens to the public in the summer.

Getting there and getting around

Geneva is the main arrival airport; from there it is about an hour and a half by car to Megève. Scheduled bus service runs from the Geneva airport.

Trains run to Sallanches, 13 km. away, where bus and taxi services are available. The TGV makes the run from Paris in only five hours. A bus from the Sallanches train station to Megève will cost about €4.50.

If you drive into town, there are three large parking garages—two right in the center of town—so parking is no hassle. The free local bus system gives access to the different hotels and the lift base areas—Rochebrune, Jaillet, Mont d'Arbois and Cote 2000.

For more picturesque views, hire a horse-drawn cart from the Place de L'eglise.

Tourist information

Office du Tourisme, rue Monseigneur Conseil, F-74120 Megève
Telephone 450 21 27 28, fax 450 93 03 09.
E-mail: megeve@megeve.com Internet: www.megeve.com

Office du Tourisme, F-74920 Combloux
Telephone 450 58 60 49, fax 450 93 33 55.
Office du Tourisme, F-74190 Le Fayet; 450 93 64 64.

Office du Tourisme de St. Gervais, F-74170 St. Gervais
Telephone 450 47 76 08; fax 450 47 75 69.

Morzine/Avoriaz

Portes du Soleil, France

About an hour and a half from Geneva just south of the lake, Morzine and Avoriaz anchor the French side of Portes du Soleil. This region vies for the title "largest ski area in Europe," with 206 interconnected lifts servicing a mind-boggling 650 km. of runs sprawling across 14 areas – eight in France and in Switzerland. There are 286 marked ski runs as well as 243 km. of cross-country trails.

Traditional Morzine is the largest settlement of Les Portes du Soleil, with 3,000 residents, 54 hotels, 39 restaurants and 25 ski shops. Although Morzine is at a relatively low 3,000 feet, a network of lifts reaches the panoramic Chamossière at 6,006 feet. And Avoriaz, at 7,080 feet, is a mere cablecar ride away. Free shuttles now connect the center of Morzine with all the lift systems.

Morzine attracts an English-speaking crowd, so rudimentary English is widely spoken, a plus for Americans who don't want to grapple with French.

The old part of town, dating back to the 16th century, rises to a 19th-century church and the tumbling Dranse River. With its own Gallic identity, the town is a pleasant place for walking and relaxing. Although nightlife lacks the glamour of Megève or Courchevel, there is plenty to do with two discos, two cinemas, many bars and an ice-skating arena that has hosted the world's top skaters.

Most out-of-towners come in for the standard Saturday-to-Saturday week. Be sure to stop by the Tourism office all day Sundays for free hot chocolate and local cheeses. This is a good time to get the weekly entertainment brochoure and any maps you may need for the week. During the high seasons (Christmas and Febuary), you may want to check out the "History of Skiing" program at Pleney every Tuesday, night skiing every Thursday, or the *Decente au Flambeaux* when at the end of the day the ESF instructors ski down the mountain with flaming torches.

Avoriaz 1800

More than just a lodge or restaurant at the top of the cablecar, car-free Avoriaz (pronunciation: Avoriah) sits perched above steep rock cliffs at 5,400 feet with a racy angular outline that the French call "integrated architecture." By any name, it's visually spectacular; a village in the snow, where sleighs and skis replace cars and where the condominiums, hotels, restaurants, shops and cafés are all truly ski-in/ski-out.

Jean Vuarnet, the sunglass king, returned to France with a gold medal from the 1960 Olympics at Squaw Valley and persuaded a big real estate agency to invest in the altitudinous Avoriaz 1800. The original structures of 1966 have now grown to a cluster of 42 modern condos, a Club Med, three hotels and 30 restaurants.

Avoriaz's Children's Village, managed by Olympic-medalist Annie Famose and a staff of 120 instructors, is acclaimed for teaching youngsters age 3-16 to ski.

Avoriaz 1800 is at the center of the Les Portes Du Soleil wheel, the main link between France and Switzerland. The question becomes, "Do you go there to ski, for a meal, for a drink and a look around," or "Do you stay?" In the old days, getting there meant climbing into a cablecar and then taking a reindeer-drawn sled to your room. Today, there are a number of choices. A road climbs up from Morzine – 14 km. and a half-hour drive away for those with cars. For those without, a gondola and two ski lifts reach from the heart of Morzine up to the Avoriaz hub – a 25-minute trip on skis. You can also take a free bus from Morzine to the cablecar base. The cablecar runs every 15 minutes and continues well into the evening for those who want to explore one town or the other. Finally, those planning an extended stay in Avoriaz may choose to arrive by bus from Geneva and avoid the parking fees and hassle of having a car here since you really don't need a car here.

Mountain layout—Skiing

Morzine-Avoriaz is a good base from which to explore the Portes du Soleil area. As well as easy access to the Les Crosets/Champoussin sector via the Swiss Wall, Avoriaz has easy access to Plaine Dranse, which has perhaps the most enjoyable and varied skiing of the region. The slopes directly above Avoriaz will challenge skiers of every level. Another plus: Avoriaz has been aggressively replacing older lifts with high-speed quads and six-seated lifts, which make lines rare here. You can easily spend a couple of days just on the Morzine/Les Gets slopes, which offer a nice mix of terrain and are especially popular with families. Beginners go to Le Pleney, which is a one-stop ascent by cablecar. Nyon has a nice mix of black, red and blue descents. Chamossière has outstanding views, good long black runs and some fine cruising through the Col de Joux Plane. Le Ranfolly has four side-by-side red runs while La Rosta is ideal for parties of different abilities. Mt. Chéry, reached by a ground connection from the Les Gets base, is best for advanced skiers.

Some of the most enjoyable and challenging skiing of the entire Portes du Soleil is best accessed from Morzine and Avoriaz. In France: Pointe de Nyon, Chamossière and Col du Fornet; and in Switzerland: Planachaux, Grand Paradis, and Champéry are all classic higher altitude alpine peaks, each with difficult descents. There are many places in the Portes du Soleil where a simple 15-minute hike can get you expert couloirs and powdery bowls. If you are looking for the most expert terrain in these mountains, plan to go with an avalanche-savvy guide. Otherwise, try The Wall of Death between Avoriaz and Switzerland. Appropriately named for it's difficulty, this descent can be exciting. It can be skied by an intermediate when the snow cover is good because there are broad segments for traverses and turns. Fearful skiers can take the chairlift down. The Swiss Wall at the top of Chavanette in Switzerland is another difficult descent. Be sure your knees are up to it, though, because this run is one of the longest mogul fields in the area. Be forewarned that the lifts on the Swiss side have not been updated like their French counterparts. When skiing from one side to the other, allow plenty of time to return. It's a long, expensive cab ride back if you get stuck.

In Morzine there is night skiing and riding at the Pléney from 8 –10 p.m. It is free for anyone with a lift ticket.

Mountain layout–Snowboarding

Morzine/Avoriaz has everything a boarder could want: few drag lifts, quality snow parks, endless off-piste opportunities and well-groomed trails for all caliber riders. Les Portes du Soleil also devotes five or six runs every year to boardercross courses.

The Portes du Soleil stations are well connected; there are few cat tracks and no tough traverses. You will never have to take your board off to hike. As a boarder, you can go all over the area without having to worry about time spent "getting there" because wherever you go, you will be riding good slopes the whole way. If you are looking for some good tree riding, hit the open forests under the Prolays, Brocheaux and Lindarets lifts in Avoriaz, or, when there is enough snow, much of the lower runs in Champery in Switzerland. For backcountry riding, hire a guide to take you down into La Vallee de la Manche, the valley between the Avoriaz 1800 and the Morzine mountain masses. After a little hike from the top of Pointe de Nyon or from Col du Fornet, above Avoriaz 1800, the descent is remote and fresh tracks are easy to find. Either way, the beginning of the run is one big powder field, and the end finds you bouncing through open forests. Don't go without prior preparations for a ride back waiting for you at the bottom of the run.

Riders now have a new boardercross course at Nyon near Morzine. Most will head to the wide-open snowfields above Avoriaz where there are three snowparks as well as halfpipes to keep riders very busy. Snowboarders also have a special pass for Avoriaz allowing access to the snowpark and the cablecar.

For anyone looking for riding through trees, the place to head is the region above Les Gets where trees drop down to the town.

Mountain Rating

The sheer size of Les Portes du Soleil allows for anyone to find his or her niche at the areas. A good mixed bag of skiing opportunities awaits, and most trails can be enjoyed by an intermediate. With wide, above-treeline slopes and trails that descend to the village through the forest, this region lets you enjoy the full experience of skiing.

Morzine is a very good place for beginners — relaxed and wide-open. The variety of lifts and terrain makes sometimes less than challenging runs interesting.

Avoriaz has some of the best beginner facilities in the Portes du Soleil region. For experts, Avoriaz has what locals call *sauvage* or wide open, all-terrain, all-condition descents. Intermediates will never have to ski the same run twice. (See Mountain Rating in the Swiss Portes du Soleil chapter.)

Cross-Country and snowshoeing

There are four cross-country areas accessible from Morzine, Avoriaz and the surrounding area: the Manche Valley with 25 km. of challenging circuits, the Morzine-Avoriaz sector with 47 km. for all levels, Lake Montriond with 10 km. of Canadian-style runs, the Pléney - Chavannes sector with 8.5 km. of forest runs. There is no cross country trail fee, but you must buy a special cross-country pass to use the ski lifts which provide access to these sectors.

The ESF (Ecole de Ski Français; 450 79 13 13), the Ecole Ski Snowboard et Aventures (450 79 05 16), Franck Herbron (450 79 02 32), Relief - Véronique Fillon - Olivier Druelle (450 75 74 33) and Alpi'Raquette – Hervé Lesobres (619 42 95 57), Damien Trombert (630 36 46 53) organize **snowshoe treks** starting from Morzine. Tours range from half-day hikes to all-day adventures ending with cheese fondue in a high-mountain chalet.

In Avoriaz, the E.S.F. (450 74 05 65) or Ecole de Ski Internationale (450 74 02 18) offer snowshoe tours starting at €22 for a half-day. Price includes equipment.

Ski school (2006/07 prices)

There are eight ski schools in Avoriaz and Morzine. The Ecole de Ski Francais (ESF) has locations in both Morzine (450 79 13 13, fax 450 79 17 70, info@esf-morzine.com) and Avoriaz (450 74 05 65, fax 450 74 10 14, info@esf-avoriaz.com). In Morzine, there are 140 instructors who teach one quarter of Morzine's visitors. The office and meeting place is at the bottom of the Pleney cablecar. In Avoriaz, you can sign up for lessons in the Place du Telepherique, in the Tourist Office or in the Cap-Neige building near Fontaines Blanches. The meeting place is either at the Place du Telepherique (at the bottom of the Plateau chairlift) or on the Plateau near the Plateau chairlift and the Dromonts ski lift. Ski passes are not included in the lesson prices, and the prices do not vary much between Morzine and Avoriaz.

The following are the prices for the Ecole de Ski Francais (ESF) **Avoriaz**.

Group lessons: Half days 9:30 a.m.–noon or 2:30 p.m.–5 p.m. for adults cost €31 in the afternoon and €28 in the morning. Six mornings are €111 and six afternoons are €122. A full day costs €39. For children (during the school holiday period), the price is €25.50 in the afternoon and €23 in the morning. Six mornings are €100 and six afternoons are €108. A full day costs €32.

Private lessons: One hour costs €38 for one or two skiers; €48 for three to five skiers. If you take private lessons during group lesson hours the price jumps to: one hour, €38 for one or two skiers; €48 for three to five skiers.

Snowboarding lessons for adults cost €110 for six half days and €30 for one half day. For children, they cost €96 for six half days and €25 for one half day.

Freeriding lessons cost €150 for three and a half hours of guided touring across the Portes du Soleil region for one to five people. Cross-country lessons cost €26 in the afternoon and €21 in the morning. Six mornings are €88 and six afternoons are €115.

Morzine

Ecole de Ski & Snowboard International (E2SA; 450 79 05 16, fax 450 79 09 36) in Morzine is slightly more expensive than ESF, as lessons are taught in smaller groups (maximum of eight people). The office is a few doors down from ESF, and meeting points vary according to the kind of lesson.

Freeride lessons: (ski or snowboard) €60 for one day (two and a half hours) or €150 for five days (two and a half hours).

They offer good guides for the Valee Blanche and other off piste trips in France and Switzerland. They also have half and full days of heliskiing.

Lift tickets (2007/08 prices)

The lift ticket system in the Portes de Soleil is a hands-free pass (price: €3) that you can keep in a pocket. Simply pass by a scanner that picks up data from a computer chip on the ticket and ride. This system makes it easy to add time or regions to your ski pass electronically at any ticket office.

	Portes du Soleil		
	Adult	**Child**	**Senior**
1 day	€39	€26	€31
3 days	€108	€72	€86
5 days	€165	€111	€132
7 days	€211	€141	€169

	Morzine/Les Gets			Avoriaz		
	Adult	Child	Senior	Adult	Child	Senior
1 day	€28.20	€22	€23.60	€32	€21.50	€24.70
3 days	€103	€69	€60.90	**	**	**
5 days	€157	€105	€96.50	**	**	**
7 days	€179	€120	€126.30	**	**	**

The age for children is 5–15 years old. Identification is required for skiers age 12 and older. Seniors are age 60 and older. Children younger than age 5 ski free.

AXA Snow Risq Neige assistance insurance costs €2.90 per day for an adult and €2.40 per day for a child.

Snowboarders can get a lift pass that gives them access to a few chairlifts around the snowparks in Avoriaz.

Accommodations

Rates: half-board for one based on double occupancy with half board. €€€=€125+; €€=€75–€124; €=less than €75.

Our recommended hotels in Morzine:

Les Airelles (450 74 71 21; fax 450 79 17 49; €€€) is modern, well-designed, and centrally located, with a big swimming pool, and toilet and phone in each of its 55 rooms. It has a big swimming pool and a fitness room.

Le Champs Fleuris (450 79 14 44; 450 79 27 75; €€€) has an indoor pool, tennis, a sauna and a fitness room.

Le Dahu (450 75 92 92; 450 75 92 50; €€€) has similar amenities to Le Champs Fleuris for just a bit less per night.

Le Tremplin (450 79 12 31, fax 450 75 95 70; €€€) has a friendly atmosphere and a pleasant sitting area and bar next to the slopes.

La Bergerie (450 79 13 69, fax 450 75 95 71; €€) is a residence hotel without a restaurant, but has rooms with kitchenettes as well as telephone, television, a parking garage, sauna and an outdoor swimming pool.

Just outside downtown, **Chalet Philibert** (450 79 25 18; €€) has 18 rooms – including three suites – all with television, safe, radio, hairdryer and telephone. It also has a pool, sauna, Jacuzzi, fitness room and an excellent dining room.

Le Carlina (450 79 01 03; fax 450 75 94 11; €–€€) is near the center of town and the lifts.

Le Sporting (04 50 79 15 03fax 450 79 11 25 €) is also near the center of town and has a pool, sauna and fitness room.

Similar but just outside of town is **Le Petit Cheval Blanc** (450 79 13 89). Enjoy a nice swim in the pool after coming in from the slopes. Here, your day will start out right with a complimentary breakfast that hits the spot.

Bel 'Alpe (04 50 79 05 50; fax 450 79 22 76; €), **Hermine Blanche** (450 75 76 55; fax 450 74 72 47; €), and **Les Côtes** (450 79 09 96; fax 450 75 97 38; €) are all affordable excellent places to stay.

Also in Morzine is **Le Mas De La Coutettaz, the "Farmhouse"** (450 79 08 26; fax 450 79 18 53; €€), an 18th-century manor house. It's the oldest building in the valley with six spacious rooms. English tea is served in the afternoon, and at night guests sit around an expansive table for a family-style four-course dinner with wine.

In nearby Les Gets (part of the Portes du Soleil region) try **Hotel Labrador** (450 75 80 00; fax 450 79 87 03; €€) with an indoor pool and great views. **Nagano** (450 79 71 46; fax 450 79 71 48; €€)is a great bargain. **Alpages** (450 75 80 88; fax 04 50 79

76 98; €€) has one of the best affordable restaurants. And **Bellevue** (450 75 80 95; fax 450 79 81 81; €€) is the best bargain of all for a simple hotel.

There is a great **youth hostel** in Morzine, equipped with 76 beds, car & cycle parking, luggage storage, credit card acceptance, a bar and a pool. It is located just outside of the center of town and very close to the lifts. A reservation is strongly recomended during December, February and Easter.

Avoriaz:

This is primarily a resort of condos. The two hotels do not take groups. High season, when rooms are toughest to get and prices are highest, are Christmas, Easter and February.

Hotel les Dromonts (494 979 191, fax 494 971 149; €€–€€€) has 31 rooms and is a symbol of Avoriaz architecture. **Hotel de la Falaise** (450 74 26 00, fax 450 74 26 20; €€–€€€) has 29 rooms with accommodations for one to four per room/suite.

Ski Chalets: Crystal, Crystal, Thomas Cook/Neilson. (See page 16 for phone, fax and Internet addresses.)

Apartments, condominiums, flats

This is what accommodations in Avoriaz 1800 is all about. The tourist board will send you a list of rental agencies who will make arrangements.

Approximate prices (for one week) with agency contact:

Immobiliere Des Hauts-Forts (450 74 16 08; fax 450 74 06 33; online reservations at www.avoriaz-holidays.com): studio for four, €343–€817; two-room for five, €600–€1,525. Ski Chalets for eight to fourteen people are also available for €3,431–€6,028 per week.

Pierre et Vacances (450 74 35 35; fax 450 74 01 82) has a two-room studio for four to five, €735–€1407; four rooms for eight people, €1,015–€2,688.

Immobiliere des Dromonts (450 74 00 03; fax 450 74 05 94; email agence.drom onts@wanadoo.fr) offers a studio for four persons €350–€790; two-rooms for four to five persons is €400–€1,100. Chalets are also available from €3,200–€5,500.

Avoriaz Location (450 74 04 53; fax 450 74 02 56; email info@avoriaz-location.com) has three rooms for seven people, €880–€1,840; five rooms for ten people, €1,500-€2,395.

Selectis Vacances (450 74 26 95; fax 450 74 26 98) offers two rooms for four people, €360-€870; three rooms for five people , €880-€2,050.

In Morzine, contact Morzine reservation at 450 79 11 57, fax 450 74 73 18, email reservation@morzine.com.

Dining

In Morzine, **La Grange** (450 75 96 40) prepares gourmet and Savoyarde specialties and serves them in an intimate setting that's both elegant and rustic. Fixed-price menus range from €30–€50.

At **La Chamade's,** owner Thierry Thorens has trained with celebrated chef Paul Bocuse. Most folks order the pizzas, but don't ignore other items on the menu.

More typical of the regional and traditional food with raclette and fondue is **L'Etale**, where a meal will run €15–€20. There is a disco downstairs.

Restaurant **Le Clin D'Oeil** (450 79 03 10) is a good choice for traditional regional foods as well as pizza. It's tucked away in Le Bourg section of Morzine, next to the post office. A three-course menu is €15–€25.

Les Sapins (450 75 90 56) with a spectacular view of Lake Montriond is known for its home cooking. Roger Muffat, father of the owner, prepares everything himself including dried meat and ham. A five-course meal is €18–€30.

Nearby Les Gets has good affordable meals at the **Alpages Hotel** (450 75 80 88) and **Hotel Regina** (450 75 80 44) where daily menus start at less than €15.

Avoriaz 1800 has a good collection of restaurants, but book in advance. The three-star **Christophe Leroy Restaurant** in Hotel Dromonts charges about €50 for a three-course meal; **Crepy** runs €20–€25. **La Reserve** serves good fish or cheese dishes for about €35. **Bistro** prepares mountain specialties that with a bottle of wine will cost about €22. For late-night fare try **Shooters**.

Since Avoriaz is on the mountain, its restaurants qualify as mountain restaurants. However the tiny village of Les Lindarets, on the other side of the ridge, has a wonderful collection of small restaurants. They are all good but **Les Marmottes, Pomme de Pin**, **Crémaillère** and **La Terrasse** stand out.

On the slopes of Super Morzine, **Les Cretes de Zorre** (450 79 24 73) serves hearty regional food such as Beignet de Pomme de Terre (potato fritters) and Croute du Valais (fried bread pieces covered with melted cheese and wine accompanied with green salad and roasted ham). No one leaves without a "squirt" of Pschit (pear brandy) right out of a squirt bottle. Parties of 10 or more may book the cabin for an evening.

For a true alpine atmosphere and a grand view of Mont Blanc, lunch at **Le Belvedere** (450 79 81 52) at the top of the Mont Chéry gondola in Les Gets. Menu is about €12. For a taste of Switzerland, enjoy a lunch of croute at **Chez Gaby** in Champousson, overlooking the Dents du Midi.

The Pass'Gourmet is a culinary treat in which numerous restaurants in the Portes du Soleil have decided to highlight their own special recipes or dishes. Each of these recipes is based on Savoyard cooking — salted products; polenta; eggs; and traditional spices such as cumin, juniper, safran, cinnamon and cloves. These recipes and restaurants are listed in a free tourist office guide.

Après-ski/nightlife

Generally low-keyed and relaxed, Morzine is no jet-set town crammed with sports cars. It is, however, good for pleasant wandering and window shopping, with several opportunities to stop for a hot chocolate or beer. **Opéra Rock** disco attracts locals and young people. **Dixie Bar** is a nicely decorated piano bar near the church. **Le Café Chaud** attracts young swingers. **Boudha Café** and **Le Crépuscule** are also a good time.

If you do go for a stroll in Morzine, watch out for cars on the narrow, winding streets of the upper part of town. This area lends itself to a pedestrian village, but no such luck yet.

Avoriaz has plenty of action: **The Place, Yak, The Fantastic Bar** and **The Shooter's** are fun and begin filling up after midnight.

Child care (2006/07 prices)

In **Morzine**, kindergarten l'Outa (450 79 26 00; haltegarderie@outa-morzine.com) welcomes children and infants from ages 3 months to 5 years who aren't taking ski lessons. The chalet is in the center of the resort near the slopes and ski school. There is a playroom for indoor activities, a nursery and a very large yard where instructors give first lessons to the youngest. Parents can bring a meal or take advantage of the special menu. L'Outa pricing is €18 for a half day, €97 for six half days, €32 for a full day, and €169 for six full days. Meals are €5.50 each for children age 2 and older. Meals are €2.50 each for children younger than age 2. Reservations required.

Club des Piou Piou (450 79 13 13) welcomes children ages 3–12 who want ski lessons. Costs are €76 for a full day including lunch and €343 for six full days with meals. Half days cost €39 without meal; six half days cost €254 with lunch and €170 without lunch. Instructors speak English.

Avoriaz's Village des Enfants takes care of children and teaches them to ski. The Children's Village (450 74 04 46) in the center of Avoriaz is open 9 a.m.–5:30 p.m. and accepts youngsters age 3–16. Children not taking lessons can play in the snow playground. Half days are €27; full days, €47 (€39 without lunch); six half days in the morning, €134; six half days in the afternoon, €120; six days, €233 (€196 without lunch). The Snowboard Village is for children ages 8–16. Rates are €27 for a morning,€23 for an afternoon, €47 for a full day (€39 without lunch); €134 for six mornings, €120 for six afternoons and €233 for six full days (€196 without lunch).

Avoriaz also has a nursery, Les Pétits Loups (450 74 00 38; fax 450 74 26 96), for children ages 3 months to 5 years. It's open Sunday–Friday, 9 a.m.–6 p.m. Rates are €21.50 for a half day (up to four hours) and €37.80 for a full day. Six consecutive days cost €188.70 and six consecutive half days cost €107. Lunch costs an additional €5.50 per day.

Other activities

The arena complex at Morzine offers **skating, ice hockey, horse-drawn carriage tours, dogsleigh rides, helicopter tours, mountain biking on the snow,** a **weight room, dancing** and **gymnastics**. **Painting exhibits, figure skating, ice dancing, hockey** games and **movies** are also scheduled. For information, call 04 50 74 72 72.

Fruitiere de Morzine is a frommagerie or **cheese-making** facility open to the public Wednesdays and Thursdays at 9 a.m. to watch cheesemaker Nicolas Baud make Abondance, Reblochon, Tomme and other cheeses that are sold in the shop upstairs.

At the turn of the century, more than 200 men worked in Morzine's **slate mines,** today only four men still do. Miner Franc Buet explains the process and demonstrates slate-cutting tools on Fridays at 11 a.m. The one-hour program is conducted primarily in French but with some English explanation. The mine is on the Route Des Ardoisieres, which is the road to the Avoriaz cablecar just past the rotary with the turn-off to Avoriaz resort. Look for the fish sign; while you're here, you can also **catch your dinner.**

At Avoriaz, all in a small radius and easy to find are **parasailing; night sledding; trampolining; ice diving; hot air ballooning; helicopter tours;** a **fitness center** with exercise machines, weights, sauna and whirlpool tubs; **skating** rink; **dog sleighs; horse sleighs;** a **cinema** and **bowling** alley.

The tourist office publishes a regular schedule of **movies**. A multi-activities card, available for €23 per person/week or €20 with a six-day Portes du Soleil ski pass, provides unlimited entrance to the ice-skating rink, including skates, the fitness center and the Turkish bath. A weekly entertainment program is also offered. It may include balloon sculptures, skate-dance parties and children's programs; most of which are free.

Getting there

The nearest airport is in Geneva. From the airport a bus runs daily. The tourist office at the airport has the schedules.

Avoriaz and Morzine can be reached by a train/bus combination. Trains from Paris and Geneva arrive several times a day, and then the bus makes the 40-km. climb.

Driving: Take the Geneva-Mont Blanc autoroute and then take exit 18, Morzine/Avoriaz. Morzine is 60 km. from Geneva and Avoriaz is only 15 km. further.

Open-air parking in Avoriaz costs about €43 for a week; covered parking for a week is about €76. Transfers, available 24 hours a day from the parking lots in the town center, cost €5–€13 for one to four people; luggage costs an extra €2.

Parking in the Morzine lot at the bottom of the cablecar is free. Avoriaz is a 20-minute drive from Morzine. Cablecars leave every 15 minutes, 7 a.m.-9 p.m.; on Friday and Saturday it closes at 1 a.m. Those with lift passes ride free 9 a.m.-5 p.m.; otherwise the charge is €5.50.

Tourist information

Morzine-Avoriaz Tourism Office
Place de la Crusaz, 74110 Morzine-Avoriaz, France; 450 74 72 72;
fax 450 79 03 48
Internet: www.morzine-avoriaz.com
E-mail: info@morzine-avoriaz.com
Avoriaz Tourism Office
Place Centrale, 74110 Avoriaz, France; 450 74 02 11;
fax 450 74 24 29
Internet: www.avoriaz.com
Email: info@avoriaz.com

Tignes

The group of towns on the Tignes side of Espace Killy is a very good, built-for-skiing resort. The series of modern villages string from 5,000 to 6,900 feet with the main village, Tignes le Lac at 6,825 feet. Les Brevieres, Lavachet, Les Boisses and Val Claret are the four other villages at the base of one of Europe's largest Glaciers, La Grande Motte. The villages, which are really clusters of apartment buildings with shop arcades and restaurants on the first floors, were built in the 1950s after the old town of Tignes was flooded by the construction of the Chevril dam. With door-to-slopes skiing in mind, the layout of the buildings and lift-systems gives skiers 24 different lifts that leave from within the five towns.

The average visitor to Tignes stays in one of more than 15,000 apartment beds as there are only a mere 1,500 beds in the 19 hotels. Reservations are required, especially during the February French school holidays. To avoid the busiest times in any French resort, make sure to plan around the kids.

At a glance, it is hard to appreciate how big this area really is. Tignes is connected seamlessly with Val d'Isere, one of Europe's most famous resorts, to create Espace Killy. The combined network features 300 kilometers of runs linked by 102 lifts. Continuous drops of more than 5,000 feet is one reason Tignes attracts so many skiers.

Tignes is very proud of the Grand Motte glacier. They even built a six-minute, underground funicular from Val Claret to the glacier, which operates in all weather conditions year-round. The funicular has capacity of over 3,000 skiers per hour.

The runs at Tignes are primarily geared towards intermediate cruisers, while the off-piste terrain ranges from classic, difficult couloirs to peaceful, rolling snowfields. There is enough physical space that you could not cover even half the resort trails in a three-day stay. Au contraire, if you are into tricks and jumps, you could easily spend all day at the two-and-a-half-kilometer long snow park. An efficient shuttle bus system allows you to end your day in any of the towns and make it quickly home.

The resort is quite international, with plenty of British skiers and riders. From ski school to take-out pizza, you probably won't have trouble communicating. The après-ski tends to be a little cliquish, as the bars often end up uniligual.

An important thing to know is the bus schedule. Free shuttle buses run around and between the towns every 10 minutes from 8 a.m. to 8 p.m.; every half-hour from 8 p.m. to midnight; and every hour from midnight to 8 a.m.

Parking is taken rather seriously in Tignes. Any cars left on the streets are consistently and diligently towed. Since legal parking is only available in the lots and indoor garages, the bus system is usually your best way to get around.

Mountain layout—Skiing

The ski area can be broken into five main sectors. If La Grande Motte is directly in front of you, La Tovière/Lavachet is on your left and the Palet/Aiguille Percée/Palafour areas rise on your right. A few lifts rise from the villages of Les Brévières and Les Boisses 1,640 feet lower.

The skiing in La Tovière/Lavachet area is a steep 1,950-foot vertical drop back into town. There are some great off-trail runs over the back side of Lavachet into Val d'Isère or around the cliffs back into Tignes.

At Le Grande Motte, skiing on the glacier is wide open and relatively mellow—this sector offers the only lower intermediate terrain. The run under the cable car is a good intermediate test of stamina, and experts can go off the trail over the Rochers de la Grande Balme into the Palet sector. Many skiers come to Tignes and never leave this section of the mountain since there is so much variety. On the expert slopes there is often avalanche danger, so check with guides.

The Palet/Aiguille Percée offers relatively mellow terrain under the Col du Palet, with relatively tough intermediate runs down from the Aiguille Percée. Experts have a wide swath of off-trail possibilities, as well as itineraries over the Col du Palet or over the back side of Aiguille Percée down Vallon de la Sache to Les Brévières.

Night skiing is also available in Le Lac, Le Lavachet and Val Claret. Your lift ticket for the day takes care of the costs.

Mountain rating

It's easy to see why the area has been rated as tops in every category. Just the expanse of snow is mind-boggling. With a vertical drop of more than a mile and a third, coupled with 30,000 acres of terrain, there is something for everyone. Beginners and intermediates can cruise all over the upper reaches.

Experts can push themselves on extensive off-trail and powder runs. It is best, at least for a day, to take a guide along who will show you the best places to test your skills. Before skiing off-piste, check with ski school for the latest on snow conditions.

Mountain layout—Snowboarding

Intermediate to expert snowboarders will be more than satisfied with Tignes. With the majority of runs above tree level, the trails in Tignes are wide and bordered by easily accessible off-piste terrain. For those who buy the Espace Killy lift ticket, the backside of Col de Fresse in the Val d'Isère section supplies a natural off-piste terrain park. For serious shredders craving some of the best backcountry in the Alps, there are ample treks and traverses leading to intense chutes and powder fields well worth hiking for. Of course, Avalanche Victim Locators are required for any serious off-piste excursions. Evolution 2 Ski and Snowboard School provides the best guides for backcountry; a half day is €50 and four half days are €175. Unfortunately, Tignes is not the best resort for never-ever or beginner boarders. They officially list only one green run in the entire Tignes area, compared with a total of twenty greens in Espace Killy.

The snowpark itself, largest in the world, is a reason to go to Tignes. Covering 1,600 vertical feet, the 2-1/2-km.-long park sports a quarterpipe and halfpipe, a boardercross course and a plethora of table-tops for skiers and boarders alike. The best riders in

Europe come to Tignes to compete and practice.

During the summer and early winter before the park above Tignes le Lac is built, head up to the La Grande Motte, where another half-pipe and more tabletops are kept in shape year around.

Cross-Country

There are a total of 52 km. of slopes in Tignes and Val d'Isère. Tignes has four loops, three of which are in the main resort at 2100 meters and are easy and flat. The fourth loop in Tignes Brévières winds around the lake. It is surrounded by trees and is a little more challenging, In summer, there's also a 4-km. loop on the Grande Motte Glacier, where cross country teams come to train.

Ski school (2006/07 prices)

The Ecole du Ski Francais has four offices: In Tignes le Lac, call 479 06 30 28; in Val Claret, call 479 06 31 28; in Lavachet, call 479 40 08 84; and in Rond Point des Pistes call 479 06 56 08. Combined they have a total of 220 instructors for any level of skier. English is spoken by many of the instructors, so mention that you'll need an English-speaking instructor when signing up.

Private lessons: A lesson (three skiers maximum) for two hours is €89; for three hours, €125.50; and a full day, €266. The services of a certified guide for powder and off-piste for a group of no more than five people cost €266 per full day.

Group lessons: Three-hour courses are given during the mornings or afternoons. Five days of half-day lessons are €121.50 for adults (students age 13 and older) and €117.50 for children. Five days of full-day lessons costs €179 for adults and €171.50 for children.

A full-day, off-piste class for good skiers from 8:30 a.m. to 6:00 p.m. costs €61. This class might traverse between Tignes, La Plagne and Les Arcs.

There are seven other ski/snowboard schools. **Evolution 2** in Le Lac, 479 06 43 78; Val Claret, 479 40 09 04; and Lavachet, 479 06 35 76. **Les Marmottons** in Val Claret, 479 06 37 12 and Lac Rosset, 479 06 51 67. In Le Lac, **Tetra Hors,** 479 41 97 07 and **Bureau des Guides** 479 06 42 76. In Val Claret, **333 Ski and Snowboard,** 479 06 20 88; **Surf Feeling,** 608 48 64 30 and **The Snocool** 479 40 08 58.

Lift tickets (2007/08 prices)

The prices below are for **Tignes only,** which includes 47 lifts serving 65 runs. There's a 1,900 meter drop and 150 km. of runs.

	Adult	Children (5-13) & Senior (60-74)
half day	€28.50	€23
one day	€36	€29
six days	€174	€140
seven days	€197	€158

Tignes has a limited local pass for snowboarders and freeskiers called **Snowspace** that includes 20 lifts in the southern part of the ski area. It also includes the famous snow park complete with jumps, a halfpipe and a freestyle zone. Lifts for this area cost €25 for a half day and €32 for a full day.

The prices below are for **l'Espace Killy,** which includes 97 lifts serving 140 runs in the interconnected Tignes/Val d'Isère area and more than 300 km. of runs.

	Adult	Children (5-13) & Senior (60-74)
half day	€30.50	€24.50
one day	€42	€33.50
six days	€202.50	€162
seven days	€231	€185

Children younger than 5 and seniors ages 75 and older ski free.

Starting in the 2007/08 season, lift tickets will be in the form of the electronic Smart Card. Also, the new Pass'Tignes program will give five percent discounts on Espace Killy ski passes and on parking fees.

For tickets valid for more than two days a photo is needed. Six- to 21-day tickets are valid for one day of your stay on La Plagne, or Les Arcs ski lifts. The tickets are also good for a day at Trois Vallées and a day at Valmorel, a half-price pass at Sainte Foy and a special price on the San Bernado espace.

Note: Insurance is not required but strongly recommended. The fee covers the cost of rescuing you and taking you down off the slopes. The cost is €2.50 per day per person for adults and €2 per day per person for children and seniors.

Accommodations

A special, low-season-only program has been organized by the tourist office and hoteliers. Low season normally runs from the end of September to Christmas week, for most of January except New Year, and late April and May. Check with the office for exact dates. Tignes is very affordable.

Hotels are rated by price. These designations are based on daily high-season (but non-holiday) cost per person based on double occupancy with half board. €€€—€125+; €€—€75–€124; €—less than €75.

Val Claret — Oftentimes hotels boast "on the slopes" when really they should say "a tough five-minute outdoor adventure to get to the nearest lift." Well, have no fear, for at Tignes the worst that could happen is that the ski runs might creep under your door. Both Val Claret and Le Lac are navigated by pedestrians, skiers and snowboarders alike.

Ski D'Or (479 06 51 60; fax 479 06 45 49; €€€) in Val Claret is the classiest four-star hotel in the Tignes/Val d'Isère area. Room 23 is the honeymoon suite; ask whether it's available, if you like. Each of the rooms is tastefully and uniquely decorated, and the restaurant is excellent.

La Vanoise (479 06 31 90, fax 0479 06 37 06; €€) is another great option; less pricy but highly regarded. It offers a package of seven nights with half-board and a six-day ski pass for €534–€782.

Hotel Diva (0479 06 70 00; fax 0479 06 71 00; €€) is the third option up in Val Claret. It's slightly more expensive than La Vanoise but has amenities such as a fitness room, sauna and child care center (18 months to 11 years old).

In Tignes Le Lac — You can choose from 10 different hotels, ranging in ritziness from the youth hostel **Auberge de Jeunesse Les Clarines** (04 79 41 01 93) in Les Boisse to the four-star suites in the **Village Montana**.

The **Suites du Montana** (0479 400144, fax 0479 400403; €€–€€€), the largest and most accommodating complex in all of Tignes, has everything a four star hotel can offer: an extensive spa/fitness center, a great restaurant, and a few cozy spots to hang out in its large, beautiful lobby.

You can choose a three star: **L'Aiguille Percèe** (0479 06 52 22, fax 0479 06 35 69; €); **Gentiana** (0479 06 52 46; fax 0479 06 35 61; €€); **Alpaka Lounge** (0479 06

45 30, fax 0479 06 58 09; €€); **Les Campanules** (0479 063436, fax 0479 06 35 78; €€); **Le Lèvanna** (0479 06 32 94, fax 0479 06 33 18; €€); or **Le Refuge** (0479 06 36 64, fax 0479 06 33 78; €). On a budget? Try these two-star hotels: **L'Arbina** (0479 06 34 78, fax 0479 06 32 99; €); **Le Paquis** (0479 06 37 33, fax 0479 06 36 59; €€).

For rock-bottom prices, stay in the village of Les Brévières. The **Relais du Lac** (479 06 40 03; €) is quiet and out of the way, but a gondola takes you to the Tignes' lift system. Another bargain spot is **Les Seracs** (479 06 03 61, fax 479 06 17 90; €).

Ski Chalets: Crystal, Thomas Cook/Neilson (see page 16 for phone, fax and Internet addresses).

Apartments, condominiums, flats

When you learn that Tignes has only 1,200 beds in hotels but almost 15,000 in apartments, you realize the importance of the rental system. The tourist office acts as a clearinghouse, providing a listing of rental apartments.

A typical sample of apartment rates from AB Immobilier, per week per apartment, is provided below. The centrally located units are only about 100 meters from the lifts. The easiest means to finding an apartment that is a good fit for you is to communicate with the tourism office.

	high season	mid season
studio: two persons	€556	€367
2BR four persons	€944	€560
3BR six persons	€1235	€745

In many cases, linen is not included but can be rented from the apartment owners or agencies. The normal linen fee is €15 a week per person.

Most agencies and individual owners offer apartments in a similar price range. Note the differences between high and mid seasons—even in high season lodging costs will be only about €33 a day per person, based on four people sharing a two-bedroom apartment. Cable TV is available with CNN, Sky Channel and the BBC.

Dining

There are more than 70 restaurants spread through the resort. Visitors can find everything from gourmet and bistro French to fine Italian and pizza to Tex/Mex to Japanese.

Val Claret — The restaurant in the **Hotel Ski d'Or** (479 06 51 60) serves exceptional gourmet meals and is relatively expensive. The restaurant **Le Caveau** (479 06 52 32) is also excellent and considered by many as the best in town. **l'Indochine** (479 06 08 07) serves good Chinese and Vietnamese dishes. For Savoyard decor and food try **Grattalu** (479 06 30 78) or **Brasserie du Petit Savoyard** (479 06 36 23). For crêpes try **La Datcha** (04 79 06 35 39). For good pizzas head to **Pizzeria 2000** (04 79 06 38 49) or **Roma** (04 79 06 36 25). For Tex-Mex (well a French version) head to **Daffy's Cafe** (04 79 06 38 75).

Tignes le Lac — Try **L'Eterlou** (479 06 33 53) or **Le Bistro** (479 06 49 75) for typical Savoyard cooking. **Carlings** is very English in the Hotel Alpaka (479 06 32 58) or test the restaurant **Escale Blanche** (479 06 45 50).

Le Lac Le Rosset/Les Almes — If you are looking for big and busy, **L'Escale Blanche** (04 79 06 45 50) should be your journey's end. Right off the Aeroski gondola, regional specialties are ski-in/ski-out during the day. Just less than 50 meters away, **L'Arbina** (04 79 06 46 83), on the second floor of the Arbina hotel, serves plenty of fish and a daily menu for €25. Warm yourself by the fireplace at another hotel restaurant, **La Montagne**

(04 79 06 31 30). Don't leave without having a crepe or a gallette. For a different kind of experience, head to **Le Clin d'Oeil** (04 79 06 59 10). This small, cozy joint seats only 26 people and charges €30 for the fixed menu. This popular food is worth every penny if you are able to reserve ahead of time. The larger **Le Paquis** (04 79 06 37 33) has a spacious view over town. The €21-fixed menu is enjoyed peacefully overlooking the slopes. **Les Chanterelles** (479 40 01 44) in Village Montana is excellent, and **La Chaumiere** in the same hotel has reasonable meals.

Le Lavachet — Dining in this area is more sparse than the other divisions of the towns, but it does host the **Le Brasero** (04 79 06 30 60), a good place for a variety of meat dishes. They also offer a €22 buffet of regional Savoyard specialties on Tuesday evenings. The alternative is **Le Grenier** (04 79 06 37 79), a straight up typical Savoyard restaurant. Standard regional specialties start from €13.80.

On the slopes — Head to **Le Panoramic** (04.79.06.60.11) at the foot of the glacier it boats spectacular, panoramic views. The snack bar is overpriced, but the view is worth the pause. The gastronomic restaurant is excellent with a Savoyard evening meal on Thursdays.

Le Bollin is on the slopes but only a short walk from Val Claret. Bring your credit cards without a limit. The dining is, as they say in France, *tres cher*!

Savouna, at base of the Col de Palet lift, is easy to reach.

 ## Après-ski/nightlife

If your vacation resolutions include paying as much respect to the nightlife as the skiing, stay at Val Claret (or be sure to at least visit). The hottest spots are right in the center of town, around the corner from the Office de Tourisme. Val Claret is much more compact that Tignes Le Lac, so finding each hub shouldn't be very hard. Get jiggy at the **Crowded House** with a variety of good dance music, a social atmosphere and occasional theme nights. **L'@robaze Café** (0479 06 49 94) kicks it off at 4 p.m. with hot chocolate and warm wine and keeps its bar open until 1:30 a.m. You can use the Internet here at €8 per hour, shoot pool, or dress up for theme night (two nights a week). **Daffy's Café/Tex Mex** (0479 06 38 75), decked out with Mexican/Western decorations, is great for the boisterous (or hungry!). It serves snacks and drinks from 4 p.m. to 1:30 a.m. You should at least swing through **Grizzly's Bar** (0479 06 34 17). If the light, warm atmosphere, comfy seats, or vast fireplace entice you, stay for a while. The **Mover Café** (0479 06 32 64), where the young and British seem to gather, sports a layout just right for groups of party people.

At the foot of the Tufs chairlift, you can choose from three beers on tap at the **Fish Tank** (0479 06 46 60), which tends to be mostly an après-ski destination (don't miss happy hour everyday from 4 p.m. to 6 p.m.). It boasts a couple of large-screen TVs that show sporting events from 8:30 am to 1 a.m. and offers mixed drinks and snacks too. Drop into the **Roadhouse Café** (0479 06 35 91) for some pool, drinks and live music, on occasion.

If you are staying at Tignes le Lac, you'll find almost all the action at **Le Bec Rouge** on rue de la Poste. **Le Café de la Poste** (0479 06 36 10) is a spacious bar/nightclub with fun employees and a billiard table. You may find live music and a dance floor that should be hoppin' until the early morning. This is one of the places the seasonals like to party. Stacked right on top, **La Grotte du Yeti** (0479 40 07 36) invites those 18 and older to hang out in a wide open, rustic, wooden après-ski bar. It attracts young people from across Europe. Across the street you'll find the **Powder Café** (0479 40 07 36), a small internet café/snack-bar. Alongside the café, **Le Bar American** (0479 06 37 80) is a quiet, well-lit, pizzeria/café/bar that serves crepes and pizzas.

Nestled within the Bec Rouge, the **Embuscade Café** (0479 06 59 51) usually hosts an older crowd. Best suited for conversation or billiards, it is a dim bar with a high ceiling. On the east side of the apartment grouping (within which there is a fairly extensive gallery of shops and restaurants), there is another hub of nightlife. **Le Bowling** (04 79 06 39 95) consists of a simple little bar alongside 10 bowling lanes, which are open from noon to 2 a.m. seven days a week. A few steps away, beside the video arcade (also open from noon to 2 a.m.) is **Jack's Club** (0479 06 54 84), a typical pub/bar and disco open from 9 p.m. to 4 a.m. **Yorin Café** (0479 06 55 20) shows freeride videos all day long for hearty après-skiers, and then through the night the in-house DJ lays down the tunes.

If you're still energized when the bars close, head to the discos that don't even begin to crank until around midnight. **Melting Pot** pumps euro-dance music and regularly hosts celebrity DJs. It's a big place with plenty of space to either sit or dance. **Le Blue Girl** (0479 06 51 53) plays music just as loud as the Pot and hosts excellent DJs.

Censored in Le Lavachet is a stop in from the cold. With a warm fireplace and warm people, this joint is always a good stop after a long day of skiing. Live bands entertain the international crowd three nights a week. People in Le Lavachet not looking to bus to the other towns tend to gravitate towards Censored.

Also in La Lavachet is **Le Petit Pub**, a small apres-ski sports bar where a good game is always showing. Head to **TC's Bar** (0479 06 46 46) for their 4 to 6 p.m. happy hour or for snacks anytime. Check out www.TCSBAR.com for more info on special events and on theme nights.

The bus system runs into the night, but the stops change to pick people up in front of the discos.

Child care (2006/07 prices)

Les Marmottons in Tignes le Lac (479 06 51 67) and Val Claret (479 06 37 12) accept kids 3–8 years old for a combination of skiing lessons and snowplay in their sizeable outdoor kindergarten. The facilities are open Monday through Saturday, 9 a.m. to 4:45 p.m. Five half days cost €120; with lunch, €190. Six half days cost €130; with lunch, €205. Five full days cost €210; with lunch, €275. Six full days cost €230; with lunch €305. Equipment rental is extra.

Ecole de Ski Francais also has locations in both Tignes le Lac (479 06 30 28) and Val Claret (479 06 31 28). Both areas have Club des Piou-Piou which accepts children age 4 -12. Five half days (three hours) €117.50; six half days cost €125.50. Five full days (six hours) cost €171.50; six full days cost €184. Lunch with the ski instructor is €12.

Five half days of snowboarding lessons for kids 8-12 are €117.50; six half days cost €125.50.

Accomplished child and adult skiers can take the Competition course, which teaches technical skills and racing techniques. It includes videos, free skiing and powder techniques. The five-day program is €199 and the six-day program is €219.50.

Other activities

In addition to skiing that's available 365 days of the year, Tignes has several interesting activities for those who want to spice up a weeklong visit or for non-skiers. In March and April, if the conditions are right, Evolution 2 Ski and Adventure School leads **scuba diving tours under the ice** of the small lake in Tignes Le Lac.

At the Hotel Village Montana there is a three-star (04 79 40 05 12) and a four-star (04 79 00 21 01) **spa**. Both offer full services, from massages and steam rooms to Jacuzzis and tanning rooms. The three star spa has an outdoor heated pool (€20 for adults, €15 for kids) open every day from 10 a.m. to 8 p.m., but it closes at 7 p.m. for kids younger than 15.

The **bowling** alley in Tignes le Lac is the highest in Europe. It has ten lanes and games are €7.60. Kids can **ice skate** on the lake for €4.30 from 2 p.m.–8 p.m. A day of ice climbing costs €110.

For a truly unique activity, try **ice diving** in Lake Tignes. Led by an instructor along an underwater guideline, you can dive during the day or night. Through the openings that have been cut in the ice, you can catch spectacular glimpses of the mountain peaks.

Spend an afternoon in **Le Lagon**, the aqua center in the heart of Tignes which affords panoramic views of the town, lake and mountains. Le Lagon has an array of pools: a 25-meter competition-sized pool; a fun pool with water slides, whirlpool seat, geyser, waterfall and more; and a paddling pool for toddlers. If you ever get tired of playing in the pools, the facility also has a fitness area and a wellness area with a Turkish bath, 3 saunas and 8 different types of showers.

Getting there

The closest international airports are Lyons (150 miles from the resort) and Geneva (about 86 miles). A smaller airport that offers some flights is Chambéry. A daily bus to Tignes from Geneva airport (00 41 900 57 15 00 for reservations) and weekend service from Lyons airport operate in winter.

TGV trains now run directly from Paris to Bourg-St. Maurice in 4-1/2 hours. A bus connection gets you to Tignes. A joint rail/bus ticket is available at the railway station or from travel agents.

If you drive, the best route from Geneva is autoroute A41 to Annecy and then N90 to Albertville. From there, follow signs to Bourg-St. Maurice and on to Tignes. From Lyons, take autoroute A43 to Albertville, then follow the signs to Moutiers, Bourg-St. Maurice, and on to Tignes.

Tourist information

Office du Tourisme, BP 51, 73321 Tignes Cedex, France
Telephone 479 40 04 40; fax 479 40 03 15.
Internet: www.tignes.net
E-mail: information@tignes.net

For hotel and apartment booking, call Tignes Reservation at 479 40 03 03; address is the same as above.
Internet: www.tignesreservation.net

Les Trois Vallées

Courchevel, Méribel, Les Menuires, Val Thorens

All skiers dream of virtually endless slopes and trails at any resort where they plan to vacation. The Trois Vallées is about as close as anyone can come to that dream chance to wake up each morning and choose a different village to explore, mountain to schuss or scenic vista to capture. If it is the call of an endless ski safari that you hear, then the epicenter of that siren song is France's Trois Vallées region.

The four main villages comprising Les Trois Vallées — all purpose-built for skiing — are Courchevel, Méribel, Les Menuires and Val Thorens. Newly-built La Tania near Courchevel and the traditional town of St. Martin de Belleville near Les Menuires are also important parts of this region.

On paper the area is overwhelming; in person it is mind-expanding. Two hundred ski lifts on a single pass, 600 km. of ski runs, 130 km. of cross-country trails, 1,500 snow cannons, 360 ski patrollers, 1,200 lift attendants.

Even with all the lifts providing access to virtually every point in the valley, the region is so vast that intrepid skiers can head off into the hinterlands and ski for thousands of vertical feet without ever seeing a lift and in some cases without seeing another skier. If you are someone who feels comforted by lifts within sight, you will have your fill. If you are the type of skier or snowboarder who wants to feel you are alone in the winter wilderness, the Trois Vallées has plenty to offer.

Skiing just doesn't get any better served than that found in this region. When you gaze at the mountains from any valley, what you can see you can ski—and it is most likely lift-served to some degree. Mountain restaurants are plentiful and the food is as good as anyone imagines when they conjure up French cooking. Make sure to test the tasty local specialties such as tartiflette, fondue and raclette.

Another way to look at the expanse of this region is to take a look at how many of the largest ski resorts in the United States can fit into the Trois Vallées region. The former *Snow Country* magazine concluded that the six largest ski areas in the United States could fit inside Les Trois Vallées. That means that Killington, Vail, Heavenly, Steamboat, Squaw Valley and Park City could all fit inside the space covered by Les Trois Vallées with almost 10,000 acres left over. So you can throw in Jackson Hole, Taos, Sun Valley, Keystone, Crested Butte, Alta, Solitude, Cranmore and Stowe and still have room. The expanse is breathtaking. The scenery is spectacular. And the overall skiing is unmatched.

Each resort is covered separately, since they large enough to be treated as separate resort. Courchevel, Méribel, Les Menuires and Val Thorens sections follow.

Lift tickets (2007/08 prices)

Each area offers three lift-ticket combinations: one covers only the lifts in the resort area, the second covers lifts in the individual valley; and a third is a full Trois Vallées lift ticket.

Skiers who are staying for a week or more will want to purchase the Trois Vallées combination ticket. This ticket gives unlimited access to all the lifts and runs in the region. It also entitles holders to a day in another Olympic resort—Val d'Isère, Tignes, La Plagne, Les Arcs, Peisey Vallandry, Pralognan la Vanoise and Les Saisies.

Hands Free Lift Ticket System: Les Trois Vallées is using chip cards for all ski passes that allow automatic access to lift facilities. Unlike other resorts, skiers will not be asked to pay a additional deposit and will not have to pay a small supplement on top of the daily cost. Keep the receipt that comes with the lift ticket in a separate place, since it will be the key to a replacement tickets should you lose the original. A replacement ticket costs €10. Keep your lift ticket in a safe place. The inner pocket on your left side is perfect. Beware: It is a light plastic card that can easily be forgotten or misplaced.Prices for Les Trois Vallées combination pass are:

	Adults	Children (age 5–12)	Seniors (age 65-75)
one day	€44	€33	€38
three days	€130	€97.50	€110.50
six days	€220	€165	€187
seven days	€251	€188	€206
13 days	€455	€332	€368

Children younger than age 5 and seniors older than age 75 ski free.

Carte Neige Ski Insurance, which pays for evacuation from the mountain and immediate medical care should you get injured skiing or riding, can be purchased for €2.50 a day for adults and for €2 a day for children younger than age 13.

The Three Valleys Family Ski Pass costs €704 for two parents and two children younger than age 18 to ski for six days. Each added child costs €165.

Getting there

The closest airports are Geneva (149 km.), Lyon (180 km.) and Chambéry (110 km.). A welcome desk is operated by the region at the Geneva Airport. This season regular air service will connect Courchevel with Geneva three times a day, four days a week.

Buses and trains leave daily from the Geneva airport. The cost is about €64 one-way or €109 round-trip. Call Société Touriscar (04 50 43 60 02). Weekend bus service connects the region with Lyon for about €86 round-trip on Satobusalps (04 37 25 52 55). The Chambéry bus with Transavoie Transport (04 79 35 21 74) costs €70.13 round trip.

Rail reaches Moutiers, 37 km. away (a 40-minute drive). Buses and taxis are available from the station. Buses cost approximately €15 and taxis run about €75.

If driving, follow the signs to Chambéry and Albertville, then take the four-lane road to Moutiers and up to the Les Trois Vallées.

For those piloting a private plane or helicopter, Courchevel and Méribel have small mountain airports as well as heliports with charter service.

Once at the resorts, shuttlebuses move you efficiently within each valley, but moving between valleys is inconvenient and expensive. For example, a taxi from Courchevel to Val Thorens is more than €140 or a time-consuming bus via Moutiers would cost about €25. Plan on skiing between resorts and don't get stuck in Val Thorens when the lifts close if you need to be in Courchevel to spend the night. It will be expensive.

Tourist information

Courchevel Tourisme, Le Coeur de Courchevel, B.P. 37, 73122 Courchevel, France
Telephone 04 79 08 00 29; fax 04 79 08 15 63.
Internet: www.courchevel.com. E-mail: info@courchevel.com
For reservations:
Courchevel Réservation, La Croisette, BP 33, 73122 Courchevel
Telephone 04 79 08 14 44; fax 04 79 08 33 59.
E-mail: info@courchevel-reservation.com

Méribel Office du Tourisme, 73550 Méribel, France;
Telephone 04 79 08 60 01; fax 04 79 00 59 61.
Internet: www.meribel.net; E-mail: info@meribel.net
Telephone reservations: 04 79 00 50 00; fax 04 79 00 31 10.
E-mail reservations: info@meribel-reservations.com

Les Menuires Office du Tourisme, 73440 Les Menuires, France;
Telephone 04 79 00 73 00; fax 04 79 00 75 06.
For reservations only, call 04 79 00 79 79; fax 04 79 00 60 92.
Internet: www.lesmenuires.com.
E-mail: lesmenuires@lesmenuires.com.

Saint Martin de Belleville Office du Tourisme
73440 Saint Martin De Belleville, France;
Telephone: 04 79 00 20 00; fax 04 79 08 91 71.
Internet: www.st-martin-belleville.com
E-mail: stmartin@st-martin-belleville.com

Val Thorens Office du Tourisme, 73440 Val Thorens, France;
Telephone; 04 79 00 08 08; fax 04 79 00 00 04.
Internet: www.valthorens.com. E-mail: valtho@valthorens.com
Reservations are handled by Val Thorens Reservations;
Telephone 04 79 00 01 06; fax 04 79 00 06 49.
Internet: www.valthorens.com. E-mail: reserver@valthorens.com

La Tania Office du Tourisme, 73125 La Tania, France;
Telephone 04 79 08 40 40; fax 04 79 08 45 71
Internet: www.latania.com E-mail: info@latania.com

Brides les Bains Office du Tourisme,
BP 73572 Brides les Bains Cedex
Telephone: 09 79 55 20 69; Fax 09 79 55 20 90
www.brides-les-bains.com Email tourism@brides-les-bains.com

COURCHEVEL

This is perhaps the most cosmopolitan of the four villages. It was France's first real jet-set resort, created to cater to the upper crust and become the darling of those crusties in the French Riviera group who didn't flock to Megève.

Courchevel itself is really a series of smaller villages whose names reflect their heights in meters—Courchevel 1850, Courchevel 1650, Courchevel 1550 and so on. Courchevel 1300, also called Le Praz, is the quaintest, but its lower altitude may mean a sacrifice of snow for charm. There is another village, Saint-Bon on a fifth level (but with no lifts). Courchevel 1850 is the highest and priciest, but it's also where most trails run right outside your hotel or apartment door. It is where the best restaurants are found and where the nightlife continues until the sky begins to lighten with the coming day. Built for ski-in/ski-out, Courchevel 1850 really works. Its lift system covers both sides of the valley. The world's largest cablecar, heading up to La Saulire (8,885 feet), connects Courchevel to the rest of the Les Trois Vallées area.

La Tania is a small separate new resort set at the base of the ridge separating Courchevel and Méribel. It has its own relatively quiet nightlife. From La Tania it is about a half-hour bus ride to either of the larger resorts straddling the ridge.

Mountain layout–Skiing

The skiing above the various levels of Courchevel varies widely. Experts will enjoy all of the chutes dropping down from La Saulire around the left side of the telepherique and the ones that shoot down under the Suisses chairlift. On the other side of the valley at Chanrossa and Roc Merlet (2734 meters) experts to intermediates will find this whole area to their liking. Beginners will enjoy the wide-open pasture below the Saulire cablecar base station. A truly gorgeous run through the trees can be had by starting at the Col de la Loze and skiing down to Le Praz or to the newly developed resort of La Tania. The series of runs ending at La Tania offers wonderful, uncrowded cruises.

Mountain rating

Something for everyone. This vast region has some of the better intermediate cruising terrain of the entire area. Beginner terrain is next to accommodations. Experts and advanced skiers will have a grand time at the higher reaches of the resort

Mountain layout–Snowboarding

For a little warm-up, ride the Ariondaz gondola up and do a little carving. If you prefer snow parks, take either the Ecureuils or the Epicca lift to the Le Plantrey Snowpark, a hectare of tables, rails, a halfpipe and a quarterpipe. There's even a area for snowskaters.

If freestyle is more your thing, head to the canyons and dunes of Les Verdons. Boarders can have fun discovering the natural jumps and turns. Experts might prefer the area off the Saulire cablecar where they can pop some jumps on the breaks in the slope. Stay to the left on the Creux Trail for a sweet little natural halfpipe.

Ski school (2007/08 prices)

Courchevel has hundreds of English-speaking instructors. These prices are non-holiday prices from Ecole du Ski Meribel, representative of most ski and snowboard schools the valley.

Courchevel 1850 (04 79 08 07 72) private lessons are €85 for 90-minute lesson; €340 for a full day.

Group lessons cost €215 for four full days; €288 for six days. Snowboard lessons are €304 for six full days. Discovery off-piste courses cost €95 per day.

Other Courchevel ski schools are E.S.F. 1650 (04 79 08 26 08); E.S.F. 1550 (04 79 08 21 07); Ski Academy (04 79 08 11 99), Supreme Ski School (04 79 08 27 87) and Magic in Motion (04 79 01 01 81).

 ## Accommodations

These resorts have every type of lodging from luxury chalets to dormitories. Accommodations in the Courchevel villages all fall in the same price range except for Courchevel 1850, which is slightly higher. Even though prices are higher, Courchevel 1850 still offers somewhat reasonably priced accommodations in luxury surroundings, but you must be very careful to make arrangements for low season. The tourist office will send a complete list of hotels with information about White Week (discount/off-season) periods and details of making reservations.

Prices are per person based on double occupancy during February with half board. €€€—€125+; €€—€75–€124; € is less than €75.

Bellecote (479 08 10 19; €€€) This hotel is more Alpine, cozier and exclusive than the Byblos described below. Its wealthy guests are reclusive rich. Much of the furniture was imported from the Himalayas; that which is in the lobby is leather and very soft. A heated pool and a well-equipped exercise room are also here.

Le Byblos Courchevel (479 00 98 00; €€€) The mountain version of the world-famous Byblos in St. Tropez, this was conceived as an all-encompassing hotel. It caters to hedonism at its best. Here you rub shoulders with the winter jet-set elite and visit the Alp's first cigar lounge.

Hotel Trois Vallées (479 08 00 12; €€€) This, for our money, is the best of the four-star properties in Courchevel. Its designers paid special attention to the bathrooms, which are at the leading edge of design, featuring giant tubs—some marble, others black, with brass fittings—and every amenity. The hotel is only steps away from the finest restaurants, as well as the wildest nightlife.

Au Rond-Point du Pistes (479 08 04 33; €€€) This hotel is right in the middle of the action and is one of the relative bargains among three-stars.

Chabichou (479 08 00 55; €€€) Flowery on the outside with modern woodsy rooms on the inside. This hotel is cute but not cheap.

Crystal (479 08 28 22; €€€) This hotel is great for children with some of the best slopeside accommodations. It is a short walk to the downtown area.

Hotel Mercure Coralia (479 08 11 23; €€€) In the residential area, this hotel is out of the center of the "commercial" district, but right on the slopes and a lake with lovely views. The rooms are very businesslike.

Les Ducs de Savoie (479 08 03 00; €€) The best of the three-stars has spacious rooms, a swimming pool, lots of wood and it's right on the slopes and within easy reach of the gondola. At night it's a 10-minute walk to get back to the hotel, or you can take a cab.

Courcheneige (479 08 02 59; €€) A good two-star find, with 86 rooms, sauna, Jacuzzi and terrace on the slopes.

L'Aiglon (479 08 02 66; €€) This recently renovated hotel is perhaps the best two-star property in town, with exceptional rooms for comparatively low rates. Its location near the slopes is excellent and it's only a short five-minute walk into town. People who stay keep coming back.

In "1650" head to **Hotel du Golf** (479 00 92 92; €€) that offers great value, good rooms and great views right on the slopes.

Also in "1650" is **Le Portetta** (479 08 01 47; €€) which is a bit less expensive than the Hotel du Golf, not as traditional but just as convenient.

Ancolies (479 08 27 66; €) is a good example of how prices drop dramatically when you head to "1550." Rooms are about half the cost of "1850," but beautiful and the hotel is a great value.

Les Flocons (479 08 02 70; €) is a traditional hotel with a great reputation.

Les Peupliers (479 08 41 47; €€) is down in the village of Le Praz across from the Praz and La Forêt lifts; it has a wonderful following. Great value.

Ski Chalets: Crystal, Inghams/Bladon, Thompson, Thomas Cook/Neilson (go to page 16 for phone, fax and Internet addresses).

Apartments, condominiums, flats

Apartments are the French choice for accommodation. In fact, apartment beds outnumber hotel beds by at least five to one. What you get is the ability to schedule off-slope life at your own pace and a good way to avoid the high hotel prices. In most of January, two-room apartment rates in "Residences" in Courchevel 1850 at Belledonne and Chalets du Forum are about €780–€950 a week. In "1650" the rates for varying luxury with a more out-of-the-way location range from €500 to €900. In "1550" Domaines du Soleil has high season rentals for €680 to €1,050.

There are ten rental agents for apartments in Courchevel. The tourist office will send more information, a registration card and will help make reservations.

 Dining

Get ready for sticker shock in restaurants, both downtown and on the slopes. Check out a few places before settling in for dinner or lunch. For bargains try pizza spots, then Tex-Mex restaurants and raclette/fondue places.

This is considered to have the best food of any French mountain resort. The **Chabichou** (479 08 00 55) maintains a friendly rivalry with the **Le Bateau Ivre** (4 7908 36 88) for the top restaurant in town. Both rate two Michelin stars and both will end up costing about €100–€160 per person.

A meal in **La Bergerie** (479 08 24 70) shouldn't be missed, especially if you go on Friday for "Russian night." Come with plenty of money.

Aux 3 Bo (479 08 29 62) serves creative traditional French cooking (and downstairs, Japanese meals) in a country atmosphere. The small restaurant exudes class and the food is well-prepared. It ranges from warm oyster soup to Fois Gras springroll appetizers and entrees such as sea scallops with polenta and bok choy to lamb chops. In the basement a small wine cave is the perfect place to select your wine and enjoy an appertif. Expect to pay around €120 for a full meal.

La Fromagerie (479 08 27 47) has the best fondue and raclette in town and Michelin agrees, giving it a fork. Choose from cheese specialty menues ranging in price from €24–€36.

For more reasonable restaurants, try **La Saulire** (479 08 07 52) with good local specialties, two Michelin forks and an owner who likes Americans thanks to years of living in Canada. Expect to pay €35–€100 per person for dinner.

La Mangeoire looks almost Western with cowhides, wagon wheels and lanterns. The food is simple but the crowds in the evening are great. Expect to pay €23–€30. **l'Arbe** (479 08 26 03) is where the locals eat. It seems to be crowded from lunch time on, first with the lunch crowd and then with après-skiers, then with dinner folk. Another good spot for pizza is **La Smalto** (479 08 31 29).

The following were all enthusiastically recommended by locals: **La Chapelle**

(479 08 19 48) is a small place where they say you'll swear your grandma was cooking (hope that's a pleasant memory). **La Cendrée** (479 08 29 38) serves Italian meals and has one of the best Italian wine cellars in the region.

For traditional Savoyard meals try one of these restaurants: **Le Génépi** (479 08 08 63); **Le Mazot** (479 08 41 72) for raclette, fondue and tartiflette; **L'Alpage** (479 08 24 87); **Le Carnozet** (479 08 41 47); **Refuge** (479 08 36 65) has salads for €12 and tartiflette for €17; and **La Montagne** (479 08 09 85) for mountain style meals.

L'Aventure (4 79 08 35 21) next to the Croisette Center and just steps to the slopes, serves an eclectic menu with good Tartiflette and Omelette Savoyard. Expect to pay around €20-€28 for a substantial Savoyard lunch.

For great atmosphere head to **La Bergerie** (previously mentioned) or **Les Allobroges** (479 08 10 15) in a wine vault.

Courchevel 1550

Le Caveau (749 08 09 42) has an Alpine woodsy atmosphere and serves very affordable traditional meals next to the Gragettes gondola just off the slopes. They offer a menu of the day for only €11.

L'Oeil de Boeuf (479 08 22 10) is in an authentic restored barn. The meats are grilled in an open fireplace with lots of flaring flames and sizzle. The meals are affordable and the experience fun.

La Praz (Courchevel 1300)

Le Bistrot du Praz (479 08 41 33) in Courchevel 1300 serves some of the best foie gras and local specialties in the area. The French country atmosphere adds a special flavor to the experience.

Across the lane in the Hotel Peupleirs is La Table de Mon Grand-Pere (479 08 41 42) which exudes atmosphere. The lunch menu price is around €25 and dinner will range from €40 to €60 with a reasonable wine.

On the slopes

Stop at the **Chalet de Pierres** (479 08 18 61) if you want to see and be seen. Bring your credit cards—the menu and wine runs €40 or more for lunch. **Le Panoramic** (479 08 00 88) has one of the best 360-degree view in the Alps from its deck at the top of the Le Saulire tram. Downstairs is a self-service restaurant with meals from tartiflette to sausages to polenta. Upstairs is a full sit-down restaurant.

Child care (2007/08 prices)

The tourist office, your hotel or apartment manager can put you in touch with qualified private baby sitters who provide child care services at any time of the day or night.

Courchevel has six ski schools for children. Children's lessons are offered by the E.S.F. 1850, E.S.F. 1650, E.S.F. 1550, Ski Academy, Magic in Motion and the Supreme Ski School.

The children's program for those ages 3–12 costs €150 for five mornings, €105 for five afternoons and €208 for five full days. Lifts are not included in these prices. Lunch costs an additional €16–€21.

Two nursery programs for children 18 months and older are available in Courchevel 1850 at Le Village des Enfants (479 08 08 47) and Courchevel 1650 at Les Pitchounets (479 08 33 69). Both are open from 9 a.m. to 5 p.m. Prices will be about €25 half day and €60 for a day plus €16 for lunch. Five full-day programs cost €166.

Après-ski/nightlife

The best spots for apres-ski in Courchevel 1850, where English speakers gather, are **Bar le Jump** across from the slopes at the Croissette Center attached to Hotel de la Croisette, and **Bar l'Equipe**. **Le Tremplin** and **Le Kalico** also pulse with crowds when the slopes close.

In Courchevel 1650 head to the **Space Bar, Rocky's, the Bubble Bar** or **Moriond Lounge** as the slopes close for a good party before dinner.

In Courchevel 1550 the the places to be for apres-ski are **Barouf**, **Channossa** or **The Bar.**

Courchevel has an upscale nightlife scene. The **Purple Bar** in Courchevel 1850 just pulses with techno music, and serves cocktails from 7 p.m. to 2 a.m. Either folks come here for early nightlife or warm up for early morning adventures at Le Cave or La Grange. There is also the **Milk Pub**, in the center of Courchevel 1850. TJ's is a bar run by one of the English tour companies and is packed from around 10 p.m. until 2 a.m.

After midnight, the **Mangeoire** restaurant becomes a dance floor. Guarentee yourself a spot on the floor by making dinner reservations. Eat, drink and then be one of the first ones on the floor merrily dancing off the calories. Also recommended are the two discos: the ultra VIP **Les Caves** and **"La Grange."**

In Courchevel 1550, the **Barouf** throws Brazilian and other cultural parties. In Le Praz, L'Escorchevel purposes special shooters.

Other activities

Courchevel has a **bowling alley, hotel indoor swimming pools, saunas, squash courts** and an Olympic-size **skating rink, hang-gliding, ski jumping, paragliding, deltagliding, mountain flying courses,** climbing, helicopter sightseeing rides, horse-drawn sleigh riding, hot-air ballooning, karting on ice, snowmobiling, snowshoeing, tobogganing and even **archery**.

Tourist information

Courchevel Tourisme, Le Coeur de Courchevel, B.P. 37, 73122 Courchevel, France
Telephone 04 79 08 00 29; fax 04 79 08 15 63.
Internet: www.courchevel.com. E-mail: info@courchevel.com
For reservations: Courchevel Réservation, La Croisette
Telephone 04 79 08 14 44; fax 04 79 08 33 59.
E-mail: info@courchevel-reservation.com

MÉRIBEL

Méribel has developed into a first-rate ski resort, at the same time taking pains to retain a semblance of the traditional mountain architecture of the French Alps. From a skier's point of view, the resort has two sections. There is Méribel that basically stretches from La Chaudanne at 4,757 feet elevation with traditional village atmosphere with a major lift center and the tourist office, to the Altiport, a small area at 5,577 feet on the mountain with a runway and lot for pilots who have their own small planes. (Pilots must have special training to use the altiport.) About four km. up the valley is Méribel-Mottaret, a smaller village with a larger lift hub and more ski-in/ski out accommodation. These villages are set in the central valley of Les Trois Vallées. There are 53 lifts in the valley, 18 of them that start in the village and link up with another 200 lifts in Les Trois Vallées.

Old Méribel center, La Chaudanne, was founded by the British; it still retains many of its British trappings and English is spoken almost everywhere. Above this original center rises the rest of Méribel with 750 vertical feet of hotels and chalets built up the side of the valley toward Courchevel. It has excellent ski slope access. It is about a 10-minute ride from the Altiport and Rond Point des Pistes down to the tourist office.

Half as old and still growing, Méribel-Mottaret is higher up in the same valley. It has more direct lift access to Les Menuires, Courchevel and Val Thorens via the Cote Brune chairlift. Méribel-La Chaudanne is about a 10-minute ride from Méribel-Mottaret. They are linked by a free bus.

The lift to La Saulire provides the best access to the Courchevel valley and the lifts to either Roc des Trois Marches (8,868 feet) or Mont de la Challe (8,448 feet) provide the best connections to Val Thorens and Menuires.

 ## Mountain layout–Skiing

The skiing on both sides of the Allues valley, home to Méribel and Méribel-Mottaret, ranges from easy to hair-raising difficult. Though a trail map won't provide black run thrills, runs marked as intermediate here would be considered black-diamond runs at most American resorts.

One of the key advantages to this area is most in evidence in this section of the Trois Vallées: bottom-to-top cablecars that not only take you to long, undisturbed cruisers, but also can get you across the valley very quickly. Experts and advanced intermediates shouldn't miss the very worthy runs and wide-open off-piste opportunities down both sides of Mont Vallon.

Mow down Mont Vallon in the morning after the sun has had a bit of a chance to soften the snow, then for gut-sucking action, mogul-busters should try the short drop under the third stage of the Plattieres lift. Advanced beginners and intermediates will find the run below the final two sections of the Plattieres lift both gentle and extended. Off-piste possibilities for intermediates abound in the area between Roc de Fer, site of the women's Olympic downhill, and Méribel for those interested in dropping into the Vallées des Belleville from the top of Roc de Fer more intermediate skiing awaits.

The snowfields stretching beneath Saulire are wonderful with varying pitches that will delight both lower intermediates and experts. The chutes directly beneath the gondola, reached only by a scramble and the wide couloir to the left of the ascending gondola, make for expert runs that will be the subject of conversations for years.

The sector near the Altiport is an intermediate's delight. With more and more families skiing there recently, Méribel installed a new high-speed eight-seat chairlift to move skiers. There is plenty of lift capacity in that section now.

Off Piste: In the Méribel valley the best off-piste skiing is in sectors between Mont de la Chambre and Les Plattieres as well as from the top of Mont Vallon. Watch out, however, for the national wildlife refuge surrounding Mont Vallon. Skiing is now prohibited here and skiers have been given merciless fines since enforcement began in July 1990. Another off-piste gem is free skiing from Roc de Fer along the ridge, then dropping down to Le Raffort or Les Allues. The slopes as far as Le Raffort normally have adequate snow. For Les Allues, check on snow conditions.

Mountain rating

This valley, as in all other valleys of this region, has something for everyone. No beginner will go wanting for good practice slopes. No intermediate will long for more cruisers. No expert will feel like there is not enough. It doesn't get better than this.

Mountain layout—Snowboarding

There are two snowparks in this valley. One is in Méribel and the other in Méribel-Mottaret. In Méribel-Mottaret the total area of the snowpark is 15 acres. It is 5,000 feet long and the vertical drop is almost 1,000 feet. There is also a halfpipe, a babypipe, two quarterpipes and tables, spines and a boardercross course.

In Meribel the Arpasson snowpark is 4,000 feet long with a vertical drop of 660 feet. There is a competition halfpipe, another beginner halfpipe and a 3.3 km. boardercross course with whoops, tables and obstacles.

Ski school (2007/08 prices)

Méribel has only one ski school. **The French Ski School** (479 08 60 31) is exceptional with children and lessons from private to group and cross-country to powder skiing. It has 500 alpine ski instructors who speak French, English, German, Spanish and Italian and 10 cross-country instructors. Group lesson cost €216 for five full days days; €143 for five mornings; €120 for five afternoons. Morning private lessons (from 9:30 to 12:15) cost €143 for one to four skiers. A full day private instructor will cost €318. Snowboarding lessons for five half days costs €115.40–€141.20.

Children pay €185 for five days of group lessons.

Special lessons for powder skiing, snowboarding, mono-skiing, ski ballet and freestyle skiing are available. There are also racing clinics and a ski kindergarten. A special accompanied ski adventure through Les Trois Vallées and another tour through the 12 valleys of the Tarentaise—including the resorts of Val Thorens, La Plagne, Les Arcs, Val d'Isère and Tignes—are also offered.

Accommodations

Méribel has every type of lodging from luxury chalets to dormitories. The tourist office will send a complete list of hotels with information about White Week periods (discounted, off-season) and special packages for both hotels and apartments. Call Méribel Réservations (www.meribel-reservations.com) at 479 00 50 00; fax 479 00 31 19 or e-mail: infos@meribel-reservations.com.

Prices are per person based on double occupancy during February with half board. €€€—€125+; €€—€75–€124; € is less than €75.

Le Grand Coeur (479 08 60 03; fax 479 08 58 38; €€€) This hotel is filled with fine antiques, paintings and furnishings. There is normally a list of returning clientele, so make reservations early. The lounge, built around a large stone fireplace and the dining room have sweeping views.

Allodis (479 00 56 00; fax 479 00 59 28; €€€) This beautiful hotel features a combination of modern color and design, with traditional classical architecture featuring arches and columns. Perfectly located for skiing, it is not close to town.

Mont Vallon (479 00 44 00; fax 479 00 46 93; €€€) In Méribel-Mottaret, this is a real luxury hotel with rustic lodge-like flavor. You have everything here: pool, exercise room, Jacuzzi, sauna, squash courts and spectacular rooms. Walk out the door and onto the lifts, but take a shuttlebus or taxi to the center of town.

Hotel de l'Altiport (479 00 52 32); fax 479 08 57 54; €€€) This hotel is at the top of the resort. Access to the slopes is perfect. The exterior exudes Alpine charm and the interior has classic touches.

Alpen Ruitor (479 00 48 48; fax 479 00 48 31; €€) Beautiful lobby and modern rooms with a new emphasis on hotel meals and a larger dining room. Ask for a room with a view of the valley rather than the parking lot.

Marie Blanche (479 08 65 55; fax 479 08 57 07; €€) A small intimate hotel in a residential district only steps from the slopes and a stairway from the center of town.

Adray Telebar (479 08 60 26; fax 479 08 53 85; €€) This hidden treasure has a mountain-lodge feel. The 26 country-style rooms all are unique, the owners charming and the food out of this world. Visit for the food even if you're not staying here.

l'Hotel du Moulin (479 00 52 23; fax 479 00 58 23; €€) A one-star hotel on the outskirts of Méribel with seven rooms in an old flour mill. You'll have to take the bus to the slopes, but it's the best bargain you'll find.

Hotel La Tarentaise (479 00 42 43; fax 479 00 46 99; €€) In Méribel-Mottaret, right on the slopes with a big British clientele. Enjoy great barbeque on the terrace. Rooms are bland but it has a great location.

Les Arolles (479 00 40 40; fax 479 00 45 50; €+) Also in Méribel-Mottaret on the slopes, this hotel also has a large group of British skiers, especially families. Basic modern rooms, nice pool and on-slope location.

Hotels l'Eterlou/Le Tremplin/La Chaudanne (479 08 61 76; fax 479 08 57 75; €€) A complex of hotels and condos smack in the middle of the Méribel-La Chaudanne section and steps from the lifts. Rooms are decorated in warm wood, the restaurants are very good, and all amenities are shared between the properties.

le Yéti (479 00 51 15; fax 479 00 51 73; €€) This great value hotel is highly recommended. Its once-small rooms have been expanded recently. It is near the previous two hotels—steps from skiing and a shuttlebus ride from the town center.

Le Parc Alpin (479 08 29 63; fax 479 08 25 21) is a chalet hotel in Altitude 1600, close to the pistes and many excellent restaurants. Rooms are decorated with a mountain spirit, and each individual room is named after an alpine bird or animal.

l'Orée du Bois (479 00 50 30; fax 479 08 57 52; €) This hotel provides good value; it is on the slopes but is far out of the center of town for nightlife and restaurants.

Le Merilys (479 08 69 00; fax 479 08 68 99; €) This is a cozy B&B with an Alpine flavor at the upper reaches of the resort near the Altiport. Great slope access, but a long walk downtown. There is a public shuttle service, however.

Croix Jean-Claude (479 08 61 05; fax 479 00 32 72; €) in the small village of Les Allues has very comfortable traditional rooms, and a great restaurant. Reach the slopes by gondola or bus.

Ski Chalets: Crystal, Inghams/Bladon, Simply Ski, Thompson and Thomas Cook/Neilson (see page 16 for phone, fax and Internet addresses).

Apartments, condominiums, flats

Apartments are the French choice for accommodation. In fact, apartment beds outnumber hotel beds by at least five to one. What you get is the ability to schedule off-slope life at your own pace and avoid high hotel prices. The descriptions in the brochures are based on maximum skiers per apartment. We have found that for the American/British market, more room is expected. Ask about the number of bedrooms carefully.

According to one realtor, apartment prices for a week's rental in Méribel-Mottaret during most of January start from €310 for a studio for two to €813 for a three-room place that will hold six. In February, prices jump to €657 and €1413 respectively.

The tourist office will send more information and a registration card and will help make reservations.

 ## Dining

Meribel has excellent restaurants. Our routine is to eat on the slopes for about €10 to €15 for a great lunch and then cook in the apartment for dinners. However, there is no shortage of places to dine like a king.

Le Grand Coeur (479 08 60 03) has a view over the chalets of the town. The experience is hard to beat, with excellent fish as well as local specialties. Expect to spend €40 per person.

Make the effort to dine at the **Hotel Allodis** (479 00 56 00). The restaurant, especially during lunch, is wonderful. The evening dining room offers meals in an architectural harmony of modern and classic lines. Expect to pay €40 per person.

Le Plantin (479 04 12 11) on the road between Meribel Village and La Tania, serves posh rustic meals for lunch and dinner. During the day the restaurant shuttles diners to their dining room from La Tania lifts or Meribel lifts if they call.

Chez Kiki (479 08 66 68) is the Méribel version of Courchevel's original Bergerie. The rustic atmosphere is cozier downstairs near the fireplace. For an adventure during the meal find the Alice in Wonderland door in the basement. Meal costs about €40 apiece.

Le Yeti Restaurant (479 00 51 15) in the hotel of the same name has an excellent kitchen and elegant dining room with a menu that offers traditional French cooking. A full dinner will cost around €55 plus wine. Lunches with the Plat du Jour and a dessert are about €28.

La Fromagerie is a traditional fromagerie where cheese and wine are kept at the perfect temperature in the basement. Head here for the best fondue and raclette in the valley.

On the road between Meribel-Center and the Altiport served by regular free shuttlebusses, **Cro Magnon** (479 00 57 38) is a nice place for more affordable French fare but not cheap: careful or the meal price might creep up to €60 or so. **La Cava** (479 00 31 29) beneath the Hotel Oiree de Bois serves bistro meals ranging from salad and pasta to soups and steaks. This place can be very affordable with pizza from €8.50 regional specialties from €17. Meal cost can easily stay below €35.

For more affordable meals in the middle of Meribel-Center try **Evolution** (au Tremplin) (479 00 44 26) for country French meals. **Le Flambé** (479 00 31 70) is the resort's original Italian place and is still considered the best. **La Kouisena** (479 08 89 23) prepares excellent Savoyard specialties.

For pizza and the least wallet damage try **Scott's** in Meribel-Center nest to the tourist office.

Méribel-Mottaret

Le Grain de Sel (479 06 12 17) in Meribel-Mottaret at the base of the Table Vert chairlift serves excellent French traditional meals. The wine cellar here has more than 70 different wines.

Au Temps Perdu (479 00 36 64) is a cellar restaurant in Meribel-Mottaret. The French meals are excellent and relatively moderate. Try the home-made blueberry sorbet with brandy and whipped cream. Expect to pay around €50-€55 per person with wine.

La Baleine (479 00 42 87) where you can have a wonderful duck fondue for two for only €20. The restaurant has tables that are easily reached from the slopes for wonderful lunches. The reasonable prices attract the locals.

Pizzeria de Mottaret (479 00 40 50) for more upscale pies and atmosphere. This is far more than the normal pizzeria. Wood-fired pizzas start at €12 or choose from beef, pork, pastas, risotto or cheeses in the cellar restaurant.

Three good restaurants sit side by side at **Mottaret Chatelet** — **La Belle Savoie** (479 00 53 90), a family place featuring local trout; **La Rastro** (479 00 41 51) a British favorite with food and fun; and **Le Zig Zag** (479 00 47 40) that is one of the valley bargains with a 3-course menu for only €17 and it is known for its Jagertee.

In Les Allues, try **La Croix Jean-Claude** (479 08 61 05) for excellent meats, mushrooms and vegetables. Great dinners and lunches. Reservations required. In the same village try **La Chemina** (479 01 12 70) or **l'Arbe** (479 01 12 70) which is very reasonable, specializes in Savoyard meals. **En'K** (479 01 13 75), in les Allues, is a tiny restaurant built in an old slaughterhouse that serves up inexpensive meals. Dine in the tiny spot at one of about six tables or take out your food. If staying in Les Allues, this is a great deal for a meal to take back to the flat.

On the mountain, a good affordable fixed-price menu is served at **Les Choucas** just below the middle station of the Burgin Saulire gondola. If you are staying in Méribel, a nice stop on the way home is the **Bar Rhododendrons**.

Après-ski/nightlife

Méribel-Centre now has a Trois Vallées version of the famous and successful **Dick's Tea Bar** from Val d'Isère. That spot promises to be hoppin' just like in Val d'Isère. It will be staying open until 4 a.m. It opens at 9 p.m. and entry is free until 1 a.m. Cocktails before midnight are 2 for 1.

Scott's is an apres-ski gathering spot. It has live music every Wednesday from 10:30 p.m., happy hours every day from 4 to 6 p.m. **Doron Pub** (The Pub) is another good apres-ski spot with live music most afternoons and then again starting at 10:30 p.m. This is also a good sports bar. **Barometer**, right in the center of town, serves beers, wines and coffees in a more tranquil atmosphere. Plasma TVs are, however, switched on for big games. It is open from 2 p.m. until 2 a.m.

Another late night spot is the **Le Loft**, Meribel's top nightclub. It is open until 4 a.m. and is the gathering place for the beautiful people who want to see and be seen.

Try **Le Poste de Secours** that claims the spot as the most sophisticated bar in downtown Meribel, with an international beer selection and a cellar of different champagnes. Cocktails range from mojitos to Sex on the Snow.

Jack's Bar, opposite the Olympic Center, claims the resort's largest selection of beers and really cranks up for apres-ski. Bands play most afternoons and in the evenings comedians and comic dress events make for an interesting time.

Meribel-les Allues — In this small town, just down the hill from Meribel Centre, **La Tsaretta** is open from 4:30 p.m. to 1 a.m. with a good collection of beers with music several nights a week.

Méribel-Mottaret — has its sophisticated late-night spot Le Privilege, a cellar disco, for dancing from 11 p.m. to 4 a.m. **Le Rastro Bar,** just past the Plattieres lift station, has been featured on British TV as one of the best party spots in Europe. The place rocks with lots of 60s, 70s and 80s music. Later in the night head to **Le Zig Zag** for a spot of Jagertee made with real Austrial Stroh Rum.

Child care (2007/08 prices)

The tourist office, your hotel or apartment manager can put you in touch with qualified private baby sitters who provide child care services at any time of the day or night.

Méribel has a highly respected child-care program. **Le Club Saturnins** (479 08 66 90) accepts children between 18 months and 3 years. It is associated with the French Ski School and ski lessons are offered to children ready to ski. Le Saturnins costs €22.10–€24.60 for a half day; €43.10 for a full day. A five-day week costs €184.50. Supervised lunch costs €21.50 a day or €102.50 for a five-day week from noon to 2 p.m. A birth certificate is required at time of reservation.

Also associated with the ski school, the **Jardin des P'tis Loups** accepts ages 3–5 for child care and has a ski playground to encourage beginners. Les P'tits Loups costs €22.60–€25 for a half day; €43 for a full day. A five-day week costs €185.

Other activities

Méribel facilities include an **indoor swimming pool, bowling alleys** and an **Olympic ice skating rink**. The rink has public skating daily and two nights a week. Figure skating lessons are available. Entrance fees: Adult €4.60, skate hire, €3.10.

An olympic-sized swimming pool is open daily and two nights per week. There is free entrance for children younger than 5; adults pay €4.30; children (ages 5 to 13) pay €3.40.

A **climbing wall** is available in the Olympic Center open from 2 p.m. to 7:30 p.m. Excellent walking trails criss-cross the entire valley. **Discovery tours** of the valley on **skimobiles** are organized daily. **Paragliding** with instructors is offered by three organizations. You can even find a six-lane **bowling alley** in the Olympic Center. Mountain **flying lessons** are offered as well as **sightseeing flights**. Call the Aéro-Club at 479 08 61 33.

The tourist office has all phone numbers and contacts.

Tourist information

Méribel Office du Tourisme, 73550 Méribel, France; Telephone 479 08 60 01; fax 479 00 59 61. Internet: www.meribel.net; E-mail: info@meribel.net For reservations: Telephone 04 79 00 50 00; fax 04 79 00 31 10. E-mail: info@meribel-reservations.com

LES MENUIRES

Les Menuires started as a cluster of high-rise apartment buildings constructed for the sole purpose of the pursuit of skiing. Today that original cluster is a small part of a far larger resort that has expanded dramatically over the past decade.

The new construction has been carefully reviewed to create an Alpine atmosphere with plenty of wood and peaked roofs. Chalets have been built sheltering spacious apartments and shops without the square apartment complex feel. The expanded village has been created to keep cars out of the way. It offers one of the best family spots in the Les Trois Vallées.

The new town plan calls for a halt to new buildings and owners are being awarded grants to rennovate the existing buildings. Where rennovation is not cost effective, the resort is demolishing buildings and constructing new complexes on the same footprint. This new approach is part of the resorts commitment to protecting the environment from further intrusion.

The the resort center, La Croisette, still serves as the resort focus and is a convenient meeting place for ski schools and children's programs. Here the reort unfolds onto the crescent boardwalk of the central shopping mall and below the bus station acts as the village's transporation hub. Across from the station, the new sports center provides an excellent indoor swimming pool for families.

Above la Croisette is the massive apartment building that makes us the section of the resort known as Brelin.

Down valley, the area of Preyerand is filled with apartments for both visitors and local workers as well as a handful of hotels.

The newer up-valley satellite sections of Reberty-Les Bruyeres and Reberty have concentrated on smaller buildings built in community clusters.

The village of St. Martin de Belleville with its Baroque churches and pastoral aura, 8 km. down-valley from Les Menuires, offers hotel and pension accommodations and plenty of apartments. It is now connected with the entire Trois Vallées area with convenient lifts.

 ## Mountain layout

Les Menuires area has excellent expert and intermediate skiing from the top of La Masse. These runs are often less crowded here. On the other side of the valley above both Les Menuires and Val Thorens, the runs are generally intermediate, rather wide-open cruisers with an expert run named after Marielle Goitschel, the Olympic darling of the valley. One of our absolute favorite runs for intermediates is the mogul-studded connector path leading down to Méribel from Mont de la Chambre above Les Menuires.

In Les Menuires you will find skiers traveling with families and those looking for the steeps. The skiing is wide open on the west-facing slope with lifts running up toward Val Thorens. An abundance of beginner and intermediate runs pass picturesque shepherd huts on the way down the valley toward the traditional village of St. Martin de Belleville. The east-facing side of the valley offers more challenging skiing from Pointe de la Masse (9,213 feet), which can be reached rapidly by riding a combination of two high-speed lifts. In the afternoon the area is deserted as skiers follow the sun. The off-trail skiing from here and nearby Cîme de Caron is exceptional, especially in spring when skiers can drop over the backside of these mountains with certified guides.

The lift taking skiers to the Roc des Trois Marches and the new Le Roc Des Trois Marches gondola (installed for the 2005/06 season) taking skiers to Mont de la Chambre provide the best connections to Méribel and the rest of Les Trois Vallées.

Off Piste: Always-present avalanche danger makes skiing with a guide very advisable and with a friend a common-sense requirement. Experts who want to explore the path less traveled should head for the Val Thorens/Les Menuires valley. Besides the aforementioned fourth valley, there is also excellent off-piste skiing above the Pointe de Thorens. At this point, be prepared to shed your skis and hike up to the glacier du Bouchet or in the other direction toward either the Glacier de Gébroulaz or to the Aguille de Péclet.

The summits of La Masse and Cîme de Caron, also in the Val Thorens/Les Menuires valley, are the richest sources of off-piste skiing in the entire Three Valleys circuit. From the top of both there are long off-piste trails down by Lac (lake) du Lou. Take particular notice of the ski hut at the peak of La Masse—a steep initial descent from this hut intimidates most and conceals desolate, expert terrain leading more directly toward Lac du Lou than the itinerary routes. From the top of La Masse there is more serene off-piste skiing to be found by heading down to La Gratte via either the Les Encombres route or the Le Chatelard route. Make arrangements for a taxi or a car to pick you up and bring you the short distance to the St. Martin de Belleville.

Snowboarding: The old Snowpark and Snowcross, which had previously been on two separate sites have been combined in the Combes-Becca sector. At 2,500 meters, the Combes-Becca Snowpark and Snowcross will receive enough snow to keep its raised turns, slides, quarters, pyramids and tables open all season. Weekly boarding competitions are organized on the halfpipe just at the side of the Boyes piste.

Mountain rating

C'est magnifique! This area is so vast and varied that no skier should have trouble finding the perfect slope for his or her ability. The basic rules here are that intermediates can stick to the slopes dropping from the Meribel ridge down to Les Menuires. Experts and advanced skiers will want to head to the other side of the valley to drop down from La Masse.

Expert skiing is everywhere however. What you can see, you can ski. No expert will go wanting. In the Val Thorens/Les Menuires valley. Here, on the Cîme de Caron and descending from Pointe de la Masse, experts can find the best steeps, the best powder and the smallest crowds

Ski school (2007/08 prices)

All of the area's resorts have good instructors and offer skiing, cross-country and snowboarding lessons. There are 120 English-speaking instructors in the Les Menuires ski school (04 79 00 61 43).

Private lessons are €40 per hour for one to two persons; €58 per hour for three to five skiers.

Group lessons are held from Sunday through Friday. Morning lessons last for nearly three hours and afternoon lessons last for two-and-a-half hours. They cost €29 per adult and €27.50 per child for a morning lesson; and €24 per adult and €22 per child for an afternoon lesson.

For skiers looking for a guide, the ski school forms groups that ski all day Monday through Friday. This is highly recommended. You will be put into a group with similar skiers.

Beginner skiers can purchase a special ski pass that includes six half-day lessons and access to 16 ski lifts starting at €159 for adults and €139 for children.

Special lessons for powder skiing, snowboarding, mono-skiing, ski ballet and freestyle skiing are available. There are also racing clinics and a ski kindergarten. A special accompanied ski adventure through Les Trois Vallées and another tour through the 12 valleys of the Tarentaise—including the resorts of Val Thorens, La Plagne, Les Arcs, Val d'Isère and Tignes—are also offered.

A **snowboard school** has morning lessons for experienced boarders. It costs €130 for six a.m. lessons for intermediates and six p.m. lessons for beginners cost €100.

A **cross-country lesson** costs €27 for morning lesson and €129 for six consecutive morning lessons.

 ## Accommodations

These resorts have every type of lodging from luxury chalets to dormitories. The tourist office will send a complete list of hotels with information about White Week periods and details on making reservations.

Prices are per person based on double occupancy during February with half board. €€€=€125+; €€=€75-€124; €=less than €75.

Chalet Hotel Kaya (479 41 42 00) is the newest hotel and the resorts only four-star establishment. It sits at the top of the Reberty section of the resort at the 2000 level. The decor is what we might call mountain modern with a shift away from the traditional wood-everywhere decor. Rooms are spacious and there is a swimming pool, fitness center and spa. The restaurant is one of the bargains of the mountain for the time being, expecially during lunch.

Hotel l'Ours Blanc (479 00 61 66; fax 479 00 63 67; €€) is run by a young English lady and her French husband who does the gourmet cooking. The interior woodwork was finished by the father and child care is free for guests.

Hotel Lattitudes (479 00 75 10; fax 479 00 70 70; €€) Has a great location in Les Bruyeres. After a total rennovation in 2006, rooms are modern with great views. Again, this hotel has a mountain-modern approach to decor with little wood and traditional touches. It is right on the slopes next to the 12-person gondola.

Hotel Le Menuire (479 00 60 33: fax 479 00 60 00; €€) This is a small, clean hotel on the road entering the complex. It is a good upscale hotel.

Chalet 2000 (479 00 60 57; fax 479 00 22 25; €€) in one of the upper Reberty sections right below the Club Med has a wonderful terrace with good slope location.

Le Pelvoux (479 00 61 09; fax 479 00 28 80; €) is right in the center of the modern village. Again don't expect tradition. You get great location with small rooms.

Hotel du Soleil Pierre Blanche (479 01 37 37; fax 479 00 69 60; €) has 68 rooms in the Brelin area above Le Croisette, the main modern village. This area is non-Savoyard and very modern, but with good location.

Hotel Carla (479 00 73 73; fax 479 00 73 76; €) This is a two-star hotel in La Croisette just beneath the main modern center.

St. Martin de Belleville

In the village of St. Martin de Belleville the **Hotel Saint Martin** (479 00 88 00; fax 479 00 88 39; €€; photo above) is a perfect spot, in chalet style and only steps from the lifts.

Les Chalets du Gypse (479 09 45 00; €€€) is an apartment hotel with full service and luxury accommodation.

The **Alp-Hotel** (479 08 92 82; fax 479 08 94 61; €€) near the Hotel Saint Martin. It connects with the Trois Vallées system and offers a nest of traditional architecture.

Also in St. Martin de Belleville try **l'Edelweiss** (479 08 96 67; fax 04 79 08 90 40; €€; photo right) for simple accommodation and good food but a bit of a walk to the lifts.

In the three-bedroom, tow-suite **La Bouitte** (479 08 96 77; fax 479 08 96 03; €€€), you can sleep like a king in a two-person room for €121-€183 per person B&B.

All-in-one weekly packages in St. Martin de Belleville including lifts and half-board cost €681–€750 in three-star hotels during January and the first week of April.

Ski Chalets: Neilson.

Apartments, condominiums, flats

Apartments are the French choice for accommodation. In fact, apartment beds outnumber hotel beds by at least 5 to 1. What you get is the ability to schedule off-slope life at your own pace and an excellent way to avoid the high hotel prices.

During all-in-one white week package periods in Les Menuires, for example, a two-bedroom apartment that will sleep four people for a week in January costs €204–€248. A 3-Valley ski pass costs €215 for a week. Low season per person costs between €415 and €475 a week with ski pass.

For four-person apartment in February high season, expect to pay €1,134–€1,520. Rates vary based on the luxury and location of the apartment. Individuals sharing flats during the high season periods will pay approximately €500-€600 per person for a week with Three Valleys skipass.

Gorgeous apartments that will sleep six to eight in Les Montagnettes, as well as the brand new Les Alpages de Reberty or Les Chalets du Soleil, cost approximately €1,350 in most of January and spike up to €2,260 for the holidays.

The tourist office will send more information and a registration card, and will help make reservations.

Dining

The local dining star is **La Bouitte** (479 08 96 77) in St. Marcel, next door to St-Martin de Belleville, is probably the best restaurant in the valley with a one-star Michelin rating.

Both in St-Martin de Belleville: **The Hotel Saint Martin** (479 00 88 00) restaurant is excellent; **Etoile des Neiges** (479 08 92 80) next to the church is highly rated by Michelin.

Le Montagnard (479 01 08 40) in Saint Martin des Belleville is a traditional restaurant with original decor that serves excellent savoyard specialties.

In Les Menuires -- La Croisette:

Just above La Croisette and reached by a short walk is the **L'Etoile** (04 79 00 75 58) with tables around a giant fireplace. It has one of the region's best chefs. The waitstaff dresses in traditional mountain costume adding a nice effect to the experience.

Au Coin du Feu (479 09 97 52) is a traditional restaurant next to the bus station and just below the tourist office. They serve us a specialty called "la tartifle" that translated into English means baked potatoes. They are baked in the open fireplace and then slathered with the toppings of choice.

Most of the La Croisette restaurants are simple but good value. Try (in no particular order) **Le Belleville** (479 00 68 93), **Le Chaudron** (479 00 60 11), **La Grange** (479 00 23 58) and **l'Isard** (479 07 67 03).

In Les Menuires — Reberty:

Le K (479 41 42 02) is the gourmet restaurant of the Hotel Kaya. The lunches, right on the slopes, are an exceptional value and the presentation will elicit oohs and aahs from diners. Dinner is a top-rated affair. **Hotel L'Ours Blanc** (479 00 61 66) is considered one of the best in Les Menuires, according to locals.

La Ferme de Reberty (479 00 77 01) in Reberty 2000 has a welcoming interior which opens onto a large terrace on the slopes and has extensive lunch and dinner menus. The restaurant takes reservations for a 7 p.m. or 9:30 p.m. seating. Though this one of the top three places in Les Menuires, the fixed-price menu can be relatively affordable at about €25 for appetizer, entree and dessert.

Baroc Cafe (479 55 48 41) owned by the same chef that runs the Michelin-star Oxalys up in Val Thorens, might be called the cusine laboratory of the better know sibling. The focus here is cutting edge experimental cooking at a high gourmet level.

In Les Menuires -- Les Bruyeres:

La Marmite du Géant (479 00 74 75) serves great food in a modern, rustic setting near the skating rink. **La Potiniere** (479 00 61 01) serves excellent family meals with meats, pizzas, Savoyard specialies and fish). It is a good value. **Les Sonnailles** (479 00 74 28) has excellent tartiflette, fondue and raclette together with grilled meats in a very traditional atmosphere complete with accordian music. The owner's wife has an interesting collection of her paintings that create a unique atmosphere.

On the slopes

Try **Chalet des Neiges** (479 00 60 55) at the top of the Roc des 3 Marches lift where you'll get simple good food for €15–€20. **Chalet du Cairn** (479 00 19 81 or 686 72 89 62) has a spreading deck and traditional meals near Chalet des Neiges. The view across to La Masse is spectacular. **Le Grand Lac** (479 08 25 78) at the base of the new Les Granges six-seater chairlift has a perfect position on the slopes with good traditional sit-down meals. It is high on the ridge separating Les Menuires from Meribel and about halfway to St-Martin de Belleville. **Les Roches Blanches** (479 00 60 22) on La Masse is a rustic chalet serving a menu of the day, pizza and spaghetti.

Restaurant La Loy (479 08 92 72) is above the town of St-Martin de Belleville. During the day it is a wonderful place to stop for lunch or a drink alongside the run. Right at the end of the day skiers stop here for the start of a Savoyard fondue adventure complete with appertif, wine, cheese fondue, fondue bourguignon, dessert and coffee for a fixed price of only €35. Skiers who arrived at 5 p.m. can then continue skiing down to the town by the light of the moon or the headlights of a snowmobile. Visitors arriving from the town are picked up at 6 p.m. and brought to the cozy mountain restaurant by snowmobile or four-wheel drive. **Le Chalet de Corbeleys** (479 08 95 31) at the top of the gondola from St-Martin de Belleville serves good mid-day meals.

 ## Après-ski/nightlife

Les Menuires has two small discos packed with the very young, tucked into the basement of the massive apartment buildings. The best is **Leeberty** in Les Bruyeres.

 ## Child care (2007/08 prices)

The tourist office (click here for more information), your hotel or apartment manager can put you in touch with qualified private babysitters who provide child care services at any time of the day or night.

Les Menuires is part of the national "Famille Plus" program that is part of certified children's day care and teaching system. The day care has a miniclub, ski school, entertainment throughout the day and a sledding hill.

The program, **Les Piou-Piou Club**, is divided into three sections: 3 months to 2 1/2 years (nursery), 2-1/2 to 3 years (mini-club) and 3 to 6 years (leisure centre). The nursery costs €14 for lunchtime supervision and a meal; €134 for six half days; and €202 for six full days. Children old enough to join the mini-club and leisure centre have a combination of care and ski instruction. Both programs cost €14 for lunchtime supervision plus meal; €130 for six half days; and €196 for six full days. Reservations and medical certificates are necessary (479 00 63 79).

The ski school also runs special programs for kids 4 years and older. The lessons are coordinated with the **Schtroumpfs' Village** to allow children to spend the time after and before lessons at the child care facility. Six morning lessons cost €137 for four and five year olds and €168 for five and six year olds. Six afternoon lessons cost €102 for ages 4 and 5; and €133 for older children. A free, adult-supervised, shuttlebus is provided every morning (except the weekends) for children in the "Ourson," "Flocon" and "1ère Etoile" lessons.

A second kindergarten, also **Les Piou-Piou Club**, in the Les Bruyères area takes children 2 1/2 to 6 years (479 00 69 50).

Other activities

There is a **heated outdoor pool** open daily from 2:30–7:30 p.m., in les Bruyères. In la Croisette in front of the bus station a new 4,500 square meter **sport and leisure centre** will be opening for the 2005/06 winter season. It will offer everything from Finnish saunas, steam bath, Jacuzzis, hydro-massage jets, swimming pools to sports hall and ultra modern gym. Entrance fees to the aquaclub are from €7.80 to €11.80 for adults and from €3.90 to €5.70 for children. The **outdoor skating rink** in Bruyères is open from 4 p.m.–8 p.m. Call 479 00 69 98. The resort also has two fully equipped **fitness centers**, Espace Tonic and Chalet du Capricorne. There are 28 km. of **cross-country trails** surrounding the resort as well.

For **parasailing** call Adrénaline Sports (479 00 62 49). **Snowshoeing** and **ice climbing** and **extreme skiing** are organized by the ski school. Call 479 00 61 43.

Take a **dog sleigh ride** along the path that follows the Doron River in Saint Martin des Belleville. Choose between a 30-minute circuit and an hour-long circuit that includes a visit of the completely renovated, traditional mountain Burdin Mill. Call 479 00 20 00 or 479 00 73 00 for more information.

Scheduled to open Christmas 2005, the **sports and fitness center** in Les Menuires will have saunas, hammam, Jacuzzis, swimming pool, water jets and paddling pool. It will also feature a large hall as well as areas for dancing, gymnastics, beauty treatments and weight training.

Tourist information

Les Menuires Office du Tourisme, 73440 Les Menuires, France; Telephone 04 79 00 73 00; fax 04 79 00 75 06.
For reservations only, call 04 79 00 79 79; fax 04 79 00 60 92.
Internet: www.lesmenuires.com.
E-mail: lesmenuires@lesmenuires.com

Saint Martin de Belleville Office du Tourisme, 73440 Saint Martin de Belleville, France; Telephone 04 79 00 20 00;
fax 04 79 08 91 71. Internet: www.st-martin-belleville.com
Email: stmartin@st-martin-belleville.com

VAL THORENS

None of the Trois Vallées villages is more attuned to the single-minded pursuit of winter sport than Val Thorens. From the moment you park your car in indoor parking near this cluster of high-rise apartments and hotels, you can feel the hum of sport activity. At 7,546 feet, Val Thorens is designed for the young and restless, or at least for the young-at-heart and active. Its altitude is the highest of any European resort. Besides some of the best winter skiing offered anywhere, there's a huge newly renovated indoor sports complex and Aqua Club where you can play tennis on one of three courts, work out in the gym or try your hand at squash.

Outside, the crowd is one teeming mass of rainbow-colored movement: snow-mobilers, skiers, snowboarders, parasailors and monoskiers riding high-speed lifts and winding through the apartment and hotel complexes. The real claim to fame is the atmosphere of sport, sure snow and the lofty location of this fun town.

The neon signs, bright splashy ads and general carnival atmosphere of Val Thorens makes it feel like a video arcade. In some Alpine resorts they play acoustic oom-pah, but here it's bass-heavy "Techno Euro-Rock" blaring from speakers. After a slight decompression period, however, the look feels in sync with the area's character: fun-loving, sporting and slightly outrageous. If you're looking to have a drink of wine and a laugh with the locals, then you'll fit right in. If you want to be waited on and pampered by lift attendants and polite locals alike, better to book St. Moritz.

 ## Mountain layout

Even with the high altitude of Val Thorens, one of the biggest capital improvements has been the continued installation of snowmaking. Though this resort gets plenty of snow, the strong sun during the spring makes snowmaking on the southern-facing slopes desirable. It is one more example of the region trying to make the skiing experience as good as possible.

As the highest resort in the Alps, Val Thorens is wide-open, bowl-type skiing above treeline. The Péclet cablecar takes skiers up to the glacier with winter skiing for intermediates and above. While most of the skiing in the bowl-shaped area is intermediate and advanced, experts can find plenty of challenges.

The cablecar ride to the top of Cîme de Caron, the highest point in the three valleys, is spectacular if you are lucky enough to be blessed with clear weather and limited winds. The view alone is worth the trip. From here you can take a black run straight down or a slightly easier advanced intermediate. True experts will want to ski over the ridge to the little-used fourth valley and then take the Rosael quad chair that will bring you back. There are some newly developed trails in this valley with a new chairlift just added. When skiing Val Thorens be ready for changeable weather. At this altitude the winds can pick up in an instant and clouds can move in quickly. Dress for winter conditions, even if the skies are clear and the sun strong when you leave the base area for Cime Caron.

If you want to explore the rest of Les Trois Vallées, hop on the Funitel Bouquetin, a lift which has been specifically designed to transport skiers between Val Thorens and the rest of Les Trois Vallées even in bad weather conditions.

Mountain rating

No one will have any problem finding the perfect skiing for their level. Beginners will be able to stick close to the village. Intermediates will have the run of all the slopes surrounding the town. Advanced and expert skiers will have off-piste opportunities and plenty of steeps to challenge them.

Ski school (2007/08 prices)

All of the area's resorts have excellent instructors who teach Alpine skiing, cross-country and snowboarding. There are more than 140 in Val Thorens. Val Thorens has four different ski schools. The French Ski School or E.S. F. (479 00 02 86), Pro-Neige (479 01 07 00), Ski Cool (479 00 04 92) and Ski School International (479 00 01 96).

At the French Ski School, **private lessons** start at €38 per afternoon hour and €45 for a morning hour. Private guides cost €320–€340 for a full day for five skiers.

Group lessons (age 12 and younger) cost €138 for six mornings, €127 for six afternoons and €198 for six full days.

Children's lessons (age 4 to 12) cost €125 for six mornings, €91 for six afternoons and €260 for six full days with meals (€175 for six full days without meals).

Snowboarding lessons cost €135 for six mornings or €110 six afternoons.

For skiers looking for a guide, the ski school forms groups that ski all day Monday through Friday. The cost for the full week group is about €260.

Accommodations

Val Thorens has a sporty feel. This is not luxury hotel territory, however there are several excellent hotels that have virtually every ammenity. Prices are per person based on double occupancy during February with half board. €€€—€125+; €€—€75–€124; € is less than €75.

Fitz Roy (479 00 04 78, fax 479 00 06 11; €€€) The luxury hotel in town. Some rooms are split level other are traditional. many have fireplaces. There is a lucious spa. Meals are a quantum leap above those of the rest of Val Thorens except Oxalys.

l'Oxalys – Chalet (479 32 75 31; €€€) is a new luxury option with 25 apartments for four to eight persons. Each has a fireplace and most hotel services. The hotel restaurant has one Michelin star. Make reservations to insure a seat. It is very popular with the Courchevel crowd who ski over for lunch.

Le Val Thorens (479 00 04 33, fax 479 00 09 40; €€) For American tastes this is perhaps the best hotel in town. The breakfast is not the usual croissant and coffee but a full buffet complete with eggs. Walk out your door and onto the slopes.

Hotel Bel Horizon (479 00 04 77; fax 479 00 06 08; €€) Right on the edge of the complex with south-facing rooms, this hotel offers good-sized rooms but a very French atmosphere, limited English speaking help and excellent food.

Le Sherpa (479 00 00 70, fax 479 00 08 03; €€) It is family-run and offers excellent value for money, with excellent food and 14 new luxury rooms.

Les Trois Vallées (479 00 01 86, fax 479 00 04 08; €€) In the center of action with a good bar and good service.

Novotel (479 00 04 04, fax 479 00 05 93; €€€) The resort's biggest with 104 rooms complete with most ammenities but no pool.

Le Portillo (479 00 00 88; fax 479 00 05 65; €€) has 15 rooms and every one is different. It just was raised from a two-star to a three-star property.

La Marmotte (479 00 00 07; fax 479 00 00 14; €) Sparsely furnished, very basic.

Les Montagnettes du Soleil (479 00 20 51; fax 479 00 24 39; €€) only has suites for up to four. This apartment with hotel services for foursomes, is a big bargain.

Ski Chalets: Crystal, Thompson, Thomas Cook/Neilson (go to page 16 for phone, fax and Internet addresses).

Apartments, condominiums, flats

Apartments are the French choice for accommodation. In fact, apartment beds outnumber hotel beds by at least five to one. What you get is the ability to schedule off-slope life at your own pace and a way to avoid the high hotel prices.

Val Thorens has a bevy of "residences" that are basically apartments with hotel services. You have a restaurant, and beds will be made up upon arrival but there is no housekeeping or room service.

The **Village Montana** (479 00 21 01), is one of the most luxurious and costs about €700 a week for a two bedroom with living room and kitchen from mid-January to mid-February. The **Chalet Altitude** (479 00 85 00) with similar amenities is around €950 for about the same space during the same timeframe.

Less expensive locations are the **Balcons de Val Thorens** (479 00 90 70) and **Pierre et Vacances** (479 09 30 30).

The tourist office will send more information and a registration card and will help make reservations. Make sure to impress on them that you are Americans or British and want a larger apartment. If you are four people and you pay for an apartment for five, it is probably worth the extra money. Nothing is worse than being stuck in a room about the size of one found on a cruise ship when you have all your ski equipment.

Dining

Val Thorens now has a Michelin-star restaurant, **l'Oxalys** (479 00 12 00) that is right on the slopes is anchored by their chef Jean Sulpice.

Lovers of fine French food should head for the **Fitz Roy Hotel** (479 00 04 78). The atmosphere is romantic and the surroundings plush.

The restaurant **Restaurant des Trois Vallees** (479 00 01 86), serves excellent French cuisine. A full meal from the fixed menu can be enjoyed from €30.

Next on the list in descending order are **Le Bellevillois** (479 00 04 33), **Auberge du Sherpa** (479 00 00 70), and **La Grange de Pierette** in the Portillo Hotel.

Le Vieux Chalet (479 00 07 93) has wonderful typical upscale Savoyard specialties from omelettes to raclette and fondue.

For more local blue-collar Savoyard specialties, try the **Galoubet** (479 00 00 48). **La Fondue** (479 00 04 33) has cheese fondue and raclette. **La Luna** (479 00 05 75) has its fans as well.

El Gringo waiters decked in cowboy gear serve the highest altitude Tex-Mex dinners in Europe with killer margaritas. **Le Choucas** (479 00 04 98) serves specialties from the south of France as well as typical Savoyard meals. Tartiflette will cost €17 and delicious Breast of Duck is served for €17.50. **Les 3 Pachas** (479 00 05 84) has very affordable lunch meals (€12) and is packed even on slow days at the resort.

Blanchot (479 00 55 78) is a wine bar with good dinners.

La Paillote (479 00 01 02) is rustic family place with very affordable meals and pizzas. Plat du Jour is normally about €12 and basic wine sets you back €13.

The best pizza—and for that matter the best deal—in town is at **Le Scapin** (479 00 05 94).

Val Thorens has an exceptional Savoyard gourmet shop, la **Belle en Cuisse** (479 00 04 30) that sells dried mountain meats and sausages as well as regional jams, honey and pates. The owner has an almost mystical connection with the local foods and will suggest different combinations that will delight any palate. For anyone staying in an apartment, the ingredients for fondue costs €29 for four; raclette ingredients per person cost €10; and the fixings for tartiflette cost about €8 per person.

Après-ski/nightlife

The nightlife in Val Thorens used to be limited, but now you can choose from three discos that don't start until after midnight and keep on throbbing until 4 a.m., or you can drink in one of ten pubs. Those hot to trot head for **Beach Mountain** nightclub, which has a €15 cover (one drink included). Prepare yourself for outrageous prices, by U.S. standards, if you plan on drinking much. **Bar Malaysia** just outside the tourist office is a surprise. Don't let the small entranceway fool you: the bar itself is underground and very classy. The live music tends toward the avant-garde and there are pool tables (€5–€11 per drink, no cover). **The Ski Rock Cafe**, **Gringo's**, the **Frog and Roast Beef** and the **Viking** all have lively action.

 ## Child care (2007/08 prices)

The tourist office, your hotel or apartment manager can put you in touch with qualified private baby sitters who provide child care services at any time of the day or night.

Val Thorens has two Mini Clubs associated with the ski school (479 00 02 86 and 479 00 02 38). These Mini-Club kindergartens accept children ages 3 months to 6 years. Ask about discounts for three or more children from the same family. Children age 3 months to 18 months cost €129 for six half days without meals. Children age 18 months to 3 years cost €129 for six half days without meals.

The various ski schools all give children's lessons for children who are about 4 or 5 years old. Beginners lessons for ages 4 and younger at the ESF are €121 for five half days skiing or snowboarding; and €178 for five full days.

 ## Other activities

Facilities include an **indoor swimming pool, whirlpool baths, saunas, squash courts, six indoor tennis courts** and a **gymnasium**. Aerobics is offered.

Val Thorens also has Europe's highest **toboggan run** set in a natural 6-km.-long valley with a vertical drop of more than 2,200 feet. It is in the Tête Ronde sector at the foot of the Péclet glacier. The run is reached by the Funitel.

 ## Tourist information

Val Thorens Office du Tourisme, 73440 Val Thorens, France; Telephone: 479 00 08 08; fax 479 00 00 04.
Internet: www.valthorens.com. E-mail: valtho@valthorens.com
Reservations are handled by Val Thorens Reservations;
Telephone: 479 00 01 06; fax 479 00 06 49.
Internet: www.valthorens.com. E-mail: reserver@valthorens.com

Val d'Isère

Val d'Isère has long been one of the true European meccas of skiing. Although the professional ski world knew Val d'Isère, the average skier began to hear more about it after native Jean-Claude Killy won his Olympic gold in 1968. The town was also home to three other Olympic champions who won a total of nine gold medals.

The town lies at 6,070 feet (at its lowest point) and the ski area rises to 11,340 feet, with working verticals of more than 3,250 feet in all sectors of the resort. Skiers looking for the best on- and off-trail runs in the world need look no further.

Unlike many French purpose-built resorts, Val d'Isère is actually a village dating back from the 11th century. Unfortunately, when it was initially being developed, architects opted for functionally square, flat-topped hotels. Recently, though, new buildings have been constructed in the Savoyard Alpine chalet style and many of the unprepossessing buildings have been dressed up with facades to create more of a mountain atmosphere.

The ski area is linked with Tignes, creating "l'Espace Killy," with 186 miles of marked runs for every level of skier, tried-and-true off-piste itineraries for serious experts and 90 lifts, including an underground lift with an uphill capacity of more than 3,000 skiers per hour.

 ## Mountain layout–Skiing

An area as enormous as Val d'Isère/Tignes is virtually impossible to describe in words. Your first clue will be when you exit from the Funival or Bellevarde cablecar and look out over the seemingly endless fields of snow. Even the trail map, on a relatively small scale, gives no feel for the immensity of the area.

The Val d'Isère share of l'Espace Killy is divided into four sectors corresponding with the three main ridges dropping into the town and the glacier area.

Le Fornet sector is reached by Le Fornet cablecar, which rises the first 1,246 feet. From the top of the cablecar, skiers can drop back down into the town on a steep and narrow expert run directly under the cables or loop to their right around an advanced beginner trail. There are also two choices of lifts further up the mountain. The gondola leaving from the cablecar building reaches the Col d'Isèran area, which provides access to skiing on the Glacier de Pissaillas or allows skiers to take the connecting lift to the

Solaise sector. The very long Signal drag lift will take you to just under the Signal peak at 10,633 feet. From there you can take a tough intermediate trail back to the cablecar or drop into the off-trail Le Vallon powder fields, which then drop more than 3,000 feet back to the base of the Fornet cablecar.

The Solaise sector is also reached by cablecar from the village center. This area is a wide-open beginner and intermediate paradise. About 1,500 vertical feet wait for open slope cruising. Off-piste itineraries from the Solaise will keep any expert happy.

The Bellevarde sector has the best access, with four methods of getting to the top of Rocher de Bellevarde and two additional lifts serving intermediate and beginner runs from La Daille. The Funival, a high-speed subway, rises from La Daille through the rock to the top of Rocher de Bellevarde. A new cablecar, l'Olympique, carries skiers up the La Face side to the top of Bellevarde. Beginners have a series of runs at higher altitudes and a choice between two long runs with more than a 2,900-foot vertical back to La Daille. Intermediates have their choice of two more challenging drops back to La Daille. Intermediates can drop down La Face or into the valley back to the town. There are also excellent off-piste routes from the top of the Bellevarde sector. Take Le Kern around the front of the cliff and drop through powder back to town. You can also take the drag lift to the side of the Charvet rock cluster and ski around the backside of the formation entering the valley, eventually returning to town, or drop down to La Daille off-piste.

Mountain rating

There is something for everyone; the upper reaches are excellent for any skier level. Experts can test themselves on the steeps that sail into town and on extensive off-trail and powder-skiing pockets. It's a good idea to take a guide along, at least for a day, to find the best places to test your limits. Also, if you plan to ski off-trail, check with the ski school before you leave for the latest information on snow conditions.

Mountain layout—Snowboarding

Most snowboarders, based on economics and terrain, tend to spend time at Tignes rather than Val d'Isère. However, the drops into the town will thrill any rider. The main problem is the series of flats sprinkling the upper reaches of the resort mean walking or hopping along. There is a snowboard park at the top of the La Daille serviced by the Mont Blanc chairlift.

Cross-Country and snowshoeing (2006/07 prices)

L'Espace Killy has a total of 44 km of tracks. Cross country skiing circuits can be found in the Manchet valley, La Daille, near the Fornet and at the Ouillette lake.

Snowshoeing: Both the Killy Sport Shop (479 41 10 01) and the Aventure Voile Montagne (662 17 62 62) arrange "diner raquettes," hiking excursions through the mountain forests to a traditional French restaurant. The Killy Sport Shop trips take place every evening. The Aventure Voile Montagne trips are in Vanoise. Ecole du Ski Francais (479 06 02 34) also has excursions every morning from 9:30 a.m. to 12:30 a.m. which cost €29 and every afternoon from 2:30 p.m. to 5 p.m. which cost €22.50. A full day excursion costs €42.

Ski school (2006/07 prices)

The Val d'Isère French Ski School boasts Jean-Claude Killy as its technical adviser. Its ski instructors are among the most qualified in the world: three former world champions and many members of the national ski team serve on the staff. In total, there are 300 instructors including 19 mountain guides who can teach any level of skier, from the basic beginner to the Olympic caliber racer. English is spoken by many of the instructors. (If required, ask for an English-speaking instructor.)

French Ski School (ESF) offices are in the Village Center (479 06 02 34) and in La Daille shopping center (479 06 09 99).

Private lessons: A lesson lasting an hour for one to four skiers costs €40. One-and-a-half hours for one to four skiers will cost €60. Instructors or guides can be hired during high season for the full day for €295 for up to four people; €339 for five; and €359 for six skiers or more.

Group lessons: These rates apply to alpine and cross-country skiing as well as snowshoe outings. Courses cost €219 for six full days of lessons, which run from 9:30 a.m. to 12:30 p.m. and from 2:30 p.m. to 5 p.m. A full day is €42; a morning lesson is €29 and an afternoon lesson is €22.50.

Snowboarding lessons: Group lessons in the Eagle Snowboard Club are from 9:30 a.m. to 12:30 p.m. and from 2:30 p.m. to 5 p.m. A full day is €51; a morning lesson is €32 and an afternoon lesson is €25.50.

There are several other ski schools and guide organizations. Instructors are bilingual, speaking English and French. Sign up with the English section of Snow Fun, the largest non-EFS school, at the Solaise Gallery (479 06 19 79). Altimanya Ski School specializes in moguls. Alpine Experience focuses on powder instruction. Surf Rider Club is a snowboard school and Top Ski has instruction in extreme skiing.

There are also powder skiing lessons for a six-day course and day trips to La Plagne, Les Arcs and La Rosière/La Thuile for expeditions. Heliskiing is also offered. The helicopter drops you into Italy for backcountry skiing.

Lift tickets (2007/08 prices)

The prices below are for **l'Espace Killy**, which includes 97 lifts serving 140 runs in the interconnected Tignes/Val d'Isère area and more than 300 km. of runs.

	Adult	**Children** (5-13) **& Senior** (60-74)
half day	€30.50	€24.50
one day	€42	€33.50
six days	€202.50	€162
seven days	€231	€185

Insurance adds about €2.50 per day for adults and €2 per day for children.

Children younger than age 5 and seniors age 75 and older ski free. A photo is needed for all tickets two days or more and to receive the discounted rates.

Six- to 21-day tickets are valid for one day of your stay on La Plagne, Les Arcs ski lifts. The tickets are also good for a day at Les Trois Vallées and a day at Valmorel; a half-price pass at Sainte Foy; and a special price on the San Bernado espace.

The lift company will refund part of your lift ticket price if extreme weather forces closure of the lifts when you have a three- to 21-day lift ticket. Apply to the ticket office for the prorated refund.

Accommodations

The tourist office and the hoteliers have organized special weekly discount programs organized for low and shoulder season periods. Costs for the program are based on the hotel category and the package being offered. Packages include seven nights accommodation with bath or shower, seven-day lift ticket and pool pass. For instance, during mid January, a four-star hotel package will be €169 per person each day for half board; a three-star package is €126 per person each day for half board; a two-star will cost €102 per person each day for half board and the one-star hotel package is only €88 per person each day for half board.

The central reservations system, run by Val Hotel, can make arrangements unless noted otherwise. They will also provide information on the packages. Contact: Val Hotel, BP 73, 73153 Val d'Isère Cedex, France; (479 06 18 90).

The hotels listed here have all been visited by *Ski Snowboard Europe* journalists. Rates are based on double occupancy during February with half board. €€€=€125+; €€=€75–€124; €=less than €75.

Hotel Grand Paradis (479 06 11 73; €€€+) is a three-star hotel with one of the best locations in the resort—just across the street from the lifts—plus, underground parking. The hotel's beautiful 36 rooms, four suites and Le Schuss restaurant have all benefited from their recent renovations.

Hotel Maeva Latitudes (479 06 18 88; €€€+) is a four-star establishment in the village center that has a sauna, gym and two restaurants that serve traditional local fare.

Hotel Christiania (479 06 08 25; €€€) is a chalet-style, four-star hotel two minutes from the lifts and full of atmosphere. The suites available on the top floor are among the best in the resort, with beautiful bathrooms and antique country furniture.

Hotel Mercure (479 06 12 93; €€) is a three-star modern hotel in the center of the village—the perfect business hotel—clean, convenient and efficient.

Hotel La Savoyarde (479 06 01 55; €€€) is our favorite hotel in Val d'Isère. This three-star is chalet-style and has a cozy sauna and spacious restaurant. Its best feature is its location in the center of town only steps away from the lifts.

The Kandahar (479 06 02 39; €€) is a three-star lodge built over the Taverne d'Alsace.

Hotel Samovar (479 06 13 51; €€–€€€) is oozing with charm. This hotel is out of the town center facing the funicular. Its restaurant is consistently rated as one of the best in town. Rooms are weathered but comfortable. The owner says he wants to create the atmosphere of a chalet rather than a hotel. Ask for room 10—an Old World, old wood masterpiece. The buffet breakfast is sumptuous.

Hotel Les Sorbiers (479 06 23 77; €€€) is a beautiful three-star hotel built in modern chalet style in the center of the resort. The interiors are rich with golden wood and rooms are cozy with nice views of either the mountains or the village. The hotel offers only B&B arrangements.

Hotel Altitude (479 06 12 55; €€) has one of the coziest restaurants of any hotel in the village. The rooms have been recently renovated.

Chamois d'Or (479 06 00 44; €€) is a two-star hotel filled with old Alpine charm. The restaurant has a giant fireplace. Rooms vary in size, but all have ample space. The hotel is only steps away from the cablecars up to the Solaise and the Bellevarde. If you want atmosphere, this is the place.

For a quiet change of pace outside of the town try **Le Chalet du Lac** (479 06 25 47; €–€€), a new hotel alongside the lake a few kilometers outside of La Daille. This hotel offers, for those with a car, a position between Tignes and Val d'Isère.

Hotel Barmes de l'Ours (475 41 37 00; €€€+) is a four-star luxury hotel at the bottom of La Face, complete with indoor swimming pool and one of the largest spas in the Alps.

Ski Chalets: Crystal, Inghams/Bladon, Total, Thompson (see page 16 for phone, fax and Internet addresses).

Apartments, condominiums, flats

The tourist office maintains an extensive list of individuals and agencies who will rent apartments in the resort.

Aparthotels combine apartments with hotel service. The most elegant of these establishments are the **Les Domaines du Soleil** which has a swimming pool. Two similar aparthotels are **Les Chalets du Jardin Alpin** and **Eureka Val**. The **Alpina Lodge** also offers similar arrangements. Apartment prices are about €230–€762 for a studio in mid January and €495–€1,319 for a two-room apartment during the same period. In February and early March rates junp to €345–€1,020 for a studio sleeping two to four and €926–€2,324 for a two-room unit which will sleep five to six. In many cases, linen is not included but can be rented from the apartment owners or agencies.

For apartment accommodation in the region contact **Val Location** (479 06 06 60, fax 479 41 95 59).

 ## Dining

Surprisingly, Val d'Isère has few nationally recognized restaurants. The smaller places that have traditionally offered the top meals are being pressed by the local hotels that offer excellent meals at reasonable prices.

La Table de l'Ours inside Hotel Barmes de l'Ours (475 41 37 00) serves award-winning meals and has a Michelin one-star rating to prove it.

L'Atelier d'Edmond (479 00 00 82), a gourmet restaurant in the Fornet village, is owned byJacques Leprivey who is the grandson of Edmond Leprivey, Val d'Isère's first ski patroller and a do-it-yourself genius. His workshop of tools is on display in one of the theme dining areas. A second area represents a mountain refuge and a third is organised around an immense fireplace. Meticulous service, an original menu and a shuttle service for guests, make this restaurant a true dining experience.

Pier Paul Jack (479 40 10 40) in the Aigle des Neiges hotel is actually three places in one and currently one of the most popular spots in the area. Pier is the hotel restaurant. Paul is the smaller original 'world cuisine' restaurant. Jack is the bar where you can try tapas while enjoying live music.

Le Grande Ourse (479 06 00 19) still reigns as the top restaurant in Val d'Isère after decades in that position. The interior is the most beautiful of any restaurant in the region. It's almost worth the price just to eat in such surroundings. Meals here are as gourmet as they get in Val d'Isère. Expect to pay €35–€50 for meal with wine.

Hotel Savoyarde Restaurant (479 06 01 55) is consistently mentioned as the second-best eatery. The dining room has a beautiful wooden ceiling, a warm Savoyard atmosphere and a delightful menu for €30–€40, including wine.

The Hotel Bellier Restaurant (479 06 03 77) serves excellent fare. Menu prices are about €25 with wine. The dining room is an elegant and cozy Alpine spot. Reservations are recommended unless you're a hotel guest.

Both of the following restaurants are within a stone's throw of one another in the La Daille ski area. They serve good meals in some of the resort's most rustic settings.

The Samovar (479 06 13 51) in La Daille serves wholesome meals. Besides their tradional Savoyard dishes, there's also freshly baked, homemade pizza every night.

La Vieille Maison (479 06 11 76) also in La Daille serves Savoyard specialties in the atmosphere of a flickering fire, whitewashed walls and flagstone floors.

These restaurants serve up less costly meals:

Restaurant La Corniche (479 06 18 75) tucked between the stone buildings of the old village, is a new spot with a splendid dining room. Stone walls alternate with wood—this is how a modern Alpine restaurant should look. Expect to spend €20.

Taverne d'Alsace (479 06 48 49) serves up German-Alsatian cuisine, including a potent onion cake, in a very cozy bar setting.

Restaurant Bellevue, across the street from the tourist office, is a good, inexpensive restaurant where you can get away for less than €17–€20.

For pizza, try **Perdrix Blanche**. Cheese fondue (€12), fondue bourgogne (€20) and raclette (€12) are best sampled in **La Raclette** in Hotel Avancher (479 06 02 00) and **Restaurant Arolay** in Le Fornet (479 06 11 68).

On the slopes, try **La Folie Douce**; **La Fruitière** at La Daille midstation; and **Bellevarde** at the top of the funival. Also try **Cabaret des Neiges** at the midstation at Solaise; **La Datcha** at Solaise; **Les Tufs** at the base of La Daille; and **La Taniere** at the midstation of La Face.

Après-ski/nightlife

Val d'Isère has great nightlife. For après-ski head to **Moris Pub**. **Dick's Tea Bar** also has good immediate après-ski with happy hour, videos and then jazz before the disco scene cranks in. Check out the various happy hours 4–7 p.m.

For nightlife, **Dick's Tea Bar** is the main English-language hangout. New bars in town are the **Café Face** in the Christiania Hotel and **St. Hubert Pub** under the St. Hubert Hotel. Avoid these places if you are searching for a quiet spot to talk. For a real French disco, try **Le Graal**. For Scandinavian bars, try **Petit Danois** or **Victors**. **Perdrix Blanche** is normally packed with a young crowd after skiing and **Taverne d'Alsace** offers a very rustic bar and quieter après-ski for a slightly older crowd.

Child care (2006/07 prices)

There are many alternatives for child care in Val d'Isère. The hotels and the tourist office can put you in touch with private babysitting services (479 06 06 60) and the ski schools have plenty of programs.

Le Petit Poucet (479 06 13 97) is for children age 3 and older. There are indoor activities (including computers) as well as outdoor fun. Costs are €43 a day and €245 for six days. Open from 9 a.m. until 5 p.m., Le Petit Poucet has bus service that shuttles the children to care.

Another facility is the French Ski School, with an extensive programs for kids ages 4–13. The Jardin des Neiges takes ages 4 and 5 for lessons at €39 from 9:30 a.m. to 12:30 p.m.: €32 from 10:30 a.m. to 12:30 p.m.; and €32 from 2:30 p.m. to 5 p.m..

The Village des Enfants (479 40 09 81) takes kids ages 3–8 in the mornings from 9 am - 12:30 pm and in the afternoons from 2 pm - 5:45 pm. With lunch, one full day costs €50. With lunch and ski instruction, six mornings cost €215.

Other activities

The town offers good but limited activities for non-skiers. There is a covered, heated **swimming pool** open from 2 p.m. to 7 p.m., with a daily entrance fee of €4.80 for adults and €3 for children (free to holders of seven- to 21-day ski passes). Cards for 10 entries are available.

Paragliding courses are offered by Air Professionnels Parapente Val d'Isère (609 46 64 78 / 662 10 66 73) and Evolution 2 Ecole d'aventure (479 41 16 72).

Viking Snowmobile (615 19 46 29) has night **snowmobiling** at Tovière plateau.

Snowshoeing walks and lessons are offered by Pascal Bertres (613 85 64 77).

Getting there

The closest airports are in Lyon and Geneva. Geneva is about 112 miles and Lyons is 137 miles from the resort (about a three-hour drive). Rail transport via TGV is quick and easy from Paris to Bourg-St. Maurice, where a bus takes you to the resort.

Driving from Geneva, take A41 to Annecy; then N90 to Albertville; follow the signs to Bourg-St. Maurice and on to Val d'Isère. From Lyon, take autoroute A43 to Albertville and on to Val d'Isère. Direct bus service leaves from Geneva airport three or four times a day and there is weekend service from Lyon Airport to Val d'Isère.

Tourist information

For information, contact Office du Tourisme, BP 228, 73155 Val d'Isère, France; tel. 479 06 06 60; fax 479 06 04 56. **Internet:** www.valdisere.com, **E-mail:** info@valdisere.com
For hotel accommodations: phone 479 06 18 90, fax 479 06 11 88 **Internet:** www.valdisere.com, **Email:** valhotel@valdisere.com

Garmisch-Partenkirchen Germany

The Olympic city Garmisch-Partenkirchen at the base of the Zugspitze, the country's highest mountain (9,721 feet), is Germany's best and most famous ski resort. Here, Germany hosted the Winter Olympic Games in 1936. Those games were the impetus to link the two villages into one. The villagers were less than enthusiastic so Hitler gave them an alternative that was much less pleasant, so unification was quickly approved. Even though these two towns are officially unified, they unofficially still compete with each other. There are two of everything: two fire stations, two schools and so on. Only the Olympic venues are shared, but to this date the Partenkirchen side handles all the arrangements for the ski jumping competitions and keeps the proceeds. The town of Garmisch takes care of the World Cup downhill races and those riches. Even though joint towns strive to keep from being termed a city, they have a population of 28,000, and have many benefits of city life such as concerts, shows and great shopping.

Partenkirchen is cute, cozy, with narrow streets and a center filled with painted houses. Unfortunately the town has a couple of square highrises interrupting the Old-World harmony. Garmisch seems more organized with a grid of streets lined with new concrete buildings intermingled with Alpine chalets and more upscale shopping streets. The Munich/Innsbruck highway abruptly divides the two sections of the city—there is no easy transition from one to the other.

Garmisch-Partenkirchen's location, less than an hour's drive from Munich and about an hour and a half from the new Munich airport, makes it a natural tourist attraction. Since the city government purchased the Zugspitzbahn giving them control over all lifts, new alliances have been created with former competitors just over the border in Austria—Lermoos and Seefeld—to make an international series of ski areas which can be skied with one lift ticket, the Happy Ski Card.

The Garmisch-Partenkirchen lifts and slopes are not located right in the town. For the most part a car will make a vacation a bit easier, especially if you plan to take advantage of any of the Austrian resorts included in the area passes.

Hotels distribute a Visitor's Card to overnight guests that allows free use of the buses, free accident insurance, free entrance to town, free access to many venues and discounts on others. Visitors will have to ask for the best bus routes to reach the lifts. Some hotels also issue a special visitor card for weeklong guests which includes entrance to the museums; a horse-drawn-sleigh ride; ice skating; an introduction to snowboarding, telemark, or skating courses and more.

Lermoos and Seefeld are the two largest Austrian villages linked with Garmisch-Partenkirchen by a common lift ticket. Both are about a half-hour drive away, but both offer an Alpine village setting rather than the hustle of a little city. These may be considered for those planning a vacation with young children.

Mountain layout—Skiing

Garmisch-Partenkirchen offers nearly 75 miles of runs, but the rugged Alpine landscape prevents any sort of continuous ski circuit between the seven different trail systems. There are two large areas. One is on the high slopes of the Zugspitze plateau and the other is the Garmisch-Partenkirchen Classic Area at Hausberg, Kreuzeck and Osterfelder with its famous World Cup runs.

The Zugspitze plateau is reached by taking the cogwheel train or the cable car from Lake Eibsee in Grainau, a neighbor village of Garmisch-Partenkirchen. The train is more direct; the cable car more scenic. Skiing here is at its best in early November and December, and in spring—April and May—when other resorts are closing. Best of the trails is the two-mile run from the Schneefernerkopf at 9,427 feet.

Garmisch-Partenkirchen hosted the Winter Olympics in 1936, and its facilities are well maintained. The World Cup runs on the Kreuzeck and the neighboring Hausberg provide several difficult turns, but overall it's perfect terrain for intermediates.

Our favorite runs are from the Osterfelderkopf. From here you can make the only real skiing circuit in Garmisch, linking up with lifts from the Hausberg below.

For Zugspitze fans there is a new six-seater chairlift to the glacier at 9,186 feet. A tunnel from the cog railway eliminates walking and climbing, and allows direct access to the slopes. During the past years, the resort has established many new and more difficult trails on the Zugspitze. According to locals, the plateau is now great for all levels of skiers rather than only intermediates and beginners.

For another ski adventure and often shorter lift lines, take the border highway past Grainau into Austria. On the other side of the Zugspitze, less than a 30-minute drive away, you can try the slopes of Ehrwald. When Garmisch-Partenkirchen's weather is bad, the sun will sometimes be shining here. Neighboring Lermoos and Biberwier, in Austria, are popular with local skiers.

Lermoos has a great skiers' mountain. A gondola, then a high-speed quad take skiers up to a surprising wonderland perfect for intermediates. A section of the mountain called "the gumdrops" is dotted with small mounds of snow that form over bushes and provide a playground for snowboarders and kids of all ages. A day here is a must for anyone in the area.

In the other direction, at Mittenwald, the Damkar run from the 7,822-foot Karwendel summit is challenging and the mountain panorama is superb.

Telephone prefix for Garmisch-Partenkirchen: 08821
Telephone prefix for Germany: 0049

Mountain layout—Snowboarding

Snowboarders can have a blast on the Zugspitze plateau which has wide slopes and a good-size fun-park. They can make cool jumps using the varied terrain and the many natural obstacles on the plateau. Deep-snow fans will enjoy the Osterfelder region, particularly the area around the Bernadein lift.

Each year in early summer, snowboarders and freestylers meet at the "Spring in the Park" camp. This is the biggest and best-known event of its kind, closing out the season with perfectly shaped terrain, a fun park with kickers and rails, coaching, material testing, a relax-and-test area, popular programs, and legendary parties.

Mountain rating

Garmisch-Partenkirchen is intermediate country but with new trails is becoming a good spot for advanced and expert skiers. The challenging parts of red runs might be considered black in other areas. The Zugspitze has added advanced terrain and the difficult World Cup sections on the Kreuzeck and Hausberg tests upper-level skiers.

The advanced beginner and intermediate will find it the place to be. Beginners could not come to a better place for outstanding ski instruction.

In nearby Austria, Lermoos has great intermediate trails and is snowboarder heaven. Seefeld has mellower trails but offers a larger Austrian village atmosphere.

Garmisch has excellent cross-country trails. There are 29 km. of maintained trails in the area. Nearby Seefeld in Austria is considered by many to be the premier cross-country area in Europe. It was twice the site of Olympic competitions. Lermoos, Ehrwald and Biberwier also are connected with a 60-km. tracked cross-country network and linked with another 40 km. of trails in the surrounding region.

Ski school (2006/07)

Garmisch-Partenkirchen's ski school program includes off-trail touring instruction, snowboarding and an outstanding climbing school. Eight schools offer instruction in the area. The following are the prices for the **Skischule Garmisch-Partenkirchen** (76260 or 4931) at the Hausberg slope.. Rates for the various schools are all within five Euros of each other.

Private lessons for skiing, snowboarding and cross-country skiing for one hour are €40; two hours are €75 and three hours are €105.

Group ski lessons for one day cost €35 (three hours); for three days, €85; for five days, €110. Group snowboarding lessons cost €35 for a day; €65 for two days; €85 for three days; €100 for four days; and €110 for five days.

Group cross-country skiing lessons cost €26 for one day; for two days, €50.

All the following ski schools have good reputations, but their locations may play a role in your choice. The schools also offer cross-country instruction and most have snowboarding equipment for lessons for every level and age.

Skischule Thomas Sprenzel (1496) near Hausberg.

Skischule Flori Wörndle (58300) At the Hausberg cable car station.

Erste Skilanglaufschule (1516) Cross-country school at the Olympic stadium.

Bergsteigerschule Zugspitze (58999) Mountain climbing and ski touring instruction with skins and ice climbing.

Lift tickets (2007/08 prices)

A day ticket for the Garmisch-Partenkirchen Classic area (excluding the Zugspitze) is €31.50 for adults, €25.50 for youth ages 16-17 and

€19.50 for kids from ages 5–15.

Zugspitze Area lifts cost €37.50 for adults, €27 for youths, €22.50 for children. You also can also buy a Twin-Ticket for €65 and ski for two days in Zugspitze or ski for one day in Zugspitze and the other day at Garmisch-Partenkirchen Classic Area.

An all-inclusive lift ticket for Garmisch-Partenkirchen lifts and several of the surrounding towns called the Happy Ski Card, is available. It is good for transport on all 101 lifts in the Zugspitze region, including the Zugspitze itself. It includes skiing at the following resorts—Garmisch-Partenkirchen, Seefeld, Reith, Mittenwald, Ehrwald, Lermoos, Biberwier, Bichlbach, Berwang and Heiterwang.

	Adults	**Youth** (ages 16-18)	**Children** (ages 6–15)
three days	€91	€83.50	€54.50
six days	€169.50	€156	€101.50
thirteen days	€285.50	€262.50	€171

 Accommodations

You can quickly find a place to stay, anywhere from a farmhouse or an ultra-luxurious hotel. The tourist office offers a series of inclusive one-week vacation plans that combine hotel, lifts and local transportation. Prices range from about €300 for a room in a private home without private bath, to €664 for lodging in a luxury hotel.

Hotel Sonnenbichel (7020; fax 702131) and the **Dorint Resort & Spa Hotel** (7060; fax 706618) are considered by many to be the best in town. But these international hotels are are out of town and lose much of the Bavarian flavor of a vacation in Garmisch-Partenkirchen.

Visitors should try to take advantage of the wonderful hotels in the middle of the towns. These lodges are full of atmosphere and will provide a memorabele vacation.

Posthotel Lidwigstr. 49, Partenkirchen (93630; fax 9363222)

Reindls Partenkirchner Hof Bahnhofstr. 15, Partenkirchen (58025; fax 73401)

Clausings Posthotel Marienplatz 12, Garmisch (7090: fax 709205)

Garmischer Hof Chamonixstr. 10, Garmisch (9110; fax 51440)

Hotel Staudacherhof Höllentalstr. 48, Garmisch (9290; fax 929333)

Other excellent lodging with easy USA reservations is available at **Best Western Hotel Obermühle** (7040; fax 704112) €67–€95 per person per night with breakfast. It has one of the resort's best restaurants.

Aschenbrenner (58029; fax 4805) €40–€60, is B&B only.

Hotel Hilleprandt (943040; fax 745448) €37–€47, is a quiet, family-run hotel within walking distance of the Hausberg ski school. Lower priced rooms begin at approximately €180 a week. It's a good choice for the budget plan.

Haus Hohe Tannen (54647) is run by a great family. They have wonderful rooms from €26–€34 and speak excellent English.

Hotel Schell (95750; fax 957540) €23–€46, is a B&B that is very close to the station. None of the rooms have baths so guests share one down the hall.

Apartments

The popularity of apartments has increased in Garmisch in recent years. The Garmisch-Partenkirchen tourist office provides an accommodations booklet, which not only lists available apartments but also includes pictures of some of them. Of those we saw the most interesting were the apartments in the Husar section with furnished apartments for two to six people. Prices start at €30 a day and range up to more than €120 a day.

Telephone prefix for Garmisch-Partenkirchen: 08821
Telephone prefix for Germany: 0049

Dining

All visitors here should have their fill of the Bavarian experience. Garmisch-Partenkirchen is full of great old Bavarian restaurants where lederhosen is part of the uniforms; beer runs freely and *Schweinhaxen mit Knodln* is the meal of choice. Here is a rundown on the best of the middle-of-the-road Bavarian spots. The first two restaurants have live Bavarian music and dancing.

Fraundorfer, Ludwigstr. 24, Partenkirchen (2176 or 9270). Closed Tuesday.

Werdenfelser Hof, Ludwigstr. 58, Partenkirchen (3621). Closed Monday.

Braüstüberl, Fürstenstr. 23, Garmisch (2312).

Zum Schatten, Sonnenbergstr. 10, Partenkirchen (2432). Closed Wednesday.

Zum Rassen, Ludwigstr. 45, Partenkirchen (2089). Closed Monday.

Drei Mohren, Ludwigstr. 65, Partenkirchen (9130).

For slightly more upscale and expensive Bavarian restaurants try **Husar** at Fürstenstr. 25 (1713) and **Clausings Posthotel** (7090) at Marienplatz 12 in Garmisch, the **Post Hotel Partenkirchen** (93630) or the **Reindl Grill Restaurant** (58025) in the Partenkirchner Hof in Partenkirchen on Bahnhofstraße.

You can eat less expensively, surrounded by an international group, at the **Chapeau Claque** bistro, Mohrenplatz 10, (71300) which has a French flavor. **Grand-Café**, Klammstr. 14, (79699) serves cuisine with an Asian flare and has vegetarian menus and a quaint bar. **Café Max**, Griesstr. 10, (2535) cooks excellent German meals as well as international dishes. **Mukkefuck Bistro**, Zugspitzstr. 3, (73440) serves wonderful salads, sandwiches on bagettes and good pasta. **Kurpark-Pavillion**, Am Kurpark 2, (3179) serves excellent German fare in a modern setting on the top shopping street.

Italian food is a mainstay in Germany and Garmisch-Partenkirchen has good spots to enjoy it. **La Baita**, Zugspitzstr. 16, (78777) has good pizzas and pastas. **Colosseo**, Klammstr. 7, (52809) upstairs above the Spar Supermarket, has excellent Italian meals. **Da Elia**, Sonnenstr. 3, (73740) serves creative Italian and French bistro foods. **Da Roberto**, Griesstr. 12, (2829) is a cozy Italian restaurant where you get great value. **Bruno's Pizza Flizza**, (1209) has affordable food mixed with great music during the Friday night jam sessions, plus they deliver to the hotels. The **Rose'n Crown** at Zugspitzstr. 70 (51282) has a British pub flavor with good pub grub. **Cerveceria** on Von-Brug-Str. 18 (912668) serves tapas, Argentinian steaks and fancy cocktails.

Another **Hotel Post** (08825-211) in Wallgau, about 12 miles from Garmisch is worth the trip for the meals amidst traditional Alpine decor.

Après-ski/nightlife

Garmisch-Partenkirchen rocks when it comes to après-ski. In Zugspitze, the brand new Gletschergarten is where everybody meets for a little après-ski before going back down to Garmisch-Partenkirchen in the cogwheel train. In the Classic Area, try the Café Bar Kandahar at the Kreuzeck cable car.

Of course you are in Bavaria, home of great beer and of knee-slapping oom-pah-pah fun. For a basic Bavarian floor show try dinner at **Fraundorfer** (2176), or head to **Werdenfelser Hof** (3621). They are both on Ludwigstrasse in Partenkirchen.

Somewhat elegant après-ski can be found in the big hotels such as the Partenkirchner Hof at **Enoteca - Michel's Weinbar** (58025), **Tenne**, the **Post-Taverna** (51067) in the Posthotel Partenkirchen, the **Mühlradl** (7040) in the Obermühle Hotel or **Post-Hörndl** (709126) in Clausing's Posthotel.

Otherwise, après-ski means a trip to the **Irish Pub** at the corner of the Hauptstrasse and Bahnhofstrasse (78798). This place has a great international crowd and plenty of suds and singing. For a late-night spot to party with a good bar crowd and live music, duck into the **Zirbelstub'n** at Promenade 2 (71671).

Late night disco action pulses at **Exit** (4710) at Chamonixstr. 1a and **Evergreen** (55098) at Klammstr. 47 by the swimming pool.

Child care (2006/07 prices)

Larger hotels provide day care services. In addition, check with the tourist office for a listing of babysitters in the area.

Most of the ski schools also provide some kind of child care or children's lessons. Prices are within €10 of each other so check around for the best deal.

The Skischule Garmish-Partenkirchen (4931 or 74260) has ski kindergarten and ski courses for youths available. Ski school for children ages 3 and older costs €35 for three hours of lessons. Three days of lessons (three hours a day) costs €85.

Kinderbüro, Brunntalstr. 2, 28467 (798025; fax, 798027) is open Monday - Friday from 9 a.m.-12:30 p.m. and Thursday from 2 p.m.- 4:30 p.m.

Other activities

The resort has an excellent **swimming pool**, the Alpspitz-Wellenbad (753313), with a wave machine, diving platforms up to 15 feet, kids pool, baby pool, solariums, saunas and hot tubs. The pool is open from 9 a.m. to 9 p.m. on weekdays and closes at 7 p.m. on weekends. Entrance is included for one day with your visitor's card. Then it will cost around €3.60 for three hours or €4.60 for an unlimited admission. Kids pay €2.10 for three hours or €2.80 for unlimited stays. Prices are higher on Sundays. There are reductions for 10-day tickets and families. Saunas cost €5.20 alone or €7.20 when combined with swimming.

The ice stadium offers **ice skating** during the season. Two hours of skating costs €2.60 and rentals cost €3. Call 753291 for information.

Garmisch-Partenkirchen also has an excellent English-language **movie theater** that shows first-run films.

Within an hour's drive are world-famous attractions. Chief among them is **Munich**, the Bavarian capital. **Oberammergau**, site of the famed Passion Play, is about a half-hour away by bus or car. Visit dozens of **woodcarving shops** displaying the work of artisans, many of them trained in Oberammergau's woodcarving school. Along the road to Oberammergau, take a trip up the Graswang valley to **Schloss Linderhof**, the ornate palace built by Ludwig II, the Mad King of Bavaria. Also consider a full-day trip to **Neuschwanstein**, the most famous of Ludwig's castles (near Füssen) and to Berchtesgaden.

Getting there

Munich's Airport II is only an hour and a half away by car on the autobahn. Get there early if you are departing from this airport—it's massive. Innsbruck is about an hour's drive. Rail travelers will find connections to Garmisch from Munich excellent.

Tourist information

Tourist Information, Richard-Strauss-Platz 2, D-82467 Garmisch-Partenkirchen, Germany; (08821-180700; fax 08821-180755).
E-Mail: tourist-info@garmisch-partenkirchen.de
Internet: www.garmisch-partenkirchen.de

Italy

Italy, geographically, has more of the Alps than any other country. Mont Blanc, the highest mountain in Europe, straddles the French-Italian border, and the Matterhorn is right on the Swiss-Italian border.

Italy also has the entire Dolomite range, which many consider the world's most spectacular mountains. Italian ski areas here are world class, and the skiing is augmented by the Italian love of life and world-class cuisine and wines. If the weather changes, there is always a beautiful city such as Milan, Turin, Verona or Venice just a few hours away from the slopes.

The border regions of Italy have distinct influences from both the French and the Germans. The cooking in the northwest has distinct French overtones and the wines of Piemonte are more like beefy French reds than the lighter Italian wines. In the far northeast, the Italian and German languages share the limelight—both are spoken with ease. The cuisine is a pleasant mixture of German and Italian taste as well. Here, the locals work with German efficiency and live life with Italian enthusiasm.

This is a land where the people go out to enjoy life as much as they can in the mountains. No one seems to take skiing seriously, even the Italian Olympic and World Cup champions. Relax. Enjoy long, long lunches. Or, if you aren't into massive mid-day meals, use the time to ski—the slopes empty between 1 and 3 p.m. Once you get into the Italian swing of skiing, you will have the time of your life. Remember, you can always squeeze that next run in tomorrow, or next year for that matter.

Phones: In Italy you still must always dial the complete phone number—it will start with a zero. When you call into Italy dial the country code 0039 followed by 0.... The old prefixes have been incorporated into the phone numbers.

When are the seasons?

Some Italian resorts have adopted a rather complicated series of mini-seasons. Basically, the high and low seasons remain, but are sometimes separated by in-between seasons. If you follow these season breakouts for planning you will not go too far wrong:

High season: Christmas and New Year holidays, and all of February and March to mid-April.

Low season: January after New Year holidays.

Pre-season: 6 December to Christmas.

Bormio

Tucked in Italy's far north — along the craggy Swiss border, not too far from glitzy St. Moritz, above the vineyards of the temperate Valtellina, past spectacular Lago di Como – lies Bormio. This medieval town, which was orginally settled by the Romans, has been forgotten by most Italian guidebooks.

The middle-aged town center has a warren of narrow, cobble-stoned streets; Romanesque churches; crenulated guard towers; and frescoed stone houses. It has a pedestrian zone with small town shops, restaurants, markets and offices that are surrounded by busy streets that lead to the best hotels, restaurants and the lifts. And as if those things weren't enticing enough, the entire town sits encircled by the majestic Alps with their world-class trails and facilities.

Bormio has thrived for centuries because of its thermal waters discovered and developed first by the Etruscans and Romans and eventually enjoyed by succeeding civilizations. There is an ancient spa which has developed through Roman, Medieval and the Imperial eras. A new modern spa with the same thermal waters has been built in the town.

 ## Mountain layout

Four different ski areas surround the town allow skiing and snowboarding during both winter and summer. The Bormio trails are the most convenient. The Santa Caterina Valfurva trails are around the mountain and down the valley. The Valdidentro/Colombano trails are across the valley from Bormio, visible from the Bormio trails. Stelvio is glacier skiing and used only in the summer.

The trails directly above Bormio are the most challenging in the region and they have the best lift systems and the longest cruising trails. Stick with the modern lifts and your day of skiing and riding will go much faster. Be advised that on weekends with the crowds from Milan, trails can get packed.

Most skiers and snowboarders tend to stay in the section directly above Bormio. This is home to one of the longest continuous vertical drops in Italy, 5,879 feet. A modern lift system takes skiers from the base area altitude of about 4,000 feet up to almost 9,789 feet. The higher trails above Bormio 2000 tend to be above treeline. Those dropping down to the town are cut through trees, almost like in New England.

The marked trails are, for the most part, intermediate and advanced at the top half of the mountain and intermediate and beginner near the top of the Bormio 2000 gondola. In fact, this is the home of Bormio's learning center. The wide-open beginner trails make up almost half of the resort's marked trails.

Intermediates will love the very long (14 km./9 miles), heavenly trails that trace about a mile of vertical drop. This is an intermediate's playground with plenty of sun and wonderful visuals. All trails eventually glide down to the base area, so there is little concern for carefully mapping out your route from the top of the mountain. Let yourself fly.

That said, skiing and snowboarding off-piste is acceptable in fresh snow. A guide can take skiers down into the surrounding valleys. What you can see, you can ski or ride. The marked expert trails tend towards advanced but provide some good continuous high-speed cruising. Those looking for the steep and deep should go elsewhere.

For snowboarders — try the Bormio Snowpark, which extends 600 meters along the side of the Alpine Star run. It is an enclosed area dedicated to boarders and free-style skiers. Its eleven zones are divided into areas for beginners, intermediates and advanced/expert. It also has quite a few features including an 120-meter long superpipe, double kinks and a mega rainbow box.

The other areas of Santa Caterina and Valdidentro/San Colombano are mainly for families and those looking for easier runs through the forests. Neither section is particularly easy to reach from town. However, there are buses. Both areas have some above-treeline skiing, but most is through the trees. Don't look for tree skiing. In Europe that has not been developed as it has been in the U.S.A. and Canada.

Passo Stelvio is glacier skiing and riding and is Italy's largest summer skiing area; however, it is not accessible in winter.

Livigno, about an hour by free bus from Bormio is right next to the Swiss border in a duty-free zone. It has excellent, sunny intermediate skiing. Anyone staying in Bormio should plan a day or two at Livigno.

Ski school (2006/07 prices)

The following lesson prices include the 10 percent discount from the Sui Corsi Collettivi Welcome Card. The lower prices are for low season; the higher prices for high season.

Private lessons for skiing and snowboarding cost €35-€40 an hour for one and each additional person costs €10.

Group lessons for skiing are from 9 a.m. to 11 a.m. and 11 a.m. to 1 p.m. with a minimum of four skiers per group. Three mornings are €45-€60 in low season and €60-€70 in high season. Three afternoons are €60-€75 in low season and €80-€85 in high season.

Group lessons for snowboarding are also a minimum of four skiers per group for a six-day course (two hours per day). Cost is €125 both high and low seasons.

Lift tickets (2007/08 prices)

These are the Alta Valtellina Ski Pass (valid in Bormio, Livigno, Santa Caterina and Valdidentro/San Colombano) high season rates.

	Adults	Children & Seniors
two days	€73	€58
four days	€141	€103
seven days	€206.50	€144

These are the high season rates for the Skipass 4 Valli which covers Bormio, Santa Caterina, Vadidentro/San Colombano.

	Adults	Children & Seniors
one day	€34	€29
four days	€122.50	€91
seven days	€179	€126.50

Children are those born in 1994 and after. Seniors (60 years or older) are those born in 1948 and before. Proof of age required.

Skipasses are free for babies born in 2000 and after if accompanied by an adult who buys a skipass of the same duration at full price – minimum length 3 days. Proof of age required.

There is a €5 deposit required for the hands-free ski pass called the Key Card.

The lift rates are divided into high season, season and promotional season. High season is 12/22/07 - 01/ 06/ 08 and 02/02/08 - 03/28/08. Season is 01/07/08 - 02/01/08. Promotional season is from resort opening to 12/21/07 and from 03/29/08 until the resort closes.

 Accommodations

Bormio's hotels are concentrated in three separate places: at the base of the lifts, in the old town and just outside the old town (a bus ride away). With so much to do in town in the evening and an excellent shuttle system, staying at the base of the lifts is not necessarily a major bonus.

Prices are high season half-board per person double occupancy: €€€=€125+; €€=€75-€124; €=less than €74.

At the base of the lifts, **Hotel Genzianella** (0342-904485; €€) offers subdued elegance. Most of the common areas have been remodeled with blond cirmiolo wood from the Alps. Meals are excellent. A great value with sauna, gym and waterfall shower.

Hotel Alú (0342-904504), **Hotel Funivia** (0342-903242), **Larice Bianco** (0342-904693) and **Hotel Nevada** (0342-910888) are all excellent properties right at the base of the gondola. **Hotel Alú** is the best of this group with superior food. (All €€)

On the slopes, at the top of the Ciuk lift, **Baita de Mario** (0342-901424; €€) has 22 rooms, spectacular views and great food. It's well worth the 5 km. drive into town. A week of full pension is about €574.

In the middle of the old town, **Hotel Posta** (0342-904753; €€) provides all the amenities and excellent service. **Hotel Silene** (0342-905455; €) is right on the pedestrian main street. This small 15-room, family-run hotel is a find in the town. **San Lorenzo Hotel** (0342-904604; €€) is also in the Old Town only about a dozen steps from the pedestrian zone. Built in a former church, the hotel has an Old-World feel.

Just outside of the old center, the hotels are excellent with good shuttle service to the slopes and only a few minutes' walk from the Old Town.

Hotel Baita Clementi (0342-904473; €€), only a few steps from the center of the old town, provides excellent facilities including a fitness room, indoor golf driving range and a children's play area. The rooms are spacious and leave little to be desired. The shuttle bus to the slopes stops in front of the hotel, otherwise it is about a 10-minute walk from the lifts. Food for the hotel guests is excellent.

Hotel Sant Anton (0342-901906; €€), just across the street from the new Bormio Spa, is beautifully finished with touches of pine. It has a wellness center including sauna and hot tub. Most rooms have balconies.

Baita dei Pini (0342-904346; €€) is between the old town and the slopes. The views in both directions are fabulous. The hotel has every comfort and great food.

Apartments

Bormio's stock of apartments is somewhat limited but often offers bargains. The regional tourism organization has an excellent website with packages as well as a telephone service that will assist with reservations — 0342-902765.

For an apartment that sleeps four to six expect to pay €650-€750 per week. During the holiday periods prices range up to €1,300 for a week.

 # Dining

Bormio is an exceptional area for dining. The Valtellina, just to the south, is one of Italy's little-known, wine-growing regions and the surrounding orchards produce excellent fruits. This, combined with the mountain flair for cheeses, sausages, dried meats and grappa, makes for a delicious mixture.

Try the Valtellina wines. *Sassella*, *Inferno*, *Valgella* and *Grumello* are all excellent red wines. The *Sforzato* (or *Sfursat*) wines are dessert wines made from dried grapes. Try it with fruit and cheese in front of a fireplace, the glass warmed in your hand.

The *bresaola*, or aged, salted, dried beef, is an excellent mountain specialty. *Pizzoccheri*, the regional dish of buckwheat noodles with melted cheese, potatoes and cabbage is a hearty meal. Test the *sciatt*, a cheese-filled buckwheat donut hole. Enjoy excellent local cheeses such as *Casera*, *Scimudin* and *Bitto*. Other local foods are their game, river trout, porcini mushrooms, sausages, hams, polenta, honey and jams.

Most hotels provide breakfast and dinner. Some of the hotel restaurants are exceptional, but for a special meal try one of the following:

The best restaurant in town is **Al Filo** (Via Dante 6, 0342-901732, closed Mon.) set in on old house cellar in the middle of the old town. It can only seat about 40 people. A local tasting menu costs about €27 and goes excellently with one of the local Valtellina wines. Finish off with Sassella Nera grappa.

On the slopes, at the top of the Ciuk lift, have a lunch at **Baita de Mario** (0342-901424) and enjoy some of the best-prepared specialties of the valley.

A rustic old barn of a restaurant, **La Rasiga** (Via Marconi 6, 0342-901541, closed Mon.), provides atmosphere in spades. Dine on local foodstuffs surrounded by wood and old sawmill and farming tools.

 # Après-ski/nightlife

Italians don't have a tradition of wild nightlife. They normally head back to the hotel after skiing. Some bars at the base of the lifts will fill up. **Bar Clem** is the place to see and be seen in the evening. **Joy's and Zeta** are friendly pubs that fill with tourists and locals. **Mozart** lives up to its name. **Sunrise** is a disco which heats up on Friday and Saturday nights.

Child care (2006/07 prices)

Ski school is an excellent option for children ages 4 and older. Few cultures deal with children better than the Italians. Most of the instructors speak enough English to communicate with children. **Scuola Sci Contea di Bormio** (0342 911605) has a kindergarten that runs from 10 a.m. to 4 p.m.. Children ages 3 and older will be under the care of qualified staff. There's an outdoor park for snowplay and an indoor kindergarten. Children can also enjoy the new ski-tubing system provided of "tape-roulant". They provide supervised lunches as well. A six-day pass for the kindergarten costs €140; a three-day pass is €95; a day costs €35; half-day is €20. Hourly supervision is €10. Child care with two hours of ski school is also available for €195 for a six-day program and €135 for a three-day program. A supervised lunch costs €6.

Other activities

At the top of anyone's list is the Bagni Vecchi (0342-910131), the **Old Spa**, about 3 km. from town, open 10 a.m. to 8 p.m. This fascinating spa has been in operation since the Roman Days, perhaps longer. It is fed by nine thermal springs with water gushing out of the earth at a temperature between 100 and 115 degrees. The baths are divided into six experiences: the sweating cave, Medieval bath, Imperial bath, Roman bath, an outdoor pool and aroma therapy. An afternoon here is an experience that one thinks Disney may have designed with spectacular vistas, dark caves, thermal waterfalls and mud baths. Make reservations.

The new **Thermal Baths**, in town, are less evocative, but the services are top flight and a bit less expensive than the ancient baths. You have a spectacular view of the Stelvio slope, especially at night when the slope is floodlit. There is a thermal a sauna and turkish bath, both powered by naturally heated waters. There also is a new outdoor area for families which includes an outdoor swimming pool with a thermal-water slide . The newer baths have all the normal spa treatments such as hydromassage and fango wraps.

Bormio also has an **indoor skating rink**. It's speed skating team is one of the best in Italy.

The downtown area is wonderful for aimless wandering and focused shopping.

Getting there

There is no easy way to get to Bormio. It is a 200-km. (124-mile) drive from the Milan airport. Expect about a 4-hour drive with traffic, especially on weekends. The drive along the banks of Lago di Lecco and Lago di Como, through long tunnels and down the Valtellina is beautiful, passing vineyards on the south-facing slopes, orchards in the valley, farms and castles.

If you're not up to driving, Mtbus (www.mtbus.it) and Ski&bike (www.bormio-viaggi.it) run shuttles from the Milan Airports in Orio al Serio and Malpensa from Dec. 1, 2007 to April 10, 2008.

Tourist information

Consorzio Turistico Bormio, via Roma 131/A, 23032 Bormio (Sondrio). Tel. 0342.902765; 0342-903300; and 0342-902769. Email: info@bormio.to; Internet: www.bormio.to

Cervinia

Walt Disney's film "Three Men on the Mountain," about the dangerous climb of the Matterhorn, had an image of grandeur that characterizes the best of the Alps. It, along with many works in all media, added to the mystique of the Matterhorn and Zermatt, but there is another side to the mountain—the Italian side. Cervinia, Zermatt's Italian opposite number, is the prototype purpose-built resort in Europe.

Despite being ravaged by architects and developers in infancy, Cervinia manages to delight skiers year after year. The wide-open slopes, the reliable snow and the chance to ski Zermatt on the cheap bring Germans, British and Americans who zip across the slopes during the week until the weekend hordes from Milan and Turin arrive for their days in the snow.

One other important point to note—the dramatic improvement of lifts from the village to Testa Grigia. Once some of the worst lifts in Europe, the old cable cars have been replaced by sleek six- and twelve-person gondolas and a 140-person cable car.

 ## Mountain Layout

To the Italians the Matterhorn is *Il Cervino*, and Cervinia is the village at the base of the Italian side of the mountain. Cervinia has prices about 25 percent lower. The longest run covers more than 20 km.—from Plateau Rosa to Val Tournenche—with a vertical drop of nearly 5,000 feet.

Skiing here is wide open and virtually all intermediate. The descent to Zermatt starts from Plateau Rosa. Special lift tickets for use on the Swiss side should be purchased before you go up the mountain; otherwise, expect to pay double for the lifts back up the Swiss side. The Zermatt side has much steeper terrain and narrower trails. An expert can have a field day on the Swiss side, while the beginner and intermediate can find enough easy runs to make the trip enjoyable.

In Cervinia experts can drop from Plateau Rosa, or try out the lifts above the Cristallo Hotel. Cervinia is paradise for beginner and lower intermediate skiers—the gentle, wide-open snow fields above Plan Maison build confidence.

Snowboarding: Snowboarders are allowed everywhere, and there's also the Indian Park Snowpark with jumps, a halfpipe, slalom runs and a few boarder-cross runs.

Mountain rating

The Cervinia/Valtournenche slopes support beginner and intermediate skills. Wide open and excellent for practice, they offer a number of challenging steeps.

Expert skiers can enjoy several great days of cruising the wide slopes, but may also become bored. However, should a group of experts invest in the services of a ski instructor, they'll find the most challenging slopes Cervinia has to offer. Experts will also have a great time on the Zermatt side, and this is part of the allure of Cervinia as a resort: it lets you take advantage of the savings made possible by staying in Italy and skiing the wilder-and-woolier Swiss side.

Ski school (2006/07 prices)

There are three excellent ski schools in Cervinia – Scuola Di Sci Del Breuil (phone/fax 0166-940960); Scuola Di Sci Matterhorn Cervinia (0166-949523, fax 0166-949885); and Scuola Di Sci Nuova Cielo Alto (0166-948451, fax 0166-949990). Make arrangements at any hotel reception desk, or visit one of the schools. Ask for an English-speaking instructor.

The main ski school, and most convenient for most, is the Scuola di Sci del Cervino. Its prices follow.

Private lessons cost approximately €33 an hour for one; €43 for two persons; €50 an hour for three, and €55 for four.

Group lessons (are from 10 a.m. to 12:45 a.m. with about five to nine skiers per group). Three mornings cost €100. Five mornings cost €145. Five mornings plus one afternoon costs €155.

Lessons are available for cross-country, racing (six-day course), off-piste skiing and summer skiing. Groups require a minimum of five participants.

Lift tickets (2006/07 prices)

Prices are for the Cervinia/Valtournenche area only covering 31 lifts:

one day	€34	six days	€182
three days	€97	seven days	€201

The supplement added to the Cervinia ski pass to ski in Zermatt costs €21.

A **combination Cervinia/Zermatt ski pass** is available for all lifts in Zermatt and Cervinia.

six days (all lifts)	€238
seven days (all lifts)	€270

Stick with the Cervinia pass and then purchase the supplement whenever you want to head to Switzerland unless you are here for a week.

Accommodations

All rates are based on high season double occupancy, with half board. €€€—€125+; €€—€75-€125; €—€74-.

Hermitage (0166-948998, fax 0166-949032; €€€+) This beautiful hotel is the best choice in Cervinia. Everyone who stays here loves it.

Bucaneve (0166-949119, fax 0166-948308; €€€+) Center-of-town location with a woodsy elegance. In the evening a piano player entertains.

Punta Maquignaz (0166-949145, fax 0166-948055; €€) has a spectacular lobby with a massive stone archway and unfinished wide wood floors. Elegant touches of wood are everywhere except in the rooms which are quite modern.

Europa (0166-948660, fax 0166-949650; €€) In the center of town, just a few minutes' walk from the lifts. Clean and modern with parking.

Breithorn (0166-949042, fax 0166-948363; €) furnished in knotty pine, this hotel is about 200 yards from the lifts and has one of the better restaurants in town.

Excelsior Planet (0166-949426, fax 0166-948827; €€) is modern and convenient to the slopes. It has a tiny swimming pool as well as steamroom and sauna.

Fosson (0166-949125, fax 0166-949720; €€), a family-run hotel, also has a small steamroom, sauna and fitness room. **Mignon** (0166-949344, fax 0166-949687; €€–€€€) is very small and cozy, just minutes from the lifts. The casual family atmosphere is hard to beat. **Lyskamm** (0166-949074; fax 0166-948692; €–€€) is as close as one can get to the base of the Cretaz lift, one of the two main access lifts. **Fürggen** (0166-948928, fax 0166-948929; €–€€) is B&B only above the town. It's ski-in/ski-out, however, inconvenient to the town. **Perruquet** (0166-949043; fax 0166-940014; €) is another B&B in the town center that's clean and roomy.

Apartments

Cervina's stock of apartments is somewhat limited but often offer bargains. The rental agencies in town are Il Cervino, tel/fax 0166-949510; La Maison de Vacances, tel/fax 0166-948267; Nuova San Grato, 0166-949442, fax 0166-949644; La Tour, 0166-940216; Studio Breuil Cervinia, tel/fax 0166-940238; and Pierre et Vacances, 0166-949242, fax 0166-949732.

 ## Dining

One of Cervinia's best restaurants is the **Hotel Hermitage** (0166-948998). It is head and shoulders above the rest of the pack when it comes to fine cuisine. But let's face it, most of us would rather have a good typical meal in a traditional setting in the mountains. Here Cervinia has plenty to offer.

Maison de Saussure (0166-948259) gets rave reviews from the critics and even locals have to make advanced reservations to get a seat for a cozy traditional mountain meal. It only seats about 30 people, so, call before you get here.

After asking locals, several restaurants seemed to be mentioned time and again. We'll start with three which are on the slopes but reachable with a van or jeep if you call ahead—**Baita Cretaz** (0166-949914), **Les Clochards** (0166-948273) and **La Bricole** (0166-948274), Baita Layet (333.3420657). **La Nicchia** (0166-949842) serves good local fare with a larger menu in a more modern and elegant atmosphere.

Try *bagna cauda*, vegetables covered with an anchovy sauce; *tomino*, a delicate riccota, normally covered with parsley or peppers; *bresaola*, smoked ham from the mountain regions; or *lardo d'Arnaz*, a fatty bacon that has been cured in a secret mountain concoction.

We were also told that **Le Blason - Da Mario** (0166-940039) and Hotel Maquignaz's **Ymeletrob Restaurant** (0166-949145) serve excellent meals. Just off the slopes next to the Cielo Alto chairlift, **Casse Croute** (0166-948783) provides good basic fare either for a slopeside lunch or a dinner later in the evening.

Many of the hotels such as **Hotel Fosson**, **Mignon**, **Breithorn**, **Bucaneve**, and **Excelsior Planet** are open to the public and have excellent kitchens.

Other recommended inexpensive eateries are **Le Vieux Grenier** (0166-948287), **Matterhorn** (0166-948518), **Pavia** (0166-949010) and **Copa Pan** (0166.949140). These were recommended by plenty of tourists and several British tour guides for good cheap fare and lots of it.

On the slopes, everyone seems to agree that **Chalet Etoile** (0166.940220) is the place to have lunch. They serve a full meal in a rustic mountain atmosphere.

 ## Après-ski/nightlife

Cervinia does not have a lot to choose from; however, there is growing English-speaking clientele at the few spots in town.

The town has two discos—**The Etoile**, which attracts an older group, and the **Bianconiglio.**

The four most popular bars are the **Yeti** and the **Dragon Pub,** just across from the slopes, and **Pub Grivola** and the **Ymeletrob Bar,** across the street from each other. You'll find plenty of English-speakers, be they from England, Scotland, Wales, Ireland, Sweden or the Netherlands. All bars have good happy hours and all are within five minutes' walk of each other.

For a more elegant and quiet après-ski try the **Samovar Tea Room** for drinks, tea and pastries. Head to **Le Bistrot de L'Abbé,** a rustic winebar only a few steps away in the Hotel Meynet. Or try a drink in **the Lyskamm Bar.**

Child care

New this season: the Baby-Club takes kids age 8 and younger every day from 9 a.m. to 5 p.m. Contact the Centro Sociale Sportivo of Breuil Cervinia (0166-940201) for more information.

Babysitting services and special ski classes for children are available. Contact the Baby-Club for more information.

Getting there

You can drive here easily from either Geneva or Milan airport. From Geneva come through the Mont Blanc tunnel. The resort can also be reached from Geneva via the Great St. Bernard Tunnel. From Milan and Turin, take the A5 Torino-Aosta motorway; the Cervinia exit (Châtillon Saint-Vincent) is only 27 km. from the resort.

Buses make the trip between Cervinia and Milan three times a day with a change in Châtillon.

Other activities

The Club Med (0166-944600) has An Olympic-size pool the with sauna, hammam, and jacuzzi. People who are not guests of the hotel must make a reservation in order to use these facilities. A public swimming-pool with sauna is open at the Giomein (0166-949271).

Cervinia has an ice-skating rink and bowling alleys. Day trips can easily be made to Geneva, Lausanne, Milan or Turin.

The ski trip over the Alps to Zermatt is a must-do side trip.

Heliskiing and Ski-Doos are available. Call 0166.949267 or 0166.940127.

On January 30 and 31 every year, the Fair of Sant'Orso, one of the largest craft fairs in Italy, takes place in Aosta. Fantastic wood carvings and other crafts can be purchased at great savings.

During *Carneval* the town of Ivrea is one of the wildest places in Italy. Costumed residents fight a "Battle of the Oranges." A castle defended by bad guys, besieged by good guys hurling about a ton of oranges, makes for pre-Lenten fun.

Tourist information

In Cervinia: Via J.A. Carrel, 11021 Cervinia, Italy. 0166.949136; fax 0166.949731.
In Valtournenche: Via Roma, 49, 11028 Valtournenche, Italy. 0166.92029; fax 0166.92430.
E-mail:breuil-cervina@montecervino.it
or valtournenche@montecervino.it
Internet: www.montcervino.it

Cortina d'Ampezzo

Since hosting the 1956 Winter Olympics, Cortina's wide, sunny valley in the eastern Dolomites has been one of the world's top ritzy ski resorts, attracting celebrities of all types.

The town's picturesque square is framed by two massive mountain ridges: to the east lies the connected area formed by Cristallo (9,613 feet) and Faloria (7,690 feet); to the west, Tofana (9,317 feet) and Pocol and Socrepes (7,487 feet) form another connected area, accessible from the town. Further to the west, approaching the Falzarego Pass (6,906 feet), the areas of Cinque Torri (8,438 feet) and Lagazuoi (9,009 feet) beckon the adventurous skier.

These areas are loosely connected by a system of inexpensive buses and taxis.

 ## Mountain layout

Cortina has what amounts to eight semiconnected ski areas. All eight areas are connected by ski bus. However, the Faloria and Cristallo as well as the Cinque Torre and Passo Giau areas are also interconnected by lifts. The main Cortina area Pocol-Tofana rises to the west of the town to Tofane at its highest point stretching to Pocol on the far left as you look up the mountains. This is the best area for intermediates and those graduating from beginner. Eighteen lifts that include three spectacular cable cars lace the area providing excellent capacity with few lines. The entire area between Duca d'Aosta and Pocol is excellent for any intermediate and most beginners. The higher area just under Tofane is more difficult and the connecting run down from Tofane to Duca d'Aosta is a tough expert run that can be made by most intermediates with plenty of traversing.

Faloria and Cristallo are linked at the Tre Croci pass. Skiers either take the bus to Tre Croci and then ski from there or they can ride from town to Faloria on the cable car. Many skiers come here and ski the Cristallo area in the morning. During the midwinter it gets earlier sun. Then for lunch they head up to Faloria from Tre Croci. The best restaurant there for an elegant lunch is Capanna Tondi or skiers can drop down to the lower self-service at Faloria. After lunch, ski Faloria's handful of intermediate trails through the trees. Take the long run back into Cortina or glide down on the cable car at the end of the day.

The Falzarego, Cinque Torri, and Passo Giau are about a 15 km. drive out of downtown Cortina. They will take care of plenty of skiing for a day. Cinque Torri has a new quad chair that opens up a good skiing bowl as well as two or three good trails to the base area. From the top of the quad chair at Cinque Torri a snowcat pulls skiers to the small rifugio which sits at the top of the Averau. *(Rifugi*—or rifugio, singular—are mountain huts found on the slopes, where skiers can find shelter and taste a few good typical dishes. Some of them are real mountain restaurants, but most of them still have the feeling of cozy mountain retreats. Rifugi are very popular places for après-ski, and some even provide lodging.) Skiers can drop down open slopes from the Averau (off the trail map) and take a double chairlift back to the top of Cinque Torri.

Just up the road from the Cinque Torri base area is the incredibly spectacular Falzarego-Lagazuoi cable car. This lift takes skiers to the top of a cliff where solid intermediate trails lead back to the parking lot, or where skiers can ski down toward the Val Badia. The run off the back of the Lagazuoi, dropping in the direction of Armentarola, is basically a beginner/intermediate rolling trail but the views must be seen to be believed. Plus, the first highlight of this run is a stop for lunch (plan for it) at the Rifugio Scotoni halfway down the run. This rifugio is known for its excellent grilled meats. You can also order simple pastas, soups and raclette, then enjoy them on the deck if the weather permits. After lunch continue down toward Armentarola. You'll pass the Capanna Alpina, but don't stop there. Keep going for the second big adventure on this run—being pulled by horses along the runout to Armentarola. This is more fun than a ride at Disneyland. About two dozen skiers hold onto a long rope trailing behind a team of two or three horses, then the horses begin to pull the skiers along the trail. Many might be expecting the trip to be slow and uneventful; the team drivers have a different idea. They whip the horses into a run with this snake of skiers whooping and screaming behind them. This is an experience that is hard to find anywhere else in the skiing world. In the U.S.A. no area would do this for fear of being sued. From the base at Armentarola taxis wait to take skiers back to the Falzarego pass. There will be a charge for the taxi back up the pass of about €3.50 in a full taxi.

Whatever your choice, there is plenty of skiing.

Mountain rating

This area is an intermediate and advanced paradise. With the exception of a few slopes, it is probably a bit too challenging for most beginners.

The intermediate will find Tofana, Faloria and Cinque Torri enjoyable areas. Beginners should stick to the Pocol-Socrepes area and the lower lifts on Cristallo, as well as several at Faloria. Experts will enjoy shooting down the Lagazuoi. The cable car ride to the peak is a thrill in itself. Other good expert areas are the Tofana and the upper lift of the Cristallo section. The off-trail skiing is exhilarating, although it should be done with a good guide or instructor along to get the most out of your day.

Ski school (2007/08 prices)

Cortina has seven ski and snowboard schools that have courses for all skill levels. These are the three main ski schools. The ski school "Cortina" is headquartered in Corso Italia (0436-2911, fax 0436-3495), Scuola di Sci Azzurra at Ria de Zeto, 8 (0436-2694) and Ski School Cristallo-Cortina, (0436.870073, fax 0436-2694, fax 04364828). Ask for an instructor who speaks English.

Low season for lessons is early December, the January after the New Year holiday and late March. Prices are competitive. The prices that follow are current at both schools within a couple of Euros.

Private lessons are €48 an hour in high season and €43 per hour in low season.

Group lessons are organized for six day classes with a minimum of four people per group. A four hour morning lesson costs €480 in high season and about €370 in low season. Six consecutive days of full day lessons cost €750 in high season and about €500 in low season.

Lift tickets (2007/08 prices)

Local area lift tickets can be purchased. However, the difference in price between these tickets and the Super Ski Dolomite pass is small (about 10 percent). The prices listed below are for the Super Ski Dolomite lift pass.

	Low Season	High Season
one day	€37	€42
two days	€72	€82
three days	€105	€119
six days	€184	€209
seven days	€195	€222
thirteen days	€319	€363

Note: Children and seniors get 11 to 30 percent discounts. Make sure you have proper identification and be sure to ask for the discount. Ski passes for eight days or more will require a photograph. Long lines are the norm for obtaining these passes on Saturday—it's quicker on Sunday afternoon and Monday morning.

Cortina-only passes cost €34 in low season and €38 in high season.

Accommodations

Cortina is a mature resort. The quality of room size and furnishings can be uneven: when checking in, check the room before accepting it. If you have a reservation, ask to see several rooms to choose from.

The hotels listed below are centrally located, offer good value, and have been visited by a *Ski Europe* representative. Based on half-board during high season per person based on double occupancy: €€€—€125+; €€—€75–€124; €—€74-.

Hotel Miramonti (0436-4201; fax 0436-867019; €€€) The most luxurious and elegant hotel in Cortina is a bit out of the center of the town. This hotel is a massive Old-World hotel left over from the days of understated elegance (not that understated). They have a beautiful pool, full fitness room and more lobbies than we could count. One can get lost in this place. The main drawback to the Miramonti is its distance from town. One of the joys of Cortina is having time to enjoy the beautiful town and its stores, restaurants and bars. Some tour groups offer rooms here for excellent rates, but for my money we'd stay in town.

Hotel Ancora (0436-3261; fax 0436-3265; €€€–€€) Our favorite hotel in Cortina is directly on the central square. This place now provides a cozy haven for those who demand pampered luxury. Normal clients are served half-pension meals in a beautiful arched dining room, but for those looking for true gourmet meals, the intimate **Petit Fleur** restaurant in the basement is hard to beat. Every motif of this beautiful hotel reflects its Alpine heritage from the intricate massive wooden ceiling that hangs overhead in the entranceway and the radiating ceramic stove to the pale blue paintings on the rooms' ceilings and the arched canopy of the Café Vienesse. This hotel is also one of the mainstays of the art scene in the region. You will probably have the opportunity to see an exhibition by one of Italy's top artists. According to top art organizers, Hotel Ancora supports the arts more than any other spot in Cortina. Staying at the Ancora is an experience you will savor long after your vacation. Make sure to meet the proprietress, Signora Flavia, who speaks good English and will make sure your stay is memorable.

Hotel Montana (0436-862126; fax 0436-868211; €) B&B only but smack in the center of town; only 30 rooms, Michelin-rated, affordable with top notch service.

Hotel Oasi (0436-862019; fax 0436-879476: €) is a B&B with 10 rooms at the edge of the old town, but near the lifts and Dolomite RR. It has impeccable service and modern rooms in a beautifully restored old house.

Hotel Cortina (0436-4221; €€–€€€) The lobby is big and plain, a step above a big cafeteria, but the location, smack in the middle of town, is hard to beat. Reports from tourists staying there indicated rooms were nothing special and ranged from sizeable to closets. The food reports for the half-pension meals are mediocre.

Parc Hotel Vitoria (0436-3246; fax 0436-4734; €€€–€€), at the southern end of the walking street (Corso Italia), is a bit long in the tooth and could use some tender loving care, but the public areas, especially the wooden barrel-vaulted lobby filled with antiques is a joy. On the night we checked out this spot the music was playing and the clients were dancing up a storm. It can't be all bad.

We have visited the following as well. **Europa** (0436-3221; €€€–€€) Good basic hotel in the center of town. **Hotel de la Poste** (0436-4271; €€€) In the middle of town with great food; Michelin rated. **San Marco** (0436-866941; fax 866940; €€) An absolutely beautiful hotel that was recently restored with fantastic woodwork. Don't let the inexpensive price fool you. **Hotel Aquila** (0436-2618; €€) Still family-run, is great value for money. **Hotel Italia** (0436-5646; fax: 0436-5757; €) This two-star serves hugh portions of well-prepared food and it is right across the street from the Faloria cable car. **Hotel Impero** (0436-4246; fax 0436-4248; €) B&B only; some rooms have kitchenettes.

Apartments, condominiums, flats

There are beds for 18,000 visitors and a special rental apartment list. Prices for rooms are €13 to €20 per person in low season, €20 to €28 per person in high season. For more information, contact the tourist office.

 Dining

If you get a chance, don't miss a lunch high above Cortina at **Capanna Tondi** on Monte Faloria (0436-5775). They serve excellent full-service meals in a chalet setting at 7,677 feet with wide views of the town and surrounding mountains. Call for reservations, especially on weekends. The same family has been running this refuge for more than half a century. The current proprietess, Signora Rosie, is a striking blond bundle of energy who ensures every detail is handled perfectly. The dining room is built with wrought iron and wood brought from Austria, then carried up the mountain on mule back and assembled before anyone dreamed of a cable car lift. A full meal here with wine, starter, main course and dessert will run about €30–€35. The view is priceless.

Just below the Tondi is another less intimate, more modern mountain restaurant with self service as well as regular service. It is frequented by tour groups since it is right at the top of the Faloria lift from Cortina.

Another excellent mountain lunch accessible by virtually every skier is the **Rifugio Scotoni** on the Lagazuoi-Armentarola trail. Head there for excellent grilled meats, raclette and local specialties.

The following restaurants, recommended by several local residents, have excellent food. Expect to pay around €13–€15 in a pizzeria and up to €60 in the top restaurant, including house wine.

Tivoli, Lacedel 34; (0436-866400) Overlooking Cortina, and rated as one of the best in town with prizewinning, home-made *tortelli di patate.* Try the deer and other mountain specialties. This is the only Michelin-star restaurant in town. Call before coming to the resort for reservations. Closed Monday.

El Toulá, Ronco 123; (0436-3339) A once-upon-a-time hayloft converted to cozy restaurant boasts three Michelin forks (not quite a star). It is considered one of the most chi-chi restaurants in town. Hence, it is expensive, very expensive—this restaurant will push the €60 price if the meal has starter, first and second course and dessert with wine. Closed Monday.

The Petite Fleur (0436-3261) in the basement of Hotel Ancora has wonderful gourmet local Cortina fare (Cucina Ampezzana) in a small elegant room.

Lago Ghedina (0436-860876) has a great setting on the lake and good food but you need a car to get there.

Da Beppe Sello (0436-3236) One of the best. Must have a car or take a taxi and it is expensive. Another two-fork Michelin spot.

Baita Fraina, Fraina, 1; (0436-3634) Hard to get to but very worth it. Michelin gives this place two forks. Closed Monday.

Lago Scin, At Lago Scin (0436-2391) is another Michelin recommended restaurant with two forks. Closed Wednesday.

Siesta (0436-867857) serves homemade food with medium prices.

Mezcal (0436-866283) Here you find Mexican food in the center of town at affordable prices where the food is served with Latin spirit. They dance on the tables until the wee hours.

Ristorante Amadeus, Verocai 73, (0436-867450) serves affordable meals with a fixed-price menu of €25 including house wine on Thursday and Friday evenings.

Ra Stua, Via Grohmann 2, (0436-868341) Great ambiance good food. Closed Wednesdays.

El Zoco, Cadamai, 18; (0436-860041) gets good reviews. Closed Monday.

For pizza try **Al Ponte, Croda Caffé,** Corso Italia, 163 (0436-866589, closed Tuesday); **Cinque Torre,** Via Stazione, 3 (0436-866301 closed Thursday); or **Da Pino** that is very elegant pizzeria with prices to match.

 Après-ski/nightlife

For all its jet-set reputation, Cortina is relatively quiet at night after the *passeggiata* (Italians, dressed to the hilt in furs and the latest styles) stroll to see and be seen.

An old wine bar, the **Enoteca** (0436-862040), is normally packed with merrymakers. Enoteca has a room where can buy wine by the bottle together with cold cuts and cheese. The best part is still the narrow original bar room.

Head to **Terrezza Viennese**, attached to the Hotel Ancora. Here they serve rich Austrian pastries and coffee with a background of soft piano music. In the evening they offer crepes flambé.

The Hotel Savoia has the **Ballads Piano Bar. Bar Arnika** (0436-3266; 102 Corso Italia—down a passageway between 85 and 106) serves scores of pure Scotch Whisky malts. It is a good place for a restrained evening.

Birreria Hacker Pschorrz (0436-867625), a Bavarian-style beer place, serves liters of beer for around €3.50 and has live electric oom-pah-pah music from about 10 p.m. onward. This spot fills up early. Closed Mondays.

Discos don't really start up until midnight. The disco at the Europa hotel, **VIP Club** (0436-3221), seems to be the main action place. **Metro Club** gets a pretty good group of Americans and Brits on tour groups. The **Bilbo Club** (0436-5599) mainly caters to a young crowd earlier in the evening and an older group later on. It is erratic regarding clientele—it really depends on hitting them on the right night.

Child care

Child care in Cortina is not a school affair. There are scores of private babysitters and services available through the hotels or private homes where skiers stay. Child-care services are relatively inexpensive, and children seem to get more than their share of affection from the Italians who take care of them. The ski school also runs a children's ski course for those old enough to begin skiing.

Other activities

Regular tours to Venice and other towns are scheduled most days. There is excellent **ice skating, bobsledding, World Cup ski races, ice hockey,** and **indoor tennis.** An hour of **horseback riding** (0436-860441) in the snow costs €18. Cortina is also known for the **curling** championships, but if you'd like to try curling yourself call the Curling Center (338-6604480) for equipment and lessons. The tourist office publishes a list of activities, and the local paper, *Il Notiziario di Cortina*, provides daily activity summaries in Italian.

Getting there

We suggest going by car. The nearest airport is Venice, about a two-hour drive. The closest train station is in Calalzo, with a regular bus service to Cortina. Trains from Innsbruck and Munich arrive at Dobbiaco, a 50-minute bus ride from Cortina. A daily bus service also connects Cortina with Venice and takes about four hours. Check with your travel agent, because there are some packages that include meeting incoming skiers at Milan and Venice airports, and busing them directly to Cortina.

Tourist information

The main office is located on Piazzetta S. Francesco 8, 32043 Cortina d'Ampezzo, Italy. A second, smaller information office is on Piazza Roma. Call 0436-3231 or 0436-2711; fax 0436-3235.
Internet: www.dolomiti.org or www.infodolomit.it
Email: cortina@infodolomiti.it

Madonna di Campiglio

One of the jewels of the Brenta Dolomites in Trentino is Madonna di Campiglio. This resort has become Italy's largest resort in terms of beds, runs and lifts.

The town has grown significantly. Whereas downtown Madonna was once where the hotels were concentrated, growth has given Madonna thousands of new rooms in the Palu section and above in the Campo Carlo Magno. These new hotels, especially those in the far reaches of Palu, are a bit of a walk from the lifts which remain centered around the original village. The hotels at Campo Carlo Magno have good lift service but are separated from downtown's shopping and nightlife.

The Brenta massif is typified by wild limestone rock formations and multicolored rocks that are as stark and beautiful during the winter as they are in the summer. These mountains, just like those in the sister Dolomites across the Adige River, have to be seen to be believed. They are truly castles and fortifications built by God. The Val di Genova is one of the most beautiful in the region and is only minutes from Madonna di Campiglio. When the road is open, a trip up to the 300-foot-high Nardis waterfalls is worth the effort.

The Campo Carlo Magno gets its name from a reported visit from Charlemagne while he was Holy Roman Emperor. Today it is part of the extended lift ticket area. The Great Rock (*Pietra Grande*) is impressive.

Mountain layout–Skiing

One of the best parts of skiing here is that the majority of the folk come for nature and relaxation rather than for all-out skiing. Another plus—the town has aggressively built new lifts. This translates into very few places where skiers will have to wait at lifts. In fact, even when the town seems packed, the slopes can seem deserted with a few slow-lift exceptions.

This is also one of the best-groomed group of trails in Italy. Here the clientele demands pool-table smooth slopes that help them look beautiful when they slip down the trails.

The skiing areas surround the town. For lift purposes it can be divided into four areas: 5 Laghi, Pradalago, Grosté and Spinale. Pradalago and Grosté are the easiest. Spinale and 5 Laghi have more challenging terrain. Little at Madonna will scare away any competent intermediate.

The most development over the past few years has been in the Pradalago region of the resort where wide cruising trails predominate. This sector is served by a gondola from town and a quad lift rising from Fortini, near Campo Carlo Magno.

As always, one way to approach a resort is to follow the sun. This means starting your day taking the 5 Laghi cablecar (if the resort is crowded this cablecar can be a bottleneck—it carries only 465 skiers an hour) or taking the Miramonti chairlift (also slow). Once up the mountain, you'll find a handful of intermediate and decent expert runs are served by a high-speed quad. They will provide a good start to the day and you will find any early morning sun. This area has about 1,600 feet of working vertical with great pitch. A looping intermediate run called Trampolino will take you over to the Pradalago section.

Pradalago has some good upper intermediate and advanced ungroomed terrain dropping down the mountainside facing 5 Laghi. On the other side of the ridge, a series of lifts yo-yos skiers to the connection point with Folgarida. A drop down the Pradalago Diretta then Zeledria brings skiers to the quad chairlift that brings them back to the top of the Pradalago section or to the base of the Fortini chair.

From Fortini, skiers and boarders can also head to the other side of the valley by taking the Grosté gondola that rises about 2,500 feet in two stages to the top of the Passo Grosté. Here, high above treeline, the mountaintop visuals are spectacular and skiing is easy. Six lifts keep skiers above treeline on the wide-open slopes.

The drop into the village from this area is very flat along the Poza Vecia trail. To avoid lots of pushing, take the Boch chairlift then drop down the Nube D'Oro trail and then Fortini or Spinale Diretta to get back to town. The Spinale runs that are linked to Grosté by the Boch chairlift offer more challenge than Grosté. The expert Spinale Direttissima trail is the toughest in the area.

Most of the original village hotels are at the base of the slopes, making them convenient both for lunch breaks and quitting time.

Madonna di Campiglio is linked with two other smaller ski areas, Folgarida and Marilleva. The Folgarida and Marilleva areas add another 25 lifts and 50 km. of prepared slopes to the overall region..

The highest lift-accessible point is Grosté at 8,235 feet.

Madonna has most of its slopes covered with snowmaking.

 ## Mountain layout–Snowboarding

From Fortini, boarders can head to the other side of the valley by taking the Grosté gondola that rises about 2,500 feet in two stages to the top of the Passo Grosté. Here, high above treeline, the mountaintop visuals are spectacular and boarding is easy.

The Ursus Snowpark in the Grosté area has a boardercross layout which includes 1 main kick, 4 intermediate kicks, 2 funboxes, 1 spina, 1 quarter, 5 rails, 2 kink rails, 1 kink rail box, 2 flat rail boxes, 1 double-up-down rail box.

Mountain rating

The area is good for beginners and intermediates. There is a lot of mountain perfectly suited for learning from top to bottom and intermediates will feel like experts with some challenge. Overall, let's call this ego-boosting terrain for everyone. While the 3 Tre, Amazzonia and Spinale runs will give experts some good exercise, the area deserves an overall rating of mellow. Experts ski off-trail (the lift system doesn't really support off-trail skiing—you'll end up climbing a lot) or go ski mountaineering, but there really isn't enough expert or advanced skiing to make a trip worthwhile.

Ski school (2007/08 prices)

Private lessons (per hour) cost for one person, €39; for two, €50; for three skiers, €63.

Check with your hotel for recommendations about the best English-speaking instructors. There are a total of 150 instructors.

Group lessons (eight people maximum) are two hours each day for six days for €135.

Children's lessons are given three hours each day for six days. Maximum of ten per group. Cost: €150.

Lift tickets (2007/08 prices)

The Super Skirama Dolomiti Adamello Brenta Pass includes unlimited runs on the following lifts: Funivie Madonna di Campiglio S.P.A. and on the Campo Carlo Magno S.P.A. ski lifts and Funivie Folgarida-Marilleva (which are connected), Pinzolo, Pejo, Ponte di Legno-Tonale-Presena, Andalo-Fai della Paganella, Monte Bondone, Folgaria-Lavarone. For adults, it costs (main season/low season) €38/€35 a day; €199/€ 176 for six days; and €213/€187 for seven days. For juniors and seniors, it costs (high season/low season) €31/€29 a day; €160/€142 for six days; and €168/€150 for seven days.

These are the high/low lift ticket prices for the Madonna di Campiglio Skipass.

	Adults	**Children/Seniors**
one day	€36/€33	€29/€27.50
three days	€102/€96	€78.50/€73
six days	€175/€166	€134/€128
seven days	€189.50/€178.50	€147/€135

Note: Main season is from Dec. 22, 2007 to Jan. 7, 2008 and from Jan. 26, 2008 to Mar. 9, 2008. Low season is fom opening to Dec. 21, 2007; from Jan. 7, 2008 to Jan. 25, 2008; and from Mar. 10, 2008 to end of season. Children are those born after November 30, 1998 or those shorter than 120 cm. Seniors are those born before Nov. 30, 1942. Juniors are those born after November 30, 1991.

Cross-Country and snowshoeing

Cross-country skiers will find this region enjoyable. Carisolo is about 20 minutes away and has a 4-km trail. The Campo Carlo Magno boasts one of the world's best expert cross-country courses with 21 kilometers of terrain which start from Adamello Brenta Natural Park in Campo Carlo Magno. The 500-m test path, the 2-km baby path, the 5-km sprint path and the 7.5-km World Cup path are in this area.

Between Caderzone and Carisolo, passing through Giustino and Pinzolo, there are 20 km. of paths — three of which are floodlit in the evenings — on which runs and training sessions take place.

With snowshoes you can explore the snow-covered nature around Val Rendena's resort, in search of new paths in the nearby valleys or up to a mountain top.

Accommodations

Madonna's hotels are for the most part modern. There probably is not a bad hotel in the bunch. Even the least aesthetic provide good-sized rooms and good food. This resort does not have the overflowing complement of restaurants that seem to be found in many resorts. Hence, taking half pension is a good idea and will save money.

Hotels listed here were visited by a *Ski Snowboard Europe* representative.

Prices are high season, half-board, per person double occupancy: €€€=€125+; €€=€75-€124; €=less than €74.

Only the first three hotels have swimming pools.

Relais Club Des Alpes (0465-446238; fax 0465-440104; €€€) is traditionally, the best hotel; built around the former hunting lodge of the Austrian emperors. But the size is large and the staff is limited, so those demanding perfect service may be less than satisfied. The 5 Laghi and Pradalago lifts are only a couple of minutes walk away.

Spinale Club Hotel (0465-441116; fax 0465-442189; €€€) tops Des Alpes in terms of tip-top service. It is smaller and more intimate than its competition. A ski lift takes skiers to the top of the Spinale area just out the back door.

Hotel C. Magno Zeledria (0465-441010; fax 0465-440550; €€) is out of the center of town, but provides luxury. It's only a short walk from the lift system.

Hotel Golf (0465-441003; fax 0465-440294; €€€) This elegant hotel outside of the village center in Campo Carlo Magno has good access to the lifts.

These hotels are in the original village with the best lift access to 5 Laghi:

Oberosler (0465-441136; fax 0465-443220; €€€), where the lift is in its back yard and the old downtown is only two minutes away, has an outdoor skating rink stretched out below the front.

Majestic (0465-441080; fax 0465-443171; €€) It is a small intimate hotel, across from the 5 Laghi lift. The hotel is owned by a family that once lived in the U.S.A.

Savoia Palace Hotel (0465-441004; fax0465-440549; €€€) This is one of the originals in the town still providing good service in the right location.

Hotel Cristallo (0465-441132; fax 0465-440687; €€€) which overlooks the foot-ball-field sized ice-skating rink, is only about two minutes from the 5 Laghi lift.

Hotel Milano (0465-441210; fax 0465-440631; €€) This is very plain, nothing fancy, with simple food, but a great location.

These hotels are in the original village center with the best access to the Prad-alago gondola: **Bertelli** (0465-441013; fax 0465-440564; €€€) **Alpina** (0465-441075; fax 0465-443465; €€); **Ariston** (0465-441070; fax 0465-441103; €€); **Hotel Laura** (0465441246; fax 0465-441576; €€€) our favorite during our first visit a decade ago—now only better; **Campiglio Bellavista** (0465-441034; fax 0465-440868; €€); **La Baita** (0465-441066; fax 0465-440750; €€); **Miramonti** (0465-441021; fax 440410; €€€).

The following hotels are in the original village with the best lift access to the Spi-nale gondola: **Cerana** (0465-440552; fax 0465-440587; €€€), just a few yards uphill from the Spinale lift, is close to everything. **Grifone** (0465-442002; fax 0465-440540; €€€) with a light pine motif, is across the street from the Garni Palu.

Recommended bed & breakfasts: **Garni Palu** (0465-441695; fax 0465-443183; €€) is a cozy, warm and beautiful B&B about a five-minute walk to the nearest lift (Spi-nale). **St. Hubertus** (0465-441144; fax 0465-440056; €) is cozy, clean and right across from 5 Laghi lift. **La Montanara** (0465-441105; fax 0465-441105; €) is equidistant from the 5 Laghi (downhill) and Pradalago lifts (uphill). **Cristiania** (0465-441470; fax 0465-443310; €), **Arnica** (0465-442227; fax 0465-440377; €) and **Dello Sportivo** (0465-441101; fax 0465-440800; €) are all near the Pradalago gondola.

Alternative Lodging: Madonna also has a series of mountain refuges where skiers can stay on the slopes. The largest is **Rifugio Graffer** (0465-441358). A week of half-board in a bunk bed costs less than €300—discounts apply for mountain club members such as AMC. Daily half-pension is about €40-€45 for mountain club members.

One refuge that is treated as a hotel is **Dosson** (441507). It's very small. A week at half-pension costs about €300.

Ski Chalets: Crystal (see page 16 for addresses, phone and fax).

Apartments, condominiums, flats

Apartments rent from Sunday to Sunday or from one Saturday to Saturday.

The **Alpen Suite Hotel**, previously the Residence Roch, (0465-440100 ; fax 0465-440409) has been remodeled. New suites are available for €125-€320 depending on the luxury and time of year. The price includes a breakfast buffet, dinner, access to the fitness center, internet, satellite and SKY-TV, and covered parking.

Residence Perla (0465-446010; fax 0465-440879) is the most luxurious, but at the far end of town. **Torre del Brenta** (0465-441078; fax 0465-441078) is the newest construction right next to the Pradalago gondola.

The tourist board can provide additional listings of apartments in the town. There are six other flat rental agents in Madonna with two additional sets of apartments in Campo Carlo Magno. As always make your selection based on location.

 ## Dining

Madonna di Campiglio isn't up to par with resorts such as Courmayeur and Cortina when it comes to on-mountain dining. The refugi serve good risotto and meat you can grill on hot rocks, but they don't have a gourmet flair. You can, however, have a very good meal at Malga Montagnoli with full service.

With that said, one of the best experiences at this resort is taking a snowcat ride for a dinner up on the mountain at **Malga Montagnoli** (0465-443355), **Boch** (0465-440465), **Malga Ritorto** (0465-442470) or **Cascina Zeledria** (0465-440303). The latter may serve the best food, but all are excellent and great fun.

Down in the town recommended restaurants are:

Da Alfiero (0465-440117) gets the nod as top dog in town from Michelin and has average prices of about €45. **Al Sottobosco** (0465-440737), about a km. out of town where meals will set you back about €40, sports a newly awarded Michelin fork. Another of the top spots to try is **Sartini** (0465-440122) where you can expect to pay €40. **Locanda degli Artisti** (0465-442980) has wonderful ambiance and affordable food with a fixed price menu for around €18. Both **Belvedere** (0465-440396) and **Pappagallo** (0465-442717) also have good food. A very plain place but a good value for meals is **Ristorante al Sarca** (0465-440287) where the fixed-price menu is €18. **Lanterna d'Oro** (0465-442104) serves good basic local cooking. Two good pizzerias are **Le Roi** (0465-443075) and **Antico Focolare** (0465-441686).

 ## Après-ski/nightlife

This town is very Italian in terms of après-ski—eccentric and very late. It all starts with the scene at **Bar Suisse, La Cantina del Suisse** or **Franz Josef's Stube**. If you are in Campo Carlo Magno, head to **La Stalla**.

There are only three discos in the area. Crowds are mixed from the young to a more middle-aged clientele. The **Des Alpes** has a pricey disco, as well as a very cozy piano bar where you can nurse a drink for as long as you want. Evening cabarets are presented in the restored Hapsburg ballroom. The **Zangola** (which translates to butter churn) with male strippers and dancing babes all in a restored cow-bar atmosphere is legendary in Italy, but you need a car to get there.

 ## Child care (2006/07 prices)

Contact the tourist office for babysitter information or check with your hotel about child-care facilities.

There are also children's ski classes. Scuola Italiana Sci Adamello Brenta (0465 443412) runs a kindergarten from 9:30 a.m. to 4 p.m. which includes lessons, meal and snowplay in the Campilandia funpark. It costs €170 for three days and €320 for six days. Scuola Italiana Sci Rainalter (0465 443300 , fax 0465 446990) also runs a similiar kindergarten from 10 a.m. to 4 p.m.

 ## Other activities

For **ice skating** call 0465-440503. Entrance is about €5 or €10 with rentals. They have lessons and discounts for Madonna hotel guests.

Once you are in Madonna, it is not an easy task to get out of the region—the drive to the autostrada is along a twisting-and-turning mountain road. But if you insist on breaking away, you can get to Venice in about three-and-one-half hours. Verona, with its giant Roman amphitheater and Romeo and Juliet balcony, is about two hours away. Vicenza with the wonderful Paladian villas is also about three hours away.

During the drive to Madonna, enjoy the multitude of castles that dot the Trentino countryside. The town of Trento has the Castello del Buon Consiglio (Castle of Good Counsel) that used to be home to prince-bishops. Today it is the Provincial Art Museum. The cathedral towers over a cobbled square and the Via Belenzani is lined with Venetian-styled palaces.

During Carnevale just before Lent, Madonna di Campiglio hosts many costume balls and special events.

 ## Getting there

By car: Madonna di Campiglio is two hours north of Verona. The closest airports are in Milan, Verona and Venice. All have rental car services. From Verona take the Trento exit and follow the signs for Madonna di Campiglio. From Milan take the Brescia exit and follow the signs for Lago Idro, Tione, and Campiglio.

The southern route from Trento or from Rovereto to Riva and then up to Madonna Via Pinzolo is the most visually dramatic. Another road leaves the autostrada just north of Trento at San Michele and goes north toward Cles through the Valle di Non and crosses one of the deepest gorges in Italy.

The Passo di Mendola to Bolzano is tortuous.

By bus: A shuttle bus connects Madonna with the main airports in Verona and Milan once every Sunday. Round trip from Verona is €40. Round trip from Milan is €45. For booking and information call 0465-447501 or fax 0465-440404 or check with your hotel.

By train: Go to Trento and transfer to a bus (about 50 yards from the Trento station), which runs on a regular schedule.

 ## Tourist information

The tourist information office, or *Azienda per il Turismo*, in Madonna di Campiglio is located in the center of the resort in the Centro Rainalter. Its staff is well organized with information.

Tourist Office, Centro Rainalter, 38086 Madonna di Campiglio (TN), Italy; 0465-447501, fax 0465-440404.
E-mail: info@campiglio.to
Internet: www.campiglio.to

MUSEO ALPINO

Courmayeur

At the Italian end of the Mont Blanc tunnel, Courmayeur enjoys a phenomenal resort location. Mont Blanc, the highest mountain in Europe, guarantees snow; the Alps here are among the most spectacular in the range; and Courmayeur lies at the junction of Switzerland, France and Italy. If a skier tires of skiing the Courmayeur slopes, Cervinia and La Thuile in Italy are within striking distance; Chamonix in France and Verbier in Switzerland can also be reached for a full day of skiing.

Courmayeur is a small, picturesque Italian village with the ski area across the valley. The village provides a cozy atmosphere with a warren of narrow cobblestone streets, small bars and fabulous restaurants. The slopes are reached by cable cars stretching across the valley, and the short return to town is by bus. During the past three years, the resort has invested heavily in snowmaking to ensure good snow conditions on the Val Veny side of the resort. But, its star quality is found in the restaurants, where Italians seem to spend far more time than on the slopes.

 ## Mountain layout

The major ski area is on the opposite side of the valley from Mont Blanc. Half of the area is centered around the Plan Chécrouit and the other half drops down to the Val Veny. The Plan Chécrouit is a transfer point for the cable cars from the town to the lifts servicing the major ski areas. This ski area is split by a ridge. One side offers a northeast exposure and the other a northwest exposure. After stepping off the cable car, there is about a 100-yard walk to the three main lifts that take skiers to the upper slopes. Most skiers will want to head directly to the gondola and go to Col Chécrouit. From there another smaller cable car heads to the Cresta Youla. The skiing from Cresta Youla at almost 8,700 feet is excellent, but the wait for the cable car can take more than half an hour even on relatively good days.

The highest lift arrives at Cresta Arp at 8,954 feet; however, the skiing from that point is for experts only, and only with the assistance of guides. The highest skiable point for the run-of-the-mill skier is the Cresta Youla. From here you can ski a good, tough, intermediate trail that ends up at the base of the cable car. Skiers can then either drop down a long cruising run to the base of the Plan de la Gabba chair lift at about 6,800 feet, or drop down narrower steeper terrain and several cat tracks to Zerotta at about 5,000 feet. Either run will allow you to ski greater vertical than 90 percent of the resorts in North America.

Much of the skiing on the Val Veny side of the ridge is through trees. The drops off the ridge line are relatively steep. Unfortunately, skiers will have to return to town via this cable car or by a short bus ride from the base of the Val Veny lifts. It's a hassle.

Off-piste adventures include skiing around the back of the Cresta d'Arp and dropping down a wide-open bowl then winding through the Val Veny; or skiers can traverse from Cresta d'Arp to Dolonne or Pré-St-Didier. Skiers with a guide and return transportation, can strike out down to La Balme and end up near La Thuile.

Otherwise expect to have a bland intermediate and beginner playground. Real beginners will be a bit cramped with limited facilities at Plan Chécrouit. They may be happier at one of the other baby slopes in Val Veny or below at Dolonne.

The second major skiing area at Courmayeur is Mont Blanc itself. Here a cable car carries skiers in three stages to almost 11,000 feet where they can ski off-piste back down toward Courmayeur, over the mountain to Chamonix or take some time skiing on the glacier accompanied by a guide.

Snowboarding: Every square inch of terrain that is open to skiers is open to snowboarders. Construction plans for a snow park and boardercross area are underway. Contact the Courmayeu Mont Blanc Cablecar Society (0165 846658; fax 0165 842347) for more details.

Mountain rating

If you are an absolute beginner this is probably a mountain you should avoid. Although there are some beginner areas, the terrain is steep enough to take the fun out of skiing if you are over your head. For the intermediate this is heaven. There are plenty of semi-steeps to make the intermediate feel like an expert and enough moguls to keep his or her head from swelling. The expert can find some challenging slopes off-piste. The ski instructors can take experts down slopes that will keep them coming back for more. Even the marked trails are good enough for a good day of cruising.

 ## Lift tickets (2007/08 prices)

The Courmayeur Mont Blanc Pass has the following benefits:

All passes valid for 3 to 5 consecutive days can be used for 1 day in the area of the Aosta Valley.

All passes valid for 6 to 10 consecutive days can be used for 2 days in the area of the Aosta Valley.

All passes valid for more than 10 consecutive days can be used for 3 days in the area of the Aosta Valley.

All passes valid for 3 to 14 consecutive days can be used for 1 day in Flaine Grand Massif.

All passes valid for 3 to 14 consecutive days can be used for 1 day in Chamonix excluding: cable car Chamonix-Plan de l'Aiguille, cable car Plan de l'Aiguille-Aiguille du Midi, train Chamonix-Montenvers, cable car Croix de Lognan-les Grands Montets, gondola Mer de Glace. It is possible to use all the lifts by paying a supplement of €10 per day.

You need a photo taken without sunglasses or ski hat. Your pass must be shown at each resort for a ski pass outside the Chamonix valley. Those skiing for four days or more must purchase the Hands Free Badge which costs €3.

These are the regular season prices for the Courmayeur Mont Blanc pass. There is approximately a 10% discount for skiing in early or late season.

	Adults	Seniors (age 65 and older)	Children (age 6-12)
three days	€106	€79.50	€53
four days	€138	€103.50	€69
six days	€199	€149	€99.50
fourteen days	€375	€281	€187.50

Ski school (2007/08 prices)

There are two ski schools: the **Monte Bianco Ski & Snowboard School** (0165 842477, fax 0165 846488) and the **Courmayeur Ski & Snowboard School** (0165 848254, fax 0165 845549). They have over 100 instructors who speak English, French and German.

Lessons are given every day. These are high-season prices for the Monte Bianco Ski & Snowboard School.

Private lessons for both skiing and snowboarding cost from €35-€44 depending on the time of day and €11 for each additional person. A ski instructor for an entire day costs €270 and €50 per additional person.

Group ski lessons require a minimum of four people. One day costs €51. Three days cost €125. Five days cost €175. Group snowboard lessons require a minimum of four people. One day costs €51. Three days cost €135. Five days cost €195.

Accommodations

The recommended hotels and apartments in Courmayeur are all close to the town center. €€€—€125+; €€—€75-€125; €—€74-.

If you are looking for the most luxurious, head to **Hotel Pavillon** (0165.846120, fax 0165.846122; €€€) one of the best in Courmayeur, with indoor pool, sauna, garage and TV. It is only 100 yards to the lifts and ski school. **Hotel Gran Baita** (0165.844040, fax 0165.844805; €€€) has a heated pool. The **Royal and Golf** (0165.831611, fax 0165.842093; €€€) in the middle of town also has a heated swimming pool.

These hotels show up in tour operator brochures and are excellent. **Hotel Les Jumeaux** (0165.846796, fax 0165.844122; €€€), a brand new, first-category hotel with sauna, TV and exercise room, is closest to the lifts . **Hotel Cresta et Duc** (0165.842585, fax 0165.842591; €€), **Hotel Cristallo** (0165.846666, fax 0165.846327; €€), and **Hotel Lo Scoiattolo** (0165.846721, fax 0165.843785; €€) are all good. **Hotel Walser** (0165.844824; €€) is a good place for kids, but about a 10-minute uphill walk to the Via Roma après-ski and nightlife.

For B&Bs, try **Bouton d'Or** (0165.846729; €€) or **Croux** (0165.846735; €€).

Apartments, condominiums, flats

This is a relatively new development for Courmayeur. There is one very basic group of apartments in town—**Le Grand Chalet** (0165.841448; fax 0165.848183).

In Pre-St. Didier, **Residence Chécrouit** (0165.844477), **Residence Courmaison** (0165.846815) and **Residence Universo** (0165.87066; fax 0165.87087) feature several types of rooms, including studios for two or three people and two-room apartments for up to five. All are equipped with TV and complete kitchen equipment. A free shuttlebus takes guests to the lifts. In the same town, **Chécrouit** (0165.844477; fax 0165.844995) has condos. In La Thuile head to **Planibel** (0165.884541; fax 0165.884535). This large apartment grouping sits at the base of its own ski area that connects to France.

Contact the tourist office for a listing of private flats available for rent.

Dining

This is a town dedicated to eating. On the slopes you can't go wrong at any one of 59 different restaurants. Even the self-service at Plan Chécrouit is good, filling and cheap. The **Christiania** (0165.843572, fax 0165.846381) serves incredible pizzas and pastas as well as full meals. The owner, originally from the island of Elba, prides himself on fish dishes; however, they are only cooked to order—call ahead. **Maison Vieille** (337230979) has a wood-fired oven. **Château Branlant** (0165.846584, fax 0165.846363) is worth the dining experience if only for its tasty desserts. Dropping down into the Val Veny try to find **La Grolla** (0165.869095, fax 0165.869783) at Peindeint for a great (and expensive) meal. Or head to the base of the Zerotta lift and grab a bite at the **Petit Mont Blanc** (0165.869066).

Most of the hotel restaurants are good. If you want to get out and explore the local restaurants, follow the old rule: if it is crowded with locals, then it must be the place. Try **Cadran Solaire**, a diner's delight, on the main street (tel./fax 0165.844609). **La Palud** (tel./fax 0165.89169) serves excellent fresh fish and **Pierre Alexis 1877** (tel./fax 0165.843517) on Via Marconi also has fine dining. Or try the very reasonable **Mont Fréty** (0165.841786, fax 0165.845095) at 21 Strada Regionale. **Le Coquelicot** (0165.846789, fax 0165.845500) has a French owner and therefore French fare. **Pizzeria Tunnel** has great pizzas and is normally packed.

Outside of town try **La Maison de Filippo** (0165.889797, fax 0165.889705) in Entrèves where, for a fixed price (about €30), you are served some 40 courses. The stream of food seems never to end, with servings of antipasti, pasta, sausages, contorni, salads, various meats, and baskets of nuts and breads. It used to be exceptional, but has grown far too crowded over the past decade.

Chalet Proment Da Floriano (0165.897006, fax 0165.897900), known locally as Da Floriano, is an out-of-the-way, romantic and traditional spot next to the cross-country area La Val Ferret. The owner prides himself on his local specialties of *boudin*—blood sausage with beets, fontina cheese, marinated smoked pork and excellent wines. Across from Da Floriano is the **Miravalle** (0165.869777, fax 0165.869729) which receives rave reviews from many local chefs. It has a selection of more than 120 local wines. Val Ferret also has **La Clotze** (0165.869720, fax 0165.869785) which has been awarded two Michelin forks.

The local red wines are excellent. Try *Donnas*—a strong heavy dry wine; and *Enfer d'Arvier*—lighter and fruitier. A good grappa or *genepy* finishes off the meal in Val d'Aosta style.

Après-ski/nightlife

Here Courmayeur shines. Après-ski is a long, drawn-out affair with several elegant bars. Start with the **Bar Roma** on the main street. Here in an old-world atmosphere enjoy mixed drinks, wine and beer with substantial snacks (put out from about 6:30 to 8:30 p.m.). A bit down the Via Roma is the **Café della Posta** that is just as full of old-world charm but with the addition of a massive fireplace surrounded by couches in the back room behind the bar. A newer spot, but just as crowded, is the **Cadran Solaire**, a wine bar in a cozy wine cellar atmosphere. The **American Bar** is a more traditional bar. If you can push through the crowd at the bar, you will discover a hidden room with comfortable seats and a fireplace. Above the American Bar is a tapas bar called **Le Privé**. It is a cozier version of the Café della Posta with top-shelf drinks and tapas. Just beyond the church and under the Museo Alpino is the **Bar des Guides**—one half is *bierkeller-esque* with long tables and the other half has couches around a crackling fire.

The most popular discos are **The Jimmy Night Cafe**, **Poppy's Pub**, **Planet Disco Bar** and **Music Bar I Maquis**.

Child care (2007/08 prices)

Hours for the children's program (0165.844036) are 9 a.m.–6 p.m. and children as young as 9 months are accepted.

The Ski School Monte Bianco (0165.842477) runs the Mini-Club for children age 10 and younger. When whether permits, children are allowed to play games in the snow outside in a park filled with balloon characters and inflatable slides and castles. Prices include lunch and care. Day and week rates do not apply to children age 2 and younger, so parents must pay the hourly rate of €15 per hour.

One hour of care costs €15; one day (from 4 to 7 hours) €45; three days €120; five days €187. Care and skiing lessons for five days cost €290; care and snowboarding lessons for five days €313. Entrance to the inflatable park costs €8.

Other activities

Geneva, Milan and Turin offer excellent **sightseeing** and museums. Aosta Valley is spectacular and features one of the best collections of castles in Italy, as well as excellent **Roman ruins** in Aosta, the capital city.

On January 30-31, the **Feast of St. Orso** is held in Aosta. It is one of the largest crafts fairs in Italy, with fantastic wood carvings and other handicrafts.

During *Carneval*, the town of Ivrea is one of the wildest places to be in Italy. The residents are decked out in costumes reminiscent of "Star Wars." They participate in the Battle of the Oranges, which features a castle defended by the bad guys being assaulted by the good guys who hurl over a ton of oranges during the siege.

A sports center (0165.844096) is open from 10 a.m. to midnight daily with **tennis** and **squash courts**, **ice skating**, **fitness club**, **curling**, **indoor golf** and a **climbing wall**.

Other activities in Courmayeur include **snowbiking**, **dogsledding**, **paragliding**, **snowshoeing, heliskiing, heliboarding, golfing in the snow, archery, riding** and **fishing**.

The valley also boasts a **casino** in St. Vincent. Milan, in addition to its sights, features La Scala, the largest **opera house** in Italy and one of the greatest opera companies in the world.

Getting there

The closest airports are Geneva and Milan. Both are within a two-hour drive. Train and bus services connect Milan and Turin with Courmayeur. Car rentals are available at both airports.

Tourist information

For any additional information, contact: Tourist Office (Azienda Informazione e Accoglienza Turistica Monte Bianco) Piazzale Monte Bianco #13, 11013 Courmayeur, Italy. Call 0165.842060; fax 0165.842072.

Internet: www.aiat-monte-bianco.com
Email: info@aiat-monte-bianco.com

Torino Olympic Region
Sestriere and Sauze d'Oulx

Along the border of Italy with France, the Alps rise majestically, the Italian dolce vita blends with French laissez faire and the regional cuisine draws from the best of Italy and France. This region, the Piemonte, owes its French/Italian lineage to the continuous shifts of the international borders for centuries between nobles pledging allegiance alternately to French and Italian kings.

The hilltops and valleys bear witness to the warfare that marked relations along this mountain border. Massive castles and fortifications lie along mountain ridges and protect narrow valley entrances. But for all this defensive posturing, valleys and towns still shifted sides based more on politics and religion than military might.

These mountains that once formed a natural boundary today are linked by hundreds of km. of ski and snowboard trails and web of gondolas, chairlifts, pomas and cable cars. This is the region that hosted the 2006 Winter Olympic Games.

The Games spread throughout the region. Sestriere hosted most of the men's downhill events. Cesana-San Sicario was the site of women's downhill, biathlon, bobsled, skeleton and luge. Sauze d'Oulx showcased the freestyle events. Bardonecchia claimed the snowboard venues.

For American and British tourists, the best towns to use as a base for discovering this area of Piemonte are Sestriere and Sauze d'Oulx. Though these resorts are linked by snow-covered trails there is a dichotomy in village flavor. Sestriere is on the main road, modern, bustling, surrounded by lifts and fashionable. Sauze d'Oulx is a traditional village laced with a warren of narrow cobbled streets, tucked at the end of a winding mountain road with at least a dozen switchbacks, with limited lift access to the far-reaching trails. Sestriere is very Italian with a rhythm that reflects traditions of coffee, apres-ski at the hotels and some late-night disco action. Sauze d'Oulx is packed with British, Dutch, Irish and other European tourists and its pubs positively rock when the lifts close.

 ## Mountain layout

This overall ski area, the Via Lattea, or Milky Way, comprises more than 129 lifts and 400 km. of interconnected skiing. The main areas are Sestriere, Sauze d'Oulx, Sansicario, Cesana-Claviere and Mont Genevre (in France).

This is a major area, and though the lifts have improved dramatically for the Olympics, it is very difficult to even ski all the regions in one week. the distances between the resorts by snow are much less , in most cases, than by road.

There is plenty of skiing and riding for those searching for long cruising runs. Most of the area trails have been cut for beginners and intermediates. There are a few black trails here and there, but for the most part, Italians come to ski for enjoyment rather than challenge. These resorts reflect that state of mind. That said, real expert skiers and riders can keep themselves busy off-piste. With an area this large any real expert skier will find plenty of challenge.

Sestriere, by far, has the best access to the slopes and the most challenging skiing in terms of marked terrain. A dozen lifts—six of them quads—take skiers from the town to the upper reaches of the mountain. Monte Sises has more advanced and expert trails. Monte Motta/Banchetta is a bit mellower filled mainly with intermediate cruisers and some advanced trails. Much of this sector is above tree line.

Take the Col Basset gondola to connect with Sauze d'Oulx and the rest of the Via Lattea. That one lift or a shuttle bus is the only connection for most skiers and riders.

Sauze d'Oulx has beautiful winding trails through forests. The best skiing and lift service is higher on the mountain. Access to the town, whether skiing down or trying to get a lift up, is torturous. New lifts being installed for the Olympics will help, but all skier and riders from Sauze d'Oulx need to catch one of two double chairs, neither of which is convenient, or a quad lift that is hike or bus ride from the center of town. This is a town where getting to the lifts is a chore, but finding a wild bar is child's play. Almost all of the trails are intermediate and beginners don't really have an easy time of it. There are beginner trails winding down snow-covered mountain roads. Expert can make their own challenge by ducking off-trail whenever they choose.

Sansicario, a purpose built resort, lying on a mountain face between Sauze d'Oulx and Sestriere has excellent intermediate and beginner trails. The lift access from the hotel areas is fine with two quads and a triple from the base. There is also a new gondola that takes skiers and snowboarders from Cesana to the hotels of Sansicario.
The rest of the Milky Way can be reached by a series of five lifts rising from Cesana-La Comba in the direction of France. Here long trails drop through the trees. At the top of mountain range the lifts interconnect with the French sector, Montgenevre. This is a different world. The French lift systems are space-age compared to most of the Italian side of the Milky Way. From Cesana to Montgenevre is very full day of skiing.

Ski school (2007/08 prices)

As in all European resorts, there are several ski schools. One of the main ski schools in Sestriere is the **Scuola Nazionale Sci** (0122-77060). Prices are competitive at the other regional ski schools.

Private lessons during high season cost €40 an hour for a person; €12 for each additional person. Low season prices are €36 for one and €12 for additional skiers.

Group lessons are from 10 a.m. to 1 p.m. with about five to nine skiers per group and have a video analysis included. Six days cost €150. One day is €35.

Lift tickets (2007/08 prices)

Prices are for high season covering the entire Via Lattea:

one day	available locally	six days	€175
three days	€89	seven days	€197

Accommodations

Pricing: €€€=more than €80; €€=€50-€70; €=less than €50 per person based/double occupancy with half-board in high season. Prices are for seven-day packages. Single night stays may be more expensive.

Sestriere –– If traveling without a group, try to stay at the **Hotel Savoy Edelweiss** (0122.77040; €€–€€€). This is a small intimate hotel in the midst of the oldest section of Sestriere and across the street from the lifts. Another small gem is **Hotel Sciatori** (0122.70323; €€), three km. outside of town with lift access only 300 meters away. Its packages include a six-day lift pass. **Hotel Cristallo** (0122.750707; €€€) is a modern giant with all the amenities right across the street from the lifts. **Grand Hotel Sestriere** (0122.76476; €€€) sits imposingly above the town, only a short walk to the center. **Hotel Biancaneve** (0122.755176; €€) is about five football fields from the center or the lifts. It is a chalet-style new hotel with good basic rooms, food and service. **Hotel Olimpic** (0122.77344-76010; €€) is a homey basic place with easy access to the town and about a 500-yard walk to the lifts.

Sauze d'Oulx — The best hotel in town and one of the nicest is **Il Capricorno** (0122.850273). It sits right on the slopes and is reached either by a single chairlift of by snowmobile. It is an atmospheric place with simple luxury, no fancy amenities, spectacular views, Michelin rated food, and plenty of peace and quiet. Down in the village the top spot is **Grand Hotel Besson** (0122.859785). This impressive building has beautiful views, a swimming pool and an attached evocative spa. It is only a three minute walk through narrow streets to the middle of town. **Chalet Faure** (0122.859760; €€ B&B only) is a small 11-room haven in the midst of Sauze d'Oulx's old world center. Great restaurants and rollicking nightlife are only a few steps outside the door. Rooms are wonderful and new spa operated in the basement. The round **Grand Hotel La Torre** (0122.859816) looks hideous from the outside but fine once inside. Mixed reviews on the food here, the location is good for nightlife and the views wonderful. **Biancaneve** (0122.850160; €€) is a gem and a bargain. Two sisters run the place and keep it clean as a whistle and whip up some fine food. **Relais des Alpes** (0122.859747: €€), **Gran Bosco** (0122.850166; €€€), and **Stella Alpina** (0122.858.731; €€) are all good. Most of the rest of the hotels near the center work with tour operators and are hit and miss.

A few hairpin turns down the mountain road in Jouvenceaux **Chalet Chez Nous** (0122.859782; €€ B&B only) with only 10 rooms, is tucked in a narrow street in an old cute-as-can-be stone building. Parking is difficult and restaurants are a shuttle bus ride away, but the place is beautiful with lots of stone and wood. A lift serves the town.

Apartments

Each of the Via Lattea towns has a collection of apartments. Use the contact numbers for the tourist offices at the end of the chapter.

For an apartment that sleeps four people expect to pay €650-€850 per week. Prices are all over the place. Make sure to check around on the web and with different tourist offices. During the holiday periods prices range up to €1,400 for a week.

Dining

The Piemonte is an exceptional area for dining. Some of Italy's finest wines are grown in the nearby valleys surrounding Torino and the orchards are famous in Italy for their fruits and nuts. This, combined with the mountain flair for cheeses, sausages, dried meats and grappa, makes for a perfect vacation spot for a serious gourmand.

Perhaps the best restaurant for traditional local meals in the region is **Du Grand Père** (0122.755970) isolated on the side of the mountain just off the road between Cesana and Sestriere. The rustic dining room with wooden floors and fireplace in a 17th-century house set in a tiny village is perfect.

Sestriere has dozens of restaurants. The saying that it is hard to find a bad Italian restaurant is almost true in the town. Most visitors to Sestriere have half-board. For a night on the town we recommend the following.

La Baita (0122.77496) run by Cavaliere Giancarlo and his wife Marisa, looks modest but the dishes such as penne with a venison and pork sausage sauce was extraordinary. It was followed by a phenomenal deer scallopini sautéed in rosemary. The beef Bourguignon made with local Barolo wine melted on my mouth. the father and his son Luciano hunt for game that is served in the restaurant.

Other good restaurants are **Colombiere** (0122.76323), one of the more expensive in town; **Al Braciere** (0122.76129), and **Last Tango** (0122.76337); and **Pinky Restaurant** (0122.76441) for simple plates and pizza. On the slopes just above Grangesises is the tiny **La Brua Restaurant** that reeks of atmosphere.

The best restaurant in Sauze d'Oulx is **Il Capricorno** (01212.850273) sitting on the slopes. Try to reserve a table here for lunch. Or, get there in the evening by chairlift or snowmobile. Next on the list of fine dining is Il Cantun del Barbabuc (0122.858593) and Old Inn 0122.858541. Del Borgo, Orto dei Frate 347.7612439 and Peccora Nera 0122.858577 and **Per Bacco** are also excellent.

Kali, who owns the **Godfather Restaurant** (0122.850291), is a controversial fixture in the town. His place has lots of wonderful southern Italian cooking and also opens from 2-7 a.m. in the morning to serve the hard-core partiers before they crawl back to their hotels.

 ## Après-ski/nightlife

Sestriere isn't much of a party town. For apres-ski head to the Pinky, the Sestriere and Baraba. Al Kovo is the spot for late night action.

Sauze d'Oulx is one of Europe's top party towns. For a bite before apres-ski or dinner head to Bar Miravallino where crepes, sandwiches, pasta and cold dishes are serve up much like tapas in Spain. They also have good mixed drinks such as mojitos and rum and coke. The list of party-hearty pubs is lengthy and each draws its own crowd. The Cotton Club, Moncrons, Paddy McGinty's, Derby, Ghost and Crowded are packed with revelers. Later in the night Vagabondi starts to fill and a live band starts the dancing. If not dancing at Vagabondi try Shuss or Bandito.

After dragging yourself out of the pub or disco stop by for a quick bite at Godfather Restaurant, the only place open from 2-7 a.m.

 ## Child care

No resort in this area has developed good child care. Italians haven't reached the point where they send children off to someone else. Family fills the role when needed.

The ski schools are excellent for children age 4 and older. Few cultures deal with children better than the Italians. Most of the instructors speak enough English to communicate with children. Prices for children's lessons are the same as adult prices.

 ## Other activities

This region is filled with history. The castles and forts are exceptional. Try to visit Exilles, a museum of military fortifications; Bramafam, in

Bardonecchia; and Fenestrelle, the largest stone fortification other the Great Wall of China. The imposing church Sacra di San Michele perched on a rock outcropping, just outside of Torino at the start of the Susa Valley, at 3,100 feet is a Benedictine Abbey. Building on this church began in the 900s and finished in the 16th Century. There is also a group of villages with extraordinary frescos. The Roure region has more than 50 frescos in four villages; Salza has 32 murals inspired by Italian songs; and Usseaux has a series of frescos depicting mountain life.

Those who love excellent, traditional foods should stop at one of the Albergian shops in the region. They sell everything from local liquors to honey and from jams and juices. They have stores in Sestriere and Progelato as well as five other villages.

 ## Getting there

Fly into Torino if possible. From there the drive is only about 1 hour and 45 minutes. From Milan the trip is about an hour longer. Trains run from Milan and Torino to Oulx. From Oulx, frequent buses head toward Sestriere.

We suggest getting a car to move around the area. It gives you far more flexibility; however, those planning on staying in one village will find the car of little use while at the resorts.

 ## Tourist information

The main regional tourist office is under the name **Montagnedoc** in Oulx, Piazza Garambois, 2, tel. 0039-0122-831596, email oulx@montagnedoc.it.

Sestriere Office: Via Louset, tel. 0038-0122-755444, email sestriere@montagnedoc.it

Sauze d'Oulx Office: Piazza Assietta, 18, tel. 0039-012-858009, email sauze@montagnedoc.it

Val Gardena

While a trip through the spectacular Italian Dolomite mountain range is worthwhile in itself, when combined with the experience of skiing one of the largest interconnected lift systems in the world, a vacation in the Dolomites rates as tops. The natural panoramas found in the Dolomites around virtually every bend in the road and ski trail are hard to properly describe. And Val Gardena, with some of the best prices in Europe, is hard to beat.

The Ladin culture is centered in the five main Dolomite valleys, in eastern Switzerland and in Italy's far northeast. Val Gardena is a stronghold of the culture, and its residents speak Ladin, a Latin derivative, as their first language. They also speak German and Italian.

The people of this region have a Germanic passion for detail and hard work, so everything works perfectly. They also have the Italian love of life, so they play as hard as anyone in the world and enjoy great music and food. The cooking is a wonderful marriage of creativity with Italian pastas and wines and German meat and potatoes.

The Gardena valley has three main villages. The first and largest, coming from Bolzano, is Ortisei. The second is S. Cristina, and the third, just at the start of the Gardena Pass and Sella Pass is Selva Gardena. S. Cristina is spread out along the highway and does not have much of a town center in which to congregate after skiing, so book your accommodations in Ortisei or Selva Gardena if après-ski is a priority. Selva Gardena, smaller and closer to the other Dolomite slopes, has improved in terms of nightlife over the last few years. It's rumored to now have more après-ski than Ortisei which is further away from the interconnected ski areas. The atmosphere in the entire valley is more German than Italian, with a beer-hall flavor.

Whichever resort you choose you will have a great vacation and you will have the opportunity to move easily between the towns on the five-euro shuttle service which links Ortisei, Selva Gardena and S. Cristina.

Mountain layout – Skiing

The interconnected Dolomite Superski lift system, with 450 lifts, reaches more than 1,200 km. of prepared slopes, and hundreds of kilometers of off-piste skiing through rocky crags and spectacular mountain scenery. Seceda, directly above Ortisei, is the highest elevation on the lift system in the Gardena region at 7,740 feet.

Perhaps the biggest draw for the region, besides the panoramic views, is the Sella Ronda, a 26-km. section of interconnected runs which allow you to ski around the Sella mountain group. This full-day expedition involves visiting eight different ski areas. The runs are well marked and the Sella Ronda can be skied either clockwise or counterclockwise. Any reasonably competent skier can complete the basic circuit. Better skiers will find many opportunities for adventurous detours.

The major requirement for doing the entire Sella Ronda in one day is stamina. Intermediates should allow about 5-1/2 to 6-1/2 hours of skiing time, starting early enough to get back over the last passes before the lifts close from 4 p.m.–5 p.m. If you are planning to do the Sella Ronda, the best day according to locals is Saturday, when most vacationers are either leaving or arriving.

Mountain layout—Snowboarding

Snowboarders will probably be happiest on Piz Sella or the Alpe di Siusi where there is a manmade half pipe off the Laurin chair lift.

There are two boardercross courses: one at Passo Sella (chair lift Grohmann-Cavazes); and the other in the area Comici/Piz Sella (open from the middle of January to the end of the season).

A natural half pipe is near the Sotsaslong lift.

Mountain rating

Judged solely on the extensiveness of its skiing opportunities, this area might be considered one of the best. However, expert skiers will have to go off-piste for real excitement. While there are some hair-raising runs above Selva Gardena and S. Cristina, experts in search of off-trail action should hire the services of a good guide. Try the Sassolungo or the Passo Pordoi at your own risk. If you decide to go without a guide, be sure to check in with the ski school for a word about your proposed route, snow conditions and avalanche warnings.

The intermediate and the beginner will find ample suitable terrain—when skiers tire of one area, they can just head over to another for variety. The Alpe di Siusi above Ortisei is a beginner's paradise.

Cross-Country

Val Gardena is a special treat for cross-country skiers. The Vallunga in Selva Gardena, the Monte Pana in S. Cristina and the Alpe di Siusi offer an unique, fantastic panorama. The valley offers more than 100 km. of well-prepared trails.

Selva Gardena-Vallunga — From Selva Gardena, Vallunga provides a total of 12 km. of trails that lead from the Carabinieri Sports Centre to the end of the valley. There is the Selva Gardena Ski & Snowboard School and a ski hire at the start of the trail.

S. Cristina-Ortisei — S. Cristina also has a variety of facilities for cross-country skiers. From the Monte Pana Mountain Lodge there is an easy 25 km.-trail that descends gradually to Alpe di Suisi.

Ortisei — In Ortisei begin on the 1 km long practice trail on the Minert field, at the eastern end of the Promenade. On the Pinei Saddle (5 km. from Ortisei on the road to Castelrotto) there is a fine 4 km. long trail for beginners and advanced skiers.

Alpe di Siusi — Nearby Alpe di Siusi is a real paradise for the more ambitious cross-country skier, with over 60 km. of prepared trails and superb views at every turn. Cross-country skiers will find a paradise up on the Alpe di Siusi, one of Europe's highest Alpine meadows with an altitude ranging 6,500–7,150 feet.

Ski school (2006/07 prices)

There are eight ski schools in Val Gardena. Two schools are in Ortisei — Ski & Snowboardschool "Saslong" (0471 786258; fax: 0471 789457) and Ski & Snowboardschool Ortisei (0471 796153 fax: 0471 797907). Three schools are in Selva Gardena — Selva Gardena Ski & Snowboard School (0471 795156; fax: 0471 794257); Top Ski School (0471 794099; fax 0471 771028); and Ski & Snowboard School "2000" (0471 773125; fax: 0471 773283). Two schools are in S. Cristina — Ski & Snowboardschool S. Cristina (0471 792045; fax: 0471 790053) and Ski & Snowboard School Cir (0471 790184, fax 0471 791010). They bring the number of instructors in the valley to almost 400. Prices are relatively uniform throughout the valley.

These are the prices for Ski &Snowboardschool S.Cristina. Make sure to ask for an English-language instructor.

Private lessons (per hour) are €31–€35.

Group lessons are €159–€182 for five full days with a maximum ten people.

Snowboarding lessons are €160-€170 for five days.

Cross-country skiing lessons are €99-€106 for four days.

Children's Ski School (4–12 years) for five full days with lunch, costs €186–€204. Children age 4 and younger have 10-hour courses (from Sunday until Friday) at the cost of €111–€115.

Lift tickets (2007/08 prices)

The prices listed are for the Dolomite Super Ski lift pass. Local area lift tickets can be purchased. However, the difference in price between these tickets and the Dolomite Super Ski pass is small (about 10 percent). This is the mega-pass for the whole of the Dolomites which is valid on 450 lifts and cableways, giving access to almost 1,220 km. of slopes, including the famous Sella Ronda and many other Dolomite ski tours.

Season is 01/06/08 to 02/02/08 and 03/25/08 until the end of the season. High season is 12/23/07 to 01/05/08 and 02/03/08 to 03/24/08.

	Season	High Season
one day	€37	€42
three days	€105	€119
six days	€184	€209
fourteen days	€336	€382

Note: Children younger than age 8 ski free. Children ages 16 and younger get 30 percent discounts. Seniors age 60 and older get 15 percent discounts. Ski passes for eight days or more require a photograph. Long lines are the norm for obtaining these passes on Saturday—it's quicker on Sunday afternoon and Monday morning.

Accommodations

The following hotels and pensions come recommended by locals. They are listed in descending order of luxury.

All rates are per-person based on double occupancy with half-board. €€€ indicates luxury hotel with high-season prices more than €125. €€ notes hotels with most high-season prices from €75–€124. € indicates hotels and pensions with high-season prices less than €75 per person for half-board.

In Ortisei: Head to **Adler** (0471-775000; €€€), one of the best, in the center of town; **Genziana-Enzian** (0471-796246; €€€); **Grien** (0471-796340; €€+); **Hell** (0471-

796785; €€); or **Cavallino Bianco** (0471-783333; €€€), right in the middle of town. **La Perla** (0471-796421; €€) is our favorite in the area—beautiful and a bit out of town, but there's bus service to the lifts and a pool. Then there's **Gardena** (0471-796315; €€€); **Villa Luise** (0471-796498; €€) with 13 rooms, which is out-of-the-way but has panoramic views. Lastly, try **Cosmea** (0471-796464; €); or **Stua Catores** (0471-796682; €), which was recently renovated and a bit out of the way, but has local flavor.

Far above Ortisei, in the tiny dorf (village) of Bulla, the 10-room **Uhrerhof-Deur** (0471-797335; €€) provides a quiet and affordable retreat with wonderful views above the town and a great kitchen open only to guests. Also in Bulla, **Sporthotel Platz** (0471-796935; €) is a great bargain with beautiful views. This is a perfect spot for cross-country skiers and walkers.

In Selva Gardena: The best are **Hotel Tyrol** (0471-774100; €€€); **Genziana** (0471-772800; €€€), with a great restaurant; or **Alpenroyal Sporthotel** (0471-795555, €€€). The next level is **Gran Baita** (0471-795210; €€) and **Chalet Portillo** (0471-795205; €€€). Then head to **Mignon** (0471-795092; €€) or **Laurin** (0471-795105; €€). The least expensive, but still Michelin-rated, is the quiet **Pozzamanigoni** (0741-794138; €) which is somewhat out of the way. All of these hotels are excellent—it just depends on the level of service you demand. For an inexpensive B&B try the **Eden** and **Somont**.

In S. Cristina: Try the **Diamant** (0471-796780; €€€), **Interski** (0471-793460; €€), **Sporthotel Maciaconi** (0471-793500; €€), or **Villa Martha** (0471-792088; €).

Ski Chalets: Inghams and Thompson (see page 16 for contacts).

Apartments, condominiums, flats

The tourist office has an extensive listing of vacation apartments that can be rented for a minimum of one week.

General descriptions included in its brochure indicate TV, garage, balcony, etc. The apartments all have fully furnished kitchens, but not all provide bedding, which may entail a small, extra cost. Weekly prices start with two beds from €200; four beds from €250; and six beds from €350.

Private rooms: A great chance to save money. Rooms rented in private homes include breakfast. The price ranges for a room with bath (per person, per day) are: low season €20–€30; high season €25–€35.

Dining

For an authentic Ladin meal, head off to the **Stua Catores** (0471-796682) on Sacunstrasse 47 in Ortisei. The food is hearty and the atmosphere rustic and unpretentious. Don't be afraid to ask among the restaurant patrons for someone who speaks English and can help you with the menu selection. Another typical Ladin restaurant is **Tubladel** in Str. Trebinger 22.

Some of our suggestions are *crafuncins*, a type of ravioli; *panicia*, a barley soup with a type of bacon; *jufa*, a puréed version of polenta; *patac cun craut*, potatoes and sauerkraut; *anes enzucredes*, pancakes with anise and sugar; *ribl da furmenton*, a buckwheat pancake; *bales da furmenton*, a buckwheat dumpling; and *crafons* for dessert.

Other recommended Ortisei restaurants:

Concordia, Romstr. 41, Ortisei (0471-796276), for ravioli in truffle sauce and game. This restaurant gets two forks from Michelin and has affordable daily menus.

Waldrand Furdenanstr. 9, Ortisei (0471-796385), for game. Reserve ahead.

Restaurant Cascade, Str. Promeneda 1/1, Ortisei (0471-786465), serves traditional meals and pizza. Its vinotheque has a good and varied choice of wine.

Restaurant Anna Stuben in Hotel Gardena, Vidalongstr., Ortisei (0471-796315).

Mar Dolomit Str. Promeneda 2, Ortisei (0471-797352), has local and traditional Italian specialties with an open wood-fired pizza oven.

Mesavia (0471-796299) and **Vedl Mulin** (0471-796089) have an excellent mix of Germanic and Italian food and are reasonably priced.

In Selva Gardena try:

Hotel Tyrol, Str. Puez 12 (0471-774100), has won prizes for its local fare.

Armins Grillstube, Str. Mëisules 161 (0471-795347), has great lamb.

Des Alpes Stuben, Str. Mëisules 157 (0471-772700), is somewhat upscale and has chateaubriand and fondues.

Gérard, Str. Plan de Gralba 37 (0471-795274), has a Michelin fork and is noted for its very affordable daily menus. The views of the Sassolungo are awe inspiring.

For fondue and cheese dishes try **Gardenia, Dorfer** (0471-795204) or **Olympia** (0471-795145).

Sal Fëur (0471-794276) at Str. Puez 6, for pizza.

Bargain meals can be found at the self-service **Dopolavoro FF.SS** in Selva at 46 Plan (0471-795165).

In S. Cristina head to:

Uridl, Str. Chamun 43 (0471-793215), for wine, venison and pumpkin ravioli.

Plaza, Str. Cisles 5 (0471-793463), serves Tirolean dishes and fine fresh trout.

For pizza try **Bruno**, **Da Peppi** (0471-793335) and **Pizzeria Iman** (0471-793793)..

On the Sella Ronda try lunch at the **Sellajoch** right at the Sella pass.

 ## Après-ski/nightlife

There is a collection of good bars with some local music, and several small discos crank up late at night. In Ortisei, try **Soviso** and **Siglu Bar in the Hotel Adler** which often have an early crowd. Later head to **Mauriz.**

In S. Cristina try **Crazy Pub,** which starts cranking about when the lifts close.

The Selva crowds can head to **Igloo**, **Laurinkeller** or **Speckkeller**. Later bars are **La Bula** and **La Stua**. **Piz5** is also popular. Dance at **Dali** and **Heustadl.**

 ## Child care (2006/07 prices)

Eight ski schools accept children from the age of 4 and offer courses that run 9:30 a.m.–4 p.m. with midday supervision. Prices are slightly lower than those for adults. Register at your ski school of choice.

The **Ski School S. Cristina** offers a kindergarten service for children 18 months and older, everyday from 9 a.m. to 4:30 p.m. A half day without lunch costs €24 (€29 with lunch); full day with lunch costs €42; and five full days with lunch costs €190.

The **Ski School Ortisei** looks after children from 2 years of age in the Mini-Club which features snowplay for children who don't ski. The Mini-Club is open weekdays from 8:30 a.m.to 4:30 p.m and costs €25 for a half day without lunch; €36 for a half day with lunch; €44 for a full day with lunch; €160 for a five full days with lunch.

Casa Bimbo (0471-793013) has qualified personnel who care for children as young as 4/5 months to age 7/8 years old.

Dolomiti Adventures - Rock and Snow (0471 770905) has a junior club that offers supervision, equipment (snow blade, big foot, ski fox, board, shoes, sticks, helmet) and drink for children age 11-18. The program takes place every Thursday and daily on request. There's a minimum of 4 people. Half day costs €36; full day €69

Mini Club Selvi for children from ages 4 and younger at the Ski School "Ski-factory" Selva Gardena, is open Sunday to Friday, from 9 am-4 pm. You will need to bring: a complete change of clothes, diapers, snow suit, warm boots, hat and gloves, non-slip socks, and food/bottles for babies younger than a year old. It costs €10 for one hour; €30 for three hours; abd €50 for seven hours. Weekly packages are also available: €230 for five days (7 hours a day); €180 for six days (5 hours a day).

Other activities

Val Gardena is a **woodcarving capital** with thousands of artisans. Browse through the stores for carvings of everything from figurines to bowls and utensils.

The music society schedules **concerts** in the winter.

Horse-drawn sleighs glide on the Alpe di Siusi, Monte Pona and Vallunga.

There is a **swimming pool, a new public sauna** and **steam bath** in Ortisei. Covered **tennis** courts and **ice skating** are found in Ortisei and Selva Gardena.

The tourist office or your hotel will provide a free schedule of events, including **folk nights, band concerts, film evenings, ice hockey games** and **toboggan races**.

Getting there

The closest airports are in Verona (about a three-hour drive), Milan (about a four-hour drive), Munich (about a three- to four-hour drive), Bolzano (about one-hour drive), Innsbruck (about two-hour drive). Major rental car companies have offices at the airports.

Trains come to Bolzano and Bressanone, connected to Val Gardena by about 10 buses daily. A taxi to Val Gardena from Bolzano costs a maximum of about €130.

Tourist information

Val Gardena
Tourist Office, Str. Dursan 80c, I-39047 S. Cristina
Telephone: 0471-777777
Fax: 0471-792235
Internet: www.valgardena.it
E-mail: info@valgardena.it
Ortisei/St. Ulrich
Tourist Office, Reziastr. 1, 39046 Ortisei
Telephone 0471-796328, fax 0471-796749.
S. Cristina
Tourist Office, Chemunstr. 9, 39047 S. Cristina
Telephone 0471- 7777800, fax 0471-793198.
Selva Gardena
Tourist Information Office, Mëisules 213, 39048 Selva Gardena
Telephone 0471-795122, fax 0471-794245.

Norway

Among Norway's many draws for tourists is its spectacular. largely unspoiled, natural beauty. Forested hills and lush dales run nonstop from the Swedish border to the North Sea and from the Oslo harbor to north of the Artic Circle. Along the North Sea coastline, the fjords knife into the mainland and create fairytale views that elicit audible gasps from virtually everyone.

Oslo

Even the capital city has more than two-thirds of its area dedicated to nature. Building is forbidden here. The glades are manicured, and all laced with trails for cross-country skiing in the winter and walking in the summer. Outdoors is an everyday part of life for Norwegians; even the city folk embrace it.

On a Sunday morning, more locals walking toward the train station had cross-country skis over their shoulders and were wearing cross-country garb, than carrying a paper under their arm to leisurely read over a cup of coffee.

From downtown Oslo, the cross-country trails are only minutes away. Some good downhill skiing is also available at Holmenkollen, site of the Olympic Games, less than half an hour from the Viking ships in the harbor. At Holmenkollen, the Ski Museum presents the history of skiing. Afterwards, climb (or take the elevator) to the top of the ski jump to see a unique bird's-eye view of Oslo and its surroundings.

Downtown Oslo has enough sites to keep any intrepid tourist busy. The Münch Museum is filled with art by the man who painted The Scream (though the most famous version of that painting is in the National Gallery). The polar exploration ship, Fram, is open for viewing. The Norwegian Folk Museum provides a glimpse of life in the olden days. Viking ships are preserved from the 9th century and the Kon Tiki raft sits inside its own museum.

Bergen

On the North Sea coast is Norway's other major city, Bergen, clinging to a spit of land jutting from the crenulated shoreline and surrounded by yet more islands and headlands. To describe the setting as 'fantastically picturesque' is to do it injustice. However, with some 300 days of rain annually, some visitors will have to take our word for the panoramas.

Bergen was one of the major trading stations of the Hanseatic League from the 1300s to the 1600s. This organization of traders controlled commerce in the North Sea for centuries. Young German executives would come alone to Bergen for a year or two to handle accounting, warehousing and barter for timber, fish and pelts with the Norwegian natives.

The medieval warehouse district where they lived and worked, the Bryggen, has been declared a UNESCO World Heritage site. There is an excellent museum that relates the story of trade in the region. There are also plenty of shops and restaurants along the harbor. A trip up the nearby funicular provides great views over the harbor. And along the quay, past the Bryggen, is Halikon Hall, the remains of the old Viking castle that once dominated this city.

Still a trading town, Bergen now focuses on oil, which the Nowegians pump from beneath the North Sea. The center of Bergen is filled with shops, many hidden inside massive, modern shoppping malls constructed within the walls of turn-of-the-century buildings. On the outside, one might imagine dour bank offices within the walls. But from the inside, brass and glass on multilevels with soaring escalators conjures shopping fantasies.

Both Oslo and Bergen have tourist cards that will allow free or discounted entrance to all museums, use of the public transportation and (if you can find it) free on-street parking. Cards can be purchased for 24, 48 or 72 hours.

Cross-country skiing

For the real cross-country enthusiasts, Norway is Nirvana. Here, cross-country skiing is not simply a sport, it is a lifestyle, a way of transportation, a social affair and everyday exercise. In North America and the Alps, cross-country skiing is in some respects the poor cousin to downhill skiing and snowboarding. Americans and other Europeans have never developed the excitement that Scandinavians have for the Nordic sports.

From the capital city, cross-country trails can literally take a skier to every corner of Norway. Trails are measured in tens of kilometers or miles in Colorado, Wyoming, California and New England. Even in the Alps, loops are carefully measured and trails shoot across a lake here or there. But in Norway, the network is measured in thousands of kilometers. For that matter, the distances don't really matter, when the entire country is accessible on cross-country skis.

In Lillehammer, trails lead right from the city through the woods surrounding the town. They connect to more trails that connect to Hafjell where the cross-country area criss-crosses the top of the mountain before descending into the dale. In Kvitfjell, the downhill course slashes down the mountain that is surrounded by caressing tracks set for kicking and gliding.

In Geilo, trails trace their path along the valley floor and then rise and cross many of the downhill tracks on the high plateau above the ski lifts. In Hemsedal, the network wanders through rich forests past small huts while the downhill skiers are far above treeline. Every area has a stated length of their trail system, however those statistics only refer to the trails that their region maintains.

Meals and drinks

Get ready for sticker shock when you order your first beer or take a close look at a wine list. Meals and drinks in Norway are far more expensive than what most American, British and European visitors are used to paying.

A beer is normally about US$6 at a minimum. A bottle of mediocre wine is $50–$60. A bargain meal might be pizza or pasta that will end up costing about $25. Moderate meals in restaurants will run about $35. The expensive places start at around $50 per person. An impeccable gourmet meal with wine will cost about $100-$120.

That said, the level of cuisine in Norway is extraordinary. Even the simplest restaurant serves excellent meals. When the prices for some of the near-gourmet creations are measured against the cost of sandwiches, pizza and pasta, the difference one would have to pay for fine dining seems slim. A fine meal in Norway (without wine) ends up costing about the same as a fine meal back home with a moderate wine.

The reindeer (reinsdyr) and elk (elg) dishes are wonderful as are the fish that arrives fresh everywhere. Try the monkfish or turbot (piggvar), the fish soup (fiskesuppe) and their version of catfish (steinbit). Make sure to enjoy these meals at least once during a stay in Norway.

Finish your meal with a unique experience, cloudberries (multer) picked north of the Arctic Circle. They normally will be served with vanilla ice cream or cream.

Geilo

If ski and snowboard resorts could be warm and fuzzy, that would describe Geilo. This gentle resort was the first in Norway. It was built at the halfway point on the Oslo-Bergen rail line. The downhill trails are decidedly friendly — intermediate and beginner. Cross-country trails loop along the top of the hills. The hotels are Old World, plush and comfortable. The staff is smiling and helpful. And this is considered one of the best family resorts in Norway.

One Norwegian Krone is worth about 17¢. Or, US$1 = NOK6.

 ## Mountain layout– Skiing

The trail system is split into the north and south side, both served by a free ski bus that shuttles between hotels and the lifts. The largest trail system is north of the town across the railroad tracks. Here, seven lifts rise from the town to open a series of interconnected, looping trails that drop back through the trees to town or traverse across the mountain. Trails from the top of the mountain drop over the backside down to another lift nexus. Two lifts take skiers to the top elevation of the area, 3,830 feet, for skiing above treeline.

On the south side, the Geilolia Ski Centre has expanded and now connects to the Kikut area. Pause a minute to enjoy the awesome view of Hallingskarvet Mountain before carving down one of Kikut's six slopes.

This area is good for beginners, which is probably why it is also the home of the children's ski area. The children's ski kindergarten, nursery and tobogganing run are also situated here.

 ## Mountain layout– Snowboarding

Geilo has three terrain parks. Check out the improvements in Fugeleleiken terrain park and Geilolia Snowpark. The Fugeleleiken terrain park, one of Norway's biggest terrain parks, is the home of Northern Europe's largest half pipe –5.7 meters high and 150 meters long. It's been upgraded with new jumps and rails.

The Geilolia Snowpark drops down from the top of the Vestliheisen lift. This snowpark, opened during the 2006/07 season, starts with two jumps of 10-15 metres, one after the other, and then the path splits into two runs. The run to the right is "slope-style". It starts with two flat rails followed by three 10- to 15-meter jumps. The snow park concludes with another 8-meter flat/down railbox. The area even has a floodlit mogul run for evening skiing.

Ski school (2007/08 prices)

Three ski and snowboard schools provide group and individual lessons. There are also courses for terrain park tricks.

Private lessons cost NOK455 for 55 minutes for one person; NOK640 for two people; and NOK750 for three people. Private lessons for 110 minutes are NOK800 for one person, NOK940 for two people and NOK1,110 for a group of three people. A personal trainer for three hours costs NOK1,295.

Group lessons are for three or more days. Three days costs NOK765; four days, NOK970; and five days, NOK1,120

Lift tickets (2007/08 prices)

An adult full day pass is NOK325; three day pass, NOK825; five days, NOK1,225. Youth, ages 7–15 pay NOK245 for a full day; NOK620; five days, NOK920. Children younger than 6 ski free.

Cross-Country

Geilo maintains 215 km. of cross-country tracks in the Geilo/Ustaoset area. There are 40 km. of wooded trails, 175 km. of trails in the high mountains, 26 km. dedicated to skate skiing and 5 km. for floodlit for night skiing. The floodlit tracks are next to the Geilo Sports Hall and are open until 10 p.m. every night. Night skiing is also available in Dagali (2.5 km.), Skurdalen (3 km.), Hovet (4 km.) and Hagafoss (3.5 km.).

Accommodations

Geilo has a stellar collection of hotels, anchored by **Dr. Holm Hotel** (32095700) which is considered by some the best hotel in Norway. It exudes Old World elegance and tradition. The dinners are sumptuous affairs and breakfast is served in a skylit courtyard. The hotel has the only Shisedio SPA and wellness area in the Nordic countries and is served by a ski lift just steps from the hotel doors. The entertainment in the evenings in the lounge is delightful.

Bardola Hoyfjellshotel (32090400) is every bit as elegant as Dr. Holms, but doesn't have the slopeside location. It is about a kilometer outside of town. The Friday evening seafood buffet is beautifully presented. The attached bakery has great coffees and sweets.

Highland Hotel (32096100) is between the two ski areas only steps from the small town. **Norlandia Geilo Hotel** (32090511) was the first hotel in Geilo and is very comfortable. **Vestlia Resort** (32090611) is right at the base of Geilolia Ski centre and a good walk from the town. It has an exclusive 1000-square-meter spa. **Ustedalen Hotel** (32096700) is a family hotel that lies close to the Geilo Ski lift and is a kilometer from the centre of Geilo.

Dining

Hallingstuene (32091250) is the best restaurant in town and one of the best and most famous in Norway. It occupies an antique wooden house and has a distinct mountain house décor. The walls are covered with various landscapes. The fireplace is draped with pots and baskets. The refined and rustic meals are created from locally available ingredients. Expect dishes such as reindeer medallions, mountain stream trout, venison carparccio, forest mushrooms and, for dessert, pale cloudberries (a Scandinavian treat) picked above the Arctic Circle and served with vanilla ice cream.

The restaurants in **Dr. Holm's** and **Bardola** are also exquisite. The buffets that are laid out each evening are mind-boggling.

Après-ski/nightlife

You can't go wrong with either of the bars in the Dr. Holms Hotel. The **Skibaren** is the hotel's main bar that is well-know for its après-ski. During the night, it becomes a cosy piano bar which is a popular spot for the more mature crowd. **Recepten Pub** has lively après-ski from 3-7 p.m., a big-screen TV and a dance floor. They also have parties throughout the winter season.

Lille Blå Cafè & Bar is a sport's bar with a big-screen and several TVs that show sports every night. It has internet access and is the only bar in Norway with an indoor climbing wall.

Child care (2006/07 prices)

Trollklubben kindergarten (next to the Geilolia Skisenter) with its friendly troll theme, is perfect for children ages 7 and younger. This is one of the best family resorts in Norway. There are scores of activities for families and children including an adventure cabin where children can listen to fairytales in three languages, sing songs, paint and dance. There's also a canvas tent with barbeque, an outdoor playground for children ages 2-6 and a children's toboganning run. Parents must bring diapers, a change of clothes and clothes for snowplay. Daycare and ski kindergarten programs are also available.

One child costs NOK80 an hour; NOK190 for 2.5 hours; NOK360 for five hours; NOK410 for a day; NOK930 for three days; and NOK1,350 for five days.

Other activities

The resort has **sleigh rides, kite skiing, dogsledding, reindeer sledding, snowmobiling, snow rafting,** and more other activities. Bardola, Dr. Holms, Ustedalen, Vestlia and Park hotels have **pools**.

Getting there

Geilo is exactly halfway between Bergen and Oslo. Train access is excellent. Train fare from either Bergen or Oslo is about NOK350 and the ride in each direction takes around three hours.

Driving from Oslo is easy. Follow Hwy. R-7 to Geilo. Oslo is 239 km. from the resort. Bergen is 273 km. from the resort.

Tourist information

Geilo Tourist Office, Vesleslaattaveien, 13, N-3580 Geilo. Tel. 32095900. Email: turistinfo@geilo.com; Internet: www.geilo.no.

Hemsedal

Hemsedal is Norway's largest ski and snowboard resort. The mountain looms above the treeline with wide-open snowfields at the higher altitudes and trails tracing paths through the trees to the base area. Some 48 trails wind down 2,600 feet of vertical drop.

Though the skiing and snowboarding is good, the facilities at the area are sparse to say the least. The town of Hemsedal may define a one-horse town. Don't expect anything traditional or cozy here. Functional seems to be the rule of the resort. The scraggly collection of hotels and restaurants along the main street seems more of an industrial area rather than a resort center.

The town does function well, however. The mountain provides skiing and riding for everyone. Shuttle buses carry skiers from their hotels to the base of the lifts. Hotels are packed with merry makers. Discos pulse with noise. And restaurants manage to serve excellent meals.

One Norwegian Krone is worth about 17¢. Or, US1 = NOK6.

Mountain layout—Skiing

This is a big mountain. No doubt about it. The base area sits at two levels, with ticket offices and rental shops at both levels and parking lots in between. Short lifts connect the two base areas.

Beginners: This area, between the two base areas, is where beginners start life on skis and where the kindergarten plays. After mastering the elementary basics, there is another beginner lift above the upper base that serves mainly children's ski school classes. Beginners have a trail that stretches from the very top of the mountain and meanders down more than 2,000 feet of vertical across snowfields and then through trees.

Intermediates will find wide-open skiing from the top of Totten and Hamaren with an opportunity to stretch their abilities by skiing down gullies, draws and through tight trees. Anyone focused on cruising will have a field day on the wide runs at the upper reaches of the resort and down the classic cruising trails that cut through the trees.

Experts have the center of the mountain that drops down to the upper base area. These steep trails through the trees offer opportunities to ski or ride the woods at every turn. The expert trails are served by a chair and a drag lift that ensure short lines and plenty of vertical.

Mountain Layout–Snowboarding

A dedicated quad lift serves the snowboard area that stretches down almost a thousand feet of vertical where boarders will find Norway's biggest terrain park and halfpipes. Hemsedal's 600-meter long main park is definitely for advanced and expert riders. It has several elements like 1/2 pipes, jumps, tabletops, corner, 1/4 pipe, big jump, wood boxes and rails.

The Blue park, which runs next to the old "Turisten," is suitable for beginner skiers and snowboarders. The park has several features like jumps, tabletops, rails and a halfpipe.

Cross-country

In Hemsedal, 133 km. of groomed tracks wind around the valley and forest. Another 80 km. of trails can be found on the mountain. To reach the Gravset cross-country area, (800 meters above sea level) drive to Ulsåk and take a right towards Lykkja (about 8 km). Parking and restrooms are on the right and left sides of the road. A bus shuttles skiers to Gravset in the morning and afternoon.

The High Mountain tracks are less predictable than the valley trails. Make sure to check the local weather/ski report or call Hemsedal Skisenter/Tourist Office for their conditions before you head up the mountain. Night skiing is also offered until 11 p.m. on two circular tracks: one near Hemsedal Centre and the other at Gravset.

Ski school (2007/08 prices)

The Hemsedal Ski School (32 05 53 90) provides group and individual lessons with video analysis. There are courses for snowpark tricks as well as normal snowboarding.

Private lessons cost NOK545 for an hour for one person; NOK670 for two people; and NOK795 for three people. Private lessons for two hours are NOK745 for one person, NOK995 for two people and NOK1,245 for a group of three people. You can receive a twenty percent discount off these prices if you book the first lesson of the day.

A personal trainer for three hours costs NOK1,345.

Group lessons: Four-day, 90-minute sessions are NOK660-NOK8255. The first and last lessons of the day are the cheapest.

Lift tickets (2007/08 prices)

In Hemsedal ski centre you must buy a Ski*Direct card for all lift passes. The price is NOK45 and the actual card can be reused next time you are in Hemsedal or at any of the other SkiStar resorts. The following are the prices for the Hemsedal Ski centre and Solheisen ski centre ski pass.

	Adults	**Youth (age 7–15)**
half day	NOK295	NOK235
one day	NOK335	NOK275
three days	NOK930	NOK755
six days	NOK1,455	NOK1,190

Children age 6 and younger ski for free. Seniors age 62 and older ski for youth prices. When you buy a pass for four days or more, you get a 15% discount during: 12/16/07, from 1/7/08-2/8/08 and from 4/14/08-5/4/08.

Night skiing is available on Tuesday, Wednesday, Thursday and Friday from 6-9 p.m. from 12/04/07 03/14/08. It costs NOK 110 for adult and NOK 90. for youth.

www.skisnowboardeurope.com

Accommodations

In the town of Hemsedal, the **Norlandia Skogstad Hotell** (32055000), right on the main street, is consider to be the best hotel, but the hotel full-board meals are passable at best. There is a pub and disco. If staying on the weekend, ask for a room away from the nightlife noise.

Perched on a rock outcropping, with spectacular views is the **Skarsnuten Hotel** (32061700) set in a small village reached by a toll road or chair lift. The rooms are simple and modern. Prices (per person double occupancy with full pension) range from NOK1,200 midweek to NOK1,500 on weekends. The common area and restaurant are exceptional. The hotel also has a collection of cozy apartments. **Scarsnuten Fjellandsby** (32055060) condominiums, in the same mountain village, are excellent as well.

Most of the other nearby accommodations are aparthotels. Rooms are clean and modern. **Rogjin Apartments** and **Hemsedal Resort Fjellandsby** (32055060) have a collection of condominiums near the base area. The **Molla Sportell** (32055060) is a collection of 56 cabins at the base of the lifts.

About 30 minutes from Hemsedal, up a winding dirt road, **Harahorn** (32062380) is an exclusive resort hotel that is more suited to a quiet private retreat, a family getaway or a corporate meeting. It is an elegant collection of 20 small authentic farmhouses that have been brought to the mountain complex. The oldest building is centuries old with a sod roof. The central building has the dining room and several guest rooms. Otherwise visitors stay in the old houses, which have been beautifully restored and modernized. The meals are considered by the locals to be exquisite.

 ## Dining

Skarsnuten Hotel (32061700) has an exceptional dining room. Soaring glass walls cut high above the rock cliffs seem almost ready to take flight. The dining room epitomizes clean Scandinavian design — plain wooden tables and chairs — minimalist with an amazing panorama. The wines and gourmet meals are as exceptional as the setting.

We started with seared fois gras over caramelized apples accompanied by a German Riesling. Next was poached trout over a bed of peas with lobster fricasee and a white Macon wine. The veal fillet was served over a bed of lentils smothered with sauteed green beans matched with a Dolcetto d'Alba full red wine. Cheese followed and then poached plums with prune ice cream.

The à la carte restaurant **Bistro Anden Etasje** in Hotel Skogstad (32055000) is excellent as well. The restaurant prepared reindeer medallions with mushrooms and green beans, pacific sole with capers and beets, and a dessert of apple cake with peach sherbet, strawberries and cherries.

Other recommended restaurants in Hemsedal are at the **Hemsedal Café** (32055410) and the **Oxen Bar & Grill** (32055850).

For a special experience make the trip out to **Harahorn** (32062380) for dinner. Call for reservations a day ahead since they have to shop for fresh ingredients for your meal. Cost will be about NOK500 for dinner and NOK250 for lunch.

 ## Après-ski/nightlife

The town claims a dozen bars and pubs. For apres-ski try the **Hemsedal Cafe, Skistua, Loftet, Experten Sportsbar, Garasjen, Fanitullen** and **Askeladen**. The **Skogstad Hotell** is the real downtown center of apres-ski and late night dancing. Other spots to check out for nightlife are the aforementioned **Loftet**, and **Experten Sportsbar** as well as **Hemsen Nightclub**.

Child care (2007/08 prices)

Hemsedal has excellent child care programs and overall family programs. The Trollia child care center (32 05 53 20) is open from 9 a.m. until the lifts close. Babysitting for children age 6 months to 1 year costs NOK100 an hour. Babysitting for children age 1 year and older costs NOK75 an hour. A one day program (2 hours) or children age 6 months to 1 year is NOK200; three days NOK400, five days NOK600. A one day program (3-6 hours) for age 1 year and older is NOK200; three days NOK400, five days NOK525. Siblings gets a 50% discount. Meals are not provided. Parents must pick up the children for lunch.

The ski area also arranges programs for children such as night skiing, tobogganing, children's racing and parties.

Other activities

The resort has **sleigh rides, ice climbing courses, kite skiing, dog sledding, snowmobiling, winter golf, paragliding** and an activity center with **bowling, a golf simulator, billiards** and **darts**. The Skogstad Hotell has a nice **pool**.

Getting there

Two buses depart Oslo airport on Sunday and Friday during the season. The ride is about three hours and costs NOK375. Book in advance by calling 32055030.

From Oslo or Bergen, trains stop at Gol, 30 km. from the resort. There is also regular bus service. Buses from Oslo or Bergen come directly to Hemsedal.

A free shuttlebus takes visitors from their hotels to the slopes. Buses run nine times in the morning and twelve times in the afternoon. The bus to the cross-country ski area leaves twice a day and costs NOK20.

Driving from Oslo is easy. Follow Hwy. R-7 to Gol, then R-52 to Hemsedal. Oslo is 220 km. from the resort. Bergen is 273 km. from the resort.

Tourist information

Hemsedal Tourist Office, Postbox 3, N-3561 Hemsedal.
Tel. 32055030; fax. 32055031
Email: info@hemsedal.com
Internet: www.hemsedal.com

Lillehammer Region
Hafjell and Kvitfjell

Lillehammer was the site of the 1994 Winter Olympic Games. The town got a lot of press and TV coverage. Lost, however, was the fact that the downhill ski and snowboard slopes are not located in or even near the small city. Lillehammer served as the base for the Olympics and the media focus, but for Alpine skiing or riding, a car or bus ride is necessary to get to the distant slopes.

The two resorts, Hafjell and Kvitfjell (fjell means mountain), are outside of Lillehammer. Hafjell is about a 20-minute trip and Kvitfjell is around 45 minutes from Lillehammer. Though the downhill facilities are not in the town of Lillehammer, combining these two resorts means the region has 40 lifts and 80 downhill runs.

One Norwegian Krone is worth about 17¢. Or, US$1 = NOK6.

 ## Mountain layout

Hafjell: The Hafjell lift system includes two high-speed quad chairlifts, a fixed grip quad chair, a gondola and T-bars. The majority of the trails can be reached by sticking to the high-speed lifts. The strengths of the area are the magnificent panoramas, excellent grooming and the ability of skiers of all abilities to ski together for most of the day with easy bypasses around the steeps.

Experts will not find the area very challenging. The black runs have pitch but are very wide and well-groomed — perfect for intermediates progressing to advanced.

Intermediates will have a mountain where they can ski and snowboard themselves giddy. The wide trails through deep green forests provide the ideal pitch to perfect a carved turn. These trails keep intermediate skiers feeling at the top of their game.

Beginners have long meandering trails that loop down the mountain from the topmost lift providing a top-of-the-mountain experience most novices don't get. There is also a separate beginner and first-timer area to the left of the main lift.

Snowboarders should check out the 900-meter Hafjell Snowboard Park.

Kvitfjell: This was the site of the Olympic downhill events. The downhill run is the only real expert terrain in the area with some good drops and parallel trails that allow skiers to double and triple their fun.

This small ski area has two chairlifts and five drag lifts. For a small area, it is an amazingly good time. The long and mellow west side is perfect for wide-open cruising in the afternoon. The trails spreading to the right side of the downhill course weave through thick forests with great views.

Cross-Country

The excellent cross-country trails at and around the Birkebeiner Ski Stadium are suitable for both adults and children. The 5-km-long lighted trail is popular all winter, and is lit up until 10 p.m. every evening. The stadium is the ideal starting point for trips into the local mountains, and is connected to a 450-km.-long trail of cross-country tracks.

Plus there are more than 1,500 km. of cross-country trails around Lillehammer, across the top of Hafjell and through the woods bordering Kvitfjell. These trails never end. Intrepid cross-country skiers can head over to the North Sea or back to Oslo.

Ski school (2007/08 prices)

Both the Hafjell Ski School (61274777, fax 61274776) and Kvitfjell Ski School (61283680) have similar prices.

Private lessons for all levels and disciplines cost NOK655 for 90 minutes for one person; NOK415 apiece with two people; and NOK310 apiece with three people in the class.

Group lessons for skiing and snowboarding last 90 minutes and classes require a minimum of three students. Three days cost NOK655; four days, NOK735; and five days, NOK805.

Lift tickets (2007/08 prices)

The Trollpass is good in Hafjell, Kvitfjell, Skeikampen and Gala. There is a mandatory key card price of NOK75. NOK50 will be refunded to you once you return the card.

Who skis free: Children ages 7 and younger.

	Adults (ages 16 and older	Children (ages 8-15)
one day	NOK325	NOK260
three days	NOK795	NOK600
five days	NOK1,165	NOK860

Passes valid for 2 days and more also include night skiing– Tue. - Wed. - Thu. 5: 30 p.m. – 8 p.m. There is no night-skiing Dec. 25, 26 and Jan. 1, 2008. The last night for night-skiing is Mar. 13, 2008.

Accommodations

Many stay in Lillehammer for the shopping, nightlife and additional restaurants. But, those coming for the snow should stay right in Hafjell or Kvitfjell rather than facing the daily shuttlebus to the ski area.

The main hotels in the Hafjell area all have half-board rates for about NOK600 per person double occupancy (ppdo) Sunday-Thursday and NOK700 ppdo Friday and Satuday; bed and breakfast rates are about NOK100 less.

Hafjell Hotel and Apartments (61285550; fax 61285551) is an 800-meter walk from the base of the lifts, but served by the local shuttle as well. It has 61 rooms, which can best be described as Norwegian kitsch with lace curtains, canopied beds and lots of room to spread out. There is also a swimming pool and sauna. Dining is cafeteria style.

Quality Hotel Hafjell (61277777) is right off the highway, 1,000 meters from the slopes and served by ski shuttle each morning. The rooms are modern Scandinavian.

Quality Hotel Hunderfossen, (61274000) is across the river near the base of the bobsled run. This modern hotel has larger rooms than its brethren across the river and is more isolated but served by a ski bus each morning at least twice a day.

Nermo Hotel (61275580; booking@nermohotell.no) – a plain, large, barn-like building – houses welcoming rooms with farm antiques and blond-wood walls. It is about a mile from the trails, but is served by ski shuttle three times each morning.

Ilsetra is an aparthotel where apartments are combined with hotel services. This property is near the top of the mountain road and close to Gaiastova Restaurant.

In Kvitfjell, stay at the **Hotel GudbrandsGard** (61284800). This is one of the top mountain hotels in Europe. It is right on the slopes and has just about every amenity one desires, plus the dining is fabulous. Full board rates are about NOK1,200 (ppdo).

Next door, **Kvitfjell Hotel** (61282902) is much simpler and less expensive. It also has small cabins for rent that will sleep from four to eight people. Hotel rooms with half pension cost about NOK650-750 during the week and NOK1,500 on weekends. A cabin for four with two bedrooms will cost about NOK5,000 for a week.

Hotels in Lillehammer

Most tourists stay in Lillehammer. The city has much more to do and has some excellent restaurants, bars and nightlife. These hotels are all in the range of NOK400-550 a night per person double occupancy.

First Hotel Breiseth (61247777) is near the train station and bus terminal. **Hotel Mølla** (61269294) is in an old mill silo — one of the most unusual buildings in town. **Clarion Collection Hotel Hammer** (61267373) has good rooms and is right on the main shopping street. **Rica Victoria Hotel** (61250049) is next to the pedestrian district. For bargains, head to **GjesteBu Overnatting** (61254321) where rooms are only NOK175; or **Mary's Guest House** (61248700) where prices are about NOK375.

 # Dining

In **Hafjell**, **Elgen Restaurant** (02636) and **Hafjell Lodge** were suggested as the best places to dine in town. The restaurants at the **Quality Hotel Hafjell** and **Hafjell Hotel and Apartments** both were recommended. Otherwise there are several pizza spots and cafés. Dining in **Kvitfjell** is in your hotel.

Restaurants in Lillehammer

Paa Bordet (61250000) is the gourmet class act in town. Each evening, in a small wooden building, it serves a fixed-price, six-course menu for NOK505 or a three-course version for NOK405. Diners are also free to order individual courses. However, those six courses make up the entire menu. The six courses consist of a starter, a fish plate, a palate cleanser, a meat plate, cheese and dessert. The dining is rated as tops in Norway — leave plenty of time and save your appetite for an adventure. The main meat courses vary from reindeer to elk to lamb. Desserts are exquisite. Wines here are priced to encourage diners to select excellent wines with their meals. Expect to pay NOK300-450 for a good bottle of wine. Call for reservations.

Café Banken (61250030), on one floor of an old bank, serves a creative menu in a casual atmosphere. Closed on Mondays when you might find locals pushing the tables back and learning to tango.

Bryggerikjellern (61270660) was an early 19th century brewery that has been transformed into a restaurant and is normally packed. It is open for dinner only.

Blåmann Restaurant (61262203) is the home of Mexican/Norwegian fusion cuisine set alongside the river. Try the reindeer burritos and quesadillas. But the best courses are pure Norwegian — soups, mountain trout and reindeer.

Egon Restaurant (61269294) was Hilary Clinton's preferred restaurant during the '94 Olympics. The dining room sits alongside the river and is packed with antiques. The menu looks like it was designed by the same folks who created Denny's or Applebee's menu. There is not a Norwegian dish on the menu, but plenty of steaks, burgers, tacos and baked potatoes. You can also order Sutter Home wine for around US$50.

Svare & Berg (61247430) (and the co-located **Nikkers** with lighter fare) was recommended repeatedly by locals. Again, the fusion of Mexican and Norwegian food is tasty, but the best meals are Norwegian reindeer and salmon.

Vertshuset Solveig (61262787) is a rambling farmhouse. It is one of Lillehammer's oldest restaurants and is casual and rustic. Its menu features Norwegian standbys such as trout, reindeer and lamb. Prices are as down to earth as the atmosphere.

 ## Après-ski/nightlife

At the base of **Hafjell**, **Woody's** is a British-styled pub. In fact, it is run by the British tour agency, Norwegian Woods Travel. The tour operator realized that one of the area's drawbacks was the high cost of beer. They solved the problem by starting their own pub and selling pints for about the same price as in London. Beers here are about 40 percent less than in normal Norwegian bars.

The other main après-ski spot is up at the **Gaiastova** restaurant at the upper village, plus **Number 1** and **Quality Bar** in the main village.

In **Kvitfjell** the one apres-ski bar is in the middle of the slopes. Getting home when inebriated is a trick on the slippery slopes. Otherwise, apres-ski is in the hotels.

Apres-ski in Lillehammer

Brenneriet (The Distillery) is the largest and best-known disco in town. It is attached to the Bryggerikjellern Restaurant. **Felix** is where heavy rock holds sway. It serves only beer and has a crowd from age 18 to 80. **Blå Rock** is one of the most popular spots with DJs and the occasional live band. **Lille Blå** has two levels with the disco upstairs. **Nikkers** is a cafe with big windows opening onto the main street where many Norwegians gather for a beer or coffee just after skiing. **Bingon** is packed with young students drinking cheap beer. **Retro** is for the very young and is where most of the 18- to 20-year-olds hang out. For late-night nightclub action, head to **Tut ankh Amon** and play like Ramses and Cleopatra.

 ## Child care (2006/07 prices)

Both resorts have a kindergarten. At Hafjell Ski School (+47-61-27-47-35) the kindergarten is open from 10 a.m. to 3 p.m. and takes kids ages 2 to 7. Costs are NOK45 for one hour; NOK85 for three hours; and NOK125 for five hours.

Hafjell Ski School also has children's clubs for various ages (Call for pricing.): TROLL CLUB offers snowplay and lessons for children ages 4-6 years who have never skied. KNERTE CLUB provides lessons for children ages 4-6 years who have skied before and know how to snowplow. SNOW CLUB is for beginnier skiers ages 7-10. JUNIOR CLUB is meant for 11-15 year-olds who are beginners or intermediates. There's also a Jibbing Clinic for children ages 10 and older who want to master different terrain-park tricks and elements.

In **Kvitfjell** there are private babysitters for about NOK60 an hour.

Kvitfjell Ski School (61283680) has child-care programs and facilities including Bamsebo, a small cabin dedicated to very young skiers. At Bamsebo children can watch movies, play or read a book.

Sleighing is taught in Bob-landet. It is open every day and once a week, during peak season, there will be a sleighing test, where the children will receive a "sleighing license" and a diploma.

During the peak season children can take part in Miljøvennene, an activity that educates children about environmental thinking. This acitivity is for free and all children who participate will receive a button and a painting book.

 Other activities

Lillehammer's Olympic Park has **bobsled rides**. Cost is about NOK170 for adults and NOK85 for kids ages 10-11 accompanied by an adult. Minimum age for the bobsled is 10.

There is an excellent 200-meter **tobogganing** run in Sjusjoen that is open until 9 p.m. each evening. There are also **doglsed rides, snowshoeing, ice skating, horse-drawn sleigh rides** and a "**Moose Safari.**"

Lillehammer has one of Norway's most important **art museums** with more than a thousand works. **Maihaugen** is Norway's oldest open-air museum founded in 1887. The indoor museum here traces Norwegian history back to 10,000 B.C. The **Olympic Museum** traces the history of the Olympics. The **Road Museum** outlines the development of the highway network.

 Getting there

From Oslo, trains reach Lillehammer in about two-and-a-half hours. They run almost hourly. The Lillehammer train station is only a short walk from almost every hotel and taxis are easy to find.

Getting to the slopes: Shuttlebuses link Lillehammer with Hafjell with three departures each morning and another five or so during the rest of the day. There is also a bus that links the town with the Nordseter/Susjoen cross-country ski areas. A rental car is required to get to Kvitfjell.

Driving from Oslo is easy. Follow Hwy. E6 all the way to Lillehammer.

 Tourist information

Lillehammer Tourists AS, Postbox 44, Jernbanetorget 2, N-2601 Lillehammer. Tel. 0047.61289800; info@lillehammerturist.com; www.lillehammerturist.no.
Hafjell Alpinsenter, N-2636 Oyer. Tel. 0047.61274700. info@ hafjell.no.
Kvitfjell Alpinanlegg. Tel. 0047.61283600; kvitfjell@kvitfjell.no.

Spain

The ski scene in Spain is split between the north and the south. In the north, the rugged Pyrénées provide an effective border with France and very good skiing. The resort of Baqueira-Beret in the Valle de Arán, in the midst of these mountain, anchors the northern resorts. It is well-run with good snow conditions and acres of snowmaking coverage. The valley Baqueira-Beret calls home preserves one of the most fascinating cultures still existing in Spain. Other Pyrénées resorts such as formidable Formigal, traditional Panticosa, extensive La Molina and purpose-built Supermolina all provide good, if limited, skiing.

In the south, Sierra Nevada, rising above the town of Granada, provides a study in contrasts. Within an hour of the snow-covered slopes, swimming in the Mediterranean is possible and verdant golf courses beckon.

Spain has come a long way in the last decade in terms of skiing. The biggest change is the installation of snowmaking equipment that has provided much more of a guarantee of acceptable conditions for skiing.

Spain has always provided excellent value for money. Lift tickets are reasonable, the ski schools (when English-speaking instructors can be found) are a bargain, and it is hard to beat the values to be found in Spain for dining and enjoying excellent Spanish wines.

One of the biggest changes for U.S., Canadian and British skiers is the change in time zones. I'm not speaking about normal time zones, but the shift in dining and après-ski/nightlife timing. Dinner doesn't start until 9 p.m. and can easily last past midnight. And nightlife doesn't even start to flicker until at least midnight, normally by about 1 a.m. and can last until 4 or 5 a.m.

The Spanish Internet web site for tourism information is: www.spain.info.

Baqueira/Beret
The Spanish Pyrenees

The remote Valle d'Arán lies tucked hard against the French border in the rugged Pyrenees range midway between the Atlantic and the Mediterranean. This Spanish valley is virtually cut off from the rest of the country by jagged mountains. In fact, geographically it should be part of France since it lies on the northern side of the Pyrenees' tallest peaks. It is accessible only by bus or car along a winding road dwarfed by waterfalls and narrow canyons watched over by grazing goats and shaggy cattle.

The drive is arduous, but beauty unfolds with every turn as you pass a string of timeless villages and Romanesque churches. The surrounding peaks are the tallest in the Pyrenees. In the eastern section of the valley, ski lifts rise to a spreading series of runs with ridges and spines traced by trails and off-piste opportunities. The original village is starkly modern, but the newer developments echo the old Pyrenee stone architecture.

The valley oozes with wood and stone charm and the restaurants are among the best in Spain, even Europe. This is a valley that has developed in a cocoon of sorts — nestled between Spain and France over centuries. The first automobile road was only cut over the Bonaigua Pass in 1925 and a tunnel connecting the valley with the south was completed in 1948. Until those developments, Valle d'Arán was self-governing and isolated from Spain with better connections to France.

Val d'Arán has its own language, Aranés with connections to Ladin, spoken in parts of southern France and Switzerland and the Dolomites in Italy. Its traditional cuisine borrows from both the French and the Spanish.

 ## Mountain layout–Skiing

Baqueira/Beret, covering 4,270 acres, is an expansive series of trails with four main access points. The vertical drop in this resort is 3,282 feet. The trails are served by 30 lifts inlcuding two new high-speed six-person chairs. More than 500 snow cannons provide dependable snow coverage on 35 km. of the trails even when faced with poor natural snow cover.

The village center of Baqueira is the main center with a gondola lifting skiers from nearby hotels up to the 5,000-foot level where the ski school operates and the main beginner slopes welcome those starting with the sport. Beret is a cluster of facilities — ticket offices, restaurant, day care and ski school that anchors what is considered the wide open area of the resort. Between Baqueira and Beret, a new development of apartments and hotels, Tanau, is served by an old double chair that reaches the Altitude 1800 area as well. At the far eastern edge of the valley, a small building at the top of the Bonaigua Pass sells tickets and has parking, day care, restaurants and rentals.

The network of lifts and runs above Baqueira is dense and should keep most intermediates busy for days. The runs in the Beret section are much more widespread with lots of off-piste possibilities. The Bonaigua sector runs are well marked, and even without a map it is fairly easy to navigate.

Altitude 1800 above Baqueira is reached by the Bosque Lift, a detachable quad from the edge of town. This brings skiers to a lower plateau where beginners learn on what are called the "pastures" and four more lifts take skiers to the upper reaches of the mountain. Head to the left of the restaurant and take the detachable quad lift. This allows experts and good intermediates the option of dropping down to the new six-passenger chair or heading to the Luis Arlas lift that will bring them back up to the Cap de Baqueira peak. Intermediates can enjoy the Isards and Mirador runs back to the lower plateau or go all the way into the valley to the De la Choza chair lift. There is also an exciting off-piste itinerary, called Escornacrabes, off the back side of the Cap de Baqueira that loops back to the front side of the mountain and eventually back to the village. Beginners should stay to the right side of the restaurant, where a chair lift and a drag lift open up a practice area.

Vall d'Aneu extends Baqueira toward Bonaigua with a new access from Alt Aneu.. The Bonaigua area is really an extension of the Baqueira section that drops down to the Bonaigua pass. This is for the most part intermediate terrain with expert touches. Baqueira and Bonaigua share the steep Manaud trail from the top of the Manaud lift.

To get to the Beret section of the resort take the connecting Vista Beret lift. It is slow but is well worth the ride. When you get off the lift stay high on the trail and ski over toward Beret. If you begin to drop down the trail, you arrive back at the base of the lift and will have to take the lift again to connect with Beret. Once in Beret get ready to cruise almost anywhere.

The Beret area is served by five lifts, but its terrain allows skiers to ski virtually anywhere and choose from beginner to expert. The trails here are an intermediate heaven with good beginner terrain laced throughout. Further to the left, two triple chairs open more difficult terrain with the most difficult trails dropping from the top of the Dossau lift. The high-speed quad lift, Blanhiblar, opens up all-new terrain on the opposite side of the valley below Cap de Blanhiblar and Tuc de Costarjàs. A small drag lift links with this chair and opens extensive off-piste opportunities down into the valley.

The link from Beret back to Baqueira is made by using the high-speed six-person chair. From the top of this lift the long trail takes skiers back to the base areas.

Mountain Layout — Snowboarding

The Bonaigua attracts snowboarders with plenty off piste and couloirs only for experts.The Peulla chairlift has opened more opportunities in this region and the resort added a boardercross and halfpipe.

Mountain rating

For intermediates, there is plenty of skiing and enough challenge to leave you feeling pushed beyond your normal limits. Every lift has good intermediate skiing. Absolute beginners have plenty of area to practice their turns, then strike out for long easy trails. With good snow, experts will find plenty to keep them busy. With powder in the bowls, the slopes beneath Costarjas, the off-piste itineraries and the chutes dropping off the ridges running through the Baqueira and Bonaigua sections of the resort provide more than enough challenge. With poor snow, experts will be left wanting.

Ski school (2006/07 prices)

Baqueira/Beret has more than 200 ski teachers, about 10 of whom speak English. Be sure to request an English-speaking instructor if you don't speak Spanish. Ski lessons start for children who are age 3 and older. Discounts for children apply to those 11 years and younger.

Private lessons for one person cost about €45–€55 for one hour.

Group lessons cost about €115–€145 for six days and €109–€132 for five days.

There are different **ski/snowboarding schools** in the area with similar prices. Check with them for the availability of English-speaking instructors.

Era Escuola (973-645126) has offices in Baqueira, Beret and Salardu.

Escuola Snowboard Val d'Aran (973-645881) focuses only on snowboarding.

Cross-Country

Cross-country skiing is limited. There is a 7 km. loop in Beret and other cross-country opportunities in Ruda and Aiguamoix. The ski school has guides and lessons.

Lift tickets (2006/07 prices)

	Adults	Children (age 11 and younger)
one day	€40.50	€27
three days	€114	€72
six days	€508	€132

Children younger than age 6 and seniors age 70 and older ski free.

Accommodations

Lodges are spread throughout the valley. This may appear inconvenient at first, but staying in such a beautiful valley is arguably a plus.

The most convenient place to stay for skiing is, of course, in Baqueira or in Tanau next to the slopes, but nightlife and restaurants are, for the most part, a drive away. Arties offers the best concentration of restaurants and nightlife and has exceptional hotels. Vielha has the valley's largest pool and skating complex, excellent après-ski and restaurants but is short on late nightlife. Otherwise stay along the road linking Vielha and Baqueira. With a car, the valley facilities can be easily reached.

€€€—€125 per double room; €€—€75-124; €—less than €75. Rates are per person, double occupancy, in February with half board.

Lodging at the slopes:

In the resort of Baqueira there are three hotels, all clustered at the base of the runs and the lifts. The most sought-after rooms are in the **Val de Ruda** (973-645258; €€), a small three-star hotel with heavy wood accents and lots of mountain atmosphere. The **Tuc Blanc** (973-644350; €€), a big modern hotel, is closest to the lifts with the only

Country code: 0034

covered swimming pool in the village as well as a steamroom. It seems like Grand Central Station when the lifts close at the end of the day. **Hotel Montarto** (973-639001; €€) has rooms that are quite small by modern standards but the service is first class and you'll have a short shuttle ride to the lifts or a 10-minute uphill walk. However, it is very convenient to the discos and the restaurants.

A small village of hotels and condos, Tanau has been built above Baquiera with a dedicated lift. Here, is the **Hotel Melia Royal Tanau** (973-644446; €€€) and its associated apartments with fine restaurant, gymnasium, spa , pool facilities, a lovely view of the ski station and a location steps from the Esquiro chair lift. The nearby **Hotel Chalet Bassibe** (973-645152; €€) has pool and sauna. **Hotel La Pleta** (973-645550; €€€) is in the same Tanau cluster, but about a 200 meter walk from the lift.

Lodging in Arties (7 km. from the slopes**):**

Parador Nacional Don Gaspar de Portola, Arties (973-640801; €€€) is a four-star parador. The town of Arties is the gourmet center of the valley, with some of Spain's top restaurants. This parador has been completely renovated over the past three years. **Hotel Valarties** (973-644364; €€) is the lodging arm of Restaurant Casa Irene. Half-board here means you dine on award-winning meals every day of the week. **Hotel Besiberri** (973-640829; €€) tucked into the back of the village is tiny, comfortable and cozy.

In Vielha (14 km. from the ski area):

Vielha, has come a long way in the past three years. The old town is being renovated and once-decrepit buildings house small restaurants and bars. The town now has two new four-star lodges — **Hotel Sol Vielha** (973-638000; €€) and **Hotel Val d'Aran** (973-643233; €€). We also recommend four smaller, recently renovated hotels tucked into the narrow streets of the old town only steps from good restaurants and packed tapas bars — **Hotel Fonfreda** (973-640486; €€) and **Hotel Riu Nere** (973-640150; €€), **Hotel Ribaeta** (973-642036; €) and **Hotel Orla** (973-642260; €).

Parador Nacional Valle de Arán, Vielha (973-640100; €€) is an impressive four-star hotel overlooking Vielha. Unfortunately, it is a long walk from the town.

Hotel HUSA Tuca (973-640700; €€) at the edge of Vielha is convenient to Vielha and 13 km. from the Baqueira slopes.

Along the main road from Veilha to Baqueira:

The **Hotel de Tredos** (973-644014; €€) has a cozy atmosphere and is just down from the ski village. In Salardù, other small family-run, atmospheric hotels are **Hotel Lacreu** (973-644222; € half-board only), **Hotel Deth Pais** (973-645836; €) and **Hotel Mont Romies** (973-645820; €). **Garòs Ostau** (973-642378; €€) is very rustic and very small with only eight rooms.

Apartments, condominiums,flats

Baqueira/Beret has thousands of apartment beds. These places are small, built along the French style. We recommend two people take an apartment rated for four people and four sign up for a place for six in order to have enough space. The foldout couch counts as one of the normal sleeping places. For example, a one-bedroom unit, listed to fit four, costs €430–€520 (five-day rate in middle season with lifts tickets), only €86–€104 per person per day based on only two people sharing the unit.

In Viehla, at the other end of the valley, the new **Aparthotel Eth Refugi d'Aran** (973-643002; €€) and **Aparthotel La Vall Blanca** (973-643024; €€) in Vielha offer half-board and breakfast-only packages. **Aparthotel Eth Palai** (973-343220; €) only has condos without meals. These properties are within an easy walk of the old town.

For reservations call the tourist office in Baqueira/Beret.

Dining

If you enjoy fine food, coming to this valley will be like finding Shangri-La. The blend of French and Spanish cooking together with the mountain basics of the Valle de Arán has resulted in a unique cuisine (Aránes) praised across Europe. The valley also has a collection of gourmet restaurants that rival anything found at even top French resorts. With the highest-priced restaurants topping out at around €60 per person with wine, the best food in the world is within many skiers' budgets. Most full meals with starter, main course and dessert will end up costing between €22 and €28. Pizza and wine ends up being around €15. Even without skiing, the trip to this valley would be worth the effort for only the food.

Lunch starts at about 2 p.m. and continues until at least 4 p.m. when skiers head out to catch the last half-hour of skiing before the slopes close at 4:30 p.m. The dinner is served late by English or American standards but not as late as in Andalusia. Restaurants open around 8 p.m. and most patrons show up between 9 and 10 p.m. Reservations, several days in advance, are necessary for many of them. Don't wait till the last minute. The restaurants are spread all through the valley. However most of the restaurants covered here are scattered between the main city, Vielha and the ski resort.

Average cost of meals €€€=€35+; €€=€20-€35; €=less than €20.

Start with the food on the mountain. Baqueira/Beret has an exceptional full-service restaurant, **Altitude 1800** (973-645202; €€). The red beans were some of the best I have ever eaten and red peppers stuffed with ears and lips sound horrible, but taste heavenly; and game and fish were excellent. In the Beret sector, the **Restaurant Pla de Beret** (973-645227; €€) offers a wide variety of appetizers and good meat with table service. Call for reservations at both restaurants.

Self-service Audeth is good for a quick lunch as well.

The restaurants in Baqueira village are only a couple of minutes walk from the base of the lifts. The three best are **Ticolet** (973-645477; €€) with fine cuisine next to the Montarto Hotel and **La Borda de Lobato** (973-645708; €€) with traditional meats and fish prepared on an open grill are served in a barn atmosphere oozing with rustic charm. **Esquiró** (973-645430; €€) serves what some say is the best fish in the valley.

Cap del Port (973-250082; €€) is in a castle-like building at the crest of the Port de la Bonaigua pass. This unique spot serves high altitude meals such as medallions of goat, deer fillets and mountain mushrooms. All these mountain restaurants are open during the evening as well except the Altitude 1800 and Cafeteria Beret.

Arties is considered the cuisine capital of the region. You'll find **Casa Irene** (973-644-364; €€€) where the King and Queen of Spain dine. Irene still takes orders and chats with customers and Irene's son, Andreas, runs the kitchen. The menu is a selection of three fixed-price menus ranging from €45 to €55, each with a half-dozen selections.

Also in Arties: **Eth Taro** (973-642558; €€€) and **Candelaria** (973-642024; €€€) serve regional and international cuisine. The **Parador** (973-641103; €€€) has an excellent restaurant but is rather stuffy and formal. **Restaurant Urtau** (973-640926; €€) borders on gourmet with more reasonable prices. **Mas Pasta** (973-641619; €) serves Italian food ranging from pizzas to pasta in a very romantic, rustic converted barn. **La Sal Gorda** (973-645431; €-€€) serves delicious Basque cuisine.

In Vielha, visit **Era Coquèla de Vielha** (973-642915: €€) for an excellent meal (don't miss the chocolate soufflé for dessert). **Era Mola** (973-640868; €€) has gourmet flavors applied to some local favorites, such as rabbit and duck. **Sidreria Era Bruisha-Sorgiña** (973-642976; €€) serves excellent grilled meats and fish in Basque style.

Three small spots are within steps of each other in Vielha on Carrer Mayor. **All i Oli** (973-641757; €) is cozy and serves family-made healthy Catalan meals — the perfect

Country code: 0034

spot for vegetarians as well as those looking for barbecued meat. **Restaurant Eth Tidon** (973-640363; €) is a place for meat — lots of meat fired over glowing coals sold by the kilo. **Restaurant Basteret** (973-640714; €) has a major French clientele with delicious and reasonable food. Each day **La Lluna** has pastries, sandwiches and pizza.

Just outside of Vielha tucked on a narrow street of Betren (the village across from the Tuca Hotel) is **Era Borda de Betren** (973-640032; €€), a small restaurant that serves Aránese meals such as trout and lamb in a very cozy atmosphere .

Casa Carmela (973-645751; €€) in the tiny village of Unha, has grown from a small dining room that was packed night after night into a restaurant empire with three different levels for dining and lodging. It is listed as **Es de Don Joan Casa Carmela.** Her *cordero lechal* is exceptional as is her local soup, *Olla Aranese*.

Casa Mestres (973-644179; €€€) in Salardu is new and good.

For good typical regional Aránese food try **Casa Turnay** (973-64092; €€), **El Niu** (973-641406; €€), **Es Pletieus** (973-640709; €€) and **Casa Estampa** (973-640048; €€) in Escunhau, **Et Restrille** (973-641539; €€) in Garos, and the very reasonable **Borda de Benjamin** (973-645113; €€) in Salardu. **Zurbaran** (973-647710; €€) in Bossost is recommended for Basque cuisine with mountain touches.

You can find plenty of inexpensive pizza and Italian restaurants as well as some "combination plate" restaurants throughout the valley if you want to save money.

Après-ski/nightlife

Après-ski here means tapas. Skiers meet in the hotel bars and in some of the bars in town from around 6 p.m. to 9 p.m. Vielha has a dozen excellent tapas bars that can be packed shoulder to shoulder. **Bar Neguri** and **Dues Portes** are right on the main road through town. **Bar Era Plaça** on the town square fills with skiers going over the day's adventures. In a cluster of recently restored ancient buildings on Carrer Mayor and nearby alleys, try **Eth Petit Basteret**, **Eth Paer** and **Era Canaula** (ask for directions, it's tucked away).

In Arties, for tapas go to **Bar Urtau** — an experience that shouldn't be missed.

There is just not overwhelming late nightlife to choose from. The major disco at the resort is **Pacha** and **Pub Tuc Nere**. They attract an older crowd (25 and up) with Pacha tending toward the younger set. The **Vielha** and **Elurra** discos in Vielha have a younger crew. Eth Clot is a music bar that gets packed on weekends.

There are four late-night music spots in Arties — **La Luna, Millenium, Devino** and **De Net**. No one really shows up until midnight or later and the gyrations continue until three or four in the morning.

Child care (2006/07 prices)

There is babysitting service starting from 3 months old.

The resort has four child care centers accepting children from 2 to 8 years of age: a newly renovated center in Beret that across from the check tower; one in Bonaigua, close to the services center; one in Baqueira 1800 across from the Bosque chairlift; and one in Baqueira 1500. Children can learn to ski or just play in the snow and watch movies. In Park 1800, Beret and Bonaigua, an hour of care costs €14; a half day with lunch, €36; a full day with lunch, €41; five half days with lunch, €156; and five full days with lunch is €175.

The Park de Neige for the Baqueira 1.500 Children's Center (973 64 54 48, fax 973 64 48 74) is close to the Hotel Montarto. They take infants from 3 months to two and a half years old. An hour of care costs €15; a half day with lunch, €44.50; a full day with lunch, €48; five half days with lunch, €176; and five full days with lunch is €206.

Other activities

Helicopter skiing (973-645797 and 629-352326) and **dogsledding** (670-536654) are available. Two heated **swimming pools** and an **ice skating** rink are open at the Palau de Gel (973-642864) in Vielha; hours vary with skating every evening and swimming in the mornings and evenings. There are **thermal baths** originally discovered by the Romans about 35 minutes away in Banys de Tredós (973-253003), accessible only by four-wheel drive in the winter, and toward France in Baronía de Les (973-648717).

The **Aran Valley Museum** in Vielha, a collection of romanesque churches and unspoiled villages provide a glimpse of valley history. The restored Joanchiquet farmhouse in Vilamòs (normally closed in winter but open by appointment) is fascinating. Contact the valley tourist office (973-642915) for information and reservations.

Getting there

This is not one of the easier spots on the earth to reach. There are no trains or planes. That means bus or rental car. The nearest airports are Toulouse in France 166 km. away, and San Sebastian and Barcelona in Spain, about 250 km. and 350 km. away respectively. From Toulouse take the autoroute west and exit at Montrejeau then follow signs to St. Beat and Val d'Arán. From Barcelona take the autopista to Lleida and then head north through Pont de Suert to Val d'Arán.

The bus ride between Vielha and Barcelona is about six hours with departures three times a day. It is not recommended.

The new Autoroute across southern France connecting Bayonne and the Mediterranean coast is also an excellent alternative to beating your way through the Spanish mountains. The airport in Biarritz or San Sebastian ends up being closer in driving time than Barcelona. The drive from Toulouse, France, is less than two hours.

Once in the valley, a car is the best way to move throughout the area. However, there is a bus system that links Baqueira and Veilha with buses heading to the resort hourly in the mornings and returning about every half hour starting from about 4 p.m. Tickets cost €0.85 per ride or €7 for 10 rides. Gas is cheaper in Spain than France.

Tourist information

Oficina de Turismo de Baqueira/Beret, Apartado 60, 25530 Vielha-Lleida, Spain; information is open 9 a.m.–7 p.m.
Telephone 973-639010, fax 973-644488.
Reservations is open 9 a.m.–1 p.m. and 3 p.m.–7 p.m.
Telephone 973-639000.
E-mail viajes@baqueira.es; baqueira@baqueira.es
Internet: www.baqueira.es. Snow reports (in Spanish) 973-639025.

☎ *When calling from outside Spain dial the country code then the phone number. From within Spain you must always dial 973 even for local calls.*

Sierra Nevada

Hard to believe, but there is skiing in southern Spain about a half-hour drive from Granada. The Sierra Nevada resort has skiing at an altitude of over 10,000 feet and brilliant sunshine most of the winter. When storms arrive, life at the top of this tree-less mountain stops and visitors either drop down to Granada or curl up with a good book. With good weather the views are spectacular — almost unbelievable. From the top of the Veleta peak, skiers can see across the Mediterranean to the Atlas Mountains of Morocco.

The resort town itself, basically a sparse cluster of hotels and apartments at the base of the first series of lifts, is modern with a hint of traditional charm. It is purpose-built. It is here only for skiing and has been well located for that pursuit. It is not a traditionally Spanish enclave, nor does it appear in any sense Alpine; however, if you want to find snow in southern Spain, this is the place to be. When it does snow, it comes down light and dry because of the low humidity in Southern Spain. When it doesn't snow, Sierra Nevada has one of Europe's most advanced snowmaking systems.

What Sierra Nevada does exude is the intoxicating Spanish love of the good life. There are lively tapas bars, quaint shops and elegant hotels climbing the mountainside. No one who comes here forgets good food and spirited nightlife.

In preparation for the the 1996 World Cup, Spain improved virtually every aspect of the village including the access road from Granada. Even the old original mid-60s modern hotels have been given a facelift and more of an traditional facade.

 ## Mountain layout

To be honest, it would be hard to get lost on this mountain unless faced with white-out conditions. The skiing range is not that extensive, but it is wide open and the runs are long and gentle. This is a true cruisers' delight. The resort boasts an above-treeline vertical of 3,757 feet.

The first lifts take all skiers to the main hub, Borreguiles, about 1,500 feet above the main village. Borreguiles is surrounded by beginner terrain and great teaching slopes.

High-speed quad chairs serve every major section of the mountain, limiting lift lines. In total, 22 lifts open this mellow mountain to skiers. Intermediates can have fun in every fold of the resort, beginners have plenty of space and only experts will find the resort limited.

At Borreguiles, the mid-station of the cablecar rising from the town, the restaurant, café and the main ski school are grouped together. The restaurant has been expanded to handle the midday crowds. The beginner area surrounds this mid-mountain station and the ski school.

If you take the Veleta lift and ski back down toward Borreguiles, you cruise through an intermediate bowl. This route takes skiers past the World Cup race course and the snowboard park. A far traverse to the right will swing you along a ridge that offers some fancy off-piste runs into the Valle de San Juan. But don't drop too far. You'll have to get back over the ridge to descend some wide-open faces back to Borreguiles or right back into the main village. Choose your line. If you can see it, you can ski it.

The more spectacular trails are reached by a traverse a little to your right toward the Olimpica run that slices down the Laguna de Yeguas bowl. Here, 2,300 vertical feet of more challenging intermediate terrain and wide-open snowfields beckon. The visuals are dramatic with cliffs ringing the bowl and the stunning snow. There are trails packed by snowcats, but the real dream is diving into the ungroomed powder. This is an excellent off-piste itinerary called Tajos de Virgen that provides great views and challenge.

Below Borreguiles, when the snow is good, better skiers can drop down the Loma Dilar section of the resort and find some acceptable steeps or search for short steeps below the Borreguiles midstation.

 ## Mountain layout–Snowboarding

Snowboarding is allowed on the entire mountain, but limited in the designated beginner ski area. There is a snowboard school and plenty of snowboard rentals. There is a snowboard park above Borreguiles that can be fun, but real riders strike out for the Laguna de Yeguas to head off-piste and play on the ridges and natural banked sides. After cruising down Laguna de Yeguas take the Dilar charilift to the ridge and choose your spot to drop back into the bowl carving beneath the chair you just rode.

Mountain rating

As always, experts can find the tough stuff anywhere. Sierra Nevada has some good challenges in the far bowls and is delightful for strong skiers in the ungroomed areas. Intermediates will be ecstatic. For the most part, this is a mellow beginning and inter-mediate paradise when sticking to groomed trails. If you enjoy long gentle cruising carving big giant-slalom turns, you will think you are in heaven. You'll quickly discover that the object here is pure enjoyment, so relax and enjoy the sun.

High season in Spain occurs at early December, Christmas/New Year, mid February and Easter. Middle season is mid January, early and late February and March (except for Easter week). Low season is most of April. In addition, Saturdays, Sundays and holidays draw premium rates.

country code: 0034

Ski school (2007/08 prices)

There are few places that are this perfect for learning to ski. The Spanish temperament makes for great initial instruction. What's more, most of the mountain can be handled by beginners after three or four days of instruction. There are 13 ski schools (958-480168, 958-480011 or 958-480142) that have more than 300 instructors and have offices in the main square of the town and at Borreguiles at mid-mountain. About a quarter of the instructors speak English.

Private lesson for one adult costs €35 and an additional €6 per additional person up to a maximum of four.

Group ski lessons for adults and children cost €115 for five days. Classes are held three hours each day in groups of eight to 10 skiers or riders.

Saturday/Sunday courses are available for €40 with two hours of instruction each day.

There are different ski/snowboarding schools in the area with similar prices: Spanish Ski School (958-480168); Official Ski School (958-480011); and the International Ski School (958-480142). Check with them for the availability of English-speaking instructors.

Lift tickets (2007/08 prices)

mid-season/high season	Adults	Children
half day**	€27.50/€34	€16.50/€22
one day	€32.50/€40	€19.50/€26
three days	€93/€114	€55.50/€74
five days	€138.50/€180	€83/€117

**Half day skipass is valid from 1 p.m.

Night skiing costs €10 a day.

The high season here is every weekend as well as the Christmas and Easter holiday periods. Mid-season is Monday through Friday, except during holidays. There is also an early and late season, but snow conditions should be carefully checked when coming to Sierra Nevada in the shoulder season.

 # Accommodations

All the hotels are relatively new. Add 16 percent value-added tax to each of these rates.

All these hotels have good rooms with bath. They are listed in descending order of luxury. Rates are per person, double occupancy with half board in February. €€€—€125+; €€—€75–€124; €—less than €75.

Hotel Maribel (958-249111, fax 958-249146; €€€) is a small place with with quiet luxury and only 31 rooms. It is considered the best place to stay on the mountain.

El Lodge (958-480600, fax 958-481314; €€€) is one of the top spots right on the slopes with ski-in/ski-out.

Hotel Kenia Nevada (958-480911, fax 958-480807; €€€) This four-star hotel provides some of the town's best accommodations in a rustic Alpine style, all within walking distance of the slopes and most shops and restaurants.

Hotel Melia Sierra Nevada (958-480400; fax 958-480458; €€€) This four-star hotel is located at the Plaza Pradollano and only steps away from shopping, restaurants and the ski slopes. The lobby is cozy with heavy wooden beams and a stone floor that give it a Nordic atmosphere.

Hotel Ziryab (958-480512, fax 958-481415; €€) is in center-village and has impressive rooms. The hotel meals are all buffet-style, and it still is rated by Michelin!

Hotel Melia-Sol y Nieve (958-480300, fax 958-480458; €€€) is one of the original standbys with all the basics and a great location.

Hotel GHM Monachil (958-481450 or 902-481100, fax 958-48101; €€–€€€), formerly Hotel La General. This hotel right on the main town square — 30 meters from the first stop of the Parador chairlift and 40 meters from the Maribel slope — has a restaurant with a solarium.

Other hotels to consider in descending order of luxury are: **Rumaykiyya** (958-481400, fax 958-480032; €€), **Hotel Nevasur** (958-480350, fax 958-480365; €€), **Casa Alpina** (958-480600, fax 958-480506; €€), **Mont Blanc** (958-481212 fax 958-481358; €€) and a B&B named **El Ciervo** (958-249409, fax 958-249461; €€).

There are also a series of Apartment-Hotels. These are basically condos with cleaning service. The two most luxurious are **Aparthotel Cumbres Blancas** and **Aparthotel Ginebra** (958-480456, fax 958-480438).

Cheap student lodging can be found at **Albergue Universitario** (958-480122), **Albergue Juvenil Sierra Nevada** (958-480305), **Albergue Militar** (958-481227) or **Residencia Pradollano** (958-480114).

Accommodations in Granada

Granada is only about a half-hour drive away from the resort, assuming no traffic and no bad weather. On most days, the commute to ski is not bad. It is recommended that skiers planning on staying in Granada rent a car and try to stay outside of the warren of narrow streets that make up the center of town unless they really want the full atmosphere. Also, try to stay in a place that has parking, since it comes at a premium in this city. The weather in Granada can be 65 degrees while it is freezing up at Sierra Nevada. Staying here is perfect when coming for late-season skiing.

€€€—€125+; €€—€75–€124; €—less than €75 per room with breakfast.

Dauro II (958-221581; fax 958-222732; €) good affordable place right on the main tapas street of town. Nightlife and wonderful restaurants are outside the door.

Casa Morisca (958-221100; fax 958-215796; €€) is a B&B in the Moorish quarter and full of atmosphere that will take visitors to days of yore with a columned patio and breakfast in the old stables.

Casa de los Migueletes (958-210700; fax 958-210702; €€) is a B&B in a 17th-century house with a tucked-away patio and rustic furnishings. It is just off the main square at the edge of the Gypsy quarter with nearby parking. Closed most of January.

Hotel Kenia (958-227506; €€) is built in an old manor building furnished with antiques and with a nice garden. It is only a short walk to the Campo de Principe, one of the tapas, dining and nightlife centers.

Hostal Suecia (958-225044 fax 958-227781; €) is a small place near the Hotel Kenia. Make sure to ask for a room with private bath — some rooms have shared baths.

These three hotel are on the hill near the Alhambra. Not as convenient to downtown, they are convenient to the back way out of town for a quicker trip to the slopes.

Hotel Guadalupe (958-223423 fax 958-223798; €€) is up behind the Alhambra with almost a country feeling.

Los Alixares (958-225575 fax 958-224102; €€) is modern and without much charm and it is a bus ride out of downtown.

Alhambra Palace (958-221468, fax 958-226404; €€€) offers a different luxurious, Old World experience. The views from the high-ceiling rooms over the town are wonderful.

Dining

This tiny village has plenty of restaurants that put on a good meal. Make reservations if you are planning to eat anywhere between 10 p.m. and midnight—these places can get packed.

Ruta del Veleta (958-486134) is a favorite of Spain's King Juan Carlos and features excellent Andalusian cuisine. Michelin rates this place with three fork—almost a star. Call for reservations and expect to pay about €35-€40.

Traditional Spanish cooking can be found at **Casablanca** (958-480830), **Rincón de Pepe Reyes** (958-480394) and **Mesón Alcazaba** (958-480129). **Restaurant La Bodega** (958-249133) serves an excellent paella and other good rice dishes.

Restaurant la Carihuela, named after the old fishermen's district of Torremolinos, in the Edelweiss building is considered to serve the town's best fish dishes.

Tito Luigi (958-480882) serves excellent pizza and inexpensive Italian cooking. **Andalusi** (958-480206) is a pizza joint with other pasta as well. **Creperie La Gauffre** (958-480445) has a Spanish version of French crêpes. For Chinese food try **Restaurante Chinatown** (958 480433).

A great place for breakfast or a sweet is the **Croisanteria La Gauffre** where there are wonderful breads, rolls and pastries.

On the slopes, the best place to head for an excellent sit-down lunch is **Restaurant Tia Maria** (958-340432) in the Borreguiles building. Call for reservations. Good places for fast food are **Bocadilleria El Campanario** and **Restaurante Monahcil** in the same complex.

Down in Granada try **San Nicolas** (958-804262) in a classic house in the Albayzin; **Pilar del Toro** (958-223847) on Plaza Nueva; **Cunini** (958-250777), a classic restaurant on the walking streets near the Cathedral; and **Lago di Como** (958-226154), an Italian place on Campo del Principe, a hot nightlife spot.

Après-ski/nightlife

This is a small resort, so you should be able to find out if anything is going on rather quickly. Though the village may be small, the nightlife is charged with that special Spanish spirit that takes advantage of the moment and normally stretches that moment into the wee hours of the morning.

El Golpe and **Soho Bar de Copas** both have hot action immediately after skiing. These are the spots to make contacts with other tourists who you can follow up on later in the night. Try **Mango** and **Sitcky Fingers** as well. Any place surrounding the main square will be packed as skiers come off the mountain.

The discos start pumping around midnight but may only get crowded around 1 or 2 a.m. Try **Nevada 53** in the Hotel Meliá Sierra Nevada, **La Chimenea** in Edificio Primaverall and **La Chicle** where the younger crowd gathers in Edificio Bulgaria. **Mango** has good disco action when the resort is packed. The older nightlife crowd tends to congregate in the **Sala Muley,** at the Hotel Meliá Sierra Nevada, or at **Crescendo** in the Telecabina building.

Expect to pay hefty cover charges, but remember these cover charges normally include one or two drinks. You'll quickly learn why party folk here don't swig down drinks at a fast pace. Most nurse their drink for the entire evening.

In **Granada**, the nightlife centers around tapas. The discos are expensive and filled with youth and blaring music. For a great evening of tapas-hopping try the Calle Navas right in the middle of town or head to Campo de Principe about a 15-minute walk from Navas.

Child care (2007/08 prices)

Spanish culture revels in children — you can be sure children will be well cared for here. Child care is available at Guarderia Infantil in the new village area next to the Telecabina Al-Andalus. The facility is well equipped and staffed by certified care providers. The guarderia has plenty of toys and videos with activities planned throughout the day. Children from 3 years of age are accepted. Hours are 10 a.m.–4 p.m. Children are accepted for a half day as well. Prices are about €31 for a half day, €51 per day, €118 for five half days and €10 per hour (a.m. or p.m. sessions).

Other activities

Snowtubing is available for €15 for three rides. **Dogsledding** can be arranged at a cost of €38 for a half-hour trip. **Snowmobiling** is also possible for around €42 for a 20-minute jaunt on your own, or €32 if you go with a guided group.

The location is what makes this resort so special. Within an hour you can reach **Granada** and visit the fabulous Alhambra and the old center of the city. Malaga is only about two hours away and the **Costa del Sol** —i ts chalk-white towns like Salobreña clutching small hilltops — is even closer. Excursions can be made to **Jaen**, with its massive cathedral and Moorish baths, or **Gaudix** and **Purullena** with their troglodyte villages. At nearby **Lacalahorra castle** you will have to find the gate-keeper in the town below the castle before heading up the hill.

During the spring, **golf** is one of the major activities of this area. There are more than 30 courses lining the Costa del Sol within a two-hour drive.

Getting there

Granada is 31 km. away. There is only one road from the city to the ski area that will take about a half-hour to drive. Traveling by car is highly recommended — it gives you much more freedom and allows exploration of Granada and the surrounding towns. Buses leave Granada from the Station Buses of Granada each day at 9 a.m., 10 a.m. and 5 p.m and return at 9 a.m., 4 p.m. and 6:30 p.m..

The airport is 17 km. from Granada. It has flights to Madrid, Barcelona, Valencia, Palma de Mallorca, Tenerife and the Canary Islands. Taxis are available from the airport to Sierra Nevada. Call Tele Taxi at 958-280654 or Radio Taxi at 958-151461. Expect to pay €45–€55 for a taxi from the airport to the resort.

Tourist information

For reservation center and information contact
Cetursa Sierra Nevada, Plaza de Andalucia, 4, Sierra Nevada, Monachil-Grenada. Telephone 958-249111 or 958-249100; fax 958-249146 or 958-249122 Internet: www.sierranevadaski.com
Email: reservasmadrid@cetursa.es or reservasplaza@cetursa.es
The provincial tourist office in Granada has responsibility for the resort. Write Patronato Provincial de Turismo de Granada, Pl. Mariana Pineda, 10-2, Granada, Spain (958-223527).
Internet: www.dipgra.es Email: turismo@dipgra.es
The telephone country code for Spain is 34.

country code: 0034

Andorra Grandvalira —

Canillo, Soldeu, El Tarter, Pas de la Casa, Encamp & Grau Roig

A surprising haven for skiers and smugglers lies along the border of France and Spain. This tiny country andorra, a leftover from the glory days of the Catholic Church and nobility, has survived for centuries as an independent state wedged between two of Europe's largest powers. This is the country that has been the home of the Catalan language over the centuries when it was suppressed by Spain and France. Today it still uses Catalan as its official language, but with French and Spanish spoken liberally in every valley.

For years, beneath jagged mountain peaks and between narrow passes andorra has thrived as a smuggling and shopping mecca. This is the original duty-free store. The entire country is a duty-free store. Thousands of Europeans come here to purchase much less expensive cigarettes, cigars, whiskeys, jewelry and virtually every luxury that is faced with high taxes in their homelands. Andorra, faced with a new unified European Community, has been forced to begin to find alternative economic activities to smuggling.

Many years ago andorrans also realized that they had an abundance of snow. In the 1930s they were some of the first developers of ski areas in Europe. However, these resorts remained relatively small and were not interconnected because of small-country politics. Recently, some of the log-jam regarding linking of resorts has broken free. A group of lifts serving the Valls de Canillo, the original Andorran ski resort, has linked up and more interconnections are on the way.

Today Valls de Canillo can compete with virtually any ski area in Europe. Millions have been invested in new hotels, gondolas, high speed lifts, grooming machines and facilities to make Andorra a true world-class destination.

It is still dependent on much group tourism. However, in a revolutionary move, the country is developing areas of the valleys that will not cater to group tourism and that have semi-private ski areas and private upscale restaurants. It is a daring move, but should play well with the upscale skiers from around the world and from Barcelona and Toulouse that flock to here on weekends and holidays.

Andorra already has a reputation for world-class, upscale shopping. Now, it is adding the element of extensive snowmaking, rustic restaurants, topnotch lodging and modern lifts.

This section focuses on the Valls de Canillo where we spent most of our time. We have included a short section on the other major ski and snowboard areas closest to Andorra la Vella, Pal-Arinsal, starting on page 341. These areas offer another inter-connected collection of trails with a slightly different experience.

At the risk of generalizing, Canillo and El Tarter are visited by more Spanish skiers; Soldeu is packed with British skiers; and Pas de la Casa/Grau Roig has more of a French flair.

Mountain layout

Closest to the capital city of Andorra la Vella is the enclave of Canillo that provides the name for the main valley. Canillo is being developed for individual tourism and has established a club concept that limits the number of skiers on their section of the mountain. A massive and modern base lodge/gondola station is the portal for this section of the resort. The slopes of Canillo also can be reached from the main Soldeu-El Tarter ski area via a drag lift. Canillo has newly cut swooping trails slicing through thick forests and provides an excellent place to ski when visibility is poor. The trails offer something for everyone and were designed by the same resort architects who have created many of the trails in Courch-evel, France. Here at Canillo there is also a dedicated ski school with a magic carpet and individualized instruction.

After the village of Canillo the road winds upward to El Tarter, which together with the next town up valley, Soldeu, anchor the main ski area. El Tarter is filled mainly with Spanish visitors and has two chairlifts taking skiers above treeline to the Pla Riba Escorxada hub. From this hub, lifts rise to Cap de Clots. From Cap de Clots a snowcat (included in the lift ticket price) takes skiers to off-piste adventures down ungroomed vertical. Also from Cap de Clots a drag lift links El Tarter with Canillo. One new six-seater chairlift brings skiers from the Riba Escorxada hub to the top of the resort at 8,398 feet where the entire Soldeu El Tarter area spreads beneath the summit.

Soldeu is the main group tourist town and is invaded by British skiers during much of the season. From January through March there is a better chance of hearing English spoken than Spanish, French or Catalan. Gondolas depart directly from the rear of hotel and apartment complexes and other older chairlifts rise as well to Pla dels Espiolets that serves as the hub of the Soldeu section. From Pla dels Espiolets several high-speed chairlifts take skiers to an elevation of more than 9,186 feet and serve almost 850 meters of vertical drop in virtually any direction. The fields of snow are dramatic when viewed from the peak of Alt del Griu.

At the French extreme of this region lies the town of Pas de la Casa with its linked lift hub of Grau Roig. The Pas de la Casa/Grau Roig area has a total of 100 km. of terrain and is linked by a gondola from the village of Encamp. Despite the fact that Pas de la Casa/Grau Roig and Soldeu El Tarter are adjacent and seemingly have interconnected lifts that would make transfer between Pas de la Casa/Grau Roig and Soldeu El Tarter relatively easy, they are separate areas that require separate lift tickets. Before you plop yourself on a lift, check to make sure your lift ticket is valid for the area.

Telephone country code and prefix: 00376

Mountain rating

Canillo/Soldeu-El Tarter/Pas de la Casa has a bit of something for every skier or boarder. Beginners have an excellent learning area near the main restaurants with a long looping trail back to the base area that can be negotiated with difficulty because of zigzagging skiers barreling down the same trails. A safer bet may be to download on the gondola. In Canillo, return to the base area is via gondola for most skiers.

Intermediates have the entire mountain. There are only a few off-piste areas where they can get into trouble, and most intermediates won't venture that far off the trails. Experts can push themselves as far as they want to go.

In an area this large, any expert worth his or her salt can find challenges. Next to the lift connecting Soldeu with Canillo there is a free snowcat that carries off advanced and expert skiers and boarders for excellent off-piste adventures dropping down from Pic d'Encampandana to Pla Riba Escorxada above El Tarter.

Cross-country

The main cross-country center for Andorra is La Rabassa in Sant Julià de Lòria (759798) south of Andorra la Vella. Cross-country skiing trail fees are €7 for adults and €4.50 for children. Tobogganing is available for a fee of €1.80 per run and €8 for six runs down a prepared run. Cross-country lessons are €15 per person per hour and €30 for two to five persons per hour.

Ski school (2007/08 prices)

Excellent ski and snowboard schools are available at every resort center; however, the Soldeu El Tarter ski school naturally has the most English-speaking ski instructors. For reservations call (376) 890501. Lesson costs are almost identical between Pas de la Casa and Soldeu El Tarter.

These prices are for Soldeu El Tarter.

Private lessons for one or two skiers cost €40 per hour during high season and €36.50 per hour during low season.

Group lessons for adults, based on 15 hours of lessons, cost €105 during high season and €101 during low season. Fifteen hours of children's lessons cost €99.50 for high season and €91 for low season.

Lift tickets (2006/07 prices)

These are prices for Soldeu El Tarter and Pas de la Casa.

High season is Christmas/New Years, most of February, Easter week and all the weekends. Low season is most of December other than holidays, January after New Years and most of March and April other than holidays.

high/mid-season prices	Adults	Children
one day	€39/€36.50	€30/€27.50
three days	€102/€97.50	€76/€71.50
five days	€156.50/€152.25	€119/€114

There is also a **Ski Andorra ski pass** that is good for five days at all resorts in Andorra including Soldeu El Tarter, Pas de la Casa/Grau Roig, Pas-Arinsal and Ordino-Arcalis. You can only ski one resort per day. The high season cost is €168 for adult and €130 for children for five consecutive days. The low season cost is €157.50 for adults and €125 for children for five consecutive days.

Children younger than age 6 and adults older than age 70 ski free at all Andorra resorts. Adult from ages 65–70 pay €15 per day for lift tickets anywhere in Andorra.

Accommodations

Canillo

Hotel Ski Plaza (739444; fax 739445) is a new luxury hotel five minutes from the lifts in quaint and traditional Canillo. It is dedicated to high standards and will focus on individual clients rather than groups.

Hotel Bonavida (851300; fax 851722) An excellent hotel undergoing renovation floor by floor. Rooms are large, and the location across the street from the gondola building is hard to beat.

Roc de Castell (851825; fax 851707) Very simple accommodation but clean and modern with a good location only about five minutes' walk from the gondola in Canillo.

Tarter

Hotel Llop Gris (851559; fax 851229) is a large hotel right at the base of the lifts with excellent spa facilities and a fine swimming pool. The owner's wife used to work with a circus. They purchased the circus wagon where she once lived and turned it into a special spot for a quiet drink and a cigar.

Hotel del Clos (851500; fax 851554) is in a good location across the main road from the lifts. It is modern with blond wood features, good sized rooms and a nicebuffet dinner each evening.

Hotel del Tarter (802080; fax 802081) Away from drunken pub crawlers and the disco crowd and is good for families.

Soldeu

Sport Hotel (870600; fax 870666) is filled with group tours but is quite nice. One of the main pubs in town is here, so crawling home is no problem. This together with the Sport Hotel Village are probably as good as group tour accommodations get in Andorra.

Sport Hotel Village (870533; fax 870533) across the road from the Sport Hotel is bigger, more luxurious, with a massive lobby and direct access to the lifts.

Hotel Xalet Montana (739333; fax 739331) sits on the opposite side of the street from the lifts and caters to more and more individual skiers. It is new and modern.

Hotel Naudi (739300; fax 852022) is a small family-run hotel that caters to individual tourists. The building has been constructed in the old valley style with lots of stone and wood.

Piolets (871787; fax 871788) is a run-of-the-mill group hotel with some good meeting facilities. If price is a consideration, this will offer adequate accommodations right in the middle of the nightlife action and direct access to the lifts.

Austria Hotel (735555; fax 735556) is a small place right on the main road. It is one of the less expensive hotels in town but is a long walk from Soldeu if you are planning on heading home late and not staying in this hotel. It has one of the more popular discos in town.

Pas de la Casa/Grau Roig

Grau Roig (755556; fax 755557) is as beautiful as a mountain hotel gets. This hotel is nestled in a hollow in the mountains that also serves as one of the main lift junctions for the region. The location is ideal and romantic, rooms are dramatic, the main restaurant is excellent, the lifts are steps outside your door, the pool and spa sparkling, parking is plentiful and the hotel works exclusively with individual tourists

Telephone country code and prefix: 00376

and has a long list of return visitors. Make reservations early. Full board here runs approximately €100 a day.

Other recommended hotels (that we did not have the opportunity to visit) over the pass in Pas de la Casa are **Font d'Argent** (739739; fax 739800) and **Guineu** (856661; fax 856662).

Apartments

Condos and flats are available throughout Andorra for weekly rentals. The normal rentals take place from Sunday through Saturday. Prices range from €200 per person for a studio for a week in low season to €450 a person in high season. Pricing, naturally, depends on location and level of luxury.

Dining

Soldeu/El Tarter/Canillo Pas de la Casa/Grau Roig

Borda de l'Horto (851622) in Canillo is a rustic spot just outside of the village. On a nice night it is about a 20 minute walk from the gondola building, otherwise call a cab.

Cort del Popaire (851211) in Soldeu is built in a rustic old barn and is full of atmosphere. The grilled meats are exceptional. The owner tells great jokes as well.

Cantina dels Racons (852607), in Canillo just down the road from the village, has good grilled meats on the main road.

Sangria in Meritxell (851327) is quite touristy but has excellent grilled meats.

Canut in Escaldes has excellent cooking.

Can Manel (822397) in Andorra la Vella is very typical with excellent snails.

L'Ermita in Meritxell (852500) is a typical restaurant in the same town as the church dedicated to the patron saint of Andorra.

Try pizza and other Italian fare at **la Fontanella** (871787) in the Hotel Piolet.

On the slopes

There is a new group of mountain restaurants above Canillo. One serves traditional Andorran meals, the second is a gourmet restaurant and the third has cafeteria service.

Gall de Bosc (890500) right on the slopes can't be beat on a sunny day when you dine on the deck with great food and fine wines.

Espiolet (851176) above Soldeu and **Riba Escorxada** (852900) both are good sit-down restaurants where you can linger over a meal.

Hotel Grau Roig's **La Marmita** is one of the best restaurants in the region. It is perfect for a long lunch prepared from local fresh produce and game.

Other recommended mountain restaurants are **Llac dels Pessons** (321683), **Solanellas** (344017) at the top of the Encamp gondola, and **Costa Rodona** above Pas de la Casa/Grau Roig ski area open for lunch only (800870). There is also a **Pizza Hut** at the Grau Roig ski lift hub.

Dining – Pas de la Casa

Restaurant **Marisqueria Campistrano** (856488) is the place to head for the most upscale gourmet dining. Expect to pay about €40-50 for a meal.

Dining – Arinsal/Pal

Borda Raubert (835420) is a very rustic, cozy and traditional restaurant in la Massana where a meal will be about €25 with wine.

El Rusc (838200) also in la Massana is an upscale gourmet restaurant where meals run about €40. It specializes in Basque cooking with lots of fish and lamb cooked on the grill.

El Surf in Arinsal serves Argentinean beef.

 ## Après-ski/nightlife

In Soldeu: The scene is virtually all English-speaking. **Aspen** and **Piccadilly** are wild pub scenes packed with Brits and Irish drinking pints as quickly as they can. The disco **Capital** in the Hotel Piolet and **Pussycat** up the hill behind Aspen have loud, loud music and late night/early morning dancing.

In Bordes d'Envalira: Bar Cheyenne is a place where drinks are mixed with table soccer and pool. It is more of a family and hotel guest atmosphere.

In Tarter: Disco Arthur's is the place to go for much of the same, however the crowd here is Spanish-speaking. Many of the ski instructors go here for their nightlife.

In Canillo: The place to see and be seen is the unassuming **Pub Camping Pia**. This bar has great music and good drinks. Open from 8:30 p.m. to 4 a.m., it fills up around midnight with Spanish speakers. English is occasionally heard. The other watering hole in Canillo is **Pub la Roda** but it doesn't generate the same energy. It opens from 5 p.m. to 8 p.m. for après-ski, then reopens at 10:30 p.m. and closes around 4 a.m.

Down in **Andorra la Vella** the largest nightlife venues pump out dancing and music until the early morning hours. The languages are mainly Catalan, Spanish and French and the experience is different from that of Soldeu. The best according to locals are **Satellit Pub, Chic, Borsa Pub** and **Festa Andorra**.

In Arinsal: Head to the **El Surf** or to the **Rocky Mountains** for nightlife and disco action.

 ## Child care (2007/08 prices)

Child care and nursery facilities are also provided at every resort in the valley.

In the Soldeu El Tarter Ski Station, there are three nurseries which welcome children age 2 and older in the Canillo and Soldeu areas and children age 3 and older in the El Tarter area. There are also three snow kindergartens in Pla dels Espiolets, Riba Escorxada and El Forn in Canillo.

Prices for the nursery in Soldeu El Tarter are €16.50 for two hours; €25 for a half day; €37 for a full day; €61 for five half days; and €111 for five full days.

The snow kindergarten for ages 3–5 is available five days for a charge of €117 and €67 over a weekend.

 ## Other activities

Palau de Gel (800840) in Canillo has **ice skating, hockey,** an Olympic **swimming pool, fitness rooms, indoor tennis, squash courts** and classes in everything from **aerobics** to **skating** to **stretch** to **swimming**. On Fridays, they offer **carting on ice** on the hockey rink.

Caldea (800995) is the largest thermal spa in Europe. The stunning glass building rises dramatically between the cliffs and apartments of Andorra la Vella. It houses a spectacular collection of lagoons and pools of differing temperatures, an outdoor thermal pool, suspended Jacuzzi tubs, baths, saunas, steam rooms, relaxation centers, massage rooms and more. Entrance is €24.50 for three hours; €65.50 for three three-hour days; and €98 for five three-hour sessions. This entrance includes use of the pools, Jacuzzis and most common areas. Bring your own swim suit and robe. Spa treatments and massages are extra. The Caldea also houses a series of upscale shops and a simulated helicopter ride over Andorra that shows off the landscape and elicits laughs, oos and aaahs from the audience.

Shopping: The entire country is duty-free. The main shopping streets are those of Andorra la Vella, the capital. You'll find every kind of luxury item as well as excellent deals on electronics and computer products.

Skidoos/snowmobiling: There are snowmobile rental shops in Port d'Envalira between Pas de la Casa and Grau Roig that also offer guided snowmobile excursions through the Pas de la Casa region and into Soldeu El Tarter. Call 324010 or 327220 for information and reservations.

The Automobile Museum (832266) is exceptional. Anyone who loves automobiles will have a blast. This museum houses one of the best and most complete collections of antique cars in the world.

Getting there

The best way to come to Andorra is to drive from either France or Spain. From Toulouse, France the driving distance is 181 km. From Barcelona airport to Andorra is 200 km. It takes about three hours traveling in either direction if all goes well. There are bus transfers directly from the airport to Andorra, however they are very cumbersome. Tour groups normally use buses from Toulouse airport passing through Pas de la Casa and then down to Soldeu.

Once in Andorra, there is a ski bus that runs between the resorts Canillo and Bordes d'Envalira that is free with your lift pass or skating rink ticket, or €1 if you have no lift pass or rink entrance ticket. It leaves every hour on the hour from Canillo and leaves Bordes d'Envalira at 20 after the hour for the return trip.

The normal Andorran bus line links Andorra la Vella and Soldeu every hour as well. The bus passes through Canillo on the way up the mountain about 20 minutes past the hour and then returns on the hour from Soldeu. It costs €2.50 for each ride. This is the best way to head into Andorra la Vella for shopping or going to the Caldea hot springs.

For local taxis call 863000.

Tourist information

Officina de Turisme Valls de Canillo, Avenida San Joan de Caselles, Canillo, Principat d'Andorra.
Telephone (376) 851002. Fax (376) 851139.
Email: vdc@andorra.ad. Internet: www.vdc.ad

Ski Andorra offices are at Av. Tarronga 58–70 Edifici les Columnes, Despatx 14 Andorra la Vella, Principat d'Andorra.

Telephone (376) 864389. Fax (376) 865910.

Email: skiandorra@skiandorra.ad.
Internet: www.skiandorra.ad.

Andorra, Pal/Arinsal & Ordino/Arcalis

These three resorts are packaging themselves with a shared lift ticket. Ordino sits by itself with a bast of 6,365 feet and summit of 8,660 feet. Pal and Arinsal are interconnected and offer a bit of a contrast. Arinsal is built-up, hodgepodge and still growing. Pal isn't even a real town, the name has more to do with the mountain. Arinsal's trails are long on treeless open slopes. Pal's runs are much shorter and wind through the woods. New lifts have breathed new lift into these resorts, whose slopes once were inconvenient and now are much more accessible.

 ## Mountain layout

For skiing Arinsal is limited to narrow east-facing mellow slopes that get lots of morning sun. Trees are nowhere to be found until you get below the midstation. A gondola takes everyone up to the midstation that is the only hub of the mountain. It is hard to get lost here, since all trails lead back to the midstation. If skiers or riders are looking for thrills and challenge, they should head elsewhere. After one or two runs, everything difficult has been covered.

For those searching for a good place to learn to ski, this is a good spot—the learning trails are out-of-the-way and have good snowmaking.

Arinsal and Pal are connected by a cablecar.

Experts will head into the trees at Pal. With a new, deep snowfall, these woods are lots of fun. In fact, the tree skiing here in Pal is relatively unusual in all of Europe which has above-treeline skiing for the most part.

Intermediates will have a blast on these trails dropping from the summit to La Caubella, El Fontanal, or down to the cablecar station.

Beginners have a good learning area in front of the base lodge with easy trails for progression.

Ordino-Arcalis is served by four chairlifts and eight surface lifts. This region offers a lot of above treline skiing and riding. Most of the marked trails are intermediate and beginner, however, the area has excellent powder skiing when conditions are right. Experts can ski where they want. Intermediates have long runs. Beginners have plenty of space to learn.

 ## Lift tickets (2006/07 prices)

These two regions share a lift ticket called Valnord. It allows skiing in Ordino-Arcalis and Pal/Arinsal.

high/low-season prices	Adults	Children
half day (from 13:00 p.m.)	€26/€22	€19.50/€16.50
one day	€33/€28	€25/€21
three days	€85.50/€71.50	€64/€54

 ## Accommodations

Most of the lodging is in Arinsal. Pal doesn't really have accommodations. The other places to stay would be in the villages of Erts or Sispony.

Telephone country code and prefix: 00376

Xalet Verdù (737140; fax 737141) is by far the best place in town.

Princesa Parc (736500) is a total leisure complex just 50 meters from the lifts. Rooms have satellite TV. The hotel provides private parking, bowling, gym, therapeutic center, sauna, sport and relaxation massages and a disco.

Hotel Solana (835127) is modern with the basic amenities and disco.

Aparthotel Crest (835866) is an impressive building with good lift access. This place is packed with tour groups and you get the basics, but no pool.

Coma Pedrosa Hotel (835123) is very basic and a bargain.

Hotel Micolau (835052) is an exceptional place. It is a departure from the over-built, modern hotels that dominate here. This rustic, stone place has only 11 rooms and is known for its wonderful cooking.

In the village of Erts, **Hotel Daina** (836005) is small with only 20 rooms but has the basics plus a small pool. A shuttle will be needed to get to the lifts. Also in Erts, the **Hotel St. Gothard** (836005) has exceptional hotel food, hot tubs and a sauna.

In the Ordino-Arcalis area the best hotel is **Hotel Coma** (736100) It has been in operation since 1932 and has one of the best restaurants in the region. Other hotels are **Hotel El Serrat** and **Hotel Boston**. Both have parking and are relatively new. **Casa Vella** and **Annapurna** offer aparthotel accommodations (small apartments with hotel services). Just outside of Ordino in Ansalonga is a small 20-room hotel, **Sant Miquel** (749000) It also has an excellent affordable restaurant.

Dining

Most of the dining in town is in the hotels where most guests have either full or half board. For a special meal head down the moutain road to La Massana and try a traditional meal at **Borda de L'Avi** (835154) where meat is grilled over glowing embers in a restored barn. The nearby, more traditionally elegant **Restaurant El Rusc** (838200) serves Basque cuisine with wonderful grilled fish and meat. For a magical atmosphere go to Borda Raubert (835420) on the road to Arinsal. It has been called the "temple of Andorran cooking."

Dine at **Hotel Coma** (736100) for the best traditional restaurant in the area or try **Sant Miquel** (749000) for very affordable and well-prepared meals.

Après-ski/nightlife

There is plenty of après action at the base of the gondola in Arinsal. The bars are crammed during high season. **Red X** has videos taken on the slopes with hilarious falls and gales of laughter from the drunk crowd. **Darby O'Gills** is a local Irish pub, but there are no Irish, only Brits. **Rocky Mountain Bar**, **Quo Vadis**, **Surf Bar, Boro Calista** and **El Cau** are legendary in the town's après-ski lore.

Tourist information

Estació de Muntanya Pal-Arinsal
Ed. El Planell, Pal-LaMassana, Principat d'Andorra.
Telephone Arinsal (376) 737020, Fax (376) 836242
Telephone Pal (376) 737000, Fax (376) 835904.
Email: pal@arinsal.ad. Internet: www.vdc.ad
Ski Andorra offices are at Av. Tarronga 58–70 Edifici les Columnes, Despatx 14 Andorra la Vella, Principat d'Andorra.
Telephone (376) 864389. Fax (376) 865910.
Email: skiandorra@skiandorra.ad. Internet: www.skiandorra.ad.

Switzerland

For many, Switzerland *is* the Alps—Switzerland *is* skiing in Europe. Of course, only part of the Alps is in Switzerland and Europe has other places to ski, but as the heart of the Alps and the home of Alpine skiing, Switzerland deserves all its superlatives. Its skiing is excellent, its resorts efficient, its tourist offices well organized, its lift systems well run and its hotels exceptional.

When is high season?

High Season: Christmas, New Year holidays and all of February through mid-April.
Low Season: January after New Year and late April.
Pre-season: December 6 to Christmas holidays

Swiss currency

All of the countries covered in this book, other than Switzerland, have switched their currency to euros. Switzerland still uses its own currency, the Swiss Franc (CHF). Prices throughout this book in the Swiss chapters, are listed Swiss Francs (CHF). According to Swiss friends of ours, Swiss ski resorts will accept euros if that's all you have for a cash payment, but the exchange rate may be well in the ski resort's favor.

One Swiss Franc equals 85¢. One US$ equals CHF 1.20

Switzerland's romantic mountain railways

The visitor whose timetable is not completely filled with skiing adventures can take a scenic ride on one of the most advanced mountain railway systems in the world. The regional Swiss railroad lines and the postbus have organized three spectacular Alpine routes.

The Glacier Express: Perhaps the most famous of the Swiss rail trips, this is advertised as the world's slowest train. Indeed the trip, some 90 miles as the crow flies, lasts seven and a half hours—spanning more than 291 bridges and burrowing through 91 tunnels—on its way from St. Moritz in Switzerland's southeast corner to Zermatt.

Trains run in both directions, leaving in the early morning and arriving in late afternoon. In their elegant dining cars a complete three-course lunch is served on the Chur-to-Andermatt leg. The full meal costs approximately €38, excluding beverages, and reservations are required. (Your wine glass on the Glacier Express has a tilted base to keep the wine from spilling on the route's many steep turns and gradients—turn it now and then to keep it tilted in the right direction.)

Bernina Express: The Bernina Express, which crosses into Italy over the Alps in Switzerland's southeast corner, is Europe's highest transalpine railway. The train trip follows the same route as the Glacier Express from Chur to St. Moritz, then strikes southward for the Bernina Pass, Poschiavo and on to Tirano in Italy.

Along one eight-mile stretch the track passes through two straight tunnels, negotiates five corkscrew tunnels, and crosses eight viaducts. The train crosses the Bernina Pass at 7,405 feet, climbing the steepest gradient of any non-cogwheel train.

The Engadin Express: This train and postbus route connects St. Moritz with Innsbruck, Salzburg and Vienna. The trip from St. Moritz to Landeck, done mostly by post-bus, lasts almost three hours and is generally felt to be one of Europe's most romantic trips.

After leaving St. Moritz, the train chuffs alongside a beautiful Swiss national park, through the village of Scuol; then the postbus takes travelers past the famous castle of Tarasp and on to Vulpera. This is the home of the fourth language of Switzerland, Ladin. The express ends in Landeck, Austria, in the Tyrol district.

Making reservations: These train trips can be booked in the United States and Britain through the Swiss National Tourist Office and online. In St. Moritz go to the Rhaetic Railway station; in Chur purchase tickets at the main train station; and in Zermatt at Zermatt-Tours.

The Swiss ski experience

The Swiss consider skiing more as an enjoyable cultural endeavor than a competitive race to measure vertical feet achieved in any certain day. They are fascinated and a bit amused by the high-tech watches that measure vertical feet skied worn by many aggresive North American skiers. The Swiss tend to measure skiing in terms of restaurants and chaise lounges, not numbers of fast runs.

Being in the mountains on vacation means enjoyment to these hard-working Swiss. They work hard and they take advantage of the sunshine and low-keyed atmosphere in the mountains to really give themselves a break.

The Swiss take advantage of sunshine by renting lounges on the mountain and enjoying the slow pace of a long, leisurely lunch. Lunch is their main daily meal and it is traditionally large and takes up to a couple of hours to consume. It might include numerous courses, beer, schnapps and coffees. They then take off to ski through the afternoon finally stopping on the trail back to the village for a late coffee and schnapps at one of the many private bistros and restaurants along the trail.

After skiing you won't find wild exuberance in the bars. The Swiss take their après-ski with restraint. Not that there's nothing going on, but the Austrian-style tea party drinking and dancing will be hard to find.

Swiss fondue and raclette

Fondue and raclette are cultural customs with an economic base. One of the Swiss mainstays is dairy farming and this country is home to some of the best cheeses that can be found. There are more than 100 different types of cheese.

Here in Switzerland, fondue and raclette are more than just a meal. They are part adventure and part ritual. They are quick meals that can be enjoyed by large groups of singing tourists or intimately by candlelight.

Raclette spread from the Valais canton of Switzerland and now can be found throughout the country. With raclette, cheese is melted in front of an open fire or under a broiler and then scraped off the wheel onto a plate. It is then served with potatoes and pickled onions and eaten immediately before the cheese sets.

Cheese fondue can be considered by many to be the national dish of Switzerland. Emmentaler and Gruyère cheeses are melted in a big pot and combined with wine and various seasonings. Then hard-crust mountain bread is cut into squares and dunked into the melted cheese.

Two other fondues without a cheese base are relatively widespread and very popular. Fondue bourguignon is made with meat and vegetables which are speared on fondue forks and then cooked in oil at the table and served with various toppings. Fondue chinoise is created from thinly sliced beef that is cooked in a broth then dipped in Oriental sauces.

The wine of choice, and normally the most affordable on the menu is Fendant, a local light white wine. Trust us. It seems to go with everything. It is the wine to order when eating out. You can't go wrong.

Traditional recipe for Swiss Fondue
2 to 3 large cloves of garlic
800 gr. or 20 oz. finely grated Switzerland cheese
(half Emmentaler, half Gruyère)
2+ cups dry white wine
1 to 2 jiggers of Kirsch Schnapps mixed with
1 teaspoon of cornstarch
dash of pepper
plenty of crusty, chewy one-inch bread cubes

Mince or crush garlic and rub the inside of your fondue pot. Leave remains in pot. Pour in white wine and 1/3 of the grated cheese. Place over medium heat on stove. Start stirring in a figure-8 motion, gradually adding the rest of the cheese. Cook over moderate heat, stirring all the time until the mixture starts to bubble. Add the cornstarch mixed with kirsch and bring once more to a boil. Season with pepper and bring to the table. Adjust the heating flame so that the fondue will simmer throughout the meal.

Spear a cube of bread and dip it into the pot, giving it a figure-8 stir each time. Serve with a dry white or sparkling white wine or tea. During the meal it is customary to drink a jigger of Kirsch Schnapps to help digestion.

Switzerland country code is 0041

Arosa

A long-established Swiss ski resort, Arosa played a part in the development of skiing as a popular winter sport. Today it is known for relatively easy, wide-open skiing and good off-slope activities. The town is beneath a circle of mountains at the end of the Schanfigger valley, above Chur.

Everything in Arosa is within easy walking distance. If you drive a car to the resort, you can park it in the public area and forget it, unless you decide to escape to some other area during your stay.

 ## Mountain layout

At 6,000 feet, Arosa's lifts fan out to reach the two major peaks in the area, the 8,241-foot-high Hörnli and the Weisshorn, at 8,704 feet. Although there are only 13 lifts, their combined capacity exceeds 21,000 skiers an hour. With the entire resort above the trees and some 60 kilometers of long, spread-out runs, there's plenty of wide-open skiing and perfect cruising.

Arosa offers 60 km. of well-prepared ski and snowboard runs of all difficulties and 40 km. of freeride slopes. Close to the middle station of the cablecar, there is a 130-meter half-pipe and an obstacle fun park.

Mountain rating

Arosa is Eden for beginners and intermediates because of its long, wide runs. When it hasn't snowed for several days, and skiers have broken new trails between the normally prepared runs, you can virtually ski across the entire mountain.

One run that does require an expert — sort of — is the descent from the top of the Weisshorn to the Carmennahütte. This very steep run is wide enough to allow a gutsy intermediate to make his way down the slope. It also offers expert-level practice on the steeps with plenty of room for error.

 ## Ski school (2007/08 prices)

The Swiss Ski School in Arosa (081-3787500; fax 081-3787508) has more than 100 qualified instructors, most of whom speak English. The ski school has special courses for children, deep-snow skiers, snowboarders and telemarkers. They also organize other events, including torchlight descents accompanied by fireworks, descents by full moon and ski races.

The following are the prices for The Swiss Ski School. They are comparable to the prices of the other ski schools in Arosa.

Private lessons for one to three people cost CHF80 per person. Two-hour lessons are offered morning, lunch and afternoon. Morning lessons from 9:45 a.m. to 11:45 a.m. cost CHF170. Lunch time lessons from noon to 2 p.m. are CHF155. Afternoon lessons from 2:15 p.m. to 4:15 p.m. cost CHF140. A full day (six hours including an hour lunch) costs CHF380. Each additional person up to a group of six people is CHF20.

Group skiing lessons (two hours) take place in the morning from 9:45 a.m. to 11:45 a.m and in the afternoon from 2:15 p.m. to 4:15 p.m.. Single lessons cost CHF55; CHF155 for three lessons; CHF245 for five lessons. Group snowboarding lessons take place mornings from 9:30 a.m. to 11:30 a.m and in the afternoon from 2 p.m. to 4 p.m.. Lessons cost CHF44 for one lesson; CHF125 for three lessons; CHF230 for six lessons. Five full days with a five-day ski pass and transportation cost CHF485.

Touring and off-piste skiing are also available.. The larger the group, the less the price is per person. One person costs CHF420; two people cost CHF210; three people cost CHF140; and four people cost CHF110.

Lift tickets (2007/08 prices)

During the off-peak season (around the first three weeks of December), lift tickets are reduced 20 percent.

Note: Proper ID is needed for children, youth and senior rates.

All lift tickets for four days or more require photos.

	Adults	Children (age 12 and younger)	Youth (age 13-17)	Seniors (age 61 and older)
one day	CHF56	CHF19	CHF37	CHF50
three days	CHF159	CHF53	CHF106	CHF143
six days	CHF259	CHF86	CHF173	CHF233
seven days	CHF279	CHF93	CHF186	CHF251

Cross-Country (2006/07 prices)

There are 26.5 km. of trails on Maran, Prätschalp/Ochsenalp, in the Isel and on the Obersee.

The Arosa Cross-Country Ski Pass can be obtained at the Cross-Country Ski School Geeser, at Arosa Tourism and on the Isla-Bus. The cost includes use of all long distance runs in Arosa, a ride on the Isla-Bus and use of the cloakrooms and waxing room. It costs approximately CHF5.00 for one full day; CHF15 for seven days; CHF25 for fourteen days.

There is also a 2-km marked snowshoe trail at Maran and guided tours every Monday and Tuesday (and Thursday if there is a large enough group).

Further information is available on cross-country skiing and snowshoeing through the Geeser Cross-Country Ski School (081 377 22 15).

Accommodations

Arosa has a hotel for everyone—from the most luxurious to the bargain one-star. Price ranges noted for each hotel are per person based on double occupancy with half board (breakfast and dinner): €€€—€125+; €€—€75-€124; €—less than €74.

Recommended five-star hotels: **Kulm Hotel** (081-3788888; €€€); **Tschuggen**

Grand Hotel (081-3789999; €€€) where you can indulge your inner diva with designer furniture and where each floor has its own color scheme.

Our recommended four-star hotels are: **Sporthotel Valsana** (081-3786363; €€) by the lake, with a good restaurant and child care; **Waldhotel National** (081-3785555; €€€) a bit back in the woods, nevertheless considered excellent; **Hotel Eden** (081-3787100; €€€).

The three-star hotels most convenient to the lifts are: **Alpina** (081-377168; €) recently restored and beautiful; **Astoria** (081-3787272; €) homey and picturesque with all the modern conveniences; **Hohe Promenade** (081-3787700; €); **Hotel Sonnenhalde** (081-377 15 31) unpretentious and one bus stop away from the village center; **Arve Central** (081-3785252; €).

Our recommended two-star hotels: **Erzhorn** (081-3771526; €); the **Hold** (081-377408; €) family-run and next to the ski instruction area; or **Carmenna** (081-3771766; €) modest and in Obersee.

Apartments, condominiums, flats

Arosa is well organized to handle tourists who want to rent apartments during the ski season, normally for a minimum of one week, Saturday to Saturday. During the Christmas season a minimum two-week rental is required.

The tourist office keeps track of available apartments. When writing, include the number of beds required, the preferred number of rooms, and your planned vacation dates. You will receive a quick response that lists a selection of apartments and prices. Pick your apartment and contact the owner.

Normally linen and kitchen utensils are provided. Other amenities, such as swimming pool, sauna, TV or room phone all add to the cost. Standard apartments rent for €35 to €60 per person a night. Prices vary significantly from low to high season.

 ## Dining

The following restaurants come recommended by locals. For a special night, take the sleigh ride up to the **Restaurant Alpenblick** (0813771428) and enjoy a special meat platter that is grilled at the table.

In Hotel Arve Central (081 378 52 52), the **ArvenStube** serves light, fresh gourmet meals made with regional and seasonal ingredients. Their fish menu changes daily.

Gspan (081-3771494) offers traditonal fair. Treat yourself to lunch on its large, sunlit terrace while enjoying the mountain backdrop.

Bündner Stübli, in the Golf- & Sporthotel Hof Maran (081-3785151), is a cozy, rustic place that was originally built in the 18th century. It specializes in fondues and raclettes.

Also try **Stüva Cuolm** and **Locanda**.

On the slopes the best spot to eat is the **Carmennahütte** beneath the Weisshorn. Get there early or late — it seems to always be crowded. The **Sattelhütte** is good as well with smaller crowds.

Après-ski/nightlife

Arosa is not the nightlife capital of Switzerland. The fun is where you make it, usually with groups that seem to form on their own on any ski trip. Arosa's après-ski activities center around the hotels in the evening. Here you'll find cozy bars with bands or piano players. There are approximately 20 such bars. Try the **Kitchen-Club** (081-3787100) in The Hotel Eden, **Nuts** (081-3773940), or **Vista** in Casino Arosa— probably the hottest discos in town.

Child care (2007/08 prices)

The Alpine Club Mickey Mouse is the major child-care program in the area. It incorporates the resort and many of the hotels. The program gives children special treatment like free lemonade in restaurants; children's menus with items less than CHF10 in many of the mountain huts; access to playgrounds; and a welcome-surprise bag if you are staying at one of the hotels that participate in the program. Children learn to ski in Donald's Ski Stadium and snowboard in Goofy's Halfpipe.

The Swiss Ski School Arosa (081-3787500; fax 081-3787508) is also a part of the Alpine Club Mickey Mouse. Children ages 4-18 are divided into groups of 4 to 8 children for lessons and other activities. A two-and-a-quarter-hour lesson for children ages 4 and older costs CHF44 for one lesson; CHF125 for three lessons; and CHF230 for six lessons. Five full days of instruction cost CHF260; and twelve days cost CHF450. There's also a package for children 6-12 that costs CHF465 for twelve days of instruction including a thirteen-day lift pass. The Junior Package is for children ages 13-18 and costs CHF365 for five days of instruction including a five-day lift pass; CHF580 for twelve days of instruction including a thirteen-day lift pass.

Hotel Arve Central (081 378 52 52) has opened a mini-club for children ages 3-12. It's open on Tuesdays and Fridays from 6:30 p.m. to 8:30 p.m. and costs CHF19 per child (meal included).

Other activities

Arosa is known for its off-slope activities. There are **indoor swimming pools**, **ice skating** on three open-air rinks and one covered rink, **chess** and **bridge** evenings, more than 60 km. of **walking trails**, **horse-drawn sleigh rides** and **tennis courts** at the Sunstar Parkhotel, the Robinson Club and the Sporthotel Valsana. The town is also active in arts and entertainment.

Swimming cost is about €5.5–€15 for adults and €2.5–€7.5 for children.

For **horse-drawn sleigh rides**, contact J. Graber (081-3774716), or Weierhof Stables (081-3774196). Costs are from €60–€140 for four persons based on the route.

Arosa offers organized one-and-a-half-hour **curling lessons** every Monday, starting in December, for CHF10 per person.

Hot-air ballooning is available. Call 076 331 86 37.

Getting there

The closest airport is Zürich; from there Arosa is less than three hours by train. Go first to Chur, where you catch a special train for Arosa. The train ride from Chur to Arosa takes about one hour and is one of the most spectacular train rides in Switzerland.

Driving from Zürich to Arosa will take about two-and-a-half hours in good weather. Follow the signs to Chur and after entering the city, follow the signs to Arosa. The road is steep and narrow and requires chains for most of the winter. Arosa has a car park for 460 cars. A free public bus in Arosa makes moving around the resort easier.

Tourist information

Arosa Tourism, CH-7050 Arosa, Switzerland; 081-3787020; fax 081-3787021). Hours: Monday–Friday 8 a.m.–6 p.m., Saturday 9 a.m.–5 p.m., Sunday 4 p.m.–5:30 p.m.

Champéry

Portes du Soleil

The Portes du Soleil ski area, nestled just south of Lake Geneva and straddling Switzerland and France, claims to be Europe's biggest ski area. Though Trois Vallées makes a similar claim, the skiing in Portes du Soleil is more unrefined. Where a skier in the Trois Vallées may be able to transfer easily from valley to valley, transfers in the Portes du Soleil area take more time and effort. Where the lift system in the Trois Vallées forms a tight web linking miles of prepared slopes, the lifts through this region are gossamer strands linking far-flung pistes.

I remember breathing heavily after a long morning of continuous skiing from Champéry in Switzerland to Châtel in France. Jean, my guide, asked me, "Do you see that peak over to the right of the stand of trees?"

"Yes," I answered.

"Do you know where that is?"

"Somewhere in France? Is it Mont Blanc?" It looked far, far away.

He chuckled. "It's not that far away. That's where we started this morning."

"Oh, come on. There's no need to exaggerate. I'm already tired enough."

"No, no, no, I'm not making a joke. I just want you to know that we have a long way to get back."

Incredulous, I forgot any notions about a relaxed afternoon cruising home.

The Portes du Soleil area is made up of about a dozen different resorts. Four lie on the Swiss side of the border: Champéry, Morgins, Torgon and Val d'Illiez-Les Crosets-Champoussin. The remaining eight are in France: Abondance, Avoriaz, Châtel, la Chapelle d'Abondance, les Gets, Montriond, Morzine and St-Jean-d'Aulps. The key resorts are Champéry in Switzerland and Avoriaz in France. More than 50 mountain restaurants dot the slopes.

Champéry is a mountain village that is waking up to the fact that it has turned into an international resort. Les Dents du Midi majestically stand watch over the valley and provide dramatic views of jagged mountain peaks. The old chalets look lived in, the odor of cow manure wafts across the main street, a plucky kid (of the goat type) prances in the back of a station wagon, the discos look like a throwback to the 1960s, and no tour buses pack the center of town.

The other main Swiss towns that are a part of the Portes du Soleil don't measure up to Champéry. Les Croset is isolated and once held promise as a resort, but today, is more fit for a skiing recluse. In the future with more stability, it has a chance of becoming a very convenient station. Morgins is far too quiet and most lodging is not very close to the two lifts up to the region.

Mountain layout

This is a real skier's area—over 650 km. of ski trails that are divided into 5 massifs. But not only is it challenging to ski the slopes; finding your way from resort to resort can test the skills of an Eagle Scout. The area does provide good maps outlining the 228 different lifts with suggested itineraries to make crisscrossing the region less difficult. (With such an expanse of skiing, no one map allows sufficient detail; when you arrive in a new section, stop and pick up the local lift map that shows runs in that area.)

NOTE: The lift system does not perfectly interconnect. In Châtel there is a shuttle-bus between the Linga and the Super-Châtel cable car.

The Portes du Soleil benefits from the fact that most of the skiable terrain is pasture land during the summers rather than rocky mountainside. This allows excellent skiing without the deep snow depth resorts such as Chamonix require. The locals claim that with only few inches of snow they can be up and running.

Experts can strike out in any direction but will most enjoy the World Cup section of Avoriaz, yo-yoing through the Plaine Dranse and Linga, and daring the Swiss Wall. No expert will feel complacent after any of these experiences. On a powder day, locals swear that since most visiting skiers stick to the trails, they can find untracked snow up to four days after a storm.

Intermediates should be ready for an endurance test of the first order. Forget any idea of skiing every run on a week-long vacation; it is just not possible. There are plenty of intermediate circuits that will provide a very full day of skiing. Try from Champéry to Avoriaz and back, or vice versa; on another day, take intermediate runs from Avoriaz to Châtel and return.

Beginners will not have a chance to really enjoy the expansive skiing of Portes du Soleil. Their best bet is to stick to the slopes of Planachaux and les Crosets on the Swiss side of the resort.

Snowboarding: Snowboarders can pick and choose from 7 diffierent snowparks which include 3 half-pipes, 4 boardercrosses, 4 snowcrosses. The snowpark in Champéry-les Crosets is 6 square kilometers and has different lines, quarters, gigantic tables, a half-pipe and a permanent boardercross.

Mountain rating

Score this one as a test for any expert, extensive enough for every intermediate on your list, and more than any beginner can handle.

Beginners taking the tram up from Champéry have a limited area in which to ski. Champoussin may be a better bet for beginners, but without the village atmosphere.

Intermediates will have a wonderful time criss-crossing the resorts on the Swiss side of the region, from Champéry to Champoussin to Le Crosets and down to Morgins.

Chavanette, also known as the Swiss Wall, between Avoriaz and Les Crosets, has lured experts for decades. Standing at the lip of the drop, skiers cannot see the slope that falls under the tips of their skis. Once dropping off the rim, it's a wide-open, expert steep with either ice or giant moguls, depending on the weather. Don't be ashamed to take the path around the Wall at this point—many skiers choose this option. The black runs above Avoriaz are good and new lifts have eliminated many of the bottlenecks.

One serious recommendation for intermediates or experts is to limit your range unless you are in good physical shape. If you are already exhausted and someone in your group points to a distant mountain and announces that you have to return to that point before quitting, you will arrive very, very tired. As we all know, that's when the snow snakes seem to strike. Be careful. This is one of the few areas in the world where you *can* ski too far to get back home.

 ## Ski school (2007/08 prices)

The Swiss Ski School in Champéry (479-1615) and the Freeride Company (024-479-2029) offer downhill lessons.

Private lessons (skiing and snowboarding): CHF140 for two hours, extra skier is CHF20. Half-day private lessons cost CHF200 extra skiers are CHF30. Full day is CHF360 plus CHF40 each extra skier.

Group lessons (skiing and snowboarding): CHF50 for a half day, and CHF200 for five half days.

A good way to get to know the area is through organized **Ski Excursions Portes du Soleil** groups of at least four skiers for €40 a day or €165 a five-day week. The groups, organized by the Swiss Ski School in Champéry, normally make a loop through Les Crosets, Champoussin, Morgins and Avoriaz, and then return to Champéry.

From Berra Sport in the center of town you can get ski rentals demo quality for about CHF145 (six days) and CHF155 (seven days). Snowboard rentals are about CHF25 (one day) and CHF105 (seven days). Rentals are also available from Freeride Company, Gonnet, Holiday and Borgeat Sports.

 ## Lift tickets (2007/08 prices)

The Portes du Soleil ski pass is for adults, age 19–59; children, age 5–15; youths, age 16-19 and students with proper identification age 24 and younger; and seniors, age 60 and older.

Photos are required for passes of six days of more. Half-day passes start at noon and children younger than age 5 are free when accompanied by a paying adult.

Limited passes are available for each region in the Portes du Soleil.

The Portes du Soleil Family Ski Pass is a bargain for families with a minimum of four people. These are the family pass prices which cover two parents with children younger than age 20.

	Adults	Children	Youth	Seniors
One day	CHF57	CHF39	CHF49	CHF46
Three days	CHF159	CHF107	CHF135	CHF127
Six days	CHF277	CHF186	CH235	CHF222
Fourteen days	CHF491	CHF329	CHF417	CHF393

 ## Accommodations

Champéry has a dozen hotels and plenty of apartments. There is also an excellent weekly program called Ski Passion, which includes seven, five or four days accommodation with half board, six- or five-day lift tickets for the entire Portes du Soleil area. Price ranges noted for each hotel are per person based on double occupancy high season with half board (breakfast and dinner): €€€—€125+; €€—€75-€125; €—less than €75.

Hotel Suisse (479-0707; fax 479-0709; €€€). Hotel Suisse is in the center of the village. All the rooms are comfortable; however, they vary significantly in size. Ask for a big room when you make reservations or when you show up at the hotel. The hotel's subterranean jazz bar, Les Mines d'Or, is a popular late night watering-hole often featuring live music. The Bar des Guides has become the nightlife haven of choice for English speakers. The manager of the hotel was a member of the Swiss Olympic ski team. He makes an effort to ski with the guests whenever possible.

Hotel des Alpes (479-1222; fax 479-1223; €€). Good hotel with a fancy and expensive à la carte restaurant which serves Ladin and Italine cuisine. Its TV room, playroom and playground are great for if you are traveling with children.

Hotel National (479-1130; fax 479-3155; €€) has 24 newly renovated rooms. It has an excellent restaurant with very affordable daily menus. The terrace off of the dining room has a panoramic view of the town and mountains.

Chalet-Hotel la Rose des Alpes (479-2303; fax 479-2306; €€) is full of mountain atmosphere and has a good restaurant as well. When you make your reservations make sure to ask for a room with a private bathroom and a full balcony.

Apartments

To reserve apartments write to the tourist office (details at the end of this chapter) or use its Web site, www.mychablais.com. You will receive a listing of available apartments, but you will have to make your reservations through a rental agency or directly with the owners. In Champéry the agencies are Agence Immobilière René Avanthay, (479-1444), Agence Mendes de Leon (479-1777) and Agence les Gaieuls (479-1885). Mendes de Leon seemed to be the most helpful.

Child care (2007/08 prices)

The ski school (479-1615) has a special Kids-Club for children aged 3–7, open 9:30 a.m. to 4:30 p.m. daily. It includes ski lessons, games and lunch. Half-day cost is CHF60; five half days will cost CHF240. A full day with lunch costs CHF120 and five full days with lunch are CHF480.

Mamans du Jour (mothers for a day) is a nanny service for ages 5 and younger, which must be booked before arrival. Rates are CHF45 for full-day service with meal and CHF20 for a half day without meal. Babysitting can also be arranged. The tourist office has phone numbers and information. (See our Champéry resort home page for tourist office addresses and phone numbers.)

Dining

Location, location, location ... Champéry's cooking benefits from its proximity to France. For the best meals in town go to the **Restaurant le Mazot** (479-0101). Try their *Pierrade* where you cook your meat on a heated stone.

These other restaurants in town are all very agreeable.

Café-Restaurant Le Nord (479-1126) at top of the High Street near Banque Cantonale. One of the more popular restaurants in the village, especially with families. Serving up an assortment of rösti, fondue, and raclette.

Café-Restaurant Le National (479 -1130) in the center of the village offers specials each day, has topnotch fish and a rustic atmosphere for very affordable prices. You can also grill your own meat to dip in one of the restaurant's delicious sauces.

Café-Restaurant La Vieux Chalet (479-1974) has lamb, fish, and meat dishes. Some nights offer music and dancing. Located at the end of High Street or just up the hill from the Téléphérique.

Café-Restaurant Le Gueullhi (479-3555) is next to the cable car and serves grilled meat, coq au vin and tripe.

Across the valley there is a raclette house called **Cantine des Rives** (479-1171, fax 479-3371). The raclette parties there are part of the resort's dining-around program for guests taking half-board at hotels or pensions. The raclette "wheel" is heated against an open fire by the chef. The restaurant also features sausage and tripe dishes.

Chez Coquoz (479 12 55) at Planachaux is the best on the Swiss side of the region. This restaurant is known for its excellent wine (over 150 selections) and cheese lists.

See the Avoriaz/Morzine chapter for restaurants on the French side.

Après-ski/nightlife

The best après-ski spot in town is **Bar des Guides** in the Hotel Suisse. There are good beers on tap and the place is packed with English speakers from the U.K., Canada, U.S.A., Holland and Scandinavia. **Mitchell's Bar** is also a favorite.

The English-style **La Crevasse Bar** run by Piste Artiste is right on the main street and has also become a focal point of English-speaking après-ski crowds until 3 a.m. **The Tarine Disco-Club** is also a popular hang-out for English-speaking après-skiers.

Café du Levant is the grunge and snowboarder hangout. Things sometimes get a little out of hand, which is this establishment's most redeeming feature.

Other activities

Champéry is just over a half-hour winding drive up the mountain from Montreux and Lausanne. Monthey, in the valley, has a covered bridge and open-air market. The town is about two hours from the airport at Geneva.

The Palladium offers **ice skating, curling** and **swimming** as well as a **fitness center, sauna** and **massage**.

Paragliding costs €66 per flight. Contact Vincent Marclay at 479-2408 or Simon Wiget at 079-306-4667. A visit to the thermal baths of Val-d'Illiez (www.thermes-parc.com) is a relaxing must with hourly train connection. Entrance is between €10 and €15.

Night skiing is also available from the end of December until Easter in Planachaux. Five kilometers of slopes are lit twice a week until 10 p.m.. Heliskiing and ski mountaineering is offered with qualified guides for €230 a day plus flight fees.

Getting there

The closest airport is Geneva. Champéry is less than 90 minutes from Geneva and only 45 minutes from Lausanne. Take the Lake Geneva motorway to Monthey, and follow the signs to Champéry. The road normally has good driving conditions year-round. Train service arrives in either Aigle or Monthey where travelers can transfer to a Postbus for the drive to the resort. The entire bus/train trip from Geneva will take approximtely three hours.

Tourist information

Champéry: Office du Tourisme, CH-1874 Champéry, Switzerland; Telephone: 024-479-2020, fax 024-479-2021.
Internet: www.champery.ch; www.mychablais.com
E-mail: info@champery.ch

Crans-Montana

Spread out on the high, broad Valais plateau 3,000 feet above the floor of the Rhone valley, the town of Crans-Montana commands a panoramic view of some of the most storied peaks in Alpine lore: Matterhorn, Mont-Blanc, the Weisshorn and the Dent-Blanche. A little too large and eclectic in its architecture to be called quaint, Crans-Montana is a modern luxury resort catering to the well-heeled, with more than 38 resort hotels and numerous boutiques sporting the haute couture of Paris and Milan.

Crans-Montana has a rich skiing history. In 1993 the resort celebrated its 100th anniversary, and in 1987 it hosted the prestigious World Alpine Ski Championships, where the Swiss swept the medals. In 1950, the first Swiss ski championships were held here. In 1911 the founder of downhill racing, Sir Arnold Lunn, organized a mass race from the highest point on the Plaine Morte glacier down to Montana that eventually developed into today's famous Kandahar race, now held each year. Crans-Montana continues this history during the 2007/08 season by hosting a leg of both the European Cup and the FIS World Cup.

Although the names are most often said in the same breath, Crans and Montana do have their differences. As mentioned, neither is a paragon of Alpine architecture. It's almost as if an architects' convention was given free reign to erect as many kinds of buildings as possible. Unappealing square concrete boxes stand beside massive triangular Toblerone-box hotels with a smattering of traditional chalets amidst the concrete and glass. Crans has the more concentrated city atmosphere. Not counting several fashion and souvenir shops and the occasional jewelry store, the shop signs in Montana read simply Cheese, Fondue, Real Estate, Restaurant. In Crans, the signs read Gucci, Louis Vuitton, Piaget and Cartier. Crans is chic and often crowded with furs. Montana is more for the family, where one is more at home in a ski outfit.

Be prepared to hike up and down hills, because both parts of the town climb the side of the mountain from their plateau above the Rhone. But this slope provides many hotels with spectacular views of the Alps in the south.

 ## Mountain layout

Four major lifts serve the ski area. From Crans, an eight-passenger gondola goes to Cry d'Err (7,173 feet), the hub of the entire area. From Montana, a six-passenger gondola whisks skiers to Cry d'Err. At Les Barzettes (a five-minute bus ride from Crans or Montana) another fast gondola takes you to Les Violettes (7,176 feet). From the base again, five minutes on the bus takes you to Aminona, where a gondola goes to Pt. Mont Bonvin (7,836 feet); here, a wide-open, above-treeline area provides fantastic uncrowded conditions.

The Cry d'Err sector of the mountain is the most crowded. Ten lifts go to Cry d'Err. After a long, flat traverse, you arrive on the Crans section of the mountain. From here the best bet is to take the Super-G/Slalom run into Crans, then catch the gondola back to Cry d'Err. The runs below Cry d'Err heading to Montana are intermediate playgrounds, but suffer from a serious bottleneck near Pas du Loup where the four trails merge through a narrow gap before widening on the way to town. At the end of the day, this bottleneck will be crowded. The Violettes area is a favorite of intermediates, featuring twisting runs down through the trees to the gondola midstation.

Across the valley from Violettes is the Aminona area and the Toula lifts. La Toula offers challenging expert runs, and Aminona boasts wide-open, uncrowded cruising. The Plaine-Morte trail starts atop the 9,843-foot-high Plaine Morte glacier. Sometime during your stay take the Funitel mountain subway up from Violettes and measure your time against the Kandahar ski pioneers, whose best time was just over one hour for the nine-mile run. It is intermediate terrain with expert tendencies.

For beginners, there is a series of baby that serve very mellow terrain surrounding the Le Signal area. Not only are there good areas to learn to ski and ride, but there is a clutch of three restaurants there for hot tea, coffee and meals. Beginners normally graduate to the easiest and widest intermediate trails up at Cry d'Err.

Snowboarders can find a 25 km. snowboard park in Arimona at La Tza. Once a week visitors can snowboard or ski at night at Cry d'Err and Verdetts.

Mountain rating

Indeed, for the intermediate skier, Crans-Montana with its excellent variety of trails may be heaven on the slopes. Long, challenging trails coupled with virtually no waiting at lifts make for a combination that most skiers will find hard to beat.

Beginners are relatively limited on this mountain. In Crans, absolute beginners should start on the golf course, which is perfect, but the next step — directly onto the mountain — is a big one. Montana beginners will likely opt for the Signal restaurant area. Fortunately, the slopes on the golf course and at Le Signal welcome beginners from both Crans and Montana. From Crans, take the bus and the cable car in Montana or Les Barzettas or Aminona. Try the blue run from the Chetzeron gondola first. In Violettes there are no beginner slopes, and the beginner sections of Aminona are for those who have been on skis at least three or four days — even then the gentle slopes are isolated in a sea of red-rated trails.

Experts will find only a few really steep sections, and there is plenty of off-trail and tree skiing. The championship runs are a good test. For steep, wide-open skiing try the run on the skier's left coming off the Les Violettes lift, or access this terrain while skiing down from the glacier. Though guides are suggested, there is also challenging off-trail skiing off the Petit Bonvin lift above Aminona.

Cross-Country (2006/07 prices)

The area has 40 km. set aside for classic style cross-country skiing and 30 km. for skate skiing, divided between the golf course and the Plaine-Morte glacier. Each of the 9 runs is groomed for both classic and skate skiing except for Plans Mayens which is groomed only for classic skiing. One day of skiing costs €5; one week costs €20. One day of skiing in Glacier Plaine-Morte costs €23 for an adult for one day; €14 for a child older than age 12.

There are 10 kilometers of marked snowshoe trails. Swiss Mountain Sports (480

44 66) offers night snowshoe excursions with fondue on Mondays and Thursdays from 6 pm-10 pm. Crans-Montana Tourism (485 04 04) also has night walks to the Colombire Alp Museum on Tuesdays. After snowshoeing up, participants sledge back down. Swiss Mountain Sports (480 44 66) has an introduction to snowshoe walking course that starts at 2.30 pm and ends at 5 pm.

Ski school (2006/07 prices)

There are five ski schools from which to choose: Ecole Suisse de Ski de Montana (027 481 14 80, fax 027 481 63 38); Ecole Suisse de Ski de Crans (0485 93 70, fax 0485 93 79); Avalanche Pro Shop & School (027 480 24 21, fax 027 480 24 20); Ski & Sky-Ecole Internationale de Ski & Snowboard (027 480 42 50, fax 027 481 04 80); and Swiss Mountain Sports (phone/fax 027 4804466).

The following are the prices for the Crans Swiss Ski School and the Montana Swiss Ski School. Prices are similar at the other ski schools.

Private lessons for skiing, snowboarding and telemarking in Crans costs CHF200 for one or two people. Three or four people cost CHF250 for a morning session in high season. An afternoon session costs CHF60 with CHF10 for each additional person. A full day of lessons for one or two people in Crans costs CHF400; three or four people, CHF 450. In Montana, one hour of lessons costs CHF60 plus CHF10 for each additional person. One day costs CHF400 plus CHF20 for each additional person.

Group lessons in Crans cost CHF55 for a half-day (three hours of lessons). A week of half-day lessons (18 hours in the morning) is CHF195. In Montana, one day of lessons (3 hours) costs CHF55 and five days of lessons (18 hours) cost CHF195. An excursion including lunch costs CHF20 for adults (with each additional person costing CHF15) and CHF10 for children.

Lift tickets (2007/08 prices)

The Crans-Montana area pass is available at the following rates:

	Adults	Children	Youth and Seniors
one day	€38	€23	€32
three days	€108	€65	€133
six days	€188	€113	€160
fourteen days	€336	€201	€286

Children must be 6-15 years old. Youths are 16-19 years old. Seniors are women age 64 and older and men age 65 and older.

Photo required for 3-day passes and longer. Families receive 10% discount. Insurance cost €2.62 per day. If the parents buy insurance children are covered for free.

Note: The Plaine-Morte glacier at the upper reaches of the mountain is reached by a Funitel, or mountain subway running from Les Violettes included in these prices.

Accommodations

Crans-Montana can be very upscale. It doesn't claim many movie stars or much of the old rich, but it is an oasis for the corporate rich. The town boasts more five-star hotels than any other Swiss resort except St. Moritz, and a dazzling selection of prize-winning, expensive restaurants. Finding the ritziest isn't difficult—digging for the good solid values for the middle-of-the-road crowd takes a bit more time. Rates are per person based on high season (February), double occupancy with half board: €€€—€125+; €€—€75–€125; €—less than €75.

Crans Ambassador (027-485-4848, fax 027-485-4849; €€€) is the best hotel on the Montana side of the town. Next to the cable cars, has good nightlife and a pool.

Royal (027-485-9595, fax 027-485-9595; €€€) in Crans is the most luxurious on this side of town and offers the Ski Soleil program.

St-George (027-481-2414, fax 027-481-1670; €€€) is more of a three- than four-star hotel. It has an English-speaking staff and is popular with the British.

Mont-Blanc (027-481-3143, fax 027-481-3146; €€€) is high on the hill with great views. It's a favorite of English-speakers and has one of the top restaurants in town.

De la Forêt (027-480-2131, fax 027-481-3120; €€€) is a bit of a walk to the downtown area but close to Les Violettes lift. This hotel has a covered swimming pool.

The Best Western National (027-481-2681, fax 027-481-7381; €€€) This hotel is near the Crans lifts. It is used by British groups, but the owner can be cantankerous.

La Prairie (027-485-4141, fax 027-485-4142; €€€) is a rustic, chalet-type hotel a few minutes outside of town with a shuttle to the lifts. We rate it a low three-star.

Teleferique (027-481-3367, fax 027-481-3309; €€) is at the base of Cry d'Err.

Apartments, condominiums, flats

With 25 major rental agencies in Crans-Montana, apartment and chalet listings in the region are overwhelming. Expect to pay €450–€550 per week for a two-bed studio in high season (Christmas, February and Easter); €625–€750 for a four-bed, two-room apartment; €1,200–€1,300 for a four-room, six- to eight-bed apartment.

Book an apartment online or write to or call the reservation office noted at the end of the chapter with details of what you want and the price range.

 ## Dining

This town, as noted above, has plenty of great eateries. These are some of our favorites—from expensive to moderate to inexpensive.

Head to **Nouvelle Rotisserie** (027-481-1885) for delicious food from its owner Mrs. Frances Massy who is renowned for her fresh food. **L'Hostellerie du Pas-de-l'Ours** (027-485-9333) in Crans has a Michelin star.

For more moderately priced meals try the rustic **Le Bistrot des Ours** (027-485-9333). **Hotel Aida** (027-485-4111) and **La Diligence** (0274-859-985) have beautiful rustic settings. Affordable hotel restaurants in Crans are **La Prairie** (0274-854-141), **Eden** (027-480-1171), **Splendide** (027-481-2056) and **Des Alpes** (027-481-3754).

In Montana head to **de la Foret** (027-480-2131) for a good meal. Also try **Mont-Plaisible** (027-480-2161). The budget crowd should indulge at the **Brasserie "Le Green"** (027-485-8787). Almost all the pizzerias have good budget dining.

On the mountain at Plans Mayens, for great meals stop at **Le Mont-Blanc** (027-481-3143) or **La Dent Blanche** (027-481-1179), which specializes in *raclette au feu de bois* (raclette in front of a fire). Make reservations. Rustic restaurant **Le Cervin** (027-481-2180) at Vermala is excellent for fondue and raclette and has an atmosphere you can't beat. Try the lunch menus at **Les Violettes, Bella-Lui** and **Chez Erwin**. The scenery from **La Plaine Morte** restaurant (027-481-3626) on the glacier and **Cry d'Err** (027-481-2410) is the stuff of which memories are made.

In the town of Bluche, just below Montana, the small **Petit Paradis** (027-481-2148) offers good basic meals at great value.

Après-ski/nightlife

By United States standards, there isn't much. Immediately after the slopes close, the only bars with a crowd are in Montana—the small, smoky **La Grange** and **Amadeus**. **The Pub Georges & Dragon** in Crans is the top

English-speaker, après-ski spot with reasonable beer. **The New Pub**, with its electronic and lottery games, is also good for apres-ski and nightlife. If you have the urge to go out between 9 p.m. and midnight, try some of the normally quiet piano bars. Our favorite is the **Memphis Bar** in Crans with its blond wood decor and raucous piano jazz. The **Punch Bar** in Crans also features Cuban music and cigars until 2 a.m.

Discos don't get going until midnight to 1 a.m. If you're determined and well-heeled, head for **Absolut** and **Le Barocke** in Crans, but expect to pay a €13–€15 cover charge, which includes one drink. **Constellation,** which is only open until midnight is a bar packed with young snowboarders. **Zapata** and **Number Two** are also good.

Child care (2006/07 prices)

Crans-Montana has four nurseries: **Crans Swiss Ski School** (027-485-9370); **Montana Swiss Ski School** (027-481-1480); **Halte-Garderie P'tits Bouts** (027 480 26 58, fax 079 660 76 20); and **Fleurs des Champs** (027 481 23 67, fax 027 481 23 68).

The tourist office provides a list of babysitters.

Other activities

Crans-Montana is a center for **hot-air ballooning, paragliding** and **hang-gliding**, with instruction in hang-gliding available. Call 027-485-0800 or 027-485-0404 for information about both. A winter meeting of **hot-air balloon** enthusiasts is held annually, usually in February. You can also find **horseback riding, snowshoeing, snowmobiling, bowling, curling, tennis, squash** and **tobogganing** (a 6 km. toboggan course runs from Petit Bonvin to Aminona). There's also a **golf-simulator** and **fitness and wellness centers**.

At the **Dabliu Beauty Farm Fitness Centre** (027-480-3481/82), next to the Grand Hotel du Golf, pamper yourself with the 'culla di olos', a package which includes a steam bath with essential oils, facial treatments, body peel and massage. There are also personalized fitness programs.

The **Wellness Centre Valaisia** in Hotel Valaisia (027-481-2612, fax 027-481-2660) is best known for its rejuvenating salt water swimming pool with massage jets, steam bath and sauna.

Getting there

You'll most likely arrive at the Geneva airport. From there it's an uncomplicated car or train ride of a couple of hours around the lake and into the mountains. From Sierre, the bus departs directly in front of the railway station and the cable car departs from around the corner.

Crossair now flies from Zürich and London to nearby Sion, only a half hour from Crans-Montana by bus or taxi.

Tourist information

Crans-Montana Tourism, CH-3963 Crans-Montana, Switzerland; 027-485-0404 or 4850800; fax 027-485-0460 or 485-0810).
Central reservations for hotels or apartments is at the same address.
Telephone: 027-485-0444, fax 027-485-0461.
Internet: www.crans-montana.ch
E-mail: reservation@crans-montana.ch;
information@cransmontana.ch for general info.

Davos

Davos is not a small quaint Alpine resort. This is a ski city—the largest ski resort in Switzerland and the highest city in Europe. The year-round population is 13,000 and the town can fill up with an additional 23,000 tourists. Davos was one of the first ski resorts to be created and is still one of the world's best.

In the southeast corner of Switzerland, Davos sits dwarfed by mountains on both sides of the valley (Davos means "behind" or "beyond" in the Romansh language). Five separate ski areas have been developed, any one of which would be enough for a U.S. resort, ensuring diversity and skiing for every skier.

Instead of wooden chalets, for the most part, square concrete hotels line the streets. but Davos still maintains a sense of comfort. Traffic moves easily along the upper and lower main arteries without buildup. The hotels have a long and distinguished tradition of excellence and practically every type of recreational activity is available.

The town was founded in 1860 by Dr. Spengler, a German physician who recognized the benefits of the dry, healthy climate in treating tuberculosis, a scourge at that time. Huge balconies seen on older houses were for patients to lie out in the sunshine. This type of treatment continued until about 1930. Thomas Mann's wife was treated at Davos, from which came his novel *The Magic Mountain*.

Development of Davos as a sports region began in 1955. Davos and Klosters (see our Klosters chapter) combined offer over 300 km. of runs, a variety of lodging, cablecars and even some yodeling accordion players. This resort was one of the first to turn skiing into a business with the construction of the Parsenn railway and the creation of the first drag lift.

At night the mix of people has unusual variety, from teenagers in town for the good skiing to elderly couples enjoying a walk in the crisp, clear mountain air and the restorative powers of an Alpine vacation. Nightlife is adequate, if restrained. Everything except the skiing seems to be done in moderation.

Mountain layout—Skiing

The five ski areas of Davos-Klosters are the Parsenn, the Schatzalp/Strela, Jakobshorn, Madrisa, Rinerhorn and Pischa.

The Parsenn: This is the best known area, almost the size of Manhattan and the major reason why Davos has become a premier European resort. It's an excellent family mountain and has fewer on-mountain bars than the other Davos ski areas.

The Parsennbahn, a cable railway, leaves every 15 to 20 minutes in ski season. It peaks at the Weissfluhjoch, the upper lift central of the Parsenn. Here the wide-open runs offer beginners and intermediates a paradise for cruising. The Parsenn has 40 seemingly endless trails, including what was once Europe's longest: the 12-km. trail from Weissfluhjoch to Küblis. Experts will want to take the cablecar which leaves the Weissfluhjoch and ascends to the Weissfluhgipfel, eventually arriving at 9,331 feet. From this point two expert runs drop to the spreading Parsenn. There are good restaurants at both the Weissfluhgipfel and Weissfluhjoch.

Lift improvements continue with high-speed chairlifts replacing many of the remaining drag lifts. A gondola stretching from the Schifer over to the Weissfluhjoch allows skiers to cruise for 20 to 30 minutes and then zip back to the top of the Parsenn.

The toughest runs back into Davos are alongside the Parsennbahn, or down the Meierhoftäli over moguls and advanced intermediate drops to Davos-Wolfgang, where you'll have to take a bus or train back into town.

Madrisa: This area is perfect for those who are looking for a place to ski with the family and for intermediate skiers who are looking for a day of cruising. Nine intermediate runs and one black run descend to Klosters-Dorf.

Jakobshorn: This is the second largest area in Davos, on the opposite side of the valley from the Parsenn. Here the trails have good pitch consistency and top-to-bottom skiing makes use of the entire vertical. It's called "The Fun Mountain," and is the favorite of most snowboarders. The area is wide and gently sloping. It's like riding down mountain pastures.

A cablecar rises from the town to the lower station of the Jakobshorn, which peaks at 8,497 feet. Here 14 marked trails will keep a skier busy for at least a day. The area is more challenging than the Parsenn, but trails are shorter and more limited.

You reach the Jakobshorn from Davos-Platz with a two-stage cablecar or with a high-speed double chairlift. Then six more lifts open up the entire side of the mountain—2,140 feet of wide-open vertical, all above treeline, with another 1,200 feet of trails through the trees. Obviously, there is plenty to ski on this side of the valley. And plenty to eat, too – both the Chalet Güggel and Clavadeler Alp are very good on-mountain restaurants. At the top of the Jazz Quattro and Jazz Junior chairs there's a "party place," with an outside bar.

If you are an expert, you have the option of skiing off-piste by dropping into the Dischma Valley to Teufi, where a bus will pick you up and take you back to Davos-Platz.

Rinerhorn: The next area is the Rinerhorn area at Glaris, just up the valley from the main town, with 13 runs and several good advanced intermediate descents. These slopes are normally uncrowded except for the ski schools, which use the wide-open slopes for classes. This is where most of the locals ski, especially on weekends.

Take the train or bus from Davos-Platz to the area. Then take the Rinerhorn-bahn up 1,900 feet and take your choice of three more lifts reaching up another 1,446 feet. This area, with its children's facilities, is perfect for families. Experts can drop down the 3.5-km. run back down to Glaris. Intermediates and beginners will have the entire upper reaches in which to practice and play.

Pischa: This area, a short bus ride from Davos, offers uncrowded runs down a 2,230-foot vertical. There isn't a lot for an expert here, but how many of us are that expert?

Pischa is one of Switzerland's largest freeride regions. Riders can take either the aerial cableway or two of the present ski lifts (Mitteltäli I and Flüelamäder) to six runs reserved for freeriding.

Mountain rating

Davos earns an A-plus when it comes to beginners and intermediates. Grooming is universally good. This is perhaps the ideal terrain for learning to ski and for perfecting your technique. For experts, the upper Parsenn terrain may become a little boring (Ah, to be so jaded!) and they might ask where the most challenging skiing—normally off the Parsenn—can be found.

Locals might suggest runs on the Parsenn from the top of the Weissfluhgipfel, the trails that drop into town alongside the Parsennbahn, or the Drostobel-to-Klosters run, which is narrow and sometimes steep. Rinerhorn has great tree skiing and good off-piste as well. The Jakobshorn has bumps and moguls to wear out any skier.

On days with good powder, it pays to hire an instructor for the morning who will take you to the special spots (off-trail) for thrills.

Mountain Layout—Snowboarding

This resort has become one of the top snowboard destinations in the world. Jakobshorn is the center for snowboard action with plenty of other action in each of the areas. There are halfpipes (one for night boarding) at the Jakobshorn as well as a boardercross park. The Jakobhorn boarderpass is only €37. The normal meeting spots for boarders are Bolgenschanze, Jatzhütte, Fuxägufer and Chalet Güggel.

Boarders congregate at the Mammut-Bar at the Jochexpress lift or at the New Bar at the middle station of the Höhenweg. The Pischa sector has a fun park near the Mitteltäli lift. And the Rinerhorn has a fun park near the training lift.

Cross-country

Davos has great cross-country skiing—the second largest cross country ski area in Switzerland—with 75 km. of classic and 40 km. of skating trails. Trails are open from 9 a.m. to 4:30 p.m., November to January and from 9 a.m. to 5 p.m., February to April. There are separate dog trails and a night trail that is lit until 9:30 p.m. Davos also has a cross country lodge with a waxing room, showers, lockers and even a small restaurant. Trail maps cost CHF3.50.

Ski school (2007/08 prices)

The Davos ski school has more than 200 instructors for skiing and snowboarding. Almost all of them speak some English.

	Private lessons	Group lessons
Half day (2 1/2 hours)	CHF220 (€137)	CHF45 (€28)
One day (about 6 1/2 hours)	CHF350 (€218)	CHF65 (€40)
Five half-days	***	CHF185 (€114)
Five full days	***	CHF265 (€165)

These are the skiing and snowboarding lesson prices for the Schweizer Schneesportschule Davos (081 416 24 54). They are similar to the prices of ski schools in the area.

There are reductions for groups of senior citizens and for children. Inquire at the ski school to see whether such a group has been organized. There is a lot of off-piste skiing in good winters and many skiers come for that experience. A guide at private instruction rates is the way to go.

Lift tickets (2007/08 prices)

Separate passes are sold for each of the areas. An adult full-day ticket for the Parsenn area costs €41; for Rinerhorn. €31; for Madrisa. €33; for Pischa, €30; for Jakobshorn, €37.

The most convenient pass to use is the Klosters-Davos Region Pass. It includes the Madrisa area, plus use of the train that runs between Davos and Klosters and as far down the valley as Küblis. It is also good on local buses in Davos and Klosters.

There are 10 percent discounts for Davos/Kloster passes purchased for three days or more before the Christmas season, (Nov. 15–Dec. 19).

	Adults	**Youth (13–17)**	**Children (6-12)**
One day	€43	€30	€15
Two days	€82	€57	€29
Three days	€114	€80	€40
Six days	€190	€133	€67
Fourteen days	€344	€241	€120

Important transportation note: The shuttlebuses that carry you from your hotel to the Parsennbahn, or down to the Jakobshornbahn, ply a route up and down the *same* one-way street. If you are in Platz and want to take the shuttlebus to the Parsennbahn, go to the main street, Promenade, which is one-way in the opposite direction. Your bus will come down Promenade in a special lane—against traffic—to take you to the lifts. If you logically head down to Talstrasse, you will have to climb back up to Promenade.

Overall, the bus system has been significantly expanded in the past seasons. Nearly all the outlying lodging is now accessible by bus. The entire system, as well as the train between Davos and the outlying villages, is free to those with guest cards.

 Accommodations

Davos hotels range from plush to plain. The following are our top recommendations in each category. The general location—Davos Dorf, Davos Platz an so on—is noted. Price ranges noted for each hotel are per person based on double occupancy high season with half board (breakfast and dinner): €€€=€125+; €€=€75–€125; €=less than €75.

Our recommended five-star hotels are:

Steigenberger Belvédère (081-415-6000, fax 081-415-6001; €€€). This is one of the grand old Alpine hotels. The view from the rooms facing the valley will beg for photography. The hotel restaurant, Romeo and Julia can be excellent and expensive. The indoor pool and spa, with steam and sauna, are very comforting.

Hotel Flüela (081-410-1717, fax 081-410-1718; €€€). A family-run hotel sits next to the Davos-Dorf station with easy access to all ski areas. A lounge with hardwood floors, comfy chairs and fireplace welcomes you. The rooms are all different.

Morosani Post Hotel (081-415-4500, fax 081-415-4501; €€€). This hotel in Davos Platz is especially popular with Swiss visitors, which speaks well of its quality, service and prices. Rooms are furnished in light pine and the interior is beautifully Alpine, even if the exterior appears cold and square.

Turmhotel Victoria (081-417-5300, fax 081-417-5380; €€€) was formerly the Hotel Cristiana. It re-opened in 1999 and is now a four-star hotel. In Davos-Dorf, it is a bit out of the way from nightlife and restaurants.

The Arabella Sheraton Hotel Seehof (081-417-9444, fax 081-417-9445; €€€), formerly the Hotel Seehof, is a renovated hotel in Davos Dorf next to the mountain railway and within walking distance of the train station.

Sporthotel Central (081-415-8200; €€€). An excellent hotel with pool and sauna in Davos-Platz. It has a cozy piano bar and lobby wth wireless Internet access.

Meierhof (081-416-8285, fax 081-416-3982; €€+). This is a hotel with a large Swiss clientele in Davos Dorf. The rooms are beautiful and the food exceptional.

Bahnhof Terminus (081-414-9797, fax: 081-414-9798) sits across from the Davos-Platz station and is the Jakobshorn base station.

Hotel Ochsen (081-415-4444, fax 081-415-4445; €) This hotel is rustic and in the center of the action with an excellent restaurant.

Edelweiss (081-416-1033, fax 081-416-5191; €) is a B&B with private bath.

The **Sports Center** in the middle of town offers budget dormitory accommodations for €50–€58 a night with half-board.

The most popular, inexpensive snowboard lodgings are the **Bolgenschanze**, **Snowboarder's Palace**, **Bolgenhof** and **Guesthaus Suvretta** near the Jacobshorn. Near the Rinerhorn most boarders stay at the **RinerLodge**.

Apartments, condominiums, flats

Rental apartments are well organized and bookings can be arranged through the tourist office (see Tourist Information). Write and provide details — when you plan to arrive, how many people will be sharing the apartment and what facilities you desire. They will respond quickly with several choices. The reservations number is 081-415-2121.

It is more convenient to stay in Davos-Platz or Davos-Dorf — Davos-Laret and Davos-Wolfgang are further out of the way. Make your selection and notify the tourist office or the individual owner, depending on the instructions from the tourist office.

Normally, linen and kitchen utensils are included in every apartment. Taxes and cleaning may be extra.

Dining

Davos has scores of restaurants. They are all relatively good. This is a town where taking half-board can be a good idea, at least when it comes to saving money. The finest restaurants here are expensive. We list some of the more reasonably priced restaurants here (except for Hubli's).

Hubli's Landhaus in Laret (081-417-1010; fax 081-417-1011) is a local nouvelle cuisine shrine adorned with a Michelin star. Make reservations early. Dinner will end up costing between €50 and €80. There is a lunch menu for only about €30.

Vinikus (081-416-5979) has a French bistro atmosphere and costs €40–€80.

The **Arabella Sheraton Seehof** (081-417-9444) serves excellent nouvelle cuisine dinners. Other hotel restaurants that are excellent with reasonable daily menus for €20–€29 are **Flüela-Stübli** (081-410-1717) and **Meierhof** (081-416-8285) in Davos-Dorf as well as **Ochsen** in Davos-Platz (081-415-4444) and the **Crystal** (081-414-0101, fax 081-414-0100) in Davos-Platz. Good 24-hour pizza and basic groceries are at **After Hours** (081-413-6376), up the stairs from the Sporthotel Central.

The **Pöstli** in the Morosani Posthotel has good local fare and **Al Ponte** serves Italian meals. The **Bündnerstübli** at Dischmastrasse in Dorf is very local, very crowded and very reasonable. Try the **Landhaus Frauenkirch** (081-413-6335) for typical Swiss specialties.

For fondue head to **Bistro Gentiana** (081-413-5649).

The best pizza in town is found at **Al Ponte** in Platz. **Zum Goldenen Drachen** (081-414-9797) in Terminus Hotel and **Zauberberg** (081-415-4200) in the Hotel Europe are the best spots for Chinese food.

Après-ski/nightlife

Davos-Platz is the place to be for any nightlife. The younger set meets at the **Cabanna Club**, which gets started at 9 p.m., or the **Cava Grischa**. Expect to hear lots of techno rock and to pay about €4.50 for a Coke, more for mixed drinks and beer. The **Ex-Bar** also hops.

The **Chämi Bar** on Promenade is where folk gather to see and be seen, drink and little else. Immediate après-ski with a bit of class is found at the **Café Schneider** in Davos-Platz or **Café Weber** in Davos-Dorf. These are more coffee and cake spots.

Piano Bar in the Hotel Europe offers changing entertainment like a blind black piano player and singer from Atlanta turning out cool tunes. Downstairs, the **Top Secret** bar is full of 20-somethings who enjoy the sound of garage bands practicing.

 ## Child care (2007/08 prices)

In Jakobshorn-Bolgen and Bünda, Schweizer Schneesportschule Davos runs **Bobo Club's** (081-416-24 54). **Kinderland Pischa** (081 416 13 13) at the top station of the Pischa aerial cableway offers child care for children ages 3 and older on an hourly basis. Youngsters can learn basic skiing skills through play and have a fun time painting and playing in the 'Spielhaus'.

In Madrisa, **The Kids Club** offers daily babycare for children ages 2 and younger as well as care for older children ages 2–6.

 ## Other activities

The sports center next to the ice stadium has a public indoor swimming pool and wellness area with saunas and a solarium. **Pool** and **wellness area** cost €14.90 a visit. **Swim** only is €5.20 a session.

There is **tennis** and **squash** in Davos-Platz with indoor courts (081-413-3131).

Europe's largest natural **ice skating** rink (081-415-3604) is open and rentals are available. Entry for adults is €2.60 and for children, €1.70. **Hang-gliding** and **tandem flight** courses are taught by Luftchraft-Flugschule Davos (079-6231970), Paragliding Davos (079-236 39 49), Flugcenter Grischa (081-422-2070) and Christian Sprecher (081-401-1414). There is also a **toboggan run** down the Schatzalp with banked turns and a total drop of over 750 feet. There is no charge for admission. Toboggans are available for rental at the base of the Schatzalp Funicular. Call 081-415-5280.

A **casino** operates in the Europa Hotel.

 ## Getting there

The closest airport is Zürich, nearly three hours away by train. You must change trains in Landquart.

By car, follow the signs to Chur on an excellent superhighway until you get to the Landquart/Davos exit. The drive from Landquart to Davos is through a narrow valley and passes through Küblis and Klosters before arriving at Davos-Platz. The distance from Zürich to Davos is just less than 100 miles.

 ## Tourist information

The tourist office is open M–F, 8:30 a.m.–6:30 p.m.; Saturday, 9 a.m. – 5:30 p.m.; Sunday, 10 a.m.–noon and 3 p.m. – 5:30 p.m.
Davos Tourismus, Promenade 67, 7270 Davos-Platz, Switzerland; Telephone: 081-415-2121, fax 081-415-2100.
Internet: www.davos.ch/ Email: info@davos.ch

Engelberg

This resort is one of the closest to Zürich and Lucerne. It has both challenging ski-ing and mellow terrain. You can come here from Zürich or Lucerne for a day or an afternoon, or you can stay for a week or longer and enjoy the scenery. Because it is central Switzerland's major resort, Engelberg is crowded on weekends. During the week, things are far less hectic.

The region is blessed by a natural beauty found in few places. On clear days, the sight of the meeting of three mountain ranges and the views of Lake Lucerne are spectacular. There are 20 hotels and 250 vacation homes.

 ## Mountain layout–Skiing

When skiing at Engelberg in central Switzerland, remember that the Gerschnialp is for beginners and the Titlis is for the advanced. The Brunni is on the sunny side of the valley, with slopes all the way up to the Schonegg, at 6,691 feet. From Schonegg it's an intermediate cruise down to the village.

The finest beginner and lower intermediate skiing is on the opposite mountain, below the Titlis glacier on Gerschnialp. Ski out the doorway of the six-person gondola station at Trübsee and down to the Gerschnialp lifts.

Everyone but the beginner eventually makes it up to the 10,624-foot-high summit of Titlis. This is where the best skiers sharpen their skills. To join them, take the gondola from the valley floor to Trübsee. Then take the unique two-section rotating cable car the rest of the way up to Klein-Titlis, at 9,908 feet. It takes about 40 minutes to get there so enjoy the view. You can see the St. Gotthard Pass off to the south. Also you can see from Lucerne, to the north past Interlaken and to the Bernese Oberland.

From the Kleine Titlis, there is a memorable run from an area that seems on clear days like the roof of Europe to Trübsee. The run crosses the snowfields below Titlis peak toward the Rotegg lift. Then it becomes a black trail, dropping steeply for most of the 2,500-foot trip to Stand. After Stand, the run mellows a bit as it tracks down to the base of the cable car. Take it easy the first time down. The glacial ice, sharp turns, and steepness of the slope can be treacherous.

After one run some intermediates choose to stay on the wider red run from Stand down to Trübsee. If you make this decision, take the horizontal chairlift across the frozen lake to Alpstübli, where you can go up to the 8,474-foot-high Jochstock. The red run down to Jochpass and Alpstübli is a good warmup for the Kanonenrohr.

The Kanonenrohr (cannon barrel) section is only a few hundred meters long, but you'll turn enough to keep your thighs burning for a while. Lower intermediates should opt for the blue trail to the left of the toughest section. To repeat the best part of the run, stop at the Untertrübsee cable car station and go back up.

The best off-trail skiing is on the Laub above the Ritz restaurant and below Titlis. The 1,000-meter vertical drop is a challenge for even experienced skiers, and a guide (for about €90) is recommended.

Mountain rating

For beginners, the slopes of the Gerschnialp and Untertrübsee are best. Intermediates will be challenged on both sides of the valley, particularly up on the glacier which tops Titlis. Experts will discover whether they really merit that classification after several runs down from the glacier summit.

Mountain layout–Snowboarding

Engelberg is a snowboarders' hill. Thousands of local Swiss kids come here to learn tricks and turns. There is excellent riding on the glacier at 10,000 feet. The 12 km. drop from the summit of Titlis to town is one of the great Swiss snowboard adventures.

The Jochpass Terrain Park on the Titlis glacier next to the Jochstock Xpress has a monster quarterpipe, BigAir, several kickers and a variety of rails. This park was specifically designed with graduating degrees of difficulty to help freestylers improve their skills. The Surfers' Paradise next to the Jochpass Mountain Hotel overlooks the terrain park, so spectators can kick back and relax, snack and listen to DJed music.

Cross-Country (2007/08 prices)

The longest course through the Engelberg valley is the 25-km Engelberg Valley trail that ascends to Herrenrüti. The leisurely 10-km Gerschnaialp-Untertrübsee course extends from Gerschnialp to the Untertrübsee with both sharp and mild ascents. The 4-km Trübsee trail has more uneven terrain for the more experienced skier. The 1.5 km Floodlit course is an extended World Cup route that runs by the Sporting Park.

Snowshoeing: For the Gerschnialp - Untertrübsee trail – From the Gerschnialp top station walk through the forest, parallel to the road, as far as the Ritz restaurant. This is the beginning two snowshoeing loops.

Ski school (2006/07 prices)

The Engelberg Titlis Ski School (041-639-5454) offers ski, snowboard, freestyle, cross-country and Telemark lessons.

Private lessons for skiing and snowboarding cost €107 for two hours; €140 for a half day (three hours); and €200 for a full day (five hours). Each additional person costs €20. **Cross-country** and **Telemark lessons** are all private.

Group lessons are offered in a full-day block, Monday to Friday with a minimum of four people in a group. The following rates include video analysis and a 10% discount on lift pass. For skiing lessons an adult full day costs €40; three days, €103; five days, €137. For snowboarding an adult full day costs €53; three days, €137; five days, €183.

Lift tickets (2007/08 prices)

The Trübsee-day pass which is valid in Engelberg-Trübsee and on all the lifts on Gerschnialp, Hopper, Starterland, Älplerseil and includes the Untertrübsee lift. Adults and seniors cost CHF32; youth cost CHF 22; and children cost CHF13 for a full day ticket.

The Engelberg ticket is good for all 25 lifts in the area, opening about 82 km. of trails. Lift tickets four days or more are discounted 10% for skiers with an Engelberg guest card. Note: These prices include VAT.

	Adults	Children(6–15)	Youth (16–19)	Senior (63+)
one day (Mon. - Fri.)	€53	€21	€37	€42
one day (Sat. - Sun.)	€59	€24	€41	€59
two days (Mon. - Fri.)	€100	€40	€70	€80
two days (Sat. - Sun.)	€108	€43	€76	€108
three days	€145	€58	€102	€116
six days	€260	€104	€182	€208

Who skis at a discount: Prices drop a few euros per hour after 12 p.m.

Accommodations

Engelberg is a relatively small town (3,300 residents) with a major tourist capacity. There are nearly 17,000 beds available in hotels, guest houses, pensions, private homes and apartments. Check with the Tourist Center for all reservations. Call 041-639-7777 or fax 041-639-7766. Price ranges noted for each hotel are per person based on double occupancy with half board (breakfast and dinner): €€€—€125+; €€—€75–€124; €—less than €75.

Berghotel Trübsee (041-637-1371, fax 041-637-3720; €€€) hotel has a phenomenal setting halfway up the Titlisbahn. The panoramas are unparalleled and the meals are fantastic. The cafeteria is open to the public during the day, but the wonderful dinners are for hotel guests only. **Hotel Regina Titlis** (041-637-2828, fax 041-637-2392; €€€) is the most luxurious in town. **Hotel Schweizerhof** (041-637-1105; €€) has a covered pool and is in the middle of town. **Hotel Engelberg** (041-637-1168, fax 041-637-3235; €€) is a pleasant hotel in the city center with an excellent restaurant. **Garni Sunmatt** (637-2045, fax 041-637-1533; €) is a B&B only but a delight. **Hotel Crystal** (041-637-2122, fax 041-637-2979; €) has an exceptional kitchen with very pleasant rooms at bargain prices. **Hotel Central** (041-637-3232, fax 041-637-3233; €€) stands in an ideal spot in town with its own pool and sauna.

If the hotels in Engelberg are fully booked, as they often are in peak season, the lakeside city of Lucerne is a good alternative. It is only 30 minutes from the slopes by car. It is a perfect arrangement for the non-skier/rider traveling with a skier/rider.

Apartments, condominiums, flats

Engelberg has good apartment accommodations. Prices start at €250 a week for a one-bedroom apartment. The average apartment for four costs about €410 in January and in February about €475. Prices include cleaning and bed linens. The tourist office (041-639-7777 or fax 041-639-7766) has a computerized listing of available apartments.

Dining

The **Dorfstübli** on the first floor of the Hotel Engelberg is highly recommended. The menu of the day will run about €22 and ordering à la carte can cost twice as much. **Restaurant Spannort** (041-637-2626) has local fare.

Restaurant La Strega (041-637-2828) in the Hotel Regina Titlis has great Italian meals, but at a price—daily menu runs around €40. As mentioned in the hotel section, **Hotel Crystal** has an excellent and affordable restaurant.

Après-ski/nightlife

Drop into the **Spindle** in the cellar of the Alpenclub Hotel. It's crowded with the 18- to 25-year-old set. Our favorite is **Dream Life**, an English pub at the Central Hotel. The **Bierlialp Chalet** disco has dancing in the center of town. Try **Yucatan** in Hotel Bellevue. They have a Happy Hour every day during the winter season from 5 p.m. to 6 p.m.

Child care (2006/07 prices)

The Engelberg-Titlis Ski School (041 639 54 54) operates a ski kindergarten for kids ages 2 years and older and non-skiers.

For kids 3 to 5 years of age (Monday to Friday from 9:30 a.m. – 3 p.m.) the ski school offers morning lessons, supervised lunch and afternoon care.

Group lessons for kids ages 6–15 are: full day, €53; three days, €137; five days, €183. These rates include lessons, supervision during lunch, lift tickets and ski test. A supervised lunch which includes drink and dessert costs €9.

Many of the hotels also offer babysitting services and day care.

Contact the tourist office for a list of local babysitters. Prices range from CHF5 – CHF10 per hour.

Other activities

Engelberg is sunny most of the year. The biggest non-skiing pursuits are **hiking** and **sightseeing**.

Engelberg has a sports center with indoor and outdoor **ice skating**, **indoor tennis courts**, a **fitness center**, a **curling** competition area, **billiards**, **darts** and **table tennis**. **Horse-drawn sleigh rides** are available throughout the winter; January through March, Friday-night sleigh rides are a tradition.

The **Engelberg Talmuseum** has been set up in the Wappenhaus. Visitors will get a good idea of what life is and was like in these high Alpine valleys.

The most scenic local excursions other than the ride up the Titlisbahn, is **a trip to Schwand**, about five miles away, for a great view of the ring of mountains.

Getting there

By air: From Zurich International Airport, you either drive or take a train to Engelberg. Driving time from Zürich is about one-and-a-half hours. If possible, make a sightseeing stop in Lucerne along the way.

By train: From Lucerne, direct, hourly local trains run to Engelberg. In addition, regular, comfortable Intercity or Eurocity trains run to Lucerne.

By car: Engelberg is easily accessible from all directions by car. There are motorways from Geneva via Bern; or from St. Gallen via Zurich to Lucerne (Gotthard route). Leave the A2 motorway at the Stans-Süd exit16 km after Lucerne and it's about a 20 km.-drive to Engelberg.

Tourist information

Engelberg-Titlis Tourism, CH-6390 Engelberg, Switzerland.
Telephone 041-639-7777, fax 041-639-7766.
For hotel and apartment reservations contact the tourist center.
Internet: www.engelberg.ch. E-mail: welcome@engelberg.ch.

Flims Laax Falera

Flims Laax Falera, the Alpenarena, is still one of the undiscovered ski areas in Switzerland as far as American and British skiers are concerned. The ski area, in the southeast part of Switzerland across the valley from Arosa, was discovered by the Swiss and the Germans, who know a good area when they see it. Nevertheless, in recent years it seems more and more British are discovering the area. The Alpenarena enjoys excellent British and American ski club patronage and the recent 2005 British Ski and Snowboard Freestyle Championship was held here.

Flims is a small village in the traditional sense. The ski lifts start from the village center (about 3,600 feet altitude) and the major hotels are spread throughout the village. Laax, a couple of kilometers down the road, has built a new part with various hotels and apartments, at the base of the Crap Sogn Gion cable car. Not only are the major hotels centered here but also the major nightlife. The more traditional and historic part of Laax with restaurants, hotels, the sport center and the museum is based around a lake a few kilometers away.

Falera, the third and smallest village in the Alpenarena, has only one hotel but various apartments to rent.

Flims is perhaps the more Swiss; Laax is a purer ski vacation experience; Falera is best suited for those who want skiing and solitude.

It is hard to describe the incredible expanse of ski area that surrounds a skier as he or she gazes from the station at the top of the Crap Sogn Gion cable car that rises from Laax. This is a wide-open area that cries out for all-day skiing.

 ## Mountain layout

One major lift from each town carries skiers to the snowfields, which are in turn linked by an extensive far-flung lift system. These lifts are not tightly packed, but they service the trails belonging to four major sections: Cassons Grat, La Siala, Crap Sogn Gion and Vorab.

Above Laax the cable car reaches the Crap Sogn Gion, at 7,283 feet, and a second continues to Crap Masegn, 650 feet higher. From here, skiers can shoot back into the valley toward Falera or to the lower cable car station. Other runs drop into the opposite valley, where more lifts bring skiers up to the La Siala area above

Flims. High-altitude buffs head to the Vorab area, which at 9,842 feet presents great panoramas and skiing.

Snowboarding: Snowboarders will find a boarder park with two monster pipes, kickerlines, and various rails on the Crap Sogn Gion. From the Café No Name which is directly above the park, there is a perfect view of the whole park. During the glacier season, there are also two halfpipes and a snow park on the Vorab glacier.

A special snowboarders lift ticket (2004/05 prices) called the Park and Pipe Ticket is available for €26 per day. It gives access to the 2 Monsterpipes, the NoName Cafe, Freestyle Park, one ride on the Crap Sogn Gion Aerial cable car.

Mountain rating

The beginner will find the best areas on Nagens and on Crap Sogn Gion and on Foppa, the first stage of the way up the Cassons Grat.

Intermediates will be overjoyed with the Crap Sogn Gion section and can find more than enough challenging runs anywhere in the resort area.

The expert skiers can stay busy when the mood strikes them, especially beneath the Crap Sogn Gion cable car, the back side of the Vorab and through the Cassons Grat powder and trails. But they will have to pick their spots.

Ski school (2007/08 prices)

Swiss Ski School Flims Laax Falera has classes in all the villages. For the office in Laax, call 081 927 7171. For the office in Flims, call 081 927 7181. For the office in Falera, call 081 921 30 30.

Private instruction: One to two people costs CHF200 for two hours and CHF20 each additional person; CHF350 for four hours and CHF40 each additional person; CHF425 for five hours and CHF50 each additional person.

Group lessons for adults: CHF240 for three full days; CHF320 for five days.

Group lessons for children: CHF50 for a half day; CHF200 for five half days.

The ski school offers special classes in freeriding, carving, skicross, and park and pipe to help intermediate skiers improve their technique. Call for prices.

Snowboard lessons are available throught the Snowboard Fahrschule in Laax-Murschetg (081-9277155), Falera (081-9213030) and Flims Dorf (081-9277156). Group lessons are CHF90 for a full day and CHF395 for five days. Private lessons are CHF200 for one to three boarders for two hours. Four-hour lessons for one to three boarders costs CHF380.

Lift tickets (2007/08 prices)

A combination ticket that allows unlimited skiing in the Flims Laax Falera area costs as follows (a photo, which they take at the lift station, is required for lift passes of six days or more):

	Adults	Children (6–12)	Youth (13-17)
one day	CHF64	CHF21	CHF43
two days	CHF127	CHF42	CHF85

Seniors, males 65+ and females 62+ geet 10 percent discount on adult prices..

Discount cards: With a Jackdaw Youth Card, kids ages 13–17 receive a 50 percent reduction on the basic adult price. Senior citizens, who have the Pioneer Card and are skiing for six days or more, get 20 percent off the basic price for adults . Check out www.alpenarena.ch/clubcard/eng/ to see how you can get these discount cards by registering on the Internet or call 081 927 70 02.

Accommodations

Rates noted below are based on double occupancy during the high-season (February) with half pension:

€€€—€125+; €€—€75–€124; €—less than €75.

Prices are around 20 percent less in low season. All-inclusive White Week packages are available during special weeks throughout the winter season. They include seven nights accommodation, six days of lifts and five days of lessons.

Park Hotel Waldhaus (081-9284848; fax 081-9284858; €€€) The best hotel in Flims. A beautiful hotel that is almost its own small village. The buildings are interconnected by covered paths and underground walkways. You can be elegant and formal or casual in this complex in the woods.

Adula (081-9282828; fax 081-9282829; €€€) In Flims, this runs a close second to the Park Hotel Waldhaus. In fact, many people prefer it because it is cozier and smaller. It has an indoor pool, sauna, fitness room and a new spa. Its Barga restaurant is considered one of the best in the region. The Italian restaurant La Clav costs about half as much.

Albana Sporthotel (081-9112333; fax 081-9113109; €€) is next to the lifts.

Hotel Curtgin (081-9113566; fax 081-9113455; €€–€€€), an exceptional hotel, is also near the lifts and features light, modern cuisine.

Hotel Bellevue (081-9113131; fax 081-9111232; €€-) is only about 150 yards from the lifts and has one of the best traditional Swiss restaurants in town, Bundnerstube, nestled in the hotel's four-century-old cellar.

Arvenhotel Waldeck (081-9281414; fax 081- 9281415; €€) In Flims/Waldhaus this hotel is known for its restaurant that features very affordable daily menus. Rooms are done in knotty pine and the ambiance is casual.

Hotel Grischuna (081-911-1139; fax 081-911412; €€) 50 yards from the lifts.

Alte Säge (081-9112807; fax 081-9112841; €), only a five-minute walk from the lifts, is packed with boarders paying only €23 with breakfast in dormitory rooms. Dinners cost about €13.

In Laax the best places to stay are up at Laax-Murschetg near the lifts. Try the surprisingly affordable **Hotel Laaxerhof** (081-9208200; fax 081-9208210; €€) and **Sporthotel Signina** (081-9279000; fax 081-9279001; €€). The Laaxerhof has an indoor pool. The Sporthotel Signina has indoor tennis.

Hotel Rancho Laax (081-9271800; fax 081-9271899; €€) is, for lack of a better description, a condo-hotel. Some apartments are rented out with half-pension, others are rented as simply self-catered condos. This complex has an indoor swimming pool, fitness center and covered parking.

Garni Casa Selva (081-9212829; fax 081-9212827; €€) a B&B near the lifts.

Budget boarders and skiers can check out dormitory beds at the **Riders Palace** (081-9279700, fax 081-9279701; €) where bunks can go for only €20.

Down in the village of Laax-Dorf, stay in either **Arena Alva** (081-9272727; fax 081-9272700; €€) or **Hotel Bellaval** (081-9214700; fax 081-9214855; €€).

For a unique experience you can stay at the highest hotel in the Alps, **Crap Sogn, Gion Mountain Hostel** (081-9277373; fax 081-9277374; €€€). Sleep at an altitude of 7,309 feet in the summit station of the cable car.

Apartments, condominiums, flats

Flims, Laax and Falera are well organized to handle apartment rentals. Apartments are normally rented out for a minimum stay of one week, Saturday to Saturday; in the Christmas and Easter seasons a minimum two-week rental is often required.

The tourist office keeps a computerized, updated listing of available apartments. When writing, include the number of beds required, the preferred number of rooms, and your planned vacation dates. You will receive a quick response that lists a selection of apartments and prices. Select your apartment and contact Flims Tourism.

Normally, linen and kitchen utensils are provided. Other communal or private amenities, such as swimming pool, sauna, TV or room phone all add to the cost. Apartments rent for CHF40–CHF300 per person a night.

 ## Dining

Area restaurants are reasonably priced and most feature a good selection of international and regional specialties with some exceptionally fine dining available in both valleys.

The best in Flims, according to Gault Millau, is the **Restaurant La Cena** (081-9284848) in the Park Hotel Waldhaus. The **Fidazerhof** (081-9113503), filled with Swiss tradition, is rated by Michelin as the best in Flims.

In Laax, the **Posta Veglia** (081-9214466) is highly recommended for traditional Swiss cooking and has a two-Michelin-fork rating. The restaurant at the **Hotel Des Alpes** (081-9110101) comes highly recommended with affordable daily menus starting some days at less than €10 for three courses. For pizza try **Pizzeria Pomodoro**.

From Laax head directly to Sagogn about two-and-a-half km. from the village, for a dining treat at **Da Veraguth Carnetg** (081-9276464; fax 081-9213698). This place rates one Michelin star and dining is in an elegant rustic setting. Try the special ravioli, meatcakes and lobster with fennel. This is a gourmet treat that will cost about €65–€85. Make reservations early.

Other excellent restaurants in Laax-Murschetg are those at the **Hotel Laaxerhof** (081-9208200) and **Sporthotel Signina** (081-9279000) where both restaurants feature very affordable daily menus starting at about €13.

 ## Après-ski/nightlife

The best meeting spot in the area is the **Iglu Bar** in Flims that caters to a younger crowd earlier in the evening. An older crowd congregates for the special shows that start around midnight. The **Legna Bar** next to the Iglu also has good après-ski for the younger set. A few steps away from the Station there is the **Living Room** and the newly renovated **Stenna Bar**. Further away in Flims Waldhaus, there is the **Flem Massiv Bar**.

In Laax, the **Camona** offers action reminiscent of big city discos. The **Casa Veglia** in Laax has a somewhat older crowd and is more sedate. The younger crowd usually head to the basement of the **Rider's Palace**. You'll pay about €7 for a beer and €10 for a mixed drink.

The **Crap Bar** and the **Granite Bar** are hotspots for snowboarders.

 ## Child care (2007/08 prices)

Kindergartens associated with the famous Swiss Ski School operate in the area. In Flims and Laax, the children's ski school and kindergarten is open from 8:30 a.m. until 4 p.m.

Rates are CHF50 for a half day (3 hours); CHF70 for a full day; CHF200 for five half days; and CHF280 for five full days. Lunch is served, but must be requested at the time of booking. Supervised lunch is CHF20 per day.

Other activities

Ice skating is €4 a half day (€8 including skate rental). Play **tennis** in the Park Hotel Waldhaus in Flims and in the Hotel Signina in Laax. There are varying court prices for guests and non-guests depending on the time of day, ranging from €13–€26 per hour.

Six heated hotel **pools** are open to the public—Park Hotel Waldhaus, Schweitzerhof and Adula in Flims, and the Laaxerhof and Signina in Laax.

There is a public swimming pool in Laax. Entrance is €5 for adults and €3 for children.

Getting there

The closest airport is Zürich. From there you can take a train to Chur, where you must change for a postbus to Flims, Laax or Falera. The entire trip takes about three hours.

If driving, take the main road to Chur and continue until you see signs for Flims to the right. Driving time is about two hours. Do not try to approach Laax, Falera and Flims from the west—the Oberalp pass is closed in winter.

Tourist information

Office Flims, Alpenarena.ch, CH-7017 Flims, Switzerland; tel. 081-920-9200; fax 081-920-9201. Hotel and apartment booking: tel. 081-920-9202.

Office Laax, Alpenarena.ch, CH-7031 Laax, Switzerland; tel. 081-920-8181; fax 081-920-8182.

Office Falera, Alpenarena.ch, CH-7153 Falera, Switzerland; tel. 081-921-3030; fax 081-921-4830.

Internet: www.alpenarena.ch

E-mail: tourismus@alpenarena.ch

Gstaad-Saanenland

Mountain Rides

People associate Gstaad more with the jet set than with good skiing, and that's a mistake, because it has outstanding slopes for beginners and intermediates.

This Alpine village tucked into a scenic valley just east of Lac Leman (Lake Geneva), two hours from Geneva and 90 minutes from Interlaken, is part of a thriving ski circuit called Gstaad Mountain Rides. When you buy a lift ticket in Gstaad, or at one of the 10 smaller resorts in the area, you can use any of 62 lifts opening up about 250 km. of prepared trails. The other villages lie stretched along the railway line from east to west: St. Stephan, Zweisimmen, Saanenmöser, Schönried, Gstaad, Saanen, Rougemont, Chateau d'Oex, Les Moulins. Lauenen, Gsteig and Reusch are accessible by bus up the valleys fanning from Gstaad. If you're taking the train from Geneva, treat yourself to the special Golden Panoramic train that operates from Montreux to Gstaad and beyond. It doesn't take much longer, but the observation cars have huge windows to take in the views of Lake Geneva, the vineyards and the Alps.

 ## Mountain layout

The skiing in the immediate area of Gstaad is fragmented. Trail maps detail skiing in six "sektors," with most of the trails found in sektors 1 through 4. Sektor 1 is comprised of Saaenmoser, Schonried, Zweisimmen and St. Stephan, Gstaad-Rougement, Gstaad-Wispile and Gstaad-Wasserngrat; Sektor 3, Chateau-d'Oex; and Sektor 4, Glacier 3000, Les Diablerets.

Sektor 1 — The Hornberg section is the largest interconnected grouping of lifts in the region. It is not directly connected with Gstaad, but is easily reached by bus or train (both included with your ski pass). Take either the Horneggli lift from Schönried or the Saanerslochgrat gondola from Sannenmöser. Both lifts are opposite the respective railway stations, making it impossible to get lost. This area, a lower-intermediate paradise, is served by 14 lifts, which keeps waiting time to less than five minutes.

For more challenging runs, head for the St. Stephan lifts connected with Hornberg. Take the Saanerslochgrat gondola and ski down to Chaltebrunne.

Then take the chairlift up to the Parwengesattel, which sits at the top of the St. Stephan section. The face of the mountain from Parwengesattel down to Chaltebrunne is an enjoyable wide-open slope. There is something for everyone, from advanced beginner to expert. Time it right for lunch and eat at the Chemi Hütte at Lengebrand on the slopes above St. Stephan, at the top of the chairlift from town.

Opposite the Hornberg section is the Rellerligrat (6,285 feet) with what many claim is the most beautiful view of Gstaad. The slopes face the sun and so are the first to lose snow. Mornings can be icy and afternoons slushy, but skiing here on sunny days is a joy. The restaurant at the top is one of the best in the area. The runs back into the valley are long cruising trails, with a long black run under the gondola for experts.

Zweisimmen offers a relatively isolated ski area flanked on the left by St. Stephan and on the right by the Hornberg lifts. A new lift from Rinderberg to Saanersloch now connects this area with the rest of the trails. The gondola from town to the Rinderberg opens up seven prepared runs served by five lifts. It is pleasant for a day's skiing. Most of the people who stay in Zweisimmen take the train to ski the Hornberg section.

The relatively low Eggli (5,494 feet) is interconnected with the peak of Videmanette and the towns of Saanen and Rougemont.

The Wasserngrat (6,365 feet) and the Wispile (6,397 feet) are the two other totally separated areas. The Wasserngrat is the most challenging of the three areas, but it has only one lift. Still, the skiing is superb and there is rarely a line. If the Eggli is crowded, this area offers skiing with no waiting. It should be noted that beginners and lower intermediates may be slightly out of their league here.

The Wispile is not as difficult as the Wasserngrat and is closer to town. This is a good intermediate area with limited lifts but long, enjoyable runs; wide stretches of the slopes are left unprepared for powder hounds. It also has short lines and is within walking distance of the Eggli lifts. The Swiss Ski School is located at its base and the drag lift is used mainly by the ski school.

The Eggli shows one black run and an intermediate should seldom feel anxiety here. The run through the trees from the chair lift at Eggli Stand to the ground Mojo station in neighboring Saanen has enough moguls and turns for an expert.

There is some genuine skiing adventure above Gstaad. The finest is La Videmanette. Ski over the Eggli and down to the Les Gouilles chair lift to reach the area above neighboring Rougemont. You can also drive there. From Rougemont, four-passenger gondolas ascend past rocky pinnacles to the La Videmanette summit at 7,071 feet. The run down through the rocks off the back side is strictly for experts.

On the Videmanette front side, the first 300 meters straight over the edge is also an eye-opener. Skittish types can take the traverse around the rim of the bowl. There's a difficult mogul field to negotiate before beginning the remainder of the 3.5-mile intermediate run to Rougemont. Alternatively, ski around the corner to the top of the Les Gouilles lift and cruise the 3.5-mile-long schuss into the valley.

Sektor 3 — Chateau d'Oex is another area included in the regional ski pass. Here the La Braye gondola lifts skiers over a ridge behind the town to a mellow area of about a dozen runs also serviced by a couple of T-bars. This is a great family area that actually skis bigger than it is, and there's also an Alpine sled ride; fun!

Sektor 4 — The head-swiveling views are reason enough to ride the Col du Pillon cable car to Glacier 3000's 10, 637-foot summit, yet another reason is for lunch. The best reason is for the glorious advanced run from the cable-car summit at Scex Rouges down to Oldenalp. Stay on the groomed sections or venture off into the powder. Before trying that route, take a few runs on the glacier, serviced by three tows and one chairlift. The wide-open slopes are easy and short, the views extensive.

Descend to Col du Pillon base on trails or via the cable car. From the base, catch a bus to Les Diablerets, which has two sections: Isenau and Meilleret, both dominated by beginner and intermediate terrain.

From Meilleret, connect to the Villars-Gryon ski region. You can spend at least the better part of a day making your way across the mountains. requires the Villars-Gryon-Les Diablerets lift ticket which covers 36 lifts and 100 km. of terrain. Travel to Bretaye with an on-mountain train stop, then on to Villars, a large village with extensive shopping and dining. The expansive terrain is primarily intermediate and advanced. Stop for lunch or a break at any of the outdoor restaurants. Trails also connect to Les Chaux, which has a handful of intermediate and advanced runs and a terrain park at the summit. They connect to two beginner runs, one down to Gryon, the other meandering over to Villars.

Snowboarding: The Super Ski Region has freeride zones in Lengenbrand and Wispile-Feutersoey and four snow parks: Vanille Noir Park in Saanersloch-Saanenmöser, which has a kickerline, rails, a boardercross, a snowskate park and a barbecue zone; Snow Park in Glacier 3000, which opens in early October as soon as the Old-enegg-Reusch slope is passable; Schneefall Park in Rinderberg-Zweisimmen; and Snow Park La Braye in Château d'Oex.

Mountain rating

If you are a beginner, Gstaad is an excellent destination. There are plenty of gentle inclines to practice snowplows and turns. The finest beginner run is the 1.253-km.-long Skilift Schopfen slope from the gondola station on the Eggli.

Intermediates will be overjoyed at the variety. Just when you think you've mastered it all, you can cut through the woods or go over the edge of a mogul field you've been bypassing and suddenly realize you have more to learn.

Experts can enjoy Gstaad if they place more emphasis on technique than thrills.

 # Ski school (2007/08 prices)

Gstaad, with more than 100 instructors, has a good reputation for English-speaking ski instructors and for private lessons. It is open 8:30 a.m.-noon and 2:30 p.m.-6 p.m. The Gstaad Saanenland region has ten ski schools in various towns.

The following are the prices are for Gstaad Snowsports (033 744 18 65) to use as a price guide. The ski schools are pretty competitive and prices should be within CHF5 of each other.

Private lesson rates: one hour (one to four persons), CHF75; one hour (5 or more people), CHF80; full day (one to four persons), CHF320; full day (5 or more people) CHF350.

Group lesson rates: half day, CHF45; full day, CHF65; five days, CHF259.

Snowboarding lessons cost CHF75 for one hour and CHF320 for one day.

 # Lift tickets (2007/08 prices)

Lift tickets can be purchased for one Sektor or for the entire region. These multiday tickets are good for the entire Gstaad Mountain Rides area covering 62 lifts and 250 km. of runs for all lift tickets purchased for at least two days. They cover every town and slope mentioned in this chapter.

	Adults
one day (per region)	€22–€36.50
two days	€72.50
six days	€178.50

The one-day tickets are good in the particular sector where they are purchased. Lift tickets are also are good on the railroad, on buses and for entrance to the covered pool in Gstaad. Children age 9 and younger ski free.

Cross-Country (2006/07 prices)

Gstaad has 135 km. different runs; 81 km. of classic cross country trails and 54 km. of skating trails. Moreover dog lovers have the Hundeloipen in Saanenmöser and Schönried. Night skiers have the Schönried trail.

Tickets can be purchased at the tourism offices and on the course. Tickets cost: CHF8 for a Saanenland day ticket; CHF40 for a weeklong pass (7 days) for Saanenland and Sparenmoos; CHF65 for a Saanenland season ticket; and CHF100 for a cross-country skiing passport for all of Switzerland.

Accommodations

All hotels in the region offer special weekly programs running throughout the season except for holiday periods. These packages include seven nights' accommodation with half board, a six-day ski pass, cross-country or snowboarding pass, plus local transportation and entrance into the indoor swimming poolnights'.

Price ranges noted for each hotel are per person based on double occupancy high season with half board (breakfast and dinner): €€€–€125+; €€–€75–€124; €–less than €75. For information call 748-8181.

Gstaad Palace (033-748-5000, fax 033-748-5001; €€€) is the best place in town where you might get the chance, if you can afford the entrance, to rub shoulders with the movie, fashion and jet-set world.

Grand Hotel Park (033-748-9800, fax 033-748-9808; €€€) has an elegant and rustic restaurant, indoor salt-water pool, heated outdoor pool, fitness center, squash and tennis courts. The hotel is only two minutes' walk from the center of Gstaad.

Le Grand Chalet (033-748-7676, fax 033-748-7677; €€€) is a small, charming hotel on the hill with a magnificent view of Gstaad.

Bernerhof (033-748-8844, fax 033-748-8840; €€€) is centrally located with swimming pool, spacious rooms, great restaurant, good service and a good kindergarten.

Hotel Arc-en-Ciel (033-748-4343, fax 033-748-4353; €) is best for skiing the Eggli since it's near the gondola station. It's quiet, with a good restaurant.

Hotel Gstaaderhof (033-748-6363, fax 033-748-6360; €) has a good location relatively near lifts, station and downtown. It is known for good, affordable meals.

Hotel Alphorn (033-748-4545, fax 033-748-4546; €) is good for skiers; near the lift for the Wispile. It is a good place for meals.

Posthotel Rössli (033-748-4242, fax 033-748-4243; €) is one of the hotel prizes in town, but is small and booked very early. The restaurant is one of the best.

Sporthotel Victoria (033-748-4422, fax 033-748-4420; €) serves excellent food; has two restaurants and a pizzeria. The most reasonable hotel in town.

Saanen

Hotel Steigenberger in Gstaad/Saanen (033-748-6464, fax 033-748-6466; €€€) is a deluxe hotel with pool, sauna, good disco and two restaurants.

Landhaus (748-4040, fax 748-4049; €€) offers good, middle-priced rooms in the town center with a well-respected restaurant.

Saanerhof (033-744-1515, fax 033-744-1323; €€) is a 23-room hotel with a noted restaurant that offers affordable daily menus.

Alpine Lodge (033-748-4151, fax 033-748-4152; €€) features a Salomon rental shop, computers in every room, 24-hour Internet access, pool and fitness room.

Saanenmöser

Hotel Hornberg (033-748-6688, fax 033-748-6689; €€€) is everything a good ski hotel should be. It's near the lifts, has a pool and sauna and an owner who helps his clients.

Schönried

Hotel Alpenrose (033-744-6767, fax 033-744-6712; €€€) is a Relais et Châteaux property. Many claim the hotel restaurant is the best in the area.

Hotel Bahnhof (033-744-4242; fax 033-744-6142; €€) includes a ski school. This is the lowest priced major hotel in town with nice rooms and it's close to the station.

Chateau d'Oex

This town down the tracks toward Montreux from Gstaad is significantly less expensive than the Saanenmöser-Gstaad-Saanen area. The town is in the French part of Switzerland. It is not as charming nor as "Alpine" as Gstaad. But for overall savings of about 25 percent, this might be the place to stay if you don't mind the half-hour train ride to the major slopes above Gstaad and Schönried. Good English is spoken here.

Hostellerie Bon Accueil (026-924-6320, fax 026-924-5126; €€), built in an 18th-century chalet, is considered the best in town.

Residence La Rocaille (026-924-6215, fax 026-924-5249) is a tiny nine-room hotel with a wonderful restaurant that serves affordable meals daily.

Hotel de Ville (026-942-7477, fax 026-924-4121; €) is one of Switzerland's bargains with good meals thrown in for good measure.

Hotel Beau-Sejour (026-924-7423, fax 026-924-5806; €) is very conveniently situated across from the train station and the cable car to the Chateau d'Oex area.

Hotel Ours (026-9242279, fax 026-9242270; €) sits in the center of town about three minutes from the lift and train station.

Rougement

The four-star **Hotel Rougement** (026-925-8080, fax 026-925-9185; €€€) has an indoor pool, exercise room and restaurant and is within walking distance of the tiny village's shops and restaurants. The morning croissants alone are worth the visit.

Villars

Eurotel Victoria (024-495-3131, fax 024-495-3953; €€€) has an inhouse restaurant, bar, game room, sauna and indoor pool. It is in town and just steps from the base of the slopes.

Apartments, condominiums, flats

Vacation apartment rentals are available in every village. Information on rentals is provided by the tourist offices. In middle season an apartment with one bedroom, living room and furnished kitchen costs approximately €450–€900 a week. Ample room for four people is typical. Call 033-748-8184 for reservations.

 # Dining

Even with Gstaad's jet-set reputation, the best restaurants are just outside town. Naturally, the Palace has several world-class restaurants, but then again most of us are not up to Palace prices.

The Cave in the Olden Hotel (033-744-3444) in the center of town has excellent dining by anyone's standards. Expect to pay top price, but you'll never know with whom you'll rub shoulders.

Always vying for best gourmet restaurant in town, and winning according to Michelin, is the one-star **Chesery** (033-744-2451, fax 033-744-8947) serving phenomenal Asian-influenced cuisine. Open your wallet wide.

The **Sonnenhof** (033-744-1023) in Saanen-Unterbord has mouth-watering meals with vistas that are hard to beat. You must call for reservations.

The best Italian meal is at **Rialto** (033-744-3474). The menu will run about €27. The **Arc-en-Ciel** opposite the Eggli gondola is stark but serves excellent Italian food at low prices. The **Rössli** across the main street from the Olden has typical Swiss cooking at its best.

Out-of-Gstaad Places

Schönried has the **Alpenrose** (033-744-6767) with a Relais et Châteaux gourmet restaurant. This small nouvelle cuisine restaurant is one of the tops in Switzerland. An exceptional traditional Swiss restaurant is the **Bären** (033-755-1033) in Gsteig on the road from Gstaad to Les Diablerets.

Down the road from Gsteig try the **Rössli** in Feutersoey (033-748-4242). In tiny Lauenen enjoy a meal at the **Wildhorn** (033-7653012). In Rougement, the cozy **Cafe du Cerf** (026-925-8123) prepares traditional fondue and raclette as well as local meats, and serves them in a 300-plus-year-old chalet where traditional music is played.

Finally, don't miss the 17th-century **Restaurant Chlösterli** (033-748-7979) outside town on the road to Gsteig. In Villars, Chef Joel Quentin's **Peppino** at the Eurotel Victoria (024-495-3131) is a real treat, with emphasis on native Alpine herbs, flowers and produce. Beyond that, there are pizzas, pastas and local beef.

On the slopes

The best mountain restaurants above Gstaad are at the Eggli and Kalberhöni. Above Schönried, try the **Hornberg** restaurants—one is slightly more upscale, the other has wonderful *rösti* and plenty of pasta. Both have great terraces to enjoy the sun. **The Rellerli Mountain Restaurant** on the opposite side of the valley from Hornberg enjoys a storybook view of Gstaad. Try the **Chemi Hütte** at Lengebrand above St. Stephan.

In Château-d'Oex make sure to stop at **Chamois** for a wonderful meal and a panorama from 3,753 feet. **Restaurant Botta 3000** tops Glacier 3000. The views are endless; the traditional fare superb.

 ## Après-ski/nightlife

The place for après-ski just off the slopes is the **Olden Bar**. It's normally packed. Otherwise, even on Friday night, this town snoozes until midnight.

The **Chesery Bar** and the **Stöckli Bar** in the Bernerhof were recommended as the best places to have a beer or drink, but both are very quiet. **VIVA** in the Hotel Victoria is popular. **The Grotte** in the Hotel Alpin Nova is a good disco.

The well-heeled enjoy an après-ski drink in the **Palace Hotel** lounge above the city. Take money if you want to join them. For starters, the Palace disco cover is €6.

After dark there's a lively crowd and live music at the **Chlösterli** disco outside town. Also try the **GreenGo** at the Palace Hotel for dancing.

Gstaad also has a swanky casino.

 ## Child care

The Gstaad Tourist Office can help with child care arrangements. Call 033-748-8181. The ski schools all have programs – call 033-744-1865 in Gstaad or 033-748-8160 in Saanen.

In Chateau d'Oex, call Mme. Blati at Les Clematites, 026-924-

7351. She cares for children from 2 months old. The ski school has children's lessons, 026-924-6848.

Other activities

Gstaad has an excellent covered **swimming pool**. The town is in a good spot for train or auto **excursions** to Montreux, Geneva, Lausanne, Interlaken and Bern which are all about two hours by train.

There are world-class **toboggan runs** here. Eggli-Grund is 6 km. Turbach is 2 km. and Chinnetritt-Gsteig is 6 km. That's a long way to slide. **Ballooning** over the Alps provides a once-in-a-lifetime thrill, and Chateau d'Oex is renowned for it. Balloon rides can be arranged through the tourist office (033-748-8181). The price is €325–€350 per person for about two hours. **Paragliding, ice skating**, **curling** and **horseback riding** are available (033-744-2460).

Rougement has three claims to fame: cheesemaking, découpage and the Rougemont Church. You can purchase locally-made cheeses in town (look for the "produits authentiques" stamp). Don't miss the opportunity to visit with some of the fine papercutters and view their exquisitely detailed works. The Romanesque church dates back to 1080 A.D.. Three of its four bells date from the 15th century; the fourth was cast in honor of the 900th anniversary of Rougement.

In Chateau d'Oex, the Musée de Vieux Pays-d'Enhaut is a small, wonderful museum with emphasis on the region's history and culture. Visit the Caves de L'Etivaz, where fromage d'Alpage is made. Les Diablerets has a **tubing park**, a 7-km. **sledding run**, 30 km. of **winter walking** and 15 km. of **snowshoe** trails.

Getting there

Zürich international airport is about three-and-a-half hours by train to Gstaad. Rental cars are also available in Zürich. You may also arrive in Geneva which doesn't have as convenient train connections, but is closer by rental car. The Golden Panoramic Train from Montreux to Rougement and on to Gstaad is a treat. Villars is around 2 hours from Geneva via train.

Tourist information

Information on the Ski Gstaad Region is through
Gstaad Saanenland Tourist Association,
CH-3780 Gstaad, Switzerland.
Telephone 033-748-8181; fax 033-7488133.
Tourist Office Chateau d'Oex: 026-9242525.
Internet: www.gstaad.ch E-mail: info@gstaad.ch

Office du Tourisme Rougemont,
CH-1659 Rougemont, Switzerland
Telephone 026-925-1166; fax 026-925-1167
Internet: www.rougemont.ch E-mail: info@rougemont.ch

Tourist Office Chateau d'Oex, 026-9242525.

Office du Tourisme Villars, CH-1884, Villars, Switzerland
Telephone 024-495-3232; fax 024-495-2794
Internet: www.villars.ch E-mail: information@villars.ch

Jungfrau Region

Grindelwald, Wengen, Mürren

The spectacular and far-flung Jungfrau region is near Interlaken on the map; for intermediate skiers it is at the end of the Alpine rainbow. A network of 213 km. of trails spreads over a vast expanse of slopes, set in two majestic valleys about an hour's drive from Bern, the Swiss capital. The backdrop created by the Jungfrau, Mönch and Eiger mountains is one you see on posters the world over. This series of valleys is the definition of picture-postcard beautiful.

The Jungfrau region has three major ski areas accessible from its twin-valley towns. The best-known resort is Grindelwald, a settlement at the foot of 10,000-foot peaks about 30 minutes by train or car from Interlaken. Wengen is a car-free resort, reached only by cog railway from Lauterbrunnen, that shares many of Grindelwald's ski areas. And Mürren is another car-free town on the opposite side of the Lauterbrunnen Valley tucked beneath the Schilthorn.

Skiing is more or less divided into three regions. Grindelwald has skiing at Grindelwald First (First, in this case, means peak), which in its day had Europe's oldest operating chairlift. Ironically, this is also the location of the first chairlift in Switzerland.

The second area (actually two well-connected areas), Kleine Scheidegg and Männlichen, is effectively shared between Grindelwald and Wengen lying just beneath the brooding Eiger.

The third ski area, Mürren/Schilthorn, is across the Lauterbrunnen Valley and is also reached only by cog train or cablecar. Mürren is a tiny village, as perfect as a movie set. In fact it was, for James Bond in *On Her Majesty's Secret Service*.

 ## Mountain layout

The Jungfrau Winter Region has scores of lifts including railway routes up the mountain. Grindelwald and its surrounding hills and mountainsides are divided into seven pie-slice pieces radiating out from the center of town.

The 9,609-foot Schwarzhorn, on your left as you enter town from Interlaken, is the backdrop for the **Grindelwald First** slopes. It used to be a real pain to reach even for those staying in Grindelwald. However, the creaky chairlift sideways ride was an experience. Alas, no more. Or should we say, Hooray! A gondola now leaves from the city core of Grindelwald, about 50 yards off the main street, taking skiers to the upper reaches of the area that is a beginner and intermediate playground.

First offers plenty of skiing on its own. In the U.S. any resort would be overjoyed to have this much terrain and vertical drop (4,705 feet—more than any resort in the United States). There are 50 km. of prepared trails here, with good limitless off-piste runs.

Most skiers stay at the higher altitudes, on the runs under the Oberjoch and the trails served by the Schilt and Grindel chairlifts. This area is shielded from the wind and provides the most varied skiing.

Kleine Scheidegg is reached by taking the cog train from Grindelwald. It takes about 35 minutes to reach this Alpine ski village trisected by railway tracks. Across from the parking lot of the Grund station is the Männlichenbahn, a gondola lift.

If you take the cog train you can yo-yo your way across towards Männlichen on the Arven, Honegg, Gummi, Tschuggen and Läger lifts. The skiing gets progressively more difficult as you work your way across, until you arrive at the Männlichen area.

From the Kleine Scheidegg station take the lift to the top of the Lauberhorn and then either ski back toward Kleine Scheidegg or loop around to the Wixi lift and Wengen, more or less following the famous Lauberhorn downhill race course. It's a delightful ski experience, with a seemingly endless variety of dips, turns, mogul fields and occasional ice patches—perfect territory for the advanced intermediate. Try the run from the Lauberhorn to the Wixi chairlift, picking your way through the mogul fields. When the snow is good, this run is exceptional.

The cog train takes skiers up to the next stop, Eigergletscher, where several steep runs drop back down toward Wixi and Wengen and over-the-ridge runs also descend toward Grindelwald alongside the Salzegg lift.

At the end of your day, there is a marvelous 30-minute run to Grindelwald that passes the Arvengarten lift base before reaching a network of intermediate trails that offer a touch of adventure—there is always an easier way around the tough places for the less advanced. This run to the car park of the Männlichen gondola or to the Grund cog train station may be the highlight of your stay in the Jungfrau region, unless you're counting the chills of Mürren's 007 Run as a fun experience.

Männlichen is reached by taking the gondola from Grund directly to Männlichen. You will rise 4,223 feet of vertical, which can be skied in one long expert run or one long intermediate run.

Most skiers remain at the upper level of the Männlichen and play on the wide-open slopes served by the Männlichen and Läger chairlifts. From the Läger chair skiers drop down to the Gummi chairlift and work their way over to Kleine Scheidegg. These runs between Männlichen and Kleine Scheidegg are a delight for all skiers.

Wengen: The town sits at the base of the cliff dropping from the Männlichen and the Lauberhorn areas. There is a choice of taking either the cablecar from town to the Männlichen area, or the cog train around the Lauberhorn to the Kleine Scheidegg area. The only way back to town without parachute or hang-glider is around the Lauberhorn under the Wixi lift, down to the Bumps T-bar, then along the trails to the town.

Mürren: For ski challenges in this region, savvy downhillers head for the Schilt-thorn, the mountain above Mürren, across the gorge from Wengen. Take the cog train from Lauterbrunnen to Mürren and then go by cablecar the rest of the way; or take a direct cablecar from Stechelberg, outside Lauterbrunnen.

There is less good skiing but more challenges on the Schilthorn than at any of the other areas. The eye-opener is the black run from the 9,748-foot Schilthorn. Start by quaffing an extra-strong cup of espresso or have lunch in the Piz Gloria revolving restaurant atop the Schilthorn, then tackle the famed Inferno, also called the 007 Run.

The lower section, called the Kanonenrohr (Cannon Barrel), sends you hurtling down a series of narrow, steep, bumped-up, rutted and often icy trails. Actually, good intermediates can make it haltingly down the entire run. The Engetal area, approximately a third of the way down from the Schilthorn, offers plenty of wide-open skiing, with the option to take the last stage of the Schilthorn cablecar up to the top for another chance to carve your way down. It's below the Engetal area that the series of narrow and steep spots come into play.

Adventurous skiers also tackle the black runs from the 7,035-foot Schiltgrat. This area has excellent bumps and some super-steep off-piste skiing. Intermediates stay on the flat top of the ridge. Connecting lifts take skiers to the Winteregg and Allmendhubel, the mountain's other two ski areas, where intermediate skiing—with an occasional black run—is the rule. The best intermediate run leads down to the base of the Winteregg chair, where you can lunch at an excellent restaurant.

If coming up from Lauterbrunnen on the train for Mürren, get off at the stop at the Winteregg chair and work over to Allmendhubel and the Schiltgrat and Schilthorn.

Snowboarding: The Grindelwal First area has always been somewhat of a snowboarders' hangout with a snowpark and a superpipe together with some good off-piste trails from the Oberjoch. And has become even more so with the addition of another boarder's park at the Bärgelegg ski lift. Mürren has a funpark with a halfpipe. Klein Scheidegg / Männl also has a snowpark that features bumps.

Mountain rating

Grindelwald First: This is an intermediate and beginner playground with some expert flashes. The panoramas toward the Eiger and the Schilthorn are spectacular.

Kleine Scheidegg: Working one's way around the mountain toward Männlichen from Kleine Scheidegg requires good skills, but can be handled by most intermediates. The Lauberhorn can get bumped up, but still can be skied by any intermediate. The Wengen side with the Lauberhorn run is perhaps the most challenging. The runs dropping from the Eigergletscher down to the Wixi are expert territory, and intermediates can also make the drop down the Salzegg side.

Männlichen: The wide-open area at the top of the gondola is perfect for every level of skier. Intermediates and experts will have a blast playing on the trails that wend over to Kleine Scheidegg. The long run to the base of the gondola is a joy.

Wengen: The nursery slopes surrounding this town are the best in the valley. If you are a beginner or traveling with a beginner, Wengen is the best village to stay in. It's also the sunniest of the ski areas.

Mürren: Don't plan to ski Mürren extensively if you're a beginner. There are some intermediate slopes that the absolute beginner may be able to handle after a few days, but just barely. Intermediates will be pushed. Experts will find that the slopes of the Schilthorn and the Schiltgrat are the most challenging in the entire Jungfrau area.

Cross-Country and snowshoeing (2006/07 prices)

Grindelwald: This area has approximately 15.5 km of cross country trails including a few sunny runs up on Bussalp and skating and cross-country runs in Grindelwald Grund. Use of the slopes are free although it is recommended that you buy a €16.60 weekly cross country sticker as a donation to for the maintainance of the trails.

Wengen and Mürren: Wengen does not have a cross-country run, but cross-country skiers are well catered for in the lovely Lauterbrunnen Valley. The 12 km Lauterbrunnen - Stechelberg piste glides along the banks of the Weisse Lütschine River into the far end of the valley, catering for both classic and skating styles. In Blumental, high above Mürren, you'll find the sunny 2 km Mürren -Sonnenberg run.

The ski and snowboarding schools, the Tourist Office and sports shops organize snowshoeing treks including a one day trek around snow covered villages or a two day trek with a fondue evening and an overnight Alpine hut stay.

 ## Ski school (2007/08 prices)

All major resorts in the region have ski schools offering downhill, snowboarding and cross-country instruction. The prices for the various ski schools are similar. Some of the programs vary. These prices are for the Grindelwald Swiss Ski and Snowboard School (033-854-1280).

Private skiing lessons

one hour	CHF75
half-day (2.5 hours)	CHF210 (a.m.); CHF190 (p.m.)
full day (5 hours)	CHF330

Group skiing lessons

full day	CHF105 (Mondays only)
three days (12 hours)	CHF275 (Mon. to Wed.)
five days (20 hours)	CHF395 (Mon. to Fri.)

Grindelwald also has the Buri Sport Private Ski- and Snowboard School (033-853-1427), Felix children ski school (033-853-1288), Privat-Ski.ch (033-853-0473) and Swiss Ski and Snowboard School Kleine Scheidegg (033-855-1545).

Wengen has the Schweizer Ski School Wengen (033-855-2022), the Privat Ski and Snowboard School (033-855-5005) and the Ski and Snowboard School Kleine Scheidegg (033-855-1545). **Mürren** has the Schweizer Skischule Mürren (033-855-1247).

 ## Lift tickets (2007/08 prices)

The Jungfrau Winter Region Sportpass for a two-day minimum includes Mürren, Schilthorn, Männlichen, Kleine Scheidegg and Grindelwald First, as well as all cog trains and ski buses. Sportpasses good only for individual areas and group passes are also available.

Note: Children must be accompanied by a parent. Children age 6 and younger ski free with parent. Also, all seniors and teenagers and adults who want to purchase sport-passes for 10 days or longer must have a photo I.D. Prices includeVAT. An additional CHF5 per Sportpass is required as a deposit on the reusable electronic KeyCard.

Jungfrau region	Adults	Teenagers (16–19)	Children (6–15)	Seniors (62+)
two days	CHF123	CHF98	CHF62	CHF111
three days	CHF169	CHF135	CHF85	CHF152
six days	CHF295	CHF236	CHF148	CHF266
fourteen days – (with photo)	CHF487	CHF390	CHF244	CHF438

Grindelwald/Wengen	Adults	Teenagers (16–19)	Children (6–15)	Seniors (62+)
one day	CHF57	CHF46	CHF29	CHF51
two days	CHF107	CHF86	CHF54	CHF96
six days	CHF265	CHF212	CHF133	CHF236

	Adults	Teenagers (16–19)	Children (6–15)	Seniors (62+)
Mürren/Schilthorn				
one day	CHF57	CHF46	CHF29	CHF51
two days	CHF105	CHF84	CHF53	CHF95
six days	CHF250	CHF200	CHF125	CHF225

Accommodations

Price ranges noted for each hotel are high season (February) per person based on double occupancy with half board (breakfast and dinner): €€€—€125+; €€—€75–€124; €—less than €75.

Grindelwald

Grindelwald has 49 hotels, and 45 of them are owned and managed by families. Many of the hotels are 100 years old, and most are smaller than 100 beds.

Grand Regina Alpine Wellfit Hotel (033-854-8600, fax 033-854-8688; €€€) Grindelwald's only five-star hotel, with excellent location by the Jungfrau cog railway station is as luxurious as it gets in this town. Jacket and tie worn in the candlelit dining rooms. Old-World elegance. Has a new wellness center.

Hotel Schweizerhof (033-853-2202, fax 033-853-2004; €€€) A chalet-style hotel with downtown location near the Jungfrau cog railway station.

Sunstar Hotel and Sunstar-Adler (033-854-7777, fax 033-854-7770; €€) This is a modern hotel across from the Grindelwald-First lifts. One side faces First; the other side faces the Eiger and Kleine Scheidegg.

Hotel Spinne (033-854-8888; fax 033-854-8889; €€).

Derby Bahnhof Hotel (033-854-5461; fax 033-854-2426; €€) Hotel with an excellent location handy to the Jungfrau cog railway station.

These hotels (with 25 or fewer rooms) are recommended—**Bodmi** (033-853-1220, fax 033-853-1353; € €), **Caprice** (033-854-3818, fax 033-8543819; €€), **Fiescherblick** (033-854-5353, fax 033-854-5350; €€), **Glacier** (033-853-1004, fax 033-853-5004; €€), and **Alpenhof** (033-853-5270, fax 033-853-1915; €€).

The following Garni or B&Bs are also recommended—**Grindelwalderhof** (033-854-4010, fax 033-854-4019; €), **Cabana** (033-854-5070, fax 033-854-5077; €), **Hotel Bernerhof** (853-1021, fax 853-4646; €€) and **Bellevue Garni** (tel/fax 033-853-1234; €) in the middle of town—ask for a room with bath.

Wengen

Beausite Park Hotel (033-856-5161, fax 033-855-3010; €€€) This is now the most elegant and upscale hotel in Wengen. It has indoor pool and sauna. It overlooks the wide-open beginner slopes and is near the Männlichen cablecar. With good snow, you can ski right back to the front door.

Hotel Silberhorn (033-855-5131, fax 033-855-5132; €€€) One of the first hotels in Wengen, directly across the street from the station. Recent renovations have all rooms with light pine furniture, sauna and whirlpool. Known for healthy servings at the dinner table, you can choose from four different dining rooms.

Wengener Hof (033-856-6969, fax 033-856-6970; €€) Popular with ski racers, particularly during Lauberhorn race week, but a bit out of the center of town.

Hotel Eiger (033-856-0505, fax 033-856-0506; €€) By the station, this is a locals' place, too, not as Alpine-looking on the inside as it seems from the outside.

Hotel Berghaus (033-855-2151, fax 033-855-3820; €€) A very pleasant hotel next to the Beausite Park and the Männlichen lift. All rooms have TV.

Alpenrose (033-855-3216, fax 033-855-1518; €€) Noted for its setting and traditional meals.

Hotel Hirschen (033-855-1544, fax 033-855-3044; €€) This is a charming mountain inn with one of the best kitchens in Wengen. The rooms are small, but each has a modern shower and toilet squeezed in.

Ski Chalets: available through Crystal (see page 18 for contact information).

Staying on the mountain above Grindelwald and Wengen

Scheidegg Hotel (033-855-1212; fax 033-8551294; €€+) is a bit worn, but for overall experience, the finest lodging in the area for the skier; overlooks Kleine Scheidegg station in the shadow of the Eiger. Thirty minutes by train into the mountains from Grindelwald. Reserve well ahead.

Skiers looking for very basic accommodation can stay in a dorm above Scheidegg train station, Silvi's Mountain Lodge, for €20 per person €25 with breakfast or €36 with half-board. Rooms are €35 with breakfast and €47 with half-board.

Hotel Jungfrau (033-855-1622, fax 033-855-3069; €€€) sits at 6,234 feet altitude, in Wengeneralb, with wonderful views of the Jungfrau. Reached by the cog railway, it only has 22 rooms. Skiers can stop here for lunch, but dinner is only for residents.

Mürren

Hotel Eiger (033-856-5454, fax 033-856-5456; €€€) This is the class act in Mürren as far as hotels go. The owner is delightful and the perfect hostess. This hotel can stand as a definition of excellent service. The restaurant is one of the best in town, and the bar is a gathering spot for locals.

Hotel Alpenruh (033-856-8800, fax 033-856-8888; €€€) As close to the lifts as you can get. This is a restored chalet with great views and exceptional decor in the old Swiss style. The restaurant presents Mürren's best nouvelle cuisine.

Jungfrau (033-855-4545, fax 033-855-4549; €€€) This hotel looks absolutely Gothic, with spires and peaked roof, but you step through the door into a time warp—everything is so modern, guests at first may have trouble finding the elevator button. Right in the center of town, near the sports center with its indoor pool.

Hotel Blumental (033-855-1826, fax 033-855-3686; €€) A three-star hotel not far from the center of the small town.

Hotel Alpina (033-855-1361, fax 033-855-1049; €–€€) Good hotel with family discounts. Excellent view and a quiet setting, but a long walk from the lifts.

Hotel Alpenblick (033-855-1327, fax 033-855-1391; €) Small hotel with great views, two minutes from the cog-train station but a long way to the Schilthorn lifts.

For unusual places to stay up on the mountain, Mürren has two guest houses in the middle of the slopes that get rave reviews from those who know them. These are the **Pension Flora-Suppenalp** (033-855-1726; €) and the **Pension Sonnenberg** (033-855-1127; €). Neither has private baths. They have only a handful of rooms, but both have dormitory space and are filled with atmosphere.

Eiger Guesthouse (033-856-5460; fax 033-856-5461) Swiss-Scottish run, cozy and relaxed hotel near the BLM Train Station with splendid view of Eiger, Mönch and Jungfrau. Offers comfortable budget accommodation, restaurant, bar and gameroom.

Lauterbrunnen

Hotel Silberhorn (033-856-2210, fax 033-855-4213; €) Ten minutes' walk from the cog trains to Kleine Scheidegg and Mürren. Great views.

Hotel Schützen (033-855-3025, fax 033-855-2950; €) Comfortable and only eight minutes' walk from the cog train.

Staying in Interlaken

Interlaken has begun to emerge as a hotel center for skiers planning to ski the Jungfrau area. It is only a 45-minute bus ride from the lower lift stations and as a relatively large city it has nightlife and good dining. Two reasons for staying in Interlaken may be persuasive for some visitors.

First: Interlaken hotels and ski packages are much less expensive than those of Wengen, Mürren and Grindelwald. In general, Interlaken menu prices are about one-quarter less than Grindelwald's. (**Piz Paz** is a satisfying Italian restaurant, in the medium price zone. At **Yelp Beers & Comics** on Centralstrasse, 400 brands of beers are available.) Second: If you are traveling with a non-skier, Interlaken has more to offer than the liveliest Jungfrau resort, Grindelwald, and is in a perfect position for day trips to many Swiss cities such as Bern, Lucerne, Zürich and even Zermatt.

If neither of these considerations applies, then head into the mountains. If you are a real skier, this city is probably too far from the mountains to keep you happy. If you're sharing a vacation with a non-skier, it's perfect.

Apartments, condominiums, flats

There are many apartments and chalets for rent in the Jungfrau region. The local tourist offices have prices and locations, and will assist in booking.

A typical apartment in Grindelwald, Wengen or Mürren with one bedroom for two, living room (with sleeping space for two more people), kitchen and all utensils costs about €800 a week in high season; €600 in midseason. The only extra is tax.

Dining

Grindelwald

In Grindelwald you can choose from more than 50 restaurants. For a very special (and expensive) meal, try the dining room, **Pendule d'Or**, in the **Grand Hotel Regina** (033-854-8600); it may serve the best meals in town. Chateaubriand for two costs about €85. The **Hotel Spinne** restaurant has good Swiss and international specialties, and a full wine cellar. The most crowded eatery in town is normally **Barry's Restaurant** (Hotel Eiger; 033-854-3131) which has Swiss and new cuisine. **Ristorante Mercato** has a good Spaghetti Rustico for €12. A Hopfenperle Bier brings the minimal meal to €15. Pastas, usually Bolognese or Milanese, and pizzas are the best dining value in local restaurants. The pastas are about €8–€12. A decent wine will cost at least €12.

At the Hotel Schweizerhof, the **Schmitte Restaurant** (033-853-2202) has surprisingly affordable specials of the day. **La Marmitte** and **Hilty-Stübli** at the Hotel Kirchbühl (033-854-4080) has excellent affordable meals. The restaurant at Fiescherblick, **Swiss Bistro** (033-854-5353), has daily menus for about €23.

Other good affordable spots are the **Adlerstube** (033-854-7777) in the Hotel Sunstar, **Memory**, in the Eiger (033-854-3131), the **Kreuz und Post** restaurant (033-854-5492), the **Alpina** (033-854-3344) and the **Glacier** (033-853-1004).

Wengen

The best restaurant town is **Chez Meyer's** (033-856-5858) in the Hotel Regina. Call for reservations. One of the best typical meals and excellent fondue *chinoise* is found at the **Hirschen** (033-855-1544). The best fondue and raclette can be found in the **Bernerhof**. **Restaurant Eiger** in the Hotel Eiger (033-856-0505) serves good fare with a nice outdoor dining area for sunny days. The **Bären** (033-855-1419), **Sunstar** (033-856-5111), **Schönegg** (033-855-3422) all have Michelin recommended affordable menus in ascending order of cost. Some of the best fish dishes are found at **Berghaus**.

Sina's and **Pizzeria da Salvi** have good pizza.

Mürren

In town the **Alpenruh** (033-856-8800) serves the best nouvelle cuisine in a beautifully rustic setting. The **Edelweiss** (033-856-5600) is also recommended for an affordable daily menu. The **Eiger** (033-856-5454) has excellent traditional Swiss fare, real U.S. cut steaks, and the best fondue—either Chinoise or Bourguignonne—in town. The **Palace Hotel Mürren** and the **Stägerstubli** both have excellent cheese fondue. The restaurant in the **Hotel Blumental** is perhaps the most rustic and atmospheric spot to enjoy Swiss specialties. The **Eiger Guesthouse** (033-856-5460) offers good moderate meals at similar prices. For Italian try **Peppino** at the Hotel Palace or **Taverna**.

Lauterbrunnen

A meal at the **Silberhorn** (033-856-2210) is excellent and affordable. **Schützen** (033-855-2032) serve good meals at massive wooden tables.

On the slopes

Enjoy at least one midday meal inside the **Piz Gloria**, a revolving restaurant (033-8552141) on the Schilthorn. Lower down, stop in at **Restaurant Allmendhubel**, tiny, cute and filled with locals; or at the new **Winteregg Restaurant**, which has great lunches and excellent après-ski. The **Flora-Suppenalp** or the **Sonnenberg** serve excellent stick-to-your-ribs mountain meals.

At the **Berghotel Männlichen**, even the cafeteria fare is served on china plates. For sun worshipping, a lounge chair and blanket rent for €3.50. **Mary's Cafe** on the trail down to Wengen has a great raclette at lunch. The restaurant at the railway station at Kleine Scheidegg has excellent meals at good prices.

Interlaken

This is an international tourist center and starting point for excursions in the Bernese Oberland, one of Switzerland's most beautiful regions. No-smoking restaurants are an extreme rarity in Switzerland, and McDonald's in Interlaken is one of the few.

 Après-ski/nightlife

Grindelwald

The **Gepsi-Bar** and **Expresso Bar** (try Kaffe Fertig with Schnapps) are the singles' meat market and the hottest immediate après-ski hangouts, where folk squeeze in and stay for the duration. **Le Plaza Club** disco in the Sunstar Hotel is the hottest spot for nightlife and gets crowded. **Mescalero** in the cellar of the Hotel Spinne is not as packed but gets interesting, depending on which groups are in town. For Country & Western music try the **Challi Bar** in the basement of the Kreuz & Post Hotel. The **Bodenwald** and the **Glacier** have traditional music and entertainment. For quieter conditions, try the **Alte Post Bar**, the **Hotel Wolter Terrace** or the **Hotel Kreuz Terrace**.

Live music or a DJ for dancing and listening are offered nightly in the **Hotel Grand Regina** and the **Challi Bar**. The **Mescalero Club** under the Hotel Spinne and the **Plaza Club** under the Hotel Sunstar are both open to 2:45 a.m.

A nighttime adventure you will remember is sledding from the tiny Gasthaus at **Bussalp** back down into Grindelwald. A bus will take you up and sleds will be waiting after a fondue or other Swiss dinner. Call the tourist office for prices and to make your sled and dinner reservations. (033-854-1212).

Wengen

Check out the Eiger Hotel's **Pickel Bar**, the **Tanne Bar, Hot Chili Peppers** and the **Silberhorn** terrace on sunny days for good après-ski. Nightlife is more limited here, since after dark only the group staying on the mountain will usually be around, although trains run until late evening. Try the **Tiffany Disco** in the Silberhorn, or **Carrousel** in Hotel Regina for dancing or head to piano bars for a quiet evening. The **Tanne Bar** and **Rocks Cafè and Bar** are good late night get-together spots.

Mürren

For immediate après-ski, head to the base of the **Winteregg**, to the old and rustic **Stägerstübli** filled with grizzled locals and a handful of tourists, the **Bellevue** across from the ski school, the pub in the **Eiger Guesthouse** for socializing, or hang out on the terrace of the **Jungfrau Bar**. For later nightlife in Mürren, head to the Hotel Eiger's **Tächi-Bar**. This bar gets a crowd aged around 27 and up. The **Inferno Disco** has a mixed clientele ranging from age 18 to 27. The **Bliemlichäller** in the cellar of the Hotel Blumental, with video games, attracts a younger, virtually all-teenage crowd.

Child care (2006/07 prices)

Grindelwald: The Swiss Ski and Snowboard School Grindelwald (033-854-1280) runs the Bodmi Kinder-Club. Bodmi is open from Monday to Friday, from 9:30 a.m. to 4:00 p.m. and takes care of children age 3 and older. Prices are €14 for one morning; €14 for one afternoon; €34 for a full day; and €14 for a supervised lunch and nursery care.

For children age 3-5, the Swiss Ski School has the Bambini program. Prices are €27 for a half day; €80 for three half days; and €120 for five half days.

Children age 6 and older can also take ski lessons. Half day prices are the same as for the Bambini program. Full day lessons cost €50 for a full day; €129 for three days; and €178 for five days.

The Grindelwald ski school will take care of and feed kids at lunch for €8.

On top of First and Männlichen there are also nurseries that provide hourly or daily care.

Wengen: The Playhouse Wengen (033-855-1414) is open from Sunday to Friday from 9 a.m. to 5 p.m. Children age 18 months or older are welcomed. Lunch is at the Hotel Sunstar. Wengen, with its no-traffic environment, is one of the premier resorts for families with children. It has good nursery slopes and plenty of easy tracks back to the town.

Mürren: The Snowgarden for Children takes little ones from 9:30 a.m.–4 p.m. They provide a pick-up service, lunch and a full day's care. Lunch is from noon to 1 pm. Call the tourist office for more information.

Private babysitters are also available call 033-855-3706 or check with the tourist office or your hotel for assistance.

Other activities

Fully 30 percent of winter visitors to Grindelwald are non-skiers, and there is plenty for them to do. Hikers, skinny skiers and snowshoers have their own trails throughout and around the ski areas. They're even groomed, to a width of about eight feet, and good for **sledding**. You can **hike** or ride a lift up. There is even a restaurant above First, to which the lifts don't even come close—you'll have to walk, but as Mark Twain said in *A Tramp Abroad,* "There is no opiate like Alpine pedestrianism."

The smart shops in Bern and the really charming Old-World center of the capital city merit a side trip.

Grindelwald offers the widest range of non-skiing activities such as **ice skating, curling, hang-gliding, sledding, swimming** and **hiking**.

The Grindelwald Winter Festival in mid-January has snow sculpture contests feature four-member teams from around the world.

The sports center, on the main street of Grindelwald, is excellent, with **swimming, sauna complex, fitness rooms, climbing room** and **ice skating**.

There are great toboggan runs from Bussalp—Bussalp to Grindelwald is eight km., the race course is 4.5 km. and Faulhorn to Bussalp to Grindelwald is 15 km. The postbus connects Grindelwald with Bussalp. Bus fare is €13.20.

The Jungfraubahn cog railway

The Jungfraubahn that takes skiers up the mountain is also a delightful outing for the non-skier. It bores through the Eiger's north face to the Jungfraujoch. The entire route through the mountain took 14 years to build and was finished in 1912.

A stop inside the mountain allows passengers to look through windows at the precipitous mountain face. At the top, the train arrives at 11,333 feet, the highest railway station in Europe. A spectacular building houses a restaurant, an ice palace carved into the glacier and outdoor observation platforms with views down over the glacier.

Be careful navigating your next path if you're in ski boots! It's an entanglement of pathways carved through an ice tunnel. Glittering passages, mysterious niches and stairways pass ice sculptures sprinkled along the route and end up at an ice bar where typical Swiss ice wine is served to giddy singing, playful children in adult bodies.

Piz Gloria

Piz Gloria and its revolving restaurant were chosen as the villain's lair in the James Bond movie, *On Her Majesty's Secret Service*. The movie features a wild chase on skis from the restaurant to the car-less village of Murren below.

A series of cablecars and cog trains haul you up to the Schilthorn, a 9,748-foot- tall peak surrounded by a sea of 200 spectacular snow-covered Alps with a view of France, Germany, and of course, much of Switzerland. Along with a 200-mile-radius view on a clear day, the Piz Gloria restaurant offers a special local dish: rare, local mountain mushrooms or "steinpilz" over pasta. It's as fabulous as the vista.

Getting there

The most frequently used international airports are Geneva and Zürich. Rail connections are frequent and excellent to Interlaken and on to Grindelwald, Wengen or Mürren.

Tourist information

Wengen Tourismus, CH-3823 Wengen, Switzerland; Telephone (033) 855-1414, fax (033) 855-3060. Email: info@wengen.ch Internet: www.wengen-muerren.ch

Grindelwald Tourismus, CH-3818 Grindelwald, Switzerland; Telephone (033) 854-1212, fax (033) 854-1210; Email: touristcenter@grindelwald.ch. Internet: www.grindelwald.ch.

Mürren Tourismus, CH-3825 Mürren, Switzerland; Telephone (033) 856 8686, fax (033) 856 8696. Email: info@muerren.ch Internet: www.wengen-muerren.ch.

Jungfrau Winter Region, CH-3800 Interlaken, Switzerland; Telephone (033) 828-7233, Fax (033) 828-7260; Email: info@jungfrau.ch. Internet: www.jungfrauwinter.ch.

Klosters

A small and traditional village, Klosters offers the low-key atmosphere and relative obscurity that make it the perfect hideaway. The English royal family, most notably Prince Charles, has chosen Klosters as their winter ski center for several years. They come for the excellent skiing and the relaxed elegant atmosphere. You will probably like Klosters for the same reasons. The houses surrounding the town proper are a bit more elaborate than most other places you'll visit, giving an immediate tipoff that Klosters is a cut above. The central town area is small and quaint, but packed with specialty stores.

Think of Klosters, little more than a suburb of Davos, as Davos' little sister resort, the beauty of the family who has been kept hidden. Both resorts share the Manhattan-sized, wide-open expanse of the Parsenn, but Klosters has the more challenging runs into town. Klosters also has its own ski runs and lift system in the Madrisa area, on the opposite side of the valley from the Parsenn. The entire Klosters-Davos ski area offers 200 miles of runs served by more than 50 lifts.

 ## Mountain layout—Skiing

From the village center, 3,937 feet high, the lift system takes you to 9,330 feet on the Parsenn side at the Weissfluhgipfel, and up to about 7,874 feet on the upper lift of the Madrisa.

The Parsenn is the best-known area and is reached by the Gotschna cable car, which leaves every 15 to 20 minutes in ski season. The cable car lets you off at the Gotschnagrat, where you can either traverse to the Parsenn or ski under the cable car to a T-bar and chair lift. The Parsenn reaches its peak at the Weissfluhgipfel (9,330 feet) where it drops into two expert runs. Here it is wide open, offering both beginners and intermediates a paradise for cruising. The Parsenn has 40 seemingly endless runs, including what was once Europe's longest—from Weissfluhjoch to Kublis. If you like carefree cruising, you will love the Parsenn.

The Madrisa area is much smaller: some 30 miles of runs served by seven lifts. The area is reached by cable car from Klosters-Dorf, an outlying hamlet, which is a hike from the center of town. The area runs are mostly beginner and intermediate. When the sun is out, the Madrisa slopes are bathed with warming rays the entire day, something to remember when it's cold but sunny. The longest and most scenic Madrisa run is from Glatteggen, 8,340 feet down to the Schlappin overlook, then down to the Madrisa cable car.

For the jaded, Madrisa is a springboard for an exciting ski mountaineering trek to Austria, which combines both skiing and climbing. The Swiss Ski School can line you up with a guide for this adventure if the snow quality is good.

Mountain layout–Snowboarding

The Sunrise Snowpark at 2,599 meters above sea level has various rails and rolls, two kicks and a quarterpipe. In the center of the park is the 110-meter-long, 5.5-meter-tall Nidecker Monsterpipe. Boadercross-Parcours on Madrisa has snakes, jumps and turns and is situated about 200 meters below the top station of the Schaffürgli lift.

There's also a relatively new free-style park at the Selfranga Lift which has rail-boxes and kickers. The park is also lit for nighttime boarding on Tuesdays from 7-9 p.m. and Fridays from 9-10 p.m.

Mountain rating

Klosters earns an A-plus from beginning and intermediate skiers. The Parsenn is perhaps the ideal terrain for learning to ski and perfecting your technique.

Experts may find the Parsenn terrain somewhat boring and should ask instructors where the most challenging skiing can be found. The best expert runs on the Parsenn are from the top of the Weissfluhgipfel. Otherwise, stick to the trails that drop into town alongside the Parsennbahn, or take the Drostobel-to-Klosters run, which is narrow and sometimes steep. The Wang trail, which runs directly under the Gotschna cable car, is one of the toughest expert runs in Europe. Unfortunately, it seems to be closed more often than open, but if it's open and there is no avalanche danger, you're in for an experience. Watch yourself here: This is the spot where Prince Charles narrowly escaped an avalanche and his aide was killed while skiing out of bounds.

The Madrisa area is strictly for intermediates, beginners and sun-worshippers.

Cross-Country & snowshoeing (2006/07 prices)

The area has 35 km. of trails for skating and classic skiing, including 7 km. of dog trails and 3 km. of night cross-country ski trails from the Aeuja Bridge on Tuesdays and Thursdays from 6 p.m.-9:30 p.m.

The use of the cross-country ski trails is free. For more information, call 081-4152133 or 081-4102020.

Snowshoeing: The Swiss Ski and Snowboard School Klosters (081-4102828, fax 081-4102829) offers guided tours on a set schedule. Price per person, 4 people or more, is €43 for a night tour including snowshoes. There's also a tour every Wednesay, call for prices. The Alpine Adventure Graubünden (081-332 32 42, fax 081-3223573) provides individually guided snowshoe tours.

Ski school (2006/07 prices)

The Swiss Ski and Snowboard School Klosters (081-4102828) is divided into six levels and also offers special children's courses and cross-country instruction. Classes meet either on the Madrisa or near the Gotschna. There is also the Ski and Snowboard School Saas in Klosters Dorf

(081-4202233). Duty Swiss Snowboard School Klosters (081-4226660) offers extreme snowboarding, freestyle and racing lessons. Nordic Ski School (081-4221040) offers cross-country skiing lessons.

These prices are for the Swiss Ski and Snowboard School Klosters.

Private lessons for one to two skiers or boarders cost €57–€60 for one 50-minute lesson; €140–€147 for one half day (two-and-a-half hours in the morning or afternoon); and €213–€227 for a full day (four-and-a-half hours). There is an additional fee of €13 for each extra skier or boarder.

Group lessons (full-day courses only) cost €157 for a three-day course and €48 for each addtional day. Lessons for a group of 4–8 snowboarders cost €213 for a three-day course that includs board and boots and €48 for each additional day.

 ## Lift tickets (2007/08 prices)

Separate passes are sold for each of the five areas.

An adult day ticket for the Parsenn area costs €41; for Madrisa, Riner-horn and Pischa, €33; for Jakobshorn, €37.

The most convenient pass to use is the Klosters/Davos all-inclusive pass (REGA). It includes the Madrisa side of the valley, plus use of the train that runs between Davos and Klosters and as far down the valley as Kublis. It is also good on local buses in Davos and Klosters.

	Adults	Children (6-12)	Teen (13-17)
one day	€43	€15	€30
two days	€82	€29	€57
three days	€114	€40	€80
six days	€190	€67	€133
fourteen days	€344	€120	€241

Children younger than 5 ski free. There are 10 percent discounts for REGA passes purchased for three days or more before Christmas season.

Accommodations

The best time to ski Klosters is during one of its special organized Ski Weeks. These weeks are normally held in early December, the last three weeks of January through the first week of February, and late March through April. Contact the tourist office for the special rates, which include lift tickets together with room and board.

Rates based on per person, double occupancy with half-pension in February are €€€—€125+; €€—€75–€124; €—less than €75.

The **Hotel Alpina** (081-4102424; fax 081-4102425; €€€) has great location, indoor pool, nice staff, and reservations can be made through Best Western.

Perhaps the most traditional hotel is the **Chesa Grischuna** (081-4222222, fax 081-4222225; €€€). It is part of the Romantic Hotel chain, but though it has ambiance, the rooms are small and there is no pool.

At the upper end of the scale is the four-star **Hotel Pardenn** (081-4232020, fax 081-4232021; €€€+). A hike from the ski shuttlebus and 10 minutes walk from town. It has plenty of five-star comfort—pool, sauna and fitness room. The **Sunstar Albeina** (081-4232100; fax 081-4232121; €€) is recommended by Michelin and is a bit less expensive than the Pardenn. Other recommended hotels are the **Steinbock** (081-4224545; €€) and **Silveretta Park** (081-4233435; €€€), only a short walk from the lifts.

The tiny, 11-room **Hotel Rustico** (081-4221212; fax 081-4225355; €€–€€€) is only steps from the lifts and downtown. It gets rave reviews from locals and tourist press for meals and comfort. **Sporthotel Kurhaus** (081-4224441; fax 081-4224609; €–€€) with 30 rooms is highly recommended for both meals and rooms. The **Cresta** (081-4232600; fax 081-4232610; €€+) also has a very good restaurant.

Sonne (081-4221349; €), a traditional B&B, is inexpensive and convenient.

The less expensive lodging is in Klosters-Dorf, near the lifts for the Madrisa area but a hike or shuttlebus ride from the Parsenn lifts. Try **Jost** (081-4223344; €), **Büel** (081-4222669; €) and **Casa Erla** (081-3225275; €), a group of condos with kitchenettes for only €34 a night per person.

Apartments, condominiums, flats

Apartments are normally rented out for a minimum of one week, Saturday to Saturday. In the Christmas holiday season a two-week minimum rental is required.

The tourist office keeps track of available apartments. Write and let them know the number of beds required, preferred number of rooms and dates of your stay. You'll get an immediate response from apartment owners with a choice of apartments and prices. Select the apartment you want and return their forms.

Normally, linen and kitchen utensils are provided, while extras, such as swimming pool, sauna, TV or room phone all add to the cost. Standard units rent for €22 to €39 per person a night.

Dining

The **Walserhof** (081-4102929; fax 081-4102939) is in a class by itself. If you want to eat here, make reservations very early. Expect to pay €50–€100 for your meal.

Highly recommended and much more traditional and rustic with quite affordable fixed-price menus are **Chesa Grischuna** (081-4222222), **Hotel Alpina** (081-4102424), **Restaurant Steinbock** (081-4224545), **Rustico** (081-4221212), **Sporthotel Kurhaus** (081-422-4441) and **Cresta** (081-4232600). Try the **Alte Post Aeuja** (081-4221716) for fondue specialties such as fondue bourguignon and enjoy the very traditional atmosphere. Full meals can be enjoyed at all these restaurants for as little as €15.

A bit out of town by taxi or sleigh ride is **Höhwald** in Monbiel (081-4223045) with a wonderful rustic setting. The **Hotel Wynegg**, open only during the winter season, also has a good restaurant with reasonable prices and is packed with Brits. In Madrisa head to **Bahnhof Restaurant** or **Pizzeria Al Berto**. Also try the new **Pizzeria Fellini** (081-422221) in Klosters Platz.

Après-ski/nightlife

On the way off the slopes stop at the **Serneuser Schwendi Hut** for a great time. Ski down to **Gaudi's Graströchni** at the end of the slope for après-ski.

Klosters' nightlife centers around its major hotels. **Casa Antica** is in the Silveretta Park. In Klosters-Dorf head to **Rufinis** or **Madrisa Pub**.

Pizzeria Fellini has a fabulous après-ski tea as does the **Chesa Grischuna**. The bar in the **Pardenn** for a late evening visit is intimate and relaxing, but a bit stuffy. Better still is the bar of the **Chesa Grischuna** where there is quiet piano entertainment.

Also recommended: **Rossli Bar** and the **Gotschnabar** in Klosters Center.

Child care (2006/07 prices)

Madrisa Kids' Land (081-4102330) (076-4977224) has a fun park with amusing obstacles and magic carpets. Also on Madrisa mountain, there is a child's tubing run, a mini-kids' area for ages 2 and younger, as well as a restaurant. Children ages 2- 6 are welcome. It's open from 9:30 a.m. to 4 p.m. and costs CHF10 for the first hour and CHF5 for each additional hour. Lunch costs CHF8.

The Swiss Ski and Snowboard School in Klosters (081-4102828) provides a Snowgarden in the Snowli Swiss snow Kids Village for children, with a magic carpet, pony lift and tepee, located just opposite the sports centre and right in the centre of Klosters Platz. A supervised lunch including meal and drink costs CHF20 per day, per child. Children's ski and snowboard lessons cost CHF46 for one morning; CHF124 for three mornings; CHf195 for five mornings; CHF67 for a full day; CHF179 for three days; and CHF272 for five days.

Children ages 3-12 who are guests of the Silvretta Parkhotel can join the Flipper-Club. From late December until the end of April and from early June until mid-October, the Flipper-Club provides supervised care for children in either the indoor playroom or outside in the area around the hotel. One day including lunch costs €23. A half day (9 a.m. to noon or 1-5 p.m.) costs €13.

A detailed list of babysitters with addresses is obtainable from Klosters Tourismus. Prices vary between CHF10– CHF20 per hour.

Other activities

Klosters is rather quiet. Visitors looking for other activities should take the train to Davos, only 15 minutes away. Klosters has an open-air **skating rink, horse-drawn sleighs** and **tobogganing**. There are five covered hotel **pools** in town; check with the hotel for the facility rates.

Getting there

The closest airport is Zürich. Klosters is two-and-a-half hours by train, with a change in Landquart.

If you decide to rent a car, take the Zürich-Chur road as far as the Landquart/Davos exit. The drive from Landquart to Klosters is through the narrow valley and passes through Kublis before arriving at Klosters-Dorf and then Klosters. The distance from Zürich is about 90 miles.

Tourist information

Tourist Office, CH-7250 Klosters;Telephone 081-4102020, fax 081-4102010. E-mail: info@klosters.ch. Internet: www.klosters.ch Normal hours are Monday through Friday, 8.30 a.m.– 6 p.m. It is also open 9 a.m.–noon and 1– 6 p.m. on Saturdays and 9a.m. – noon and 1 p.m. – 4 p.m. on Sundays .

Saas-Fee

Saas-Fee is a village of very narrow streets, wooden chalets, small hotels and year-round skiing. It's for serious skiers—the ones who care more about the number of black-rated runs on the mountain than the number of discos in the village. Nestled in the next valley from Zermatt, Saas-Fee allows no private cars in town; you park on the outskirts and take public transportation.

The town occupies a magnificent site at 5,904 feet, ringed by 13 separate peaks of 13,000 feet or more. Snowcaps on these mountains are permanent, as is skiing on the Allalin. Saas-Fee also has its own snowmaking equipment on the beginner slopes below. That, combined with the glacier runs above, means that your vacation will never be in danger from poor snowfall.

 ## Mountain layout—Skiing

Saas-Fee's nearly 100 km. of downhill trails are superbly divided between beginner, intermediate and expert. Absolute beginners start on the Saas-Fee town lifts, where they usually stay for about three days. Later they ski either the Plattjen lift or the Felskinn.

The first area to get the morning sun is the Spielboden/Längfluh. These runs are on good intermediate to expert terrain. From Längfluh down to the chair lift is intermediate country. If you ski past this middle station, get ready for the steep and narrow.

From the top of the Längfluh cable car there is a drag lift right on the glacier. This lift connects the two main ski areas of Längfluh and Felskinn/Mittelallalin.

The Felskinn/Mittelallalin area is the most popular section of Saas-Fee's trails. Two small lifts tow skiers from town to the lower station of the Felskinn cable car.

Once at the top of the Felskinn cable car, you're whisked up another 1,600 feet on the underground Metro Alpin to Mittelallalin. Here, stop to enjoy the magnificent panorama of dozens of 13,000-foot peaks. Intermediates, and beginners brave enough to come this far, should traverse to the left, and experts should cross to the right, in front of the revolving restaurant. Skiers have a choice of doing several runs or heading back to the Metro Alpin underground and the Felskinn area.

To the left of the Felskinn cable car, a drag lift opens to a delightful smaller area—the Egginer. Strong intermediates will be satisfied with the Egginerjoch lift.

The rest of the Felskinn runs crisscross under the cable car back toward town. The area between the middle station and the top of the Felskinn is a beginner and intermediate playground. The drop back into the village steepens considerably, and experts have a challenge on the Kanonenrohr and Bach trails.

The final section of Saas-Fee's ski domain, the Plattjen, catches the last of the day's sunshine. This area is served by a long top-to-bottom six-person gondola. The gondola takes skiers up from town (5,910 feet) to Plattjen (8,430 feet), resulting in a run with a little more than a 2,500-foot vertical drop. There are uncrowded trails for all abilities.

One interesting point for anyone searching for a place to go summer skiing, the new lifts have opened 20 km. of slopes on the glaciers at 11,811 feet above sea level. Saas-Fee has constructed a year-round snowboarding park on its glacier complete with halfpipes, quarterpipes, rails, tables, gaps and a high jump for professionals.

Mountain layout–Snowboarding

Snowboarders have a snow park with jumps, five rails, a halfpipe and a triple kicker line. In the Saas valley, there are four snowboard schools as well with lessons covering all aspects of the sport.

Mountain rating

Experts will never complain about the runs at Saas-Fee. There's enough black to make things interesting.

Intermediates may think that the lift network and trails were laid out with them in mind: most trails above Saas-Fee start with an intermediate or beginner stretch, often with the option of taking an expert plunge.

Beginners can work toward becoming advanced beginners on the Saas-Fee town slopes; then the slopes above the valley beckon.

Cross-Country (2007/08 prices)

There are 32 km. of cross-country trails through forests and along the Vispa River.

The 26 km.-long Saas Valley trail goes from Saas-Balen via Saas-Bidermatten, Saas-Grund, Unter den Bodmen, Saas-Almagell and Zermeiggern to Eiualp. Depending on snow conditions, there are also 10–16 km. of skating pistes available in addition to the 26 km. of trails groomed in the classical style. There are bus-stops at regular intervals so that you can ski the whole trail or just individual sections. A one-day pass is €4 (€6 with bus); and a one-week pass is €22 (€32 with bus).

The 6 km. groomed cross-country trail in Saas-Fee is free of charge.

Ski school (2007/08 prices)

The Skischule Saas-Fee (027-9572438) has approximately 100 instructors. English is no problem.

Private lessons cost €46 an hour for one person and €53 for two persons. An hour for three persons cost €60 and €66 for four people. Five hours of lessons including lunch break cost €220 for one or two persons and €254 for three or four people.

Group lessons (three hours a day) are €36 for a day; €125 for five days.

Special **ski mountaineering off-trail adventures** have been organized in the past for climbs to the top of the Alphubel and Allalin. These treks start with a two- to four-hour climb and end with long, high altitude powder cruises through virtually virgin snow. Tours are limited by both the weather and the availability of qualified instructors. From mid-February through the end of the season the treks depart approximately once a week.

"The Haute Route" is a classic ski adventure tour between Saas-Fee, Zermatt, Courmayeur and Chamonix. These trips are organized from mid April to the end of May. For this tough, physical trek participants should be in good shape and must be able to ski in deep snow. The mountain climbing school conducts a different special tour from early May until the first week in June. Contact: Mountain Life Office, CH-3906 Saas-Fee; (027-9574464, or the tourist office at 027-9581858). The classic "Haute Route" costs approximately €1,000, including guides, accommodations in mountain huts, meals, hotel expenses during the tour, and mountain railway and bus.

 ## Lift tickets (2007/08 prices)

	Adult	Youth (age 17-18)	Child (age 10-16)
one day	€42.50	€36	€21
three days	€128	€108	€42
six days	€215	€182	€114
fourteen days	€383	€326	€210

New for winter 2007/2008, children age 9 and younger ski free when accompanied by a parent.

Beginners can purchase tickets for only the village lifts. These tickets are valid for unlimited travel on all the facilities in Saas-Almagell, Saas-Grund, Saas-Balen and Saas-Fee and include the post buses until 7 p.m.

The resort also offers a ticket for five of seven days costing €185 for adults and €98 for children; and 10 of 14 days for €304, adults and €167 children.

Accommodations

Price ranges noted for each hotel are per person based on double occupancy during February with half board (breakfast and dinner): €€€—€125+; €€—€75–€124; €—less than €75.

Ferienart Resort and Spa (027-958-1900, fax 027-9581905; €€€) The best hotel in town. For a splurge, try the suite with round bed, white marble bath and sauna.

Allalin (027-9571815, fax 027-9573115; €€) This four-star hotel has hand-carved wooden furniture. It is at the far end of town from the lifts, but has ski storage facilities at the lifts. They have some of the best food in town.

Mischabel (027-9572118, fax 027-9572461; €€€) At the entrance of the town, about a seven-minute walk to most lifts.

Au Chalet Cairn (027-9571550; fax 027-9573380; €€€) A rustic gem with only 16 rooms and a traditional atmosphere.

Hotel Waldesruh (027-9586464, fax 027-9586465; €€) Near the Plattjen and Längfluh gondola ground stations. Caters to families and has a wonderful, affordable restaurant.

Hotel Marmotte (027-957-2852, fax 027-9571987; €–€€) This hotel shines because of its owner, Karl Dreier, who makes everyone feel at home. Karl, who doubles as the chef, cooks some of the best hotel food we've eaten. There is a free ski storage arrangement with the Waldesruh Hotel opposite the Felskinn lift, and a free baby sitting arrangement with Hotel Alphubel, a good hotel for children.

Derby (027-9572345, fax 027-9571246; €€) Good family hotel near Felskinn and Plattjen.

Hotel Europa (027-9589600; fax 027-9589696; €) Small hotel for those planning to do some hiking on the Hannig.

Mühle (027-9572676, fax 027-9572677; €) Small basic hotel.

Feehof (027-9579700; fax 027-9589701; €) (Garni only) Inexpensive. No telephone, no public restaurant and no credit cards accepted.

Ski Chalets: Crystal, Inghams/Bladon (see page 16 for contact information).

Apartments, condominiums, flats

Apartments are the way to go if you really want to save money. Saas-Fee has about 1,500 chalets and apartments for rent. Write to the tourist office and ask for apartments that will be available when you plan to be in Saas-Fee. Include details on the number of people in your party. The office will send a list of available apartments and a map showing locations. Select the apartment you want and write to the tourist board or to the owner. The reservation line for apartments is 027-958-1868.

The apartments normally include linen and kitchen utensils. You will be charged a visitor's tax, and there may be an extra charge for the electricity and heat you use.

Expect to pay €20–€35 per person per night, based on location and the number of people sharing the apartment.

Dining

The best restaurant in the region is the **Fletschhorn** (027-9572131; fax 027-957-2187), a 30-minute walk from town or a 10-minute taxi ride. It is considered one of the best in Switzerland and features nouvelle cuisine. The 2007 "Chef of the Year" award was given to the Waldhotel Fletschhorn and it also received its 18th Gault & Millau point. Make reservations early. Meals will range from €85–€115.

Perhaps the second-best eatery is the **Hohnegg** (027-9572268), just about a 10-minute walk above the town (or call for its taxi service). Also nouvelle cuisine in a Swiss country atmosphere. It features a daily menu selection starting at less than €15.

Le Mandarin Thai restaurant in the Ferienart Resort and Spa (027-9581900) serves Asian cuisine for €30–€60. The Italian restaurant in the same hotel, **Del Ponte** is highly recommended with meals from €25–€55 and pizzas for only €10–€13.

For excellent traditional local Walliser food, try the **Golfhotel Saaserhof** and the **Schäferstube**. For cheese and Swiss specialties the top recommendations are the **Käse-Keller** (027-9572120) and the **Arvu Stuba** (027-9572747).

For good, less expensive meals, try the **Hotel Allalin** (027-9571815)—a rebuilt 300-year-old room with wooden beams and hand-carved chairs that make it magical by candlelight; **Hotel Dom** (027-9575101) for great *rösti*. **La Gorge** (027-9581680) and the **Du Glacier** (027-9581600) also have excellent fondue and raclette. **Chüestall** has various steaks (027 958 91 60).

For pizza, try the restaurant **Spaghetteria da Rasso** or the **Boccalino**, in front of the Saaserhof. Pizza or pasta is €10–€13.

On the slopes, have at least one lunch in the revolving restaurant on the **Allalin**. The prices are down to earth. The mountain restaurant **Berghaus Plattjen Terminus**, is great for a late lunch when the area catches the sun. It has great *rösti*.

The mountain restaurant **Meeting-Point Morenia**, at 2, 500 meters next to the Alpin Express and Snowpark serves a wide variety of foods buffet-style.

On the opposite side along the Längfluh run, where it meets the Gletschergrotte trail cutting off from the Kanonenrohr, is the **Gletscher-Grotte**, which catches sun most of the day.

A good lunch with beer and coffee at most spots on the mountain costs €15–€18. Fondue is about €24 and a normal three-course dinner will be about €24.

In Saas Grund try the **Hotel Dom** (027-9572233) for magical setting and very affordable meals.

Après-ski/nightlife

Saas-Fee is known as a town for young skiers and those who think young. The **Crazy Night** in the Metropol has good music with an 18–25 crowd. **Pic Pic** is a Swiss locals' spot; the **Alpen Pub** and the **Popcorn** (young crowd and snowboarders) normally have a good crowd; **Feeloch** under the Du Glacier and the **Go-Inn Bar** and **Poison** attract the young lively crowd.

Après-ski, as the slopes close, is an early affair because the sun drops behind the mountains quickly. If you're off the mountain at around 3 p.m., the terrace bars at the **Derby, No. 1 Bar, Mühle, Rendezvous** and **Christiania** do a great business. After 4 p.m., when the sun drops out of sight, the crowd evaporates. Most gather in bars like **Chemi Stube** in the Christiania, the **Saaserhof, Nesti's,** the **Black Bull** or the **Rendezvous**.

Child care (2007/08 prices)

The Kids Fun Park at the Saas-Fee sports field combines snowplay with skiing lessons. The Fun Park is for children age 4 and older and is open Monday to Friday from 9:30 a.m. to 3:15 p.m. It has a magic carpet that makes it easier for children to go up the hill; funny figures on the slalom course; a snow carousel that pulls children around in circles; and tubing.

The Swiss Ski and Snowboard School Saas-Fee (027-9572348) offers activities for children. One full day (including lunch) costs €55 and one week (including lunch) costs €230. Mornings from 10:00 a.m. to 1 p.m. cost €36 for one morning and €125 for a week of mornings.

The school also offers both the Pulvo ski course and the Junior ski course. The Pulvo is a beginners only course for children age 4 and older, Monday to Friday from 1:45 p.m. to 3:15 p.m. and cost €24 per day. The Junior ski course is for children aged 5 and older, Monday to Friday from 10 a.m. to 1 p.m. and costs €36 per day or €125 for a week.

Other activities

The Hannig area is now closed to skiers. It gets good early morning sun and is now the location of a 5-km. **toboggan** run. Tobaggans can be rented from the sports shops or at the Hannig cable car station.

Visit the **Saaser Museum**, packed with photographs of the old Saas valley, and old tools, kitchen utensils and furniture of mountain people. Open from 2–5 p.m., the museum charges €3.50 for adults, €1.50 for children to age 16.

The **Bielen sports and leisure center** has been newly renovated. It offers an 25-meter, heated indoor swimming pool, an indoor tennis court, billiards and table tennis, exercise room, whirlpools, steam bath and coed sauna. Tennis court should be reserved. Open all week from 10 a.m. to 9 p.m. The indoor pool costs €9.50 for adults and €5.50 for children. The sauna area costs €14 for adults. Every Tuesday morning from 7–10 a.m. they also offer breakfast.

Getting there

By train: From Zürich airport via Bern, Spiez, through the Lötschberg tunnel to Brig. From Geneva, trains run directly to Brig. Travelers by rail reach the Saas valley via Brig or Visp, and change into the post-car with direct destination "Saas Fee." There are connections every hour until 8:05 p.m. from Brig or 8:25 p.m. from Visp.

On December 9, 2007, the base tunnel through the Lötschberg will open making the trip tfrom the north into the Valais considerably shorter. There will also be a new junction at Visp, which will shorten travelling time by about an hour. Post bus service will leave for Saas-Fee every 30 minutes from Visp.

By car: Private car travelers from the north approach via Bern through the Lötschberg tunnel (railway car ferry). Trains transit the tunnel every half-hour from 5:35 a.m. to 11:05 p.m. The trip takes only 15 minutes. Cost per car (including nine-seat vans) is €13–€16. From Goppenstein, drive to Visp, then on to Saas-Fee.

From the east and south via the Furka and Simplon.

From western Switzerland you reach Saas-Fee via Lausanne, and along the Rhone valley to Visp. Motorway until Siders East.

Park in the public lot at the town entrance. Call your hotel for pickup, or take a taxi. Taxis from the parking lot and bus station to town cost about €10.

Tourist information

Saas-Fee Tourism, CH-3906 Saas-Fee, Switzerland
Telephone 027-958-1858; fax 027-958-1860.
Reservations: 027-958-1868.
Internet: www.saas-fee.ch or www.saastal.ch
E-mail: to@saas-fee.ch

Verbier

Seen from below in the fading day, the flickering lights of Verbier beckon as if from Olympus. This quaint Swiss town rests in the saddle of majestic mountains nearly 5,000 feet above the valley floor. It is the crux of Switzerland's renowned "4 Valleys," a vast, interconnected web of Alpine valleys and towns that comprises over 402 km. of ski runs and 93 individual ski-lifts. With some of the most challenging ski terrain and scenic vistas in the Alps, a southwesterly orientation that maximizes sun exposure, and the 850-year history of the surrounding "Val de Bagnes" region, Verbier epitomizes the kind of adventure unique to the European "superski" networks.

Though sizable at nearly 15,000 beds, Verbier is dominated by chalet-style houses and mid-size hotels, giving it a traditional Swiss feel that is at odds with the multi-story hotel blocks and modern atmosphere typical of many major French resorts. This is the French-speaking region of Switzerland, but thanks to its standing as one of the most popular Alpine destinations for British tourists, Verbier also hangs out an "English is spoken" plaque for its visitors.

 ## Mountain layout—Skiing

This resort is at one end of the Four Valleys area. It links with Thyon, Veysonnaz and Nendaz. Verbier has the best skiing for experts and advanced skiers, a decent beginner area, and new intermediate trails.

The Savoleyres area is the smallest of the Verbier sectors. A gondola takes skiers up to mellow trails. This area doesn't get too many crowds, is full of sunshine all day long, and the lift lines stay manageable for the most part. During the early season, skiing back to Verbier is relatively easy, however during the late season the snow coverage requires most skiers to download on the gondola.

The main Verbier area is on the north-facing slopes with the main lifts rising to Ruinettes and Attelas. This section gets crowded and at the lower levels skiers need to be careful to keep from running into each other.

From the Attelas upper station, cablecars rise to the Mont Gelé glacier. The problems here are: weather, which closes the area many days, and the long lift lines, which can be a pain.

One intermediate secret is the Bruson area that is connected with the rest of the Four Valleys by a 15-minute bus trip from the lower station of the Châble cablecar. The trails here are far from the maddening crowds. On powder days, this is a wonderful spot to practice turns and perfect technique.

Experts and advanced skiers will have the time of their lives with virtually limitless off-piste possibilities. Many of the formerly black runs have been redefined as itineraries. They are not groomed or marked, but have so much traffic, they may as well have been marked by the resort as they once were. A guide is highly recommended in this area to get the most out of the mountain.

Mountain layout–Snowboarding

Like some other meccas of free ride, Verbier's snowboarding depends heavily on snow conditions. If it hasn't snowed in more than a few days, boarders will find themselves faced with crowded groomed slopes due to the unappealing chopped up and moguled off-piste. Especially during the high seasons, you will find all the best descents from Mont Gelé and Mont-Fort totally covered with moguls. After a good dump of snow, though, be ready for extraordinary powder rides that can take you from the 10,925-foot peak of Mont-Fort all the way down to Verbier at 4,921 feet, with a few cuts around the gondola line of Médran 1&2. On good snow days, the Bruson area can also host good off-piste terrain.

The other three valleys connected to Verbier have good variety and nice slopes, but getting there and back on a snowboard is not only a pain, but also dangerous; if you don't make it up the lifts back to Verbier in time, you're stuck. In general, the lifts at Verbier are faster and of better quality than in the other parts of the four Valleys, so you aren't missing anything by spending most of your time just in the Verbier section.

Unfortunately, the main Verbier ski area offers little haven to never-ever and beginner boarders. If you fall in to one of these categories, stick to either the Bruson or Savoleyres areas, which are excellently connected to the Verbier village.

Intermediate snowboarders will be able to find slopes matching their abilities all over the mountain except from Mont-Fort and Mont-Gelé. For the most variety and best scenery, we recommend hitting the lifts set around La Chaux, Les Ruinettes, and Attelas. From here challenge yourself on a steeper run, or take a break on a nice cruiser.

Advanced and expert riders will have a ball hitting the challenging slopes of Mont Fort and Mont Gelé. After a good snow, the itineraries from either peak all the way down to Tortin can keep you happy all day long.

The Neipark 1936 Snowpark at La Chaux, depending on snow conditions, is comprised of many table tops, rails, and one big-air jump sure to test your guts. On sunny days the park can be a nice place to hang out, take some jumps, and listen to some new French and Swiss music.

Mountain rating

Verbier has a solid reputation as the Promised Land for advanced and expert skiers. The twin and only runs down the Mont-Fort Gondola — steep, mogully, and ... did we say steep already? — make this among the most difficult marked descents from a gondola station (10,925 feet) in all of the Alps. The Tortin descent from either Col des Gentianes or Chassoure is also renowned for its steepness: if you fall, as we have learned from personal experience, you can slide what seems forever. All of the areas beneath Mont Fort and Mont Gele above Verbier—Attelas, La Chaux, Les Ruinettes—offer challenging runs for experts as well as good terrain for advanced and intermediate skiers.

In truth, any area this large offers something for every skier. Intermediate skiers will greatly enjoy the top-to-bottom runs down to towns such as Nendaz, Veysonnaz, or Les Collons. All are long, well-groomed trails with good pitch. Be forewarned, however, that you must time your touring to reach the Tortin lift back to Verbier before it closes at the end of the day, or you could be stuck on the wrong side of the mountain ridge and facing a long bus ride.

Advanced beginners will prefer the La Tzoumaz/Savoleyres area just above Verbier. The slopes on this side of the mountain tend to be wide-open and well-groomed. There are also many gentler slopes across the valley at Mayens-de-Bruson.

Cross-country

Verbier, Bagnes Valley and their nine surrounding areas have a total of 45 km. of terrain. There are 4 km. of cross-country skiing near the Sports Center, and another 5 km. at 2,200 meters at Les Ruinettes/Le Chaux. We recommend, however, taking the gondola down and accessing the 8 km. of cross-country trails in the Valley de Bagnes below. Further nformation is available at the tourist office or at www.sentiers-raquettes.com.

Ski school (2007/08 prices)

There are eight ski schools in the town. Verbier Sport Plus (027-7753363), which houses the Swiss Ski School Verbier and the Swiss Snowboard School Verbier, has approximately 120 instructors. Le Fantastique can be reached at 027-7714241. For Adrenaline, call 027-7717459. For Altitude, call 027-7716006. For European Snowsport, call 027-7716222. For Powder Extreme, call 076-4798771. For New Generation, call 027-7711181.

These are the prices for Verbier Sport Plus and are similar to other ski schools in the area. Euros are accepted, but we list Swiss Francs here for more exact pricing.

Private lessons

one or two persons (2 hours)	CHF190 (morning) CHF155 (afternoon)
one or two skiers for a half day	CHF 220 (morning or afternoon)
one or two skiers for a full day	CHF 400

Group lessons Lessons run from 9:15 a.m. to 11:45 a.m.

five consecutive days (adults)	CHF 240
five consecutive days (child)	CHF 225

Lift tickets (2007/08 prices)

Family vacationers should be sure to ask about discounts. Calculate discounts at www.televerbier.ch. Euros are accepted, but we list Swiss Francs here for more exact pricing.

Four-Valley with Mont-Fort	Adult	Child	Junior/Senior
one day	CHF64	CHF32	CHF51
two days	CHF124	CHF62	CHF99
six days	CHF331	CHF166	CHF265
fourteen days	CHF624	CHF312	CHF500

Verbier only	Adult	Child	Junior/Senior
one day	CHF56	CHF28	CHF45
two days	CHF109	CHF55	CHF87
six days	CHF331	CHF145	CHF231
fourteen days	CHF624	CHF280	CHF449

Note: Ski passes for three days or more are issued on computer-chip cards. These rechargeable cards cost approximately €3.50 each and are non-returnable.

Fifty percent-off tickets are available for children born from 1994 to 2001. For juniors born from 1989 to 1993 and for seniors from 1932 to 1943 there is twenty percent discount. Children born before 2001 and seniors born before 1932 are free.

Accommodations

The approximate daily high-season rate with half pension, based on double occupancy, is noted after each hotel. €€€=€125+; €€=€75–€125; €=€74-. A complete list of hotels is available at www.verbier.ch.

Chalet d'Adrien (027 771 62 00; fax 027 771 62 24; €€€) dominates Verbier. There is something for everyone here and visitors pay a hefty price for it. This hotel also has apartments with hotel service. It is next to the Savoleyres gondola.

Montpelier (027 771 61 31; fax 027 771 46 89; €€€) is in an imposing chalet near the sports complex. It has an exceptional restaurant.

Rhodania (027 771 61 21; fax 027 771 52 54; €€) in a chalet-style, four-star hotel in the middle of town that's ideal for families.

Les 4 Vallées (027 775 33 44; fax 027 775 33 45; €€€) is a B&B with 20 rooms across from the Rosalp.

La Rotonde (027 771 65 25; fax 027 771 27 12: €€) is a B&B in the heart of the town with each room decorated in a different style. It is next to the swimming pool.

Vanessa (027 775 28 00; fax 027 775 28 28; €€€) has all the creature comforts of a four-star hotel including a restaurant, piano bar and a guest-only sauna-whirlpool.

Ermitage (027 771 64 77; fax 027 771 52 64; €€) can't be more centrally located. It is across from the tourist office in the center of town.

There is a bomb shelter turned cheap hotel called **The Bunker** (027 771 66 02, fax 027 771 66 03), inside the sports center with rates of about €25 per night for bed; breakfast; whirlpool, ice-rink and pool access; digital TV and video; showers; and locker. A nearby public bus stop takes you to the ski area. Bring your own sleeping bag and for a few euros more you can also have access to a sauna; tennis and squash; public telephone; internet access; and the bar.

Ski Chalets: Crystal, Inghams/Bladon, Simply Ski, Chalet World, Thomas (go to page 16 for phone, fax and Internet addresses).

Apartments, condominiums, flats

For a list of apartments and their availability. go to www.verbier.ch and enter details on the number of beds required, the preferred number of rooms, and the dates you plan to be there. Select the apartment you want and contact the owner directly. Minimum stays are normally one week, Saturday to Saturday (in Christmas season the minimum is two weeks).

Bed linen, towels and kitchen utensils are usually provided. Other communal or private amenities, such as swimming pool, sauna, TV or room phone, all add to the cost. Apartments rent for €450–€550 per person per week in high season. Prices vary significantly by season.

Dining

Given the strong French influence and regional culinary traditions in Verbier and the surrounding Val de Bagnes region, it is difficult to find a poorly prepared meal. Prices, of course, will depend on the establishment's relative position on the luxury scale. Be sure to try the local raclette, a soft, melted cheese that is continually replenished on your plate, and typically served with potatoes, pickles, vegetables and assorted meats. Raclette is especially nice when accompanied by one of the crisp, dry white wines of the local Valais region.

At **Au Vieux Verbier** (027-7711668) you'll find good service, exquisite food, and a unique mountain class. Prices for dinner range from €30–€60. **La Grange** (027-7716431), in a space resembling an old Valais barn, has very affordable menus at lunch ranging from €11–€16. A full meal at dinner will run €35–€65. **Au Vieux Valais** (027-7753520), in the quintisential Swiss chalet, has a nice terrace, next to the Medran lift, with lunch menus for as little as €15. The full meal in the evening starts at about €25. **L'Ecurie** (027-7712760) in the center of the village serves traditional meals with a very affordable daily menu. Iron lamps and stone and stucco walls add Swiss atmosphere. We especially liked **The King's Restaurant** (027-7752035), a trendy restaurant with stuffed leather couches, roaring fireplace and arched windows. The candle-lit atmosphere matches its sophisticated menu of game, fish and innovative salads.

Borsalino Pizzeria (027-7711750) across from the Hotel Bristol has excellent pizzas from a wood-burning oven. The food in **Le Fer à Cheval** (027-7712669) is inexpensive and good, with a lively atmosphere where English is usually the common language. For a cheap burger, head to **Harold's Hamburger** (027-7716243), where you can check your email while you wait for your order.

In terms of on-mountain dining during the day, Verbier offers the wide variety typical in Europe. Gondola-station buffets share duty with numerous private restaurants dotted about the slopes. At least two restaurants, however, merit a special mention. At the **Chez Dany** (027-7712524) chalet just above Verbier, visitors enjoy unsurpassed vistas of the valley below from the outside deck. Try the "Croute au Fromage," a piece of locally baked bread topped with ham and smothered in melted Swiss cheese, with a fried egg on top. Those skiing the Savoleyres area should try lunch at **Le Marmotte** restaurant halfway down the slope. The specialty-of-the-house pasta is röstis and the view from the outside deck is equally rewarding.

 ## Après-ski/nightlife

With 17 bars and discotheques, Verbier boasts some of the best après-ski and nightlife in the Swiss Alps. After stepping out of your boards, stop at the **Pub Mont-Fort** near the gondola, a favorite of the British crowd. The crowd is raucous and eclectic. If you're staying in the center of town, however, remember it's a long, wavering walk down with skis and ski boots. The English accent is carried over at the **Big Ben Pub**, nearer to the gondola, and down in the center of town at **The Nelson Pub**. Le Fer a' Cheval (the "horseshoe") halfway between the center of town and the gondola also rocks after the lifts close, and you can pass the time checking out the endless license plates from all over the world that are plastered on the wall. The **Offshore** has a funky, well, right off the shore theme, and serves mostly as a before dinner après-ski hang-out. A favorite bar before hitting the discos is the **New Club**.

We've been told that you may find a Swede wearing a football helmet banging his head against the wall at **Bar'Jo**, under Chez Martin, after they have imbibed a few cement mixers made with aquavit.

When dinner is done and the leg-strong still have dancing on the mind, the **Casbah Club** and **Club Taratata** play techno-music, largely for a younger crowd of 20-somethings. The **Farm Club** in the Hotel Rhodania caters to an older, more sophisticated crowd, many of them up from Geneva to visit their chalets. The scores of vodka bottles on the wall with names on them are for the regulars who come back every weekend. The atmosphere is nice, with stuffed couches and a smallish dance floor, but the prices will make your eyes roll. The **Ice-Box Club** is also popular with a slightly older, local crowd sprinkled with British visitors.

Expect to pay about €13–€15 for entry to most clubs, with drinks at the more swanky spots costing roughly the same.

Child care (2007/08 prices)

The Kids Club Verbier, run by the Verbier Sport (027 775 33 63), offers care and beginners lessons for children that are 3- 6 years old. It has an escalator and baby-lift for beginners and a small restaurant. The Kids Club is open from the middle of December to April. Hours are from 8:30 a.m. to 4:30 p.m. A half day costs CHF 55; six half days for CHF 250; one full day for CHF 105 (with lunch); six full days for CHF 495 (with lunch). Verbier Sport Plus also has a nursery that runs from 7:45 a.m. to 6 p.m, every day.

Other activities

Verbier has an extensive sports center, which features an **indoor swimming pool, ice rink, curling rinks, squash courts, whirlpools, saunas,** and **solariums**. Pool entry is about €5 for guests staying in a hotel in Verbier. An hour of tennis costs €16. Ice skating is €5 and squash courts cost €9.60 per half-hour. There are also **tandem paragliding** flights offered at Verbier. Call the Centre de Parapente, 027 771 68 18; Fly Time 079 606 12 64; Max Biplace 027 771 55 55; or Verbier Summits 079 313 56 77.

For **tobogganing**, check for the signposted 10 km. run from Savoleyres to la Tzoumaz. There are 25 km. of groomed, marked trails. Maps are available at the tourist office.

In Medran Parc, go on an adventure trail consisting of more than 800 m. of hanging bridges, Tyrolean traverses, rope ladders and assisted climbs. Supervision by professionals from the Maison du Sport.

Getting there

The closest airport is Geneva. Train service runs from Martigny. Then you must take a small train to Le Chable, where you can either take the cablecar to Verbier or a direct bus from the station in the winter. The drive from Geneva takes about two hours. Follow the signs to the St. Bernard Pass (home of the famous St. Bernard dogs) until Sembrancher; turn left there, up the hill to Verbier.

Tourist information

Tourist office, CH-1936 Verbier, Switzerland; tel. 027 775 38 88; fax 027 775 38 89.
Internet: www.verbier.ch
E-mail: info@verbier.ch

ITALIAN TOURIST OFFICES

Canada

Italian Government Travel Office
175 Bloor Street East , Suite 907 - South Tower
Toronto, Ontario, M4W 3R8
Phone: +1 (416) 925-4882
Fax: +1 (416) 925-4799
Brochure Hot Line: +1 (416) 925-3870
e-mail: enit.canada@on.aibn.com

United Kingdom

Italian State Tourist Board
1, Princess Street
London W1R 9AY-1
Phone: +44 (20) 73551557 or 73551439
Fax: +44 (20) 74936695
e-mail: enitlond@globalnet.co.uk

United States

New York

Italian Government Travel Office
630 Fifth Avenue, Suite 1565
New York NY 10011
Phone: +1 (212) 245-5618 or 245-4822
Fax: +1 (212) 586-9249
e-mail: enitny@italiantourism.com

Chicago

Italian Government Travel Office
500 North Michigan Avenue, Suite 2240
Phone: +1 (312) 644-0996
Fax: +1 (312) 644-3019
e-mail: enitch@italiantourism.com

Los Angeles

Italian Government Travel Office
12400 Wilshire Blvd., Suite 550
Los Angeles, CA 90025
Phone: +1 (310) 820-2977, 820-1898, or 820-1959
Fax: +1 (310) 820-6357
e-mail: enitla@earthlink.net

GERMAN NATIONAL TOURIST OFFICE

Canada

German National Tourist Office
175 Bloor Street East
North Tower, Suite 604
Toronto, Ontario M4W 3R8
Phone: +1 (416) 968-1570
Fax:+1 (416) 968-1986
e-mail: gntoyyz@d-z-t.com

United Kingdom

German National Tourist Office
P.O. Box 2695
London W1A 3TN
Phone: +44 207- 317-0908
Fax: +44 20-495-6129
e-mail: gntolon@d-z-t.com

United States

New York

German National Tourist Office
122 East 42nd Street, 52nd Floor
New York, NY 10168-0072
Phone: +1 (212) 661-7200
Fax: +1 (212) 661-7174
e-mail: gntonyc@d-z-t.com

Chicago

German National Tourist Office
German National Tourist Office Chicago
P.O. Box 59594
Chicago IL, 60659-9594
Phone: +1 (773) 539-6303
Fax:: +1 (773) 539-6378
e-mail: gntoch@aol.com

Los Angeles

German National Tourist Office
P.O. Box 641009
Los Angeles, CA 90064-1009
Phone: +1 (310) 234-0250
Fax: +1 (310) 474-1604
e-mail: gntolax@aol.com

SCANDINAVIAN TOURISM

United Kingdom
Norwegian Tourist Board
5th Floor, Charles House, 5 Regent Street
(Lower)
London SW1Y 4LR
Phone: +44 (0)207 839 6255
Fax: +44 (0)207 839 6014
e-mail: greatbritain@ntr.no

United States & Canada
P.O. Box 4649, Grand Central Station
New York, NY 01063
Phone: (212) 885-9700
Fax: (212) 885-9710
e-mail: info@goscandinavia.com

SWISS NATIONAL TOURIST OFFICE

Canada
Switzerland Tourism
926 The East Mall
Toronto, Ontario M9B 6K1
Phone: +1 (416) 695-2090 (English)
Phone: +1 (514) 333-9526 (francais)
Fax: +1 (416) 695-2774
e-mail: info.caen@switzerlandtourism.ch
(English)
e-mail: info.cafr@switzerlandtourism.ch
(francais)

United Kingdom
Switzerland Tourism
Swiss Centre, Swiss Court
London W1V 8EE
Phone: +44 (0171) 734-1921
Fax: +44 (0171) 437-4577
e-mail: stlondon@switzerlandtourism.ch

United States
Switzerland Tourism
Swiss Center, 608 Fifth Avenue
New York, NY 10020-2303
Phone: +1 (212) 757-5944
Toll-free phone: 1-877-SWITZERLAND

TOURIST OFFICE OF SPAIN

Canada
Tourist Office of Spain
2 Bloor Street West, 34th Floor
Toronto, Ontario M4W 3E2
Tel.: + 1 (416) 961-3131
Fax : + 1 (416) 961-1992
e-mail: toronto@tourspain.es

United Kingdom
Spanish Tourist Office
22-23, Manchester Square, London W1M 5AP
Phone: +44 20 7486-8077
Fax: +44 20 7486 8034
e-mail: londres@tourspain.es

United States

New York
Tourist Office of Spain
666 Fifth Avenue, New York, NY 10103
Phone: + 1 (212) 265-8822
Fax: + 1 (212) 265-8864
e-mail: oetny@tourspain.es

Chicago
Tourist Office of Spain
Water Tower Place, Suite 915 East
845 North Michigan Avenue, Chicago IL 60611
Phone: + 1 (312) 642-1992
Fax: + 1 (312) 642-9817
e-mail: chicago@tourspain.es

Los Angeles
Tourist Office of Spain
8383 Wilshire Blvd, Suite 960
Beverly Hills, CA 90211
Phone: + 1 (323) 658-7188
Fax: + 1 (323) 658-1061
e-mail: losangeles@tourspain.es

Miami
Tourist Office of Spain
1221 Brickell Avenue, Miami, FL. 33131
Phone: + 1 (305) 358-1992